The Contemporary Middle East
A Documentary History

A Documentary History

John Felton

The Contemporary Middle East:
A Documentary History

John Felton

CQ PRESS

A Division of Congressional Quarterly Inc.
Washington, D.C.

CQ Press
1255 22nd Street, NW, Suite 400
Washington, DC 20037

Phone: 202-729-1900; toll-free, 1-866-4CQ-PRESS (1-866-427-7737)

Web: www.cqpress.com

Primary document credits and acknowledgments can be found on page 703, which constitutes a continuation of the copyright page.

Cover design: Diane Buric

∞ The paper used in this publication exceeds the requirements of the American National Standard for Information Sciences—Permanence of Paper for Printed Library Materials, ANSI Z39.48-1992.

Printed and bound in the United States of America

10   09   08   07   1   2   3   4   5   6

Library of Congress Cataloging-in-Publication Data

Felton, John.
    The contemporary Middle East : a documentary history / John Felton.
       p. cm.
    Includes bibliographical references and index.
     ISBN 978-0-87289-488-4 (hardback : alk. paper)   1. Middle East—History—20th century—Sources.   I. Title.

DS42.F44 2008
956.04—dc22   2007033104

Contents

About the Author

John Felton is a freelance writer specializing in foreign affairs. He has reported on U.S. foreign policy for *CQ Weekly* and was a foreign affairs editor for National Public Radio. He is the co-editor of CQ Press's acclaimed Historic Documents series and the author of *Global Connections: America's Role in the 21st Century*.

Preface

The Contemporary Middle East: A Documentary History centers around speeches and diplomatic agreements, UN and other resolutions, and additional texts that effected or reflect important events and remain of enduring significance. In some cases, the documents are of no immediate urgency to events today, but examining the role they played in the past is essential to a full understanding of the contemporary world. Such examples include the secret agreement in which Britain, France, and Israel decided to invade Egypt in 1956 to seize the Suez Canal. Other documents remain as compelling today as when they were originally produced. Examples of these include the treaties that brought peace (or at least the absence of war) between Israel and two of its immediate neighbors, Egypt and Jordan. These treaties—reflective of decisions by Arab leaders to come to terms with Israel's existence in exchange for the return of captured land and other concessions—continue to influence the course of events in the region on a daily basis.

"Foundations of the Contemporary Middle East," the introduction to chapter 1, sets the stage for all subsequent chapters by examining the events of the World War I era that played such an important role in the creation of today's Middle East. The other chapters deal with the conflicts involving Israel and its Arab neighbors, Afghanistan, Iran, Iraq, Lebanon and Syria, and Turkey. The table of contents for each chapter features part titles to identify periods of conflict and trends in foreign policy and diplomacy. A comprehensive chronology of major events since 1914 provides additional historical context for the documents and is followed by a bibliography.

An introduction precedes each document or set of related documents, establishing context with a brief explanation of the relevant history. For comprehensive histories, readers should consult the bibliography and other available resources on the Middle East elsewhere. Most of the documents are presented in their entirety, but for reasons of space, some of the longer ones have been excerpted but retain their essence. Editorial notes and wording added for clarity appear in brackets.

Original source documents have been used whenever possible. In other cases, however, the primary source documents are difficult or nearly impossible to obtain or exist only in their original (non-English) language. These latter documents have been retrieved from the most reliable secondary sources accessible. In contrast to some recent publications, *The Contemporary Middle East* cites the sources of the documents reproduced. For ease of access, many of these sources include a Web site address where a copy of the full document can be found. Although the Internet has made many documents accessible, reliable sources can sometimes be difficult to locate. Thus, before selecting a particular document for this volume, it was sometimes necessary to compare various versions before settling on the most reliable and accurate of them.

Few contemporary or historical subjects are as fraught with controversy as the Middle East. Because the lands of the Middle East hold great historical, religious, and economic importance for so many people, almost everything that happens in the region arouses passions; these are amplified by the tendency to view events there through decidedly partisan lenses. Without a doubt, much of the conflict in the Middle East results from and persists because of the refusal of participants and their supporters even to consider the possible validity of views different from their own. History demonstrates the difficulty of debating with, much less settling differences with, someone who believes his or her views to be ordained by God. People willing to consider alternative viewpoints almost never rise to power, and in the Middle East those with open minds often pay for such a perspective with their lives. This book does not espouse any particular point of view. Even so, some readers undoubtedly will believe that they detect biases of one kind or another.

Many people helped make this book possible. CQ Press acquisition editors Mary Carpenter and Marc Segers along with Andrea Pedolsky, chief of acquisitions, conceived it and had the persistence to push it through to its end. Also at CQ Press, assistant development editors Andrew Boney and Scott Kuzner contributed invaluable assistance as researchers, Robin Surratt copyedited the volume, and Nancy Matuszak oversaw production. Two editorial assistants, Sarah Abdelnaby and Zina Sadek Sawaf, helped track down documents, often at the risk of being inundated by dust in libraries.

Archivists, librarians, scholars, and fellow journalists helped me find what I needed, always cheerfully and in the spirit of making knowledge more widely accessible. Among them are Gail Fithian at the Boston Public Library; Michal Saft at the Israeli State Archives in Jerusalem; Hana Pinshow at the David Ben-Gurion Archives in Sde Boker, Israel; Christopher M. Murphy at the Library of Congress; Ömer Faruk Gençkaya, assistant professor of political science at Bilkent University in Ankara, Turkey; Kemal Gozler, associate professor of constitutional law at Kroc University Law School in Istanbul; and Ian S. Lustick, professor of political science at the University of Pennsylvania in Philadelphia. Also, I wish to thank Anne Garrels, Mike Shuster, and Ivan Watson, three of my former colleagues at National Public Radio whose assistance and insights into contemporary events they cover each day proved invaluable.

Finally, I want to thank my wife, Marty Gottron, who endured many days of my being focused on 1919 or 1937 rather than the daily tasks of contemporary life. Marty also happens to be the best editor I know, and her comments greatly improved the initial drafts.

Any errors of fact, interpretation, or omissions are mine.

Introduction

For the better part of a century, the Middle East consistently has been a focal point of armed conflict and political tension. Although constituting only a small percentage of the world's landmass and population, the region has endured and has produced far more than its share of turmoil. *The Contemporary Middle East: A Documentary History* illustrates the reasons for the focus of the world's attention on this area by presenting documents central to the region's past and thus ultimately to its future.

This volume takes as its starting point World War I, or the Great War, which ended the old ways of life in Europe but as a byproduct also opened a new chapter of increased international intervention in the Middle East. In the early twenty-first century, many aspects of major news events—from sectarian divisions in Iraq and Lebanon to the seemingly endless conflict between Israelis and Palestinians—stem directly from the decisions made by world leaders, most of them in London and Paris, during and shortly after that war.

Since the first events documented here, conflict has been chronic in the areas of the Middle East where international intervention has been most intense. One obvious example stands out—the establishment of Israel as a Jewish state in the midst of a region otherwise dominated by Arab Muslims. The current round of conflict between Arabs and Jews is now nearly a century old, and despite progress on some fronts, it shows no sign of abating. Iraq and Lebanon represent examples of countries torn by internal sectarian conflict resulting from European decisions after World War I in creating new countries comprised of disparate societies with no unifying, common national interest. The consequences of intervention after the postwar period can also be seen in today's headlines. For example, Iran's reported determination to acquire nuclear weapons is partially driven by memories of U.S. intervention a half century ago, and the Western-sponsored attempt to implant democracy in Afghanistan follows nearly three decades of war resulting from an invasion by the Soviet Union.

This litany of international intervention is not to say that the people of the Middle East always have been the hapless victims of outside powers. The view of the West imposing strife on otherwise innocent people does, however, stand as a central element in some of the self-serving explanations for the region's problems as developed, notably, by Islamists, ranging from Hasan al-Banna, founder of the Muslim Brotherhood in Egypt, to the current leaders of Iran and al-Qaida's Osama bin Laden. As with any one-size-fits-all accounting of complex historical forces, this finger-pointing at Western treachery absolves the people of the Middle East—if not their rulers, who are often portrayed as Western dupes—of all responsibility for their own plight, making it that more difficult for them to shoulder the burden of creating a better future.

The documents reproduced in this book, along with the essays placing them in historical context, tell the stories of political leaders and nations grappling with the results of their own actions and those of others. Because of the focus on events and conflicts relating to politics, the documents primarily consist of speeches, treaties, official agreements, and reports generated by leaders and public institutions. Such texts tell only part of the story behind a series of events, but they often express the hopes and expectations—some fulfilled, some not—essential to the story.

The issues of terrorism and the advocacy of extremist religious or ideological views provide a backdrop to much of the material in *The Contemporary Middle East*. Of course, the use of violence to advance a cause is not unique to the Middle East, or even to recent history, but in the contemporary, world violent acts of terrorism have become particularly associated with that region. Within living memory, the Middle East has been plagued by the violence of Jewish gangs fighting British mandatory authorities in Palestine before World War II, airplane hijackings in the 1970s, and suicide bombings in Lebanon in the 1980s and in Israel and the occupied territories starting in the 1990s, and more recently the daily carnage of sectarian killings in Iraq under U.S. occupation. In some cases, the violence helped the perpetrators achieve their goals; for example, the British tired of the attacks against them in Palestine, opening the way for the creation of Israel as a Jewish state. Other uses of terrorism and violence have been less successful, notably, the failure of the Palestinians to achieve either their previous goal of driving Israel into the sea or their later goal of an independent Palestinian state.

In a similar vein, oil also features in the background of several chapters. Since the first major oil strike in Iran in 1908, international reliance on abundant oil and natural gas has been a contributing factor in the Middle East's frequent bouts of turmoil. Britain's conflict with Iran in the early 1950s (after Tehran nationalized a British oil company) and the Persian Gulf crisis and war of 1990–1991 are but two examples in which nations have gone to extraordinary lengths to ensure the supply of Middle Eastern oil.

This book focuses on a range of countries and territories in the Middle East that have seen some of the greatest turmoil of the past century. As might be expected, Israel features prominently in several chapters simply because the conflict between Jews and Arabs has been a dominant factor in the region for almost the entire period since World War I. The Palestinians are the other half of the equation that for some four decades has been called the Israeli-Palestinian conflict, a cycle of violence interrupted occasionally by failed diplomacy, that neither side seems able to win or bring to a conclusion. Afghanistan, Iran, Iraq, Lebanon, and Turkey are the other countries on which the volume concentrates. Each has experienced chronic political turmoil and outright war.

Although on the periphery of the Middle East, Afghanistan has experienced the types of foreign intervention, sectarian conflict, and ideological extremism common to much of the rest of the region. Once the center of a mighty Persian Empire, Iran spent much of the twentieth century almost as a vassal state to outside powers, only to rise in importance after 1979 because of the powerful ideas generated by its Islamic revolution. Iraq and Lebanon share similar histories as neocolonial creations in which disparate ethnic and religious groups found themselves as part of nation-states with artificial boundaries. Iraq for nearly three decades has been at the center of much of the region's turbulence, while Lebanon would seem to have "Intervene Here" signs posted on the borders with its neighbors. Turkey is included here because its unique history as the center of the Ottoman Empire so intimately intertwines it with the rest of the region, and its attempts at modernization of an Islamic society have been echoed, with varying success, elsewhere. What happens in each of these countries continues to be of regional and potentially global importance.

It is difficult to be optimistic about the near-term future of most of the countries covered here. Iran, Israel, the Palestinian territories, Lebanon, and Turkey all face serious internal political challenges arising from historic disputes as well as differing visions for the future. The Palestinian territories are experiencing yet another period of intense upheaval, one resulting as much from internal stresses as from the long-term conflict with Israel. The Western-backed governments of Afghanistan and Iraq are fighting for their lives against insurgencies that use classic guerrilla techniques as well as the tools of terrorism (notably suicide bombs) that in recent years have become hallmarks of civil conflict in the region. Predicting the future in the Middle East is risky business, but if the past is any guide, one prediction is almost a certainty: the production of more documents offering the peace and prosperity that many of those in this book also promised but failed to deliver.

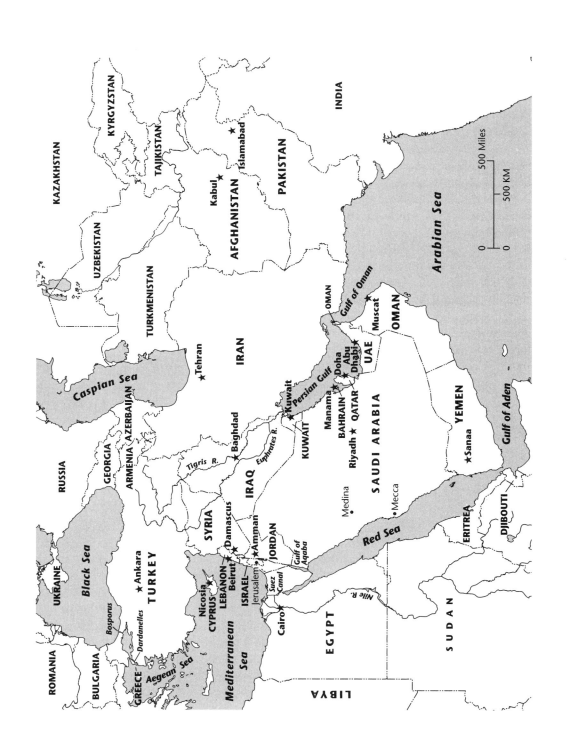

Foundations of the Contemporary Middle East

CHAPTER 1 DOCUMENTS

Overview

For better or worse, the Middle East of the early twenty-first century was largely shaped by decisions made by European leaders during and shortly after World War I. Their decisions, motivated by political or strategic considerations, had little to do with the cultural, geographic, historical or other realities in the region. Moreover, residents of the Middle East had only modest influence over what leaders in London and Paris decided.

The most important of these decisions involved the division of the Arabic-speaking portions of the former Ottoman Empire into virtual colonies of Britain and France and Britain's commitment to promote the region of Palestine as a "national home" for the world's Jews. These actions ultimately led to the creation of the modern states of Iraq, Israel, Jordan, Lebanon, and Syria. After the Ottoman Empire collapsed in the ashes of World War I, its Turkish core emerged as the modern state of Turkey. In turn, the creation of countries along artificial boundaries—without regard to the differing ethnicities and relations of the peoples who lived there—set the stage for much of the conflict that has since roiled the Middle East (see map, The Ottoman Empire at World War I, p. 4).

World War I was important in the emergence of the twentieth-century Middle East. Although it raged primarily in Europe, from 1914 to 1918, the conflict also affected much of the eastern Mediterranean. Britain, France, Russia, and (starting in 1917) the United States allied themselves against Germany and the declining empires of Austria-Hungary and the Ottoman Turks. The outcome of the war remained uncertain until the United States intervened, which helps explain the eagerness of leaders on both sides to gather as many allies as possible, even in places as remote from the front lines as the deserts of Arabia.

In 1915 Britain sought out Arab allies for a military campaign to put pressure on the Ottoman Empire from the south. Britain found an ally in the person of Sharif Hussein ibn Ali, who held the prestigious post of guardian of the Islamic holy sites in Mecca. Over the course of seven months during late 1915 and early 1916, Hussein secretly exchanged letters with Sir Henry McMahon, the senior British official in the

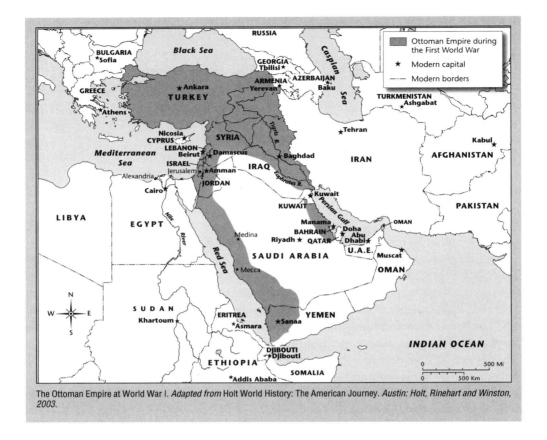

The Ottoman Empire at World War I. *Adapted from* Holt World History: The American Journey. *Austin: Holt, Rinehart and Winston, 2003.*

Middle East. Believing that McMahon had assured him of British backing for an independent Arab state under his leadership after the war, Hussein agreed to foment an "Arab revolt" against the Ottoman Empire. Begun in June 1916, the revolt consisted of a small army of Arabs who accompanied a much larger British army led by General Edmund Allenby. One of Hussein's sons, Faisal, led the Arabs, who were advised by British agents, including army captain T. E. Lawrence, who gained fame as "Lawrence of Arabia." The British and their Arab allies captured Jerusalem in December 1917 and then moved on to Damascus, which fell in October 1918, just before the Ottomans surrendered to the allies.

As Hussein and McMahon exchanged letters in 1915–1916, British and French diplomats met in London to divide the spoils of the Ottoman Empire in anticipation of the war's conclusion. Chief negotiators Mark Sykes of Britain and François Georges Picot of France eventually settled on a complex arrangement under which Britain would assume direct or indirect control of much of modern-day Iraq and Jordan while France would control modern-day Lebanon and Syria. The region of "Palestine"—modern-day Israel and the Palestinian territories—would come under international supervision once the war ended. The Sykes-Picot Agreement eventually became the basis for key postwar peace treaties affecting the Middle East.

Yet another document from this period set in motion the series of events that would lead to the establishment of the state of Israel three decades later. Believing that Jewish businessmen and other leaders in Germany, Russia, and the United States might be able to influence the outcome of the war, the British government aligned itself with the relatively new movement called "Zionism," which advocated the establishment of a Jewish homeland in Palestine.

On November 2, 1917, Britain's foreign secretary, Arthur James Balfour, sent a letter to Lionel Walter, Lord Rothschild, a Zionist leader in Britain, pledging that the government would support creation of a "Jewish national home" in Palestine. This pledge came just weeks before General Allenby's military expedition captured Jerusalem, thus putting Britain in control of Palestine. Balfour's letter, known ever since as the Balfour Declaration, swung British diplomatic and political weight behind Zionism, which previously had gained little backing in world capitals and was even controversial among Jews.

Chaim Weizmann, the Zionist leader largely responsible for persuading British officials to adopt Zionism as official policy, also sought to win Arab support for the cause. In 1918 and early 1919, Weizmann met repeatedly with Faisal, Sharif Hussein's son, and the two men signed an agreement calling for Arab-Jewish cooperation in the founding of a Jewish homeland in Palestine. Except for its historical importance as an idealistic vision of pan-Semitic harmony, the agreement never amounted to anything of substance, in part because Faisal later renounced it.

The Mandates

The end of World War I in November 1918 launched numerous rounds of international diplomacy that lasted longer than the war and resulted in the ratification of most of the decisions about the Middle East taken in London and Paris during the war. Of note, in July 1922 the newly founded League of Nations assigned mandates giving Britain and France virtual colonial power over the Arabic-speaking portions of the former Ottoman Empire. The mandate for British control of Palestine incorporated the language of the Balfour Declaration calling for the creation of a Jewish national home on that territory.

In theory, the mandates required Britain and France to lay the groundwork for self-governance in the territories they ruled, but London and Paris showed little interest in this aspect of their control. In fact, they suppressed Arab nationalist movements that demanded greater say in local decision making. Rising nationalist sentiments and the tumultuous events of World War II brought an end to the mandates, leaving in their place the independent Arab states of Iraq, Jordan, Lebanon, and Syria and the Jewish state of Israel.

In forming Iraq and Lebanon, the European powers drew boundaries that brought together disparate groups that shared no common sense of nationhood. The French detached Lebanon from Greater Syria for the benefit of their Maronite Christian allies who predominated in the Mount Lebanon area. Minorities of Shiite and Sunni Muslims also were included within the new Lebanese boundaries, later necessitating arrangements for uneasy power-sharing among the three communities. Britain similarly created Iraq from the former Ottoman provinces of Basra (in the south, dominated by Shiites), Baghdad (in the center, dominated at the time by Sunnis), and Mosul (in the north, with a population that included Kurds). The artificial nature of Iraq and Lebanon bred problems years later, beginning in the 1950s, when Lebanon experienced the first of its internal conflicts, and continuing into the 2000s, when the

United States ousted Saddam Hussein from power in Iraq and Lebanon's sectarian communities began a new round in the struggle to control the government.

Turkey and Iran, both nations with long histories, emerged in new guises in the wake of World War I. Turkey, which had been the core of the Ottoman Empire for some four hundred years, came under the dynamic leadership of former general Mustafa Kemal (later named Ataturk). Turkey regained large pieces of territory, including Istanbul, that the victorious allies had severed from the former Ottoman lands. In 1919 Kemal advocated positions incorporated into a statement known as the National Pact, which has since served as a basis for Turkish policy. The pact abandoned Turkey's claim to most Arab lands but insisted that all Turkish-speaking regions rightfully belonged to the new Turkish state.

Persia also emerged from World War I with a new identity and a new monarchy. Reza Khan Pahlavi, a former army commander, worked his way to power in the 1920s and renamed the country Iran to emphasize the Aryan background of most of its people. While Kemal guided Turkey to genuine independence from foreign powers, Pahlavi proved unable to do the same for Iran because of Iran's strategic location and international interest in its oil resources. Britain and Russia exerted substantial control over Iran until after World War II, and a British-run oil company dominated the national economy. In the 1950s, the United States became the dominant outside power in Iranian affairs, a position it would retain until the late 1970s.

World War I also launched the processes leading to independence for Egypt and the creation of Saudi Arabia, two of the most important nations in the Middle East. Although not strictly a colony, Egypt had been under effective British control since the late nineteenth century. Egyptian nationalists took seriously Britain's promises of independence. Discovering after the war that these promises were empty, nationalists launched a popular uprising in 1919 that forced London to begin easing its grip. Britain granted limited autonomy to a local Egyptian government in 1922 and a greater degree of independence in 1936. On the Arabian Peninsula, Sharif Hussein lost his bid for pan-Arab primacy in 1924, when he suffered military defeat by the armies of Abd al-Aziz ibn Saud, a rival tribal leader. Saud established a monarchy in a new country named after his family.

A New Era

Despite the diplomacy of the European powers during and after World War I, the Middle East quickly became an unruly place. The postwar revolt against British rule in Egypt was followed by successive clashes in Afghanistan, Iraq, Palestine, and Syria. Taken together, these events demonstrated that Britain and France lacked the military resources to pacify completely their regional domains and that many locals resented having their destinies plotted in faraway European capitals.

In Afghanistan, a new king, Amanullah, sought in 1919 to assert his country's independence from London by launching a surprise attack on British forces across the border in imperial India. A brief war ended in a draw but brought British recognition of the high cost of imposing their will on the Afghan kingdom. A treaty signed in August 1919 gave Afghanistan its independence, after which the king established closer relations with the new communist leaders in Moscow.

The first of many modern-day conflicts in Palestine took place in April 1920, during a festival honoring Moses, when Arabs—frustrated by Jewish immigration—rioted against Jews in Jerusalem. Fewer than ten people died in the violence, but several hundred were wounded and the experience convinced British officials to replace its military government in Palestine with a civilian administration dedicated to improving relations between the two communities.

Britain's attempt to create the unified state of Iraq out of the disparate provinces of Baghdad, Basra, and Mosul received a rude shock in June 1920, when rural tribes revolted and proclaimed an Arab government. The imperial army took more than eight months to suppress the revolt, and it lost approximately 450 soldiers in the process. Britain allowed Iraq to become independent in 1932 but maintained significant influence in part through the retention of military bases there.

Meanwhile, France faced difficulties of its own in Syria, where it was to govern under a still-pending League of Nations mandate. With British support, Faisal had established a government in Damascus. In 1919 he gathered Arab notables from Greater Syria—that is, Lebanon, Palestine, and Syria—for a meeting known as the General Syrian Congress. They demanded a completely independent Syrian state, with Faisal at its head. Britain and France ignored them, and a year later the French sent an army to Damascus, forced Faisal from office, and established a colonial-style government. France also designated coastal Lebanon as a separate entity because of its interest in trade there and its Christian majority.

Widening regional resentment of European domination after World War I also contributed to the growth of Arab nationalism and an Islamic resurgence, broad-based movements that over decades would grow in importance. The concept of Arab nationalism had developed late in the nineteenth century, but not until the collapse of the Ottoman Empire did Arab intellectuals and leaders began to agitate for independent nation-states. The often heavy-handed reactions by the British and French to local demands merely increased the desire for independence as illustrated by the spate of violence in the years immediately after World War I. Movements to revive a "pure" form of Islam similarly gained new traction in areas of the Middle East in part as a response to European domination. The founding of the Muslim Brotherhood in Egypt in 1928 represents one of the more prominent examples of attempts by some Arab Muslims to assert cultural, rather than just political, independence from an outside world that they believed to be corrupt and illegitimate. The better part of a century later, Arab nationalism has lost much of its appeal, having produced a host of authoritarian regimes in the region without improving the lives of average Arabs. By contrast, Islamist movements have grown in influence and popularity in much of the Middle East in part in response to the dominance of the United States, which after World War II assumed some aspects of the role played by European powers after World War I.

Toward Arab Independence

Few aspects of modern Middle Eastern history have been as hotly disputed as the correspondence of 1915–1916 between Sharif Hussein ibn Ali, a leading Arab figure of the time, and Sir Henry McMahon, Britain's chief diplomatic representative in the region. Many Arab leaders and some Western historians contend that the correspondence committed Britain to supporting Arab control of key territories, including the portion of Palestine that is now Israel. Most British officials, Jewish leaders, and other historians insist that the correspondence was deliberately vague and made no such commitment to the Arabs. The dispute has never been resolved and probably never will be. In any event, the correspondence remains an important marker, in part because many Arabs still view it as demonstrating Western treachery.

Hussein, the amir of Mecca, initiated the correspondence with McMahon, the British high commissioner in Egypt, which at the time was under British control. In a letter dated July 14, 1915, Hussein demanded that Britain acknowledge the independence of an Arab kingdom (to be headed by Hussein) comprising most of the Arabian Peninsula, the provinces then known as Greater Syria (consisting of present-day Israel, Lebanon, Jordan, and Syria), and much of present-day Iraq. In making this demand, Hussein was essentially endorsing proposals advanced by other Arab figures (including dissident officers in the army of the Ottoman Empire) who hoped to gain support from either the British or the Ottomans for the idea of an independent Arab state.

Hussein's letter created controversy among senior British officials, some of whom saw it as an opportunity to gain Arab support in World War I, while others opposed any dealings with Arabs, whom they regarded as untrustworthy and inconsequential to the war. Officials in London eventually authorized McMahon to send Hussein a generally positive reply.

After another exchange of letters, McMahon's reply came in a vaguely worded and generally noncommittal letter, dated October 24, 1915, that endorsed "the independence of the Arabs" in some but not all of the regions Hussein had cited. McMahon excluded the coastal region of present-day Syria and most of Lebanon by arguing that the districts west of a line stretching from the town of Aleppo on the north to Damascus in the south "cannot be said to be purely Arab." He did not say as much, but this exclusion was intended to preserve the option for France, Britain's war-time ally, to assume control of that part of Syria and Lebanon.

McMahon also excluded from a potential Arab state what he called the "districts" of Mersina (now Mersin in southwestern Turkey) and Alexandretta (now Iskenderun, a Mediterranean port city in Turkey). In addition, McMahon wrote that Britain would have to maintain what he called "special administrative arrangements" for the provinces of Baghdad and Basra, much of what is present-day Iraq. He did not define what he meant by these arrangements, though the language almost certainly was intended to assert that Britain should control those parts of Iraq. McMahon also did not directly address the status of Palestine, portions of which would become Israel three decades later. He told Hussein that a new Arab state would need the services of British advisers—in effect putting the Arabs under some degree of British control—and expressed hope for an alliance between Britain and the Arabs that he said would lead to "the expulsion of the Turks from Arab countries." At the time of this correspondence, several other British officials stated privately that McMahon had made no formal or binding commitments to Hussein, offering only a vague pledge to support Arab independence in an area yet to be defined.

In a reply dated November 5, 1915, Hussein challenged McMahon's exclusion of coastal Syria and Lebanon from an independent Arab state, calling French claims to those areas "quite out of the question." Hussein and McMahon exchanged three subsequent letters, but failed to resolve the question of what lands would be included in an Arab state. Instead, the two sides agreed to postpone the matter until after the war.

Although Hussein's request for formal British recognition of an independent Arab state had produced mixed results at best, Hussein in June 1916 proceeded to carry out his part of the bargain: an "Arab revolt" against Ottoman rule. Westerners know about this uprising primarily because of the role played by T. E. Lawrence, a British army officer known in the movies and popular literature as Lawrence of Arabia. The revolt produced one significant military victory in the ousting of Ottoman troops from Aqaba, the port at the head of the Gulf of Aqaba. An Arab army led by Hussein's son Faisal contributed to the British capture of Damascus in October 1918.

Early in 1916, some aspects of the Hussein-McMahon correspondence were taken into account (though most were ignored) when senior British and French diplomats negotiated to divide much of the Middle East among themselves after the war. Again, in 1917, Britain ignored the thrust of the Hussein-McMahon correspondence when it asserted that portions of Palestine should be a "national home" for the Jewish people (Sykes-Picot Agreement, p. 14; Balfour Declaration, p. 24).

The Hussein-McMahon correspondence remained secret until 1938, when it appeared in The *Arab Awakening*, a book by the Lebanese-Egyptian historian George Antonius, who argued that Britain had "betrayed" its promises to Hussein and thus to the Arabs. The British government formally published the correspondence the following year, when a parliamentary committee reviewed the history of British diplomacy on the Middle East during World War I.

Hussein never became the king of the Arabs, as he apparently envisioned himself. In fact, he lost control of Mecca and the surrounding Hijaz region in 1924 to his chief rival, Abd al-Aziz ibn Saud, who went on to incorporate most of the Arabian Peninsula into a new kingdom, Saudi Arabia. Two of Hussein's sons eventually served as British-appointed leaders of Arab states created by the peace treaties that ended World War I. In 1920 Faisal briefly headed a government in Damascus before being ousted by the French. A year later, Britain installed Faisal as Iraq's first king, a position he held until his death in 1933. Also in 1921, Britain installed Faisal's older brother Abdallah as amir of the new country of Transjordan (present-day Jordan), which remains a monarchy ruled by his descendants to this day. Abdallah's grandson Hussein served as king from 1953 until his death in 1999, when Hussein's son became King Abdallah II.

Following are the texts of two letters dated July 14 and October 24, 1915, that were exchanged by Sharif Hussein ibn Ali, the amir of Mecca, and Sir Henry McMahon, the British high commissioner in Cairo.

DOCUMENT

Letter from Hussein to McMahon

JULY 14, 1915

Whereas the whole of the Arab nation without any exception have decided in these last years to live, and to accomplish their freedom, and grasp the reins of their administration both in theory and practice; and whereas they have found and felt that it is to the interest of the Government of Great Britain to support them and aid them in the attainment of their firm and lawful intentions (which are based upon the maintenance of the honor and dignity of their life without any ulterior motives whatsoever unconnected with this object);

And whereas it is to their (the Arab's) interest also to prefer the assistance of the Government of Great Britain in consideration of their geographical position and economic interests, and also of the attitude of the above-mentioned Government, which is known to both nations and therefore need not be emphasized;

For these reasons, the Arab nation see fit to limit themselves, as time is short, to asking the Government of Great Britain if it should think fit, for the approval, through her deputy or representative, of the following fundamental propositions, leaving out all things considered secondary in comparison with these, so that it may prepare all means necessary for attaining this noble purpose, until such time as it finds occasion for making the actual negotiations:—

Firstly,— England to acknowledge the independence of the Arab countries, bounded on the north by Mersina and Adama up to the 37th degree of latitude, on which degree all Birijik, Ufa, Mardin, Midiat, Jezirat Amadia, up to the border of Persia; on the east by the borders of Persia up to the Gulf of Basra; on the south by the Indian Ocean, with the exception of the position of Aden [Yemen] to remain as it is; on the west by the Red Sea, the Mediterranean Sea up to Mersina. England to approve of the proclamation of the Arab Caliphate of Islam.

Secondly,— The Arab Government of the Sharif to acknowledge that England shall have the preference in all economic enterprises in the Arab countries whenever conditions of enterprise are otherwise equal.

Thirdly, — For the security of this Arab independence and the certainty of such preference of economic enterprises, both high contracting parties to offer mutual assistance, to the best ability of their military and naval forces, to face any foreign Power which may attack either party. Peace not to be decided without agreement of both parties.

Fourthly,— If one of the parties enters upon an aggressive conflict, the other party to assume a neutral attitude, and in case of such party wishing the other to join forces, both to meet and discuss the conditions.

Fifthly,— England to acknowledge the abolition of foreign privileges in the Arab countries, and to assist the Government of the Sharif in an International Convention for confirming such abolition.

Sixthly,— Articles 3 and 4 of this treaty to remain in vigor for fifteen years, and, if either wishes it to be renewed, one year's notice before lapse of the treaty to be given.

Consequently, and as the whole of the Arab nation have, praise be to God, agreed and united for the attainment, at all costs and finally, of this noble object, they beg the Government of Great Britain to answer them positively or negatively, in a period of thirty days after receiving this intimation; and if this period should lapse before they receive answer, they reserve to themselves complete freedom of action. Moreover, we (the Sharif's family) will consider ourselves free in word and deed from the bonds of ⟨ our previous declaration which we made through Ali Effendi [the messenger]

SOURCE: Parliamentary Papers, Command No. 5957, House of Commons Sessional Papers, 1939, pp. 3–4.

[McMahon responded on August 30, with a letter expressing hope for "harmony" between Great Britain and the Arab people but also that it would be "premature" to discuss the boundaries of a potential Arab state. Sharif Hussein replied on September 9 with a letter expressing disappointment with what he called McMahon's reluctance to discuss borders and repeating his assertion that the Arab people were waiting for a positive sign from Great Britain.]

DOCUMENT

Letter from McMahon to Hussein

OCTOBER 24, 1915

I have received your letter of the 29th Shawal, 1333 [September 9, 1915], with much pleasure and your expressions of friendliness and sincerity have given me the greatest satisfaction.

I regret that you should have received from my last letter [dated August 30, 1915] the impression that I regarded the question of limits and boundaries with coldness and hesitation; such was not the case, but it appeared to me that the time had not yet come when that question could be discussed in a conclusive manner.

I have realised, however, from your last letter [dated September 9, 1915] that you regard this question as one of vital and urgent importance. I have, therefore, lost no time in informing the Government of Great Britain of the contents of your letter, and it is with great pleasure that I communicate to you on their behalf the following statement, which I am confident you will receive with satisfaction.

The two districts of Mersina and Alexandretta and portions of Syria lying to the west of the districts of Damascus, Homs, Hama, and Aleppo cannot be said to be purely Arab, and should be excluded from the limits demanded.

With the above modification, and without prejudice to our existing treaties with Arab chiefs, we accept those limits.

As for those regions lying within those frontiers wherein Great Britain is free to act without detriment to the interests of her ally, France, I am empowered in the name of the Government of Great Britain to give the following assurances and make the following assurances and make the following reply to your letter:

(1) Subject to the above modifications, Great Britain is prepared to recognize and support the independence of the Arabs in all the regions within the limits demanded by the Sherif [Sharif] of Mecca.

(2) Great Britain will guarantee the Holy Places against all external aggression and will recognize their inviolability.

(3) When the situation admits, Great Britain will give to the Arabs her advice and will assist them to establish what may appear to be the most suitable forms of government in those various territories.

(4) On the other hand, it is understood that the Arabs have decided to seek the advice and guidance of Great Britain only, and that such European advisers and officials as may be required for the formation of a sound form of administration will be British.

(5) With regard to the *vilayets* [districts] of Bagdad [Baghdad] and Basra, the Arabs will recognize that the established position and interests of Great Britain necessitate special administrative arrangements in order to secure these territories from foreign aggression to promote the welfare of the local populations and to safeguard our mutual economic interests.

I am convinced that this declaration will assure you beyond all possible doubt of the sympathy of Great Britain towards the aspirations of her friends the Arabs and will result in a firm and lasting alliance, the immediate results of which will be the expulsion of the Turks from the Arab countries and the freeing of the Arab peoples from the Turkish yoke, which for so many years has pressed heavily upon them.

I have confined myself in this letter to the more vital and important questions, and if there are any other matters dealt with in your letters which I have omitted to mention, we may discuss them at some convenient date in the future.

It was with very great relief and satisfaction that I heard of the safe arrival of the Holy Carpet [a decorative covering for the sacred Kabah in Mecca] and the accompanying offerings which, thanks to the clearness of your directions and the excellence of your arrangements, were landed without trouble or mishap in spite of the dangers and difficulties occasioned by the present sad war. May God soon bring a lasting peace and freedom of all peoples!

I am sending this letter by the hand of your trusted and excellent messenger, Sheikh Mohammed ibn Arif ibn Uraifan, and he will inform you of the various matters of interest, but of less vital importance, which I have not mentioned in this letter.

SOURCE: Parliamentary Papers, Command No. 5957, House of Commons Sessional Papers, 1939, pp. 7–9.

Post–World War I Division

While the Hussein-McMahon correspondence took place, Britain and France in November 1915 began negotiating a division of the Middle East once World War I ended. François Georges Picot represented France, and starting in December 1915, Mark Sykes, an official of the British War Office who had come to view the Middle East as central to the war effort, acted as the chief British negotiator. In January 1916, they reached what came to be known as the Sykes-Picot Agreement. It was then formally laid out in an exchange of letters among British, French, and Russian diplomats in April and May 1916. The core of the agreement called for the Arabic-speaking areas of the Ottoman Empire to be divided into five zones as illustrated in a map incorporated into the agreement:

- a section of southeastern Asia Minor (or Anatolia, present-day Turkey) and most of the coastline of the eastern Mediterranean Sea south of Asia Minor (the present-day Syrian coast and Lebanon), to be under direct French control;
- the interior regions of present-day Syria and much of northern Iraq (including the city of Mosul), to be an independent Arab state or confederation under indirect French control;
- Palestine (present-day Israel, the West Bank of the Jordan River, and the Gaza Strip), to be under an undefined international administration, but with Britain controlling the ports of Acre (Akka) and Haifa;
- most of present-day Jordan, western Iraq, inland portions of Kuwait, and eastern Saudi Arabia, to be an independent Arab state or confederation under indirect British control; and
- the southern half of Iraq (including Baghdad and Basra), along with the rest of Kuwait, to be under direct British control.

Other provisions protected each power's commercial interests in the Middle East. For example, British goods could be shipped duty-free to and from the port of Alexandretta (present-day Iskenderun on the Turkish coast), and the same held for French goods passing through the port of Haifa.

In effect, the agreement allowed Britain and France to control the parts of the Middle East that each country wanted to control for reasons of its own. Britain sought to protect its interests in the Suez Canal and the principal land route between Europe and British-held India, while France wanted to assert its longstanding trade and other interests in Lebanon and coastal Syria.

The Sykes-Picot Agreement was kept secret at the time, but became public knowledge nearly two years later, after the new Bolshevik leaders in Russia discovered a copy in foreign ministry files and decided to renounce it, along with other wartime pledges of the czarist regime. The agreement, once revealed, angered key constituencies affected by it: Sharif Hussein of Mecca and other Arab leaders believed the agreement contravened the British promise of an "independent" Arab state; some Zionist leaders believed the agreement would hamper their plans for a Jewish homeland in Palestine; Italy wanted to assert its territorial interests in the Middle East, notably concerning the southwestern coast of Asia Minor; and the United States generally opposed all forms of colonial expansionism.

Many British officials, including Sykes, later came to regret the agreement for various reasons, not the least of which was a desire to thwart French ambitions in the Middle East. A year and a half after reaching the agreement, Britain issued the Balfour Declaration favoring a Jewish "national home" in Palestine, effectively repudiating the part of the Sykes-Picot Agreement placing Palestine under international control (Balfour Declaration, p. 24).

The Sykes-Picot Agreement ultimately established the parameters for the postwar division of the former lands of the Ottoman Empire outside Turkey: France gained direct control of Lebanon and indirect control of the new Syrian state; Britain established the new states of Iraq and Jordan under its sponsorship and controlled Palestine through a League of Nations mandate; and other powers that had territorial designs on the Middle East, notably Italy and pre-revolutionary Russia, ultimately were excluded.

Following is the text of a letter dated May 16, 1916, from British foreign secretary Sir Edward Grey to the French ambassador to London, Paul Cambon, incorporating the Sykes-Picot Agreement for the division of Arabic lands of the Ottoman Empire following World War I. The agreement also had the endorsement of Russian foreign minister Sergei Sazanov, representing the third major Entente ally in the war. It is therefore sometimes referred to as the Sykes-Picot-Sazanov Agreement.

DOCUMENT

Sykes-Picot Agreement

MAY 16, 1916

Letter from Grey to Cambon

I have the honor to acknowledge the receipt of your Excellency's note of the 9th instant, stating that the French Government accept the limits of a future Arab State, or Confederation of States, and of those parts of Syria where French interests predominate, together with certain conditions attached thereto, such as they result from recent discussions in London and Petrograd on the subject.

I have the honor to inform your Excellency in reply that the acceptance of the whole project, as it now stands, will involve the abdication of considerable British interests, but, since His Majesty's Government recognize the advantage to the general cause of the Allies entailed in producing a more favorable internal political situation in Turkey, they are ready to accept the arrangement now arrived at, provided that the co-operation of the Arabs is secured, and that the Arabs fulfill the conditions and obtain the towns of Homs, Hama, Damascus, and Aleppo.

It is accordingly understood between the French and British Governments—

1. That France and Great Britain are prepared to recognize and protect an independent Arab State or a Confederation of Arab States in the areas (A) and (B) marked on the annexed map, under the suzerainty of an Arab chief. That in area (A) France, and in area (B) Great Britain, shall have priority of right of enterprise and local loans. That in area (A) France, and in area (B) Great Britain, shall alone supply advisers or foreign functionaries at the request of the Arab State or Confederation of Arab States.

2. That in the blue area France, and in the red area Great Britain, shall be allowed to establish such direct or indirect administration or control as they desire and as they may think fit to arrange with the Arab State or Confederation of Arab States.

3. That in the brown area there shall be established an international administration, the form of which is to be decided upon after consultation with Russia, and subsequently in consultation with the other Allies, and the representatives of the Sharif of Mecca.

4. That Great Britain be accorded (1) the ports of Haifa and Acre, (2) guarantee of a given supply of water from the Tigris and Euphrates in area (A) for area (B). His Majesty's Government, on their part, undertake that they will at no time enter into negotiations for the cession of Cyprus to any third Power without the previous consent of the French Government.

5. That Alexandretta shall be a free port as regards the trade of the British Empire, and that there shall be no discrimination in port charges or facilities as regards British shipping and British goods; that there shall be freedom of transit for British goods through Alexandretta and by railway through the blue area, whether those goods are intended for or originate in the red area, or (B) area, or area (A); and there shall be no discrimination, direct or indirect against British goods on any railway or against British goods or ships at any port serving the areas mentioned.

That Haifa shall be a free port as regards the trade of France, her dominions and protectorates, and there shall be no discrimination in port charges or facilities as regards French shipping and French goods. There shall be freedom of transit for French goods through Haifa and by the British railway through the brown area, whether those goods are intended for or originate in the blue area, area (A), or area (B), and there shall be no discrimination, direct or indirect, against French goods on any railway, or against French goods or ships at any port serving the areas mentioned.

6. That in area (A) the Baghdad Railway shall not be extended southwards beyond Mosul, and in area (B) northwards beyond Samarra, until a railway connecting Baghdad with Aleppo via the Euphrates Valley has been completed, and then only with the concurrence of the two Governments.

7. That Great Britain has the right to build, administer, and be sole owner of a railway connecting Haifa with area (B), and shall have a perpetual right to transport troops along such a line at all times.

It is to be understood by both Governments that this railway is to facilitate the connection of Baghdad with Haifa by rail, and it is further understood that, if the engineering difficulties and expense entailed by keeping this connecting line in the brown area only make the project unfeasible, that the French Government shall be prepared to consider that the line in question may also traverse the polygon Banias-Keis Marib-Salkhab Tell Otsda-Mesmie before reaching area (B).

8. For a period of twenty years the existing Turkish customs tariff shall remain in force throughout the whole of the blue and red areas, as well as in areas (A) and (B), and no increase in the rates of duty or conversion from ad valorem to specific rates shall be made except by agreement between the two Powers.

There shall be no interior customs barriers between any of the above-mentioned areas. The customs duties leviable on goods destined for the interior shall be collected at the port of entry and handed over to the administration of the area of destination.

9. It shall be agreed that the French Government will at no time enter into any negotiations for the cession of their rights and will not cede such rights in the blue area to any third Power, except the Arab State or Confederation of Arab States without the previous agreement of His Majesty's Government, who, on their part, will give a similar undertaking to the French Government regarding the red area.

10. The British and French Governments, as the protectors of the Arab State, shall agree that they will not themselves acquire and will not consent to a third Power acquiring territorial possessions in the Arabian peninsula, nor consent to a third Power installing a naval base either on the east coast, or on the islands, of the Red Sea. This, however, shall not prevent such adjustment of the Aden frontier as may be necessary in consequence of recent Turkish aggression.

11. The negotiations with the Arabs as to the boundaries of the Arab State or Confederation of Arab States shall be continued through the same channel as heretofore on behalf of the two Powers.

12. It is agreed that measures to control the importation of arms into the Arab territories will be considered by the two Governments.

I have further the honor to state that, in order to make the agreement complete, His Majesty's Government are proposing to the Russian Government to exchange notes analogous to those exchanged by the latter and your Excellency's Government on the 26th April last. Copies of these notes will be communicated to your Excellency as soon as exchanged.

I would also venture to remind your Excellency that the conclusion of the present agreement raises, for practical consideration, the question of the claims of Italy to a share in any partition or rearrangement of Turkey in Asia, as formulated in article 9 of the agreement of the 26th April, 1915, between Italy and the Allies.

His Majesty's Government further consider that the Japanese Government should be informed of the arrangement now concluded.

SOURCE: Library of Congress, Foreign Affairs Division, *A Select Chronology and Background Documents Relating to the Middle East: [Prepared for the] Committee on Foreign Relations, United States Senate,* 2nd rev. ed. (Washington, D.C.: Government Printing Office, 1975), 132–135.

Arab-Jewish Dialogue

DOCUMENT IN CONTEXT

One of the most intriguing, if ultimately fruitless, documents of the World War I era is an agreement signed by World Zionist Organization president Chaim Weizmann and Amir Faisal ibn Hussein, a leader of the British-inspired "Arab revolt" against the Ottoman Empire.

At the instigation of the British, Weizmann traveled to Faisal's desert camp near Aqaba, on the Gulf of Aqaba, in June 1918. The two men exchanged pleasantries and appeared to agree on the need for cooperation between Arabs and Jews, including on the question of Jewish immigration to Palestine. They met again in January 1919 in Paris, at the international conference to draft the terms of peace formally ending World War I. Weizmann was in Paris to press negotiators to recognize Zionist claims to Palestine, while Faisal sought recognition of his claim, on behalf of the Arabs, to Syria.

In Paris, the two men signed a document with many of the features of a formal agreement between two governments. Now known alternately as the Faisal-Weizmann Agreement or the Weizmann-Faisal Agreement, the document committed each side to recognizing some of the demands of the other. For his part, Faisal agreed to recognize the Balfour Declaration and to accept increased Jewish immigration to Palestine. In return, Weizmann committed the World Zionist Organization to sending a commission of experts to Palestine to examine prospects for economic development, apparently including for its Arab residents. On its face, the agreement did not commit Faisal to supporting any form of a Jewish political entity in Palestine, although numerous Zionist commentators over the years have insisted that it did.

Faisal added a stipulation stating that his concurrence depended on the Arabs obtaining "independence," which he demanded in a separate memorandum to Britain dated January 4, 1919. If the Arabs were not granted independence, Faisal asserted, his agreement with Weizmann would be deemed "void and of no account or validity. . . ." Years later, Faisal insisted that he had no recollection of signing the agreement with Weizmann.

The exact date of this agreement has been the subject of some dispute. Most accounts contend that it was signed on January 3, 1919, but Faisal's stipulation referred to his January 4 memorandum, leading some observers to argue that the entire agreement, or at least Faisal's stipulation, dates to January 4 or later. The agreement was not made public at the time, but versions were subsequently published.

Fourteen months later, in March 1920, Faisal was crowned king of Syria, a territory that he and other Arab leaders considered to include Palestine. Faisal's rule from Damascus lasted only four months. On July 24, 1920, a French army unit took control of Damascus, and Faisal fled into exile. In August 1921, the British government installed Faisal as king of the new country of Iraq.

In terms of historical significance, the Weizmann-Faisal Agreement stands primarily as a curiosity, and for some observers, is one of the great "what ifs" in Middle Eastern history. Whether the agreement, if adhered to by Arabs and Jews, could have led to any degree of reconciliation over Palestine is a matter of conjecture. In any event, nothing similar was achieved for nearly six decades, until 1978, when President Jimmy Carter gathered Egyptian and Israeli leaders at Camp David and pressed them into accepting the first real peace agreement between an Arab state and Israel (Camp David Peace Process, p. 118).

Following is the text of the Weizmann-Faisal Agreement, signed in January 1919 by Amir Faisal ibn Hussein, who later became the king of Iraq, and Chaim Weizmann, president of the World Zionist Organization.

DOCUMENT

The Weizmann-Faisal Agreement

JANUARY 1919

His Royal Highness the Emir Faisal, representing and acting on behalf of the Arab Kingdom of Hedjaz, and Dr. Chaim Weizmann, representing and acting on behalf of the Zionist Organization, mindful of the racial kinship and ancient bonds existing between the Arabs and the Jewish people, and realizing that the surest means of working out the consummation of their natural aspirations is through the closest possible collaboration in the development of the Arab State and Palestine, and being desirous further of confirming the good understanding which exists between them, have agreed upon the following:

Article I

The Arab State and Palestine in all their relations and undertakings shall be controlled by the most cordial goodwill and understanding, and to this end Arab and Jewish duly accredited agents shall be established and maintained in the respective territories.

Article II

Immediately following the completion of the deliberations of the Peace Conference, the definite boundaries between the Arab State and Palestine shall be determined by a Commission to be agreed upon by the parties hereto.

Article III

In the establishment of the Constitution and Administration of Palestine, all such measures shall be adopted as will afford the fullest guarantees for carrying into effect the British Government's Declaration of the 2nd of November, 1917.

Article IV

All necessary measures shall be taken to encourage and stimulate immigration of Jews into Palestine on a large scale, and as quickly as possible to settle Jewish immigrants upon the land through closer settlement and intensive cultivation of the soil. In taking such measures the Arab peasant and tenant farmers shall be protected in their rights and shall be assisted in forwarding their economic development.

Article V

No regulation or law shall be made prohibiting or interfering in any way with the free exercise of religion; and further, the free exercise and enjoyment of religious profession and worship, without discrimination or preference, shall forever be allowed. No religious test shall ever be required for the exercise of civil or political rights.

Article VI

The Mohammedan [Muslim] Holy Places shall be under Mohammedan control.

Article VII

The Zionist Organization proposes to send to Palestine a Commission of experts to make a survey of the economic possibilities of the country, and to report upon the best means for its development. The Zionist Organization will place the aforementioned Commission at the disposal of the Arab State for the purpose of a survey of the economic possibilities of the Arab State and to report upon the best means for its development. The Zionist Organization will use its best efforts to assist the Arab State in providing the means for developing the natural resources and economic possibilities thereof.

Article VIII

The parties hereto agree to act in complete accord and harmony on all matters embraced herein before the Peace Congress.

Article IX

Any matters of dispute which may arise between the contracting parties shall be referred to the British Government for arbitration.

Given under our hand at London, England, the third day of January, one thousand nine hundred and nineteen.

Chaim Weizmann
Faisal Ibn-Hussein

Reservation by the Emir Faisal

Provided the Arabs obtain their independence as demanded in my Memorandum dated the 4th of January, 1919, to the Foreign Office of the Government of Great Britain, I shall concur in the above articles. But if the slightest modification or departure were to be made I shall not be bound by a single word of the present Agreement which shall be deemed void and of no account or validity, and I shall not be answerable in any way whatsoever.

SOURCE: United Nations Information System on the Question of Palestine, http://domino.un.org/unispal.nsf/ 9a798adbf322aff38525617b006d88d7/5bff833964edb9bf85256ced00673d1f!OpenDocument.

General Syrian Congress and the King-Crane Commission

DOCUMENT IN CONTEXT

Deliberations at the Paris peace conference early in 1919 made clear the fundamentally different views of Britain and France, the two main European Allies of World War I, and the United States on how to approach the former lands of the soon-to-be defunct Ottoman Empire. The British and French were determined to carry through with their wartime plans to divide much of the Middle East between themselves, creating virtual colonies. President Woodrow Wilson earnestly hoped to promote his dream of "self-determination" for all the world's nationalities, which would have meant the end of all forms of European colonialism.

British ambivalence about giving France responsibility for Syria complicated the deal. Prime Minister David Lloyd George appeared, at times, to want Syria for Britain. Wilson suggested, to the apparent annoyance of the Europeans, that the Arabs of Syria should be asked for their views on the matter. Wilson then appointed Henry C. King, the president of Oberlin College in Ohio, and Charles R. Crane, a Chicago businessman, as a "commission" to look into the matter. In June 1919, the two men traveled to Damascus, where Amir Faisal (temporarily) held power. With British support, his government arranged for the convocation of the General Syrian Congress, consisting of notables from Lebanon, Palestine, and Syria, to present a unified front to the U.S. delegation. The congress was far from representative of the broad spectrum of opinion in Greater Syria and was intended to bolster Faisal's claim as the region's new ruler.

Meeting on July 2, the congress adopted a declaration calling for Syria (including Lebanon and Palestine) to be a fully independent "democratic civil constitutional monarchy." If the participants at the Paris peace conference prohibited such an outcome, the declaration said, the United States should be entrusted with providing the "technical and economic assistance" to guide Syria to independence. The declaration rejected French rule of Syria "under any circumstances" and opposed Zionist plans to establish a Jewish home in Palestine.

King and Crane included this declaration in their report to Wilson on August 29, 1919, and they cited it as supporting their own proposal for the United States, rather than France, to supervise Syria for a limited period of time. The commissioners also opposed what they called the "extreme Zionist program" for a Jewish national home in Palestine. According to most accounts, Wilson never saw the King-Crane Commission report, which was filed away and played no role in subsequent peace conference negotiations. The full report was first made public in 1922 by *Editor and Publisher*, a U.S. newspaper industry trade magazine. Along with the Faisal-Weizmann Agreement earlier in 1919, the King-Crane Commission report and the declaration of the General Syrian Congress stand as historical curiosities demonstrating the views of some of those who sought to influence the course of events in the Middle East. The

Syrian declaration also represents one of the first modern attempts by Arab leaders to adopt a united position on the great issues affecting the region, including Zionism.

Following is the text of the declaration of the Syrian General Congress adopted on July 2, 1919.

DOCUMENT

Statement by the General Syrian Congress

JULY 2, 1919

We, the undersigned, members of the General Syrian Congress, meeting in Damascus on Wednesday, July 2, 1919, made up of representatives from the three Zones, viz., the Southern, Eastern, and Western, provided with credentials and authorizations by the inhabitants of our various districts, Moslems, Christians, and Jews, have agreed upon the following statement of the desires of the people of the country who have elected us to present them to the American Section of the International Commission; the fifth article was passed by a very large majority; all the other articles were accepted unanimously.

1. We ask [for] absolutely complete political independence for Syria within these boundaries. The Taurus [Mountain] System on the North; Rafeh [Rafah] and a line running from Al-Juf to the south of the Syrian and the Mejazian line to Akaba [Aqaba] on the south; the Euphrates and Khabur Rivers and a line extending east of Abu Kamal to the east of Al-Juf on the east; and the Mediterranean on the west.

2. We ask that the Government of this Syrian country should be a democratic civil constitutional Monarchy on broad decentralization principles, safeguarding the rights of minorities, and that the King be the Emir Feisal [Faisal] who carried on a glorious struggle in the cause of our liberation and merited our full confidence and entire reliance.

3. Considering the fact that the Arabs inhabiting the Syrian area are not naturally less gifted than other more advanced races and that; they are by no means less developed than the Bulgarians, Serbians, Greeks, and Roumanians at the beginning of their independence, we protest against Article 22 of the Covenant of the League of Nations, placing us among the nations in their middle stage of development which stand in need of a mandatory power.

4. In the event of the rejection by the Peace Conference of this just protest for certain considerations that we may not understand, we, relying on the declarations of President Wilson that his object in waging war was to put an end to the ambition of conquest and colonization, can only regard the mandate mentioned in the Covenant of the League of Nations as equivalent to the rendering of economical and technical assistance that does not prejudice our complete independence. And desiring that our country should not fall a prey to colonization and believing that the American Nation

is farthest from any thought of colonization and has no political ambition in our country, we will seek the technical and economic assistance from the United States of America, provided that such assistance does not exceed twenty years.

5. In the event of America not finding herself in a position to accept our desire for assistance we will seek this assistance from Great Britain, also provided that such assistance does not infringe the complete independence and unity of our country, and that the duration of such assistance does not exceed that mentioned in the previous article.

6. We do not acknowledge any right claimed by the French Government in any part whatever of our Syrian country and refuse that she should assist us or have a hand in our country under any circumstances and in any place.

7. We oppose the pretensions of the Zionists to create a Jewish commonwealth in the southern part of Syria, known as Palestine, and oppose Zionist migration to any part of our country; for we do not acknowledge their title, but consider them a grave peril to our people from the national, economical, and political points of view. Our Jewish compatriots shall enjoy our common rights and assume the common responsibilities.

8. We ask that there should be no separation of the southern part of Syria, known as Palestine, nor of the littoral western zone which includes Lebanon, from the Syrian country. We desire that the unity of the country should be guaranteed against partition under whatever circumstances.

9. We ask complete independence for emancipated Mesopotamia and that there should be no economical barriers between the two countries.

10. The fundamental principles laid down by President Wilson in condemnation of secret treaties impel us to protest most emphatically against any treaty that stipulates the partition of our Syrian country and against any private engagement aiming at the establishment of Zionism in the southern part of Syria, therefore we ask the complete annulment of these conventions and agreements.

The noble principles enunciated by President Wilson strengthen our confidence that our desires emanating from the depths of our hearts, shall be the decisive factor in determining our future; and that President Wilson and the free American people will be supporters for the realization of our hopes, thereby proving their sincerity and noble sympathy with the aspiration of the weaker nations in general and our Arab people in particular.

We also have the fullest confidence that the Peace Conference will realize that we would not have risen against the Turks, with whom we had participated in all civil, political, and representative privileges, but for their violation of our national rights, and so will grant us our desires in full in order that our political rights may not be less after the war than they were before, since we have shed so much blood in the cause of our liberty and independence.

We request to be allowed to send a delegation to represent us at the Peace Conference to defend our rights and secure the realization of our aspirations.

SOURCE: "Paris Peace Conference, 1919," *Foreign Relations of the United States* (Washington, D.C.: Government Printing Office, 1947), 12:780–781.

A Jewish National Home

DOCUMENT IN CONTEXT

Few twentieth-century documents concerning the Middle East have had consequences as momentous as a brief statement issued in a 1917 letter by the British government. Universally referred to as the Balfour Declaration, it put Britain on record as favoring a "national home for the Jewish people" in Palestine.

Much of the credit for the Balfour Declaration goes to Chaim Weizmann, a Russian-born Jew who settled in Britain in 1904 and became one of the country's most active and influential advocates of the Zionist movement, which aspired to resettle Jews in Palestine. President of the World Zionist Organization and a chemist who developed a process used in the manufacture of munitions, Weizmann had a remarkable ability to develop friendships with people in high places, among them Lord Arthur James Balfour, the British foreign secretary in the last years of World War I. By 1917 Weizmann, along with other Zionist leaders in Britain, had convinced Balfour, Prime Minister David Lloyd George, and other senior officials that Jewish support could be vital to the Entente Allies in the war, which was then stalemated. Hoping to gain Jewish backing, the government agreed to endorse the Zionist cause.

The government's decision proved to be controversial, even among some Jewish leaders. Not all Jews were Zionists, and some Jewish leaders feared that the designation of Palestine as *the* national home for the Jews would lead to pressure on Jews in Europe to leave their home states and move there. Edwin Montagu, the sole Jew in the British cabinet, stood among those who resisted Zionism for this reason. Other British officials opposed endorsing it for different reasons, some arguing, for example, that Britain siding with the Jews would cause trouble in what was certain to become a conflict with the Arabs already living in Palestine.

After considerable debate over wording, the war cabinet on October 31, 1917, approved a declaration of support for a Jewish homeland in Palestine. It was then incorporated into a letter dated November 2, signed by Balfour, and addressed to Lionel Walter Lord Rothschild, the president of the British Zionist Federation. The text of Balfour's letter was not made public until November 7, by coincidence the same day that Vladimir Lenin and his fellow Bolsheviks seized power in Russia.

The British government's internal debates had resulted in a carefully worded declaration that took into account some of the concerns expressed by Montagu and others. The declaration referred to a Jewish "national home" in Palestine, reflecting terminology the Zionists preferred with the intent of allaying fears about a Jewish state. The declaration also said the Jewish national home would be "in" Palestine, a formulation suggesting that the Jews might not occupy all of that ill-defined territory. In addition, the declaration made vague statements about protecting the rights of Arabs in Palestine and of Jews in other countries.

Before issuing the declaration, the British government sought to secure an endorsement from the United States, which had entered the war six months earlier. According to most accounts, the administration of President Woodrow Wilson initially opposed Britain's plans to issue the declaration but relented after an appeal to the White House by Louis Brandeis, one of the country's most prominent Jewish leaders and an active Zionist whom Wilson had appointed to the Supreme Court in 1916.

Although the Balfour Declaration was never intended as an unconditional endorsement of Jewish aspirations in Palestine, Zionist leaders embraced it as the single most important step to date toward the advancement of their cause. Many Arab leaders were correspondingly angry, viewing the declaration as retreat from what they viewed as British pledges to support an Arab state that included Palestine.

The Balfour Declaration ironically had little impact in the one area that had been uppermost in the minds of some British leaders. Lloyd George and some of his colleagues had hoped that issuing the declaration would reassure Jews in Russia and encourage them to use their perceived influence to keep Russia in the war against Germany. In the event, Lenin's new communist government quickly withdrew Russia from the conflict. The longer-term impact of the Balfour Declaration was that it committed the British government to supporting Zionist claims on Palestine during postwar peace negotiations in Paris. When President Wilson publicly embraced the declaration in 1918, the United States became committed to that goal as well. The essence of the Balfour Declaration was incorporated into the 1922 League of Nations mandate that ratified British control of Palestine (League of Nations Mandate for Palestine, p. 27).

Subsequent British governments often appeared ambivalent in their commitment to Zionism, in part because of the inherent contradiction in the Balfour Declaration of encouraging Jews to move to a land already inhabited by others. Some of this ambivalence was reflected in the government's June 1922 White Paper, the next significant statement on the matter, issued by Winston S. Churchill, the colonial secretary. The White Paper sought to assure the Arabs of Palestine that "Jewish nationality" would not be imposed on them. Even so, the Balfour Declaration pointed the way toward a policy that led not only to a Jewish "national home" in Palestine but to the creation three decades later of the State of Israel.

Following is a copy of the Balfour Declaration, issued in a letter dated November 2, 1917, from British foreign secretary Lord Arthur James Balfour to Lionel Walter Lord Rothschild of the Zionist Federation.

DOCUMENT

Balfour Declaration

NOVEMBER 2, 1917

Dear Lord Rothschild,

I have much pleasure in conveying to you, on behalf of His Majesty's Government, the following declaration of sympathy with Jewish Zionist aspirations which has been submitted to, and approved by, the Cabinet.

"His Majesty's Government view with favor the establishment in Palestine of a national home for the Jewish people, and will use their best endeavors to facilitate the achievement of the object, it being clearly understood that nothing shall be done which may prejudice the civil and religious' rights of existing non-Jewish communities in Palestine, or the rights and political status enjoyed by Jews in any other country".

I should be grateful if you would bring this declaration to the knowledge of the Zionist Federation.

Yours sincerely,
(Signed) Arthur James Balfour

SOURCE: Library of Congress, Foreign Affairs Division, *A Select Chronology and Background Documents Relating to the Middle East: [Prepared for the] Committee on Foreign Relations, United States Senate*, 2nd rev. ed. (Washington, D.C.: Government Printing Office, 1975), 136.

Mandate for Palestine

DOCUMENT IN CONTEXT

Immediately after World War I, the division of the lands of the Ottoman Empire—which had collapsed in all but name—stood as one of the most difficult tasks facing the victorious Allies. In the Sykes-Picot Agreement of 1916, Britain and France had already settled on a basic formula for dividing the Arabic-speaking portions of the empire between them, and in the Balfour Declaration of 1917, Britain had advocated that Palestine become a "national home" for the Jews. It would take another three years of diplomacy and political maneuvering after the war before the European powers would gain official control of the lands of the Middle East (Sykes-Picot Agreement, p. 14; Balfour Declaration, p. 24).

Britain had placed Palestine under military rule following Gen. Edmund Allenby's capture of Jerusalem in December 1917. After a violent riot between Arabs and Jews in Jerusalem in April 1920, London installed a civil administration headed by Herbert Samuel, one of Britain's most senior Jewish politicians. The violence in Jerusalem coincided with (and may have been intended, in part, to influence) an international conference held in the Italian resort town of San Remo. One of several conferences held to settle the details of postwar peace agreements, the San Remo meeting dealt with the assigning of "mandates" to European powers for governing the remnants of the Ottoman Empire. The delegates essentially implemented the agreements that Britain and France already had reached between themselves: Britain would govern Palestine (including the territory east of the Jordan River that later became Transjordan) and Iraq (defined as the three Ottoman-era provinces of Baghdad, Basra, and Mosul), while France would govern Syria, including Lebanon. In August 1920, the terms of the San Remo conference were incorporated into the broader Treaty of Sèvres, which imposed harsh terms on the Ottoman Empire, including international control of Istanbul and the strategic Bosporus and Dardanelles straits. (The aspects of that treaty dealing with Turkey were replaced by the more conciliatory Treaty of Lausanne, signed in July 1923. See Turkish National Pact, p. 634.)

In the meantime, Britain and France each took actions that would affect their presumed mandates. In July 1920, France ousted Faisal Ibn Hussein, an ally of Britain who had proclaimed himself king of Syria, ending the first-ever attempt to form an independent Arab state. (Two years later, Britain would install Faisal as the first king of Iraq). Britain in 1921 created Transjordan by separating the large expanse of territory east of the Jordan River from the rest of Palestine. The British transformed the East Bank area, at the time largely uninhabited desert, into a protectorate under the leadership of Faisal's older brother Abdallah, who established the Hashimite monarchy that remains in power to this day. (The name of the country was changed to Jordan in 1949.)

The League of Nations formally approved the British and French mandates on July 24, 1922. Part of the delay after San Remo stemmed from the need for consultations with the United States, which had refused to join the League but nevertheless was an increasingly important power on the world stage. The mandates gave the two European powers complete administrative responsibility, along with the task of preparing the local populations to eventually "stand by themselves" as independent countries. Britain and France took seriously their governance of these mandates but generally ignored their responsibilities to create conditions for self-government.

In historical terms, the mandate for Palestine is important because of its incorporation of the language of the Balfour Declaration, thus affixing an international seal to what had been a unilateral British policy favoring a Jewish "national home" on that territory. The mandate also formalized the separation of Transjordan from Palestine (thus eliminating Zionist dreams of controlling the area east of the Jordan River), encouraged the immigration of Jews into Palestine, and decreed that Hebrew join English and Arabic as the official languages of Palestine. The mandate made no reference to the Arabs of Palestine directly, referring to them only as the "existing non-Jewish communities."

Before the official approval of the mandate for Palestine, Britain, on July 1, 1922, had published a White Paper, a document articulating its vision of how the mandate would be administered. Among its key features, the White Paper sought to assure the Arab population that Britain would not impose "a Jewish nationality" upon them and that Jewish immigration would not be allowed to exceed the "economic capacity of the country." Zionist leaders accepted the document, although some of them viewed it as a retreat from the promise of the Balfour Declaration. Arab leaders in Palestine rejected the White Paper, arguing that it would strip the Arab population of its rights.

Between 1922 and the establishment of the State of Israel in 1948, Britain governed Palestine with an increasingly uneasy hand, troubled by the inherent contradiction between the legal and moral promises that it had made to Arabs and Jews. Rounds of violence made it clear that important elements of the two communities were not prepared to live in peace with one another. The British government's frequently clumsy efforts at controlling or containing the situation merely heightened tensions. After the end of World War II, London, searching for a route out of Palestine, turned for help to the newly established United Nations (Official Summary of the Palestine Royal Commission, p. 45; UN General Assembly Resolution 181, p. 59).

Following is the text of the mandate, approved on July 24, 1922, by the Council of the League of Nations, giving Great Britain the power to govern the territory of Palestine. The mandate officially began on September 29, 1923, and remained in effect until May 14, 1948, when Britain withdrew from Palestine and Zionist leaders proclaimed the establishment of Israel.

DOCUMENT

League of Nations Mandate for Palestine

JULY 24, 1922

The Council of the League of Nations:

Whereas the Principal Allied Powers have agreed, for the purpose of giving effect to the provisions of Article 22 of the Covenant of the League of Nations, to entrust to a Mandatory selected by the said Powers the administration of the territory of Palestine, which formerly belonged to the Turkish Empire, within such boundaries as may be fixed by them; and

Whereas the Principal Allied Powers have also agreed that the Mandatory should be responsible for putting into effect the declaration originally made on November 2nd, 1917, by the Government of His Britannic Majesty, and adopted by the said Powers, in favor of the establishment in Palestine of a national home for the Jewish people, it being clearly understood that nothing should be done which might prejudice the civil and religious rights of existing non-Jewish communities in Palestine, or the rights and political status enjoyed by Jews in any other country; and

Whereas recognition has thereby been given to the historical connection of the Jewish people with Palestine and to the grounds for reconstituting their national home in that country; and

Whereas the Principal Allied Powers have selected His Britannic Majesty as the Mandatory for Palestine; and

Whereas the mandate in respect of Palestine has been formulated in the following terms and submitted to the Council of the League for approval; and

Whereas His Britannic Majesty has accepted the mandate in respect of Palestine and undertaken to exercise it on behalf of the League of Nations in conformity with the following provisions; and

Whereas by the aforementioned Article 22 (paragraph 8), it is provided that the degree of authority, control or administration to be exercised by the Mandatory, not having been previously agreed upon by the Members of the League, shall be explicitly defined by the Council of the League of Nations;

Confirming the said mandate, defines its terms as follows:

Article 1

The Mandatory shall have full powers of legislation and of administration, save as they may be limited by the terms of this mandate.

Article 2

The Mandatory shall be responsible for placing the country under such political, administrative and economic conditions as will secure the establishment of the Jewish national home, as laid down in the preamble, and the development of self-governing institutions, and also for safeguarding the civil and religious rights of all the inhabitants of Palestine, irrespective of race and religion.

Article 3

The Mandatory shall, so far as circumstances permit, encourage local autonomy.

Article 4

An appropriate Jewish agency shall be recognized as a public body for the purpose of advising and co-operating with the Administration of Palestine in such economic, social and other matters as may affect the establishment of the Jewish national home and the interests of the Jewish population in Palestine, and, subject always to the control of the Administration, to assist and take part in the development of the country.

The Zionist Organization, so long as its organization and constitution are in the opinion of the Mandatory appropriate, shall be recognized as such agency. It shall take steps in consultation with His Britannic Majesty's Government to secure the co-operation of all Jews who are willing to assist in the establishment of the Jewish national home.

Article 5

The Mandatory shall be responsible for seeing that no Palestine territory shall be ceded or leased to, or in any way placed under the control of, the Government of any foreign Power.

Article 6

The Administration of Palestine, while ensuring that the rights and position of other sections of the population are not prejudiced, shall facilitate Jewish immigration under suitable conditions and shall encourage, in co-operation with the Jewish agency referred to in Article 4, close settlement by Jews on the land, including State lands and waste lands not required for public purposes.

Article 7

The Administration of Palestine shall be responsible for enacting a nationality law. There shall be included in this law provisions framed so as to facilitate the acquisition of Palestinian citizenship by Jews who take up their permanent residence in Palestine.

Article 8

The privileges and immunities of foreigners, including the benefits of consular jurisdiction and protection as formerly enjoyed by Capitulation or usage in the Ottoman Empire, shall not be applicable in Palestine.

Unless the Powers whose nationals enjoyed the afore-mentioned privileges and immunities on August 1st, 1914, shall have previously renounced the right to their re-establishment, or shall have agreed to their non-application for a specified period, these privileges and immunities shall, at the expiration of the mandate, be immediately reestablished in their entirety or with such modifications as may have been agreed upon between the Powers concerned.

Article 9

The Mandatory shall be responsible for seeing that the judicial system established in Palestine shall assure to foreigners, as well as to natives, a complete guarantee of their rights.

Respect for the personal status of the various peoples and communities and for their religious interests shall be fully guaranteed. In particular, the control and administration of Wakfs shall be exercised in accordance with religious law and the dispositions of the founders.

Article 10

Pending the making of special extradition agreements relating to Palestine, the extradition treaties in force between the Mandatory and other foreign Powers shall apply to Palestine.

Article 11

The Administration of Palestine shall take all necessary measures to safeguard the interests of the community in connection with the development of the country, and, subject to any international obligations accepted by the Mandatory, shall have full power to provide for public ownership or control of any of the natural resources of the country or of the public works, services and utilities established or to be established therein. It shall introduce a land system appropriate to the needs of the country, having regard, among other things, to the desirability of promoting the close settlement and intensive cultivation of the land.

The Administration may arrange with the Jewish agency mentioned in Article 4 to construct or operate, upon fair and equitable terms, any public works, services and utilities, and to develop any of the natural resources of the country, in so far as these matters are not directly undertaken by the Administration. Any such arrangements shall provide that no profits distributed by such agency, directly or indirectly, shall exceed a reasonable rate of interest on the capital, and any further profits shall be utilized by it for the benefit of the country in a manner approved by the Administration.

Article 12

The Mandatory shall be entrusted with the control of the foreign relations of Palestine and the right to issue exequaturs to consuls appointed by foreign Powers. He shall also be entitled to afford diplomatic and consular protection to citizens of Palestine when outside its territorial limit.

Article 13

All responsibility in connection with the Holy Places and religious buildings or sites in Palestine, including that of preserving existing rights and of securing free access to the Holy Places, religious buildings and sites and the free exercise of worship, while ensuring the requirements of public order and decorum, is assumed by the Mandatory, who shall be responsible solely to the League of Nations in all matters connected herewith, provided that nothing in this article shall prevent the Mandatory from entering into such arrangements as he may deem reasonable with the Administration for the purpose of carrying the provisions of this article into effect; and provided also that nothing in this mandate shall be construed as conferring upon the Mandatory authority to interfere with the fabric or the management of purely Moslem sacred shrines, the immunities of which are guaranteed.

Article 14

A special Commission shall be appointed by the Mandatory to study, define and determine the rights and claims in connection with the Holy Places and the rights and claims relating to the different religious communities in Palestine. The method of nomination, the composition and the functions of this Commission shall be submitted to the Council of the League for its approval, and the Commission shall not be appointed or enter upon its functions without the approval of the Council.

Article 15

The Mandatory shall see that complete freedom of conscience and the free exercise of all forms of worship, subject only to the maintenance of public order and morals, are ensured to all. No discrimination of any kind shall be made between the inhabitants of Palestine on the ground of race, religion or language. No person shall be excluded from Palestine on the sole ground of his religious belief.

The right of each community to maintain its own schools for the education of its own members in its own language, while conforming to such educational requirements of a general nature as the Administration may impose, shall not be denied or impaired.

Article 16

The Mandatory shall be responsible for exercising such supervision over religious or eleemosynary bodies of all faiths in Palestine as may be required for the maintenance of public order and good government. Subject to such supervision, no measures shall be taken in Palestine to obstruct or interfere with the enterprise of such bodies or to discriminate against any representative or member of them on the ground of his religion or nationality.

Article 17

The Administration of Palestine may organize on a voluntary basis the forces necessary for the preservation of peace and order, and also for the defense of the country, subject, however, to the supervision of the Mandatory, but shall not use them for purposes other than those above specified save with the consent of the Mandatory. Except for such purposes, no military, naval or air forces shall be raised or maintained by the Administration of Palestine.

Nothing in this article shall preclude the Administration of Palestine from contributing to the cost of the maintenance of the forces of the Mandatory in Palestine.

The Mandatory shall be entitled at all times to use the roads, railways and ports of Palestine for the movement of armed forces and the carriage of fuel and supplies.

Article 18

The Mandatory shall see that there is no discrimination in Palestine against the nationals of any State Member of the League of Nations (including companies incorporated under its laws) as compared with those of the Mandatory or of any foreign State in matters concerning taxation, commerce or navigation, the exercise of industries or professions, or in the treatment of merchant vessels or civil aircraft. Similarly, there shall be no discrimination in Palestine against goods originating in or destined for any of the said States, and there shall be freedom of transit under equitable conditions across the mandated area.

Subject as aforesaid and to the other provisions of this mandate, the Administration of Palestine may, on the advice of the Mandatory, impose such taxes and customs duties as it may consider necessary and take such steps as it may think best to promote the development of the natural resources of the country and to safeguard the interests of the population. It may also, on the advice of the Mandatory, conclude a special customs agreement with any State the territory of which in 1914 was wholly included in Asiatic Turkey or Arabia.

Article 19

The Mandatory shall adhere on behalf of the Administration of Palestine to any general international conventions already existing, or which may be concluded hereafter with the approval of the League of Nations, respecting the slave traffic, the traffic in arms and ammunition, or the traffic in drugs, or relating to commercial equality, freedom of transit and navigation, aerial navigation and postal, telegraphic and wireless communication or literary, artistic or industrial property.

Article 20

The Mandatory shall co-operate on behalf of the Administration of Palestine, so far as religious, social and other conditions may permit, in the execution of any common policy adopted by the League of Nations for preventing and combating disease, including diseases of plants and animals.

Article 21

The Mandatory shall secure the enactment within twelve months from this date, and shall ensure the execution of a Law of Antiquities based on the following rules. This law shall ensure equality of treatment in the matter of excavations and archaeological research to the nationals of all States Members of the League of Nations.

(1) "Antiquity" means any construction or any product of human activity earlier than the year 1700 A.D.

(2) The law for the protection of antiquities shall proceed by encouragement rather than by threat.

Any person who, having discovered an antiquity without being furnished with the authorization referred to in paragraph 5, reports the same to an official of the competent Department, shall be rewarded according to the value of the discovery.

(3) No antiquity may be disposed of except to the competent Department, unless this Department renounces the acquisition of any such antiquity.

No antiquity may leave the country without an export license from the said Department.

(4) Any person who maliciously or negligently destroys or damages an antiquity shall be liable to a penalty to be fixed.

(5) No clearing of ground or digging with the object of finding antiquities shall be permitted, under penalty of fine, except to persons authorized by the competent Department.

(6) Equitable terms shall be fixed for expropriation, temporary or permanent, of lands which might be of historical or archaeological interest.

(7) Authorization to excavate shall only be granted to persons who show sufficient guarantees of archaeological experience. The Administration of Palestine shall not, in granting these authorizations, act in such a way as to exclude scholars of any nation without good grounds.

(8) The proceeds of excavations may be divided between the excavator and the competent Department in a proportion fixed by that Department. If division seems impossible for scientific reasons, the excavator shall receive a fair indemnity in lieu of a part of the find.

Article 22

English, Arabic and Hebrew shall be the official languages of Palestine. Any statement or inscription in Arabic on stamps or money in Palestine shall be repeated in Hebrew and any statement or inscription in Hebrew shall be repeated in Arabic.

Article 23

The Administration of Palestine shall recognize the holy days of the respective communities in Palestine as legal days of rest for the members of such communities.

Article 24

The Mandatory shall make to the Council of the League of Nations an annual report to the satisfaction of the Council as to the measures taken during the year to carry out the provisions of the mandate. Copies of all laws and regulations promulgated or issued during the year shall be communicated with the report.

Article 25

In the territories lying between the Jordan and the eastern boundary of Palestine as ultimately determined, the Mandatory shall be entitled, with the consent of the Council of the League of Nations, to postpone or withhold application of such provisions of this mandate as he may consider inapplicable to the existing local conditions, and to make such provision for the administration of the territories as he may consider suitable to those conditions, provided that no action shall be taken which is inconsistent with the provisions of Articles 15, 16 and 18.

Article 26

The Mandatory agrees that, if any dispute whatever should arise between the Mandatory and another Member of the League of Nations relating to the interpretation or the application of the provisions of the mandate, such dispute, if it cannot be settled by negotiation, shall be submitted to the Permanent Court of International Justice provided for by Article 14 of the Covenant of the League of Nations.

Article 27

The consent of the Council of the League of Nations is required for any modification of the terms of this mandate.

Article 28

In the event of the termination of the mandate hereby conferred upon the Mandatory, the Council of the League of Nations shall make such arrangements as may be deemed necessary for safeguarding in perpetuity, under guarantee of the League, the rights secured by Articles 13 and 14, and shall use its influence for securing, under the guarantee of the League, that the Government of Palestine will fully honor the financial obligations legitimately incurred by the Administration of Palestine during the period of the mandate, including the rights of public servants to pensions or gratuities.

The present instrument shall be deposited in original in the archives of the League of Nations and certified copies shall be forwarded by the Secretary-General of the League of Nations to all Members of the League.

Done at London the twenty-fourth day of July, one thousand nine hundred and twenty-two.

SOURCE: Library of Congress, Foreign Affairs Division, *A Select Chronology and Background Documents Relating to the Middle East: [Prepared for the] Committee on Foreign Relations, United States Senate*, 2nd rev. ed. (Washington, D.C.: Government Printing Office, 1975), 144–149.

Arabs and Israelis

CHAPTER 2 DOCUMENTS

Part III: Steps toward Peace, 1975–2002

Overview

AL-Nakba—[handwritten annotation]

For many Jews, the establishment of the State of Israel was the symbolic build-ing of a "third temple" in Jerusalem to replace King Herod's second temple, which the Romans had destroyed nearly 2000 years earlier. For most Arabs, the creation of Israel was al-nakba, the "disaster" imposed on them by self-interested out-side powers. From whatever perspective, the establishment of Israel in 1948 is one of the most important events of the twentieth century. Six decades later, it continues to reverberate every day in the region and on a regular basis around the world.

Arabs and Israelis have fought a half-dozen or so wars—depending on how one counts their confrontations—since Zionist leader David Ben-Gurion proclaimed Israel's independence on May 14, 1948, and to this day continue to engage in seem-ingly endless cycles of violence. Tens of thousands of people have been killed, thou-sands more wounded, and energies diverted from more productive enterprises. Some people have long believed that the two sides could settle their differences and live in peace if only they would talk responsibly to each other, rather than past one another. Dozens of peace plans have attempted to achieve such a goal, occasionally with some success. Wounds of victimization, however, remain too raw on both sides, and vio-lence often has been too convenient an outlet in their expressions of grievance.

During the second half of the twentieth century, Israel developed a vibrant econ-omy and one of the world's most contentious democracies, while economic and polit-ical development lagged far behind in the neighboring Arab states. For decades, most Arab countries experienced a succession of military coups or assassinations and were ruled by dictators or monarchs, few of whom had much interest in promoting such Western concepts as democracy and the rule of law. Although national and per capita incomes were high in the few Arab countries with large oil resources, the majority of Arabs at the beginning of the twenty-first century were only marginally better off than were their ancestors a century earlier.

Arabs and Jews had been a combustible combination even before the establishment of Israel. The arrival of thousands of Jewish settlers in Palestine from the late nine-teenth century through the 1930s had led to repeated outbreaks of violence, largely contained (though with difficulty) by the British, who after World War I exercised neocolonial powers over much of the Middle East between the eastern Mediterranean and the Persian Gulf. Officials in London sent numerous delegations to Palestine to inquire into the reasons for the violence and what could be done about it. One of the most diligent inquiries, the Palestine Royal Commission, or Peel Commission, in 1937, became so alarmed by the "irrepressible conflict" that it advocated the "partition" of Palestine between Arabs and Jews. The British government rejected that option, but the logic of it became so compelling that the newly established United Nations (UN) embraced the idea a decade later, when Britain decided it could no longer afford to govern Palestine. The splitting of Palestine became the very basis for the founding of Israel despite the continuing objections of some Arabs and Jews to this day.

When Ben-Gurion and his fellow Jewish leaders proclaimed Israel, they knew war would result. The first of the wars between Arabs and Israelis began the day after their declaration. Over several months, a carefully prepared, well-led Israeli army fighting to preserve the new state fended off the uncoordinated armies of five Arab states. After the war, the United Nations opened the first of many attempts to mediate an end to the Arab-Israeli dispute. That effort led to armistice agreements between Israel and its neighbors, but it failed to resolve the underlying conflict or the many problems created by it. One of these problems was the dislocation of about 700,000 Palestinian Arabs who had fled or been pushed by the Israelis from their homes in what had become Israel. The United Nations General Assembly in December 1948 adopted a resolution insisting that the refugees be allowed to return to their homes or compensated for their lost property. Within a few years, Israel allowed nearly 100,000 of the refugees back but has since refused to accept any more. The surrounding Arab countries to which the Palestinians fled were poor and could not offer the refugees much by way of assistance. Palestinians, thinking that they would soon return to their homes chose to remain in camps, which over the years became permanent. Six decades later, the United Nations counts 4.4 million Palestinian refugees and their descendants. More than 1.3 million of them live in dilapidated UN-run refugee camps around the region.

The next big challenge to peace in the region came in 1956, at least partly in response to a phenomenon that mirrored Zionism: Arab nationalism, as embodied by Gamal Abdel Nasser, the charismatic leader of Egypt. Angered by what he perceived as slights by the United States and Britain, and seeking to assert Egyptian authority over the Suez Canal, the country's prime economic asset, Nasser in June 1956 nationalized the waterway, which had been controlled by British and French interests. Britain and France plotted to take back the canal and brought Israel in on the conspiracy. On October 29, four days after leaders from the three countries secretly agreed on a plan, Israel invaded Egypt. It was supposed to be the first step leading to British and French seizure of the canal, the ousting of Nasser, and an Israeli takeover of much of the Sinai Peninsula. The careful planning went awry, however, when the two superpowers—the United States and the Soviet Union—intervened to halt the attack on Egypt. An angry President Dwight D. Eisenhower, believing he had been misled by the three conspirators, used U.S. influence to force them to back down. Israel's subsequent foot-dragging in acceding to international demands that it withdraw from the Sinai led to one of the lowest points in U.S.-Israeli relations.

In the long history of Arab-Israeli wars, the one fought in 1967 was perhaps the most decisive. After three years of heightening tension resulting from cross-border attacks and competition for water resources, Arab armies massed on Israel's borders in early June 1967. Israel attacked on June 5, decimating the air forces of Egypt, Jordan, and Syria and launching ground attacks that quickly drove the Arab armies back. In six days, Israel captured the entire Sinai Peninsula (to the eastern banks of the Suez Canal) and the Gaza Strip from Egypt, the West Bank and East Jerusalem from Jordan, and the Golan Heights from Syria. The Arabs' defeat demonstrated Israel's military dominance and left Israel in control of Arab territory, which continues to have consequences four decades later.

About two weeks after the war, President Lyndon B. Johnson put forward the first of many U.S. peace plans for the region. His proposal dealt with some of the specific grievances that led to the war, but not the underlying conflict between Arabs and Israelis. In September, Arab leaders meeting in Khartoum adopted a resolution endorsing "three noes": no negotiations, no peace, and no recognition of the Jewish state. The UN Security Council sought two months later, in November, to address the basic issue of the conflict. Its Resolution 242 articulated the "land-for-peace" formula that has been at the heart of nearly all subsequent peace initiatives: It calls for Israel to return the lands it captured in 1967 in exchange for Arabs making peace with Israel.

Nasser died three years after the 1967 war, depriving the Arab world of its most dynamic leader. He was succeeded by a fellow former army officer, Anwar al-Sadat, who sought to regain Arab honor and some of the lost Arab lands—by inflicting even a small defeat on Israel. After careful planning and a military buildup facilitated by the Soviet Union, Egypt and Syria launched a surprise attack against Israel on October 6, 1973, which was Yom Kippur, the holiest day of the year for Jews. The Arab armies acquitted themselves very well in the early stages of the fighting, but Israel eventually recovered and counterattacked with force after being resupplied by the United States. By the time the UN Security Council imposed a cease-fire on October 22, the Israeli army had crossed the Suez Canal to within sixty miles of Cairo and had driven the Syrians off the Golan Heights and advanced to within twenty miles of Damascus. Psychologically and militarily, the war ended in a draw: the Arabs had regained their pride by challenging the Israelis and avoiding outright defeat, but Israel remained in control of important sections of Arab land. UN Security Council Resolution 338, which ended the war, spoke of the need for a "durable peace" and became linked with Resolution 242, from the 1967 war, making them the twin pillars of international diplomacy for the Arab-Israeli conflict.

In Israel, political squabbling over who was to blame for the success of the Arab surprise attack contributed to the election in 1977 of a new government headed by Menachem Begin, a right-wing hawk who insisted on Israel's entitlement to all the land between the Mediterranean Sea and the Jordan River. Begin seemed an unlikely candidate to lead his country to its first peace treaty with an Arab nation, but circumstances put him in that position. The circumstances arose from a decision by Sadat to reach out to Israel to regain by diplomacy the territory that Egypt's armies had been unable to secure through war. Sadat also hoped that economic benefits would follow and help lift Egypt from chronic poverty.

On November 19, 1977, Sadat flew to Jerusalem, where he was greeted by Begin and other Israeli leaders; it was the first public meeting between an Arab leader and an Israeli leader. The drama of that event did not, however, open the floodgates of peace. It would take direct and persistent intervention the following year by U.S. president Jimmy Carter before Egypt and Israel could settle their differences. Carter invited Begin and Sadat to Camp David, the presidential retreat in Maryland, and for nearly two weeks pushed and cajoled them to compromise until they reached a deal. At the White House on September 17, 1978, Carter, Begin, and Sadat signed two "frameworks," documents portending a formal peace treaty and an effort to settle the Palestinian problem. More tough bargaining, including several bouts of brinksmanship, followed, but on March 29, 1979, the two sides signed a treaty on the White House lawn. The peace between Israel and the largest Arab nation has since held although often strained. Angry that Sadat had signed a separate peace agreement, the other Arab leaders expelled Egypt from the Arab League. Two years later, in 1981, radical Islamists assassinated Sadat. In April 1982, Israel removed the last of its settlers and soldiers from the Sinai Peninsula.

Also in the early 1980s, Israel turned its attention to its northern neighbor, Lebanon, where thousands of Palestinians, many of them armed guerrillas, had fled after being expelled from Jordan in 1971 following fighting with government forces. The presence of the Palestinians had been a major factor in the outbreak of civil war in Lebanon in 1975, and the guerrillas established themselves in southern Lebanon and used bases there to launch artillery and rocket attacks against Jewish communities in northern Israel. In June 1982, Israel invaded Lebanon to push the Palestinians from the south. Israeli forces continued north, eventually surrounding Beirut and forcing Palestine Liberation Organization (PLO) chairman Yasir Arafat along with thousands of Palestinian fighters and supporters to evacuate the country. In September, the bloody conflict in Lebanon led President Ronald Reagan to propose a new peace plan that focused on the Palestinian issue. As with so many other peace plans over the years, nothing concrete came of it; it did, however, set out principles that would be useful in later diplomatic efforts. Meeting in Fez, Morocco, a week after Reagan announced his plan, Arab leaders ignored the specifics of that plan but for the first time offered tentatively that Israel's existence might one day be accepted.

The 1991 Persian Gulf War resulted, directly and indirectly, in rounds of Arab-Israeli peacemaking that were more successful than previous efforts. Determined diplomacy—and weeks of round-the-world travel—by Secretary of State James A. Baker III resulted in the first sustained series of meetings between Arab and Israeli officials. They began with the convening of the Madrid peace conference in October 1991 and lasted for more than a year. In a move that produced more concrete results, a left-of-center Israeli government entered into secret negotiations with PLO leaders resulting in a landmark agreement and signing in September 1993. The so-called Oslo Accords, reached with the mediation of Norway, appeared to offer the first real prospect for ending or at least diminishing what nearly everyone agreed had become the core of the Arab-Israeli conflict: violence and animosity between Israel and the 3 million-plus Palestinians living under Israeli occupation in the Gaza Strip, West Bank, and East Jerusalem.

The agreement between Israel and the Palestinians also provided political cover and room to maneuver to Jordan's King Hussein. Over the years, Israeli and Jordanian diplomats secretly had negotiated the essence of a peace deal, so they quickly struck a political agreement, which Hussein and Israeli prime minister Yitzhak Rabin signed at the White House in June 1994 with President Bill Clinton looking on. The two leaders signed a formal treaty the following October at a border crossing between their countries. Clinton again was there to help seal the peace.

Clinton tried in July 2000 to replicate Carter's success at Camp David, this time by attempting to force Israeli and PLO officials to agree to a peace deal ending their dispute. In this case, Israeli prime minister Ehud Barak offered concessions, but they were not enough for Arafat, and the effort failed. Two months later, Palestinians launched a widespread uprising against Israel that resulted in thousands of deaths and extensive destruction over the next several years. Nonetheless, Clinton's aides tried again to wrest a deal. Israeli and Palestinian negotiators met in Washington in December and in Taba, Egypt, in January 2001. They again came close to reaching agreement, but in the context of the violence and an impending Israeli election, it was not close enough. As part of this exercise, Clinton presented to Israel and the Palestinians what he called "parameters" for an eventual peace between them, but neither side fully embraced them before Clinton left office. Many people on both sides believe that Clinton's ideas remain the most logical basis for such a peace.

In March 2002, with the worsening of Israeli-Palestinian violence, Saudi Arabia's de facto ruler, Crown Prince Abdallah, introduced a plan in which Arab nations would make peace with Israel if it abandoned the territories occupied since 1967. Arab leaders embraced the plan at an Arab League summit in Beirut, but a Palestinian suicide bombing in Israel overshadowed their acceptance. Israel dismissed the Arab initiative at that point, only to give it a cautious endorsement nearly five years later when the United States suddenly seized on Abdallah's ideas as offering the potential for yet another round of diplomacy.

The Peel Commission

DOCUMENT IN CONTEXT

Great Britain administered Palestine for more than thirty years, between its capture of Jerusalem from the Ottoman Empire in December 1917 and the establishment of the State of Israel in May 1948. Throughout this period, the British government struggled to reconcile the seemingly incompatible elements of policies that it had articulated during World War I and that the League of Nations had officially adopted in the mandate for Palestine. The central policies involved promoting the establishment of a Jewish "national home" in Palestine while protecting the rights of the Arabs who had lived there for centuries. In 1920 waves of violence, much of it generated by Arabs increasingly frustrated by what they viewed as British favoritism toward the Jews, began to plague Palestine. In response to the violence and other events, the British government repeatedly tinkered with its policies for Palestine. Britain often enraged the Arabs as well as the Jews, but it remained officially committed to a Jewish national home.

Immigration and land quickly became the core issues of dispute among the British, the Arabs, and the Jews. Britain was officially committed to supporting the emigration of Jews (predominantly from Eastern Europe) to Palestine. During the first decade of the mandate, the Jewish population in Palestine more than doubled, to about 175,000, while the Arab population grew steadily but more slowly to slightly less than 900,000. Zionist leaders made no secret of their plans to push for even more immigration so that Jews eventually would become a majority in Palestine, thus justifying the creation of a Jewish state. To provide homes and livelihoods for these immigrants, the Jewish National Fund purchased (mostly from wealthy Arab landowners) thousands of acres of land, much of which in turn was given or sold at a discount to newly arrived Jews. In many cases, Arab tenants were evicted after the land was sold from under them.

The first wave of Arab violence against Jews erupted in 1920–1921, just as London began finalizing its plans to administer Palestine under the League of Nations mandate. Another round of violence occurred in 1929, sparked by a dispute over religious observances at the Western, or "Wailing," Wall of the ancient Temple of Herod in Jerusalem. The violence stemmed from growing Arab fears that the Zionists were succeeding in their plans to turn Palestine into a Jewish homeland. Nearly 250 people were killed in 1929, slightly more than half of them Jews.

In response to the violence, the British government sent two investigating commissions to Palestine. The first, headed by Sir Walter Shaw, recommended in March 1930 that the government exercise more control over Jewish immigration and that it protect Arab tenants against automatic eviction when the land they occupied was sold to Jewish interests. A second investigation, led by Sir John Hope Simpson in October 1930, also proposed an even-handed policy toward the Arabs and Jews and that immigration of Jews be limited to the ability of Palestine's economy to absorb them. The government incorporated the recommendations of this second commission into a policy statement known as the Passfield White Paper (after Lord Passfield, the colonial secretary at the time).

Zionist leaders in Britain and the United States immediately launched an intense campaign against the Passfield policies, notably the proposed limit on Jewish immigration. Their campaign succeeded. In February 1931, Prime Minister Ramsay MacDonald sent British Zionist leader Chaim Weizmann a letter essentially repudiating the Passfield White Paper by emphasizing Britain's "positive obligation" under the League of Nations mandate to facilitate Jewish immigration to Palestine.

Another outbreak of violence in the spring of 1936 led to a strike by Arabs that crippled much of Palestine's economy; more than 300 people, most of them Arabs, died in the violence over a six-month period. In an attempt to calm the situation, the British government appointed the Palestine Royal Commission headed by Lord Robert Peel, the former secretary of state for India. The commission arrived in Palestine in November 1936 and spent two months taking testimony from Arabs (who at first boycotted the proceedings) and Jews.

The commission's report, submitted in July 1937, represented a repudiation of the key elements of British policy toward Palestine during the previous two decades. Fundamentally, the commission said, the Balfour Declaration of 1917 had fostered an irreconcilable conflict between Arabs and Jews over the land of Palestine: Arabs feared being overwhelmed by Jewish economic power, backed by British policy, and that they ultimately would be driven from their homes and deprived of their livelihoods. On the other hand, the Jews assumed that they had de facto British support for creating a Jewish state in Palestine. The report offered a gloomy assessment of the prospects of accommodating both of these communities, noting that it had found "no hope of compromise" in the stated positions of Arab and Jewish leaders.

As an alternative to a future unified state in Palestine—which had been the expectation behind the League of Nations mandate—the Peel Commission proposed splitting Palestine into three sections: one for Arabs, one for Jews, and a central enclave (including Jerusalem) to remain under British control as a neutral zone. Calling this plan "partition," the commission said it would entail hardships for both communities but was the best of the available options. "The difficulties are certainly very great, but when they are closely examined they do not seem so insuperable as the difficulties inherent in the continuance of the mandate or in any other alternative arrangement," the commission wrote. "Partition offers a chance of ultimate peace. No other plan does." One of the difficulties acknowledged by the commission was that tens of thousands of people—most of them Arabs—would have to move voluntarily or be forcibly moved to create two states. The commission cited what it called a successful precedent: the transfer of more than 1.3 million Greeks from Turkey and some 400,000 Turks from Greece nearly fifteen years earlier as part of the settlement of the 1921–1922 war between Greece and Turkey (Turkey Emerges from World War I, p. 631.)

The British government initially endorsed the Peel Commission recommendations. Zionist leaders in Britain and in Palestine liked the idea of transferring Arabs from parts of Palestine that would constitute the core of a Jewish state, but they were divided on the wisdom of ceding any of the territory of Palestine to the Arabs. Arab leaders flatly rejected the concept of partition because it ratified the Zionist plans for a Jewish state on land they considered to be Arab territory, gave Jews some of the most fertile agricultural land, and required the forced transfer of many more Arabs than Jews.

In London, yet another examination of the situation led the British government to switch its policy once again. Another panel, the Palestine Partition Commission, concluded in November 1938 that the Peel Commission's plan would not work. The government then issued a statement withdrawing its earlier endorsement of partition and calling instead for an "understanding" between Arabs and Jews. Rather than bringing long-term peace to Palestine, the Peel Commission report was followed by an expansion of the violence that had led to the commission's appointment in the first place. By the time it was quelled in August 1939, three years of violence had resulted in the deaths of nearly 3,800 Arabs, 2,400 Jews, and some 600 British.

Although its precise recommendations were never carried out, the Peel Commission's report did represent an important step in the process leading up to the establishment of Israel in 1948: The commission was the first official body to advocate partition—something the UN General Assembly would endorse in 1947. In addition, its pessimistic assessment of the situation in Palestine proved to be more accurate than the often optimistic statements of senior British officials (Partition of Palestine, p. 56).

In May 1939, a new British government issued a new white paper proposing an independent, unified Palestine of Arabs and Jews within ten years; in the meantime, restrictions would be tightened on Jewish immigration to ensure that Jews remained a minority unless the Arabs agreed otherwise. Under this white paper, 25,000 Jews would be allowed into Palestine immediately, but no more than 75,000 would be allowed during the next five years. These restrictions angered Zionist leaders, who viewed them as a betrayal of British promises since the Balfour Declaration to support large-scale Jewish emigration to Palestine. One motivation for this change of policy, according to most historians, was Britain's desire to dissuade Arab leaders in the Middle East from aligning with Nazi Germany.

During the course of World War II, Britain generally enforced the immigration limits set out in the 1939 White Paper, in some cases turning away boats loaded with Jewish refugees fleeing Europe. In the most dramatic case, the SS *Struma*, carrying refugees from Romania, was refused entry to Palestine and sank in February 1942 shortly after leaving the harbor of Istanbul; 767 men, women, and children died. The incident deeply angered Zionists, who blamed the British government.

Historians have offered conflicting assessments of the actual impact of the 1939 White Paper, however. Some argue that many Jews could have been saved from the Holocaust in Europe if an escape route to Palestine had been an option. Others contend that only a massive increase in emigration would have saved large numbers of Jews, and Palestine could not absorb hundreds of thousands or millions of refugees, even in the event such an exodus could have been arranged during the war.

Following are excerpts from the "Official Summary" of the report of the Palestine Royal Commission, chaired by Lord Robert Peel, and dated June 22, 1937. The British government published the report on July 7, 1937. The summary appears as an appendix to the full report.

D O C U M E N T

Official Summary of the Palestine Royal Commission

JULY 7, 1937

[Parts I and II of the Official Summary discuss the ancient and recent history of Palestine, along with specific details of the situation faced by the British mandatory authorities in 1937.]

PART III: THE POSSIBILITY OF A LASTING SETTLEMENT

Chapter XX. The Force of Circumstances

The problem of Palestine is briefly restated.

Under the stress of the World War the British Government made promises to Arabs and Jews in order to obtain their support. On the strength of those promises both parties formed certain expectations.

The application to Palestine of the Mandate System in general and of the specific Mandate in particular implies the belief that the obligations thus undertaken towards the Arabs and the Jews respectively would prove in course of time to be mutually compatible owing to the conciliatory effect on the Palestinian Arabs of the material prosperity which Jewish immigration would bring in Palestine as a whole. That belief has not been justified, and there seems to be no hope of its being justified in the future.

But the British people cannot on that account repudiate their obligations, and, apart from obligations, the existing circumstances in Palestine would still require the most strenuous efforts on the part of the Government which is responsible for the welfare of the country.

The existing circumstances are summarized as follows.

An irrepressible conflict has arisen between two national communities within the narrow bounds of one small country. There is no common ground between them. Their national aspirations are incompatible. The Arabs desire to revive the traditions of the Arab golden age. The Jews desire to show what they can achieve when restored to the land in which the Jewish nation was born. Neither of the two national ideals permits of combination in the service of a single State.

The conflict has grown steadily more bitter since 1920 and the process will continue. Conditions inside Palestine, especially the systems of education, are strengthening the national sentiment of the two peoples. The bigger and more prosperous they grow the greater will be their political ambitions, and the conflict is aggravated by the uncertainty of the future. "Who in the end will govern Palestine?" it is asked. Meanwhile, the external factors will continue to operate with increasing force. On the one hand in less than three years' time Syria and the Lebanon will attain their national sovereignty, and the claim of the Palestinian Arabs to share in the freedom of all Asiatic Arabia will thus be fortified. On the other hand the hardships and anxieties of the Jews in Europe are not likely to grow less and the appeal to the good faith and humanity of the British people will lose none of its force.

Meanwhile, the Government of Palestine, which is at present an unsuitable form for governing educated Arabs and democratic Jews, cannot develop into a system of self-government as it has elsewhere, because there is no such system which could ensure justice both to the Arabs and to the Jews. Government therefore remains unrepresentative and unable to dispel the conflicting grievances of the two dissatisfied and irresponsible communities it governs.

In these circumstances peace can only be maintained in Palestine under the Mandate by repression. This means the maintenance of security services at so high a cost that the services directed to "the well-being and development" of the population cannot be expanded and may even have to be curtailed. The moral objections to repression are self-evident. Nor need the undesirable reactions of it on opinion outside Palestine be emphasized. Moreover, repression will not solve the problem. It will exacerbate the quarrel. It will not help towards the establishment of a single self-governing Palestine. It is not easy to pursue the dark path of repression without seeing daylight at the end of it.

The British people will not flinch from the task of continuing to govern Palestine under the Mandate if they are in honor bound to do so, but they would be justified in asking if there is no other way in which their duty can be done.

Nor would Britain wish to repudiate her obligations. The trouble is that they have proved irreconcilable, and this conflict is the more unfortunate because each of the obligations taken separately accords with British sentiment and British interest. The development of self-government in the Arab world on the one hand is in accordance with British principles, and British public opinion is wholly sympathetic with Arab aspirations towards a new age of unity and prosperity in the Arab world. British interest similarly has always been bound up with the peace of the Middle East and British statesmanship can show an almost unbroken record of friendship with the Arabs. There is a strong British tradition, on the other hand, of friendship with the Jewish people, and it is in the British interest to retain as far as may be the confidence of the Jewish people.

The continuance of the present system means the gradual alienation of two peoples who are traditionally the friends of Britain.

The problem cannot be solved by giving either the Arabs or the Jews all they want. The answer to the question which of them in the end will govern Palestine must be "Neither." No fair-minded statesman can think it right either that 400,000 Jews, whose entry into Palestine has been facilitated by the British Government and approved by the League of Nations, should be handed over to Arab rule, or that, if the Jews should become a majority, a million Arabs should be handed over to their rule. But while neither race can fairly rule all Palestine, each race might justly rule part of it.

The idea of Partition has doubtless been thought of before as a solution of the problem, but it has probably been discarded as being impracticable. The difficulties are certainly very great, but when they are closely examined they do not seem so insuperable as the difficulties inherent in the continuance of the Mandate or in any other alternative arrangement. Partition offers a chance of ultimate peace. No other plan does.

[Chapter XXI discusses, and rejects, an alternative proposal of "cantonization," which would involve dividing Palestine into provinces and cantons that would

be self-governing in matters such as immigration, land sales, and social services.
Chapter XXII reviews specific elements of the commission's proposed plan for parti-
tion, including provisions for the protection of holy places and for providing public
services.]

Chapter XXIII. Conclusion

Considering the attitude which both the Arab and the Jewish representatives adopted in giving evidence, the Commission think it improbable that either party will be satisfied at first sight with the proposals submitted for the adjustment of their rival claims. For Partition means that neither will get all it wants. It means that the Arabs must acquiesce in the exclusion from their sovereignty of a piece of territory, long occupied and once ruled by them. It means that the Jews must be content with less than the Land of Israel they once ruled and have hoped to rule again. But it seems possible that on reflection both parties will come to realize that the drawbacks of Partition are outweighed by its advantages. For, if it offers neither party all it wants, it offers each what it wants most, namely freedom and security.

The advantages to the Arabs of Partition on the lines we have proposed may be summarized as follows:—

(i) They obtain their national independence and can co-operate on an equal footing with the Arabs of the neighboring countries in the cause of Arab unity and progress.
(ii) They are finally delivered from the fear of being swamped by the Jews, and from the possibility of ultimate subjection to Jewish rule.
(iii) In particular, the final limitation of the Jewish National Home within a fixed frontier and the enactment of a new Mandate for the protection of the Holy Places, solemnly guaranteed by the League of Nations, removes all anxiety lest the Holy Places should ever come under Jewish control.
(iv) As a set-off to the loss of territory the Arabs regard as theirs, the Arab State will receive a subvention from the Jewish State. It will also, in view of the backwardness of Trans-Jordan, obtain a grant of £2,000,000 from the British Treasury; and, if an agreement can be reached as to the exchange of land and population, a further grant will be made for the conversion, as far as may prove possible, of uncultivable land in the Arab State into productive land from which the cultivators and the State alike will profit.

The advantages of Partition to the Jews may be summarized as follows:—

(i) Partition secures the establishment of the Jewish National Home and relieves it from the possibility of its being subjected in the future to Arab rule.
(ii) Partition enables the Jews in the fullest sense to call their National Home their own; for it converts it into a Jewish State. Its citizens will be able to admit as many Jews into it as they themselves believe can be absorbed. They will attain the primary objective of Zionism—a Jewish nation, planted in Palestine, giving its nationals the same status in the world as other nations give theirs. They will cease at last to live a minority life.

To both Arabs and Jews Partition offers a prospect—and there is none in any other policy—of obtaining the inestimable boon of peace. It is surely worth some sacrifice on both sides if the quarrel which the Mandate started could be ended with its termination. It is not a natural or old-standing feud. The Arabs throughout their history have not only been free from anti-Jewish sentiment but have also shown that the spirit of compromise is deeply rooted in their life. Considering what the possibility of finding a refuge in Palestine means to many thousands of suffering Jews, is the loss occasioned by Partition, great as it would be, more than Arab generosity can bear? In this, as in so much else connected with Palestine, it is not only the peoples of that country who have to be considered. The Jewish Problem is not the least of the many problems which are disturbing international relations at this critical time and obstructing the path to peace and prosperity. If the Arabs at some sacrifice could help to solve that problem, they would earn the gratitude not of the Jews alone but of all the Western World.

There was a time when Arab statesmen were willing to concede little Palestine to the Jews, provided that the rest of Arab Asia were free. That condition was not fulfilled then, but it is on the eve of fulfillment now. In less than three years' time all the wide Arab area outside Palestine between the Mediterranean and the Indian Ocean will be independent, and, if Partition is adopted, the greater part of Palestine will be independent too.

As to the British people, they are bound to honor to the utmost of their power the obligations they undertook in the exigencies of war towards the Arabs and the Jews. When those obligations were incorporated in the Mandate, they did not fully realize the difficulties of the task it laid on them. They have tried to overcome them, not always with success. The difficulties have steadily become greater till now they seem almost insuperable. Partition offers a possibility of finding a way through them, a possibility of obtaining a final solution of the problem which does justice to the rights and aspirations of both the Arabs and the Jews and discharges the obligations undertaken towards them twenty years ago to the fullest extent that is practicable in the circumstances of the present time.

SOURCES: Palestine Royal Commission, Report Presented by the Secretary of State for the Colonies to Parliament by Command of His Majesty, July 1937. Parliamentary Papers, Command No. 5479, HMSO, 1937; United Nations Information System on the Question of Palestine, http://domino.un.org/UNISPAL.NSF/9a798adbf322aff38525617b006d88d7/08e38a718201458b052565700072b358!OpenDocument.

The Arab League

DOCUMENT IN CONTEXT

Arab nationalism—the concept of Arab peoples as constituting a nation regardless of which country they call home—emerged as a force in the middle of the twentieth century but quickly faded. Aside from the brief experiment of the United Arab Republic—consisting of Egypt and Syria from 1958 to 1961—and a stillborn merger of Libya and Syria in 1980, the League of Arab States, or the Arab League, represents the chief embodiment of Arab nationalism. The league has served as a platform for Arab leaders to espouse common goals, and, indeed, its main accomplishments have been rhetorical rather than concrete improvements to the lives of the Arab people.

The Arab League was founded during a meeting of leaders from six countries held in Alexandria, Egypt, in late September and early October 1944, by which time the Middle East no longer was an important theater in World War II. The delegates from Egypt, Iraq, Lebanon, Saudi Arabia, Syria, and Transjordan (later Jordan) signed a protocol with several goals, including "to coordinate their political plans so as to insure their cooperation, and protect their independence and sovereignty against every aggression by suitable means." This protocol was transformed into a formal treaty on March 22, 1945, in time to make the Arab League an official regional organization under the rules of the newly established United Nations. Other countries joined the league from the late 1940s through the 1970s, bringing the organization's total membership to twenty-one countries, plus the Palestine Liberation Organization (PLO), which was accorded full membership in 1976.

Although the league's treaty calls for "close cooperation" among Arab states, some of the most memorable events in the organization's history have involved discord rather than harmony. One prominent case occurred in 1979, when the league voted to expel Egypt after it became the first Arab state to sign a peace treaty with Israel. This step was all the more embarrassing for the concept of Arab unity because Egypt was (and remains) the most populous Arab country and the league's headquarters were in Cairo. Member states allowed Egypt back into the league in 1989, after passions had cooled.

The league also fractured in 1990 after one member country (Iraq) invaded and announced its annexation of another member country (Kuwait). Meeting in Cairo on August 10, 1990, twelve Arab League members backed a resolution calling for troops to be sent to support Saudi Arabia, which feared that it might be Iraq's next target. Jordan, Mauritania, and Sudan also voted for the resolution with reservations, while Libya and the PLO, in effect, supported Iraq. Three other countries abstained or did not attend (see Camp David Peace Process, p. 118; Persian Gulf War, p. 455).

Opposition to Israel and offering political support for Palestinians have been the most unifying forces in the Arab League's history, with the central question often being how tough a stand to take against the Jewish state. The Arab League officially declared war against Israel immediately after its founding in May 1948, but the league played no formal role in the numerous subsequent wars involving Israel. A league meeting in Khartoum following the Arab defeat in the June 1967 war—in which Egypt, Jordan, and Syria lost territory—was the venue for the united Arab position on the "three noes" involving Israel—no recognition, no negotiations, and no peace (see Khartoum Declaration, p. 108).

With the passage of time, the league's hard-line stance gradually gave way to a grudging acknowledgment of Israel as a permanent fact of life in the Middle East. At the same time, it has demanded that Israel accept a Palestinian state consisting of the Gaza Strip and the West Bank, with a capital in East Jerusalem. Meeting in Beirut on March 27–28,

2002, Arab League leaders adopted a plan articulated by Saudi Arabia's Crown Prince Abdallah pledging to establish "normal relations" with Israel if the Jewish state agreed to several conditions, including withdrawing from all the territories it had occupied since 1967 and agreeing to a "sovereign, independent" Palestinian state. Israel rejected the plan and its prospects were overwhelmed by continued violence between Israelis and Palestinians. Even so, the Saudi plan was the most conciliatory statement ever offered to Israel by Arab leaders as a group, and in 2007 it was revivied as the basis for a possible new round of peacemaking (Arab League Beirut Summit, p. 156).

Following is the text of the charter of the League of Arab States, adopted on March 22, 1945.

DOCUMENT

The Charter of the Arab League

MARCH 22, 1945

ARTICLE I

The League of Arab States is composed of the independent Arab states which have signed this Charter. Any independent Arab state has the right to become a member of the League. If it desires to do so, it shall submit a request which will be deposited with the Permanent Secretariat General and submitted to the Council at the first meeting held after submission of the request.

ARTICLE II

The League has as its purpose the strengthening of the relations between the member-states, the coordination of their policies in order to achieve co-operation between them and to safeguard their independence and sovereignty; and a general concern with the affairs and interests of the Arab countries. It has also as its purpose the close co-operation of the member-states, with due regard to the Organisation and circumstances of each state, on the following matters:

    A. Economic and financial affairs, including commercial relations, customs, currency and questions of agriculture and industry.
    B. Communications; this includes railroads, roads, aviation, navigation, telegraphs and posts.
    C. Cultural affairs.
    D. Nationality, passports, visas, execution of judgments and extradition of criminals.
    E. Social affairs.
    F. Health affairs.

ARTICLE III

Coun'd

The League shall possess a Council composed of the representatives of the member-states of the League; each state shall have a single vote, irrespective of the number of its representatives.

It shall be the task of the Council to achieve the realisation of the objectives of the League and to supervise the execution of agreements which the member-states have concluded on the questions enumerated in the preceding Article, or on any other questions.

It likewise shall be the Council task to decide upon the means by which the League is to co-operate with the international bodies to be created in the future in order to guarantee security and peace and regulate economic and social relations.

For each of the questions listed in Article II there shall be set up a special committee in which the member-states of the League shall be represented. These committees shall be charged with the task of laying down the principles and extent of co-operation. Such principles shall be formulated as draft agreements to be presented to the Council for examination preparatory to their submission to the aforesaid states.

Representatives of the other Arab countries may take part in the work of the aforesaid committees. The Council shall determine the conditions under which these representatives may be permitted to participate and the rules governing such representation.

ARTICLE IV

For each of the questions listed in Article II there shall be set up a special committee in which the member-states of the League shall be represented. These committees shall be charged with the task of laying down the principles and extent of co-operation. Such principles shall be formulated as draft agreements to be presented to the Council for examination preparatory to their submission to the aforesaid states.

Representatives of the other Arab countries may take part in the work of the aforesaid committees. The Council shall determine the conditions under which these representatives may be permitted to participate and the rules governing such representation.

ARTICLE V

Any resort to force in order to resolve disputes between two or more member-states of the League is prohibited. If there should arise among them a difference which does not concern a state's independence, sovereignty, or territorial integrity, and if the parties to the dispute have recourse to the Council for the settlement of this difference, the decision of the Council shall then be enforceable and obligatory.

In such case, the states between whom the difference has arisen shall not participate in the deliberations and decisions of the Council.

The Council shall mediate in all differences which threaten to lead to war between two member-states, or a member-state and a third state, with a view to bringing about their reconciliation.

Decisions of arbitration and mediation shall be taken by majority vote.

ARTICLE VI

In case of aggression or threat of aggression by one state against a member-state, the state which has been attacked or threatened with aggression may demand the immediate convocation of the Council.

The Council shall by unanimous decision determine the measures necessary to repulse the aggression. If the aggressor is a member-state, his vote shall not be counted in determining unanimity.

If, as a result of the attack, the government of the state attacked finds itself unable to communicate with the Council, the state's representative in the Council shall request the convocation of the Council for the purpose indicated in the foregoing paragraph. In the event that this representative is unable to communicate with the Council, any member-state of the League shall have the right to request the convocation of the Council.

ARTICLE VII

Unanimous decisions of the Council shall be binding upon all member-states of the League; majority decisions shall be binding only upon those states which have accepted them.

In either case the decisions of the Council shall be enforced in each member-state according to its respective laws.

ARTICLE VIII

Each member-state shall respect the systems of government established in the other member-states and regard them as exclusive concerns of those states. Each shall pledge to abstain from any action calculated to change established systems of government.

ARTICLE IX

States of the League which desire to establish closer co-operation and stronger bonds than are provided for by this Charter may conclude agreements to that end.

Treaties and agreements already concluded or to be concluded in the future between a member-state and another state shall not be binding or restrictive upon other members.

ARTICLE X

The permanent seat of the League of Arab States is established in Cairo. The Council may, however, assemble at any other place it may designate.

ARTICLE XI

The Council of the League shall convene in ordinary session twice a year, in March and in September. It shall convene in extraordinary session upon the request of two member-states of the League whenever the need arises.

ARTICLE XII

The League shall have a permanent Secretariat-General which shall consist of a Secretary-General, Assistant Secretaries and an appropriate number of officials.

The Council of the League shall appoint the Secretary-General by a majority of two thirds of the states of the League. The Secretary-General, with the approval of the Council, shall appoint the Assistant Secretaries and the principal officials of the League.

The Council of the League shall establish an administrative regulation for the functions of the Secretariat-General and matters relating to the staff.

The Secretary-General shall have the rank of Ambassador and the Assistant Secretaries that of Ministers Plenipotentiary.

The first Secretary-General of the League is named in an annex to this Charter.

ARTICLE XIII

The Secretary-General shall prepare the draft of the budget of the League and shall submit it to the Council for approval before the beginning of each fiscal year.

The Council shall fix the share of the expenses to be borne by each state of the League. This may be reconsidered if necessary.

ARTICLE XIV

The members of the Council of the League as well as the members of the committees and the officials who are to be designated in the administrative regulation shall enjoy diplomatic privileges and immunity when engaged in the exercise of their functions.

The buildings occupied by the organs of the League shall be inviolable.

ARTICLE XV

The first meeting of the Council shall be convened at the invitation of the head of the Egyptian Government. Thereafter it shall be convened at the invitation of the Secretary-General.

The representatives of the member-states of the League shall alternately assume the presidency of the Council at each of its ordinary sessions.

ARTICLE XVI

Except in cases specifically indicated in this Charter, a majority vote of the Council shall be sufficient to make enforceable decisions on the following matters:

    A. Matters relating to personnel.
    B. Adoption of the budget of the League.
    C. Establishment of the administrative regulations for the Council, the committees and the Secretariat General.
    D. Decisions to adjourn the sessions.

ARTICLE XVII

Each member-state of the League shall deposit with the Secretariat-General one copy of treaty or agreement concluded or to be concluded in the future between itself and another member-state of the League or a third state.

ARTICLE XVIII

If a member state contemplates withdrawal from the League [it] shall inform the Council of its intention one year before such withdrawal is to go into effect.

The Council of the League may consider any state which fails to fulfill its obligations under the Charter as separated from the League, this to go into effect upon a unanimous decision of the states, not counting the state concerned.

ARTICLE XIX

This Charter may be amended with the consent of two thirds of the states belonging to the League, especially [in] order to make firmer and stronger the ties between the member-states, to create an Arab Tribunal of Arbitration, and to regulate the relations of the League with any international bodies to be created in the future to guarantee security and peace.

Final action on the amendment cannot be taken prior to the session following in which the motion was initiated.

If a state does not accept such an amendment it may withdraw at such time as the amendment goes into effect, without being bound by the provisions of the preceding Article.

ARTICLE XX

This Charter and its annexes shall be ratified according to the basic laws in force among the High Contracting parties.

The instruments of ratification shall be deposited with the Secretariat-General of the Council and the Charter shall become operative as regards each ratifying state fifteen days after the Secretary-General has received the instruments of ratification from four states.

This Charter has been drawn up in Cairo in the Arabic language on this 8th day of Rabi II, thirteen hundred and sixty four H. (March 22, 1945), in one copy which shall be deposited in the safe keeping of the Secretariat-General.

An identical copy shall be delivered to each state of the League.

(1) Annex Regarding Palestine

Since the termination of the last great war the rule of the Ottoman Empire over the Arab countries, among them Palestine, which had become detached from that Empire, has come to an end. She has come to be autonomous, not subordinate to any other state.

The Treaty of Lausanne proclaimed that her future was to be settled by the parties concerned.

However, even though she was as yet unable to control her own affairs, the Covenant of the League (of Nations) in 1919 made provision for a regime based upon recognition of her independence.

Her international existence and independence in the legal sense cannot, therefore, be questioned, any more than could the independence of the other Arab countries.

Although the outward manifestations of this independence have remained obscured for reasons beyond her control, this should not be allowed to interfere with her participation in the work of the Council of the League.

The states signatory to the Pact of the Arab League are therefore of the opinion that, considering the special circumstances of Palestine and until that country can effectively exercise its independence, the Council of the League should take charge of the selection of an Arab representative from Palestine to take part in its work.

(2) Annex Regarding Cooperation with Countries Which Are Not Members of the Council of the League

Whereas the member states of the League will have to deal in the Council as well as in the committees with matters which will benefit and affect the Arab world at large;

And whereas the Council has to take into account the aspirations of the Arab countries which are not members of the Council and has to work toward their realization;

Now, therefore, it particularly behooves the states signatory to the Pact of the Arab League to enjoin the Council of the League, when considering the admission of those countries to participation in the committees referred to in the Pact, that it should spare no efforts to learn their needs and understand their aspirations and hopes; and that it should work thenceforth for their best interests and the safeguarding of their future with all the political means at its disposal.

(3) Annex Regarding the Appointment of a Secretary-General of the League

The states signatory to this Pact have agreed to appoint His Excellency Abdul-Rahman 'Azzam Bey, to be Secretary-General of the League of Arab States.

This appointment is made for two years. The Council of the League shall hereafter determine the new regulations for the Secretary-General.

SOURCE: Arab League, www.arableague-us.org/charter1.html.

The Partition of Palestine

In some respects, World War II produced a temporary respite in the growing conflict among Arabs, Jews, and the British government over Palestine. The end of the war, however, swiftly brought about the events that culminated in the establishment of the State of Israel and led to even greater levels of conflict that continue to this day.

As a result of the recommendations in the 1939 White Paper, British policy during the war restricted Jewish immigration to Palestine, which had been a flashpoint during the 1920s and throughout the 1930s. Regardless, Zionists, despite their differences with the British over immigration and other issues, pragmatically sided with Britain in its struggle against Nazi Germany. In 1939 just before the war broke out, David Ben-Gurion, the chairman of the quasi-governmental Jewish Agency in Palestine, stated the Zionist position this way: "We shall fight the war against Hitler as if there were no White Paper, and we shall fight the White Paper as if there were no war."

Thousands of Palestinian Jews served in British-backed military units in Europe and in the Middle East, and the Jewish economy of Palestine rapidly industrialized to produce weapons and transport gear and other material necessary for the war against Germany. This militarization proved invaluable for the Zionist cause after the war in terms of pressuring Britain and later when the new state of Israel found itself at war with the Arabs. Meanwhile, some Palestinian Arab leaders, notably the exiled mufti of Jerusalem, Hajj Amin al-Husseini, actively sided with Germany as a way of opposing Britain, while a small number of Arabs aided the British war effort.

In the late stages of the war, the British government in Palestine announced long-term economic plans that the Zionists perceived as favoring the Arabs. This led to renewed tensions and conflict, including violence against the government by Jewish guerrilla groups. In August 1944, LEHI—also known as the Stern Gang, after its founder Avraham Stern—tried but failed to assassinate Sir Harold MacMichael, the British high commissioner in Palestine. Three months later, however, the group succeeded in assassinating Lord Moyne, the senior British official in Egypt. The attack damaged residual British support for Zionism, including that of Prime Minister Winston Churchill, who for more than two decades had been a key Zionist backer in London.

The unexpected electoral defeat of Churchill immediately after the war, in July 1945, brought a new Labor government to power in Britain, headed by Clement Attlee, who claimed to be committed to the Zionist program in Palestine. Once again, however, broader British concerns—maintaining access to the oil reserves that it had developed in the region—played a more decisive role in London's policymaking than did loyalty to the Zionists' enterprise. For the British, maintaining access to oil also meant having good relations with Arabs. After carrying out a study of the Palestine issue in late 1945, the Labor government decided on a policy of sticking with the status quo, including admitting only a small quota of Jewish immigrants to Palestine while deferring judgment on its political future.

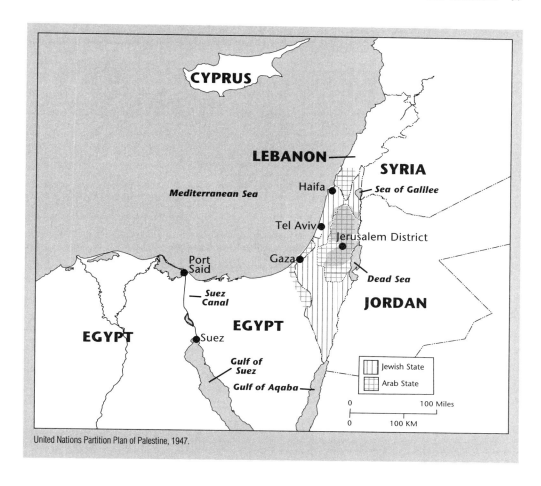

United Nations Partition Plan of Palestine, 1947.

Zionist leaders in Palestine reacted angrily to Britain's stance, which they saw as more backtracking on the Balfour Declaration. Beginning in November 1945, leaders of the Haganah, the semi-official Jewish army in Palestine, joined with LEHI and the Irgun, another paramilitary Zionist group, in planning and carrying out armed attacks against British interests. In June 1946, Haganah units blew up ten bridges, and on July 22 the Irgun, commanded by future Israeli prime minister Menachem Begin, bombed 'a wing of the famed King David Hotel in Jerusalem, where several British government offices were located. Ninety-one people died in the attack, most of them civilian British workers but also several Arabs and Jews.

By this time, Zionist leaders had turned their attention to the United States, hoping that pressure from Washington would force the British to be more accommodating to their concerns. In November 1942, a Zionist conference at the Biltmore Hotel in New York City had adopted a platform calling for unlimited Jewish immigration to Palestine and the establishment there of a Jewish-led "commonwealth," a term intended to soften the implications of statehood.

In April 1945, President Franklin D. Roosevelt died in office. For a variety of reasons, Harry S. Truman, Roosevelt's successor, was more committed to the Zionist cause than Roosevelt had been. The plight of millions of displaced Europeans, many of them Jews, deeply moved Truman. His first major action on the Palestine question was to pressure the British government, in August 1945, to allow 100,000 displaced European Jews to emigrate to Palestine. London rebuffed Truman, asserting that it intended to adhere to its White Paper policy of giving Arabs an effective veto power over large-scale Jewish immigration. Truman repeated his request in May 1946, after a joint U.S.-British committee recommended approval of it. The British again demurred, though it could not afford to maintain the status quo much longer. Exhausted and nearly bankrupt after the war, Britain found itself with more than 100,000 soldiers and policemen stationed in Palestine. Its costly security force increasingly battled the Jews, who once had been the beneficiaries of British policy toward Palestine.

Truman intervened again on October 4, 1946. In a statement addressed to the American Jewish community on the eve of Yom Kippur, Truman endorsed the partition of Palestine and called for a substantial increase in Jewish immigration there. His statement put additional pressure on the British, who were trying once more to negotiate a compromise acceptable to the Arabs as well as the Jews of Palestine. When that effort failed early in 1947, Britain conceded defeat and began to retreat from its imperial responsibilities. On February 14, 1947, Foreign Secretary Ernest Bevin announced that Britain had decided to hand the problem of Palestine to the newly established United Nations. On February 20, the government announced its intention to withdraw from India by mid-1948, and a day later it made known that Britain could no longer afford to support the governments of Greece and Turkey, which were under intense pressure from Russian-backed communists.

Significantly, Britain turned to the UN's General Assembly for help, rather than to the Security Council, where the Soviet Union's veto power could block any decision agreed to by the other members. It established the United Nations Special Committee on Palestine (UNSCOP) to assess the situation, and in summer 1947, committee members set out for Palestine on a study tour. Zionist officials cooperated with the inquiry, while local Arab leaders refused to meet with committee members or provide them proposals, apparently fearing that the United Nations was destined to support partition.

While the UN committee deliberated, another drama played out on the high seas when British authorities blocked a U.S. ferryboat renamed the *Exodus-1947*. Loaded with 4,500 European Jewish refugees, the ferry was headed from France to Palestine. After intercepting the ship, the British put the refugees aboard transport ships and sent them back to France and then to Germany, where most ended up in camps for displaced persons. The plight of the refugees captured worldwide attention and put British policy in its harshest possible light at a crucial moment.

UNSCOP's report to the General Assembly on August 31 was illustrative of the fundamental divisions over Palestine: A majority of seven committee members favored the partition of Palestine into an Arab state and a much smaller Jewish state along with a UN-controlled zone around Jerusalem. A three-member minority favored transforming Palestine into a federation composed of Arab and Jewish cantons with Jerusalem as a unified capital. The minority proposal, which restricted Jewish immigration, envisioned a united Palestine dominated indefinitely by the Arab majority.

Although numerous features of the majority position disappointed Zionist visions for a Jewish state, most Zionist groups backed it as the superior option. Arab leaders, both in Palestine and in surrounding countries, emphatically rejected both the majority and the minority positions as giving too much to the Jews in Palestine. The Arab

League, founded with British support just two years earlier, threatened war if the General Assembly adopted either proposal (The Arab League, p. 48).

Amid intense international lobbying and pressure, the General Assembly took up the proposal for partition on November 29, 1947. The key factor, according to many historians, was the united stance in favor of the partition resolution by the United States and the Soviet Union, the two countries that had emerged as the world's dominant powers after World War II. Resolution 181 passed by a vote of thirty-three to thirteen, with ten abstentions. The most prominent of the abstainers was the British government, which by that time had developed second thoughts about relinquishing Palestine and had decided to oppose any plan for the territory not supported by Arabs as well as by Jews.

The partition resolution assigned to the Jewish state only a fraction of the territory that Zionists had long claimed as the rightful Jewish heritage in Palestine. For this reason, some Zionist leaders—the Revisionist faction, intellectual predecessors to Israel's Likud Party—denounced the partition resolution as a betrayal. Even so, the UN action represented one of the greatest triumphs for the Zionist movement since the Balfour Declaration, issued almost exactly thirty years earlier. Jews seemed finally to be assured of their own state, not just a vague "national home" in Palestine, and one with the imprimatur of international law (Map, p. 57).

The Arabs' anger grew along with the belief that Jewish money and influence had swayed world leaders, particularly in the West. Some Arab leaders believed, however, that they had a trump card in any case: Their combined armies were stronger than the Jewish forces in Palestine. If partition could not be defeated through international diplomacy, it assuredly would be defeated by military force, according to this view. That expectation would repeatedly prove to be faulty in the following decades.

Following is the text of UN General Assembly Resolution 181, adopted on November 29, 1947, calling for the partition of Palestine into Arab and Jewish sectors.

DOCUMENT

UN General Assembly Resolution 181 (1947)

NOVEMBER 29, 1947

The General Assembly,

Having met in special session at the request of the mandatory Power to constitute and instruct a special committee to prepare for the consideration of the question of the future government of Palestine at the second regular session;

Having constituted a Special Committee and instructed it to investigate all questions and issues relevant to the problem of Palestine, and to prepare proposals for the solution of the problem, and

Having received and examined the report of the Special Committee (document A/364)[1] including a number of unanimous recommendations and a plan of partition with economic union approved by the majority of the Special Committee,

Considers that the present situation in Palestine is one which is likely to impair the general welfare and friendly relations among nations;

Takes note of the declaration by the mandatory Power that it plans to complete its evacuation of Palestine by 1 August 1948;

Recommends to the United Kingdom, as the mandatory Power for Palestine, and to all other Members of the United Nations the adoption and implementation, with regard to the future government of Palestine, of the Plan of Partition with Economic Union set out below;

Requests that

(a) The Security Council take the necessary measures as provided for in the plan for its implementation;

(b) The Security Council consider, if circumstances during the transitional period require such consideration, whether the situation in Palestine constitutes a threat to the peace. If it decides that such a threat exists, and in order to maintain international peace and security, the Security Council should supplement the authorization of the General Assembly by taking measures, under Articles 39 and 41 of the Charter, to empower the United Nations Commission, as provided in this resolution, to exercise in Palestine the functions which are assigned to it by this resolution;

(c) The Security Council determine as a threat to the peace, breach of the peace or act of aggression, in accordance with Article 39 of the Charter, any attempt to alter by force the settlement envisaged by this resolution;

(d) The Trusteeship Council be informed of the responsibilities envisaged for it in this plan;

Calls upon the inhabitants of Palestine to take such steps as may be necessary on their part to put this plan into effect;

Appeals to all Governments and all peoples to refrain from taking action which might hamper or delay the carrying out of these recommendations, and

Authorizes the Secretary-General to reimburse travel and subsistence expenses of the members of the Commission referred to in Part I, Section B, paragraph 1 below, on such basis and in such form as he may determine most appropriate in the circumstances, and to provide the Commission with the necessary staff to assist in carrying out the functions assigned to the Commission by the General Assembly.

B[2]

The General Assembly

Authorizes the Secretary-General to draw from the Working Capital Fund a sum not to exceed $2,000,000 for the purposes set forth in the last paragraph of the resolution on the future government of Palestine.

Hundred and twenty-eighth plenary meeting
29 November 1947

---

[1]See Official Records of the second session of the General Assembly, Supplement No. 11, Volumes I–IV.
[2]This resolution was adopted without reference to a Committee.

[At its hundred and twenty-eighth plenary meeting on 29 November 1947 the General Assembly, in accordance with the terms of the above resolution [181 A], elected the following members of the United Nations Commission on Palestine: Bolivia, Czechoslovakia, Denmark, Panama, and the Philippines.]

PLAN OF PARTITION WITH ECONOMIC UNION

PART I
Future constitution and government of Palestine

A. TERMINATION OF MANDATE, PARTITION AND INDEPENDENCE

1. The Mandate for Palestine shall terminate as soon as possible but in any case not later than 1 August 1948.

2. The armed forces of the mandatory Power shall be progressively withdrawn from Palestine, the withdrawal to be completed as soon as possible but in any case not later than 1 August 1948.

The mandatory Power shall advise the Commission, as far in advance as possible, of its intention to terminate the Mandate and to evacuate each area.

The mandatory Power shall use its best endeavours to ensure than an area situated in the territory of the Jewish State, including a seaport and hinterland adequate to provide facilities for a substantial immigration, shall be evacuated at the earliest possible date and in any event not later than 1 February 1948.

3. Independent Arab and Jewish States and the Special International Regime for the City of Jerusalem, set forth in part III of this plan, shall come into existence in Palestine two months after the evacuation of the armed forces of the mandatory Power has been completed but in any case not later than 1 October 1948. The boundaries of the Arab State, the Jewish State, and the City of Jerusalem shall be as described in parts II and III below.

4. The period between the adoption by the General Assembly of its recommendation on the question of Palestine and the establishment of the independence of the Arab and Jewish States shall be a transitional period.

B. STEPS PREPARATORY TO INDEPENDENCE

1. A Commission shall be set up consisting of one representative of each of five Member States. The Members represented on the Commission shall be elected by the General Assembly on as broad a basis, geographically and otherwise, as possible.

2. The administration of Palestine shall, as the mandatory Power withdraws its armed forces, be progressively turned over to the Commission; which shall act in conformity with the recommendations of the General Assembly, under the guidance of the Security Council. The mandatory Power shall to the fullest possible extent co-ordinate its plans for withdrawal with the plans of the Commission to take over and administer areas which have been evacuated.

In the discharge of this administrative responsibility the Commission shall have authority to issue necessary regulations and take other measures as required.

The mandatory Power shall not take any action to prevent, obstruct or delay the implementation by the Commission of the measures recommended by the General Assembly.

3. On its arrival in Palestine the Commission shall proceed to carry out measures for the establishment of the frontiers of the Arab and Jewish States and the City of Jerusalem in accordance with the general lines of the recommendations of the General Assembly on the partition of Palestine. Nevertheless, the boundaries as described in part II of this plan are to be modified in such a way that village areas as a rule will not be divided by state boundaries unless pressing reasons make that necessary.

4. The Commission, after consultation with the democratic parties and other public organizations of The Arab and Jewish States, shall select and establish in each State as rapidly as possible a Provisional Council of Government. The activities of both the Arab and Jewish Provisional Councils of Government shall be carried out under the general direction of the Commission.

If by 1 April 1948 a Provisional Council of Government cannot be selected for either of the States, or, if selected, cannot carry out its functions, the Commission shall communicate that fact to the Security Council for such action with respect to that State as the Security Council may deem proper, and to the Secretary-General for communication to the Members of the United Nations.

5. Subject to the provisions of these recommendations, during the transitional period the Provisional Councils of Government, acting under the Commission, shall have full authority in the areas under their control, including authority over matters of immigration and land regulation.

6. The Provisional Council of Government of each State acting under the Commission, shall progressively receive from the Commission full responsibility for the administration of that State in the period between the termination of the Mandate and the establishment of the State's independence.

7. The Commission shall instruct the Provisional Councils of Government of both the Arab and Jewish States, after their formation, to proceed to the establishment of administrative organs of government, central and local.

8. The Provisional Council of Government of each State shall, within the shortest time possible, recruit an armed militia from the residents of that State, sufficient in number to maintain internal order and to prevent frontier clashes.

This armed militia in each State shall, for operational purposes, be under the command of Jewish or Arab officers resident in that State, but general political and military control, including the choice of the militia's High Command, shall be exercised by the Commission.

9. The Provisional Council of Government of each State shall, not later than two months after the withdrawal of the armed forces of the mandatory Power, hold elections to the Constituent Assembly which shall be conducted on democratic lines.

The election regulations in each State shall be drawn up by the Provisional Council of Government and approved by the Commission. Qualified voters for each State for this election shall be persons over eighteen years of age who are: (a) Palestinian citizens residing in that State and (b) Arabs and Jews residing in the State, although not Palestinian citizens, who, before voting, have signed a notice of intention to become citizens of such State.

Arabs and Jews residing in the City of Jerusalem who have signed a notice of intention to become citizens, the Arabs of the Arab State and the Jews of the Jewish State, shall be entitled to vote in the Arab and Jewish States respectively.

Women may vote and be elected to the Constituent Assemblies.

During the transitional period no Jew shall be permitted to establish residence in the area of the proposed Arab State, and no Arab shall be permitted to establish residence in the area of the proposed Jewish State, except by special leave of the Commission.

10. The Constituent Assembly of each State shall draft a democratic constitution for its State and choose a provisional government to succeed the Provisional Council of Government appointed by the Commission. The constitutions of the States shall embody chapters 1 and 2 of the Declaration provided for in section C below and include inter alia provisions for:

(a) Establishing in each State a legislative body elected by universal suffrage and by secret ballot on the basis of proportional representation, and an executive body responsible to the legislature;

(b) Settling all international disputes in which the State may be involved by peaceful means in such a manner that international peace and security, and justice, are not endangered;

(c) Accepting the obligation of the State to refrain in its international relations from the threat or use of force against the territorial integrity of political independence of any State, or in any other manner inconsistent with the purposes of the United Nations;

(d) Guaranteeing to all persons equal and non-discriminatory rights in civil, political, economic and religious matters and the enjoyment of human rights and fundamental freedoms, including freedom of religion, language, speech and publication, education, assembly and association;

(e) Preserving freedom of transit and visit for all residents and citizens of the other State in Palestine and the City of Jerusalem, subject to considerations of national security, provided that each State shall control residence within its borders.

11. The Commission shall appoint a preparatory economic commission of three members to make whatever arrangements are possible for economic co-operation, with a view to establishing, as soon as practicable, the Economic Union and the Joint Economic Board, as provided in section D below.

12. During the period between the adoption of the recommendations on the question of Palestine by the General Assembly and the termination of the Mandate, the mandatory Power in Palestine shall maintain full responsibility for administration in areas from which it has not withdrawn its armed forces. The Commission shall assist the mandatory Power in the carrying out of these functions. Similarly the mandatory Power shall co-operate with the Commission in the execution of its functions.

13. With a view to ensuring that there shall be continuity in the functioning of administrative services and that, on the withdrawal of the armed forces of the mandatory Power, the whole administration shall be in the charge of the Provisional Councils and the Joint Economic Board, respectively, acting under the Commission, there shall be a progressive transfer, from the mandatory Power to the Commission, of responsibility for all the functions of government, including that of maintaining law and order in the areas from which the forces of the mandatory Power have been withdrawn.

14. The Commission shall be guided in its activities by the recommendations of the General Assembly and by such instructions as the Security Council may consider necessary to issue.

The measures taken by the Commission, within the recommendations of the General Assembly, shall become immediately effective unless the Commission has previously received contrary instructions from the Security Council.

The Commission shall render periodic monthly progress reports, or more frequently if desirable, to the Security Council.

15. The Commission shall make its final report to the next regular session of the General Assembly and to the Security Council simultaneously.

C. DECLARATION

A declaration shall be made to the United Nations by the provisional government of each proposed State before independence. It shall contain inter alia the following clauses:
General Provision

The stipulations contained in the declaration are recognized as fundamental laws of the State and no law, regulation or official action shall conflict or interfere with these stipulations, nor shall any law, regulation or official action prevail over them.

Chapter 1

Holy Places, religious buildings and sites
1. Existing rights in respect of Holy Places and religious buildings or sites shall not be denied or impaired.

2. In so far as Holy Places are concerned, the liberty of access, visit and transit shall be guaranteed, in conformity with existing rights, to all residents and citizens of the other State and of the City of Jerusalem, as well as to aliens, without distinction as to nationality, subject to requirements of national security, public order and decorum.

Similarly, freedom of worship shall be guaranteed in conformity with existing rights, subject to the maintenance of public order and decorum.

3. Holy Places and religious buildings or sites shall be preserved. No act shall be permitted which may in any way impair their sacred character. If at any time it appears to the Government that any particular Holy Place, religious building or site is in need of urgent repair, the Government may call upon the community or communities concerned to carry out such repair. The Government may carry it out itself at the expense of the community or communities concerned if no action is taken within a reasonable time.

4. No taxation shall be levied in respect of any Holy Place, religious building or site which was exempt from taxation on the date of the creation of the State.

No change in the incidence of such taxation shall be made which would either discriminate between the owners or occupiers of Holy Places, religious buildings or sites, or would place such owners or occupiers in a position less favourable in relation to the general incidence of taxation than existed at the time of the adoption of the Assembly's recommendations.

5. The Governor of the City of Jerusalem shall have the right to determine whether the provisions of the Constitution of the State in relation to Holy Places, religious buildings and sites within the borders of the State and the religious rights appertaining thereto, are being properly applied and respected, and to make decisions on the basis of existing rights in cases of disputes which may arise between the different reli-

gious communities or the rites of a religious community with respect to such places, buildings and sites. He shall receive full co-operation and such privileges and immunities as are necessary for the exercise of his functions in the State.

Chapter 2

Religious and Minority Rights

1. Freedom of conscience and the free exercise of all forms of worship, subject only to the maintenance of public order and morals, shall be ensured to all.

2. No discrimination of any kind shall be made between the inhabitants on the ground of race, religion, language or sex.

3. All persons within the jurisdiction of the State shall be entitled to equal protection of the laws.

4. The family law and personal status of the various minorities and their religious interests, including endowments, shall be respected.

5. Except as may be required for the maintenance of public order and good government, no measure shall be taken to obstruct or interfere with the enterprise of religious or charitable bodies of all faiths or to discriminate against any representative or member of these bodies on the ground of his religion or nationality.

6. The State shall ensure adequate primary and secondary education for the Arab and Jewish minority, respectively, in its own language and its cultural traditions.

The right of each community to maintain its own schools for the education of its own members in its own language, while conforming to such educational requirements of a general nature as the State may impose, shall not be denied or impaired. Foreign educational establishments shall continue their activity on the basis of their existing rights.

7. No restriction shall be imposed on the free use by any citizen of the State of any language in private intercourse, in commerce, in religion, in the Press or in publications of any kind, or at public meetings.

8. No expropriation of land owned by an Arab in the Jewish State (by a Jew in the Arab State) shall be allowed except for public purposes. In all cases of expropriation full compensation as fixed by the Supreme Court shall be paid previous to dispossession.

Chapter 3

Citizenship, international conventions and financial obligations

1. Citizenship. Palestinian citizens residing in Palestine outside the City of Jerusalem, as well as Arabs and Jews who, not holding Palestinian citizenship, reside in Palestine outside the City of Jerusalem shall, upon the recognition of independence, become citizens of the State in which they are resident and enjoy full civil and political rights. Persons over the age of eighteen years may opt, within one year from the date of recognition of independence of the State in which they reside, for citizenship of the other State, providing that no Arab residing in the area of the proposed Arab State shall have the right to opt for citizenship in the proposed Jewish State and no Jew residing in the proposed Jewish State shall have the right to opt for citizenship in the proposed Arab State. The exercise of this right of option will be taken to include the wives and children under eighteen years of age of persons so opting.

Arabs residing in the area of the proposed Jewish State and Jews residing in the area of the proposed Arab State who have signed a notice of intention to opt for citizenship of the other State shall be eligible to vote in the elections to the Constituent Assembly of that State, but not in the elections to the Constituent Assembly of the State in which they reside.

2. International conventions. (a) The State shall be bound by all the international agreements and conventions, both general and special, to which Palestine has become a party. Subject to any right of denunciation provided for therein, such agreements and conventions shall be respected by the State throughout the period for which they were concluded.

(b) Any dispute about the applicability and continued validity of international conventions or treaties signed or adhered to by the mandatory Power on behalf of Palestine shall be referred to the International Court of Justice in accordance with the provisions of the Statute of the Court.

3. Financial obligations. (a) The State shall respect and fulfil all financial obligations of whatever nature assumed on behalf of Palestine by the mandatory Power during the exercise of the Mandate and recognized by the State. This provision includes the right of public servants to pensions, compensation or gratuities.

(b) These obligations shall be fulfilled through participation in the Joint economic Board in respect of those obligations applicable to Palestine as a whole, and individually in respect of those applicable to, and fairly apportionable between, the States.

(c) A Court of Claims, affiliated with the Joint Economic Board, and composed of one member appointed by the United Nations, one representative of the United Kingdom and one representative of the State concerned, should be established. Any dispute between the United Kingdom and the State respecting claims not recognized by the latter should be referred to that Court.

(d) Commercial concessions granted in respect of any part of Palestine prior to the adoption of the resolution by the General Assembly shall continue to be valid according to their terms, unless modified by agreement between the concession-holder and the State.

Chapter 4

Miscellaneous provisions

1. The provisions of chapters 1 and 2 of the declaration shall be under the guarantee of the United Nations, and no modifications shall be made in them without the assent of the General Assembly of the United Nations. Any Member of the United Nations shall have the right to bring to the attention of the General Assembly any infraction or danger of infraction of any of these stipulations, and the General Assembly may thereupon make such recommendations as it may deem proper in the circumstances.

2. Any dispute relating to the application or the interpretation of this declaration shall be referred, at the request of either party, to the International Court of Justice, unless the parties agree to another mode of settlement.

D. ECONOMIC UNION AND TRANSIT

[This section proposes an "economic union" in Palestine, to consist of a customs union, commonly operated transportation and public utilities, joint economic development, and other functions.]

E. ASSETS

[The following section concerns the "equitable distribution" between the Arabs and Jews of the "movable assets" of the British administration in Palestine.]

F. ADMISSION TO MEMBERSHIP IN THE UNITED NATIONS

When the independence of either the Arab or the Jewish State as envisaged in this plan has become effective and the declaration and undertaking, as envisaged in this plan, have been signed by either of them, sympathetic consideration should be given to its application for admission to membership in the United Nations in accordance with Article 4 of the Charter of the United Nations.

PART II

[This section lays out the boundaries of the Arab state, the Jewish state, and the city of Jerusalem, as shown on an accompanying map, p. 57.]

PART III

[This section describes provisions for the administration, by the United Nations, of the City of Jerusalem, including neighboring towns and villages.]

PART IV

[This section requests that foreign countries renounce any special privileges (known as capitulations) that they enjoyed in Palestine in the past.]

SOURCE: United Nations Information System on the Question of Palestine (UNISPAL), http://domino.un.org/UNISPAL.NSF/a06f2943c226015c85256c40005d359c/7f0af2bd897689b785256c330061d253!OpenDocument.

Founding of the State of Israel

DOCUMENT IN CONTEXT

Most of the diplomatic maneuvering over Palestine ended with the UN General Assembly's approval of a partition plan, in Resolution 181, in late November 1947. The assembly's action also moved into high gear the attempts by Arabs and Jews to gain the upper hand through military force. In retrospect, it must be understood that the Arabs, enjoying overt support from neighboring countries and tacit support from the British government, were thought at the time to have the advantage over the Jews, who were outnumbered. At the same time, however, the Arabs were disorganized and indecisive.

After more than thirty years of neocolonial rule, Britain planned to pull out of Palestine on May 14, 1948. As this date approached, the British gradually reduced their presence in Palestine, while armed conflict escalated between Arabs and Jews and between Jews and the British government. Zionist political leaders made plans to establish the State of Israel upon Britain's withdrawal.

At the United Nations in March 1948, a final flurry of diplomacy took place when U.S. State Department officials, acting at variance to President Harry S. Truman's policies, made a last-minute attempt to head off the declaration of a Jewish state by proposing that partition be deferred. Instead, under a U.S. State Department plan submitted to the United Nations on March 19, Palestine would be placed under a UN trusteeship until a permanent settlement could be reached. This plan met with little international enthusiasm and was quietly shelved.

At this point as well, Jewish forces seized Arab towns commanding major roads and other strategic points. Arab guerrillas had cut off supplies to Jerusalem, but the Haganah, the military arm of the quasi-governmental Jewish Agency, broke the blockade long enough to move supplies into Jewish neighborhoods in the western part of the city. As British forces withdrew in late April and early May, Jewish units moved into their forts and police stations, gaining strategic control over much of the countryside.

Two of the main Arab-dominated cities, Haifa and Jaffa, fell to advancing Jewish forces, and terrorized Arab residents fled their homes. Overall, during the early days of the war, an estimated 300,000 to 400,000 Arabs fled or were forced from their homes by advancing Jewish units. (Decades later, heated debate continues concerning the number of Arabs who left of their own volition during all phases of the fighting versus those who fled in terror or were forced out by Jewish fighters). The Arab armies—factionalized and lacking anything approaching a unified political leadership—often folded in the face of advancing Jewish units. By early May, Jewish forces controlled most of the territory allocated to the Jewish state by UN Resolution 181, plus at least half of the land that had been allocated for the Arab state (UN General Assembly Resolution 181, p. 59).

The Arab village of Dayr Yassin, west of Jerusalem, came to symbolize the aggressiveness of the Jewish fighters. In the early hours of April 9, Jewish guerrillas attacked the village and killed many of its 400-some inhabitants; subsequent investigations put the number killed at between 100 and 250. News of the killings spread quickly and contributed to the growing panic among Arabs, thus achieving one of the goals of the attack. For years to come, Arabs would cite Dayr Yassin as an example of Jewish terrorism, and Israelis would bicker over who was responsible.

On the morning of May 14, the British lowered the Union Jack over their headquarters in Jerusalem, signifying the end of the mandate. At 4:00 p.m., Jewish leaders gathered at the Tel Aviv Museum, where they sat beneath a portrait of Theodore Herzl, whose writings in the late nineteenth century had inspired the Zionist movement. David Ben-Gurion read a statement declaring the establishment of the State of Israel. The declaration affirmed the historic right of Jews to live in and govern Israel, and it also included a plea to the Arabs for peace: "We appeal, in the very midst of the onslaught launched against us now for months, to the Arab inhabitants of the State of Israel to preserve peace and participate in the upbuilding of the state on the basis of full and equal citizenship and due representation in all its provisional and permanent institutions."

By then, fighting between Arab and Jewish forces had engulfed much of Palestine in the opening stages of an all-out war between Israel and its five Arab neighbors. After the declaration of the Israeli state, countries were forced to decide on recognition. Overriding his senior advisors, President Truman decided that the United States would recognize Israel and issued a statement to that effect on May 14, making the United States the first country to do so. The Soviet Union followed suit two days later. Britain waited nearly eight months, until January 30, 1949 (Founding of the State of Israel, p. 67).

Following is the declaration issued May 14, 1948, by the founders of Israel upon its creation.

DOCUMENT

Declaration of the Founding of Israel

MAY 14, 1948

ERETZ-ISRAEL [(Hebrew)—the Land of Israel, Palestine] was the birthplace of the Jewish people. Here their spiritual, religious and political identity was shaped. Here they first attained to statehood, created cultural values of national and universal significance and gave to the world the eternal Book of Books.

After being forcibly exiled from their land, the people kept faith with it throughout their Dispersion and never ceased to pray and hope for their return to it and for the restoration in it of their political freedom.

Impelled by this historic and traditional attachment, Jews strove in every successive generation to re-establish themselves in their ancient homeland. In recent decades they returned in their masses. Pioneers, *ma'pilim* [(Hebrew)—immigrants coming to Eretz-Israel in defiance of restrictive legislation] and defenders, they made deserts bloom, revived the Hebrew language, built villages and towns, and created a thriving community controlling its own economy and culture, loving peace but knowing how to defend itself, bringing the blessings of progress to all the country's inhabitants, and aspiring towards independent nationhood.

In the year 5657 (1897), at the summons of the spiritual father of the Jewish State, Theodore Herzl, the First Zionist Congress convened and proclaimed the right of the Jewish people to national rebirth in its own country.

This right was recognized in the Balfour Declaration of the 2nd November, 1917, and re-affirmed in the Mandate of the League of Nations which, in particular, gave international sanction to the historic connection between the Jewish people and Eretz-Israel and to the right of the Jewish people to rebuild its National Home.

The catastrophe which recently befell the Jewish people—the massacre of millions of Jews in Europe—was another clear demonstration of the urgency of solving the problem of its homelessness by re-establishing in Eretz-Israel the Jewish State, which would open the gates of the homeland wide to every Jew and confer upon the Jewish people the status of a fully privileged member of the comity of nations.

Survivors of the Nazi holocaust in Europe, as well as Jews from other parts of the world, continued to migrate to Eretz-Israel, undaunted by difficulties, restrictions and dangers, and never ceased to assert their right to a life of dignity, freedom and honest toil in their national homeland.

In the Second World War, the Jewish community of this country contributed its full share to the struggle of the freedom- and peace-loving nations against the forces of Nazi wickedness and, by the blood of its soldiers and its war effort, gained the right to be reckoned among the peoples who founded the United Nations.

On the 29th November, 1947, the United Nations General Assembly passed a resolution calling for the establishment of a Jewish State in Eretz-Israel; the General Assembly required the inhabitants of Eretz-Israel to take such steps as were necessary on their part for the implementation of that resolution. This recognition by the United Nations of the right of the Jewish people to establish their State is irrevocable.

This right is the natural right of the Jewish people to be masters of their own fate, like all other nations, in their own sovereign State.

ACCORDINGLY WE, MEMBERS OF THE PEOPLE'S COUNCIL, REPRE-SENTATIVES OF THE JEWISH COMMUNITY OF ERETZ-ISRAEL AND OF THE ZIONIST MOVEMENT, ARE HERE ASSEMBLED ON THE DAY OF THE TERMINATION OF THE BRITISH MANDATE OVER ERETZ-ISRAEL AND, BY VIRTUE OF OUR NATURAL AND HISTORIC RIGHT AND ON THE STRENGTH OF THE RESOLUTION OF THE UNITED NATIONS GEN-ERAL ASSEMBLY, HEREBY DECLARE THE ESTABLISHMENT OF A JEWISH STATE IN ERETZ-ISRAEL, TO BE KNOWN AS THE STATE OF ISRAEL.

WE DECLARE that, with effect from the moment of the termination of the Man-date being tonight, the eve of Sabbath, the 6th Iyar, 5708 (15th May, 1948), until the establishment of the elected, regular authorities of the State in accordance with the Constitution which shall be adopted by the Elected Constituent Assembly not later than the 1st October 1948, the People's Council shall act as a Provisional Council of State, and its executive organ, the People's Administration, shall be the Provisional Government of the Jewish State, to be called "Israel".

THE STATE OF ISRAEL will be open for Jewish immigration and for the Ingath-ering of the Exiles; it will foster the development of the country for the benefit of all its inhabitants; it will be based on freedom, justice and peace as envisaged by the prophets of Israel; it will ensure complete equality of social and political rights to all its inhabitants irrespective of religion, race or sex; it will guarantee freedom of reli-gion, conscience, language, education and culture; it will safeguard the Holy Places of all religions; and it will be faithful to the principles of the Charter of the United Nations.

THE STATE OF ISRAEL is prepared to cooperate with the agencies and repre-sentatives of the United Nations in implementing the resolution of the General Assem-bly of the 29th November, 1947, and will take steps to bring about the economic union of the whole of Eretz-Israel.

WE APPEAL to the United Nations to assist the Jewish people in the building-up of its State and to receive the State of Israel into the comity of nations.

WE APPEAL—in the very midst of the onslaught launched against us now for months—to the Arab inhabitants of the State of Israel to preserve peace and partici-pate in the upbuilding of the State on the basis of full and equal citizenship and due representation in all its provisional and permanent institutions.

WE EXTEND our hand to all neighbouring states and their peoples in an offer of peace and good neighbourliness, and appeal to them to establish bonds of cooper-ation and mutual help with the sovereign Jewish people settled in its own land. The

State of Israel is prepared to do its share in a common effort for the advancement of the entire Middle East.

WE APPEAL to the Jewish people throughout the Diaspora to rally round the Jews of Eretz-Israel in the tasks of immigration and upbuilding and to stand by them in the great struggle for the realization of the age-old dream—the redemption of Israel.

Placing our trust in the "Rock of Israel", we affix our signatures to this proclamation at this session of the Provisional Council of State, on the soil of the homeland, in the city of Tel-Aviv, on this sabbath eve, the 5th day of Iyar, 5708 (14th May, 1948).

[Signed by David Ben-Gurion and other members of the Provisional Council of State]

SOURCE: Israel Ministry of Foreign Affairs, www.mfa.gov.il/MFA/Peace+Process/Guide+to+the+Peace+Process/Declaration+of+Establishment+of+State+of+Israel.htm.

War and Refugees

DOCUMENT IN CONTEXT

The first of a half-dozen wars between Israel and its Arab neighbors began in earnest one day after Zionist leaders proclaimed Israel a state on May 14, 1948. On the morning of May 15, 1948, army units from Egypt, Iraq, Lebanon, Syria, and Transjordan (later Jordan) moved into Israel and the remainder of Palestine with the goal of defeating the new Israeli army and forcing abandonment of the Israeli state. The Arab League endorsed the attack, but each state had its own agenda and operated almost entirely on its own, depriving the Arab armies of tactical coordination. Transjordan's King Abdallah, in fact, had no intention of unseating the new Israeli government; he simply wanted to assert his authority over the Muslim holy sites in Jerusalem and much of the Jordan River valley (Declaration of the Founding of Israel, p. 69).

Subsequent Israeli mythology claimed that the Israeli army—formed around the Haganah militia—was vastly outnumbered and succeeded against the Arabs only through the miraculous, almost superhuman, efforts of its commanders and soldiers. Recent research reveals, however, that the Israelis matched or even exceeded the Arabs in numbers of fighters and outclassed the Arabs in terms of the quality of soldiers, organizational and command ability, and, in the later stages of the fighting, in weaponry. Rather than eliminating Israel, the war produced the opposite—confirming Israel's existence and its ability to ensure its own survival.

The fighting unfolded in three stages. In the first stage, between May 15 and June 11, the Arab armies attacked from four directions, but the Israelis beat them back, except in the Jerusalem area, where Transjordan's Arab Legion (led by British officers) succeeded in holding on to the eastern part of the city. A month-long truce, imposed by the United Nations, allowed both sides to regroup in preparation for another round of fighting. The

Israelis made the best use of the interval, essentially doubling the size of their forces and importing large quantities of weapons from Czechoslovakia and France.

The second stage started on July 8, when the reenergized Israeli military broke out of its defensive positions and attacked the Arabs on all fronts. The Israelis captured several towns in central Palestine that the United Nations had designated for the Arab state, but they failed to dislodge the Arab Legion from East Jerusalem and the Egyptian army from the Negev desert, in the south. Another UN-imposed cease-fire took effect on July 19 and held for nearly three months.

It was during this period on September 17 that assassins killed Count Folke Bernadotte, the UN's peace mediator, near Jerusalem. The Israeli government blamed extremist Jewish guerrillas, but never brought anyone to trial for the crime. Bernadotte had submitted a report suggesting that the Negev be turned over to the Arabs, that Jerusalem be put under international control, and that Arab refugees be allowed to return to their homes. The Israelis and the Arabs both rejected the plan.

Charging that Egypt had violated the truce, Israel on October 15 resumed its offensive in the Negev, quickly isolating the Egyptian army and ultimately driving across the international border to cut off the Egyptians' escape route. In the north, known as the Galilee, the Israelis managed to beat back the combined Arab armies in three days at the end of October. At the conclusion of the bulk of the fighting, Israel controlled all of the portions of Palestine that the United Nations had designated for partition between the Arabs and Jews, except for the Gaza Strip (a sliver of land along the Mediterranean held by Egypt) and the West Bank of the Jordan River (the potato-shaped territory in central Palestine held by Transjordan). Israelis held West Jerusalem, including the recently built section of the city called the New City, and Transjordan controlled the historic Old City, site of the most revered religious shrines, and the surrounding neighborhoods of East Jerusalem.

Many of the towns and villages in Israel formerly inhabited by Palestinian Arabs were now empty, most of their residents having fled in advance of approaching Israeli forces or having been forced out by the Jews. The United Nations estimated that about 720,000 Arabs—two-thirds of Palestine's prewar Arab population—had fled the areas of Palestine that fell under Israeli control. The largest number of refugees, about 240,000, headed for Transjordan-controlled East Jerusalem and the West Bank, while more than 50,000 crossed over the Jordan River into Transjordan. According to UN figures, another 180,000 Arab refugees crowded into the Egyptian-controlled Gaza Strip, about 100,000 went to Lebanon, 70,000 to Syria, and the remainder to Egypt and Iraq. (The Israeli government disputed most of these figures, contending that slightly more than 500,000 Arabs fled Palestine before and during the war and that most left voluntarily or were encouraged to leave by Arab governments.)

The new Israeli government quickly made clear its position that the Arabs who had fled would not be allowed to return. In a speech on August 1, Israeli leader David Ben-Gurion, said the question of refugees could be discussed only within the context of formal peace treaties between Israel and its neighbors, and even then under conditions that would make their return practically impossible. The UN General Assembly intervened on December 11, adopting Resolution 194, which created a Conciliation Commission to continue the mediation effort performed by Count Bernadotte before his assassination. The resolution also repeated past UN proposals that the Jerusalem area be placed under UN trusteeship. A key provision of the resolution stated that "refugees wishing

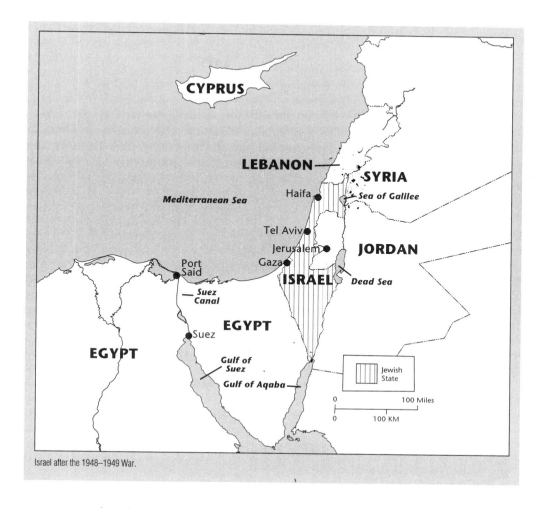

Israel after the 1948–1949 War.

to return to their homes and live at peace with their neighbors should be permitted to do so at the earliest practicable date"; those who did not return should be compensated for the property they had lost or left behind. Little came of this provision because Israel would accept only 100,000 of the refugees; in 1951 Israel offered to help pay for reset-tling the refugees in Arab countries, but nothing came of this offer. Palestinians con-tinue to cite the resolution as the legal basis for refugees' and their descendants' so-called right of return to Israel, an interpretation the Israeli government rejects.

It was not until January 6, 1949, that Egypt—the last Arab country engaged in seri-ous fighting against Israel—agreed to UN-sponsored negotiations to craft a formal armistice. The negotiations, held on the island of Rhodes, were mediated by American diplomat Ralph Bunche, who had been Bernadotte's chief assistant. The Egyptians refused at first to meet face-to-face with the Israelis, forcing Bunche to shuttle between the two delegations until the Egyptians agreed to joint meetings. Bunche secured an armistice agreement on February 24 that locked in place most of the existing lines that each country controlled. It in effect extended Israeli control over the Negev but allowed Egypt to control the Gaza Strip, recently crowded with Palestinian Arab refugees.

The armistice did not constitute a peace treaty nor, at Egyptian insistence, did it imply Cairo's recognition of the State of Israel. The agreement simply held out the prospect some day for "permanent peace in Palestine." Israel then signed similar UN-mediated armistice agreements with Lebanon on March 23, with Transjordan on April 3, and with Syria on July 20. Iraq, which had assigned its negotiating rights to Transjordan before withdrawing its remaining forces, was the lone Arab belligerent not to sign an armistice with Israel.

The United Nations was unable to translate the armistice agreements into longer-term peace treaties. The reasons for this failure were numerous, but ultimately neither the Arabs nor the Israelis were prepared for such a far-reaching step. Even so, the armistice agreements held for seven years, until the next significant round of fighting between Israel and Egypt during the Suez crisis in 1956 (Suez Crisis, p. 80).

> *Following is the text of UN General Assembly Resolution 194, adopted on December 11, 1948, establishing a Palestine Conciliation Commission and calling for the return of Arab refugees to their lands following the Arab-Israeli war.*

DOCUMENT

UN General Assembly Resolution 194 (1948) Palestine—Progress Report of the United Nations Mediator

DECEMBER 11, 1948

The General Assembly,
Having considered further the situation in Palestine,

1. *Expresses* its deep appreciation of the progress achieved through the good offices of the late United Nations Mediator in promoting a peaceful adjustment of the future situation of Palestine, for which cause he sacrificed his life; and

Extends its thanks to the Acting Mediator and his staff for their continued efforts and devotion to duty in Palestine;

2. *Establishes* a Conciliation Commission consisting of three States members of the United Nations which shall have the following functions:

(a) To assume, in so far as it considers necessary in existing circumstances, the functions given to the United Nations Mediator on Palestine by resolution 186 (S-2) of the General Assembly of 14 May 1948;

(b) To carry out the specific functions and directives given to it by the present resolution and such additional functions and directives as may be given to it by the General Assembly or by the Security Council;

(c) To undertake, upon the request of the Security Council, any of the functions now assigned to the United Nations Mediator on Palestine or to the United

Nations Truce Commission by resolutions of the Security Council; upon such request to the Conciliation Commission by the Security Council with respect to all the remaining functions of the United Nations Mediator on Palestine under Security Council resolutions, the office of the Mediator shall be terminated;

3. *Decides* that a Committee of the Assembly, consisting of China, France, the Union of Soviet Socialist Republics, the United Kingdom and the United States of America, shall present, before the end of the first part of the present session of the General Assembly, for the approval of the Assembly, a proposal concerning the names of the three States which will constitute the Conciliation Commission [France, Turkey, and the United States later were named as the three members];

4. Requests the Commission to begin its functions at once, with a view to the establishment of contact between the parties themselves and the Commission at the earliest possible date;

5. Calls upon the Governments and authorities concerned to extend the scope of the negotiations provided for in the Security Council's resolution of 16 November 1948 and to seek agreement by negotiations conducted either with the Conciliation Commission or directly, with a view to the final settlement of all questions outstanding between them;

6. *Instructs* the Conciliation Commission to take steps to assist the Governments and authorities concerned to achieve a final settlement of all questions outstanding between them;

7. *Resolves* that the Holy Places—including Nazareth—religious buildings and sites in Palestine should be protected and free access to them assured, in accordance with existing rights and historical practice; that arrangements to this end should be under effective United Nations supervision; that the United Nations Conciliation Commission, in presenting to the fourth regular session of the General Assembly its detailed proposals for a permanent international regime for the territory of Jerusalem, should include recommendations concerning the Holy Places in that territory; that with regard to the Holy Places in the rest of Palestine the Commission should call upon the political authorities of the areas concerned to give appropriate formal guarantees as to the protection of the Holy Places and access to them; and that these undertakings should be presented to the General Assembly for approval;

8. *Resolves* that, in view of its association with three world religions, the Jerusalem area, including the present municipality of Jerusalem plus the surrounding villages and towns, the most eastern of which shall be Abu Dis; the most southern, Bethlehem; the most western, Ein Karim (including also the built-up area of Motsa); and the most northern, Shu'fat, should be accorded special and separate treatment from the rest of Palestine and should be placed under effective United Nations control;

Requests the Security Council to take further steps to ensure the demilitarization of Jerusalem at the earliest possible date;

Instructs the Conciliation Commission to present to the fourth regular session of the General Assembly detailed proposals for a permanent international regime for the Jerusalem area which will provide for the maximum local autonomy for distinctive groups consistent with the special international status of the Jerusalem area;

The Conciliation Commission is authorized to appoint a United Nations representative, who shall co-operate with the local authorities with respect to the interim administration of the Jerusalem area;

9. *Resolves* that, pending agreement on more detailed arrangements among the Governments and authorities concerned, the freest possible access to Jerusalem by road, rail or air should be accorded to all inhabitants of Palestine;

Instructs the Conciliation Commission to report immediately to the Security Council, for appropriate action by that organ, any attempt by any party to impede such access;

10. *Instructs* the Conciliation Commission to seek arrangements among the Governments and authorities concerned which will facilitate the economic development of the area, including arrangements for access to ports and airfields and the use of transportation and communication facilities;

11. *Resolves* that the refugees wishing to return to their homes and live at peace with their neighbours should be permitted to do so at the earliest practicable date, and that compensation should be paid for the property of those choosing not to return and for loss of or damage to property which, under principles of international law or in equity, should be made good by the Governments or authorities responsible;

Instructs the Conciliation Commission to facilitate the repatriation, resettlement and economic and social rehabilitation of the refugees and the payment of compensation, and to maintain close relations with the Director of the United Nations Relief for Palestine Refugees and, through him, with the appropriate organs and agencies of the United Nations;

12. *Authorizes* the Conciliation Commission to appoint such subsidiary bodies and to employ such technical experts, acting under its authority, as it may find necessary for the effective discharge of its functions and responsibilities under the present resolution;

The Conciliation Commission will have its official headquarters at Jerusalem. The authorities responsible for maintaining order in Jerusalem will be responsible for taking all measures necessary to ensure the security of the Commission. The Secretary-General will provide a limited number of guards to the protection of the staff and premises of the Commission;

13. *Instructs* the Conciliation Commission to render progress reports periodically to the Secretary-General for transmission to the Security Council and to the Members of the United Nations;

14. *Calls upon* all Governments and authorities concerned to co-operate with the Conciliation Commission and to take all possible steps to assist in the implementation of the present resolution;

15. *Requests* the Secretary-General to provide the necessary staff and facilities.

Status of Jerusalem

Until the 1948 Arab-Israeli war, most international diplomacy concerning Palestine assumed that Jerusalem would come under some form of international control. Such thinking, in turn, flowed from the assumption that only a disinterested, international regime could protect the interests of the three major religions—Christianity, Islam, and Judaism—with historic holy places in or near the city.

UN General Assembly Resolution 181, adopted in November 1947, set out the most specific proposal for international control of Jerusalem while calling for the partition of Palestine into separate Arab and Jewish states. It proposed making Jerusalem and its surrounding neighborhoods a "corpus separatum" administered by a trusteeship council appointed by the United Nations. A principal task of the council would be "to ensure that order and peace, and especially religious peace, reign in Jerusalem" (UN General Assembly Resolution 181, p. 59).

The idealistic rhetoric of that resolution never came into play, however, because the 1948 war left Jerusalem and its environs split between Israel and Transjordan, neither of which had the slightest inclination to relinquish its hard-won gains. Israel controlled the western portions of the city, including the recently built-up New City, while Jordan controlled East Jerusalem and the historic Old City, where most of the important religious shrines were located. In a speech to the local Jewish advisory council in Jerusalem on December 1, 1948, Israel's first president, Chaim Weizmann, insisted that "Jerusalem is ours" and called it "utterly inconceivable" that the city could ever be placed under international control.

In mid-1949, however, the idea of international stewardship of Jerusalem resurfaced with the deliberations of the Palestine Conciliation Commission, a three-member body created under UN General Assembly Resolution 194 (passed in December 1948). In a report issued on September 1, 1949, the commission suggested a compromise: dividing the city into two zones, one Israeli and one Arab, with each side in charge of local affairs. A UN commissioner would have authority for protecting the holy places in both zones and preventing immigration that "might alter the present demographic equilibrium" of the entire city (UN General Assembly Resolution 194, p. 74).

Israel and Jordan (Transjordan's new name as of April 1949) emphatically rejected the proposal and instead began secret negotiations over practical arrangements for running a divided Jerusalem. International debate about the city continued at the United Nations, fostered in part by the Vatican's sudden endorsement of international control.

On December 5, 1949, just before a planned debate in the General Assembly on the subject of Jerusalem, Israeli prime minister David Ben-Gurion told the Knesset, or parliament, that Israel would never accept international control of Jerusalem because the city was "an organic and inseparable part of the State of Israel." Ben-Gurion's uncompromising rhetoric failed, however, to deter advocates of internationalization. On December 9, the General Assembly adopted Resolution 303, calling for Jerusalem to be placed under a "permanent international regime," by which it meant a special authority answerable to the UN's Trusteeship Council.

Israel and Jordan both acted quickly to establish facts on the ground to prevent the resolution from being implemented. On December 13, the Knesset approved a plan to move most Israeli government agencies from Tel Aviv to Jerusalem. The Knesset held its first session in the city just two weeks later, and most government offices were moved there by January 1950. On January 1, 1950, King Abdallah issued a decree granting Jordanian citizenship to residents of the West Bank, including East Jerusalem, and four months later formally annexed those areas to Jordan. Israel and Jordan conducted secret negotiations that produced several tentative agreements, but ultimately failed to reach a final settlement because neither side was able or willing to make the necessary compromises. The negotiations ended after Abdallah's assassination by a Muslim extremist on July 20, 1951.

Jerusalem remained divided until Israel captured its eastern portion from Jordan in the June 1967 war. Israel immediately annexed East Jerusalem and its majority Arab population, declaring Jerusalem as "one city indivisible, the capital of the State of Israel." The Knesset also enacted a law guaranteeing access to Jerusalem's religious shrines for Christians, Jews, and Muslims; in contrast, Jordan had refused from 1948 to 1967 to allow Jews to pray at the Western, or Wailing, Wall, the exposed portion of the remains of the Second Temple. (Despite its law, Israel often did bar young Muslim men from worshiping at the al Aqsa Mosque in the Old City, fearing that Friday prayers there could result in violence.) In later years, Israel encouraged Jewish migration to East Jerusalem and enacted regulations that "encouraged" Arabs to leave. Nearly four decades later, Jerusalem once again became a divided city when the Israeli government erected what it called a security barrier separating the main part of the city from its Palestinian neighborhoods to the east.

The United Nations has never formally accepted or recognized Israel's control of East Jerusalem, declaring in numerous resolutions that this part of the city remains "occupied Palestinian territory," along with the West Bank. Several dozen countries have established embassies in Jerusalem, but the United States and most other powers continue to maintain their embassies in Tel Aviv (although often with consulates or other satellite offices in Jerusalem). The future status of Jerusalem is considered one of the major obstacles to any final settlement of the Israeli-Palestinian conflict, as both sides claim the city as their capital. To date, the most comprehensive proposal for the city is one put forward by President Bill Clinton in December 2000. His "parameters" envisioned Jerusalem serving as the capital of Israel as well as of any new Palestinian state (Camp David and the al-Aqsa Intifada, p. 276).

Following is the text of a statement delivered to the Knesset on December 13, 1949, by Prime Minister David Ben-Gurion.

DOCUMENT

Ben-Gurion Statement on the Status of Jerusalem

DECEMBER 13, 1949

One week ago today, in the name of the Government of Israel, I made a statement on Jerusalem before the Knesset. I need hardly say to you that this statement retains its full force, and that no change in our attitude has occurred or can possibly occur.

As you know, the General Assembly of the United Nations has, in the meantime, by a large majority, decided to place Jerusalem under an international regime as a separate entity. This decision is utterly incapable of implementation—if only because of the determination and unalterable opposition of the inhabitants of Jerusalem themselves. It is to be hoped that the General Assembly will in the course of time amend the error which its majority has made, and will make no attempt to impose a regime on the Holy City against the will of its people.

We respect and shall continue to respect the wishes of all those States which are concerned for freedom of worship and free access to the Holy Places, and which seek to safeguard existing rights in the Holy Places and religious edifices in Jerusalem. Our undertaking to preserve these rights remains in force, and we shall gladly and willingly carry it out, even though we cannot lend our participation to the forced separation of Jerusalem, which violates without need or reason the historic and natural right of the people who dwell in Zion.

From the establishment of the Provisional Government we made the peace, the security and the economic consolidation of Jerusalem our principal care. In the stress of war, when Jerusalem was under siege, we were compelled to establish the seat of Government in Ha'Kirya at Tel Aviv. But for the State of Israel there has always been and always will be one capital only—Jerusalem the Eternal. Thus it was 3,000 years ago—and thus it will be, we believe, until the end of time.

As soon as the fighting stopped, we began transferring Government offices to Jerusalem and creating the conditions the capital needed—effective communications, economic and technical arrangements. We are continuing with the transfer of the Government to Jerusalem and hope to complete it as soon as possible.

When the first Knesset was opened in Jerusalem on 14 February 1949, there were no adequate facilities for its normal functioning in the capital, and it was necessary to transfer its sessions temporarily to Tel Aviv. The required arrangements in Jerusalem are on the verge of completion, and there is nothing now to prevent the Knesset from returning to Jerusalem. We propose that you take a decision to this effect.

In all these arrangements there is, of course, nothing that alters in the slightest degree any of the existing rights in the Holy Places, which the Government of Israel will respect in full, or our consent to effective supervision of these Holy Places by the United Nations, as our delegation to the General Assembly declared.

SOURCE: Israel Ministry of Foreign Affairs, www.mfa.gov.il/MFA/Foreign+Relations/Israels+Foreign+Relations+since+1947/1947-1974/7+Statement+to+the+Knesset+by+Prime+Minister+Ben-G.htm.

The Suez Crisis

DOCUMENT IN CONTEXT

Israel lived in an uneasy neighborhood after its establishment in 1948. Egypt regularly sent armed guerrillas, or *fedayeen* ("volunteers"), on raids into Israel from the Gaza Strip, and other Arab states periodically threatened more serious conflict. Israel also engaged in provocative acts, notably attacks on Egyptian forces in Gaza in February 1955 and on Syrian forces along the Sea of Galilee in December 1955. For the most part, however, Israel's first eight years of existence were relatively peaceful. All that changed in 1956, when Israel became a major actor in what the West calls the Suez crisis and in Israel is referred to as the Sinai campaign. Regardless, it was one of the most dangerous episodes of the cold war.

In 1954 Gamal Abdel Nasser emerged as the dynamic new leader of Egypt and fashioned himself the champion of a putative pan-Arab nation. Among Nasser's goals was the elimination of the last vestiges of Western imperialism from the Middle East. He made a significant step in that direction in July 1954, when Britain agreed to remove its military bases adjacent to the Suez Canal within twenty months. A year later, Nasser upset the geostrategic balance in the region when he signed an agreement to buy some $200 million worth of advanced warplanes and other weapons from Czechoslovakia, then a client state of the Soviet Union. The step appeared to herald Moscow's determination to play a greater role in the Middle East, and it frightened Israel, which was relying on France to help it retain a military edge over the Arab states.

In June 1956, Britain completed its withdrawal from the Suez Canal, and Nasser won the first of several uncontested elections for the presidency of Egypt. The following month, the United States and Britain unexpectedly backed away from their promises to provide financing for the Aswan High Dam, the cornerstone of Nasser's economic development program. The project was designed to regulate the Nile's annual floods and to generate the bulk of Egypt's electricity. Although the Eisenhower administration cited technical concerns, its principal reason was anger at Nasser's decision two months earlier to recognize the communist government of China, a step regarded as moving Egypt even deeper into the anti-Western camp. Nasser quickly responded by announcing Egypt's intent to nationalize the Suez Canal. The canal's British and French owners would be compensated, he said, but the canal henceforth would be in Egyptian hands and its profits used to subsidize construction of the Aswan High Dam.

British and French officials immediately began plotting to retake the canal militarily and, they hoped, to force Nasser from power. In October, Israel joined the operation. During a secret three-day meeting in the Paris suburb of Sèvres, senior officials from the three countries developed a detailed plan in which Israel—claiming to be responding to Egyptian attacks—would send its army across the Sinai Peninsula toward the Suez Canal; Britain and France would then intervene to separate the warring Egyptian and Israeli parties and in the process seize control of the canal. The plan, compressed into a seven-point agreement later known as the Protocol of Sèvres, was signed on October 24, 1956, by Israeli prime minister David Ben-Gurion, French foreign minister Christian Pineau, and Patrick Dean, a senior official of the British Foreign Office. The protocol remained secret for nearly forty years, until the BBC revealed its existence in 1996.

The three parties signed the document one day after public protests began in Hungary against Soviet domination; the demonstrations eventually would blossom into an uprising during the Suez crisis. Together, these two events count among the most worrisome developments of the entire cold war period, as each had the potential to explode into a full-scale confrontation between the United States and the Soviet Union.

The conspirators moved rapidly to put their plan into effect. On October 29, Israeli paratroopers landed at the strategic Mitla Pass in the central mountains of the Sinai Peninsula. A day later, Israeli ground forces moved into the peninsula along four routes, three of them in the direction of the canal. The fourth route was toward Sharm al-Sheikh, where a base at the extreme southern point of Sinai controlled access to the Strait of Tiran, the waterway leading into the Gulf of Aqaba, Israel's only direct access to the Red Sea.

Following the plan laid out at Sèvres, Britain and France on October 30 issued an ultimatum to Egypt and to Israel demanding an immediate cease-fire, the withdrawal of Egyptian and Israeli troops from the canal (Israeli forces were not yet there), and insisting that Egypt accept temporary occupation of the canal zone by British and French forces to ensure freedom of shipping. As expected, Israel accepted the ultimatum, and Egypt rejected it as a challenge to its sovereignty. Later that day, the United States submitted a draft resolution to the UN Security Council demanding that Israel withdraw from Egyptian territory; a majority of the council voted yes, but Britain and France used their vetoes to block the resolution. By this time, it had become clear to the world that Britain and France were not—as officials in London and Paris claimed—innocent bystanders, but were in fact acting in collusion with Israel.

Over the next several days, British and French troops actively joined in the fighting. Starting on October 31, the two countries launched air raids that destroyed much of Egypt's newly acquired force of Soviet warplanes, and on November 5 British and French paratroopers landed at Port Said at the northern end of the Suez Canal. Israeli ground forces had by then captured the Gaza Strip and all of the Sinai Peninsula, including Sharm al-Sheikh. Its army having retreated in the face of the Israeli advance, and its air force a shambles, Egypt responded by sinking ships in the canal, thus preventing use of the vital waterway.

Fighting continued despite the UN General Assembly's adoption of two resolutions—997 on November 2 and 999 on November 4—demanding an immediate cease-fire and the withdrawal of all forces behind the lines mandated by the 1949 armistice between Egypt and Israel. The United States and other countries had taken the matter to the General Assembly to avoid vetoes in the Security Council by Britain and France. On November 5, the General Assembly adopted Resolution 1000, authorizing a peacekeeping force to monitor a cease-fire once one took place.

The fighting ended in the early hours of November 7 after intervention by the United States and the Soviet Union. President Dwight D. Eisenhower placed angry telephone calls to British prime minister Anthony Eden and threatened to block a pending loan to Britain by the International Monetary Fund. That same day, Eisenhower also sent a stern letter to Ben-Gurion demanding that Israel withdraw from Egypt. Israel's refusal to heed the UN resolutions, Eisenhower said, "would seriously undermine the urgent efforts being made by the United Nations to restore peace in the Middle East, and could not but bring about the condemnation of Israel as a violator of the principles as well as the directives of the United Nations." An even blunter warning arrived from Soviet prime minister Nikolai Bulganin, who threatened rocket attacks against the three aggressor countries and suggested that "volunteers" would be sent to aid Egypt.

Britain and France began withdrawing their troops from Egypt on November 21, but Israel retreated slowly and grudgingly, starting with a pullback from the Suez Canal in early December. At first, Israel insisted on holding on to the Gaza Strip along with Sharm al-Sheikh and a strip of land adjacent to the Gulf of Aqaba to ensure its shipping rights. Another potential diplomatic crisis arose early in 1957 when Israel appeared to be ignoring repeated UN resolutions demanding its complete withdrawal behind the 1949 armistice lines. On February 4, 1957, Eisenhower sent another letter to Ben-Gurion stating that continued Israeli disregard for UN resolutions would "seriously damage relations between Israel and UN members, including the United States." Under congressional pressure, Eisenhower later softened his stance somewhat, saying in a nationwide radio and television address on February 20 that Israel must withdraw unconditionally and rely on assurances from the United States and the United Nations that its right of transit in the Gulf of Aqaba would be protected. Israel finally withdrew from Gaza and Sharm al-Sheikh in March 1957 under a Canadian-negotiated compromise providing for the stationing of UN monitoring forces in both locations. Shortly after the withdrawal, Egypt sent civil administrators (but not troops) into Gaza in violation of UN resolutions. Egypt also announced that it would continue its ban on Israeli use of the Suez Canal.

Without question, the principal losers in the Suez crisis were Britain and France, which suffered a humiliating diplomatic defeat when the superpowers forced them to back down from their attempt to reassert their imperial roles in the Middle East. The crisis contributed to the collapse of the French Fourth Republic two years later and emboldened rebels in Algeria fighting to gain independence from Paris. (They succeeded in 1962.) Britain, which had dominated Egypt and strategic points in the Middle East for much of a century, withdrew entirely from the region in 1971.

The results were more mixed for Egypt and Israel. The crisis exposed the weakness and incompetence of the Egyptian army, and the country's new Soviet-built air force was destroyed. Even so, Nasser deftly converted military defeat into political victory: He survived in office, retained control of the canal, and strengthened his position in Egypt and the broader Arab world. Moreover, Nasser exploited the imperialist intervention to foment a wave of Arab nationalism that crested two years later with the formation of the United Arab Republic, the short-lived political union between Egypt and Syria.

Israel achieved two of its strategic objectives: freedom of navigation for Israelbound ships in the Strait of Tiran and an end to Egyptian-sponsored guerrilla attacks from Gaza. Nasser remained in power, however, as a potent symbol unifying the Arab world against Israel, and Ben-Gurion's dreams of an Israeli-controlled Sinai Peninsula were dashed (for the time being). The Suez crisis led to one of the lowest points in

U.S.-Israeli relations. Eisenhower was furious at being misled by Britain, France, and Israel; his letters to Ben-Gurion were among the bluntest ever sent by a U.S. president to an Israeli leader.

The Suez crisis, the last gasp of European imperial intervention in the Middle East, made the United States the foremost outside actor in the region, followed closely (for a time) by the Soviet Union. Washington developed increasingly close relations with Israel and, until the 1973 Arab-Israeli war, also remained on good terms with most of the Arab world (October 1973 War, p. 112).

Following are three documents related to the Suez crisis: an English translation of the original French text of the agreement signed at Sèvres, France, on October 24, 1956, by Israeli prime minister David Ben-Gurion, French foreign minister Christian Pineau, and Patrick Dean, a senior official of the British Foreign Office; text of UN General Assembly Resolution 997, adopted on November 2, 1956; and the text of a letter from U.S. president Dwight D. Eisenhower to Israeli prime minister Ben-Gurion on November 7, 1956 (released to the public on November 8, 1956), stating his concern that Israel withdraw from Egyptian territory.

DOCUMENT

Protocol of Sèvres

OCTOBER 24, 1956

The results of the conversations which took place at Sèvres from 22 to 24 October 1956 between the representatives of the Governments of the United Kingdom, the State of Israel and of France are the following:

The Israeli forces launch in the evening of 29 October 1956 a large scale attack on the Egyptian forces with the aim of reaching the Canal Zone the following day.

2. On being apprised of these events, the British and French Governments during the day of 30 October 1956 respectively and simultaneously make two appeals to the Egyptian Government and the Israeli Government on the following lines:

A. *To the Egyptian Government*

  a) halt all acts of war.
  b) withdraw all its troops ten miles from the Canal.
  c) accept temporary occupation of key positions on the Canal by the Anglo-French forces to guarantee freedom of passage through the Canal by vessels of all nations until a final settlement.

B. *To the Israeli Government*

  a) halt all acts of war.
  b) withdraw all its troops ten miles to the east of the Canal.

In addition, the Israeli Government will be notified that the French and British Governments have demanded of the Egyptian Government to accept temporary occupation of key positions along the Canal by Anglo-French forces.

It is agreed that if one of the Governments refused, or did not give its consent, within twelve hours the Anglo-French forces would intervene with the means necessary to ensure that their demands are accepted.

C. The representatives of the three Governments agree that the Israeli Government will not be required to meet the conditions in the appeal addressed to it, in the event that the Egyptian Government does not accept those in the appeal addressed to it for their part.

3. In the event that the Egyptian Government should fail to agree within the stipulated time to the conditions of the appeal addressed to it, the Anglo-French forces will launch military operations against the Egyptian forces in the early hours of the morning of 31 October.

4. The Israeli Government will send forces to occupy the western shore of the Gulf of Aqaba and the group of islands Tiran and Sanafir to ensure freedom of navigation in the Gulf of Aqaba.

5. Israel undertakes not to attack Jordan during the period of operations against Egypt. But in the event that during the same period Jordan should attack Israel, the British Government undertakes not to come to the aid of Jordan.

6. The arrangements of the present protocol must remain strictly secret.

7. They will enter into force after the agreement of the three Governments.

(signed) DAVID BEN-GURION   PATRICK DEAN   CHRISTIAN PINEAU

SOURCE: David Ben-Gurion Archives, http://bgarchives.bgu.ac.il (Original French version). English translation published in Avi Shlaim, "The Protocol of Sèvres, 1956: Anatomy of a War Plot." *International Affairs* 73, no. 3 (1997): 509–530.

DOCUMENT

UN General Assembly Resolution 997 (1956)

NOVEMBER 2, 1956

The General Assembly,

Noting the disregard on many occasions by parties to the Israel-Arab armistice agreements of 1949 of the terms of such agreements, and that the armed forces of Israel have penetrated deeply into Egyptian territory in violation of the General Armistice Agreement between Egypt and Israel of 24 February 1949,[1]

---

[1]Official Records of the Security Council, Fourth Year, Special Supplement No. 3.

Noting that armed forces of France and the United Kingdom of Great Britain and Northern Ireland are conducting military operations against Egyptian territory,

Noting that traffic through the Suez Canal is now interrupted to the serious prejudice of many nations,

Expressing its grave concern over these developments,

1. *Urges* as a matter of priority that all parties now involved in hostilities in the area agree to an immediate cease-fire and, as part thereof, halt the movement of military forces and arms into the area;

2. *Urges* the parties to the armistice agreements promptly to withdraw all forces behind the armistice lines, to desist from raids across the armistice lines into neighbouring territory, and to observe scrupulously the provisions of the armistice agreements;

3. *Recommends* that all Member States refrain from introducing military goods in the area of hostilities and in general refrain from any acts which would delay or prevent the implementation of the present resolution;

4. *Urges* that, upon the cease-fire being effective, steps be taken to reopen the Suez Canal and restore secure freedom of navigation;

5. *Requests* the Secretary-General to observe and report promptly on the compliance with the present resolution to the Security Council and to the General Assembly, for such further action as they may deem appropriate in accordance with the Charter;

6. *Decides* to remain in emergency session pending compliance with the present resolution.

SOURCE: United Nations Information System on the Question of Palestine, http://domino.un.org/UNISPAL. NSF/9a798adbf322aff38525617b006d88d7/5b887dcdb63624f7852560df0066d4b0!OpenDocument.

DOCUMENT

Eisenhower Letter to Ben-Gurion on Withdrawal from the Sinai

NOVEMBER 7, 1956

Dear Mr. Prime Minister:

As you know, the General Assembly of the United Nations has arranged a cease-fire in Egypt to which Egypt, France, the United Kingdom and Israel have agreed. There is being dispatched to Egypt a United Nations force in accordance with pertinent resolutions of the General Assembly. That body has urged that all other foreign forces be withdrawn from Egyptian territory, and specifically, that Israeli forces be withdrawn to the General Armistice line. The resolution covering the cease-fire and withdrawal was introduced by the United States and received the overwhelming vote of the Assembly.

Statements attributed to your Government to the effect that Israel does not intend to withdraw from Egyptian territory, as requested by the United Nations, have been called to my attention. I must say frankly, Mr. Prime Minister, that the United States views these reports, if true, with deep concern. Any such decision by the Government of Israel would seriously undermine the urgent efforts being made by the United Nations to restore peace in the Middle East, and could not but bring about the condemnation of Israel as a violator of the principles as well as the directives of the United Nations.

It is our belief that as a matter of highest priority peace should be restored and foreign troops, except for United Nations forces, withdrawn from Egypt, after which new and energetic steps should be undertaken within the framework of the United Nations to solve the basic problems which have given rise to the present difficulty. The United States has tabled in the General Assembly two resolutions designed to accomplish the latter purposes, and hopes that they will be acted upon favorably as soon as the present emergency has been dealt with.

I need not assure you of the deep interest which the United States has in your country, nor recall the various elements of our policy of support to Israel in so many ways. It is in this context that I urge you to comply with the resolutions of the United Nations General Assembly dealing with the current crisis and to make your decision known immediately. It would be a matter of the greatest regret to all my countrymen if Israeli policy on a matter of such grave concern to the world should in any way impair the friendly cooperation between our two countries.

With best wishes,
Sincerely,

DWIGHT D. EISENHOWER

SOURCE: John Woolley and Gerhard Peters, The American Presidency Project, University of California, Santa Barbara, http://www.presidency.ucsb.edu/ws/?pid=10699.

The Eisenhower Doctrine

DOCUMENT IN CONTEXT

For much of the cold war period, one of the principle U.S. interests in the Middle East was keeping the Soviet Union out of the region, or at the very least minimizing Moscow's influence there. Every U.S. president from Harry S. Truman to Ronald Reagan had to contend with some degree of what Washington considered Soviet "meddling" in the Middle East, ranging from economic and military support for such favored clients as Egypt and Syria in the 1950s to the outright invasion and occupation of Afghanistan from the end of the 1970s through the 1980s.

The mid-1950s were an especially active period of U.S. concern about Soviet influence in the Middle East. Anticommunist uprisings in Hungary and Poland during 1956, the crisis over the Suez Canal that same year, and Moscow's successful launch of a satellite, *Sputnik,* in 1957 heightened cold war tensions. In the Middle East, Egyptian leader Gamal Abdel Nasser sought to play the two superpowers against one another by demanding aid from both; his strategy reaped large amounts of military aid from the Soviet Union but annoyed the United States, which provided only limited amounts of food assistance. Both superpowers came to Egypt's aid during the Suez crisis, using diplomatic pressure, including outright threats, to force Britain, France, and Israel to back down in their attempt to seize the Suez Canal and oust Nasser from power (The Suez Crisis, p. 80).

In response to the Suez crisis and broader concerns about possible Soviet intervention in the Middle East, Secretary of State John Foster Dulles developed a broad proposal for U.S. action to counter Moscow in the region. President Dwight D. Eisenhower presented the plan to a special joint session of Congress on January 5, 1957, warning that the Soviet Union was intent on "dominating the Middle East" as part of its grander scheme of "communizing the world." Moscow had no legitimate economic or other interests in the region, he said, noting for example that the Soviet Union had its own ample reserves of oil and natural gas.

To counter Soviet expansionism, Eisenhower asked Congress for the authority to provide economic and military aid, including military force if necessary, to support any nation or group of nations in the Middle East threatened by "international communism." Significantly, Eisenhower told Congress that the use of military force by the United States would be "subject to the overriding authority of the United Nations Security Council in accordance with the [UN] Charter." This was one of the few statements by any U.S. president appearing to acknowledge that the United Nations had any kind of veto power over the use of military force.

Members of both parties in Congress greeted Eisenhower's proposal, which immediately became known as the Eisenhower Doctrine, with much skepticism. Some members thought that the president had not made the case that the Soviet Union posed a genuine threat to U.S. interests in the Middle East, and others said that the administration had contributed to the Suez crisis by withholding aid that it earlier had promised for construction of the Aswan High Dam in Egypt. Despite these and other concerns, Congress gave Eisenhower the authority he requested, adopting a joint resolution on March 7 allowing for economic and military assistance to the Middle East. The resolution also authorized the president to use U.S. armed forces in the region "if the president determines the necessity" of doing so.

Eisenhower made use of the new authority slightly more than a year later when he sent U.S. marines to Lebanon to bolster that country's government, which (along with Jordan) feared the consequences of a political union between Nasser's Egypt and Syria. The marines remained in Lebanon for about three months and accomplished Eisenhower's goal of stabilizing the situation there. It was to be the first of several major U.S. military interventions in the Middle East (U.S. Involvement in Lebanon, p. 339).

Following is the text of the address to a Joint Session of Congress delivered by President Dwight D. Eisenhower on January 5, 1957.

DOCUMENT

Eisenhower's Message to Congress on the Middle East

JANUARY 5, 1957

First may I express to you my deep appreciation of your courtesy in giving me, at some inconvenience to yourselves, this early opportunity of addressing you on a matter I deem to be of grave importance to our country.

In my forthcoming State of the Union Message, I shall review the international situation generally. There are worldwide hopes which we can reasonably entertain, and there are worldwide responsibilities which we must carry to make certain that freedom—including our own—may be secure.

There is, however, a special situation in the Middle East which I feel I should, even now, lay before you.

Before doing so it is well to remind ourselves that our basic national objective in international affairs remains peace—a world peace based on justice. Such a peace must include all areas, all peoples of the world if it is to be enduring. There is no nation, great or small, with which we would refuse to negotiate, in mutual good faith, with patience and in the determination to secure a better understanding between us. Out of such understandings must, and eventually will, grow confidence and trust, indispensable ingredients to a program of peace and to plans for lifting from us all the burdens of expensive armaments. To promote these objectives, our government works tirelessly, day by day, month by month, year by year. But until a degree of success crowns our efforts that will assure to all nations peaceful existence, we must, in the interests of peace itself, remain vigilant, alert and strong.

I.

The Middle East has abruptly reached a new and critical stage in its long and important history. In past decades many of the countries in that area were not fully self-governing. Other nations exercised considerable authority in the area and the security of the region was largely built around their power. But since the First World War there has been a steady evolution toward self-government and independence. This development the United States has welcomed and has encouraged. Our country supports without reservation the full sovereignty and independence of each and every nation of the Middle East.

The evolution to independence has in the main been a peaceful process. But the area has been often troubled. Persistent crosscurrents of distrust and fear with raids back and forth across national boundaries have brought about a high degree of instability in much of the Mid East. Just recently there have been hostilities involving Western European nations that once exercised much influence in the area. Also the relatively large attack by Israel in October has intensified the basic differences between that nation and its Arab neighbors. All this instability has been heightened and, at times, manipulated by International Communism.

II.

Russia's rulers have long sought to dominate the Middle East. That was true of the Czars and it is true of the Bolsheviks. The reasons are not hard to find. They do not affect Russia's security, for no one plans to use the Middle East as a base for aggression against Russia. Never for a moment has the United States entertained such a thought.

The Soviet Union has nothing whatsoever to fear from the United States in the Middle East, or anywhere else in the world, so long as its rulers do not themselves first resort to aggression.

That statement I make solemnly and emphatically.

Neither does Russia's desire to dominate the Middle East spring from its own economic interest in the area. Russia does not appreciably use or depend upon the Suez Canal. In 1955 Soviet traffic through the Canal represented only about three fourths of 1% of the total. The Soviets have no need for, and could provide no market for, the petroleum resources which constitute the principal natural wealth of the area. Indeed, the Soviet Union is a substantial exporter of petroleum products.

The reason for Russia's interest in the Middle East is solely that of power politics. Considering her announced purpose of Communizing the world, it is easy to understand her hope of dominating the Middle East.

This region has always been the crossroads of the continents of the Eastern Hemisphere. The Suez Canal enables the nations of Asia and Europe to carry on the commerce that is essential if these countries are to maintain well-rounded and prosperous economies. The Middle East provides a gateway between Eurasia and Africa.

It contains about two thirds of the presently known oil deposits of the world and it normally supplies the petroleum needs of many nations of Europe, Asia and Africa. The nations of Europe are peculiarly dependent upon this supply, and this dependency relates to transportation as well as to production! This has been vividly demonstrated since the closing of the Suez Canal and some of the pipelines. Alternate ways of transportation and, indeed, alternate sources of power can, if necessary, be developed. But these cannot be considered as early prospects.

These things stress the immense importance of the Middle East. If the nations of that area should lose their independence, if they were dominated by alien forces hostile to freedom, that would be both a tragedy for the area and for many other free nations whose economic life would be subject to near strangulation. Western Europe would be endangered just as though there had been no Marshall Plan, no North Atlantic Treaty Organization. The free nations of Asia and Africa, too, would be placed in serious jeopardy. And the countries of the Middle East would lose the markets upon which their economies depend. All this would have the most adverse, if not disastrous, effect upon our own nation's economic life and political prospects.

Then there are other factors which transcend the material. The Middle East is the birthplace of three great religions—Moslem, Christian and Hebrew. Mecca and Jerusalem are more than places on the map. They symbolize religions which teach that the spirit has supremacy over matter and that the individual has a dignity and rights of which no despotic government can rightfully deprive him. It would be intolerable if the holy places of the Middle East should be subjected to a rule that glorifies atheistic materialism.

International Communism, of course, seeks to mask its purposes of domination by expressions of good will and by superficially attractive offers of political, economic and military aid. But any free nation, which is the subject of Soviet enticement, ought, in elementary wisdom, to look behind the mask.

Remember Estonia, Latvia and Lithuania! In 1939 the Soviet Union entered into mutual assistance pacts with these then dependent countries; and the Soviet Foreign Minister, addressing the Extraordinary Fifth Session of the Supreme Soviet in October 1939, solemnly and publicly declared that "we stand for the scrupulous and punctilious observance of the pacts on the basis of complete reciprocity, and we declare that all the nonsensical talk about the Sovietization of the Baltic countries is only to the interest of our common enemies and of all anti-Soviet provocateurs." Yet in 1940, Estonia, Latvia and Lithuania were forcibly incorporated into the Soviet Union.

Soviet control of the satellite nations of Eastern Europe has been forcibly maintained in spite of solemn promises of a contrary intent, made during World War II.

Stalin's death brought hope that this pattern would change. And we read the pledge of the Warsaw Treaty of 1955 that the Soviet Union would follow in satellite countries "the principles of mutual respect for their independence and sovereignty and noninterference in domestic affairs." But we have just seen the subjugation of Hungary by naked armed force. In the aftermath of this Hungarian tragedy, world respect for and belief in Soviet promises have sunk to a new low. International Communism needs and seeks a recognizable success.

Thus, we have these simple and indisputable facts:

1. The Middle East, which has always been coveted by Russia, would today be prized more than ever by International Communism.
2. The Soviet rulers continue to show that they do not scruple to use any means to gain their ends.
3. The free nations of the Mid East need, and for the most part want, added strength to assure their continued independence.

III.

Our thoughts naturally turn to the United Nations as a protector of small nations. Its charter gives it primary responsibility for the maintenance of international peace and security. Our country has given the United Nations its full support in relation to the hostilities in Hungary and in Egypt. The United Nations was able to bring about a cease-fire and withdrawal of hostile forces from Egypt because it was dealing with governments and peoples who had a decent respect for the opinions of mankind as reflected in the United Nations General Assembly. But in the case of Hungary, the situation was different. The Soviet Union vetoed action by the Security Council to require the withdrawal of Soviet armed forces from Hungary. And it has shown callous indifference to the recommendations, even the censure, of the General Assembly. The United Nations can always be helpful, but it cannot be a wholly dependable protector of freedom when the ambitions of the Soviet Union are involved.

IV.

Under all the circumstances I have laid before you, a greater responsibility now devolves upon the United States. We have shown, so that none can doubt, our dedication to the principle that force shall not be used internationally for any aggressive purpose and that the integrity and independence of the nations of the Middle East should be inviolate. Seldom in history has a nation's dedication to principle been tested as severely as ours during recent weeks.

There is general recognition in the Middle East, as elsewhere, that the United States does not seek either political or economic domination over any other people. Our desire is a world environment of freedom, not servitude. On the other hand many, if not all, of the nations of the Middle East are aware of the danger that stems from International Communism and welcome closer cooperation with the United States to realize for themselves the United Nations goals of independence, economic well-being and spiritual growth.

If the Middle East is to continue its geographic role of uniting rather than separating East and West; if its vast economic resources are to serve the well-being of the peoples there, as well as that of others; and if its cultures and religions and their shrines are to be preserved for the uplifting of the spirits of the peoples, then the United States must make more evident its willingness to support the independence of the freedom-loving nations of the area.

V.

Under these circumstances I deem it necessary to seek the cooperation of the Congress. Only with that cooperation can we give the reassurance needed to deter aggression, to give courage and confidence to those who are dedicated to freedom and thus prevent a chain of events which would gravely endanger all of the free world.

There have been several Executive declarations made by the United States in relation to the Middle East. There is the Tripartite Declaration of May 25, 1950, followed by the Presidential assurance of October 31, 1950, to the King of Saudi Arabia. There is the Presidential declaration of April 9, 1956, that the United States will within constitutional means oppose any aggression in the area. There is our Declaration of November 29, 1956, that a threat to the territorial integrity or political independence of Iran, Iraq, Pakistan, or Turkey would be viewed by the United States with the utmost gravity.

Nevertheless, weaknesses in the present situation and the increased danger from International Communism, convince me that basic United States policy should now find expression in joint action by the Congress and the Executive. Furthermore, our joint resolve should be so couched as to make it apparent that if need be our words will be backed by action.

VI.

It is nothing new for the President and the Congress to join to recognize that the national integrity of other free nations is directly related to our own security.

We have joined to create and support the security system of the United Nations. We have reinforced the collective security system of the United Nations by a series of collective defense arrangements. Today we have security treaties with 42 other nations which recognize that our peace and security are intertwined. We have joined to take decisive action in relation to Greece and Turkey and in relation to Taiwan.

Thus, the United States through the joint action of the President and the Congress, or, in the case of treaties, the Senate, has manifested in many endangered areas its purpose to support free and independent governments—and peace—against external menace, notably the menace of International Communism. Thereby we have helped to maintain peace and security during a period of great danger. It is now essential that the United States should manifest through joint action of the President and the Congress our determination to assist those nations of the Mid East area, which desire that assistance.

The action which I propose would have the following features.

It would, first of all, authorize the United States to cooperate with and assist any nation or group of nations in the general area of the Middle East in the development of economic strength dedicated to the maintenance of national independence.

It would, in the second place, authorize the Executive to undertake in the same region programs of military assistance and cooperation with any nation or group of nations which desires such aid.

It would, in the third place, authorize such assistance and cooperation to include the employment of the armed forces of the United States to secure and protect the territorial integrity and political independence of such nations, requesting such aid, against overt armed aggression from any nation controlled by International Communism.

These measures would have to be consonant with the treaty obligations of the United States, including the Charter of the United Nations and with any action or recommendations of the United Nations. They would also, if armed attack occurs, be subject to the overriding authority of the United Nations Security Council in accordance with the Charter.

The present proposal would, in the fourth place, authorize the President to employ, for economic and defensive military purposes, sums available under the Mutual Security Act of 1954, as amended, without regard to existing limitations.

The legislation now requested should not include the authorization or appropriation of funds because I believe that, under the conditions I suggest, presently appropriated funds will be adequate for the balance of the present fiscal year ending June 30. I shall, however, seek in subsequent legislation the authorization of $200,000,000 to be available during each of the fiscal years 1958 and 1959 for discretionary use in the area, in addition to the other mutual security programs for the area hereafter provided for by the Congress.

VII.

This program will not solve all the problems of the Middle East. Neither does it represent the totality of our policies for the area. There are the problems of Palestine and relations between Israel and the Arab States, and the future of the Arab refugees. There is the problem of the future status of the Suez Canal. These difficulties are aggravated by International Communism, but they would exist quite apart from that threat. It is not the purpose of the legislation I propose to deal directly with these problems. The United Nations is actively concerning itself with all these matters, and we are supporting the United Nations. The United States has made clear, notably by Secretary Dulles' address of August 26, 1955, that we are willing to do much to assist the United Nations in solving the basic problems of Palestine.

The proposed legislation is primarily designed to deal with the possibility of Communist aggression, direct and indirect. There is imperative need that any lack of power in the area should be made good, not by external or alien force, but by the increased vigor and security of the independent nations of the area.

Experience shows that indirect aggression rarely if ever succeeds where there is reasonable security against direct aggression; where the government disposes of loyal secu-

rity forces, and where economic conditions are such as not to make Communism seem
an attractive alternative. The program I suggest deals with all three aspects of this matter and thus with the problem of indirect aggression.

It is my hope and belief that if our purpose be proclaimed, as proposed by the
requested legislation, that very fact will serve to halt any contemplated aggression. We
shall have heartened the patriots who are dedicated to the independence of their
nations. They will not feel that they stand alone, under the menace of great power.
And I should add that patriotism is, throughout this area, a powerful sentiment. It is
true that fear sometimes perverts true patriotism into fanaticism and to the acceptance
of dangerous enticements from without. But if that fear can be allayed, then the climate will be more favorable to the attainment of worthy national ambitions.

And as I have indicated, it will also be necessary for us to contribute economically
to strengthen those countries, or groups of countries, which have governments mani-
festly dedicated to the preservation of independence and resistance to subversion. Such
measures will provide the greatest insurance against Communist inroads. Words alone
are not enough.

VII[I].
Let me refer again to the requested authority to employ the armed forces of the United
States to assist to defend the territorial integrity and the political independence of any
nation in the area against Communist armed aggression. Such authority would not be
exercised except at the desire of the nation attacked. Beyond this it is my profound
hope that this authority would never have to be exercised at all.

Nothing is more necessary to assure this than that our policy with respect to the
defense of the area be promptly and clearly determined and declared. Thus the United
Nations and all friendly governments, and indeed governments which are not friendly,
will know where we stand.

If, contrary to my hope and expectation, a situation arose which called for the
military application of the policy which I ask the Congress to join me in proclaiming,
I would of course maintain hour-by-hour contact with the Congress if it were in session. And if the Congress were not in session, and if the situation had grave implications, I would, of course, at once call the Congress into special session.

In the situation now existing, the greatest risk, as is often the case, is that ambitious
despots may miscalculate. If power-hungry Communists should either falsely or correctly
estimate that the Middle East is inadequately defended, they might be tempted to use
open measures of armed attack. If so, that would start a chain of circumstances which
would almost surely involve the United States in military action. I am convinced that
the best insurance against this dangerous contingency is to make clear now our readiness to cooperate fully and freely with our friends of the Middle East in ways consonant
with the purposes and principles of the United Nations. I intend promptly to send a
special mission to the Middle East to explain the cooperation we are prepared to give.

IX.
The policy which I outline involves certain burdens and indeed risks for the United
States. Those who covet the area will not like what is proposed. Already, they are
grossly distorting our purpose. However, before this Americans have seen our nation's
vital interests and human freedom in jeopardy, and their fortitude and resolution have

been equal to the crisis, regardless of hostile distortion of our words, motives and actions.

Indeed, the sacrifices of the American people in the cause of freedom have, even since the close of World War II, been measured in many billions of dollars and in thousands of the precious lives of our youth. These sacrifices, by which great areas of the world have been preserved to freedom, must not be thrown away.

In those momentous periods of the past, the President and the Congress have united, without partisanship, to serve the vital interests of the United States and of the free world.

The occasion has come for us to manifest again our national unity in support of freedom and to show our deep respect for the rights and independence of every nation—however great, however small. We seek not violence, but peace. To this purpose we must now devote our energies, our determination, ourselves.

SOURCE: John Woolley and Gerhard Peters, The American Presidency Project, University of California, Santa Barbara, www.presidency.ucsb.edu/ws/?pid=11007.

June 1967 Arab-Israeli War

DOCUMENT IN CONTEXT

The Suez crisis of 1956 marked the start of more than a decade of chronic tension and occasional cross-border raids between Israel and the Arabs, though not outright war. Israel spent the next decade building and developing its economy, political and social institutions, and military forces. Arab nations nursed their grievances against Israel and rebuilt their armies as well.

Tensions escalated in the early 1960s within the Arab world—where Egyptian leader Gamal Abdel Nasser attempted to assert his leadership, often to the annoyance of other Arab leaders—and between the Arabs and Israelis—as each side violated the 1949 armistice agreements, sometimes in deliberate provocations and at other times in response to real or perceived threats. Efforts by the Arab League—and in particular Nasser—to channel popular anger against Israel led in 1964 to the establishment of the Palestine Liberation Organization (PLO), a landmark event of the period. Another significant event that year was the Arab League's decision to divert the headwaters of the Jordan River to deprive Israel of freshwater, a step that Israel blocked by destroying Syrian excavating equipment (Palestinian National Movement, p. 169).

The early months of 1967 produced a sequence of events leading to a war that most leaders in the region apparently neither wanted nor expected. Israel and Syria were the primary actors prior to the outbreak of war, but Israel and Egypt emerged as the initial combatants. Tensions between Israel and Syria had been the greatest because of the latter's sponsorship of more than two years of raids into Israel by Pales-

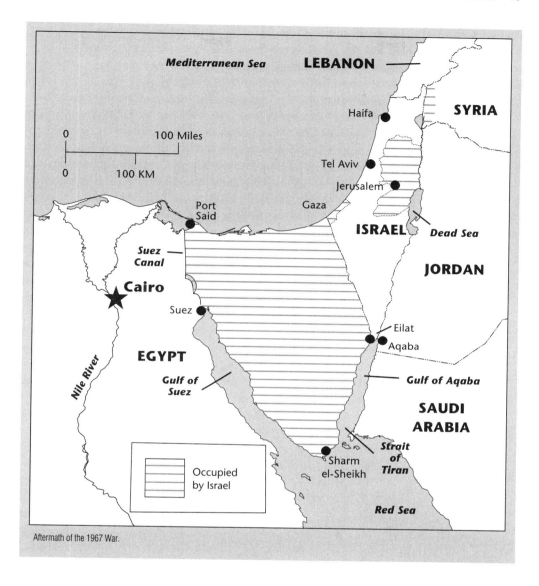

Aftermath of the 1967 War.

tinian guerrillas, usually from the West Bank, which at the time was held by Jordan. Also, Syrian shelling of farms in northern Israel had led on April 7, 1967, to an air battle in which Israel destroyed six of Syria's Soviet-supplied warplanes.

Responding in part to criticism by Arab leaders for failing to counter Israeli "aggression," Nasser on May 16–17, 1967, demanded that the United Nations Emergency Force (UNEF), a peacekeeping outfit, withdraw from its positions in Egypt along the armistice lines created after the 1948 war. When the UN forces withdrew, Nasser heightened the sense of crisis by moving some 100,000 troops into position at Egypt's border with Israel. Nasser then announced on May 22 that the Strait of Tiran would be closed to Israeli shipping, reversing one of Israel's chief gains from the Suez conflict eleven years earlier. With escalating rhetoric, the Egyptian leader on May 26 said, "If Israel wants war—well, then, Israel will be destroyed." In a speech to the Egyptian National Assembly three days later, Nasser signaled that war was at hand:

"Preparations have already been made," he said. "We are now ready to confront Israel." Israel responded by mobilizing its army reserves, adding to the sense of crisis.

At the United Nations in New York, diplomats expressed worries about the potential for war, but they were unable or unwilling to do anything to stop it. In Israel, political leaders formed a national unity government on June 1 to ensure broad backing should war break out; the chief change was a handover of the Defense Ministry to Moshe Dayan, Israel's military hero of the Suez crisis and a harsh critic of Prime Minister Levi Eshkol, who had held the defense portfolio in the previous government.

Despite a U.S. appeal to Israel to hold its fire, the Egyptian military maneuvers and the hawkish rhetoric of Nasser and other Arab leaders provided Israel the incentive to strike first: On the morning of June 5, Israeli warplanes attacked airfields in Egypt, destroying in just three hours nearly three-fourths of that country's air force and putting its runways out of service. The Egyptians had expected an attack but were caught off guard by the timing and the unusual pattern the Israel planes took on their bombing runs. As it had done in 1956, the Israeli army surged into the Sinai Peninsula in four directions, easily defeating Egyptian defenders and forcing thousands of soldiers to flee.

On June 5, with the initial attack against Egypt under way, Israeli ground forces moved into the Jordanian-held West Bank, and the Israeli air force quickly destroyed Jordan's small air force. Israel said that it had not planned an attack on its eastern front, but moved against Jordan nonetheless in response to artillery fire from its territory. Before the outbreak of hostilities, Israel had bluntly warned Jordan's King Hussein to stay out of the conflict if war erupted. Jordan's artillery attack provided Israel an opportunity, which it seized.

King Hussein had given temporary command of his army to an Egyptian general. In the face of the Israeli assault, the overmatched Jordanian army quickly withdrew from East Jerusalem, and Israeli forces moved into that part of the city early on June 7, completing what had been, from Israel's perspective, the major unfinished business from the 1948 war. By that evening, Israel also had captured Nablus, the largest city on the West Bank, and gained effective control of that territory. According to most estimates, some 200,000 to 300,000 Palestinian Arabs fled the West Bank or were pushed out by the Israeli army. Most crossed the river into Jordan.

The third front in the war involved Syria, the country that had staged the most provocative acts against Israel during the previous two years. The Syrian air force had met the same fate as those of Egypt and Jordan, also in the early hours of the war on June 5. Syrian artillery fired at Israeli military and civilian positions for the first four days of the war, but on the afternoon of June 8, Syria accepted a UN demand for a cease-fire, apparently hoping to avoid an Israeli ground invasion. With actions against Jordan complete and those against Egypt nearly so, Israel on June 9 moved its army against heavily fortified Syrian positions on the Golan Heights, a strategic plateau with commanding views of the Hula and Jordan Valleys in northeastern Israel. As Israeli tanks surged up the Golan's steep approaches, Syrian forces responded with defensive fire, but within hours the government ordered the army to withdraw to positions outside Damascus.

On June 10, Israeli units moved across the heights, encircling several small towns and capturing Quneitra, the area's administrative capital, and Mount Hermon, a 9,000-foot mountain with a view of downtown Damascus. This offensive, which appeared to have Damascus as a target, briefly threatened global repercussions, with the Soviet Union warning that it would come to Syria's defense if U.S. pressure failed to force Israel to back down. The diplomatic crisis ended in the late afternoon of June 10, when Israel accepted a UN cease-fire. Even so, Israeli forces continued to move into new positions on the Golan, capturing the last, remote, positions on June 12.

The June 1967 War—lasting six days—was one of the shortest major conflicts in recent world history, but it had profound consequences that reverberate to this day. Israel captured an enormous amount of territory—more than 40,000 square miles, some 3.5 times the size of Israel—stretching from the banks of the Suez Canal to the banks of the Jordan River and to the outskirts of Damascus. Nearly all the land that the early Zionists had dreamed of possessing decades earlier was now under Israeli control, in particular, the entirety of Jerusalem. Israel also controlled the more than 1.2 million Palestinian Arabs living in the Gaza Strip and the West Bank, many of them refugees from the first Arab-Israeli war in 1948.

Some Israelis gloated about these territorial conquests, arguing that the time had come to proclaim a Greater Israel encompassing nearly all of the captured lands. Others saw a different opportunity: the chance to trade some of this territory for a negotiated, permanent, peace with Israel's Arab neighbors. The Israeli cabinet at first adopted the latter position, voting secretly on June 19 to trade the Sinai and the Golan for peace with Egypt and Syria; both countries quickly rejected the offer, relayed by U.S. diplomats. Nearly all Israelis agreed on one thing: East Jerusalem would be kept as part of Israel's unified capital. To reinforce the point, Israel in late June officially annexed East Jerusalem and some of its immediate West Bank neighborhoods. The Israeli government evicted several hundred Arab residents from their homes and helped Jews settle in their places—the opening round of a policy that would eventually settle several hundred thousand Jews on Arab lands in East Jerusalem and the West Bank (Israeli Settlement of the Occupied Territories, p. 178).

From a military perspective, the June war was yet another overwhelming victory for Israel, this time against the combined force of three Arab countries with many more citizens. Israel quickly gained air superiority over Egypt, Jordan, and Syria, demonstrating that even Soviet-supplied weaponry could not transform Arab armies into effective fighting forces. Israel accomplished its feats while suffering only 4 percent as many casualties (dead and wounded) as its opponents.

After such a humiliating defeat, Arab rhetoric toward Israel grew even more hostile. Less than three months after the war had ended, Arab leaders met in Khartoum and, under Nasser's continued leadership, voiced what became known as the "three noes" in regard to Israel: no peace, no recognition, and no negotiations (Khartoum Declaration, p. 108). On a more practical basis, Egypt for the next three years waged a low-level "war of attrition" intended to sap Israel's will to hold on to the Sinai.

The new realities in the Middle East led U.S. president Lyndon B. Johnson to outline a peace plan for the region. Announced in a televised address on June 19, it advocated five principles, notably the "political independence and territorial integrity" of all states in the region (Johnson Plan, p. 103). A few days later, Johnson and Soviet prime minister Alexi Kosygin met in Glassboro, New Jersey, and discussed prospects for peace in the Middle East but failed to reach an agreement on how to achieve that goal. Instead of following through on this rhetoric, the United States stepped up its support for Israel, and the Soviet Union became an even more staunch backer of the Arabs.

The most important diplomatic outcome of the war was a renewed push at the United Nations for a longer-term resolution of the Arab-Israeli dispute. The Security

Council on November 22, 1967, adopted Resolution 242, one of the landmark resolutions of the conflict, urging Israel to cede the lands it had just won in exchange for peace with its neighbors (UN Security Council Resolution 242, p. 111).

Following are excerpts from a speech delivered by Egyptian president Gamal Abdel Nasser to the National Assembly on May 29, 1967, and excerpts from a statement to the UN Security Council by Israeli foreign minister Abba Eban on June 6, 1967, the second day of the June war.

DOCUMENT

Nasser Addressing the National Assembly

MAY 29, 1967

. . . The circumstances through which we are now passing are in fact difficult ones because we are not only confronting Israel but also those who created Israel and who are behind Israel. We are confronting Israel and the West as well—the West, which created Israel and which despised us Arabs and which ignored us before and since 1948. They had no regard whatsoever for our feelings, our hopes in life, or our rights. The West completely ignored us, and the Arab nation was unable to check the West's course.

Then came the events of 1956—the Suez battle. We all know what happened in 1956. When we rose to demand our rights, Britain, France and Israel opposed us, and we were faced with the tripartite aggression. We resisted, however, and proclaimed that we would fight to the last drop of our blood. God gave us success and God's victory was great.

Subsequently we were able to rise and to build. Now, eleven years after 1956, we are restoring things to what they were in 1956. This is from the material aspect. In my opinion this material aspect is only a small part, whereas the spiritual aspect is the great side of the issue. The spiritual aspect involves the renaissance of the Arab nation, the revival of the Palestine question, and the restoration of confidence to every Arab and to every Palestinian. This is on the basis that if we were able to restore conditions to what they were before 1956, God will surely help and urge us to restore the situation to what it was in 1948.

Brothers, the revolt, upheaval and commotion which we now see taking place in every Arab country are not only because we have returned to the Gulf of Aqaba or rid ourselves of the UNEF [United Nations Emergency Force], but because we have restored Arab honour and renewed Arab hopes.

Israel used to boast a great deal, and the Western Powers, headed by the United States and Britain, used to ignore and even despise us and consider us of no value. But now that the time has come—and I have already said in the past that we will decide the time and place and not allow them to decide—we must be ready for triumph and not for a recurrence of the 1948 comedies. We shall triumph, God willing.

Preparations have already been made. We are now ready to confront Israel. They have claimed many things about the 1956 Suez war, but no one believed them after the secrets of the 1956 collusion were uncovered—that mean collusion in which Israel took part. Now we are ready for the confrontation. We are now ready to deal with the entire Palestine question.

The issue now at hand is not the Gulf of Aqaba, the Straits of Tiran, or the withdrawal of the UNEF, but the rights of the Palestine people. It is the aggression which took place in Palestine in 1948 with the collaboration of Britain and the United States. It is the expulsion of the Arabs from Palestine, the usurpation of their rights, and the plunder of their property. It is the disavowal of all the UN resolutions in favour of the Palestinian people.

The issue today is far more serious than they say. They want to confine the issue to the Straits of Tiran, the UNEF and the right of passage. We demand the full rights of the Palestinian people. We say this out of our belief that Arab rights cannot be squandered because the Arabs throughout the Arab world are demanding these Arab rights.

We are not afraid of the United States and its threats, of Britain and its threats, or of the entire Western world and its partiality to Israel. The United States and Britain are partial to Israel and give no consideration to the Arabs, to the entire Arab nation. Why? Because we have made them believe that we cannot distinguish between friend and foe. We must make them know that we know who our foes are and who our friends are and treat them accordingly.

If the United States and Britain are partial to Israel, we must say that our enemy is not only Israel but also the United States and Britain and treat them as such. If the Western Powers disavow our rights and ridicule and despise us, we Arabs must teach them to respect us and take us seriously. Otherwise all our talk about Palestine, the Palestine people and Palestinian rights will be null and void and of no consequence. We must treat enemies as enemies and friends as friends.

I said yesterday that the States that champion freedom and peace have supported us. I spoke of the support given us by India, Pakistan, Afghanistan, Yugoslavia, Malaysia, the Chinese People's Republic and the Asian and African States.

After my statements yesterday I met the War Minister Shams Badran and learned from him what took place in Moscow. I wish to tell you today that the Soviet Union is a friendly Power and stands by us as a friend. In all our dealings with the Soviet Union—and I have been dealing with the USSR since 1955—it has not made a single request of us. The USSR has never interfered with our policy or internal affairs. This is the USSR as we have always known it. In fact, it is we who have made urgent requests of the USSR. Last year we asked for wheat and they sent it to us. When I also asked for all kinds of arms they gave them to us. When I met Shams Badran yesterday he handed me a message from the Soviet Premier Kosygin saying that the USSR supported us in this battle and would not allow any Power to intervene until matters were restored to what they were in 1956.

Brothers, we must distinguish between friend and foe, friend and hypocrite. We must be able to tell who is making requests, who has ulterior motives and who is applying economic pressure. We must also know those who offer their friendship to us for no other reason than a desire for freedom and peace.

In the name of the UAR [United Arab Republic, the short-lived union between Egypt and Syria] people, I thank the people of the USSR for their great attitude which is the attitude of a real friend. This is the kind of attitude that we expect. I said yesterday that we had not requested the USSR or any other State to intervene because we really want to avoid any confrontation which might lead to a world war and also because we really work for peace and advocate world peace. When we voiced the policy of non-alignment, our chief aim was world peace.

Brothers, we will work for world peace with all the power at our disposal, but we will also hold tenaciously to our rights with all the power at our disposal. This is our course. On this occasion, I address myself to our brothers in Aden and say: Although occupied with this battle, we have not forgotten you. We are with you. We have not forgotten the struggle of Aden and the occupied South for liberation. Aden and the occupied South must be liberated and colonialism must end. We are with them; present matters have not taken our minds from Aden.

I thank you for taking the trouble to pay this visit. Moreover, your presence is an honour to the Qubbah Palace, and I am pleased to have met you. Peace be on you.

SOURCE: Foreign Broadcast Information Service, Middle East/North Africa, "29 May Nasir Speech to National Assembly Members," May 31, 1967, pp. B6-B8.

DOCUMENT

Abba Eban's Statement to the UN Security Council

JUNE 6, 1967

[In the opening portions of his remarks, Eban reviewed the events leading up to the outbreak of the June 1967 War, emphasizing what he called acts of "sabotage" against Israel by Syria, Egypt's denial of Israeli access to the Strait of Tiran, and the deployment of Arab armies along Israel's borders.]

177. These then were the three main elements in the tension: the sabotage movement; the blockade of the port; and, perhaps more imminent than anything else, this vast and purposeful encirclement movement, against the background of an authorized presidential statement announcing that the objective of the encirclement was to bring about the destruction and the annihilation of a sovereign State.

178. These acts taken together—the blockade, the dismissal of the United Nations Emergency Force, and the heavy concentration in Sinai—effectively disrupted the *status quo* which had ensured a relative stability on the Egyptian-Israel frontier for ten years. I do not use the words "relative stability" lightly, for in fact while those elements in the Egyptian-Israel relationship existed there was not one single incident of violence between Egypt and Israel for ten years. But suddenly this status quo, this pat-

tern of mutually accepted stability, was smashed to smithereens. It is now the task of the Governments concerned to elaborate the new conditions of their co-existence. I think that much of this work should be done directly by these Governments themselves. Surely, after what has happened we must have better assurance than before, for Israel and for the Middle East, of peaceful coexistence. The question is whether there is any reason to believe that such a new era may yet come to pass. If I am a little sanguine on this point, it is because of a conviction that men and nations do behave wisely once they have exhausted all other alternatives. Surely the other alternatives of war and belligerency have now been exhausted. And what has anybody gained from that? But in order that the new system of interstate relationships may flourish in the Middle East, it is important that certain principles be applied above and beyond the cease-fire to which the Security Council has given its unanimous support.

179. Let me then say here that Israel welcomes the appeal for the cease-fire as formulated in this resolution. But I must point out that the implementation depends on the absolute and sincere acceptance and co-operation of the other parties, which, in our view, are responsible for the present situation. And in conveying this resolution to my colleagues, I must at this moment point out that these other Governments have not used the opportunity yet to clarify their intentions.

180. I have said that the situation to be constructed after the cease-fire must depend on certain principles. The first of these principles surely must be the acceptance of Israel's statehood and the total elimination of the fiction of its non-existence. It would seem to me that after 3,000 years the time has arrived to accept Israel's nationhood as a fact, for here is the only State in the international community which has the same territory, speaks the same language and upholds the same faith as it did 3,000 years ago.

181. And if, as everybody knows to be the fact, the universal conscience was in the last week or two most violently shaken at the prospect of danger to Israel, it was not only because there seemed to be a danger to a State, but also, I think, because the State was Israel, with all that this ancient name evokes, teaches, symbolizes and inspires. How grotesque would be an international community which found room for 122 sovereign units and which did not acknowledge the sovereignty of that people which had given nationhood its deepest significance and its most enduring grace.

182. No wonder, then, that when danger threatened we could hear a roar of indignation sweep across the world, that men in progressive movements and members of the scientific and humanistic cultures joined together in sounding an alarm bell about an issue that vitally affected the human conscience. And no wonder, correspondingly, that a deep and universal sense of satisfaction and relief has accompanied the news of Israel's gallant and successful resistance.

183. But the central point remains the need to secure an authentic intellectual recognition by our neighbors of Israel's deep roots in the Middle Eastern reality. There is an intellectual tragedy in the failure of Arab leaders to come to grips, however reluctantly, with the depth and authenticity of Israel's roots in the life, the history, the spiritual experience and the culture of the Middle East.

184. This, then, is the first axiom. A much more conscious and uninhibited acceptance of Israel's Statehood is an axiom requiring no demonstration, for there will never be a Middle East without an independent and sovereign State of Israel in its midst.

185. The second principle must be that of the peaceful settlement of disputes. The resolution thus adopted falls within the concept of the peaceful settlement of

disputes. I have already said that much could be done if the Governments of the area would embark much more on direct contacts. They must find their way to each other. After all, when there is conflict between them they come together face to face. Why should they not come together face to face to solve the conflict? And perhaps on some occasions it would not be a bad idea to have the solution before, and therefore instead of, the conflict.

186. When the Council discusses what is to happen after the cease-fire, we hear many formulas: back to 1956, back to 1948—I understand our neighbors would wish to turn the clock back to 1947. The fact is, however, that most clocks move forward and not backward, and this, I think, should be the case with the clock of Middle Eastern peace—not backward to belligerency, but forward to peace.

187. The point was well made this evening by the representative of Argentina, who said: the cease-fire should be followed immediately by the most intensive efforts to bring about a just and lasting peace in the Middle East. In a similar sense, the representative of Canada warned us against merely reproducing the old positions of conflict, without attempting to settle the underlying issues of Arab-Israel coexistence. After all, many things in recent days have been mixed up with each other. Few things are what they were. And in order to create harmonious combinations of relationships, it is inevitable that the States should come together in negotiation.

188. Another factor in the harmony that we would like to see in the Middle East relates to external Powers. From these, and especially from the greatest amongst them, the small States of the Middle East—and most of them are small—ask for a rigorous support, not for individual States, but for specific principles; not to be for one State against other States, but to be for peace against war, for free commerce against belligerency, for the pacific settlement of disputes against violent irredentist threats; in other words, to exercise an even-handed support for the integrity and independence of States and for the rights of States under the Charter of the United Nations and other sources of international law.

189. There are no two categories of States. The United Arab Republic, Iraq, Syria, Jordan, Lebanon—not one of these has a single ounce or milligram of Statehood which does not adhere in equal measures to Israel itself.

190. It is important that States outside our region apply a balanced attitude, that they do not exploit temporary tensions and divergencies in the issues of global conflict, that they do not seek to win gains by inflaming fleeting passions, and that they strive to make a balanced distribution of their friendship amongst the States of the Middle East.

191. Now whether all the speeches of all the great Powers this evening meet this criterion, everybody, of course, can judge for himself. I do not propose to answer in detail all the observations of the representative of the Soviet Union. I had the advantage of hearing the same things in identical language a few days ago from his colleague, the Soviet Ambassador in Israel. I must confess that I was no more convinced this evening than I was the day before yesterday about the validity of this most vehement and one-sided denunciation. But surely world opinion, before whose tribunal this debate unrolls, can solve this question by posing certain problems to itself. Who was it that attempted to destroy a neighboring State in 1948, Israel or its neighbors? Who now closes an international waterway to the port of a neighboring State, Israel or the United Arab Republic? Does Israel refuse to negotiate a peace settlement with the Arab States, or do they refuse to do so with it? Who disrupted the 1957 pattern of stability, Israel

or Egypt? Did troops of Egypt, Syria, Jordan, Iraq, Lebanon, Kuwait and Algeria surround Israel in this menacing confrontation, or has any distinguished representative seen some vast Israel colossus surrounding the area between Morocco and Kuwait?

192. I raise these points of elementary logic. Of course, a great Power can take refuge in its power from the exigencies of logic. All of us in our youth presumably recounted La Fontaine's fable, *"La raison du plus fort est toujours la meilleure."* But here, after all, there is nobody who is more or less strong than others; we sit here around the table on the concept of sovereign equality. But I think we have an equal duty to bring substantive proof for any denunciation that we make, each of the other.

193. I would say in conclusion that these are, of course, still grave times. And yet they may perhaps have fortunate issue. This could be the case if those who for some reason decided so violently, three weeks ago, to disrupt the *status quo* would ask themselves what the results and benefits have been. As he looks around him at the arena of battle, at the wreckage of planes and tanks, at the collapse of intoxicated hopes, might not an Egyptian ruler ponder whether anything was achieved by that disruption? What has it brought but strife, conflict with other powerful interests, and the stern criticism of progressive men throughout the world?

194. I think that Israel has in recent days proved its steadfastness and vigour. It is now willing to demonstrate its instinct for peace. Let us build a new system of relationships from the wreckage of the old. Let us discern across the darkness the vision of a better and a brighter dawn.

SOURCE: United Nations Information System on the Question of Palestine, http://domino.un.org/unispal.nsf/ 9a798adbf322aff38525617b006d88d7/f0e5cf015592d4d10525672700590136!OpenDocument.

The Johnson Plan

DOCUMENT IN CONTEXT

One of the many consequences of the June 1967 Arab-Israeli war was that it drew the United States deeper into Middle Eastern affairs. Although the United States stood as one of the two superpowers and had interests in the Middle East, it had generally played only a marginal role in the region. This changed after the June war created new opportunities for peace, as well as new dangers for conflict (June 1967 Arab-Israeli War, p. 94).

Reacting to the context of the new realities created by Israel's decisive victory, President Lyndon B. Johnson on June 19, 1967, laid out the first of numerous U.S. "plans" for peace in the Middle East. Some aspects of Johnson's plan focused on specific issues that had contributed to the war, but others had the broader aim of making the Middle East a generally more peaceful place. By coincidence, Johnson offered his plan on the same day that the Israeli cabinet voted, in secret, to return two of the newly captured territories—the Sinai Peninsula and the Golan Heights—to Egypt and Syria, respectively, in exchange for peace. The Egyptian and Syrian governments rejected the offer, and Israel withdrew it.

Addressing a conference at the State Department, Johnson laid out what he called "five great principles of peace" in the region: that every country has the "right to live" and to have that right respected by its neighbors; that refugees from armed conflicts deserve justice; that maritime rights be respected; that the "wasteful and destructive arms race" be halted or at least limited; and that all states in the area be accorded "respect for political independence and territorial integrity." Johnson did not, however, offer specific proposals for reaching any of these goals.

Subsequent U.S. policies toward the Middle East have incorporated all of Johnson's goals, though some have received greater prominence than others. Every U.S. administration since Johnson's has emphasized the first and last goals, which relate to Israel's existence as a Jewish state in a region dominated by Muslims. Protecting maritime rights also has been an important feature of U.S. policy, although it has not been severely tested since Israel made peace with Egypt in 1978–1979.

Justice for refugees and limiting the arms race in the Middle East are the two goals in Johnson's plan that have received the least attention from U.S. policymakers. The former goal refers to the plight of several hundred thousand Palestinians who fled or were forced from their homes during the 1948 and 1967 wars. Israel consistently has argued that Arab countries are responsible for the refugees, most of whom endure impoverished lives in neighboring Arab lands, and the United States rarely has pressed the Arabs or the Israelis to find permanent solutions for the refugees. The United States has routinely ignored Johnson's warnings—prompted by the Soviet Union's arming of Egypt and other Arab countries—about the dangers of a Middle Eastern arms race. Indeed, since the 1970s the United States has been the most important source of weapons in the region, selling advanced warplanes, tanks, bombs, and other equipment primarily to Israel, but also to Egypt, Iran (until the Islamic revolution in 1979), Jordan, and Saudi Arabia.

Following are excerpts from the address by President Lyndon B. Johnson to the State Department's Foreign Policy Conference for Educators on June 19, 1967.

DOCUMENT

Johnson on the Middle East

JUNE 19, 1967

. . . Now, finally, let me turn to the Middle East—and to the tumultuous events of the past months.

Those events have proved the wisdom of five great principles of peace in the region.

The first and the greatest principle is that every nation in the area has a fundamental right to live, and to have this right respected by its neighbors.

For the people of the Middle East, the path to hope does not lie in threats to end the life of any nation. Such threats have become a burden to the peace, not only of that region but a burden to the peace of the entire world.

In the same way, no nation would be true to the United Nations Charter, or to its own true interests, if it should permit military success to blind it to the fact that its neighbors have rights and its neighbors have interests of their own. Each nation, therefore, must accept the right of others to live.

Second, this last month, I think, shows us another basic requirement for settlement. It is a human requirement: justice for the refugees.

A new conflict has brought new homelessness. The nations of the Middle East must at last address themselves to the plight of those who have been displaced by wars. In the past, both sides have resisted the best efforts of outside mediators to restore the victims of conflict to their homes, or to find them other proper places to live and work. There will be no peace for any party in the Middle East unless this problem is attacked with new energy by all, and certainly, primarily by those who are immediately concerned.

A third lesson from this last month is that maritime rights must be respected. Our Nation has long been committed to free maritime passage through international waterways, and we, along with other nations, were taking the necessary steps to implement this principle when hostilities exploded. If a single act of folly was more responsible for this explosion than any other, I think it was the arbitrary and dangerous announced decision that the Straits of Titan would be closed. The right of innocent maritime passage must be preserved for all nations.

Fourth, this last conflict has demonstrated the danger of the Middle Eastern arms race of the last 12 years. Here the responsibility must rest not only on those in the area—but upon the larger states outside the area. We believe that scarce resources could be used much better for technical and economic development. We have always opposed this arms race, and our own military shipments to the area have consequently been severely limited.

Now the waste and futility of the arms race must be apparent to all the peoples of the world. And now there is another moment of choice. The United States of America, for its part, will use every resource of diplomacy, and every counsel of reason and prudence, to try to find a better course.

As a beginning, I should like to propose that the United Nations immediately call upon all of its members to report all shipments of all military arms into this area, and to keep those shipments on file for all the peoples of the world to observe.

Fifth, the crisis underlines the importance of respect for political independence and territorial integrity of all the states of the area. We reaffirmed that principle at the height of this crisis. We reaffirm it again today on behalf of all.

This principle can be effective in the Middle East only on the basis of peace between the parties. The nations of the region have had only fragile and violated truce lines for 20 years. What they now need are recognized boundaries and other arrangements that will give them security against terror, destruction, and war. Further, there just must be adequate recognition of the special interest of three great religions in the holy places of Jerusalem.

These five principles are not new, but we do think they are fundamental. Taken together, they point the way from uncertain armistice to durable peace. We believe there must be progress toward all of them if there is to be progress toward any.

There are some who have urged, as a single, simple solution, an immediate return to the situation as it was on June 4. As our distinguished and able Ambassador, Mr. Arthur Goldberg, has already said, this is not a prescription for peace, but for renewed hostilities.

Certainly troops must be withdrawn, but there must also be recognized rights of national life, progress in solving the refugee problem, freedom of innocent maritime passage, limitation of the arms race, and respect for political independence and territorial integrity.

But who will make this peace where all others have failed for 20 years or more?

Clearly the parties to the conflict must be the parties to the peace. Sooner or later it is they who must make a settlement in the area. It is hard to see how it is possible for nations to live together in peace if they cannot learn to reason together.

But we must still ask, who can help them? Some say it should be the United Nations; some call for the use of other parties. We have been first in our support of effective peacekeeping in the United Nations, and we also recognize the great values to come from mediation.

We are ready this morning to see any method tried, and we believe that none should be excluded altogether. Perhaps all of them will be useful and all will be needed.

So, I issue an appeal to all to adopt no rigid view on these matters. I offer assurance to all that this Government of ours, the Government of the United States, will do its part for peace in every forum, at every level, at every hour.

Yet there is no escape from this fact: The main responsibility for the peace of the region depends upon its own peoples and its own leaders of that region. What will be truly decisive in the Middle East will be what is said and what is done by those who live in the Middle East.

They can seek another arms race, if they have not profited from the experience of this one, if they want to. But they will seek it at a terrible cost to their own people—and to their very long-neglected human needs. They can live on a diet of hate—though only at the cost of hatred in return. Or they can move toward peace with one another.

The world this morning is watching, watching for the peace of the world, because that is really what is at stake. It will look for patience and justice, it will look for humility and moral courage. It will look for signs of movement from prejudice and the emotional chaos of conflict to the gradual, slow shaping steps that lead to learning to live together and learning to help mold and shape peace in the area and in the world.

The Middle East is rich in history, rich in its people and its resources. It has no need to live in permanent civil war. It has the power to build its own life, as one of the prosperous regions of the world in which we live.

If the nations of the Middle East will turn toward the works of peace, they can count with confidence upon the friendship, and the help, of all the people of the United States of America.

In a climate of peace, we here will do our full share to help with a solution for the refugees. We here will do our full share in support of regional cooperation. We here will do our share, and do more, to see that the peaceful promise of nuclear energy is applied to the critical problems of desalting water and helping to make the deserts bloom.

Our country is committed—and we here reiterate that commitment today—to a peace that is based on five principles:

- first, the recognized right of national life;
- second, justice for the refugees;
- third, innocent maritime passage;
- fourth, limits on the wasteful and destructive arms race; and
- fifth, political independence and territorial integrity for all.

This is a time not for malice, but for magnanimity; not for propaganda, but for patience; not for vituperation, but for vision.

On the basis of peace, we offer our help to the people of the Middle East. That land, known to every one of us since childhood as the birthplace of great religions and learning, can flourish once again in our time. We here in the United States shall do all in our power to help make it so.

Thank you and good morning.

SOURCE: John Woolley and Gerhard Peters, The American Presidency Project, University of California, Santa Barbara, www.presidency.ucsb.edu/ws/index.php?month=06&year=1967.

Arab League Khartoum Summit

DOCUMENT IN CONTEXT

Israel's overwhelming defeat of Egypt, Jordan, and Syria in the June 1967 War produced a range of reactions among Arabs, including anger, humiliation, resignation, and a determination to seek revenge. All those emotions remained on display less than three months after the war when Arab leaders met for a summit in the Sudanese capital of Khartoum. According to accounts of private meetings, the war had made some leaders—notably Jordan's King Hussein—more realistic than before about the necessity of dealing with Israel as a fait accompli. Others, however, appeared more determined than ever to insist—at least in statements to their publics—that Israel's victory would be reversed someday, somehow.

The leaders met from August 28 to September 2, and by all accounts, the sessions were among the most acrimonious in the history of often-contentious Arab League meetings. As usual during that era, attention focused on Egyptian president Gamal Abdel Nasser, who viewed himself as the preeminent Arab leader and whose rhetoric and military maneuverings in late May had given Israel the incentive and excuse to initiate war on June 5. Also as usual, Nasser proved to be a skillful politician when dealing with his colleagues. Under attack from leaders more radical than himself, including those from Algeria and Iraq, he took a hard-line on the central question of what to do about Israel. Nasser also offered sympathy to King Hussein, who was more willing to deal with Israel but who needed broad Arab support because of his own political weakness at home.

The chief product of the summit was a resolution that, on its face, appeared to voice only unrelenting opposition to Israel in all respects. News accounts at the time, and most historical reviews, focused on one part of one sentence in the resolution: "no peace with Israel, no recognition of Israel, no negotiations with it." This construction is routinely referred to as the Arabs' "three noes" toward Israel. King Hussein, however, insisted in his memoir that the Khartoum resolution took a more subtle stance toward Israel. He said, and some historians agree, that the resolution did not foreclose the possibility of using methods other than war or direct negotiations to achieve the immediate Arab goal of regaining the territories Israel had conquered. For example, the resolution did not prevent dealing with Israel through third parties, such as the United Nations or the United States or the Soviet Union, nor did it rule out intermediate steps, such as a brokered armistice leading to the demilitarization of the conquered territories. Some historians have argued that the Khartoum resolution was flexible enough to permit what subsequently occurred—a de facto peace between Israel and the Arabs most of the time, indirect negotiations through third parties, and a grudging acceptance of Israel's existence.

The Israeli government, however, chose to emphasize the rejectionist component of the Khartoum resolution, insisting that Arab leaders had once again refused to acknowledge Israel's legitimacy. The cabinet responded by reversing its still-secret decision of June 19 to exchange some of the lands acquired in the June war for a peace settlement. The Knesset in late October publicly endorsed the statement that Israel "will maintain the situation fixed by the cease-fire agreements and reinforce its position by taking into account its security and development needs." In other words, Israel would use the conquered lands for its own purposes. From that point forward, Israel's position was that any peace agreement would have to guarantee it "secure borders," signifying the retention of some captured lands as a necessity for Israel's security rather than an option open to discussion.

Following is the text of the resolution adopted on September 1, 1967, at the conclusion of a summit meeting of the Arab League, held in Khartoum, Sudan.

DOCUMENT

Khartoum Declaration

SEPTEMBER 1, 1967

1. The conference has affirmed the unity of Arab ranks, the unity of joint action and the need for coordination and for the elimination of all differences. The Kings, Presidents and representatives of the other Arab Heads of State at the conference have affirmed their countries' stand by and implementation of the Arab Solidarity Charter which was signed at the third Arab summit conference in Casablanca.

2. The conference has agreed on the need to consolidate all efforts to eliminate the effects of the aggression on the basis that the occupied lands are Arab lands and that the burden of regaining these lands falls on all the Arab States.

3. The Arab Heads of State have agreed to unite their political efforts at the international and diplomatic level to eliminate the effects of the aggression and to ensure

the withdrawal of the aggressive Israeli forces from the Arab lands which have been occupied since the aggression of June 5. This will be done within the framework of the main principles by which the Arab States abide, namely, no peace with Israel, no recognition of Israel, no negotiations with it, and insistence on the rights of the Palestinian people in their own country.

4. The conference of Arab Ministers of Finance, Economy and Oil recommended that suspension of oil pumping be used as a weapon in the battle. However, after thoroughly studying the matter, the summit conference has come to the conclusion that the oil pumping can itself be used as a positive weapon, since oil is an Arab resource which can be used to strengthen the economy of the Arab States directly affected by the aggression, so that these States will be able to stand firm in the battle. The conference has, therefore, decided to resume the pumping of oil, since oil is a positive Arab resource that can be used in the service of Arab goals. It can contribute to the efforts to enable those Arab States which were exposed to the aggression and thereby lost economic resources to stand firm and eliminate the effects of the aggression. The oil-producing States have, in fact, participated in the efforts to enable the States affected by the aggression to stand firm in the face of any economic pressure.

5. The participants in the conference have approved the plan proposed by Kuwait to set up an Arab Economic and Social Development Fund on the basis of the recommendation of the Baghdad conference of Arab Ministers of Finance, Economy and Oil.

6. The participants have agreed on the need to adopt the necessary measures to strengthen military preparation to face all eventualities.

7. The conference has decided to expedite the elimination of foreign bases in the Arab States.

SOURCE: United Nations Information System on the Question of Palestine , http://unispal.un.org/unispal.nsf/ 181c4bf00c44e5fd85256cef0073c426/1ff0bf3ddeb703a785257110007719e7!OpenDocument.

UN Security Council Resolution 242

DOCUMENT IN CONTEXT

In the weeks after the June 1967 War, the central front between Israel (and its supporters) and the Arabs (and their supporters) shifted to diplomacy at the United Nations. There, the Soviet Union, Arab nations, and the "nonaligned" bloc centered in Africa and Asia sought to pass resolutions demanding that Israel withdraw from the territories it had just conquered and reimburse its Arab neighbors for their losses during the war. The United States and its allies pressed for an approach that called for full peace between Israel and its neighbors. Diplomatic efforts to negotiate a compromise failed in the Security Council in June and in early July in the General Assembly. Diplomacy took on new urgency in late October when Egypt sank an Israeli ship and Israel responded by shelling Egyptian oil installations.

Under the leadership of Lord Caradon, Britain's ambassador to the United Nations, the Security Council in November arrived at a compromise that met the key demands of the Israelis as well as the Arabs. Adopted on November 22 as Security Council Resolution 242, it set out what came to be known as the "land-for-peace" formula: It called on Israel to withdraw from territories it had occupied "in the recent conflict," and in a clear message to the Arabs, it called for states in the region to acknowledge the sovereignty of other states and allow them to "live in peace within secure and recognized boundaries free from threats or acts of force." The resolution was further balanced by a call for freedom of navigation (thus meeting Israel's demand for the right to use the Suez Canal and other waterways) and for a "just settlement of the refugee problem" (in recognition of Arab calls for Israeli concessions to the hundreds of thousands of Palestinian Arab refugees who had fled or been forced from their homes during the 1948 and 1967 wars).

Described by historian Avi Shlaim as "a masterpiece of deliberate British ambiguity," the resolution gave the Israelis and the Arabs enough maneuvering room for each to claim diplomatic victory without forcing either side to do anything. Even the wording of the resolution was subject to conflicting interpretations. Israel and the United States pointedly noted that the official English-language version of the resolution called for Israel to withdraw "from territories," a wording that could be read as implying that Israel was not required to withdraw from *all* the territories it had captured. Arab nations preferred the French text, which called for an Israel withdrawal from "the territories," language that could be interpreted as demanding a full withdrawal.

The resolution also called on the UN secretary-general to appoint a special representative to promote a "peaceful and accepted settlement" of the Arab-Israeli dispute. Secretary-General U Thant immediately appointed the first such representative, the Swedish diplomat Gunnar Jarring, who visited the region later in 1967 and again in 1968 but failed to make any headway, in part because Syrian officials refused to meet with him but primarily because the Arab nations refused to negotiate even indirectly with Israel. Jarring also failed to meet with Palestinians, who were mentioned only indirectly in the UN resolution as "refugees."

Within a year of Resolution 242's adoption, Egypt launched a low-level "war of attrition" to sap Israel's will for holding onto the Sinai and other captured territories. This war involved dozens of artillery and air attacks, commando raids, and other actions by each side, with Egypt suffering the greatest damage. Both countries accepted a cease-fire in August 1970, and a month later, on September 28, Egyptian president Gamal Abdel Nasser died of a heart attack.

Jarring's efforts to mediate a peace settlement under the terms of Resolution 242 continued until early 1971, when the new Egyptian president, Anwar al-Sadat, agreed to further negotiations under certain conditions. Among those conditions was Israel's withdrawal from all the lands it had captured in 1967. Nothing came of Sadat's agreement, however, because the Israeli government had decided by that point to hold on to at least some of the lands, notably East Jerusalem. In October 1971, the United States offered its own plan for peace talks, including an agreement for reopening the

Suez Canal, which Egypt had closed to all traffic during the 1967 war. Egypt and Israel both demurred, and the Nixon administration abandoned the plan. Despite the failures of these (and most subsequent) peace efforts, Resolution 242 has remained the bedrock of international policy toward the Arab-Israeli dispute. In 2002–2003, the European Union, Russia, the United Nations, and the United States developed a more detailed plan, the so-called "road map" for peace between the Israelis and the Palestinians (Road Map, p. 298).

> *Following is the text of UN Security Council Resolution 242, adopted on November 22, 1967, calling on Israel to withdraw from Arab territories that it had occupied in the June 1967 War and on Arab nations to live in peace with Israel.*

DOCUMENT

UN Security Council Resolution 242 (1967)

NOVEMBER 22, 1967

The Security Council,
Expressing its continuing concern with the grave situation in the Middle East,
Emphasizing the inadmissibility of the acquisition of territory by war and the need to work for a just and lasting peace in which every State in the area can live in security,
Emphasizing further that all Member States in their acceptance of the Charter of the United Nations have undertaken a commitment to act in accordance with Article 2 of the Charter,

1. *Affirms* that the fulfillment of Charter principles requires the establishment of a just and lasting peace in the Middle East which should include the application of both the following principles:

(i) Withdrawal of Israeli armed forces from territories occupied in the recent conflict;

(ii) Termination of all claims or states of belligerency and respect for and acknowledgement of the sovereignty, territorial integrity and political independence of every State in the area and their right to live in peace within secure and recognized boundaries free from threats or acts of force;

2. *Affirms further* the necessity

(a) For guaranteeing freedom of navigation through international waterways in the area;

(b) For achieving a just settlement of the refugee problem;

(c) For guaranteeing the territorial inviolability and political independence of every State in the area, through measures including the establishment of demilitarized zones;

3. *Requests* the Secretary-General to designate a Special Representative to proceed to the Middle East to establish and maintain contacts with the States concerned in order to promote agreement and assist efforts to achieve a peaceful and accepted settlement in accordance with the provisions and principles in this resolution;

4. *Requests* the Secretary-General to report to the Security Council on the progress of the efforts of the Special Representative as soon as possible.

The October 1973 War

DOCUMENT IN CONTEXT

After the end of the "war of attrition" between Egypt and Israel in 1970, and the failure of peace initiatives by the United Nations and the United States, Egyptian president Anwar al-Sadat decided on a two-track policy toward Israel: probing behind the scenes for signs of Israeli willingness to negotiate and preparing for yet another war. Several possible openings for peace talks fell by the wayside, in each case because Egypt or Israel proved to be unable or unwilling to make the necessary concessions.

In preparing for the option of war, Sadat in July 1972 took the unexpected step of ousting the thousands of Soviet airmen, soldiers, and other military advisers who had helped rebuild the Egyptian military after its shattering defeat in the 1967 war. Moscow reportedly angered Sadat by being slow to deliver promised weapons. The Egyptian leader, realizing that the United States ultimately would play a greater role than Moscow in the Middle East, in part because of its influence with Israel, had maintained secret contacts with Washington.

Throughout 1972 and into 1973, Sadat and Syrian leader Hafiz al-Assad laid plans for an attack on Israel. According to almost all reliable accounts, Sadat and Assad had no expectation of destroying Israel in their attack, and instead hoped to regain some of the territory lost in the 1967 war and to galvanize the international community into pressuring Israel into making concessions. Two equally important goals were to restore Arab pride and strengthen their regimes domestically by inflicting a military setback on Israel.

Egypt and Syria launched their attack in the early afternoon of October 6, 1973, to catch Israelis off-guard as they celebrated Yom Kippur, the Day of Atonement or Day of Judgment, the holiest day of the year for Jews. The Arabs achieved their objective of surprise. Although Israeli intelligence services had gathered substantial information about Arab military capabilities and intentions, and Jordan's King Hussein had secretly warned the Israelis, the Israeli government believed—until a few hours before the attack—that the Arabs would not be foolish enough to risk another defeat.

The main thrust of the attack came from Egypt, which sent approximately 90,000 troops across the Suez Canal, driving Israeli forces from their supposedly unbreachable defensive positions on the eastern shore of the waterway. Rather than continuing deep into the Israeli-held Sinai Peninsula, however, the Egyptians focused on consolidating their hold on the area adjacent to the canal; eventually they controlled a strip nearly ten miles wide. In contrast to events in the June 1967 War, Israel was unable to quickly establish air superiority because the Soviet Union had provided Egypt with an extensive defensive system of antiaircraft artillery and missiles.

With matters stalled on the Egyptian front, Israel quickly shifted its attention to its northeastern front, where the Syrian military was attempting to drive Israeli forces from the Golan Heights, the strategic plateau that Israel had captured from Syria in 1967. Syrian ground forces at first achieved rapid success by pushing the Israelis from their eastern positions on the Golan. A massive Israeli counterattack stopped the Syrian advance on October 9 and appeared, for a time, to threaten Damascus, the Syrian capital.

Responding to an appeal from Assad to launch an offensive to ease the pressure on Syrian troops, Sadat on October 14 sent Egyptian forces against Israeli positions in the Sinai Peninsula. The Egyptian attack proved to be the biggest mistake of the war. In a huge battle involving nearly 2,000 tanks, the well-coordinated Israeli forces easily prevailed, forcing many of the Egyptian troops to flee. Late the next day, October 15, an Israeli commando force led by Gen. Ariel Sharon pierced Egyptian defenses at the Suez Canal and eventually crossed over to the western side. The Israelis then moved a larger force onto the west bank and on October 19 began a drive to the south in hopes of trapping the entire Egyptian Third Army, composed of about 20,000 troops.

A cease-fire vote by the UN Security Council in Resolution 338 took effect on October 22, but fighting continued for three more days, as Israel attempted to consolidate its positions, and Egypt used artillery fire in hopes of breaking the Israeli grip on both sides of the canal. In addition to demanding a cease-fire, Resolution 338 reiterated the land-for-peace formula of Resolution 242, adopted in 1967, and called for negotiations "between the parties concerned under appropriate auspices aimed at establishing a just and durable peace in the Middle East." The "appropriate auspices" language was intended to open the door to negotiations brokered by the superpowers, possibly as a substitute for the United Nations.

The war ended with Israel in control of even more Arab territory than at the beginning; indeed, Israeli forces came within twenty miles of Damascus and sixty miles of Cairo. Even so, most independent assessments, at the time and in later years, described the October 1973 war as much closer to a draw than an outright Israeli victory: Israel was caught off guard and failed to establish clear air superiority. Moreover, the Egyptian and Syrian armies achieved important gains in the early stages of the fighting, thus raising doubts about Israel's self-proclaimed invincibility against its Arab foes.

The results of the war also can be judged by the political infighting afterward in Israel: Elections the following December produced gains by rightist parties and led to the collapse of the government of Prime Minister Golda Meir, who was succeeded by former army chief of staff Yitzhak Rabin. An independent investigation faulted the

Israeli intelligence services and two key generals but did not assign blame to the political leadership. On the Arab side, political leaders boasted of their armies' achievements. Even so, the war showed once again the difficulty of defeating Israel, eventually leading Sadat to conclude that Egypt could regain its lost territory only through negotiation.

Resolution 338, officially ending the war, resulted from intense international diplomacy that included an unusual degree of cooperation as well as heightened tensions between the United States and the Soviet Union. Both superpowers rushed enormous quantities of weapons and equipment to the region in the middle stages of the war, with Moscow aiding Egypt and the United States assisting Israel at a crucial stage. Regardless, Resolution 338 was brokered during two days of negotiations in Moscow between Soviet officials and U.S. secretary of state Henry Kissinger. The Security Council adopted it unanimously early on October 22.

The continued fighting between Egypt and Israel after adoption of the cease-fire resolution resulted in a brief crisis in relations between Washington and Moscow. After Sadat appealed on October 24 for U.S. and Soviet troops to supervise the cease-fire, the Soviets hinted that they might intervene on Egypt's behalf. As a warning to Moscow, President Richard Nixon on October 25 put U.S. military forces on a worldwide alert, one of the few times the United States did so during the cold war. All sides quickly backed away from confrontation, and later that day the Security Council adopted Resolution 340 establishing an emergency UN force to supervise the cease-fire. The resolution excluded troops from the five permanent members of the council.

On November 11, Israel and Egypt signed a formal cease-fire—the first major diplomatic agreement between them since their 1949 armistice. A UN-sponsored peace conference held in Geneva in December brought together diplomats from Egypt, Israel, Jordan, the Soviet Union, and the United States but made no clear progress, in part because Syria boycotted the event.

In January 1974, Kissinger embarked on "shuttle diplomacy," trips among Middle Eastern capitals, that produced agreements for disengaging the combatants. The first agreement, signed by Egypt and Israel on January 18, 1974, obligated Israel to withdraw its forces from the western bank of the Suez Canal and establish new positions about twenty miles to the east of the canal. Kissinger returned to the region in May and brokered an agreement separating Israeli and Syrian forces; under that accord, signed on May 31, 1974, the two sides exchanged prisoners, and Israel withdrew behind a buffer zone on the Golan Heights patrolled by a UN monitoring force.

Kissinger resumed Middle East diplomacy during much of 1975, with a renewed focus on Egypt and Israel. On September 4, 1975, those two countries signed an agreement pledging to resolve their differences "by peaceful means" and establishing new positions for their respective forces in the Sinai. That agreement helped set the stage for an ambitious diplomatic initiative by Sadat two years later that led to the first formal, comprehensive peace treaty between Israel and an Arab nation (Camp David Peace Process, p. 118).

In addition to introducing an element of military balance into the Middle East conflict, the 1973 war resulted in the Arabs' first concerted use of oil as a political weapon. On October 17, just two days after the Nixon administration announced its military resupply of Israel, ministers of the Organization of the Arab Petroleum Exporting Countries (OAPEC) met in Kuwait and agreed to reduce oil production by 5 percent until Israel withdrew from occupied Arab territory. The next day, Saudi Arabia, the world's foremost oil exporter, announced its intention to cut production by 10 percent and to halt all shipments to the United States. Other Arab countries quickly announced a similar embargo of the United States and the Netherlands because of their support for Israel. The oil producers gradually increased their overall production but retained the embargo against the United States and the Netherlands until mid-March 1974. Although the embargo lasted just five months, it unleashed the enormous economic consequences of quadrupling world oil prices, exacerbating rampant inflation, and causing a worldwide recession that lasted into 1975.

Following is the text of UN Security Council Resolution 338, adopted on October 22, 1973.

DOCUMENT

UN Security Council Resolution 338 (1973)

OCTOBER 22, 1973

The Security Council,

1. *Calls upon* all parties to present fighting to cease all firing and terminate all military activity immediately, no later than 12 hours after the moment of the adoption of this decision, in the positions after the moment of the adoption of this decision, in the positions they now occupy;

2. *Calls upon* all parties concerned to start immediately after the cease-fire the implementation of Security Council Resolution 242 (1967) in all of its parts;

3. *Decides* that, immediately and concurrently with the cease-fire, negotiations start between the parties concerned under appropriate auspices aimed at establishing a just and durable peace in the Middle East.

SOURCE: United Nations Information System on the Question of Palestine, http://domino.un.org/UNISPAL. NSF/d744b47860e5c97e85256c40005d01d6/7fb7c26fcbe80a31852560c50065f878!OpenDocument.

Zionism as Racism

Although the United Nations played a significant role in the creation of Israel through its 1947 resolution calling for the partition of Palestine, relations between the Jewish state and the world body rarely have been cordial and often have been downright hostile. This was particularly true during the cold war, when the so-called nonaligned nations, including most of the Arab world, dominated the UN General Assembly. With the United States routinely blocking criticism of Israel in the Security Council, Arab nations often turned to the General Assembly as a venue for denouncing Israeli actions.

Israel hit a low point in its relations with the United Nations on November 10, 1975, when the General Assembly adopted three resolutions dealing with the Middle East. The first, Resolution 3375, insisted that the Palestine Liberation Organization (PLO) be accorded "equal footing" with other parties in any Middle East peace conferences. The second, Resolution 3376, established a committee to examine the "Exercise of the Inalienable Rights of the Palestinian People." The third, Resolution 3379, declared that "Zionism is a form of racism and racial discrimination." The General Assembly adopted Resolution 3379 by a vote of 72 to 35, with 32 abstentions. Flushed with anger, Daniel Patrick Moynihan, U.S. ambassador to the United Nations, lashed out at his colleagues, stating, "The United States rises to declare before the General Assembly of the United Nations, and before the world, that it does not acknowledge, it will not abide by, it will never acquiesce in, this infamous act."

To some degree, the General Assembly tarred Israel because of the Jewish state's warm relations at the time with the white minority government of South Africa. South Africa was a significant trading partner for Israel, and it was widely alleged that the two countries swapped technology for the development of nuclear weapons. The General Assembly in December 1973 had denounced the Israeli–South African relationship as an "unholy alliance," language it repeated in the Zionism-as-racism resolution.

Resolution 3379 remained on the books for sixteen years, until the administration of President George H. W. Bush decided, in mid-1991, to press for its repeal. After an intense diplomatic effort that included Bush himself, the General Assembly voted on December 16, 1991, to repeal the resolution. The vote this time was 111 in favor of repeal, 25 opposed, with 13 abstentions. Several major events contributed to the success of Bush's effort. After the Madrid peace conference between Arabs and Israelis in October 1991, Israel had participated with several Arab nations in a series of peace talks stemming from the defeat of Iraq in the Persian Gulf War. Also, the white minority government of South Africa in late 1991 was actively negotiating with black leaders, thereby easing the stigma of Israel's association with that country. The Soviet Union, which long had supported Arab countries and often had been hostile toward Israel, was a few days from collapsing when the resolution reached the General Assembly, and its ambassador voted for the repeal (Madrid Conference, p. 138; Persian Gulf War, p. 455).

Following is the text of UN General Assembly Resolution 3379, adopted on November 10, 1975.

DOCUMENT

UN General Assembly Resolution 3379 (1975)

NOVEMBER 10, 1975

The General Assembly,

Recalling its resolution 1904 (XVIII) of 20 November 1963, proclaiming the United Nations Declaration on the Elimination of All Forms of Racial Discrimination, and in particular its affirmation that "any doctrine of racial differentiation or superiority is scientifically false, morally condemnable, socially unjust and dangerous" and its expression of alarm at "the manifestations of racial discrimination still in evidence in some areas in the world, some of which are imposed by certain Governments by means of legislative, administrative or other measures,"

Recalling also that, in its resolution 3151 G (XXVIII) of 14 December 1953, the General Assembly condemned, *inter alia,* the unholy alliance between South African racism and Zionism,

Taking note of the Declaration of Mexico on the Equality of Women and Their Contribution to Development and Peace,[1] proclaimed by the World Conference of the International Women's Year, held at Mexico City from 19 June to 2 July 1975, which promulgated the principle that "international co-operation and peace require the achievement of national liberation and independence, the elimination of colonialism and neo-colonialism, foreign occupation, Zionism, apartheid and racial discrimination in all its forms, as well as the recognition of the dignity of peoples and their right to self-determination,"

Taking note also of resolution 77 (XII) adopted by the Assembly of Heads of State and Government of the Organization of African Unity at its twelfth ordinary session,[2] held at Kampala from 28 July to 1 August 1975, which considered "that the racist regime in occupied Palestine and the racist regime in Zimbabwe and South Africa have a common imperialist origin, forming a whole and having the same racist structure and being organically linked in their policy aimed at repression of the dignity and integrity of the human being,"

Taking note also of the Political Declaration and Strategy to Strengthen International Peace and Security and to Intensify Solidarity and Mutual Assistance among Non-Aligned Countries,[3] adopted at the Conference of Ministers for Foreign Affairs of

---

[1]E/5725, part one, sect. I.
[2]See A/10297, annex II.
[3]A/10217 and Corr.1, annex, p. 3.

Non-Aligned Countries held at Lima from 25 to 30 August 1975, which most severely condemned Zionism as a threat to world peace and security and called upon all countries to oppose this racist and imperialist ideology,

Determines that Zionism is a form of racism and racial discrimination.

[Note: The General Assembly repealed Resolution 3379 on December 16, 1991.]

SOURCE: United Nations Information System on the Question of Palestine, http://domino.un.org/unispal.nsf/ A06F2943C226015C85256C40005D359C/761C1063530766A7052566A2005B74D1!OPENDOCUMENT.

Camp David Peace Process

DOCUMENT IN CONTEXT

Egypt fought more wars—five, counting an undeclared "war of attrition"—with Israel than any other Arab country, but in 1978–1979 it became the first Arab country to reach a formal peace settlement and establish diplomatic relations with the Jewish state. The peace, often a cold one, was based on the practical self-interest of each party and failed to lead to a broader peace between Israel and its Arab neighbors. Nevertheless, the peace has held despite numerous strains and has helped prevent another full-scale Arab-Israeli war.

In many ways, the Egyptian-Israeli peace agreement flowed from the October 1973 War, the last one involving Israel and multiple Arab countries. Both sides claimed victory, but in reality neither side won a conventional victory. The war's ambiguous results forced leaders in Egypt and Israel to reconsider key aspects of their military and political strategies (October 1973 War, p. 112).

The emergence of new leaders in the United States and Israel also brought new momentum toward peace. In November 1976, former Georgia governor Jimmy Carter won a close election as president of the United States. Although lacking foreign policy experience, he brought to office an idealistic vision of peace and justice in the Middle East and a hard-headed willingness to engage in the messy diplomatic work required to transform such visions into reality. Six months later, in May 1977, Israeli voters handed power to a right-of-center coalition headed by Menachem Begin. A former leader of Jewish guerrillas in the 1940s and a long-time advocate of the most hardline Israeli policies, Begin appeared to be an unlikely candidate to lead his country to peace. His background, however, lent him the political strength necessary to make crucial concessions.

The peace initiative came from another unlikely candidate: Egyptian president Anwar al-Sadat, a former general and vice president who had assumed office following the death of Gamal Abdel Nasser in 1970 and who then launched the 1973 war against Israel in collusion with Syria. Although pleased with the Egyptian army's performance in the early stages of that war, Sadat nonetheless realized that Israel could not be defeated militarily and that some kind of accommodation with the Jewish state was inevitable. By the middle of 1977, Sadat was actively reaching out to Israel, at first indirectly, through the United States, and then directly. At each stage, Sadat ignored or overrode the objections of senior aides who thought he was moving too quickly, acting too independently of other Arab leaders, and making too many concessions to the Israelis.

In October 1977, after Carter appealed to Sadat for help in restarting long-stalled regional talks, the Egyptian president decided on a much bolder step: a trip to Jerusalem, where he would make his case directly to Israel's leaders and its people. Over the opposition of some aides, Begin responded with an invitation. Sadat flew to Jerusalem on November 19, 1977, his arrival marking one of the most dramatic events in recent Middle East history.

Sadat told Israeli leaders that his visit was simply to advance the cause of the Palestinians, not to negotiate a separate peace treaty between Egypt and Israel. In his landmark speech to the Knesset on November 20, Sadat listed several requirements for peace between Israel and the Arabs, among them "secure boundaries" for Israel but also Israel's "complete withdrawal" from the territories occupied in 1967, including East Jerusalem. Despite the symbolic importance of the occasion, Israelis interpreted Sadat's speech as confrontational rather than conciliatory. Begin responded in kind, saying that, while Israel was willing to negotiate with the Arabs, it would never give up East Jerusalem.

Sadat's gambit highlighted yet again the stark differences between Arab and Israeli self-interests and historical perspectives. Even so, the public aspects of the visit—a smiling Begin greeting a courtly Sadat—showed Egyptians and Israelis that their perceived enemies were humans, with similar hopes and fears, not the monsters portrayed by official propaganda. The event also created an opening for a serious diplomatic process, though it failed to win over hard-liners on either side, particularly among Arabs who feared that Sadat had shattered their unity against Israel. Officials from several Arab states, along with the Palestine Liberation Organization (PLO), met in Libya on December 2 to declare an economic boycott against Egypt.

A reciprocal visit by Begin to Ismailia, Egypt, on December 25, 1977, appeared to result in a hardening of positions, making clear the necessity of an outside mediator to break the impasse. At this point, the United States actively entered the picture, starting with a meeting between Carter and Sadat in Egypt on January 4, 1978. This meeting produced the Aswan Declaration, a joint statement that referred to the "legitimate rights of the Palestinian people," including their right to determine "their own future." The statement marked the United States' first formal embrace of a formula implying some kind of self-governance by the Palestinians. Carter also appeared to side with Egypt on two other significant matters. After a meeting with Sadat at the Camp David presidential retreat in Maryland on February 3, 1978, Carter said that UN Security Council Resolution 242 required Israel to withdraw from all—not just some—Arab territories, and he denounced as "illegal" Israel's construction of Jewish settlements on these lands.

U.S.-mediated efforts to bridge differences between the Egyptians and the Israelis made little headway during mid-1978, leading Carter at the end of July to take a gam-

ble of his own—inviting Begin and Sadat to Camp David to hammer out an agreement. Despite misgivings on both sides, the two leaders accepted and arrived at the
retreat on September 5.

Carter had planned for only a few days of meetings, but the sessions dragged on
for nearly two weeks and at several points appeared on the verge of collapse, as the
two leaders stuck by their long-held positions. The status of Israeli settlements in the
eastern Sinai proved to be the major stumbling block. Sadat insisted on their removal
and the return of all of Sinai to Egyptian control, while Begin vowed to keep the settlements as a "security" measure for Israel. Under pressure from Carter, and after
receiving conflicting advice from his own delegation, Begin eventually agreed to relinquish the settlements, a decision that made a deal possible.

Begin, Carter, and Sadat then traveled to the White House, where late on the
evening of September 17 they signed two documents drafted by U.S. officials. One
document, Framework for the Conclusion of a Peace Treaty between Egypt and Israel,
called for Israel to withdraw completely from the Sinai Peninsula in exchange for peace
and normal diplomatic relations with Egypt. It required that the two sides negotiate
a formal peace treaty within the next three months and implement all its measures
within two or three years. The second document, The Framework for Peace in the
Middle East, was more complex but also more ambiguous. It specified compliance with
UN Security Council Resolutions 242 and 338 as the basis for underlying peace in
the region and set out procedures for negotiations to resolve the "the Palestinian problem in all its aspects." This framework called for a "transitional" period of up to five
years, during which Israel and its neighbors would negotiate the creation of a "self-
governing authority" for the Palestinians in the Gaza Strip and West Bank. Although
it promised an unspecified form of "autonomy" for the Palestinians, the framework
did not specifically call for Israel to withdraw from the territories, and it was vague or
silent on the toughest issues, notably the status of Jerusalem.

Carter and other U.S. officials exchanged letters with the two sides offering various assurances or staking out positions on matters (such as Jerusalem) that had not
been settled in the two framework documents. In a letter to Begin, Defense Secretary
Harold Brown held out the promise of U.S. aid for two new Israeli airbases to replace
ones that would be abandoned in the Sinai.

The historic signing of the framework agreements generated decidedly mixed
reactions worldwide. In the United States and Europe, Carter and the two Middle
Eastern leaders were hailed as visionary statesmen. Key constituencies in Egypt and
Israel supported the accords as necessary, if distasteful, compromises for peace. Most
of the rest of the Arab world branded Sadat a traitor, especially Palestinians, who
believed that he had sold out their interests simply to regain the Sinai and who felt
that Sadat had no right to negotiate on their behalf. Begin and Sadat received the
1978 Nobel Peace Prize for their efforts. (Carter did not share in that prize but was
awarded the peace prize in 2002 for his many achievements, including the Camp
David agreements.)

The negotiations toward a formal peace treaty, during the winter of 1978–1979,
were as difficult as the haggling at Camp David. In fact, some aspects of these negotiations proved to be even more contentious as Begin and Sadat both came under increasing pressure from the extreme elements of their respective constituencies to reverse the
compromises they had already accepted. In January 1979, Islamists in Iran ousted Shah

Reza Pahlavi, who had been a strong U.S. ally and had supplied oil to Israel. The prospect of a greater role in Iran for Islamists provided new incentive to Egypt, Israel, and the United States to press forward with negotiations. Begin and Carter held another round of talks early in March 1979, first in Washington and then in Jerusalem, before reaching final agreement on the text of a treaty (Iranian Revolution, p. 379).

On March 26, 1979, at a sun-soaked ceremony on the White House lawn, Begin and Sadat signed (and Carter witnessed) the Treaty of Peace between the Arab Republic of Egypt and the State of Israel. The agreement embraced the land-for-peace formulation of Resolution 242 adopted nearly a dozen years earlier. It required Israel to withdraw all of its military installations and civilian settlements from the Sinai Peninsula in exchange for peace and a "normal relationship" between the two countries. The treaty also established, for the first time, an official international border between Israel and an Arab state. The status of the Gaza Strip remained unresolved, but the international border otherwise followed that of the pre-1948 boundary between Egypt and Palestine.

The treaty included three annexes establishing timetables and procedures for specific actions by both sides, including Israel's staged withdrawal (over three years) from the Sinai and the exchange of ambassadors. Begin and Sadat also signed letters to Carter pledging to conduct the talks agreed to at Camp David leading to "autonomy" for the Palestinians in the Gaza Strip and the West Bank. In subsequent years, Egypt and Israel fitfully carried out most of their respective duties under the bilateral peace treaty, but the negotiations on behalf of the Palestinians quickly bogged down and collapsed in 1982. Israel withdrew from the Sinai in three stages, completing the removal of soldiers and settlers on April 25, 1982. (Not until 2005 would Israel again dismantle all of its settlements from an Arab territory, the Gaza Strip.) Egypt and Israel exchanged ambassadors in February 1980, but other aspects of normalizing economic and political relations occurred slowly or not at all, in some cases because Israel dragged its feet on the Palestinian autonomy talks, and Egypt felt leery of appearing to make further concessions to Israel (Israeli Disengagement, p. 313).

The Arab League, which had threatened to expel Egypt if it signed a separate peace agreement with Israel, followed through on that threat on March 31, five days after the signing of the treaty. The league moved its headquarters from Cairo to Tunis and imposed diplomatic and economic boycotts against Egypt, breached officially only by Oman and Sudan. The boycott would last until May 1989, when member states agreed to allow Egypt to rejoin.

According to memoirs and statements made to colleagues, Sadat realized the personal risk of negotiating with Israel. The full extent of that risk became clear on October 6, 1981, when Islamist extremists assassinated Sadat as he reviewed a military parade commemorating Egypt's self-proclaimed victory in the 1973 war. Vice President Hosni Mubarak, like Sadat a former military officer, assumed the presidency. Begin attended Sadat's funeral four days later, and Mubarak assured him that he intended to carry out Egypt's obligations under the peace treaty.

One other legacy of the Camp David peace process has been an enormous transfer of U.S. economic and military aid to Israel and Egypt. Carter promised both sides that the United States would help shoulder the financial burden of implementing the peace treaty, and that promise translated into financial aid packages that over the next two decades would average about $3 billion a year for Israel and $2 billion for Egypt.

Following are the texts of three documents: Framework for the Conclusion of a Peace Treaty between Egypt and Israel, signed by Egyptian president Anwar al-Sadat and Israeli prime minister Menachim Begin and witnessed by President Jimmy Carter at the White House on September 17, 1978; the Framework for Peace in the Middle East, also signed by Sadat and Begin and witnessed by Carter, September 17, 1978; and Treaty of Peace between the Arab Republic of Egypt and the State of Israel, signed by Sadat and Begin and witnessed by Carter at the White House on March 26, 1979.

D O C U M E N T

Framework for the Conclusion of a Peace Treaty between Egypt and Israel

SEPTEMBER 17, 1978

In order to achieve peace between them, Israel and Egypt agree to negotiate in good faith with a goal of concluding within three months of the signing of this framework a peace treaty between them:

It is agreed that:
- The site of the negotiations will be under a United Nations flag at a location or locations to be mutually agreed.
- All of the principles of U.N. Resolution 242 will apply in this resolution of the dispute between Israel and Egypt.
- Unless otherwise mutually agreed, terms of the peace treaty will be implemented between two and three years after the peace treaty is signed.

The following matters are agreed between the parties:

1. the full exercise of Egyptian sovereignty up to the internationally recognized border between Egypt and mandated Palestine;

2. the withdrawal of Israeli armed forces from the Sinai;

3. the use of airfields left by the Israelis near al-Arish, Rafah, Ras en-Naqb, and Sharm el-Sheikh for civilian purposes only, including possible commercial use only by all nations;

4. the right of free passage by ships of Israel through the Gulf of Suez and the Suez Canal on the basis of the Constantinople Convention of 1888 applying to all nations; the Strait of Tiran and Gulf of Aqaba are international waterways to be open to all nations for unimpeded and nonsuspendable freedom of navigation and over-flight;

5. the construction of a highway between the Sinai and Jordan near Eilat with guaranteed free and peaceful passage by Egypt and Jordan; and

6. the stationing of military forces listed below.

Stationing of Forces

No more than one division (mechanized or infantry) of Egyptian armed forces will be stationed within an area lying approximately 50 km. (30 miles) east of the Gulf of Suez and the Suez Canal.

Only United Nations forces and civil police equipped with light weapons to perform normal police functions will be stationed within an area lying west of the international border and the Gulf of Aqaba, varying in width from 20 km. (12 miles) to 40 km. (24 miles).

In the area within 3 km. (1.8 miles) east of the international border there will be Israeli limited military forces not to exceed four infantry battalions and United Nations observers.

Border patrol units not to exceed three battalions will supplement the civil police in maintaining order in the area not included above.

The exact demarcation of the above areas will be as decided during the peace negotiations.

Early warning stations may exist to insure compliance with the terms of the agreement.

United Nations forces will be stationed:

1. in part of the area in the Sinai lying within about 20 km. of the Mediterranean Sea and adjacent to the international border, and

2. in the Sharm el-Sheikh area to insure freedom of passage through the Strait of Tiran; and these forces will not be removed unless such removal is approved by the Security Council of the United Nations with a unanimous vote of the five permanent members.

After a peace treaty is signed, and after the interim withdrawal is complete, normal relations will be established between Egypt and Israel, including full recognition, including diplomatic, economic and cultural relations; termination of economic boycotts and barriers to the free movement of goods and people; and mutual protection of citizens by the due process of law.

Interim Withdrawal

Between three months and nine months after the signing of the peace treaty, all Israeli forces will withdraw east of a line extending from a point east of al-Arish to Ras Muhammad, the exact location of this line to be determined by mutual agreement.

For the Government of the Arab Republic of Egypt:
Muhammed Anwar al-Sadat

For the Government of Israel:
Menachem Begin

Witnessed by:
Jimmy Carter,
President of the United States of America

SOURCE: U.S. Department of State, www.state.gov/p/nea/rls/22578.htm.

The Framework for Peace in the Middle East

SEPTEMBER 17, 1978

Muhammad Anwar al-Sadat, President of the Arab Republic of Egypt, and Menachem Begin, Prime Minister of Israel, met with Jimmy Carter, President of the United States of America, at Camp David from September 5 to September 17, 1978, and have agreed on the following framework for peace in the Middle East. They invite other parties to the Arab-Israel conflict to adhere to it.

Preamble
The search for peace in the Middle East must be guided by the following:

- The agreed basis for a peaceful settlement of the conflict between Israel and its neighbors is United Nations Security Council Resolution 242, in all its parts.
- After four wars during 30 years, despite intensive human efforts, the Middle East, which is the cradle of civilization and the birthplace of three great religions, does not enjoy the blessings of peace. The people of the Middle East yearn for peace so that the vast human and natural resources of the region can be turned to the pursuits of peace and so that this area can become a model for coexistence and cooperation among nations.
- The historic initiative of President Sadat in visiting Jerusalem and the reception accorded to him by the parliament, government and people of Israel, and the reciprocal visit of Prime Minister Begin to Ismailia, the peace proposals made by both leaders, as well as the warm reception of these missions by the peoples of both countries, have created an unprecedented opportunity for peace which must not be lost if this generation and future generations are to be spared the tragedies of war.
- The provisions of the Charter of the United Nations and the other accepted norms of international law and legitimacy now provide accepted standards for the conduct of relations among all states.

To achieve a relationship of peace, in the spirit of Article 2 of the United Nations Charter, future negotiations between Israel and any neighbor prepared to negotiate peace and security with it are necessary for the purpose of carrying out all the provisions and principles of Resolutions 242 and 338.

Peace requires respect for the sovereignty, territorial integrity and political independence of every state in the area and their right to live in peace within secure and recognized boundaries free from threats or acts of force. Progress toward that goal can accelerate movement toward a new era of reconciliation in the Middle East marked by cooperation in promoting economic development, in maintaining stability and in assuring security.

Security is enhanced by a relationship of peace and by cooperation between nations which enjoy normal relations. In addition, under the terms of peace treaties, the parties can, on the basis of reciprocity, agree to special security arrangements such as demilitarized zones, limited armaments areas, early warning stations, the presence of international forces, liaison, agreed measures for monitoring and other arrangements that they agree are useful.

Framework
Taking these factors into account, the parties are determined to reach a just, comprehensive, and durable settlement of the Middle East conflict through the conclusion of peace treaties based on Security Council resolutions 242 and 338 in all their parts. Their purpose is to achieve peace and good neighborly relations. They recognize that for peace to endure, it must involve all those who have been most deeply affected by the conflict. They therefore agree that this framework, as appropriate, is intended by them to constitute a basis for peace not only between Egypt and Israel, but also between Israel and each of its other neighbors which is prepared to negotiate peace with Israel on this basis. With that objective in mind, they have agreed to proceed as follows:

A. West Bank and Gaza
Egypt, Israel, Jordan and the representatives of the Palestinian people should participate in negotiations on the resolution of the Palestinian problem in all its aspects. To achieve that objective, negotiations relating to the West Bank and Gaza should proceed in three stages:

a. Egypt and Israel agree that, in order to ensure a peaceful and orderly transfer of authority, and taking into account the security concerns of all the parties, there should be transitional arrangements for the West Bank and Gaza for a period not exceeding five years. In order to provide full autonomy to the inhabitants, under these arrangements the Israeli military government and its civilian administration will be withdrawn as soon as a self-governing authority has been freely elected by the inhabitants of these areas to replace the existing military government. To negotiate the details of a transitional arrangement, Jordan will be invited to join the negotiations on the basis of this framework. These new arrangements should give due consideration both to the principle of self-government by the inhabitants of these territories and to the legitimate security concerns of the parties involved.

b. Egypt, Israel, and Jordan will agree on the modalities for establishing elected self-governing authority in the West Bank and Gaza. The delegations of Egypt and Jordan may include Palestinians from the West Bank and Gaza or other Palestinians as mutually agreed. The parties will negotiate an agreement which will define the powers and responsibilities of the self-governing authority to be exercised in the West Bank and Gaza. A withdrawal of Israeli armed forces will take place and there will be a redeployment of the remaining Israeli forces into specified security locations. The agreement will also include arrangements for assuring internal and external security and public order. A strong local police force will be established, which may include Jordanian citizens. In addition, Israeli and Jordanian forces will participate in joint patrols and in the manning of control posts to assure the security of the borders.

c. When the self-governing authority (administrative council) in the West Bank and Gaza is established and inaugurated, the transitional period of five years will begin. As soon as possible, but not later than the third year after the beginning of the transitional period, negotiations will take place to determine the final status of the West Bank and Gaza and its relationship with its neighbors and to conclude a peace treaty between Israel and Jordan by the end of the transitional period. These negotiations will be conducted among Egypt, Israel, Jordan and the elected representatives of the inhabitants of the West Bank and Gaza. Two separate but related committees will be convened, one committee, consisting of representatives of the four parties which will negotiate and agree on the final status of the West Bank and Gaza, and its relationship with its neighbors, and the second committee, consisting of representatives of Israel and representatives of Jordan to be joined by the elected representatives of the inhabitants of the West Bank and Gaza, to negotiate the peace treaty between Israel and Jordan, taking into account the agreement reached in the final status of the West Bank and Gaza. The negotiations shall be based on all the provisions and principles of UN Security Council Resolution 242. The negotiations will resolve, among other matters, the location of the boundaries and the nature of the security arrangements. The solution from the negotiations must also recognize the legitimate right of the Palestinian peoples and their just requirements. In this way, the Palestinians will participate in the determination of their own future through:

   i. The negotiations among Egypt, Israel, Jordan and the representatives of the inhabitants of the West Bank and Gaza to agree on the final status of the West Bank and Gaza and other outstanding issues by the end of the transitional period.

   ii. Submitting their agreements to a vote by the elected representatives of the inhabitants of the West Bank and Gaza.

   iii. Providing for the elected representatives of the inhabitants of the West Bank and Gaza to decide how they shall govern themselves consistent with the provisions of their agreement.

   iv. Participating as stated above in the work of the committee negotiating the peace treaty between Israel and Jordan.

  d. All necessary measures will be taken and provisions made to assure the security of Israel and its neighbors during the transitional period and beyond. To assist in providing such security, a strong local police force will be constituted by the self-governing authority. It will be composed of inhabitants of the West Bank and Gaza. The police will maintain liaison on internal security matters with the designated Israeli, Jordanian, and Egyptian officers.

  e. During the transitional period, representatives of Egypt, Israel, Jordan, and the self-governing authority will constitute a continuing committee to decide by agreement on the modalities of admission of persons displaced from the West Bank and Gaza in 1967, together with necessary measures to prevent disruption and disorder. Other matters of common concern may also be dealt with by this committee.

  f. Egypt and Israel will work with each other and with other interested parties to establish agreed procedures for a prompt, just and permanent implementation of the resolution of the refugee problem.

B. Egypt-Israel

1. Egypt-Israel undertake not to resort to the threat or the use of force to settle disputes. Any disputes shall be settled by peaceful means in accordance with the provisions of Article 33 of the U.N. Charter.

2. In order to achieve peace between them, the parties agree to negotiate in good faith with a goal of concluding within three months from the signing of the Framework a peace treaty between them while inviting the other parties to the conflict to proceed simultaneously to negotiate and conclude similar peace treaties with a view [to] the achieving [of] a comprehensive peace in the area. The Framework for the Conclusion of a Peace Treaty between Egypt and Israel will govern the peace negotiations between them. The parties will agree on the modalities and the timetable for the implementation of their obligations under the treaty.

C. Associated Principles

1. Egypt and Israel state that the principles and provisions described below should apply to peace treaties between Israel and each of its neighbors—Egypt, Jordan, Syria and Lebanon.

2. Signatories shall establish among themselves relationships normal to states at peace with one another. To this end, they should undertake to abide by all the provisions of the U.N. Charter. Steps to be taken in this respect include:
   a. full recognition;
   b. abolishing economic boycotts;
   c. guaranteeing that under their jurisdiction the citizens of the other parties shall enjoy the protection of the due process of law.

3. Signatories should explore possibilities for economic development in the context of final peace treaties, with the objective of contributing to the atmosphere of peace, cooperation and friendship which is their common goal.

4. Claims commissions may be established for the mutual settlement of all financial claims.

5. The United States shall be invited to participate in the talks on matters related to the modalities of the implementation of the agreements and working out the timetable for the carrying out of the obligations of the parties.

6. The United Nations Security Council shall be requested to endorse the peace treaties and ensure that their provisions shall not be violated. The permanent members of the Security Council shall be requested to underwrite the peace treaties and ensure respect or the provisions. They shall be requested to conform their policies and actions with the undertaking contained in this Framework.

For the Government of Israel:
Menachem Begin

For the Government of the Arab Republic of Egypt:
Muhammed Anwar al-Sadat

Witnessed by:
Jimmy Carter,
President of the United States of America

SOURCE: U.S. Department of State, www.state.gov/p/nea/rls/22578.htm.

DOCUMENT

Treaty of Peace between the Arab Republic of Egypt and the State of Israel

MARCH 26, 1979

Preamble

CONVINCED of the urgent necessity of the establishment of a just, comprehensive and lasting peace in the Middle East in accordance with Security Council Resolutions 242 and 338

REAFFIRMING their adherence to the "Framework for Peace in the Middle East Agreed at Camp David," dated September 17, 1978

NOTING THAT the aforementioned Framework as appropriate is intended to constitute a basis for peace not only between Egypt and Israel but also between Israel and each of its other Arab neighbors which is prepared to negotiate peace with it on this basis;

DESIRING to bring to an end the state of war between them and to establish a peace in which every state in the area can live in security

CONVINCED THAT the conclusion of a Treaty of Peace between Egypt and Israel is an important step in the search for comprehensive peace in the area and for the attainment of settlement of the Arab-Israeli conflict in all its aspects

INVITING the other Arab parties to this dispute to join the peace process with Israel guided by and based on the principles of the aforementioned Framework;

DESIRING as well to develop friendly relations and cooperation between themselves in accordance with the United Nations Charter and the principles of international law governing international relations in times of peace

AGREE TO the following provisions in the free exercise of their sovereignty; in order to implement the "Framework for the Conclusion of a Peace Treaty between Egypt and Israel":

Article I

- The state of war between the Parties will be terminated and peace will be established between them upon the exchange of instruments of ratification of this Treaty.
- Israel will withdraw all its armed forces and civilians from the Sinai behind the international boundary between Egypt and mandated Palestine, as provided in the annexed protocol (Annex I), and Egypt will resume the exercise of its full sovereignty over the Sinai.
- Upon completion of the interim withdrawal provided for in Annex I, the Parties will establish normal and friendly relations, in accordance with Article III (3).

Article II

The permanent boundary between Egypt and Israel is the recognized international boundary between Egypt and the former mandated territory of Palestine, as shown on the map at Annex II, without prejudice to the issue of the status of the Gaza Strip. The Parties recognize this boundary as inviolable. Each will respect the territorial integrity of the other, including their territorial waters and airspace.

Article III

- The Parties will apply between them the provisions of the Charter of the United Nations and the principles of international law governing relations among states in times of peace. In particular:
- They recognize and will respect each other's sovereignty, territorial integrity and political independence
- They recognize and will respect each other's right to live in peace within their secure and recognized boundaries
- They will refrain from the threat or use of force, directly or indirectly, against each other and will settle all disputes between them by peaceful means.
- Each Party undertakes to ensure that acts or threats of belligerency, hostility, or violence do not originate from and are not committed from within its territory, or by any forces subject to its control or by any other forces stationed on its territory, against the population, citizens or property of the other Party. Each Party also undertakes to refrain from organizing, instigating, inciting, assisting or participating in acts or threats of belligerency, hostility, subversion or violence against the other Party, anywhere, and undertakes to ensure that perpetrators of such acts are brought to justice.
- The Parties agree that the normal relationship established between them will include full recognition, diplomatic, economic and cultural relations, termination of economic boycotts and discriminatory barriers to the free movement of people and goods, and will guarantee the mutual enjoyment by citizens of the due process of law. The process by which they undertake to achieve such a relationship parallel to the implementation of other provisions of this Treaty is set out in the annexed protocol (Annex III).

Article IV

- In order to provide maximum security for both Parties on the basis of reciprocity, agreed security arrangements will be established including limited force zones in Egyptian and Israeli territory, and United Nations forces and observers, described in detail as to nature and timing in Annex I, and other security arrangements the Parties may agree upon.
- The Parties agree to the stationing of United Nations personnel in areas described in Annex I. The Parties agree not to request withdrawal of the United Nations personnel and that these personnel will not be removed unless such removal is approved by the Security Council of the United Nations, with the affirmative vote of the five Permanent Members, unless the Parties otherwise agree.
- A Joint Commission will be established to facilitate the implementation of the Treaty, as provided for in Annex I.
- The security arrangements provided for in paragraphs 1 and 2 of this Article may at the request of either party be reviewed and amended by mutual agreement of the Parties.

Article V

- Ships of Israel, and cargoes destined for or coming from Israel, shall enjoy the right of free passage through the Suez Canal and its approaches through the Gulf of Suez and the Mediterranean Sea on the basis of the Constantinople Convention of 1888, applying to all nations, Israeli nationals, vessels and cargoes, as well as persons, vessels and cargoes destined for or coming from Israel, shall be accorded non-discriminatory treatment in all matters connected with usage of the canal.
- The Parties consider the Strait of the Gulf of Aqaba to be international waterways open to all nations for unimpeded and non-suspendable freedom of navigation and overflight. The parties will respect each other's right to navigation and overflight for access to either country through the Strait of Tiran and the Gulf of Aqaba.

Article VI

- This Treaty does not affect and shall not be interpreted as affecting in any way the rights and obligations of the Parties under the Charter of the United Nations.
- The Parties undertake to fulfill in good faith their obligations under this Treaty, without regard to action or inaction of any other party and independently of any instrument external to this Treaty.
- They further undertake to take all the necessary measures for the application in their relations of the provisions of the multilateral conventions to which they are parties, including the submission of appropriate notification to the Secretary General of the United Nations and other depositaries of such conventions.
- The Parties undertake not to enter into any obligation in conflict with this Treaty.
- Subject to Article 103 of the United Nations Charter, in the event of a conflict between the obligation of the Parties under the present Treaty and any of their other obligations, the obligations under this Treaty will be binding and implemented.

Article VII

- Disputes arising out of the application or interpretation of this Treaty shall be resolved by negotiations.
- Any such disputes that cannot be settled by negotiations shall be resolved by conciliation or submitted to arbitration.

Article VIII
The Parties agree to establish a claims commission for the mutual settlement of all financial claims.

Article IX

- This Treaty shall enter into force upon exchange of instruments of ratification.
- This Treaty supersedes the Agreement between Egypt and Israel of Sep[t] 1975.
- All protocols, annexes, and maps attached to this Treaty sbe [should be] regarded as an integral part hereof.
- The Treaty shall be communicated to the Secretary General of the United Nations for registration in accordance with the provisions of Article 102 of the Charter of the United Nations.

Done at Washington, D.C. this 26th day of March 1979, in triplicate in the English, Arabic, and Hebrew languages, each text being equally authentic. In case of any divergence of interpretation, the English text shall prevail.
FOR THE GOVERNMENT OF THE ARAB REPUBLIC OF EGYPT FOR THE GOVERNMENT OF ISRAEL

Witnessed by Jimmy Carter,
President of the United States of America

[Note: The treaty contained three annexes, plus "minutes" that defined particular terms in the treaty and the annexes. Annex I dealt with procedures for Israel's withdrawal from the Sinai Peninsula and the establishment of a United Nations monitoring force there. Annex II was a map of the international border between Egypt and Israel. Article III contained specific provisions for the normalization of relations between Egypt and Israel.]

SOURCE: United Nations Information System on the Question of Palestine (UNISPAL), http://domino.un.org/unispal.nsf/bc8b0c56b7bf621185256cbf005ac05f/b3414a2adff4ceaf8525721200790dd1!OpenDocument.

The Reagan Plan

DOCUMENT IN CONTEXT

The war fought in Lebanon in the summer of 1982 highlighted the interconnectedness of the various conflicts in the Middle East. Israel invaded Lebanon in June 1982 to destroy the bases in southern Lebanon that Palestinian guerrillas used for launching artillery attacks against towns and villages in northern Israel. The invasion also had broader purposes including strengthening the minority Christian-led government in Lebanon and crushing the Palestine Liberation Organization (PLO), which had established its base in Lebanon after being expelled from Jordan eleven years earlier (Israeli Invasion of Lebanon, p. 334).

One of the unintended outcomes of the war was the revival of U.S. interest in promoting an overall peace settlement between the Arabs and Israelis. As had often happened, the U.S. interest proved to be fleeting, lasting only until the various parties made clear that they did not intend to follow the U.S. lead. In this case, the administration of President Ronald Reagan believed that Israel's success in forcing the expulsion from Lebanon of the PLO leadership to Tunis and the dispersal of thousands of guerrillas created an opening for a peace initiative. The administration hoped to build on the success of the 1978–1979 Camp David peace process between Egypt and Israel, which had culminated earlier in 1982 with Israel's final withdrawal from the Sinai Peninsula (Camp David Peace Process, p. 118).

Reagan announced his peace initiative in a nationally televised speech on September 1, 1982, just as the last of the PLO fighters and leaders were being transported from Lebanon. The crux of Reagan's plan was the adoption by the United States of the so-called Jordanian option: establishing a formal, governing relationship between Jordan and the Palestinian Arabs living in the Gaza Strip and the West Bank. This option had some credibility because Jordan at the time claimed sovereignty over the West Bank. Reagan argued that "self-government by the Palestinians of the West Bank and Gaza in association with Jordan offers the best chance for a durable, just, and lasting peace." The president ruled out two other options: creation of a Palestinian state and annexation of the West Bank and Gaza by Israel. Reagan also called for a "freeze" on Israeli settlements, which had been expanded rapidly in the territories during the previous decade. He said creation of Jewish settlements there "is in no way necessary for the security of Israel and only diminishes the confidence of the Arabs that a final outcome can be freely and fairly negotiated."

Reagan's plan reportedly came as a rude shock to Israeli prime minister Menachem Begin, who had hoped that Israel's intervention in Lebanon would kill any remaining prospects for the Palestinian nationalist movement led by the PLO. He was then suddenly confronted with the United States focusing on the plight of the Palestinians and a demand for eventual Israeli withdrawal from the West Bank and Gaza. Begin's cabinet firmly rejected Reagan's plan on September 2, insisting that it was not in accord with the Camp David agreements.

King Hussein had privately told U.S. officials that he supported the thrust of the plan, but he also insisted that he could not negotiate with Israel on the basis of the plan unless he had backing from other Arab leaders, including those in the PLO. Arab leaders met in Fez, Morocco, in the days after Reagan announced his plan. They took a modest step toward recognizing Israel, but failed to respond directly to Reagan's plan, which soon took its place among the long list of peace initiatives that staked out new positions but failed to bring any semblance of peace (Arab League Fez Summit, p. 136).

Following are excerpts from the nationally televised speech by President Ronald Reagan on September 1, 1982, presenting his peace plan for the Middle East.

DOCUMENT

Reagan Address to the Nation on U.S. Peace Efforts in the Middle East

SEPTEMBER 1, 1982

[Note: In the opening portions of his address, President Ronald Reagan reviewed the outcome of the Camp David peace process between Egypt and Israel, and the results of Israel's invasion

of Lebanon in summer 1982 that resulted in the expulsion of the guerrillas and leaders of the Palestine Liberation Organization (PLO) from that country.]

. . . The evacuation of the PLO from Beirut is now complete, and we can now help the Lebanese to rebuild their war-torn country. We owe it to ourselves and to posterity to move quickly to build upon this achievement. A stable and revived Lebanon is essential to all our hopes for peace in the region. The people of Lebanon deserve the best efforts of the international community to turn the nightmares of the past several years into a new dawn of hope. But the opportunities for peace in the Middle East do not begin and end in Lebanon. As we help Lebanon rebuild, we must also move to resolve the root causes of conflict between Arabs and Israelis.

The war in Lebanon has demonstrated many things, but two consequences are key to the peace process. First, the military losses of the PLO have not diminished the yearning of the Palestinian people for a just solution of their claims; and, second, while Israel's military successes in Lebanon have demonstrated that its armed forces are second to none in the region, they alone cannot bring just and lasting peace to Israel and her neighbors.

The question now is how to reconcile Israel's legitimate security concerns with the legitimate rights of the Palestinians. And that answer can only come at the negotiating table. Each party must recognize that the outcome must be acceptable to all and that true peace will require compromises by all.

So, tonight I'm calling for a fresh start. This is the moment for all those directly concerned to get involved—or lend their support—to a workable basis for peace. The Camp David agreement remains the foundation of our policy. Its language provides all parties with the leeway they need for successful negotiations.

I call on Israel to make clear that the security for which she yearns can only be achieved through genuine peace, a peace requiring magnanimity, vision, and courage.

I call on the Palestinian people to recognize that their own political aspirations are inextricably bound to recognition of Israel's right to a secure future.

And I call on the Arab States to accept the reality of Israel—and the reality that peace and justice are to be gained only through hard, fair, direct negotiation.

In making these calls upon others, I recognize that the United States has a special responsibility. No other nation is in a position to deal with the key parties to the conflict on the basis of trust and reliability.

The time has come for a new realism on the part of all the peoples of the Middle East. The State of Israel is an accomplished fact; it deserves unchallenged legitimacy within the community of nations. But Israel's legitimacy has thus far been recognized by too few countries and has been denied by every Arab State except Egypt. Israel exists; it has a right to exist in peace behind secure and defensible borders; and it has a right to demand of its neighbors that they recognize those facts.

I have personally followed and supported Israel's heroic struggle for survival, ever since the founding of the State of Israel 34 years ago. In the pre-1967 borders Israel was barely 10 miles wide at its narrowest point. The bulk of Israel's population lived within artillery range of hostile Arab armies. I am not about to ask Israel to live that way again.

The war in Lebanon has demonstrated another reality in the region. The departure of the Palestinians from Beirut dramatizes more than ever the homelessness of the

Palestinian people. Palestinians feel strongly that their cause is more than a question of refugees. I agree. The Camp David agreement recognized that fact when it spoke of the legitimate rights of the Palestinian people and their just requirements.

For peace to endure it must involve all those who have been most deeply affected by the conflict. Only through broader participation in the peace process, most immediately by Jordan and by the Palestinians, will Israel be able to rest confident in the knowledge that its security and integrity will be respected by its neighbors. Only through the process of negotiation can all the nations of the Middle East achieve a secure peace.

These, then, are our general goals. What are the specific new American positions, and why are we taking them? In the Camp David talks thus far, both Israel and Egypt have felt free to express openly their views as to what the outcome should be.

Understandably their views have differed on many points. The United States has thus far sought to play the role of mediator. We have avoided public comment on the key issues. We have always recognized and continue to recognize that only the voluntary agreement of those parties most directly involved in the conflict can provide an enduring solution. But it's become evident to me that some clearer sense of America's position on the key issues is necessary to encourage wider support for the peace process.

First, as outlined in the Camp David accords, there must be a period of time during which the Palestinian inhabitants of the West Bank and Gaza will have full autonomy over their own affairs. Due consideration must be given to the principle of self-government by the inhabitants of the territories and to the legitimate security concerns of the parties involved. The purpose of the 5-year period of transition which would begin after free elections for a self-governing Palestinian authority is to prove to the Palestinians that they can run their own affairs and that such Palestinian autonomy poses no threat to Israel's security.

The United States will not support the use of any additional land for the purpose of settlements during the transitional period. Indeed, the immediate adoption of a settlement freeze by Israel, more than any other action, could create the confidence needed for wider participation in these talks. Further settlement activity is in no way necessary for the security of Israel and only diminishes the confidence of the Arabs that a final outcome can be freely and fairly negotiated.

I want to make the American position well understood. The purpose of this transitional period is the peaceful and orderly transfer of authority from Israel to the Palestinian inhabitants of the West Bank and Gaza. At the same time, such a transfer must not interfere with Israel's security requirements.

Beyond the transition period, as we look to the future of the West Bank and Gaza, it is clear to me that peace cannot be achieved by the formation of an independent Palestinian state in those territories, nor is it achievable on the basis of Israeli sovereignty or permanent control over the West Bank and Gaza. So, the United States will not support the establishment of an independent Palestinian state in the West Bank and Gaza, and we will not support annexation or permanent control by Israel.

There is, however, another way to peace. The final status of these lands must, of course, be reached through the give and take of negotiations. But it is the firm view of the United States that self-government by the Palestinians of the West Bank and Gaza in association with Jordan offers the best chance for a durable, just, and lasting peace. We base our approach squarely on the principle that the Arab-Israeli conflict should be resolved through negotiations involving an exchange of territory for peace.

This exchange is enshrined in United Nations Security Council Resolution 242, which is, in turn, incorporated in all its parts in the Camp David agreements. U.N. Resolution 242 remains wholly valid as the foundation stone of America's Middle East peace effort. It is the United States' position that, in return for peace, the withdrawal provision of Resolution 242 applies to all fronts, including the West Bank and Gaza. When the border is negotiated between Jordan and Israel, our view on the extent to which Israel should be asked to give up territory will be heavily affected by the extent of true peace and normalization, and the security arrangements offered in return.

Finally, we remain convinced that Jerusalem must remain undivided, but its final status should be decided through negotiation.

In the course of the negotiations to come, the United States will support positions that seem to us fair and reasonable compromises and likely to promote a sound agreement. We will also put forward our own detailed proposals when we believe they can be helpful. And, make no mistake, the United States will oppose any proposal from any party and at any point in the negotiating process that threatens the security of Israel. America's commitment to the security of Israel is ironclad, and, I might add, so is mine.

During the past few days, our Ambassadors in Israel, Egypt, Jordan, and Saudi Arabia have presented to their host governments the proposals, in full detail, that I have outlined here today. Now I'm convinced that these proposals can bring justice, bring security, and bring durability to an Arab-Israeli peace. The United States will stand by these principles with total dedication. They are fully consistent with Israel's security requirements and the aspirations of the Palestinians.

We will work hard to broaden participation at the peace table as envisaged by the Camp David accords. And I fervently hope that the Palestinians and Jordan, with the support of their Arab colleagues, will accept this opportunity.

Tragic turmoil in the Middle East runs back to the dawn of history. In our modern day, conflict after conflict has taken its brutal toll there. In an age of nuclear challenge and economic interdependence, such conflicts are a threat to all the people of the world, not just the Middle East itself. It's time for us all—in the Middle East and around the world—to call a halt to conflict, hatred, and prejudice. It's time for us all to launch a common effort for reconstruction, peace, and progress.

It has often been said—and, regrettably, too often been true—that the story of the search for peace and justice in the Middle East is a tragedy of opportunities missed. In the aftermath of the settlement in Lebanon, we now face an opportunity for a broader peace. This time we must not let it slip from our grasp. We must look beyond the difficulties and obstacles of the present and move with a fairness and resolve toward a brighter future. We owe it to ourselves—and to posterity—to do no less. For if we miss this chance to make a fresh start, we may look back on this moment from some later vantage point and realize how much that failure cost us all.

These, then, are the principles upon which American policy toward the Arab-Israeli conflict will be based. I have made a personal commitment to see that they endure and, God willing, that they will come to be seen by all reasonable, compassionate people as fair, achievable, and in the interests of all who wish to see peace in the Middle East.

Tonight, on the eve of what can be a dawning of new hope for the people of the troubled Middle East—and for all the world's people who dream of a just and peaceful future—I ask you, my fellow Americans, for your support and your prayers in this great undertaking.

Thank you, and God bless you.

SOURCE: John Woolley and Gerhard Peters, The American Presidency Project. University of California, Santa Barbara, www.presidency.ucsb.edu/ws/?pid=42911.

The Arab League Fez Summit

DOCUMENT IN CONTEXT

With few exceptions, the periodic steps toward Middle East peace have been incremental ones involving small concessions by one side or the other. One such example came about early in September 1982, when Arab leaders met in Fez, Morocco, in the wake of Israel's invasion of Lebanon. As could be expected, the leaders harshly denounced the invasion, which led to the expulsion of Palestinian guerrillas and leaders from Lebanon, but at the initiative of Saudi Arabia's King Fahd, they also for the first time put forth the possibility of recognizing Israel as a legitimate presence in the region.

The Final Declaration of the summit issued on September 9 listed eight "principles" for Middle East peace. These included what had become the traditional Arab demands for Israel to withdraw from all the territories it had occupied since the June 1967 war and to allow for the "self-determination" of the Palestinians. The seventh principle departed from the standard rhetoric in calling for "the establishment by the United Nations Security Council of guarantees of peace between all States of the region, including the independent Palestinian State." The reference to "all States" implicitly includes Israel, which none of the Arab leaders present had been willing to recognize officially. At the time, only Egypt had signed a peace treaty with Israel, and it had been expelled from the Arab League for doing so.

Despite this noteworthy change in position, the Arab declaration included two caveats that made it unacceptable to Israel. One was a reference to the UN Security Council implying that any peace negotiations should take place under UN auspices, which Israel opposed because of its distrust of the organization. The other was a reference to an "independent Palestinian State," something that the Israeli government at the time adamantly opposed and said it would never allow.

Another notable aspect of this declaration was that it limited the maneuvering room of Jordan's King Hussein. The declaration referred to the Palestine Liberation Organization (PLO) as the "sole and legitimate representative" of the Palestinians. Hussein had accepted that role for the PLO in 1974, but in 1982 he still claimed sovereignty over the West Bank. On the basis of that claim, the 1978 Camp David Accords had envisioned a role for the king in negotiations on behalf of the Palestinians. In their declaration at Fez, however, Arab leaders appeared to reject the whole idea of negotiations on Palestinian issues that excluded the PLO (Camp David Peace Process, p. 118).

Following are excerpts from the final declaration of the Arab League summit held in Fez, Morocco, issued on September 9, 1982. Libya boycotted the event, and Egypt remained expelled because of its peace treaty with Israel. All other Arab states and the Palestine Liberation Organization were represented at the summit.

DOCUMENT

Fez Declaration

SEPTEMBER 9, 1982

In view of the grave and delicate circumstances through which the Arab nation is passing and inspired by awareness of historic national responsibility, Their Majesties, Their Excellencies and Their Highnesses, the Kings, Presidents and Amirs of the Arab States examined the important questions before the Conference and took the following decisions.

I. The Arab-Israeli conflict

The Conference paid a tribute to the resistance of the forces of the Palestinian revolution, the Lebanese and Palestinian peoples and the Syrian Arab armed forces, and declared its support for the Palestinian people in their struggle for the restoration of their inalienable national rights.

Convinced of the ability of the Arab nation to achieve its legitimate objectives and to put an end to the aggression, on the basis of the fundamental principles laid down by the Arab Summit Conferences, in view of the desire of the Arab States to continue to strive by every means for the achievement of peace based on justice in the Middle East region, taking account of the plan of His Excellency President Habib Bourguiba, which holds international legality to be the basis for the solution of the Palestinian question, and of the plan of His Majesty King Fahd Ibn Abdul Aziz for peace in the Middle East and in the light of the discussions and observations of Their Majesties, Their Excellencies and Their Highnesses, the Kings, Presidents and Amirs, the Conference adopted the following principles:

1. The withdrawal of Israel from all the Arab territories occupied by it in 1967, including Arab Jerusalem;
2. The dismantling of the settlements established by Israel in the Arab territories since 1967;
3. The guaranteeing of freedom of worship and performance of religious rites for all religions in the Holy Places;
4. The reaffirmation of the right of the Palestinian people to self-determination and to the exercise of their inalienable and imprescriptible national rights,

under the leadership of the Palestine Liberation Organization, their sole and legitimate representative, and the indemnification of those who do not desire to return;

5. The placing of the West Bank and the Gaza Strip under the supervision of the United Nations for a transitional period not exceeding a few months;

6. The establishment of an independent Palestinian State with Jerusalem as its capital;

7. The establishment by the United Nations Security Council of guarantees of peace between all States of the region, including the independent Palestinian State;

8. The guaranteeing by the Security Council of the implementation of these principles.

[Note: Subsequent portions of the declaration stated opposition to the Israeli invasion of Lebanon, support for Iraq in its war with Iran, and support for Somalia in its war with Ethiopia.]

SOURCE: United Nations Information System on the Question of Palestine, http://domino.un.org/UNISPAL. NSF/be65b75f931fa995052567270057d45e/a65756251b75f6ad852562810074e5f4!OpenDocument.

The Madrid Conference

DOCUMENT IN CONTEXT

After the United States and other countries drove Iraqi forces from Kuwait in the Persian Gulf War, which ended in February 1991, President George H. W. Bush sought to use what he called a "new world order" to revive the long-stalled Middle East peace process. Bush's secretary of state, James A. Baker III, spent months getting the region's leaders to agree to attend a peace conference at which great issues of peace as well as more mundane matters, such as transportation and water resources, could be discussed under the watchful eyes of the United States and the Soviet Union. The Israeli government, headed by Prime Minister Yitzhak Shamir, was the most reluctant to attend, but Shamir eventually agreed after Baker established procedures emphasizing bilateral, rather than multilateral, negotiations that met Israel's specifications (Persian Gulf War, p. 455).

The conference convened in Madrid on October 30, with delegates or observers attending from Israel and most Arab countries. At Israel's insistence, Palestinians were officially represented only as part of the Jordanian delegation, but the Palestinian delegates had been chosen by the Palestine Liberation Organization (PLO). In opening speeches, President Bush and Soviet president Mikhail Gorbachev emphasized the historic nature of the occasion and called for all parties to make the compromises necessary for peace.

Bush told the delegates that the United States would not attempt to impose agreements, but he noted that "territorial compromise" would be necessary—a warning to Israel that it would have to return most of the lands it had occupied during the 1967 war and to Israel's Arab neighbors that they would not get back every inch of the lands they had lost.

Speeches in the following days by delegates from the individual countries offered no hints of compromise, however, and the conference ended on November 4 without the convening of bilateral talks that the U.S. and Soviet sponsors had planned. A series of bilateral and multilateral talks did take place in Washington and Moscow through May 1992 but produced no firm agreements on any issues.

The Bush administration made no secret that it held Shamir's government largely responsible for the failure of the Madrid peace process. Israel refused to participate in some sessions involving Palestinians, and its expansion of Jewish settlements in the West Bank, over explicit U.S. opposition, was widely seen as a provocative act at a sensitive time.

Israeli voters defeated Shamir's right-leaning government in elections held in June 1992. The new prime minister, Yitzhak Rabin of the left-leaning Labor Party, then met with Bush and reached understandings that led to two more rounds of peace talks in August and October. Although Israel showed a new willingness to compromise, the negotiations again failed to produce a breakthrough, and the entire Madrid process collapsed after Bush lost his reelection bid that November. Even so, the year of negotiations did contribute to a changed atmosphere in Israel and among some Arabs that helped make possible the formal agreements in 1993 through 1995 between Israel and the Palestinians and Israel and Jordan (Oslo Accords, p. 213; Jordanian-Israeli Peace, p. 142).

Following are excerpts from the opening speech by U.S. president George H. W. Bush to the Middle East peace conference, hosted by the United States and the Soviet Union, held in Madrid, Spain, starting on October 30, 1991.

D O C U M E N T

Opening Statement by President George H. W. Bush at the Madrid Conference

OCTOBER 30, 1991

We come to Madrid on a mission of hope, to begin work on a just, lasting, and comprehensive settlement to the conflict in the Middle East. We come here to seek peace for a part of the world that in the long memory of man has known far too much hatred, anguish, and war. I can think of no endeavor more worthy, or more necessary.

Our objective must be clear and straightforward. It is not simply to end the state of war in the Middle East and replace it with a state of nonbelligerency. This is not enough. This would not last. Rather, we seek peace, real peace. And by real peace, I mean treaties, security, diplomatic relations, economic relations, trade, investment, cultural exchange, even tourism. . . .

Peace will only come as the result of direct negotiations, compromise, give-and-take. Peace cannot be imposed from the outside by the United States or anyone else. While we will continue to do everything possible to help the parties overcome obstacles, peace must come from within.

We come here to Madrid as realists. We do not expect peace to be negotiated in a day or a week or a month or even a year. It will take time. Indeed, it should take time: time for parties so long at war to learn to talk to one another, to listen to one another; time to heal old wounds and build trust. In this quest, time need not be the enemy of progress.

What we envision is a process of direct negotiations proceeding along two tracks: one between Israel and the Arab States; the other between Israel and the Palestinians. Negotiations are to be conducted on the basis of U.N. Security Council Resolutions 242 and 338.

The real work will not happen here in the plenary session but in direct bilateral negotiations. This conference cannot impose a settlement on the participants or veto agreements. And just as important, the conference can only be reconvened with the consent of every participant. Progress is in the hands of the parties who must live with the consequences.

Soon after the bilateral talks commence, parties will convene as well to organize multilateral negotiations. These will focus on issues that cross national boundaries and are common to the region: arms control, water, refugee concerns, economic development. Progress in these fora is not intended as a substitute for what must be decided in the bilateral talks; to the contrary, progress in the multilateral issues can help create an atmosphere in which longstanding bilateral disputes can more easily be settled.

For Israel and the Palestinians, a framework already exists for diplomacy. Negotiations will be conducted in phases, beginning with talks on interim self-government arrangements. We aim to reach agreement within 1 year. And once agreed, interim self-government arrangements will last for 5 years. Beginning the 3d year, negotiations will commence on permanent status. No one can say with any precision what the end result will be. In our view, something must be developed, something acceptable to Israel, the Palestinians, and Jordan, that gives the Palestinian people meaningful control over their own lives and fate and provides for the acceptance and security of Israel.

We can all appreciate that both Israelis and Palestinians are worried about compromise, worried about compromising even the smallest point for fear it becomes a precedent for what really matters. But no one should avoid compromise on interim arrangements for a simple reason: Nothing agreed to now will prejudice permanent status negotiations. To the contrary, these subsequent negotiations will be determined on their own merits.

Peace cannot depend upon promises alone. Real peace, lasting peace, must be based upon security for all States and peoples, including Israel. For too long the Israeli people have lived in fear, surrounded by an unaccepting Arab world. Now is the ideal moment for the Arab world to demonstrate that attitudes have changed, that the Arab world is willing to live in peace with Israel and make allowances for Israel's reasonable security needs.

We know that peace must also be based on fairness. In the absence of fairness, there will be no legitimacy, no stability. This applies above all to the Palestinian people, many of whom have known turmoil and frustration above all else. Israel now has an opportunity to demonstrate that it is willing to enter into a new relationship with its Palestinian neighbors: one predicated upon mutual respect and cooperation.

Throughout the Middle East, we seek a stable and enduring settlement. We've not defined what this means. Indeed, I make these points with no map showing where the final borders are to be drawn. Nevertheless, we believe territorial compromise is essential for peace. Boundaries should reflect the quality of both security and political arrangements. The United States is prepared to accept whatever the parties themselves find acceptable. What we seek, as I said on March 6, is a solution that meets the twin tests of fairness and security.

I know—I expect we all know—that these negotiations will not be easy. I know, too, that these negotiations will not be smooth. There will be disagreement and criticism, setbacks, who knows, possibly interruptions. Negotiation and compromise are always painful. Success will escape us if we focus solely upon what is being given up.

We must fix our vision on what real peace would bring. Peace, after all, means not just avoiding war and the costs of preparing for it. The Middle East is blessed with great resources: physical, financial and, yes, above all, human. New opportunities are within reach if we only have the vision to embrace them.

To succeed, we must recognize that peace is in the interest of all parties; war, absolute advantage of none. The alternative to peace in the Middle East is a future of violence and waste and tragedy. In any future war lurks the danger of weapons of mass destruction. As we learned in the Gulf war, modern arsenals make it possible to attack urban areas, to put the lives of innocent men, women, and children at risk, to transform city streets, schools, and children's playgrounds into battlefields.

Today, we can decide to take a different path to the future, to avoid conflict. I call upon all parties to avoid unilateral acts, be they words or deeds, that would invite retaliation or, worse yet, prejudice or even threaten this process itself. I call upon all parties to consider taking measures that will bolster mutual confidence and trust, steps that signal a sincere commitment to reconciliation.

I want to say something about the role of the United States of America. We played an active role in making this conference possible. Both the Secretary of State, Jim Baker, and I will play an active role in helping the process succeed. Toward this end, we've provided written assurances to Israel, to Syria, to Jordan, Lebanon, and the Palestinians. In the spirit of openness and honesty, we will brief all parties on the assurances that we have provided to the other. We're prepared to extend guarantees, provide technology and support, if that is what peace requires. And we will call upon our friends and allies in Europe and in Asia to join with us in providing resources so that peace and prosperity go hand in hand.

Outsiders can assist, but in the end, it is up to the peoples and Governments of the Middle East to shape the future of the Middle East. It is their opportunity, and it is their responsibility to do all that they can to take advantage of this gathering, this historic gathering, and what it symbolizes and what it promises.

No one should assume that the opportunity before us to make peace will remain if we fail to seize the moment. Ironically, this is an opportunity born of war, the destruction of past wars, the fear of future wars. The time has come to put an end to war, the time has come to choose peace.

Speaking for the American people, I want to reaffirm that the United States is prepared to facilitate the search for peace, to be a catalyst, as we've been in the past and as we've been very recently. We seek only one thing, and this we seek not for ourselves, but for the peoples of the area and particularly the children: That this and future generations of the Middle East may know the meaning and blessing of peace.

We have seen too many generations of children whose haunted eyes show only fear, too many funerals for their brothers and sisters, the mothers and fathers who died too soon, too much hatred, too little love. And if we cannot summon the courage to lay down the past for ourselves, let us resolve to do it for the children.

SOURCE: John Woolley and Gerhard Peters, The American Presidency Project. University of California, Santa Barbara, www.presidency.ucsb.edu/ws/?pid=20163.

Jordanian-Israeli Peace

DOCUMENT IN CONTEXT

Among Israel's Arab neighbors, Jordan has been one of the least belligerent toward it. In the decades after Israel's founding in 1948, however, Jordan's King Abdallah and his grandson King Hussein rested uneasily on their thrones and were reluctant to get too far in front of their Arab colleagues. A major consideration for both men was the large proportion of the Jordanian population that consisted of Palestinian Arabs who had left or had been driven from their homes in Palestine, from Israel after its declaration, and from the West Bank as a result of the wars fought in the region after 1948 (Founding of the State of Israel, p. 67).

In the decades after ascending the throne in 1953, King Hussein held numerous secret meetings with senior Israeli officials, including prime ministers. He, however, remained reluctant to be seen as too cozy with the Israelis and refused to sign a formal peace agreement with them until other Arab leaders had taken the first step. This step came in 1978–1979, when Egyptian president Anwar al-Sadat negotiated the Camp David agreements and then a formal peace treaty with Israel. Even then Hussein felt insecure because the Arab League then expelled Egypt, and Islamist extremists assassinated Sadat in 1981 (see Camp David Peace Process, p. 118).

Hussein took significant action in 1988, when, in response to the first Palestinian intifada, he renounced Jordan's claim to the West Bank, which Israel had captured from the kingdom in the 1967 war. Among other things, Hussein's action undercut Israel's policy that it would discuss the future of the Palestinians only with Jordan—not with the Palestine Liberation Organization (PLO)—because Jordan officially represented them.

A series of events—the PLO's expulsion from Lebanon in 1982, the intifada, the Persian Gulf War, the 1991 Madrid conference and peace process, and Israeli elections that brought the Labor Party's Yitzhak Rabin to office as prime minister—set the stage for peace talks between the Israelis and Palestinians (moderated by Norway) in 1993. Those talks resulted in the signing of a tentative peace agreement, the Declaration of Principles, by Rabin and PLO chairman Yasir Arafat on September 13, 1993. The next day, Israeli and Jordanian officials completed work on a long-pending "common agenda" to pave the way for a permanent peace deal between their countries.

In May 1994, Hussein and Rabin met secretly in London and pushed ahead with negotiations to complete a formal agreement. President Bill Clinton offered Hussein tangible inducements for peace, including a pledge to ask Congress to waive about $700 million in debts Jordan owed the United States.

On July 25, 1994, Hussein held his first official, public meeting with an Israeli leader, Rabin, at the White House. The two men signed the Washington Declaration, a document one step short of a formal peace treaty. The declaration expressed the two leaders' determination to finalize a treaty and proclaimed that "the state of belligerency between Jordan and Israel has been terminated." One of its notable features was Israel's recognition of Jordan's "special role" in administering the Muslim holy places in Jerusalem and promise to "give high priority to the Jordanian historic role" at those sites when the time came for negotiating a final agreement with the Palestinians. This provision was bound to annoy the PLO, which did not accept Hussein's supposed status—claimed through the Hashemite dynasty of which he was a part—as the official Islamic caretaker of those sites. The Hashemite's claim direct descent from the Prophet Muhammad.

Because so much groundwork had been laid in previous negotiations, Israeli and Jordanian diplomats quickly reached agreement on a formal peace treaty. On October 26, 1994, Rabin signed the document for Israel and Prime Minister Abdul Salam Majali signed it for Jordan at the Arava/Araba border crossing between the two countries. King Hussein, President Clinton, and Russian foreign minister Andrei Kozyrov acted as official witnesses.

The treaty contained expressions of mutual respect, noting for example that the countries "recognize and will respect each other's sovereignty, territorial integrity and political independence," as well as "each other's right to live in peace within secure and recognized boundaries." Each country pledged not to allow third parties to use its territory to attack the other; this provision applied primarily to Jordan, which before 1970 had been the launching pad for numerous Palestinian operations against Israel. The treaty also settled several specific long-standing disputes between the two countries, including conflicting claims over water resources, and Israel agreed to return to Jordan a sliver of land in the border area south of the Dead Sea that had been captured in 1967. The treaty, however, was silent on the status of the West Bank, the much larger territory that Israel had seized from Jordan in 1967 and over which King Hussein had unilaterally relinquished sovereignty in 1988.

Despite periodic crises, the treaty has remained in force since 1994, and Israel generally has enjoyed much warmer relations with Jordan than with Egypt, the only other Arab country to have signed a formal peace treaty with it. The treaty has not, however, resulted in the widespread economic benefits for Jordan that Hussein had envisioned. Trade between the two countries expanded only marginally, and Jordan experienced little of the economic growth that took place in Israel during the 1990s, when general peace prevailed between Israel and the Palestinians. Hussein died in 1999 and was succeeded by his son, Abdallah II, who continued to respect the terms of the treaty with Israel.

> *Following are two documents: The text of the Washington Declaration, signed on July 25, 1994, by Israeli prime minister Yitzhak Rabin and Jordan's King Hussein, in Washington, D.C., and witnessed by President Bill Clinton, and excerpts from the Treaty of Peace signed by Prime Minister Rabin and King Hussein on October 26, 1994, at the Arava/Araba border crossing between their two countries.*

DOCUMENT

The Washington Declaration

JULY 25, 1994

A. After generations of hostility, blood and tears and in the wake of years of pain and wars, His Majesty King Hussein and Prime Minister Yitzhak Rabin are determined to bring an end to bloodshed and sorrow. It is in this spirit that His Majesty King Hussein of the Hashemite Kingdom of Jordan and Prime Minister and Minister of Defense, Mr. Yitzhak Rabin of Israel, met at Washington, D.C., today at the invitation of President William J. Clinton of the United States of America. This initiative of President William J. Clinton constitutes an historic landmark in the United States' untiring efforts in promoting peace and stability in the Middle East. The personal involvement of the President has made it possible to realize agreement on the content of this historic declaration. The signing of this declaration bears testimony to the President's vision and devotion to the cause of peace.

B. In their meeting, His Majesty King Hussein and Prime Minister Yitzhak Rabin jointly reaffirmed the five underlying principles of their understanding on an agreed common agenda designed to reach the goal of a just, lasting and comprehensive peace between the Arab States and the Palestinians, with Israel.

1. Jordan and Israel aim at the achievement of just, lasting and comprehensive peace between Israel and its neighbors and at the conclusion of a treaty of peace between both countries.

2. The two countries will vigorously continue their negotiations to arrive at a state of peace, based on Security Council resolutions 242 (1967) and 338 (1973) in all their aspects, and founded on freedom, equality and justice.

3. Israel respects the present special role of the Hashemite Kingdom of Jordan in Muslim holy shrines in Jerusalem. When negotiations on the permanent status will take place, Israel will give high priority to the Jordanian historic role in these shrines. In addition, the two sides have agreed to act together to promote interfaith relations among the three monotheistic religions.

4. The two countries recognize their right and obligation to live in peace with each other as well as with all States within secure and recognized boundaries. The two States affirmed their respect for and acknowledgment of the sovereignty, territorial integrity and political independence of every State in the area.

5. The two countries desire to develop good neighborly relations of cooperation between them to ensure lasting security and to avoid threats and the use of force between them.

C. The long conflict between the two States is now coming to an end. In this spirit, the state of belligerency between Jordan and Israel has been terminated.

D. Following this declaration and in keeping with the agreed common agenda both countries will refrain from actions or activities by either side that may adversely affect the security of the other or may prejudice the final outcome of negotiations. Neither side will threaten the other by use of force, weapons or any other means against each other and both sides will thwart threats to security resulting from all kinds of terrorism.

E. His Majesty King Hussein and Prime Minister Yitzhak Rabin took note of the progress made in the bilateral negotiations within the Jordan-Israel track last week on the steps decided to implement the sub-agendas on borders, territorial matters, security, water, energy, environment and the Jordan Rift Valley.

In this framework, mindful of items of the agreed common agenda (borders and territorial matters) they noted that the boundary subcommission reached agreement in July 1994 in fulfillment of part of the role entrusted to it in the sub-agenda. They also noted that the subcommission for water, environment and energy agreed to recognize mutually, as a result of their negotiations, the rightful allocations of the two sides in Jordan River and Yarmouk River waters and to respect fully and comply with the negotiated rightful allocations, in accordance with agreed acceptable principles with mutually acceptable quality.

Similarly, His Majesty King Hussein and Prime Minister Yitzhak Rabin expressed their deep satisfaction and pride in the work of the trilateral commission in its meeting held in Jordan on Wednesday, 20 July 1994, hosted by the Jordanian Prime Minister, Dr. Abdessalam al-Majali, and attended by Secretary of State Warren Christopher and Foreign Minister Shimon Peres. They voiced their pleasure at the association and commitment of the United States in this endeavor.

F. His Majesty King Hussein and Prime Minister Yitzhak Rabin believe that steps must be taken both to overcome psychological barriers and to break with the legacy of war. By working with optimism towards the dividends of peace for all the people in the region, Jordan and Israel are determined to shoulder their responsibilities towards the human dimension of peacemaking. They recognize imbalances and disparities are a root cause of extremism which thrives on poverty and unemployment and the degradation of human dignity. In this spirit His Majesty King Hussein and

Prime Minister Yitzhak Rabin have today approved a series of steps to symbolize the new era which is now at hand:

1. Direct telephone links will be opened between Jordan and Israel.
2. The electricity grids of Jordan and Israel will be linked as part of a regional concept.
3. Two new border crossings will be opened between Jordan and Israel—one at the southern tip of Aqaba-Eilat and the other at a mutually agreed point in the north.
4. In principle free access will be given to third country tourists traveling between Jordan and Israel.
5. Negotiations will be accelerated on opening an international air corridor between both countries.
6. The police forces of Jordan and Israel will cooperate in combating crime, with emphasis on smuggling and particularly drug smuggling. The United States will be invited to participate in this joint endeavor.
7. Negotiations on economic matters will continue in order to prepare for future bilateral cooperation including the abolition of all economic boycotts.

All these steps are being implemented within the framework of regional infrastructural development plans and in conjunction with the Jordan-Israel bilaterals on boundaries, security, water and related issues and without prejudice to the final outcome of the negotiations on the items included in the agreed common agenda between Jordan and Israel.

G. His Majesty King Hussein and Prime Minister Yitzhak Rabin have agreed to meet periodically or whenever they feel necessary to review the progress of the negotiations and express their firm intention to shepherd and direct the process in its entirety.

H. In conclusion, His Majesty King Hussein and Prime Minister Yitzhak Rabin wish to express once again their profound thanks and appreciation to President William J. Clinton and his Administration for their untiring efforts in furthering the cause of peace, justice and prosperity for all the peoples of the region. They wish to thank the President personally for his warm welcome and hospitality. In recognition of their appreciation to the President, His Majesty King Hussein and Prime Minister Yitzhak Rabin have asked President William J. Clinton to sign this document as a witness and as a host to their meeting.

SOURCE: United Nations Information System on the Question of Palestine (UNISPAL), http://unispal.un.org/unispal.nsf/181c4bf00c44e5fd85256cef0073c426/cbceef698a7f310e85256c4f004d61b0!OpenDocument.

DOCUMENT

Treaty of Peace between the State of Israel and the Hashemite Kingdom of Jordan

OCTOBER 26, 1994

Preamble

The Government of the State of Israel and the Government of the Hashemite Kingdom of Jordan:

Bearing in mind the Washington Declaration, signed by them on 25th July, 1994, and which they are both committed to honor;

Aiming at the achievement of a just, lasting and comprehensive peace in the Middle East based on Security Council resolutions 242 and 338 in all their aspects;

Bearing in mind the importance of maintaining and strengthening peace based on freedom, equality, justice and respect for fundamental human rights, thereby overcoming psychological barriers and promoting human dignity;

Reaffirming their faith in the purposes and principles of the Charter of the United Nations and recognizing their right and obligation to live in peace with each other as well as with all states, within secure and recognized boundaries;

Desiring to develop friendly relations and co-operation between them in accordance with the principles of international law governing international relations in time of peace;

Desiring as well to ensure lasting security for both their States and in particular to avoid threats and the use of force between them;

Bearing in mind that in their Washington Declaration of 25th July, 1994, they declared the termination of the state of belligerency between them;

Deciding to establish peace between them in accordance with this Treaty of Peace; Have agreed as follows:

Article 1 Establishment of Peace

Peace is hereby established between the State of Israel and the Hashemite Kingdom of Jordan (the "Parties") effective from the exchange of the instruments of ratification of this Treaty.

Article 2 General Principles

The Parties will apply between them the provisions of the Charter of the United Nations and the principles of international law governing relations among states in times of peace. In particular:

1. They recognize and will respect each other's sovereignty, territorial integrity and political independence;

2. They recognize and will respect each other's right to live in peace within secure and recognized boundaries;

3. They will develop good neighborly relations of co-operation between them to ensure lasting security, will refrain from the threat or use of force against each other and will settle all disputes between them by peaceful means;

4. They respect and recognize the sovereignty, territorial integrity and political independence of every state in the region;

5. They respect and recognize the pivotal role of human development and dignity in regional and bilateral relationships;

6. They further believe that within their control, involuntary movements of persons in such a way as to adversely prejudice the security of either Party should not be permitted.

Article 3 International Boundary

1. The international boundary between Israel and Jordan is delimited with reference to the boundary definition under the Mandate as is shown in Annex I (a), on the mapping materials attached thereto and co-ordinates specified therein.

2. The boundary, as set out in Annex I (a), is the permanent, secure and recognized international boundary between Israel and Jordan, without prejudice to the status of any territories that came under Israeli military government control in 1967.

3. The parties recognize the international boundary, as well as each other's territory, territorial waters and airspace, as inviolable, and will respect and comply with them.

4. The demarcation of the boundary will take place as set forth in Appendix (I) to Annex I and will be concluded not later than nine months after the signing of the Treaty.

5. It is agreed that where the boundary follows a river, in the event of natural changes in the course of the flow of the river as described in Annex I (a), the boundary shall follow the new course of the flow. In the event of any other changes the boundary shall not be affected unless otherwise agreed.

6. Immediately upon the exchange of the instruments of ratification of this Treaty, each Party will deploy on its side of the international boundary as defined in Annex I (a).

7. The Parties shall, upon the signature of the Treaty, enter into negotiations to conclude, within 9 months, an agreement on the delimitation of their maritime boundary in the Gulf of Aqaba.

8. Taking into account the special circumstances of the Naharayim/Baqura area, which is under Jordanian sovereignty, with Israeli private ownership rights, the Parties agreed to apply the provisions set out in Annex I (b).

9. With respect to the Zofar/Al-Ghamr area, the provisions set out in Annex I (c) will apply.

Article 4 Security

1. a. Both Parties, acknowledging that mutual understanding and co-operation in security-related matters will form a significant part of their relations and will further enhance the security of the region, take upon themselves to base their security relations on mutual trust, advancement of joint interests and co-operation, and to aim towards a regional framework of partnership in peace.

   b. Towards that goal the Parties recognize the achievements of the European Community and European Union in the development of the Conference on Security and Co-operation in Europe (CSCE) and commit themselves to the creation, in the Middle East, of a CSCME (Conference on Security and Co-operation in the Middle East).

This commitment entails the adoption of regional models of security successfully implemented in the post World War era (along the lines of the Helsinki process) culminating in a regional zone of security and stability.

2. The obligations referred to in this Article are without prejudice to the inherent right of self-defense in accordance with the United Nations Charter.

3. The Parties undertake, in accordance with the provisions of this Article, the following:

    a. to refrain from the threat or use of force or weapons, conventional, non-conventional or of any other kind, against each other, or of other actions or activities that adversely affect the security of the other Party;

    b. to refrain from organizing, instigating, inciting, assisting or participating in acts or threats of belligerency, hostility, subversion or violence against the other Party;

    c. to take necessary and effective measures to ensure that acts or threats of belligerency, hostility, subversion or violence against the other Party do not originate from, and are not committed within, through or over their territory (hereinafter the term "territory" includes the airspace and territorial waters).

4. Consistent with the era of peace and with the efforts to build regional security and to avoid and prevent aggression and violence, the Parties further agree to refrain from the following:

    a. joining or in any way assisting, promoting or co-operating with any coalition, organization or alliance with a military or security character with a third party, the objectives or activities of which include launching aggression or other acts of military hostility against the other Party, in contravention of the provisions of the present Treaty.

    b. allowing the entry, stationing and operating on their territory, or through it, of military forces, personnel or materiel of a third party, in circumstances which may adversely prejudice the security of the other Party.

5. Both Parties will take necessary and effective measures, and will co-operate in combating terrorism of all kinds. The Parties undertake:

    a. to take necessary and effective measures to prevent acts of terrorism, subversion or violence from being carried out from their territory or through it and to take necessary and effective measures to combat such activities and all their perpetrators.

    b. without prejudice to the basic rights of freedom of expression and association, to take necessary and effective measures to prevent the entry, presence and co-operation in their territory of any group or organization, and their infrastructure, which threatens the security of the other Party by the use of or incitement to the use of, violent means.

    c. to co-operate in preventing and combating cross-boundary infiltrations.

6. Any question as to the implementation of this Article will be dealt with through a mechanism of consultations which will include a liaison system, verification, supervision, and where necessary, other mechanisms, and higher level consultation. The details of the mechanism of consultations will be contained in an agreement to be concluded by the Parties within 3 months of the exchange of the instruments of ratification of this Treaty.

7. The Parties undertake to work as a matter of priority, and as soon as possible in the context of the Multilateral Working Group on Arms Control and Regional Security, and jointly, towards the following:

    a. the creation in the Middle East of a region free from hostile alliances and coalitions;

    b. the creation of a Middle East free from weapons of mass destruction, both conventional and non-conventional, in the context of a comprehensive, lasting and stable peace, characterized by the renunciation of the use of force, reconciliation and goodwill.

Article 5 Diplomatic and Other Bilateral Relations

1. The Parties agree to establish full diplomatic and consular relations and to exchange resident ambassadors within one month of the exchange of the instruments of ratification of this Treaty.

2. The Parties agree that the normal relationship between them will further include economic and cultural relations.

Article 6 Water

With the view to achieving a comprehensive and lasting settlement of all the water problems between them:

1. The Parties agree mutually to recognize the rightful allocations of both of them in Jordan River and Yarmouk River waters and Araba/Arava ground water in accordance with the agreed acceptable principles, quantities and quality as set out in Annex II, which shall be fully respected and complied with.

2. The Parties, recognizing the necessity to find a practical, just and agreed solution to their water problems and with the view that the subject of water can form the basis for the advancement of co-operation between them, jointly undertake to ensure that the management and development of their water resources do not, in any way, harm the water resources of the other Party.

3. The Parties recognize that their water resources are not sufficient to meet their needs. More water should be supplied for their use through various methods, including projects of regional and international co-operation.

4. In light of paragraph 3 of this Article, with the understanding that co-operation in water-related subjects would be to the benefit of both Parties, and will help alleviate their water shortages, and that water issues along their entire boundary must be dealt with in their totality, including the possibility of trans-boundary water transfers, the Parties agree to search for ways to alleviate water shortage and to co-operate in the following fields:

    a. development of existing and new water resources, increasing the water availability including co-operation on a regional basis as appropriate, and minimizing wastage of water resources through the chain of their uses;

    b. prevention of contamination of water resources;

    c. mutual assistance in the alleviation of water shortages;

    d. transfer of information and joint research and development in water-related subjects, and review of the potentials for enhancement of water resources development and use.

5. The implementation of both Parties' undertakings under this Article is detailed in Annex II.

[Article 7 provides for normal economic relations between the parties.]
[Article 8 provides for negotiations, under international auspices, on the future of refugees.]

Article 9 Places of Historical and Religious Significance and Interfaith Relations
1. Each party will provide freedom of access to places of religious and historical significance.

2. In this regard, in accordance with the Washington Declaration, Israel respects the present special role of the Hashemite Kingdom of Jordan in Muslim Holy shrines in Jerusalem. When negotiations on the permanent status will take place, Israel will give high priority to the Jordanian historic role in these shrines.

3. The Parties will act together to promote interfaith relations among the three monotheistic religions, with the aim of working towards religious understanding, moral commitment, freedom of religious worship, and tolerance and peace.

[Article 10 provides for cultural and scientific exchanges.]

Article 11 Mutual Understanding and Good Neighborly Relations
1. The Parties will seek to foster mutual understanding and tolerance based on shared historic values, and accordingly undertake:
   a. to abstain from hostile or discriminatory propaganda against each other, and to take all possible legal and administrative measures to prevent the dissemination of such propaganda by any organization or individual present in the territory of either Party;
   b. as soon as possible, and not later than 3 months from the exchange of the instruments of ratification of this Treaty, to repeal all adverse or discriminatory references and expressions of hostility in their respective legislation;
   c. to refrain in all government publications from any such references or expressions;
   d. to ensure mutual enjoyment by each other's citizens of due process of law within their respective legal systems and before their courts.

2. Paragraph 1 (a) of this Article is without prejudice to the right to freedom of expression as contained in the International Covenant on Civil and Political Rights.

3. A joint committee shall be formed to examine incidents where one Party claims there has been a violation of this Article.

Article 12 Combating Crime and Drugs
The Parties will co-operate in combating crime, with an emphasis on smuggling, and will take all necessary measures to combat and prevent such activities as the production of, as well as the trafficking in illicit drugs, and will bring to trial perpetrators of such acts. In this regard, they take note of the understandings reached between them in the above spheres, in accordance with Annex III and undertake to conclude all relevant agreements not later than 9 months from the date of the exchange of the instruments of ratification of this Treaty.

Article 13 Transportation and Roads
Taking note of the progress already made in the area of transportation, the Parties recognize the mutuality of interest in good neighborly relations in the area of transportation and agree to the following means to promote relations between them in this sphere:

1. Each party will permit the free movement of nationals and vehicles of the other into and within its territory according to the general rules applicable to nationals and vehicles of other states. Neither party will impose discriminatory taxes or restrictions on the free movement of persons and vehicles from its territory to the territory of the other.

2. The Parties will open and maintain roads and border-crossings between their countries and will consider further road and rail links between them.

3. The Parties will continue their negotiations concerning mutual transportation agreements in the above and other areas, such as joint projects, traffic safety, transport standards and norms, licensing of vehicles, land passages, shipment of goods and cargo, and meteorology, to be concluded not later than 6 months from the exchange of the instruments of ratification of this Treaty.

4. The Parties agree to continue their negotiations for a highway to be constructed and maintained between Egypt, Israel and Jordan near Eilat.

Article 14 Freedom of Navigation and Access to Ports
1. Without prejudice to the provisions of paragraph 3, each Party recognizes the right of the vessels of the other Party to innocent passage through its territorial waters in accordance with the rules of international law.

2. Each Party will grant normal access to its ports for vessels and cargoes of the other, as well as vessels and cargoes destined for or coming from the other Party. Such access will be granted on the same conditions as generally applicable to vessels and cargoes of other nations.

3. The Parties consider the Strait of Tiran and the Gulf of Aqaba to be international waterways open to all nations for unimpeded and non-suspendable freedom of navigation and overflight. The Parties will respect each other's right to navigation and overflight for access to either Party through the Strait of Tiran and the Gulf of Aqaba.

Article 15 Civil Aviation
1. The Parties recognize as applicable to each other the rights, privileges and obligations provided for by the multilateral aviation agreements to which they are both party, particularly by the 1944 Convention on International Civil Aviation (The Chicago Convention) and the 1944 International Air Services Transit Agreement.

2. Any declaration of national emergency by a Party under Article 89 of the Chicago Convention will not be applied to the other Party on a discriminatory basis.

3. The Parties take note of the negotiations on the international air corridor to be opened between them in accordance with the Washington Declaration. In addition, the Parties shall, upon ratification of this Treaty, enter into negotiations for the purpose of concluding a Civil Aviation Agreement. All the above negotiations are to be concluded not later than 6 months from the exchange of the instruments of ratification of this Treaty.

Article 16 Posts and Telecommunications
The Parties take note of the opening between them, in accordance with the Washington Declaration, of direct telephone and facsimile lines. Postal links, the negotiations on which having been concluded, will be activated upon the signature of this Treaty. The Parties further agree that normal wireless and cable communications and

television relay services by cable, radio and satellite, will be established between them, in accordance with all relevant international conventions and regulations. The negotiations on these subjects will be concluded not later than 9 months from the exchange of the instruments of ratification of this Treaty.

Article 17 Tourism

The Parties affirm their mutual desire to promote co-operation between them in the field of tourism. In order to accomplish this goal, the Parties—taking note of the understandings reached between them concerning tourism—agree to negotiate, as soon as possible, and to conclude not later than three months from the exchange of the instruments of ratification of this Treaty, an agreement to facilitate and encourage mutual tourism and tourism from third countries.

Article 18 Environment

The Parties will co-operate in matters relating to the environment, a sphere to which they attach great importance, including conservation of nature and prevention of pollution, as set forth in Annex IV. They will negotiate an agreement on the above, to be concluded not later than 6 months from the exchange of the instruments of ratification of this Treaty.

Article 19 Energy

1. The Parties will co-operate in the development of energy resources, including the development of energy-related projects such as the utilization of solar energy.

   2. The Parties, having concluded their negotiations on the interconnecting of their electric grids in the Eilat-Aqaba area, will implement the interconnecting upon the signature of this Treaty. The Parties view this step as a part of a wider binational and regional concept. They agree to continue their negotiations as soon as possible to widen the scope of their interconnected grids.

   3. The Parties will conclude the relevant agreements in the field of energy within 6 months from the date of exchange of the instruments of ratification of this Treaty.

Article 20 Rift Valley Development

The Parties attach great importance to the integrated development of the Jordan Rift Valley area, including joint projects in the economic, environmental, energy-related and tourism fields. Taking note of the Terms of Reference developed in the framework of the Trilateral Israel-Jordan-US Economic Committee towards the Jordan Rift Valley Development Master Plan, they will vigorously continue their efforts towards the completion of planning and towards implementation.

Article 21 Health

The Parties will co-operate in the area of health and shall negotiate with a view to the conclusion of an agreement within 9 months of the exchange of instruments of ratification of this Treaty.

Article 22 Agriculture

The Parties will co-operate in the areas of agriculture, including veterinary services, plant protection, biotechnology and marketing, and shall negotiate with a view to the conclusion of an agreement within 6 months from the date of the exchange of instruments of ratification of this Treaty.

Article 23 Aqaba and Eilat

The Parties agree to enter into negotiations, as soon as possible, and not later than one month from the exchange of the instruments of ratification of this Treaty, on arrangements that would enable the joint development of the towns of Aqaba and Eilat with regard to such matters, inter alia, as joint tourism development, joint customs, free trade zone, co-operation in aviation, prevention of pollution, maritime matters, police, customs and health co-operation. The Parties will conclude all relevant agreements within 9 months from the exchange of instruments of ratification of the Treaty.

Article 24 Claims

The Parties agree to establish a claims commission for the mutual settlement of all financial claims.

Article 25 Rights and Obligations

1. This Treaty does not affect and shall not be interpreted as affecting, in any way, the rights and obligations of the Parties under the Charter of the United Nations.

2. The Parties undertake to fulfill in good faith their obligations under this Treaty, without regard to action or inaction of any other party and independently of any instrument inconsistent with this Treaty. For the purposes of this paragraph each Party represents to the other that in its opinion and interpretation there is no inconsistency between their existing treaty obligations and this Treaty.

3. They further undertake to take all the necessary measures for the application in their relations of the provisions of the multilateral conventions to which they are parties, including the submission of appropriate notification to the Secretary General of the United Nations and other depositories of such conventions.

4. Both Parties will also take all the necessary steps to abolish all pejorative references to the other Party, in multilateral conventions to which they are parties, to the extent that such references exist.

5. The Parties undertake not to enter into any obligation in conflict with this Treaty.

6. Subject to Article 103 of the United Nations Charter, in the event of a conflict between the obligations of the Parties under the present Treaty and any of their other obligations, the obligations under this Treaty will be binding and implemented.

Article 26 Legislation

Within 3 months of the exchange of ratifications of this Treaty the Parties undertake to enact any legislation necessary in order to implement the Treaty, and to terminate any international commitments and to repeal any legislation that is inconsistent with the Treaty.

Article 27 Ratification

1. This Treaty shall be ratified by both Parties in conformity with their respective national procedures. It shall enter into force on the exchange of instruments of ratification.

2. The Annexes, Appendices, and other attachments to this Treaty shall be considered integral parts thereof.

Article 28 Interim Measures
The Parties will apply, in certain spheres, to be agreed upon, interim measures pending the conclusion of the relevant agreements in accordance with this Treaty, as stipulated in Annex V.

Article 29 Settlement of Disputes
1. Disputes arising out of the application or interpretation of this Treaty shall be resolved by negotiations.
2. Any such disputes which cannot be settled by negotiations shall be resolved by conciliation or submitted to arbitration.

Article 30 Registration
This Treaty shall be transmitted to the Secretary General of the United Nations for registration in accordance with the provisions of Article 102 of the Charter of the United Nations.

Done at the Arava/Araba Crossing Point this day Heshvan 21st, 5775, Jumada Al-Ula 21st, 1415 which corresponds to 26th October, 1994 in the Hebrew, English and Arabic languages, all texts being equally authentic. In case of divergence of interpretation the English text shall prevail.

For the State of Israel
Yitzhak Rabin, Prime Minister

For the Hashemite Kingdom of Jordan
Abdul Salam Majali, Prime Minister

Witnessed by:
William J. Clinton
President of the United States of America

SOURCE: United Nations Information System on the Question of Palestine (UNISPAL), http://unispal.un.org/unispal.nsf/181c4bf00c44e5fd85256cef0073c426/9074e1ecb51150c485256174005a2f41!OpenDocument.

The Arab League Beirut Summit

DOCUMENT IN CONTEXT

In the decades after the June 1967 War, Arab leaders moved slowly—almost imperceptibly at times—to come to terms with Israel's existence and its control of what Arabs considered to be their lands. This gradual shift could be seen in various statements made during regular Arab summits, starting with the "three noes"—"no peace with Israel, no recognition of Israel, no negotiations with it"—at the Khartoum summit in 1967 and continuing through the 1982 declaration in Fez, Morocco, that cautiously suggested an acknowledgment of Israel's existence (Khartoum Declaration, p. 108; Fez Declaration, p. 137).

Yet another step came early in 2002, a time not particularly auspicious for Middle Eastern peace endeavors. The al-Aqsa intifada, the second Palestinian uprising against Israeli occupation, was in its third year, and the United States had just begun the political and military buildup that would culminate in the U.S.-led invasion of Iraq in March 2003. Despite, or perhaps because of, these events, Saudi Arabia's de facto ruler, Crown Prince Abdallah, chose this time to push for a new Arab opening to Israel. Abdallah caused a worldwide stir in February when he told *New York Times* columnist Tom Friedman that he was working on a peace plan under which Arab nations would "normalize" relations with Israel in exchange for several steps by Israel, including full withdrawal from the Arab territories it had occupied and acceptance of a Palestinian state. Abdallah's statement was the first hint by any prominent Arab leader of a regionwide plan for peace with Israel.

Abdallah carried his plan to a scheduled summit meeting of Arab leaders starting on March 27 in Beirut. In a speech to his colleagues that was televised in Israel and the Arab world Abdallah said that if Israel "abandons the policy of force and oppression and embraces true peace, we will not hesitate to accept the right of the Israeli people to live in security with the people of the region."

The next day, Arab leaders endorsed Abdallah's plan—the Arab Peace Initiative—which repeated standard calls for Israel to withdraw from Arab territories and to accept a Palestinian state but also contained an unprecedented reciprocal offer. If Israel took those steps, the leaders said, they would "consider the Arab-Israeli conflict at an end and enter into a peace agreement between them and Israel while achieving security for all the states of the region." They also would "establish normal relations with Israel in the context of this comprehensive peace."

The exceptionally conciliatory nature of this language was coupled with standard Arab rhetoric against Israel. The accompanying Beirut Declaration contained the same offer of peace while also condemning Israeli "massacres" of Palestinians and praising Palestinian "martyrs," a term that includes suicide bombers and others who die in the act of attacking Israel and civilians killed by Israelis. Three key Arab leaders did not attend the summit: Egyptian president Hosni Mubarak, Jordan's King Abdallah II, and Palestinian leader Yasir Arafat. Israel had confined Arafat to his government compound in Ramallah, offering to allow him to attend the summit on the condition that he not return.

On the evening of March 27 shortly after Abdallah presented his plan, a Palestinian blew himself up at a hotel in the Israeli seaside resort town of Netanya, killing twenty-eight people and wounding about 140 others; most of the victims were Israelis and tourists celebrating the first night of Passover. The Islamist group Hamas issued a statement claiming responsibility and warning of its intention to carry out similar acts of "resistance" against Israel.

Despite Hamas's assertion of responsibility, Israel blamed Arafat and sent an army contingent to Ramallah, where troops surrounded Arafat's compound. On March 29, the Israeli army moved into other West Bank cities, reoccupying them in a massive show of force and in the process destroying much of the infrastructure of the Palestinian Authority. Israel rejected the Beirut summit declaration as insufficient grounds for a peace initiative. President George W. Bush sent Secretary of State Colin Powell to meet separately with Arafat and Israeli prime minister Ariel Sharon in April; their sessions made no progress. On June 24, Bush stepped up U.S. criticism of Arafat, calling on Palestinians to elect "new leaders" as a prelude to negotiations on the establishment of a Palestinian state.

The immediate circumstances of the Palestinian-Israeli conflict frustrated Abdallah's plan to breathe new life into the long-stalled Arab-Israeli peace process, and the war in Iraq one year later made it impossible for either side to attempt a new initiative to carry the plan forward. Abdallah's peace plan appeared to take on new life in 2007, again at an inauspicious moment. Meeting in Riyadh, Saudi Arabia, on March 29, 2007, Arab leaders reaffirmed the 2002 peace plan and urged Israel to "seize the opportunity" the plan offered for direct negotiations. The Israeli government and the Bush administration responded more positively, with Israeli prime minister Ehud Olmert suggesting a regional peace conference, and U.S. secretary of state Condoleezza Rice using the Arab plan as the starting point for exploratory trips to the region. Olmert's (weakened) government, however, continued to suffer from the lingering consequences of its summer 2006 war against Hizballah, and Palestinian leaders, focused on internal political struggles caused by the election of a Hamas-led government and a Fatah-led presidency, were in no position to devise a united approach for dealing with Israel (Hizballah-Israeli War, p. 365; Hamas Government, p. 317).

Following are the texts of two documents adopted at the conclusion of the summit of the Arab League held in Beirut, Lebanon, March 27–28, 2002. The Arab Peace Initiative, based on a proposal by Saudi crown prince Abdallah, is followed by the Beirut Declaration, which incorporates the peace initiative and other statements on regional affairs.

DOCUMENT

Arab Peace Initiative

MARCH 27–28, 2002

The Summit-level Council of the League of Arab States,

Reaffirming the decision of the extraordinary Arab summit conference held in Cairo in June 1996 that a just and comprehensive peace is a strategic choice for the Arab States to be achieved in accordance with international legality and to require an equivalent commitment in this regard on the part of Israel,

Having heard the statement in which His Royal Highness Prince Abdullah bin Abdul-Aziz, Crown Prince of the Kingdom of Saudi Arabia, presented his Initiative and called for Israel's full withdrawal from all the Arab territories that have been occupied since 1967, in implementation of Security Council resolutions 242 (1967) and 338 (1973) as confirmed by the 1991 Madrid Conference and the principle of land for peace, and for its acceptance of the emergence of an independent and sovereign Palestinian State with East Jerusalem as its capital in return for the establishment by the Arab States of normal relations in the context of a comprehensive peace with Israel, Proceeding from the conviction of the Arab States that a military solution to the conflict will not achieve peace or provide security for any of the parties,

1. Requests Israel to re-examine its policies and to incline towards peace and declare that a just peace is also its own strategic choice;
2. Further calls upon it:
   (a) To withdraw fully from the occupied Arab territories, including the Syrian Golan to the line of 4 June 1967, and from the territories in southern Lebanon that are still occupied;
   (b) To arrive at a just and agreed solution to the Palestine refugee problem in accordance with United Nations General Assembly resolution 194 (III);
   (c) To accept the establishment of an independent, sovereign Palestinian State in the Palestinian territories occupied since 4 June 1967 in the West Bank and Gaza Strip, with East Jerusalem as its capital;
3. Undertakes that the Arab States shall then:
   (a) Consider the Arab-Israeli conflict at an end and enter into a peace agreement between them and Israel while achieving security for all the States of the region;
   (b) Establish normal relations with Israel in the context of this comprehensive peace;
4. Guarantees the rejection of all forms of Palestinian resettlement, which is incompatible with the special situation in the Arab host countries;
5. Urges the Government of Israel and all Israelis to accept the foregoing Initiative in order to safeguard the prospects for peace and spare further bloodshed, thus enabling the Arab States and Israel to live side by side in peace and ensuring for generations to come a secure future in which stability and prosperity can prevail;
6. Invites the international community and all its constituent States and organizations to support this Initiative;

7. Requests the Chairman of the summit to form a special committee, to include interested member States and the Secretary-General of the League, to pursue the necessary contacts to gain support for this Initiative at all levels and in particular from the United Nations, the Security Council, the United States of America, the Russian Federation, the Islamic countries and the European Union.

DOCUMENT

The Beirut Declaration

MARCH 27–28, 2002

We, the Kings, Presidents and Amirs of the Arab States, meeting as the Summit-level Council of the League of Arab States (fourteenth regular session) in Beirut, capital of the Lebanese Republic, on 27 and 28 March 2002,

Having examined the grave regional and international developments and their disturbing consequences, the challenges confronting the Arab nation and the threats posed to Arab national security,

Having conducted a thorough evaluation of these developments and challenges, and especially those relating to the Arab region and the occupied Palestinian territories in particular, and of the general war of destruction launched by Israel on the pretext of combating terrorism while exploiting the tragic events of September and the universal condemnation they have merited,

Having discussed the fate of the peace process and Israel's practices that seek to destroy it and to plunge the Middle East into anarchy and instability,

Having observed with the greatest pride the Intifadah of the Palestinian people and its valiant resistance,

Having discussed the Arab initiatives seeking a just and comprehensive peace in the region and compliance with the United Nations resolutions on the Arab-Israeli conflict and the question of Palestine,

Invoking the national responsibility and believing in the purposes and principles of the Pact of the League of Arab States and the Charter of the United Nations,

Declare that we shall undertake the following:

To continue to take action to strengthen Arab solidarity in all fields in order to safeguard Arab national security and thwart the foreign schemes to diminish Arab territorial integrity;

To acclaim with pride and admiration the steadfastness of the Palestinian people and its valiant Intifadah against the Israeli occupation and Israel's devastating military machine, its systematic repression and the massacres it commits, targeting children, women and the elderly without distinction and without any humanitarian inhibitions;

To stand in veneration and deference before the valiant martyrs of the Intifadah, and to affirm our constant and manifold support for the Palestinian people in order to sustain its heroic and legitimate struggle against occupation until it achieves its just demands, including the right to return, exercise self-determination and establish an independent Palestinian State with Jerusalem as its capital;

To act in solidarity with Lebanon in completing the liberation of its territory and to provide it with support for its development and reconstruction;

To express pride in the Lebanese resistance and in the splendid steadfastness of Lebanon that caused the rout of the Israeli forces from most of southern Lebanon and the Western Bekaa; to demand the immediate release of Lebanese detainees being held in Israeli prisons in violation of international norms and covenants; to condemn the recurring Israeli aggression against Lebanon's sovereignty exemplified by the violations by Israeli aircraft and warships of Lebanese airspace and territorial waters, which portend dire consequences because they represent incitement, provocation and aggression that might create an explosive situation along Lebanon's southern boundaries for which Israel will be entirely responsible;

To acclaim the steadfastness of the Syrian Arab citizens of the occupied Syrian Golan, to commend their commitment to their national identity and their resistance to the Israeli occupation, to affirm our solidarity with Syria and Lebanon in confronting the Israeli threats of aggression that are undermining security and stability in the region, and to regard any aggression against them as aggression against all the Arab States;

To affirm, in the light of the setback to the peace process, our commitment to suspending the maintenance of any relations with Israel and to reactivating the Office for the Arab Boycott of Israel until Israel complies with the relevant United Nations resolutions and the terms of reference of the Madrid peace conference and withdraws fully from all the occupied Arab territories to the line of 4 June 1967;

To stress that peace in the Middle East is destined never to succeed unless it is just and comprehensive and in accordance with Security Council resolutions 242 (1967), 338 (1973) and 425 (1978) and the principle of land for peace; and to affirm the inseparable character of the Syrian and Lebanese tracks and their organic link with the Palestinian track in the achievement of Arab objectives for a global and inclusive solution;

To request Israel, in the context of the sponsorship by the Council of the Saudi initiative as the Arab Peace Initiative, to re-evaluate its policies and incline towards peace and to declare that a just peace is also its own strategic choice;

To further call upon it:

(a) To withdraw fully from the occupied Arab territories, including the Syrian Golan to the line of 4 June 1967, and from the territories in southern Lebanon that are still occupied;

(b) To arrive at a just and agreed solution to the Palestine refugee problem in accordance with United Nations General Assembly resolution 194 (III);

(c) To accept the establishment of an independent, sovereign Palestinian State in the Palestinian territories occupied since 4 June 1967 in the West Bank and Gaza Strip, with East Jerusalem as its capital;

To undertake that the Arab States shall then:

(a) Consider the Arab-Israeli conflict at an end and enter into a peace agreement between them and Israel while achieving security for all the States of the region;

(b) Establish normal relations with Israel in the context of this comprehensive peace;

To guarantee the rejection of all forms of Palestinian resettlement, which is incompatible with the special situation in the Arab host countries;

To urge the Government of Israel and all Israelis to accept the foregoing Initiative in order to safeguard the prospects for peace and spare further bloodshed, thus enabling the Arab States and Israel to live side by side in peace and ensuring for generations to come a secure future in which stability and prosperity can prevail;

To invite the international community and all its constituent States and organizations to support this Initiative;

To request the Chairman of the summit to form a special committee, to include interested member States and the Secretary-General of the League, to pursue the necessary contacts to gain support for this Initiative at all levels and in particular from the United Nations, the Security Council, the United States of America, the Russian Federation, the Islamic countries and the European Union;

To welcome the assurances provided by the Republic of Iraq concerning respect for the independence, sovereignty, security and territorial integrity of the State of Kuwait, thereby obviating any possible repetition of the events of 1990; to urge the pursuit, in a framework of good faith and relations of good-neighbourliness, of policies conducive to that goal; and to urge, in this connection, the importance of halting negative media campaigns and pronouncements with a view to creating a positive climate in which the two countries can confidently uphold the principles of good-neighbourliness and non-interference in the internal affairs of others;

To demand respect for the independence, sovereignty, security, national unity and territorial integrity of Iraq;

To urge Iraq to cooperate in the formulation of a speedy and definitive solution to the issue of the Kuwaiti prisoners and hostages and the return of property, in accordance with the relevant United Nations resolutions; and to call for Kuwait's cooperation in connection with Iraq's submissions, through the International Committee of the Red Cross, concerning missing Iraqis;

To welcome the resumption of the dialogue between Iraq and the United Nations, which began in a positive and constructive atmosphere, with a view to the full implementation of the relevant Security Council resolutions;

To call for the sanctions imposed on Iraq to be lifted and for the suffering of its fraternal people to be brought to an end so that stability and security in the region can be ensured;

To reject the threat of aggression against certain Arab States, and in particular Iraq, and to affirm their unconditional rejection of a strike against Iraq, or a threat to the security and integrity of any Arab State, as a threat to the national security of all Arab States;

To affirm the sovereignty of the United Arab Emirates over its three islands and to support all peaceful measures and actions taken with a view to restoring its sovereignty over them in accordance with the principles and norms of international law, including agreement to refer the case to the International Court of Justice;

To condemn international terrorism, including the terrorist attack of 11 September 2001 against the United States of America and the exploitation by the Israeli Government of this attack in order to maintain its practice of State terrorism and to launch a devastating general war of aggression against the Palestinian people;

To stress the distinction between international terrorism and the legitimate right of peoples to resist foreign aggression; and to affirm the need to conclude an international agreement in the framework of the United Nations that lays down a precise definition of international terrorism and identifies its causes and the means to address it;

To affirm—in accordance with the repudiation of all forms of racial discrimination, the encouragement of tolerance and coexistence on a basis of mutual respect and the safeguarding of legitimate rights that are advocated by the revealed religions and by human values—the importance of interaction among cultures and civilizations; and to commend the efforts being made by the League of Arab States, the Organization of the Islamic Conference and others to communicate the facts concerning Arab and Islamic culture and civilization and to refute the false assertions made in their regard;

To expedite the introduction of the Greater Arab Free Trade Area in the light of the growing phenomenon of global economic groupings and the approaching end of the period set for the application of the World Trade Organization Agreement;

To express our great appreciation to the Lebanese Republic and to His Excellency General Émile Lahoud, President of the Republic, for their attention and solicitude and for the excellent preparations made for the summit; and to convey our deep gratitude to His Excellency President Émile Lahoud for successfully conducting and directing the work of the Arab summit with the highest degree of political skill, mature wisdom and insightful responsibility.

SOURCE: United Nations Information System on the Question of Palestine (UNISPAL), http://unispal.un.org/ unispal.nsf/181c4bf00c44e5fd85256cef0073c426/75207eec8fec65a985256c470066373b!OpenDocument.

Israel and the Palestinians

CHAPTER 3 DOCUMENTS

CHAPTER 3

Overview

Of all the conflicts in the contemporary world, none has proved to be as dangerous to broader peace as the conflict between Israel and the Palestinian Arabs. Civil wars in Northern Ireland, Southeast Asia, Sri Lanka, sub-Saharan Africa, and other places have lasted longer or killed many more people, but the dispute between the Israelis and Palestinians—over a small patch of land in what is probably the world's most volatile region—has stubbornly resisted even the most determined efforts at a diplomatic solution. As early as the 1920s, British authorities wrote reports warning that Arabs and Jews would not live quietly together in the historic land of Palestine. Events of the next eight decades proved the accuracy of their assessment.

In 1947 the newly created United Nations believed that it had solved the problem of conflicting claims to Palestine by dividing the land between the Arabs and Jews. The war that erupted in 1948 after the declaration of Israel shattered any assumption that the claims of history could be satisfied so easily. After the fighting, the Jews, now calling themselves Israelis, controlled most of the land. Israel took control of the rest of Palestine—the Gaza Strip, West Bank, and East Jerusalem—in the June 1967 war. Four decades later, in 2007, the Jewish state of Israel—which has more than 1 million Arab citizens, constituting nearly one-fifth of its population—continued to dominate the lives of more than 3 million stateless, increasingly frustrated Palestinians in the territories occupied in 1967.

Although many Israelis delighted at the expansion of their country, the occupation would not be a benign experience, by and large, for either the Israelis or the Palestinians. Various Palestinian nationalist groups soon began launching attacks against Israeli institutions, and eventually against Israeli civilians, dispelling any illusions that the Palestinians would meekly submit to Israeli authority. The Israelis improved some public services that the Jordanian government had ignored in East Jerusalem and the West Bank, but Israeli civilian and military authorities were stern, often unforgiving, rulers.

As has been the case with the broader dispute between Israel and the Arab Middle East, differing historical narratives frame the conflict between Israelis and Palestinians.

Many Israelis believe that they have a God-given right to Palestine that cannot be denied and that this overrides all other considerations. Even some Israelis who dismiss such theological claims believe that Jews deserve to rule over all or most of Palestine because of their historical sufferings, the democracy they have built amid the region's autocracies, and their success over the Arabs in war. Moreover, the official Israeli mythology asserts that Israel always has been the party offering reconciliation and the Palestinians (and other Arabs) the ones who nearly always spurn it, choosing instead to respond with terrorism and war.

The Palestinian narrative also has roots in perceived historical injustices, beginning with the British decision in 1917 to create a "national home" for the Jews in Palestine, continuing through the United Nations' efforts at partition three decades later, and culminating in Israel's occupation of Palestinian territories in 1967. Palestinians view the Israelis as the ones refusing to compromise for peace, subjugating them with their economic and military power, and wanting to gain permanent control over the territories occupied in 1967.

Some Israelis and Palestinians have acknowledged the misrepresentations in their own side's narrative and have recognized elements of the other side's grievances, but those with such views have rarely held positions of power. Most often, true believers—or leaders afraid of the true believers—have been the decision makers.

The central events in the Israeli-Palestinian conflict are the establishment of Israel in 1948, along with the resulting war that preserved the state, and the June 1967 War, in which Israel captured parts of Palestine that had remained under Arab control. These events made Israeli Jews the overseers of Palestinian Arabs who believed the land rightfully theirs. This was, and continues to form, the essence of their conflict.

The Israeli-Palestinian conflict has been a classic war between occupiers and the occupied, in some respects similar to the struggle the Jews waged against the British when they controlled Palestine during the 1930s and 1940s. As a people without a state, the Palestinians have not fought conventional battles against Israel or even had an army to defend or seize territory. Even so, the history of the conflict is one of violence, by both sides. Israel, with the strongest and most technologically advanced army in the Middle East, has caused vastly more casualties than have the Palestinians, whose weapons have included airplane hijackings, suicide bombs, car bombs, improvised rockets, and even stones. In the first Palestinian uprising, or intifada (1987–1993), and the second uprising, called the al-Aqsa intifada (2000–early 2005), about three times as many Palestinians died as did Israelis. Israel's frequent military occupation of Palestinian cities, the army's strict control of travel by Palestinians, the assassination of faction leaders, and other tactics may dampen violence on occasion, but they never stop it entirely and also add to Palestinian grievances against Israel. By 2004 Prime Minister Ariel Sharon, over the years one of Israel's chief advocates of using military power against the Palestinians, seized upon "disengagement"—the physical separation of Israelis and Palestinians—by withdrawing from Gaza and building a fence in and around the West Bank, in part as a way to solve the problem of violence. The long-term success of such measures remains in doubt, as evidenced by Palestinians' resort to rocket fire that crosses fences and borders.

Despite their respective narratives blaming each other, each side has missed or ignored opportunities for a peaceful solution to their conflict. Several such opportunities arose during the quarter-century after the June 1967 War, but the wounds from that war were too fresh for the Arabs, and Israelis were too smitten by the prospect of creating the Greater Israel of Zionist dreams—in other words, holding onto all of the territory captured from the Arabs in 1967. One potential breakthrough was Egyptian president Anwar al-Sadat's decision to reach out to Israel in 1977, an act that led to the first formal peace treaty between Israel and an Arab nation, in March 1979, but resulted in no real progress on settling the issue of the Palestinians.

Thus far, the Oslo Accords are the closest the Palestinians and Israelis have come to peace. In September 1993, the two sides signed agreements under which Israel officially recognized the Palestine Liberation Organization (PLO) as the representative of the Palestinians, and the PLO acknowledged Israel's existence. Several subsequent agreements sought to give the Palestinians authority to govern increasingly larger blocks of territory. By action or inaction, however, both sides allowed the hope inspired by Oslo to slip into the more-familiar despair. One of the greatest blows to the Oslo peace process was the assassination of Israeli prime minister Yitzhak Rabin in November 1995 by Yigal Amir, an Israeli Jew opposed to peace talks with the Palestinians. In subsequent months a series of suicide bombings by Palestinians convinced Israelis to elect a right-wing government, which stalled the peace process and expanded Jewish settlements in the Palestinian territories. Meanwhile, the new Palestinian Authority, under the leadership of Yasir Arafat, proved to be corrupt and incompetent, and it squandered the limited opportunities available to it. By the time another chance for peace arrived in 2000, attitudes had hardened again on both sides, and another cycle of violence ensued.

Throughout the years, extremists on both sides have been a driving force in the ongoing conflict. It is not surprising that in the land that produced the world's three great monotheistic religions, the hard-liners have used religion to pressure secular-oriented leaders. On the Israeli side, religious nationalists pushed successive governments to establish Jewish settlements on the lands occupied by Israel in the June 1967 War; these settlements served to affirm historical Jewish claims to the land and to make it more difficult for any government to trade the land for peace with the Arabs. Among the Palestinians, frustration with the failures of Arafat's leadership contributed to the rise in the 1990s of Hamas and other Islamist groups, which added suicide bombing to their jihad (holy war) against the Israelis.

By the first decade of the twenty-first century, the views and actions of the extremists on both sides had limited the options of their respective political leaderships. The success of Hamas in winning Palestinian legislative elections in 2006 made this dynamic all the more complex by deepening the turmoil in the Palestinian territories and allowing Israelis to argue that they had no one to talk to on the other side; the Israelis long had used this same argument when Arafat's Fatah faction controlled the Palestinian government. Yet another layer of complexity was added in mid-2007, when conflict between Fatah and Hamas erupted into something close to a Palestinian civil war, resulting in Hamas gaining full control of the Gaza Strip while Fatah held on to the West Bank. It suddenly looked as if historic Palestine might be divided into three entities—Israel and two Palestinian fiefdoms. This prospect appeared to make peace even more remote.

The international community, notably Britain through its control of Palestine for three decades, helped lay the groundwork for the eventual conflict between the Jews of Israel and the Palestinian Arabs. Ever since 1948, the great powers (often acting through the United Nations) have responded to the conflict in one of two ways: offering rhetorical support for one side or the other because its grievances seemed more compelling, or attempting to broker a compromise. By far, the most important outside actor has been the United States, which has attempted to portray itself as an "honest broker" between the two sides despite its underlying commitments to Israel. The United States has intervened at crucial points to dampen the conflict and to help negotiate peace agreements; during much of the 1990s, U.S. intervention was a major factor propelling the Oslo peace process in a somewhat forward direction. The weight of the world's only superpower could not, however, bring about a permanent agreement during negotiations in 2000, but the general absence of U.S. diplomacy in subsequent years helped ensure that the conflict would continue a while longer.

The Palestinian
National Movement

In January 1964, Arab leaders meeting in Cairo voted to establish the Palestine Liberation Organization (PLO) as the official representative of Palestinian Arabs and to carry out military operations against Israel. Egyptian leader Gamal Abdel Nasser primarily instigated the organization's founding. In his self-proclaimed capacity as leader of the Arab world, he wanted to establish control over the various Palestinian groups that had evolved since the founding of Israel in 1948; Nasser also wanted to ensure that he, not the Palestinians, determined the timing and manner of any attacks against Israel.

Ahmad Shuqary, an Arab diplomat and lawyer, became the first chairman of the PLO, which was based in Cairo. Under his guidance, a group of Palestinian leaders came together to form the Palestine National Council (PNC) and, in May 1964, drafted the Palestinian National Charter, or covenant, proclaiming the Palestinian people a distinct nation. As an umbrella organization, the PLO included a range of factions of various ideologies. Shuqary had only limited control over the half-dozen or more factions, some headed by more aggressive leaders intent on using any means of armed "resistance" to topple Israeli control of what they considered to be Palestinian territory.

One PLO faction, Fatah—the Palestine National Liberation Movement—had been founded in 1959 and was headed by Yasir Arafat, a former leader of Palestinian students in Cairo and the son of Palestinians from Gaza. Fatah guerrillas carried out dozens of attacks against Israel beginning in 1965. Although reliant on Arab countries for weapons and financial support, Arafat and other Palestinian leaders concluded after the June 1967 War that the Arab armies were incapable of defeating Israel by conventional means, so the Palestinians should take the matter into their own hands. Operating primarily from Jordan, Fatah stepped up its military operations in August 1967, declaring a "popular rebellion" against the Israeli occupation of the West Bank and Gaza Strip. Israel quickly suppressed that rebellion, killing hundreds of Palestinian guerrillas in the process.

Following a Palestinian attack on an Israeli school bus in March 1968, the Israeli army mounted an assault on Arafat's headquarters in the town of Karameh, in western Jordan. The Israelis managed to destroy much of the Palestinian camp and kill dozens of guerrillas after encountering stiff resistance from the Palestinians and the Jordanian army. They failed, however, to capture or kill Arafat and his top lieutenants. Arafat and the Jordanians trumpeted a great "victory" over the supposedly invincible Israelis, encouraging thousands of Palestinians to join Fatah as fighters or supporters. Several Arab leaders—including Egypt's Nasser, who at the time also headed the short-lived United Arab Republic—quickly sought to identify themselves more closely with the Palestinian cause.

Flush with self-proclaimed success, the Palestinians convened the first Palestine National Council meeting in Cairo in July 1968. Dominated by Fatah, the PNC amended its 1964 charter to redouble the emphasis on "armed struggle" as "the only way to liberate Palestine" from Israel. Other parts of the charter denounced Zionism as "illegitimate" and promised to eliminate it—and thus Israel—from the Middle East. Arafat succeeded Shuqary as chairman of the PLO in 1969 and remained the preeminent Palestinian leader until his death in late 2004.

In 1988 the PLO conceded the reality of Israel's existence, acknowledged that any Palestinian state would be limited to the West Bank and Gaza Strip, and officially renounced violence. In a September 9, 1993, letter to Israeli prime minister Yitzhak Rabin, Arafat pledged, "the PLO affirms that those articles of the Palestinian Covenant which deny Israel's right to exist, and the provisions of the Covenant which are inconsistent with the commitments of this letter are now inoperative and no longer valid. Consequently, the PLO undertakes to submit to the Palestinian National Council for formal approval the necessary changes in regard to the Palestinian Covenant." Three years later, the PNC followed through, voting to amend the national charter to eliminate references to "armed struggle" and the destruction of Israel. Despite that vote, language remained in official PLO copies of the charter until December 1998, when the council voted again to remove it, this time in the presence of U.S. president Bill Clinton. Even so, members of the PLO continued to use violence against Israel, notably during the al-Aqsa intifada, the second uprising against Israeli occupation following the failure of the negotiations at Camp David in July 2000 (Declaration of Principles, p. 220).

> *Following is the text of the Palestinian National Charter, as adopted July 1–17, 1968, during a meeting of the Palestine National Council. The council agreed in 1996 to amend or repeal articles 8 through 10, 15, and 19 through 23 (in italics)—key provisions dealing with Israel—and reaffirmed the decision to do so in 1998.*

DOCUMENT

Palestinian National Charter

JULY 1–17, 1968

Article 1: Palestine is the homeland of the Arab Palestinian people; it is an indivisible part of the Arab homeland, and the Palestinian people are an integral part of the Arab nation.

Article 2: Palestine, with the boundaries it had during the British Mandate, is an indivisible territorial unit.

Article 3: The Palestinian Arab people possess the legal right to their homeland and have the right to determine their destiny after achieving the liberation of their country in accordance with their wishes and entirely of their own accord and will.

Article 4: The Palestinian identity is a genuine, essential, and inherent characteristic; it is transmitted from parents to children. The Zionist occupation and the dispersal of the Palestinian Arab people, through the disasters which befell them, do not make them lose their Palestinian identity and their membership in the Palestinian community, nor do they negate them.

Article 5: The Palestinians are those Arab nationals who, until 1947, normally resided in Palestine regardless of whether they were evicted from it or have stayed there. Anyone born, after that date, of a Palestinian father—whether inside Palestine or outside it—is also a Palestinian.

Article 6: The Jews who had normally resided in Palestine until the beginning of the Zionist invasion will be considered Palestinians.

Article 7: That there is a Palestinian community and that it has material, spiritual, and historical connection with Palestine are indisputable facts. It is a national duty to bring up individual Palestinians in an Arab revolutionary manner. All means of information and education must be adopted in order to acquaint the Palestinian with his country in the most profound manner, both spiritual and material, that is possible. He must be prepared for the armed struggle and ready to sacrifice his wealth and his life in order to win back his homeland and bring about its liberation.

*Article 8: The phase in their history, through which the Palestinian people are now living, is that of national (*watani*) struggle for the liberation of Palestine. Thus the conflicts among the Palestinian national forces are secondary, and should be ended for the sake of the basic conflict that exists between the forces of Zionism and of imperialism on the one hand, and the Palestinian Arab people on the other. On this basis the Palestinian masses, regardless of whether they are residing in the national homeland or in diaspora (*mahajir*) constitute—both their organizations and the individuals—one national front working for the retrieval of Palestine and its liberation through armed struggle.*

Article 9: Armed struggle is the only way to liberate Palestine. This it is the overall strategy, not merely a tactical phase. The Palestinian Arab people assert their absolute determination and firm resolution to continue their armed struggle and to work for an armed popular revolution for the liberation of their country and their return to it. They also assert their right to normal life in Palestine and to exercise their right to self-determination and sovereignty over it.

Article 10: Commando action constitutes the nucleus of the Palestinian popular liberation war. This requires its escalation, comprehensiveness, and the mobilization of all the Palestinian popular and educational efforts and their organization and involvement in the armed Palestinian revolution. It also requires the achieving of unity for the national (*watani*) struggle among the different groupings of the Palestinian people, and between the Palestinian people and the Arab masses, so as to secure the continuation of the revolution, its escalation, and victory.

Article 11: The Palestinians will have three mottoes: national (*wataniyya*) unity, national (*qawmiyya*) mobilization, and liberation.

Article 12: The Palestinian people believe in Arab unity. In order to contribute their share toward the attainment of that objective, however, they must, at the present stage of their struggle, safeguard their Palestinian identity and develop their consciousness of that identity, and oppose any plan that may dissolve or impair it.

Article 13: Arab unity and the liberation of Palestine are two complementary objectives, the attainment of either of which facilitates the attainment of the other. Thus, Arab unity leads to the liberation of Palestine, the liberation of Palestine leads to Arab unity; and work toward the realization of one objective proceeds side by side with work toward the realization of the other.

Article 14: The destiny of the Arab nation, and indeed Arab existence itself, depend upon the destiny of the Palestine cause. From this interdependence springs the Arab nation's pursuit of, and striving for, the liberation of Palestine. The people of Palestine play the role of the vanguard in the realization of this sacred (*qawmi*) goal.

Article 15: The liberation of Palestine, from an Arab viewpoint, is a national (qawmi) *duty and it attempts to repel the Zionist and imperialist aggression against the Arab homeland, and aims at the elimination of Zionism in Palestine. Absolute responsibility for this falls upon the Arab nation—peoples and government—with the Arab people of Palestine in the vanguard. Accordingly, the Arab nation must mobilize all its military, human, moral, and spiritual capabilities to participate actively with the Palestinian people in the liberation of Palestine. It must, particularly in the phase of the armed Palestinian revolution, offer and furnish the Palestinian people with all possible help, and material and human support, and make available to them the means and opportunities that will enable them to continue to carry out their leading role in the armed revolution, until they liberate their homeland.*

Article 16: The liberation of Palestine, from a spiritual point of view, will provide the Holy Land with an atmosphere of safety and tranquility, which in turn will safeguard the country's religious sanctuaries and guarantee freedom of worship and of visit to all, without discrimination of race, color, language, or religion. Accordingly, the people of Palestine look to all spiritual forces in the world for support.

Article 17: The liberation of Palestine, from a human point of view, will restore to the Palestinian individual his dignity, pride, and freedom. Accordingly the Palestinian Arab people look forward to the support of all those who believe in the dignity of man and his freedom in the world.

Article 18: The liberation of Palestine, from an international point of view, is a defensive action necessitated by the demands of self-defense. Accordingly the Palestinian people, desirous as they are of the friendship of all people, look to freedom-loving, and peace-loving states for support in order to restore their legitimate rights in Palestine, to re-establish peace and security in the country, and to enable its people to exercise national sovereignty and freedom.

Article 19: The partition of Palestine in 1947 and the establishment of the state of Israel are entirely illegal, regardless of the passage of time, because they were contrary to the will of the Palestinian people and to their natural right in their homeland, and inconsistent with the principles embodied in the Charter of the United Nations, particularly the right to self-determination.

Article 20: The Balfour Declaration, the Mandate for Palestine, and everything that has been based upon them, are deemed null and void. Claims of historical or religious ties of Jews with Palestine are incompatible with the facts of history and the true conception of what constitutes statehood. Judaism, being a religion, is not an independent nationality. Nor do Jews constitute a single nation with an identity of its own; they are citizens of the states to which they belong.

Article 21: The Arab Palestinian people, expressing themselves by the armed Palestinian revolution, reject all solutions which are substitutes for the total liberation of Palestine and reject all proposals aiming at the liquidation of the Palestinian problem, or its internationalization.

Article 22: Zionism is a political movement organically associated with international imperialism and antagonistic to all action for liberation and to progressive movements in the world. It is racist and fanatic in its nature, aggressive, expansionist, and colonial in its aims, and fascist in its methods. Israel is the instrument of the Zionist movement, and geographical base for world imperialism placed strategically in the midst of the Arab homeland to combat the hopes of the Arab nation for liberation, unity, and progress. Israel is a constant source of threat vis-à-vis peace in the Middle East and the whole world. Since the liberation of Palestine will destroy the Zionist and imperialist presence and will contribute to the establishment of peace in the Middle East, the Palestinian people look for the support of all the progressive and peaceful forces and urge them all, irrespective of their affiliations and beliefs, to offer the Palestinian people all aid and support in their just struggle for the liberation of their homeland.

Article 23: The demand of security and peace, as well as the demand of right and justice, require all states to consider Zionism an illegitimate movement, to outlaw its existence, and to ban its operations, in order that friendly relations among peoples may be preserved, and the loyalty of citizens to their respective homelands safeguarded.

Article 24: The Palestinian people believe in the principles of justice, freedom, sovereignty, self-determination, human dignity, and in the right of all peoples to exercise them.

Article 25: For the realization of the goals of this Charter and its principles, the Palestine Liberation Organization will perform its role in the liberation of Palestine in accordance with the Constitution of this Organization.

Article 26: The Palestine Liberation Organization, representative of the Palestinian revolutionary forces, is responsible for the Palestinian Arab people's movement in its struggle—to retrieve its homeland, liberate and return to it and exercise the right to self-determination in it—in all military, political, and financial fields and also for whatever may be required by the Palestine case on the inter-Arab and international levels.

Article 27: The Palestine Liberation Organization shall cooperate with all Arab states, each according to its potentialities; and will adopt a neutral policy among them in the light of the requirements of the war of liberation; and on this basis it shall not interfere in the internal affairs of any Arab state.

Article 28: The Palestinian Arab people assert the genuineness and independence of their national *(wataniyya)* revolution and reject all forms of intervention, trusteeship, and subordination.

Article 29: The Palestinian people possess the fundamental and genuine legal right to liberate and retrieve their homeland. The Palestinian people determine their attitude toward all states and forces on the basis of the stands they adopt vis-à-vis to the Palestinian revolution to fulfill the aims of the Palestinian people.

Article 30: Fighters and carriers of arms in the war of liberation are the nucleus of the popular army which will be the protective force for the gains of the Palestinian Arab people.

Article 31: The Organization shall have a flag, an oath of allegiance, and an anthem. All this shall be decided upon in accordance with a special regulation.

Article 32: Regulations, which shall be known as the Constitution of the Palestinian Liberation Organization, shall be annexed to this Charter. It will lay down the manner in which the Organization, and its organs and institutions, shall be constituted; the respective competence of each; and the requirements of its obligation under the Charter.

Article 33: This Charter shall not be amended save by [vote of] a majority of two-thirds of the total membership of the National Congress of the Palestine Liberation Organization [taken] at a special session convened for that purpose.

SOURCE: U.S. Embassy, Israel, http://usembassy-israel.org.il/publish/peace/plo_covn.htm, as published in Leila S. Kadi, ed., *Basic Political Documents of the Armed Palestinian Resistance Movement* (Beirut: Palestine Research Centre, 1969), 137–141 (italics added).

Israel and the Question of Palestinian Statehood

During the first four and a half decades of Israel's existence, the vast majority of Israelis held to the view that no need existed for a Palestinian state because the Palestinians already had a state of their own—Jordan. Israeli leaders from David Ben-Gurion onward argued that the land formerly known as Palestine had been divided by the forces of history into the states of Israel and Jordan. According to their logic, because the majority of Jordan's citizens were of Palestinian origin, and because the majority of Palestinians were (until 1988) Jordanian citizens, Jordan was *the* state for Palestinian Arabs who were not citizens of Israel. One consideration ignored by this argument was that Jordan's Hashemite rulers were not Palestinians.

One of the clearest expressions of official Israeli government policy on this matter appears in a speech delivered by Prime Minister Golda Meir to a conference of her ruling Labor Party on April 12, 1973. Meir, one of Israel's founding leaders, served as prime minister from May 1969 until April 1974, and she routinely took a tough, uncompromising line toward the Arabs in general and the Palestinians in particular. In the speech, Meir stated that "there is room for two states only"—Israel and Jordan—between the Mediterranean Sea and the desert to the east. If the Palestinian Arabs need a state, she said, they have "every opportunity for national self-expression" in Jordan. "They need Jordan—just as Jordan cannot exist without them," she said. Meir suggested that the more than 1 million Palestinian Arabs then in the West Bank could simply move to Jordan if they wanted to live in a Palestinian state: "There are in Jordan wide spaces with a development potential in which the Palestinians can be rehabilitated."

Meir also reiterated what was then standard Israeli policy: Israel would negotiate peace with its Arab neighbors, including Jordan, but would not negotiate with the Palestine Liberation Organization (PLO) or other Palestinian groups. She described them as "organizations of murderers" and accused their leaders of seeking "to destroy the State of Israel and to establish instead a Palestinian state on the 'plundered earth.' "

In the late 1980s, official Israeli policy on Jordan's sovereignty over the Palestinians shifted as a result of events, including the first Palestinian intifada, or uprising, beginning in 1987. In large part because of the intifada, King Hussein in July 1988 renounced any Jordanian claims to the West Bank, which Jordan had controlled from 1948 until Israel captured it in the June 1967 War. Thus, in one stroke, Hussein eliminated the Jordanian citizenship of Palestinians living on the West Bank and undercut Israeli assertions that Jordan was the Palestinians' state. Hussein's action also reinforced his and other Arab leaders' acknowledgment that the PLO, not Jordan, was the sole representative of the Palestinian people (King Hussein on Relinquishing the West Bank, p. 201).

The Israeli government headed by Prime Minister Yitzhak Shamir in 1989 offered a "peace initiative," calling for Palestinians living under Israeli occupation to elect representatives who would then negotiate with Israel. That initiative went nowhere, but four years later, in 1993, Israeli prime minister Yitzhak Rabin formally recognized the PLO as the representative of the Palestinians as part of the Oslo Accords, in which Israel and the Palestinians agreed to negotiate a long-term peace (Oslo Accords, p. 213).

Following is the statement on Palestinians by Israeli prime minister Golda Meir, delivered to the Secretariat of the Labor Party on April 12, 1973.

DOCUMENT

Golda Meir on the Palestinians

APRIL 12, 1973

We Israelis make no pretensions of determining whether there is or is not a "Palestinian entity." This decision is the privilege of the Arabs themselves. As a result of the war imposed upon us in 1948, some of the Arabs of Palestine left and wandered to other places. Nonetheless, I reject the contention that "two and a half million Palestinian Arabs are wandering about the world without a homeland."

There is a complete distortion in any comparison between the Situation of the Jews in the Diaspora who are without a homeland and that of the Palestinians. The Palestinian Arabs live among their brethren, with whom they share a common religion, culture and language. The Arabs themselves declare that they are a single Arab nation—even though it is a nation which stretches over eighteen independent States.

The differences and distinction between an Arab from Judaea or Samaria [the West Bank] living today in Amman [capital of Jordan] and an Arab who has for generations lived on the East Bank of the Jordan are much less than the differences and distinction among Jews from various lands—yet we absorb these Jews and blend with them into one nation. Whoever speaks in terms of balance and analogy between the Jewish problem on the one hand and the Palestinian problem on the other is ignoring the fact that this parcel of land in which we have established the State of Israel is the only one in which the Jewish people can be sovereign and in which every Jew can live with his fellow-Jews in independence.

A non-Israeli who hears such a comparison and is persuaded by it is only a step away from accepting the concept of "the plundered earth" and everything implied by it.

The Palestinian refugee problem has not yet been solved only because the Arab States have kept it unsolved for use against us. A shocking example of this was the situation prevailing in the refugee camps in 1967 when we entered the Gaza Strip.

The Egyptian Government, for instance, did not extend Egyptian citizenship to the inhabitants of the Gaza Strip, nor did it allow them to work or to move anywhere else.

In contrast with the unfriendly behaviour of some of the Arab States, the Government of Jordan extended Jordanian citizenship to the Arabs of Palestinian origin within its territory. Citizenship was bestowed upon the residents of Judaea and Samaria as well as upon their brethren on the East Bank. All these—those on the East Bank and those in Judaea and Samaria—are thus Jordanian citizens.

The Palestinian Arabs have in Jordan every opportunity for national self expression. They need Jordan—just as Jordan cannot exist without them. There are in Jordan wide spaces with a development potential in which the Palestinians can be rehabilitated.

Some 600,000 or more citizens of Palestinian origin are now living on the East Bank of the Jordan. For many years now, never less than half of the members of the Jordanian Parliament have been of Palestinian origin, as are the majority of the members of the present Jordanian Cabinet.

Between the Mediterranean Sea and the eastern desert, there is room for two States only: a Jewish State, and an Arab State—Israel and Jordan. We oppose the establishment of an additional Arab State in the region between Israel and Jordan.

As I have mentioned, there are at least 600,000 citizens of Palestinian origin living on the eastern bank of the Jordan River. This population is bound to the Arabs of Judaea and Samaria by family ties and by a common origin. For this reason, I am glad that the policy of the open bridges is continuing, a policy that makes it possible to maintain this link between the Arabs of the administered territories and their brothers in Jordan and the Arabs in the neighbouring countries.

During the past two years, about half a million people have crossed those bridges. This figure includes some 210,000 inhabitants of the administered areas who crossed into Jordan for visits to that and other Arab countries, and about 290,000 inhabitants of Arab countries who visited the administered areas and Israel, including 260,000 who came in the framework of the summer visits. The number of Arabs crossing the bridges in both directions is increasing steadily.

We have enacted the policy of the open bridges out of consideration for the needs of the Arabs in Judaea and Samaria and their brethren living on the East Bank of the Jordan. One can imagine the suffering and distress caused this population if the bridges were barred, and with them, the opportunity to maintain family contacts and the large-scale exchange of goods between Judaea and Samaria and the East Bank of the Jordan.

Commenting in the Knesset on King Hussein's speech of 15 March 1972, I said: "We have never interfered in the internal structure or nature of the regime of any country. Should the King of Jordan decide to change the name of his kingdom to 'Falastin' or any other name, and to introduce changes in the internal structure of his realm in order to give, within his kingdom, an opportunity for self-expression to those Arabs who call themselves Palestinians, and if, in the course of negotiations between us, we should have agreed on all relevant aspects, including the territorial one, then we should not concern ourselves with taking a stand in internal affairs which are within the sovereign competence of the Arab nation that borders on Israel in the East."

We shall not negotiate with the organizations of murderers and their leaders who endeavour to destroy the State of Israel and to establish instead a Palestinian state on the "plundered earth." All the more so since the murder and terror organizations' claims of representing the Arabs of Judea and Samaria, and Arabs of Palestinian origin in other countries, lack all foundation.

The peace treaties shall include a reiteration of our readiness, which has remained valid throughout the years, to pay compensation for abandoned Arab property, and our willingness to offer all technical aid for the rehabilitation of refugees in Arab countries. The rehabilitation of those refugees who live within the borders of Israel shall be our responsibility. The problem of the Arabs who strive for a Palestinian identity can and must find its solution in the Kingdom of Jordan. At the conclusion of the peace treaties, we shall insist that the advent of peace be accompanied by an end to the Arab-Israeli conflict and that it be agreed that the Arabs shall have no further claims on Israel.

SOURCE: Israel Ministry of Foreign Affairs, "Statement by the Prime Minister on the Palestinian Issue," www.mfa.gov.il/MFA/Foreign+Relations/Israels+Foreign+Relations+since+1947/1947-1974/40+Statement+by+the+Prime+Minister+on+the+Palestin.htm.

Israeli Settlement of the Occupied Territories

DOCUMENT IN CONTEXT

Israel's capture of the Gaza Strip, Golan Heights, Sinai Peninsula, and West Bank, including East Jerusalem, from its Arab neighbors during the June 1967 War raised the prospect of the Zionist dream of "Greater Israel" becoming reality. Shortly after that war, and at an increasing pace in the 1970s, a succession of Israeli governments promoted or allowed the establishment of dozens of Jewish settlements in these territories. One idea behind the settlements was to allow Israel to tighten its hold on the land, making it politically and practically impossible to relinquish it in any peace negotiations with the Arabs. The negotiation of Israel's first peace treaty with an Arab nation proved that expectation flawed: In 1978 Israel agreed to remove a handful of settlements in the Sinai Peninsula and return the peninsula to Egypt as the price for peace with its largest Arab neighbor. In 2005 Israel unilaterally eliminated Jewish settlements in the Gaza Strip in response to the demographic and security challenges posed by the presence of some 8,000 Israeli Jews in the midst of more than 1 million Palestinian Arabs (June 1967 Arab–Israeli War, p. 94; Camp David Peace Process, p. 118; Israeli Disengagement, p. 313).

Some of the settlements in the territories occupied by Israel resulted from official policies publicly articulated by successive governments. Others, established with little or no public announcement, stemmed from the behind-the-scenes actions of the military or government agencies. Still others took hold through the actions of religious organizations, sometimes with the implicit support of the government and in other cases only after the government had tried with varying degrees of sincerity to block their establishment.

However the settlements came about, four decades later, more than one hundred of them were populated by nearly 450,000 Israeli Jews: approximately 200,000 settlers in and around East Jerusalem, some 17,000 on the Golan Heights, about 230,000 in the West Bank, and an estimated 8,000 in the Gaza Strip. (Israel dismantled its settlements in Gaza in 2005.) Israel unilaterally annexed East Jerusalem in 1967 and the Golan Heights in 1981, but the United Nations does not acknowledge these annexations as legitimate and considers these lands, in addition to the rest of the West Bank and the Gaza Strip, as occupied territory.

The Israeli government approved the first settlement in the West Bank three months after the June 1967 War. Called Gush Etzion and located south of Jerusalem between Bethlehem and Hebron, this community represents the reestablishment of the Kfar Etzion settlement, which Jews had built decades earlier but Jordan had dismantled after it conquered the West Bank in the 1948 Arab-Israeli war. Gush Etzion subsequently grew into a collection of more than a dozen settlements and by 2004 had a total population of around 15,000 settlers. Israel argued that many of the post-1967 settlements in East Jerusalem also were not new, but instead were restorations of Jewish neighborhoods that had existed in the area before the 1948 war, some for hundreds of years.

In the first few years after the 1967 war, the Israeli government focused on placing settlements in the Jordan Valley, immediately to the west of the Jordan River. It justified these settlements as part of security measures to thwart any future attack by Jordan, to the east of the river. The government used this same reasoning to establish Jewish settlements on the Golan Heights, the strategic plateau captured from Syria in 1967 that offers commanding views of northeastern Israel.

Starting in 1971, however, senior government officials put forth the broader rationale that the settlements demonstrated Israel's determination to hold onto the territories, despite the UN Security Council's call for Israel to return them to the Arabs in exchange for peace. Defense Minister Moshe Dayan made one of the boldest such statements in an August 19, 1971, speech, asserting that Israel must "create facts" in what the government called the "administered territories." Said Dayan, "We should regard our role also in the administered territories as that of the established government—to plan and implement whatever can be done without leaving 'options open' for the day of peace, which may be distant."

In July 1967, Yigal Allon, a minister in the cabinet of Prime Minister Levi Eshkol, put forth the closest thing to a "master" settlement plan in the early years of Israeli occupation. Allon proposed to divide the West Bank between Israel and Jordan: Israel would control most of the Jordan Valley (except for an enclave centering around the Palestinian town of Jericho) and the midsection of the West Bank neighboring Jerusalem; Jordan would control the rest of the West Bank, including the Arab-majority cities of Bethlehem, Hebron, Jenin, Nablus, Ramallah, and Tulkarm. Officials of the ruling Labor Party endorsed Allon's plan and several subsequent modifications of it, but the full cabinet never did.

The Allon plan influenced government policy for two decades, as successive governments adopted key elements, notably retaining control of the Jordan Valley and all of the area around Jerusalem. Allon's idea of sharing parts of the West Bank, however, lost all validity after 1988, when Jordan's King Hussein renounced his country's claim to the West Bank. Even so, the essential idea of Allon's plan—Israel keeping some of the West Bank and returning the rest to Arab control—has become the foundation of policy for some Israeli governments over the years and of many international plans for peace between Israel and the Palestinians.

In 1973 Israel Galili, a minister without portfolio in the cabinet of Prime Minister Gold Meir, drafted another semiofficial document that promoted the establishment of settlements. Known as the Galili Document, this plan called for new settlements in the Gaza Strip and the West Bank, but also promised government assistance for Palestinian refugees living in the occupied territories. Labor Party leaders also endorsed this document but never submitted it to the government for formal approval. Government officials, however, reportedly used the plan as the basis for approving at least some new settlements.

The religious nationalist movement emerged as a crucial force behind the expansion of the settlements. Its leaders argued fervently that God intended—indeed, had ordered—that Jews live in all of the lands between the Mediterranean Sea and the eastern bank of the Jordan River. An increasingly powerful voice for this argument arose in March 1974 with the creation of Gush Emunim (Block of the Faithful), a movement based on the "redemptionist" teachings of Rabbi Rav Tzvi Yehuda Kook, who argued that Jews would be redeemed, as a nation, by fulfilling God's command that they control all of Eretz Yisrael ha-Shlema (Greater Israel).

Gush Emunim devoted much of its early efforts to combating one of the implications of the unofficial Allon plan—that much of the central section of the West Bank remain free of Jewish settlements so that it could be returned to Jordan in an eventual peace settlement. For almost five years, the city of Nablus, north of Jerusalem, would be the focal point of a struggle between Gush Emunim and other settler groups and the government.

On July 25, 1974, a group of Gush Emunim adherents moved into the abandoned Sebastia train station near Nablus. The army, under orders from Prime Minister Yitzhak Rabin, forced the settlers to leave. Rabin's cabinet on July 26 issued a statement asserting that settlements only be established "solely in accordance with the government's decisions. The government will prevent any attempt at settling without its approval and decision." Explaining the government's action in a speech to the Knesset, Rabin noted that the settlers had moved into Sebastia after being told not to and therefore had evaded the "rule of law." Rabin did not argue, however, that Israelis should not live in the West Bank and the other occupied territories. "Our right to this land is indisputable," he said.

Such government intervention did not deter Gush Emunim leaders, who argued that they were acting in accordance with God's higher authority. The group made six more attempts to settle at Sebastia, and each time the army forced them out. In late 1975, however, Defense Minister Shimon Peres relented and agreed to allow the settlers to move temporarily into a nearby former army camp. This camp eventually became the Kedumim settlement, which today is home to some 3,000 settlers.

Gush Emunim was allied in its early years with the National Religious Party, one of Israel's small political movements that exercised leverage when the mainstream parties needed its votes in the Knesset. Starting in 1977, Gush Emunim and similar groups found an even more powerful patron in the rightist Likud Party, which won elections that year, and its leader, Menachem Begin, who became prime minister. After Begin agreed in 1978 to return the Sinai Peninsula to Egypt in exchange for peace, he apparently became even more determined to hang onto the Gaza Strip, Golan Heights, and West Bank by expanding the settlements there. A legal battle over the Elon Moreh settlement, near Nablus, coupled with pressure from Gush Emunim led

Begin's government in 1979 to decide to expand the scope of the settlements. A key element flowing from this decision was the creation of five large communities, known as settlement blocs, that have since grown to include the majority of Jewish settlers in the West Bank.

The official policy of every U.S. administration since the early 1970s has been to oppose Israel's establishment of settlements in the territories, referring to them as "obstacles" to peace. Every U.S. administration since that of Ronald Reagan, in the 1980s, also has called on Israel to "freeze" settlement construction, a request that Israeli governments have interpreted as applying to the construction of new settlements, not the expansion (or "thickening") of existing ones. President George W. Bush substantially altered U.S. policy in April 2004, however, by asserting that Israel should be allowed to keep its major West Bank settlements as part of any eventual peace agreement with the Palestinians. Bush's aides said his statement merely reflected reality, and they noted that Washington policymakers long had assumed that some settlements would be included in a final agreement. Palestinians were angered that the United States presumed to dictate the ultimate outcome of negotiations between themselves and the Israelis.

One of the most controversial aspects of Israeli settlement has been disputes over the ownership of land. Before the 1967 war, most of the land in the Gaza Strip, Golan Heights, and West Bank (including East Jerusalem) was owned by private individuals, some of them absentee Arab landlords who lived in neighboring countries or by Islamic charities known as *waqfs*. After 1967, the Israeli government took possession of much of the private and waqf lands in these areas through a variety of maneuvers. In some cases, the army seized land for "security" reasons, then turned it over to civilian Jewish settlers. The government also decreed that all landholdings in the territories had to be newly registered; many absentee Arab owners, including those who had fled during the war, were unable to register their lands, enabling the Israeli government to take possession of them. Over the years, the government and military also confiscated thousands of acres of Palestinian land for such public purposes as building access roads between settlements and erecting the separation barrier surrounding much of the West Bank and Jerusalem. Some Palestinians were compensated for their losses, but many were not.

In general, Israelis have moved to the settlements for one of two reasons. Members of Gush Emunim and similar groups established settlements in the West Bank and other territories primarily for religious reasons, to fulfill what they said was God's command. Thousands of other Israelis, however, were attracted by more practical considerations: the housing, tax, and other subsidies provided by the government as inducements. Most of the settlements near Jerusalem were established as suburbs for people who work in the city and desire affordable housing nearby.

The eventual fate of the settlements will depend on the state of affairs if Israel and the Palestinians are able to negotiate a "final status" peace agreement. The Israel-Palestinian agreements of 1993–1995 committed Israel to handing over the administration of Gaza and parts of the West Bank to the newly established Palestinian Authority. All prime ministers since that time have, however, said that Israel would hold on to all of East Jerusalem and the surrounding neighborhoods that Israel has annexed, plus the West Bank settlement blocs. The Palestinians have insisted on their right to designate East Jerusalem as the capital of their state. They also have argued that some of the major Jewish settlements must be dismantled so the new Palestinian state can be a contiguous unit on the West Bank.

Following are the texts of two documents. The first is a communiqué issued by the Israeli cabinet on July 26, 1974, following the expulsion of Gush Emunim members from the abandoned railway station of Sebastia, near the city of Nablus in the West Bank. The second is a speech delivered on July 31, 1974, by Israeli prime minister Yitzhak Rabin to the Knesset on the authorized establishment of settlements.

DOCUMENT

Cabinet Communiqué on Israeli Settlements

JULY 26, 1974

Settlements in the Administered territories are established solely in accordance with the government's decisions. The government will prevent any attempt at settling without its approval and decision.

The Prime Minister and the Minister of Defence are authorized to implement this policy.

The proposals put forward by the Prime Minister were passed unanimously.

SOURCE: Israel Ministry of Foreign Affairs, www.mfa.gov.il/MFA/Foreign%20Relations/Israels%20Foreign%20 Relations%20since%201947/1974-1977/17%20Cabinet%20communique%20on%20settlements%20in%20 the%20West%20B.

DOCUMENT

Statement by Prime Minister Yitzhak Rabin on Settlements

JULY 31, 1974

Mr. Speaker, Members of the Knesset,

On the Thursday of last week, when I learned the facts about the Sebastia incident, I had no doubt about the negative significance of the act. The Attorney-General was consulted and expressed the opinion that this was a breach of the law. I had no doubt that it was the duty of the government to expel the people who had occupied the location without its approval, as governments of Israel have done since the Six-Day War. I submitted the subject to the entire cabinet. The government of

Israel thoroughly discussed the matter. At the end of the discussion, the government adopted the decision proposed by the Prime Minister:

Outposts and settlements in the administered areas are established solely according to the decisions of the government. The government will prevent any attempt to occupy a location or establish a settlement without its approval and decision. The Prime Minister and the Minister of Defence are authorized to implement this policy.

I see no need to describe the course of events. The government's decision was carried out. The Israel Defence Forces acted according to orders. I cannot say that the people evacuated the place of their own free will, but their evacuation was carried out without it being necessary to adopt measures which we wished to avoid so long as it was possible to carry out the evacuation without resorting to them.

We acted irrespective of considerations of prestige, but consistently and according to plan. It was clear to the people in Sebastia that there would be no negotiations with them on settlement elsewhere before they evacuated Sebastia. In determining the timing of the operation, we took into account the observance of the Sabbath and the Ninth of Av fast. The timetable we adopted enabled the people to realize the strength of the government's determination, to consider their actions, and to choose evacuation without a clash with the I.D.F. I regard this event as a test of the inner strength of Israeli society and not as a test of strength for the I.D.F. I am glad that we have saved ourselves pain and shame—and perhaps even more.

Members of the Knesset,

In the basic principles of the government's policy, it is stated that we will work for the continuation of settlement in accordance with the decisions that the government of Israel will adopt. This undertaking is being carried out, in practice. The policy on this subject has been repeatedly clarified and the Knesset has also decided to hold a debate on the matter. I must therefore emphasize at the outset of my remarks that in this statement I shall not discuss plans and criteria, possibilities and limitations affecting our actions in the sphere of settlement.

Today, after the events of last week, the Knesset must first of all discuss the public and national significance of the incident in order to resolve once again that in the state of Israel the procedures of the rule of law shall be maintained and no one shall be permitted to violate them. This is vital for the democratic stability of Israeli society. It is vital for the continuation of responsible action in the sphere of settlement.

The Knesset cannot evade its duty to resolve once again that the law in Israel is binding on all citizens in various fields, including settlement in the administered areas. Our country protects the rights of the citizen and respects his liberty, but these precious principles cannot be preserved without meticulous compliance with the laws enacted to the Knesset.

The rules were violated in the Sebastia incident. Members of the group which concentrated in Sebastia met me and a few of my ministerial colleagues before they decided on this inadmissible act. We explained to them the policy of the government, which engages in rural and urban settlement in keeping with an order of priorities, security, political and settlement considerations, possibilities and limitations. During the meetings, principal proposals were made to them and other locations designated where the population is sparse and its reinforcement vital. They were promised consideration of specific proposals. They were not convinced. From the course of the meetings it was clear that according to their concepts they were entitled to decide where and when settlement should take place. That they believed that their will would prevail and that ultimately they would impose their decision and their plan on the government. It was in this conviction that the Sebastia operation was born. The people knew that the government would use its authority, and nevertheless they believed that they would create an accomplished fact and the government of Israel would say amen.

Thus, the argument today is not over settlement, but over the maintenance of state responsibility and authority, over the foundations of the democratic system, over the authority of the government, which is subject to the Knesset. The Knesset must reject acts whose aim is to undermine the foundations of the democratic system and governmental authority in Israel. This is vital not only as a judgement on the past, but also to secure the future. The Knesset's ruling will be of the utmost educational and political importance. Aspirations in the sphere of settlement must not serve as justification for actions against the authority of the state.

Israel is a free society which respects various views and differences of opinion. Differences of opinion exist, inter alia, regarding various aspects of the settlement issue. Every person and group holds its opinion dear, and many of us are zealous in their views. It is intolerable, however, that any group of people in Israel—whatever its motives—should take the law into its own hands in spheres which are not the private domain of the individual but are subject to the decision of the community. The people of Israel do not adopt their decisions by arbitrary will, but according to democratic rules and processes, and by the will of the majority. These rules must also apply to settlement in the administered areas, which have not been annexed to Israel, and in every act of settlement in the areas' security and political considerations must be taken into account. Every act of settlement in the areas imposes obligations on Israel's defence forces and involves national responsibility.

Only the government of Israel is authorized to decide where and when to settle, whether at one time or another, and no government can tolerate the violation of this authority.

The government's decisions can be influenced by means of the ballot box. By the Knesset's decisions, by public opinion, but not by deeds which undermine the foundations of our regime. This consciousness is binding on all sections of the community, and first and foremost on the people's representatives and emissaries.

In conclusion, under the circumstances in which Israel is placed, every new settlement requires the prior approval of the government of Israel, which is subject to the authority of the Knesset. Provocative and unauthorized initiatives in the administered areas cannot be tolerated. Settlement is not a demonstration, nor is it compatible with violation of the law. The IDF should not have security obligations stemming from irresponsible acts imposed on it. The IDF should not be burdened with tasks that disrupt its preparations and plans, and it should not be confronted with a situation wherein it is obliged to use force to prevent occupation of a location without prior and authorized sanction.

The government will, in the future as in the past, scrupulously maintain the customary procedures in the sphere of settlement. It will work for the continuation of settlement in line with its authoritative decisions. It will do whatever has to be done to prevent any attempt to exploit the ideal of settlement for an anti-democratic purpose.

Members of the Knesset,

Our right to this land is indisputable. That is not what the argument is about. The Knesset is asked today not to divert its mind from its duty.

The government calls upon the house to give its full support to this policy, which provides a guarantee for the maintenance of the rule of law and the authority of the administration and the Knesset.

SOURCE: Israel Ministry of Foreign Affairs http://www.mfa.gov.il/MFA/Foreign%20Relations/Israels%20 Foreign%20Relations%20since%201947/1974-1977/17%20Cabinet%20communique%20on%20settlements %20in%20the%20West%20B.

Arab Recognition of the PLO

DOCUMENT IN CONTEXT

In 1970 Jordan expelled the Palestine Liberation Organization (PLO) after the group sparked a brief civil war there. A few years later, on October 28, 1974, leaders of the Arab League adopted a resolution at a summit in Rabat, Morocco, recognizing the PLO as the "sole legitimate representative" of the Palestinian people. Some three weeks after that, PLO chairman Yasir Arafat addressed a regular session of the UN General Assembly, which then accorded the PLO "observer" status, allowing it to participate in the work of the organization. These measures did not bring the Palestinians any closer to their goal of an independent state, but together they accorded diplomatic legitimacy to a "national liberation" group whose most notable accomplishments had been attacks against Israel and in countries bordering Israel.

The Arab League statement was one of many declarations by Arab leaders aligning themselves with the Palestinian Arabs. Most Palestinians were refugees living in Arab countries surrounding Israel or in the Gaza Strip, the West Bank, or East Jerusalem— territories captured by Israel in the June 1967 War. (Several hundred thousand Palestinian Arabs lived in Israel as citizens.) For domestic political reasons, Arab leaders wished to be seen as championing the cause of the Palestinians, viewed by most Arabs as the foremost victims of Israel. Even so, several leaders—notably Jordan's King Hussein, who until 1988 claimed sovereignty over the West Bank—had a relationship with the Palestinian leadership that was cool, at best (Jordan Relinquishes the West Bank, p. 200).

Israeli leaders responded angrily to the Rabat summit declaration. In a speech to the Knesset on November 5, Prime Minister Yitzhak Rabin said that "the government of Israel, will not negotiate with terrorist organizations whose avowed policy is to strive for Israel's destruction and whose method is terrorist violence."

Arafat, in his speech to the General Assembly, defended the Palestinian "struggle" against Israeli Zionists, who he accused of committing acts of terrorism against the Palestinians. Arafat mixed his harsh denunciations of Israel with a description of his "noble dream" for a united Palestine, where Jews and Palestinians could live together in peace.

Arafat's speech at the United Nations is remembered more for the PLO leader's presentation than for the actual words he spoke. Wearing his trademark checkered head-dress, or *kaffiyah,* and military fatigues, Arafat also had a gun holster on his belt; some reports said Arafat carried a gun in the holster, but others said either that he had been forced to check his gun at the door or had never brought one into the U.N. building. In any event, Arafat did carry a gun rhetorically. "Today I have come bearing an olive branch and a freedom-fighter's gun," he told the General Assembly at the end of his speech. "Do not let the olive branch fall from my hand. I repeat: do not let the olive branch fall from my hand. War flares up in Palestine, and yet it is in Palestine that peace will be born." Arafat's appearance at the United Nations won praise from many Arab leaders and representatives from the "nonaligned bloc" but was denounced by the United States and Israel. In a statement the next day to ambassadors to Israel, Foreign Minister Yigal Allon said, "The voice of Arafat was and remains the voice of indiscriminate terror, the crack of the gun, without any suggestion of the olive branch of peace."

Following is the text of a resolution adopted by Arab heads of state at a summit meeting of the Arab League in Rabat, Morocco, on October 28, 1974, and excerpts from the speech delivered to the UN General Assembly on November 13, 1974, by Palestine Liberation Organization chairman Yasir Arafat.

DOCUMENT

Arab League Recognition of the PLO

OCTOBER 28, 1974

The Seventh Arab Summit Conference after exhaustive and detailed discussions conducted by their majesties, Excellencies, and Highnesses, the Kings, Presidents and Amirs on the Arab situation in general and the Palestine problem in particular, within their national and international frameworks; and after hearing the statements submitted by His Majesty King Hussein, King of the Hashemite Kingdom of Jordan and His Excellency Brother Yasir Arafat, Chairman of the Palestine Liberation Organization, and after the statements of their Majesties and Excellencies the Kings and Presidents, in an atmosphere of candour and sincerity and full responsibility; and in view of the Arab leaders' appreciation of the joint national responsibility required of them at present for confronting aggression and performing duties of liberation, enjoined by the unity of the Arab cause and the unity of its struggle; and in view of the fact that all are aware of Zionist schemes still being made to eliminate the Palestinian existence and to obliterate the Palestinian national entity; and in view of the Arab leaders' belief in the necessity to frustrate these attempts and schemes and to counteract them by supporting and strengthening this Palestinian national entity, by providing all requirements to develop and increase its ability to ensure that the Palestinian people recover their rights in full; and by meeting responsibilities of close cooperation with its brothers within the framework of collective Arab commitment;

And in light of the victories achieved by Palestinian struggle in the confrontation with the Zionist enemy, at the Arab and international levels, at the United Nations, and of the obligation imposed thereby to continue joint Arab action to develop and increase the scope of these victories; and having received the views of all on all the above, and having succeeded in cooling the differences between brethren within the framework of consolidating Arab solidarity, the Seventh Arab Summit Conference resolves the following:

1. To affirm the right of the Palestinian people to self-determination and to return to their homeland;
2. To affirm the right of the Palestinian people to establish an independent national authority under the command of the Palestine Liberation Organization, the sole legitimate representative of the Palestinian people in any Palestinian territory that is liberated. This authority, once it is established, shall enjoy the support of the Arab states in all fields and at all levels;
3. To support the Palestine Liberation Organization in the exercise of its responsibility at the national and international levels within the framework of Arab commitment;
4. To call on the Hashemite Kingdom of Jordan, the Syrian Arab Republic, the Arab Republic of Egypt and the Palestine Liberation Organization to devise a formula for the regulation of relations between them in the light of these decisions so as to ensure their implementation;
5. That all the Arab states undertake to defend Palestinian national unity and not to interfere in the internal affairs of Palestinian action.

SOURCE: Library of Congress, Congressional Research Service, Foreign Affairs and National Defense Division, *The Search for Peace in the Middle East: Documents and Statements, 1967–1979.* Report Prepared for the Subcommittee on Europe and the Middle East of the Committee on Foreign Affairs, U.S. House of Representatives (Washington, D.C.: Government Printing Office, 1979), 273.

DOCUMENT

Arafat Speech to the UN General Assembly

NOVEMBER 13, 1974

[Note: In the first portion of his address, Arafat offered his view of the ancient and recent history of Palestine and described what he termed "Zionist terrorism" against Palestinian Arabs.]

56. For the past 30 years, our people have had to struggle against British occupation and Zionist invasion, both of which had one intention, namely, the usurpation of our

land. Six major revolts and tens of popular uprisings were staged to foil these attempts, so that our homeland might remain ours. Over 30,000 martyrs, the equivalent in comparative terms of 6 million Americans, died in the process.

57. When the majority of the Palestinian people was uprooted from its homeland in 1948, the Palestinian struggle for self-determination continued under the most difficult conditions. We tried every possible means to continue our political struggle to attain our national rights, but to no avail. Meanwhile, we had to struggle for sheer existence. Even in exile we educated our children. This was all a part of trying to survive.

58. The Palestinian people produced thousands of physicians, lawyers, teachers and scientists who actively participated in the development of the Arab countries bordering on their usurped homeland. They utilized their income to assist the young and aged amongst their people who remained in the refugee camps. They educated their younger sisters and brothers, supported their parents and cared for their children. All along, the Palestinian dreamt of return. Neither the Palestinian's allegiance to Palestine nor his determination to return waned; nothing could persuade him to relinquish his Palestinian identity or to forsake his homeland. The passage of time did not make him forget, as some hoped he would. When our people lost faith in the international community, which persisted in ignoring its rights, and when it became obvious that the Palestinians would not recuperate one inch of Palestine through exclusively political means, our people had no choice but to resort to armed struggle. Into that struggle it poured its material and human resources. We bravely faced the most vicious acts of Israeli terrorism, which were aimed at diverting our struggle and arresting it.

59. In the past 10 years of our struggle, thousands of martyrs and twice as many wounded, maimed and imprisoned were offered in sacrifice, all in an effort to resist the imminent threat of liquidation, to regain our right to self-determination and our undisputed right to return to our homeland. With the utmost dignity and the most admirable revolutionary spirit, our Palestinian people has not lost its spirit in Israeli prisons and concentration camps or when faced with all forms of harassment and intimidation. It struggles for sheer existence and it continues to strive to preserve the Arab character of its land. Thus it resists oppression, tyranny and terrorism in their ugliest forms.

60. It is through our popular armed struggle that our political leadership and our national institutions finally crystallized and a national liberation movement, comprising all the Palestinian factions, organizations and capabilities, materialized in the PLO.

61. Through our militant Palestine national liberation movement, our people's struggle matured and grew enough to accommodate political and social struggle in addition to armed struggle. The PLO was a major factor in creating a new Palestinian individual, qualified to shape the future of our Palestine, not merely content with mobilizing the Palestinians for the challenges of the present.

62. The PLO can be proud of having a large number of cultural and educational activities, even while engaged in armed struggle, and at a time when it faced increasingly vicious blows of Zionist terrorism. We established institutes for scientific research, agricultural development and social welfare, as well as centers for the revival of our cultural heritage and the preservation of our folklore. Many Palestinian poets, artists and writers have enriched Arab culture in particular, and world culture generally. Their profoundly humane works have won the admiration of all those familiar with them. In contrast to that, our enemy has been systematically destroying our culture and dis-

seminating racist, imperialist ideologies; in short, everything that impedes progress, justice, democracy and peace.

63. The PLO has earned its legitimacy because of the sacrifice inherent in its pioneering role, and also because of its dedicated leadership of the struggle. It has also been granted this legitimacy by the Palestinian masses, which in harmony with it have chosen it to lead the struggle according to its directives. The PLO has also gained its legitimacy by representing every faction, union or group as well as every Palestinian talent, either in the National Council or in people's institutions. This legitimacy was further strengthened by the support of the entire Arab nation, and it was consecrated during the last Arab Summit Conference, which reiterated the right of the PLO, in its capacity as the sole representative of the Palestinian people, to establish an independent national State on all liberated Palestinian territory.

64. Moreover, the legitimacy of the PLO was intensified as a result of fraternal support given by other liberation movements and by friendly, like-minded nations that stood by our side, encouraging and aiding us in our struggle to secure our national rights.

65. Here I must also warmly convey the gratitude of our revolutionary fighters and that of our people to the non-aligned countries, the socialist countries, the Islamic countries, the African countries and friendly European countries, as well as all our other friends in Asia, Africa and Latin America.

66. The PLO represents the Palestinian people, legitimately and uniquely. Because of this, the PLO expresses the wishes and hopes of its people. Because of this, too, it brings these very wishes and hopes before you, urging you not to shirk the momentous historic responsibility towards our just cause.

67. For many years now our people has been exposed to the ravages of war, destruction and dispersion. It has paid in the blood of its sons that which cannot ever be compensated. It has borne the burdens of occupation, dispersion, eviction and terror more uninterruptedly than any other people. And yet all this has made our people neither vindictive nor vengeful. Nor has it caused us to resort to the racism of our enemies. Nor have we lost the true method by which friend and foe are distinguished.

68. For we deplore all those crimes committed against the Jews; we also deplore all the real discrimination suffered by them because of their faith.

69. I am a rebel and freedom is my cause. I know well that many of you present here today once stood in exactly the same resistance position as I now occupy and from which I must fight. You once had to convert dreams into reality by your struggle. Therefore you must now share my dream. I think this is exactly why I can ask you now to help, as together we bring out our dream into a bright reality, our common dream for a peaceful future in Palestine's sacred land.

70. As he stood in an Israeli military court, the Jewish revolutionary, Ahud Adif, said: "I am no terrorist; I believe that a democratic State should exist on this land." Adif now languishes in a Zionist prison among his co-believers. To him and his colleagues I send my heartfelt good wishes.

71. And before those same courts there stands today a brave prince of the church, Bishop Capucci. Lifting his fingers to form the same victory sign used by our freedom-fighters, he said: "What I have done, I have done that all men may live on this land of peace in peace." This princely priest will doubtless share Adif's grim fate. To him we send our salutations and greetings.

72. Why therefore should I not dream and hope? For is not revolution the making real of dreams and hopes? So let us work together that my dream may be fulfilled, that I may return with my people out of exile, there in Palestine to live with this Jewish freedom-fighter and his partners, with this Arab priest and his brothers, in one democratic State where Christian, Jew and Muslim live in justice, equality and fraternity.

73. Is this not a noble dream worthy of my struggle alongside all lovers of freedom everywhere? For the most admirable dimension of this dream is that it is Palestinian, a dream from out of the land of peace, the land of martyrdom and heroism, and the land of history, too.

74. Let us remember that the Jews of Europe and the United States have been known to lead the struggles for secularism and the separation of Church and State. They have also been known to fight against discrimination on religious grounds. How can they then refuse this humane paradigm for the Holy Land? How then can they continue to support the most fanatic, discriminatory and closed of nations in its policy?

75. In my formal capacity as Chairman of the PLO and leader of the Palestinian revolution I proclaim before you that when we speak of our common hopes for the Palestine of tomorrow we include in our perspective all Jews now living in Palestine who choose to live with us there in peace and without discrimination.

76. In my formal capacity as Chairman of the PLO and leader of the Palestinian revolution I call upon Jews to turn away one by one from the illusory promises made to them by Zionist ideology and Israeli leadership. They are offering Jews perpetual bloodshed, endless war and continuous thralldom.

77. We invite them to emerge from their moral isolation into a more open realm of free choice, far from their present leadership's efforts to implant in them a Masada complex.

78. We offer them the most generous solution, that we might live together in a framework of just peace in our democratic Palestine.

79. In my formal capacity as Chairman of the PLO I announce here that we do not wish one drop of either Arab or Jewish blood to be shed; neither do we delight in the continuation of killing, which would end once a just peace, based on our people's rights, hopes and aspirations had been finally established.

80. In my formal capacity as Chairman of the PLO and leader of the Palestinian revolution I appeal to you to accompany our people in its struggle to attain its right to self-determination. This right is consecrated in the United Nations Charter and has been repeatedly confirmed in resolutions adopted by this august body since the drafting of the Charter. I appeal to you, further, to aid our people's return to its homeland from an involuntary exile imposed upon it by force of arms, by tyranny, by oppression, so that we may regain our property, our land, and thereafter live in our national homeland, free and sovereign, enjoying all the privileges of nationhood. Only then can we pour all our resources into the mainstream of human civilization. Only then can Palestinian creativity be concentrated on the service of humanity. Only then will our Jerusalem resume its historic role as a peaceful shrine for all religions.

81. I appeal to you to enable our people to establish national independent sovereignty over its own land.

82. Today I have come bearing an olive branch and a freedom-fighter's gun. Do not let the olive branch fall from my hand. I repeat: do not let the olive branch fall from my hand.

83. War flares up in Palestine, and yet it is in Palestine that peace will be born. . . .

SOURCE: United Nations Information System on the Question of Palestine, http://domino.un.org/UNISPAL. NSF/9a798adbf322aff38525617b006d88d7/a238ec7a3e13eed18525624a007697ec!OpenDocument.

The First Intifada

DOCUMENT IN CONTEXT

The Israeli occupation of the Gaza Strip and West Bank, including East Jerusalem, has been marked by two periods of intense protest by Palestinians. Each of these uprisings, or intifadas ("shaking off"), prompted renewed international efforts to resolve the underlying conflict between the Israelis and the Palestinians.

The first intifada erupted in December 1987. The proximate cause was the death of four Palestinians, killed when a truck driven by an Israeli ran into the vehicles in which they sat at an Israeli checkpoint at the Gaza border on December 8. The next day, thousands of Palestinians turned out in Gaza for the funeral of three of the men; large demonstrations followed, eventually leading to confrontations between Palestinians—many of them wielding stones and sticks—and Israeli security forces. Conflict escalated rapidly on both sides as groups of Palestinians sought to provoke the Israelis, and the Israelis employed increasingly tough measures.

The intifada initially appeared to be spontaneous, but within days Palestinian factions began organizing the rebellion. The Unified National Leadership Command (UNLC) of the Intifada, consisting of local representatives of four groups belonging to the Palestine Liberation Organization (PLO), coalesced and began issuing regular leaflets, or communiqués, calling for collective action against the Israeli occupation. The command's third communiqué, dated January 18, 1988, is typical of others in its call for civil disobedience against the occupation and its florid praise for Palestinian "martyrs," people killed or wounded by the Israelis: "A thousand thousand salutations, endless honor and glory, exaltation and eternal life to you and our people's martyrs, heroes of the uprising, who saturate the soil of the beloved homeland with rivers of your spilt blood, hoist the banners of freedom and independence, and with your pure shed blood pave the way to victory and the independent state under the leadership of the great and powerful PLO." Among other things, this leaflet—the first to be specifically authorized by the PLO leadership—also calls on Palestinians in all sectors of society to stop working for Israelis, to boycott Israeli products, to close streets to impede the Israeli army and settlers, and to assist in aid and information operations.

The mix of tactics advocated in this and other communiqués reflects, in part, different approaches among the Palestinian factions. In addition to the Unified Command's leaflets, individual factions and for a time Hamas (formed in December 1987 after the intifada had began) disseminated their own, competing communiqués. Although Hamas did not agree with the Unified Command's program of nonviolence, it cooperated with the uprising's leadership. Regardless of the source, many of the intifada's leaflets dealt with long-term political issues, such as demands for Israel's withdrawal from the West Bank and Gaza Strip and the release of prisoners held by the Israelis.

Although most of the early communiqués stressed nonviolent resistance—such as strikes and nonpayment of taxes and fines—the emotion-laden atmosphere often resulted in violence, in part because the stepped-up presence of Israeli soldiers created flashpoints for confrontation. The Palestinians purposely avoided the use of guns against the Israelis. Instead youths confronted Israeli soldiers primarily with stones; some occasionally used knives, broken glass, and Molotov cocktails in attacks on security forces and civilians in the occupied territories. According to the Israeli military, from December 1987 through 1991 only twelve of its soldiers died as a result of confrontations with Palestinians.

The outbreak of the intifada caught the Israeli government off-guard. Despite some Israeli assertions to the contrary, the uprising clearly represented the release of pent-up grievances after two decades of military occupation, including humiliating treatment of Palestinians by Israelis on a daily basis. Defense Minister Yitzhak Rabin adopted a hard-line approach and was reported to have told his troops to "break their [Palestinian] bones," a statement Rabin later denied having made. In a speech to the Knesset on December 23, Rabin said the Palestinians' actions "will achieve nothing. . . . Here we will fight united in all our strength—and it is substantial—against any element that attempts through violence to undermine our complete rule in Judea, Samaria [Israeli terms for the West Bank] and the Gaza District."

International media coverage of Israel's harsh suppression of the intifada led to widespread outrage, even among traditional supporters of Israel in the United States and other Western countries. The UN Security Council on December 22, 1987, adopted Resolution 605, the first of several resolutions condemning the crackdown. The United States, which often vetoed resolutions critical of Israel, supported this one.

The intifada led the administration of President Ronald Reagan, which had generally avoided involvement in the Middle East following its disastrous experience in Lebanon in 1983, to mount a new peace initiative in March 1988. As outlined by Secretary of State George Shultz, it called for an international conference leading to negotiations toward self-rule by the Palestinians. The administration quickly dropped the initiative, however, in the face of reluctance by the PLO and adamant opposition by Israeli prime minister Yitzhak Shamir (U.S. Involvement in Lebanon, p. 339).

The intifada raged for more than three years before sputtering out during 1991 for a variety of reasons, including inadequate leadership by the PLO and the frustration of many Palestinians who lost their jobs, and even their family members, without any concrete gains. Although Israeli-Palestinian violence continued during the 1990s, the intifada itself ended in 1993, the year that Israel and the PLO signed a landmark peace agreement. B'Tselem, an Israeli human rights group, tallied deaths during the intifada as 1,067 Palestinians killed by Israeli security forces; 54 Israeli soldiers and policemen killed by Palestinians; 67 Palestinians killed by Israeli civilians (many of them settlers in the territories); and 97 Israeli civilians killed by Palestinians. More than 300 other Palestinians died at the hands of fellow Palestinians, in many cases for allegedly collaborating with Israeli authorities, according to B'Tselem's figures. In addition, thousands of people—most of them Palestinians—were injured during the intifada, many of them crippled for life. The intifada also had severe economic consequences for the Palestinians. Shops closed sometimes for days or even weeks at a time because of demonstrations and strikes, Israeli military actions, or threats and activities by Palestinians; fields and orchards were burned. Thousands of Palestinians went without work or were prevented from going to their jobs.

Beyond the violence, the loss of income, and the radicalizing effect on thousands of Palestinian youths, the intifada reshaped the basic landscape of relations between Israelis and Palestinians as well as those between the Palestinians and influential international forces. One of the first such changes was a decision by King Hussein in June 1988 to abandon Jordan's claim to sovereignty over the West Bank, a move that undercut Israel's insistence on using Jordan as the intermediary for any diplomatic dealings with the Palestinians. In November 1988, the PLO issued a declaration of Palestinian "independence," officially embracing the idea of a "two-state solution" to the conflict, with Israel and a Palestinian state living side-by-side. In mid-December 1988 PLO chairman Yasir Arafat for the first time renounced the use of violence against Israel, opening the way for official contacts between the United States and the PLO. Over the longer term, the intifada created the pressures that led Israel and the PLO to begin secret talks in January 1993 that produced an agreement between them in September 1993. The ultimate failure of all these steps toward peace led to a second, more violent, intifada beginning in 2000 (Jordan Relinquishes the West Bank, p. 200; Oslo Accords, p. 213; Camp David and the al-Aqsa Intifada, p. 276).

Following is the text of a statement by Israeli defense minister Yitzhak Rabin to the Knesset on December 23, 1987, and the text of "Communiqué No. 3" issued by the Palestine Liberation Organization and the United National Command of the Uprising on January 18, 1988.

DOCUMENT

Rabin on the Intifada

DECEMBER 23, 1987

For the past two weeks, we have been facing a continuous series of civil disorders, exceptional in their scope, force and intensity in Judea, Samaria, [the West Bank] and the Gaza District. At week's end, these grave events spread to Jerusalem, and two days ago, Israeli Arabs also joined the violent disorders. It is my hope that this was an exceptional event not to be repeated.

We have already experienced disturbances and terrorist attacks in the past. However, one cannot ignore the unusual severity of the events of the past two weeks—

both from the viewpoint of the large number of Arab residents who took part in some of the events, the scope of events throughout the area, and the extent of the continuity and duration of these events, which indeed have yet to end.

The tension and intense alertness in the field have not yet faded away: the atmosphere still enables the small number of extremists to incite and to draw the masses into additional riots. This is not the time or the place to enter into an analysis and assessment of the general circumstances and the specific reasons which formed the background to the outburst of the violent and unusual series of events such as we have not seen for many years. We must face this phenomenon with our eyes wide open—to recognize the fact of its existence and to find the suitable ways to end it now and prevent its recurrence in the future, with the goal of providing security for all residents.

All Israeli governments, without exception, have determined that the legal and political status of the area of Judea, Samaria and the Gaza District will not be subject to a unilateral and decisive Israeli act. This is in order to prove our desire for peace on our eastern border as well: peace that will be obtained through direct bilateral negotiations with Jordan and the Palestinian residents in the territories who are not identified as PLO [Palestine Liberation Organization] personnel. We will not hold negotiations with the PLO terrorist organization.

Since the end of the Six Day War, the territories have been under military rule through a Military Government and a Civil Administration. The policies which are carried out by the government are interwoven: an all-out war against PLO terrorism on the one hand, while maintaining public law and order for all residents, and, on the other hand, providing assistance to improve the quality of life for all those who want to live in peace.

The violent public disorders during the past two weeks broke out against a backdrop of local events, and were the fruits of spontaneous organization. The PLO terrorist organizations and activists in the territories seized on this wave of events and did everything they could, both inside and outside the territories, in order to heighten and intensify the events. The Arab media, particularly those of the extremist Arab states, were filled with calls to residents of the territories to violate law and order violently and acutely. The Arab press in East Jerusalem was full of incitement, direct and indirect, to continue the demonstrations.

The standing of the Palestinian terrorist organizations were badly damaged in the Arab world and the international community as a result of the resolutions passed at the Arab summit conference in Amman. These resolutions signalled the Arab world, and the entire world, that the priorities of the majority in the Arab world are preventing the spread of Islamic extremism of a Khomeinist stripe, and the continuation of the Iran-Iraq war. Based on the resolutions made at the Amman summit conference, handling of a solution to the Arab-Israeli conflict was downgraded on the scale of priorities.

One can add to the failure of the PLO terrorist organizations and their goal of increasing terrorist activity against Israel prior to the summit and during its meeting.

For the terrorist organizations and their leaders, the events that took place in the past two weeks were like a life line for their pan-Arab and international standing. The PLO therefore made exceptional efforts to incite and organize continued violent public disorders.

In the face of this, Israel is determined to prevent violent public disorders and to increase activity against PLO terrorist elements wherever they are found. This mission is assigned to IDF [Israel Defense Forces] forces, the Border Police, and the other security arms. The objective of the overall activity of these forces is to make unequivocally clear, both in words and in deeds, to the residents of the territories, the Arab states, and the international community that the path leading to war, threats of war, terror and violent public disorder will achieve nothing. To the contrary, the continuation of violent public disorder and terror will cause suffering, pain and hardships for those who initiate or are involved in the disorders.

Gaza and Hebron, Ramallah and Nablus are not and will not become Beirut, Sidon and Tyre. Here we will fight united in all our strength—and it is substantial—against any element that attempts through violence to undermine our complete rule in Judea, Samaria and the Gaza District. Peace on our eastern border and we all want this—will be achieved only at the negotiating table with Jordan and residents of the territories.

With the aim of bringing about calm in the territories and restoring a sense of security for all the residents living there, the security forces are acting with all the means at our disposal within the framework of, and subject to, the law. In accordance with this, security forces will apply all the means and methods against the inciters, the organizers, and those participating in the violent disorders.

I want to note some of the principal directives which exist for the IDF and the other security arms acting in the territories.

1. A concentration of large forces, as deemed necessary by the IDF command at any given time.
2. Activating relatively large forces against a violent disturbance as promptly as possible, with the goal of aborting it.
3. While dealing with violent public disorders—to warn those who are disturbing the peace and allow them to disperse peacefully. If there is no response to the warning, to employ in the first stage means such as tear gas and rubber bullets fired by the guns of IDF soldiers. And if these, too, cannot disperse a violent demonstration, and rioters are endangering IDF soldiers and Border Police in carrying out their missions, they are permitted to fire with the intention of wounding those leading the riots and throwing petrol bombs, initially at their legs, as far as this is possible, and this only after shots in the air have also failed to disperse the rioters.

As defense minister, I am responsible for the lives and well-being of IDF soldiers and the Border Police acting alongside them. It is my obligation to provide them with the ability to defend themselves while carrying out the missions they have been charged with, including the use of their weapons with intent to wound those attempting to strike at their lives and their well-being.

4. There are no restrictions on the military commanders responsible for Judea, Samaria and Gaza concerning implementation of the punishment of deportation and administrative detention against the inciters and the organizers of the violent disturbances and the terrorism. This, subject to the limitations of the legal procedures prescribed by law.

There are no restrictions on the O/C's [officers in command] of Southern and Central Commands to impose curfew for a defined period in order to prevent a violent disturbance or for any action required to maintain public law and order. In accordance with the existing regulations, greater freedom will be permitted for closing institutions which serve as hothouses for incitement to terrorism and disruption of the public order, such as educational institutions and others. At the same time, we will give full assistance to all those in the territories who wish to continue pursuing a normal life [there], and those who wish to leave for work in Israel.

I know that the depictions of the events in the territories, as these have found expression in the foreign media, are not contributing to Israel's image in many countries. Nevertheless, I am convinced that beyond the temporary problem of our image, the supreme duty incumbent upon the government, the defense establishment and the forces of the IDF, is to combat the violence in the territories and prevent it with all the means at our disposal within the framework of the law. This we shall do, and I am convinced that we shall be successful.

I want to say a few words to the Israeli Arabs. In the course of a generation you have passed the test of loyalty to the State of Israel, and with the exception of isolated and exceptional cases, you were unblemished. You were and you are part of us. I permit myself to propose to you not to be dragged after incitement, not to be tempted by calls to do harm and to demonstrate, and to remain as you have been until now: loyal, and leading a tranquil life.

In the remote past you knew a tragedy, and it will be best for you and for us if you do not revert to it or repeat it.

Even at this hour I find it needful as well as my duty to appeal to the Palestinian inhabitants in Judea, Samaria and Gaza, not to be tempted by the incitement of the leaders of the PLO terrorist organization. Your leaders, from the Mufti Haj Amin al-Husseini to Arafat, have led you from one disaster to another. Every time you followed them you encountered failures in which you, more than others, were the chief victims.

In the events to date 21 Arab residents have been killed and 158 wounded. Your life has been disrupted. In addition, 31 IDF soldiers and Border Policemen have been wounded, as well as 19 Israeli civilians. You will achieve nothing through violence and terrorism. You have no chance of coping in this manner with the Israel Defense Forces and the other security forces. The only way for a solution of the Arab-Israeli conflict, and within that framework, a solution of the Palestinian problem, is via negotiations for peace.

Members of the Knesset,

I wish to express from this rostrum my esteem and appreciation to the soldiers and officers of the IDF, the Israel Police, the Border Police and the other security branches which are operating on behalf of the government to prevent violence wherever it may be found, and to maintain the law, security and order for all the inhabitants of the territories, Jerusalem and Israel.

I call for a joint and united stand behind the IDF and the security forces in their mission. Let us strengthen them in the activity for their success, the success of us all.

SOURCE: Israel Ministry of Foreign Affairs, www.mfa.gov.il/MFA/Foreign%20Relations/Israels%20Foreign%20Relations%20since%201947/1984-1988/312%20Statement%20in%20the%20Knesset%20by%20Defense%20Minister%20R.

DOCUMENT

Communiqué No. 3

JANUARY 18, 1988

No voice will overcome the voice of the uprising
No voice will overcome the voice of the Palestinian people—the people of the PLO

Communiqué No. 3

Issued by the Palestine Liberation Organization/The United National Command of the Uprising

O masses of the magnificent Palestinian people, O masses of the stone and the Molotov cocktail, O soldiers of justice who are taking part in the uprising of our heroic people! May your arms of steel be strengthened, O heroes, may your hands be strengthened, O workers and *fellahin* [farm workers and peasants], students, merchants, and women . . . May your valiant arms be strengthened, O lion cubs of Palestine, O generation of the future, O builders of the independent Palestinian state! May your arms be strengthened, O young commanders, the new generals of our people! Blessed be this glorious people, which has registered the most magnificent spectacles of struggle, this people that heeded the call to duty, the call of the PLO and of the United National Command of the Uprising, which shook the ground from under the feet of the occupation during the past week.

Salutations of pride and honor to the masses of this struggling people, salutations of respect and admiration for the precious victims, the sacrifice in every sector of our generous people, salutations of challenge, steadfastness and pride, salutations of the resistance that the children of the stone and the Molotov cocktail are inscribing in the history of our people and the contemporary revolution.

Salutations to you, descendants of al-Qassam, salutations to the spearhead that repulses the enemy's soldiers in the byways of the camps, villages, and towns throughout our occupied homeland.

Salutations of the wound that triumphs over the knife of Shamir, Sharon, and Peres and stands proudly against their war machine, their armored vehicles, their airplanes, and their suffocating and poisonous bombs.

A thousand thousand salutations, endless honor and glory, exaltation and eternal life to you and our people's martyrs, heroes of the uprising, who saturate the soil of the beloved homeland with rivers of your spilt blood, hoist the banners of freedom and independence, and with your pure shed blood pave the way to victory and the independent state under the leadership of the great and powerful PLO.

For the millionth time we reiterate: may your hands be strengthened, heroes, in Sheykh Radwan, Kafr Nue'ima, Rafah, Bittin, Jabalya, Qalqilya, in the camps, the villages, the neighborhoods, and the byways. We reaffirm our esteem and our pride in the masses, who in an uplifted and united voice called out:

With spirit and blood we will redeem you O shahid…
With spirit and blood we will redeem you O Palestine.

To the masses of our glorious people:

On the way to the escalation and continuation of the uprising, on the way to the removal of the occupation and the realization of the slogans of the uprising, we urge the national action committees and the popular committees to ensure the escalation and advancement of the victorious popular uprising by declaring a general and comprehensive strike from the morning of Tuesday, January 19, 1988, until the eve of Friday, January 22, 1988.

Let our people remain in their houses on Wednesday and Thursday, let the prayers, the symbolic funerals, and the vociferous popular demonstrations resume on Friday to commemorate the martyrs of the uprising. Let the bells sound in the churches in all the villages and towns throughout the occupied homeland.

O heroic merchants,

You who have recorded a glorious and honorable struggle with steadfastness, you who experience the arbitrariness of the occupation and its daily repression. You who valiantly defy the closure orders, the brandished rods, the war machines, and the armed soldiers, you who maintain a commercial strike despite all the measures of the occupation, we salute you and your central role in our people's uprising and in the victories that are achieved every day.

We urge you to observe the general strike that has been called even if the army increases its presence and in spite of the measures it will take. We further urge you to continue establishing and expanding special committees for merchants in every street and city, village, and camp, in order to formulate a united stand and form a united plan that will endorse a collective abstention from paying V.A.T. With all the masses of the people and its national movement behind you, the threats and measures of the occupation, whatever they may be, will not succeed in dissuading you from implementing this slogan, which is one of the paramount slogans of our people's heroic uprising.

O masses of our people from all sectors and strata,

From this day we will begin to boycott Israeli merchandise and products that our industry also manufactures. We note especially the boycott on Israeli chocolates, milk, and cigarettes.

O masses of the Palestinian working class,

Indeed the bronzed arms of steel have succeeded, by virtue of their broad and active participation in the general strike, in bringing to a stop the production line and the wheels of industry in thousands of Israeli plants, projects, and workshops. The pioneering role of the workers in the uprising was prominent and honorable. Persist in your labor strikes in Israeli plants, our valiant workers. Do not be intimidated by the frightened threats being voiced by the Zionists, authorities, rulers, and owners. All we have to lose in our uprising are the chains, the suppression, and the exploitation that we groan under. Let the wheels of Israeli industry grind to a halt through damaging the Israeli economy and deepening the economic crisis in Israel. This is one of our weapons on the road to attaining our rights of return, self-determination, and establishment of the independent national state.

O masses of heroic pupils,

You who disturbed the rest of the occupiers for years, let us teach the occupation a lesson it will never forget, we will teach the occupation that its policy of closing down educational institutions, universities, institutes, and schools will bring it nothing but trouble. Just recently the occupation authorities closed down all the educational institutions. Let us transform the masses of students in the villages, the camps, and the cities, mobilizing them for the school of revolution, the schools of the struggle in the streets, so that they can help shake and burn the ground under the feet of the occupiers. Let us therefore organize the ranks and mobilize all the student forces from the schools of the struggle in order to escalate and advance our people's heroic uprising.

Our heroic taxi and bus drivers and owners of taxi companies,

Having seen your actions in previous strikes, the United National Command calls on you to desist from activity completely in all places on the strike days, with the exception of Friday. We urge you to cooperate with the national and popular committees and to punish the few drivers who do not accede to the obligatory call.

To the sector of doctors and health services,

We call on you to remain vigilant and to join immediately the medical committees and bodies that are organizing medical-aid activities in the camps and besieged locales that have been adversely affected. We also call on all doctors, pharmacists, male nurses, and lab technicians to take part in these aid actions in the camps and in the occupied areas where the medical situation is poor and disease is rampant due to siege, the starving of the population, and the use of noxious and suffocating gas.

To the owners of the warehouses and the drugs industry and the pharmacies,

We call on you to contribute medicines and equipment to the medical committees and the medical bodies to enable our wounded to receive free treatment.

To the owners of the national capital and all persons of means,

We call on you to take a substantial part in contributing merchandise and goods as well as funds, in order to supply food to the camps and the besieged areas that have been adversely affected. Contributions should be made to the national and popular committees and to the local supply committees [lijan al-tamwin].

To the academics and practitioners of the various professions,

The uprising needs the effort of each and every one of you. You must join the national and popular committees and the functional committees, take an active part in the uprising, in the supply and aid operations, or do literary writing, compose poems, sons, and slogans, take part in information campaigns, organize marches and sit-down strikes against the occupation policy.

The PLO and the Uprising Command take pride in the large forces of the masses that have been given expression in our people's heroic uprising. We urge you to continue escalating the uprising in accordance with the mission sand slogans already determined. We also call for the closing of all the streets—main and side streets—in the villages, camps, and towns to prevent the movement of soldiers on these streets. Likewise the closing of the roads leading to settlements in order to block the access of the settlers.

Let Palestinian flags be raised over every house and building, over the churches and the turrets of the mosques.

We say yes to our people's right of return, self-determination, and building an independent national state.

Victory to the uprising of our people, down with the occupation! Glory and eternal life to our people's virtuous martyrs!

The Palestine Liberation Organization
The United National Command of the Uprising in the Occupied Territories
January 18, 1988

SOURCE: Shaul Mishal and Reuben Aharoni. *Speaking Stones: Communiqués from the Intifada Underground.* Syracuse: Syracuse University Press, 1994.

Jordan Relinquishes the West Bank

DOCUMENT IN CONTEXT

Nearly four decades after King Abdallah declared Jordanian sovereignty over the West Bank, his grandson King Hussein formally relinquished all claims to the potato-shaped territory to the west of the Jordan River in July 1988. Hussein's action ended an often-troubled relationship between the government in Amman and the Palestinian Arabs living on the West Bank, some of whom had fled Israel at the time of the 1948 Arab-Israeli war and many of whom had relatives among the Palestinian majority of Jordan's population (Founding of the State of Israel, p. 67).

Between King Abdallah's annexation of the West Bank in 1949 and King Hussein's renunciation of it in 1988, most West Bank Palestinians held Jordanian citizenship. The Israeli occupation of the West Bank, along with the Sinai Peninsula and Golan Heights following the June 1967 Arab-Israeli war, did not alter Palestinians' citizenship status. The government of Jordan continued to pay the salaries of thousands of West Bank civil servants, and King Hussein saw himself as the legal guardian of the rights of residents on the West Bank (June 1967 Arab–Israeli War, p. 94).

The relationship between King Hussein and Palestinian leaders was often a strained one. The low point came in 1970, when Palestinian guerrillas hijacked four European airliners and flew three of them to Jordan. Hussein responded with a crackdown on the Palestine Liberation Organization (PLO) and other groups, provoking a brief civil war that almost drew in Syria. In 1971 the king drove most of the Palestinian fighters into Lebanon, where their presence would contribute four years later to the outbreak of the long and bloody Lebanese civil war (Lebanese Civil War, p. 331).

Despite his conflicts with the PLO leadership, King Hussein continued to claim to represent the Palestinian people as a whole. He lost that claim on October 28, 1974, when Arab leaders, at a summit in Rabat, Morocco, recognized the PLO as the "sole legitimate representative" of the Palestinian people (Arab Recognition of the PLO, p. 185). The severing of ties between Jordan and the West Bank arose within the context of the first Palestinian intifada, or uprising, that began in December 1987. By mid-1988, with turmoil in the Palestinian territories threatening to spill over into Jordan, Hussein decided to distance his country, and his throne, from the upheaval. On July 31, 1988, Hussein announced in a radio and television broadcast that he was breaking all "legal and administrative links" with the West Bank. The king said he was acting "in response to the wish of the Palestine Liberation Organization" as well as to what he called a "general Palestinian and Arab orientation" to "highlight the Palestinian identity" separate from that of Jordan. If only indirectly, he also acknowledged another reason for this step: "safeguarding national unity," which in the context of events meant protecting Jordan from the instability on the West Bank. Hussein remarked that "stable and productive societies are those where orderliness and discipline prevail."

The king's action immediately eliminated Jordan's subsidizing of salaries for Palestinian civil servants in the West Bank; according to one estimate, about one-fifth of the money used to pay the territory's 16,000 teachers, administrators, and other officials came from Jordan. Hussein also dissolved the Jordanian parliament, almost one-half of whose members represented the West Bank, and called for new elections to select a parliament exclusively representing Jordan.

By severing ties to the West Bank, the king also undermined any remaining Israeli hope for the "Jordanian option," returning parts of the West Bank to Jordan. Many Israelis, particularly in the center-left Labor Party, for years had advocated such an option as an alternative to the independent state being demanded by the Palestinians. Hussein said he remained eager to participate in an international peace conference, but his speech, and subsequent statements, made clear that Israel could no longer count on Jordan assuming responsibility for Palestinians and their affairs on the West Bank.

Following are excerpts from the July 31, 1988, address by King Hussein of Jordan relinquishing Jordanian control of the West Bank.

DOCUMENT

King Hussein on Relinquishing the West Bank

JULY 31, 1988

In the name of God, the Merciful, the Compassionate,
Peace be upon His Faithful Arab Messenger.

Brother Citizens,
I send you greetings and am pleased to address you in your cities and villages, in your camps and dwellings, in your institutions of learning, and in your places of work. I would like to address your hearts and minds in all parts of our beloved Jordanian land.

This is all the more important at this juncture, when we have initiated—after seeking God's help and after thorough and extensive study—a series of measures to enhance Palestinian national orientation and highlight Palestinian identity; our goal is the benefit of the Palestinian cause and the Arab Palestinian people.

Our decision, as you know, comes after 38 years of the unity of the two banks, and fourteen years after the [Arab League] Rabat Summit resolution [of 1974] designating the Palestine Liberation Organization (PLO) as the sole legitimate representative of the Palestinian people. It also comes six years after the Fez Summit resolution [of 1982] that agreed unanimously on the establishment of an independent Palestinian state in the occupied West Bank and the Gaza Strip as one of the bases and results of the peaceful settlement.

We are certain that our decision to initiate these measures does not come as a surprise to you. Many among you have anticipated it, and some of you have been calling for it for some time. As for its contents, it has been a topic of discussion and consideration for everyone since the Rabat Summit.

Nevertheless, some may wonder: Why now? Why today and not after the Rabat or Fez summits, for instance?

To answer this question, we need to recall certain facts that preceded the Rabat resolution. We also need to recall considerations that led to the debate over the slogan-objective which the PLO raised and worked to gain Arab and international support for. Namely, the establishment of an independent Palestinian state. This meant, in addition to the PLO's ambition to embody the Palestinian identity on Palestinian national soil, the separation of the West Bank from the Hashemite Kingdom of Jordan.

I reviewed the facts preceding the Rabat resolution, as you recall, before the Arab leaders in the Algiers Extraordinary Summit last June. It may be important to recall that one of the main facts I emphasized was the text of the unity resolution of the two banks of April 1950. This resolution affirms the preservation of all Arab rights in Palestine and the defense of such rights by all legitimate means without prejudicing the final settlement of the just cause of the Palestinian people—within the scope of the people's aspirations and of Arab cooperation and international justice.

Among these facts, there was our 1972 proposal regarding our concept of alternatives, on which the relationship between Jordan on the one hand and the West Bank and Gaza on the other, may be based after their liberation. Among these alternatives was the establishment of a relationship of brotherhood and cooperation between the Hashemite Kingdom of Jordan and the independent Palestinian state in case the Palestinian people opt for that. Simply, this means that we declared our clear-cut position regarding our adherence to the Palestinian people's right to self-determination on their national soil, including their right to establish their own independent state, more than two years before the Rabat Summit resolution. This will be our position until the Palestinian people achieve their complete national goals, God willing.

The relationship of the West Bank with the Hashemite Kingdom of Jordan in light of the PLO's call for the establishment of an independent Palestinian state, can be confined to two considerations: First, the principle consideration pertaining to the issue of Arab unity as a pan-Arab aim, which Arab peoples aspire to and want to achieve. Second, the political consideration pertaining to the extent of the Palestinian struggles from the continuation of the legal relationship to the Kingdom's two banks. Our answer to the question, "why now?" also derives from these two factors, and the background of the clear and constant Jordanian position on the Palestinian cause, as already outlined.

Regarding the principled consideration, Arab unity between any two or more countries is an option of any Arab people. This is what we believe. Accordingly, we responded to the wish of the Palestinian people's representatives for unity with Jordan in 1950. From this premise, we respect the wish of the PLO, the sole and legitimate representative of the Palestinian people, to secede from us as an independent Palestinian state. We say that while we fully understand the situation, nevertheless, Jordan will remain the proud bearer of the message of the Great Arab Revolt, adhering to its principles, believing in one Arab destiny, and committed to joint Arab action.

Regarding the political consideration, since the June 1967 aggression we have believed that our actions and efforts should be directed at liberating the land and the sanctities from Israeli occupation. Therefore, we have concentrated all our efforts over the past twenty-one years of occupation on that goal. We did not imagine that maintaining the legal and administrative relationship between the two banks could constitute an obstacle to liberating the occupied Palestinian land. Hence, in the past and before we took measures, we did not find anything requiring such measures, especially since our support for the Palestinian people's right to self-determination was clear.

Lately, it has transpired that there is a general Palestinian and Arab orientation which believes in the need to highlight the Palestinian identity in full in all efforts and activities that are related to the Palestine question and its developments. It has also become clear that there is a general conviction that maintaining the legal and administrative links with the West Bank, and the ensuing Jordanian interaction with our Palestinian brothers under occupation through Jordanian institutions in the occupied territories, contradicts this orientation. It is also viewed that these links hamper the Palestinian struggle to gain international support for the Palestinian cause of a people struggling against foreign occupation.

In view of this line of thought, which is certainly inspired by genuine Palestinian will, and Arab determination to support the Palestinian cause, it becomes our duty to be part of this direction, and to respond to its requirements. After all, we are a part of our nation, supportive of its causes, foremost among which is the Palestinian cause. Since there is a general conviction that the struggle to liberate the occupied Palestinian land could be enhanced by dismantling the legal and administrative links between the two banks, we have to fulfill our duty, and do what is required of us.

At the Rabat Summit of 1974 we responded to the Arab leaders' appeal to us to continue our interaction with the Occupied West Bank through Jordanian institutions, to support the steadfastness of our brothers there. Today we respond to the wish of the Palestine Liberation Organization, the sole legitimate representative of the Palestinian People, and to the Arab orientation to affirm the Palestinian identity in all its aspects. We pray to God that this step be a substantive addition to the intensifying Palestinian struggle for freedom and independence.

Brother Citizens,

These are the reasons, the considerations, and the convictions that led us to respond favorably to the wish of the PLO, and to the general Arab direction consistent with it. We cannot continue in this state of suspension, which can neither serve Jordan nor the Palestinian cause. We had to leave the labyrinth of fears and doubts, towards clearer horizons where mutual trust, understanding, and cooperation can prevail, to the benefit of the Palestinian cause and Arab unity. This unity will remain a goal which all the Arab peoples cherish and seek to realize.

At the same time, it has to be understood in all clarity, and without any ambiguity or equivocation, that our measures regarding the West Bank concern only the occupied Palestinian land and its people. They naturally do not relate in any way to the Jordanian citizens of Palestinian origin in the Hashemite Kingdom of Jordan. They all have the full rights of citizenship and all its obligations, the same as any other citizen irrespective of his origin. They are an integral part of the Jordanian state to which they belong, on whose soil they live, and in whose life and various activities they participate. Jordan is not Palestine and the independent Palestinian state will be established on the occupied Palestinian territory after its liberation, God willing. There the Palestinian identity will be embodied, and there the Palestinian struggle shall come to fruition, as confirmed by the glorious uprising of the Palestinian people under occupation.

If national unity in any country is dear and precious, it is for us in Jordan more than that. It is the basis of our stability and the cause of our development and prosperity, as well as the foundation of our national security and the source of our faith in the future. It is also a living embodiment of the principles of the Great Arab Revolt which we inherited and whose banner we are proudly carrying. It is also a living example of constructive plurality and a sound nucleus of wider Arab unity.

Based on that, safeguarding national unity is a sacred duty that will not be compromised. Any attempt to undermine it, under any pretext, would only help the enemy carry out his policy of expansion at the expense of Palestine and Jordan alike. Consequently, true nationalism lies in bolstering and fortifying national unity. Moreover, the responsibility to safeguard it falls on every one of you, leaving no place in our midst for sedition or treachery. With God's help, we shall be as always, a united cohesive family, whose members are joined by bonds of brotherhood, affection, awareness, and common national objectives.

It is most important to remember, as we emphasize the importance of safeguarding national unity, that stable and productive societies, are those where orderliness and discipline prevail. Discipline is the solid fabric that binds all members of a community in a solid, harmonious structure, blocking all avenues before the enemies, and opening horizons of hope for future generations.

The constructive plurality which Jordan has lived since its foundation, and through which it has witnessed progress and prosperity in all aspects of life, emanates not only from our faith in the sanctity of national unity, but also in the importance of Jordan's pan-Arab role. Jordan presents itself as the living example of the merger of various Arab groups on its soil, within the framework of good citizenship, and one Jordanian people. This paradigm that we live on our soil gives us faith in the inevitability of attaining Arab unity, God willing. . . .

To display any doubts that may arise out of our measures, we assure you that these measures do not mean the abandonment of our national duty, either towards the Arab-Israeli conflict, or towards the Palestinian cause. Nor do they mean a relinquishing our faith in Arab unity. As I have stated, these steps were taken only in response to the wish of the Palestine Liberation Organization, the sole legitimate representative of the Palestinian people, and the prevailing Arab conviction that such measures will contribute to the struggle of the Palestinian people and their glorious uprising. Jordan will continue its support for the steadfastness of the Palestinian people, and their courageous uprising in the occupied Palestinian land, within its capabilities. . . .

SOURCE: A Living Tribute to the Legacy of King Hussein I, www.kinghussein.gov.jo/88_july31.html.

The Founding of Hamas

DOCUMENT IN CONTEXT

A few days after the Palestinian intifada erupted in December 1987, a religious teacher, Sheikh Ahmed Yassin, and his followers and supporters in Gaza City founded the group Hamas. The name means "zeal" in Arabic and is an acronym for the group's formal name, Harakat al-Muqawaama al-Islamiyya, or Islamic Resistance Movement (The First Intifada, p. 191).

Yassin and his supporters were members of the Palestinian branch of the Muslim Brotherhood, an Islamist organization founded in Egypt in 1928. Although the Brotherhood had been active in the Palestinian territories, particularly in Gaza, for many years and had founded the Islamic University there, it had little influence among Palestinians until the late 1980s, when an increasing number of Palestinians began to grow frustrated with the failure of the Palestine Liberation Organization (PLO) to oust Israel from the territories. The rise of Hamas also reflected a growing interest among Palestinians in Islam—rather than the PLO's secular nationalism—as the solution to their problems.

During Hamas's early stages, Israel tolerated it, and even encouraged it. Apparently under the assumption that the group could be a useful means of weakening the PLO, Israel at first made no attempt to stop Hamas, and granted it an official permit to operate as an Islamic charity. Israel's permissive attitude toward Hamas changed in August 1988 when the group adopted its covenant. Laced with standard quotes from the Quran and other religious texts, the covenant also called for a jihad (holy war) against "the Jews' usurpation of Palestine," and it attributed nearly all of the world's recent troubles to the influence of Jews. The covenant did not specially advocate the use of violence, but it did call for the elimination of Israel. Its florid language expressed unrelenting hostility toward Jews in general and Israel in particular.

Although many of its supporters participated in the Palestinian intifada against Israel, Hamas as an organization did not take part in the official leadership of the intifada, which eventually was guided by the PLO. As the intifada wore on and Israel continued its crackdown, Hamas took a step toward radicalization in 1989, sponsoring dozens of shooting attacks against Israeli soldiers and civilians. In response, Israel arrested Yassin and sentenced him to life in prison. He was released in 1997 in an

Israeli effort to calm Arab anger after a botched attempt by Mossad, Israel's intelligence service, to kill another Hamas official, Khaled Meshel, in Jordan. In March 2004, during the second Palestinian intifada, the Israeli military assassinated Yassin and killed several supporters as they left a mosque in Gaza City. Less than one month after the killing of Yassin, Israel assassinated his successor, Abd al-Aziz Rantisi.

In 1991, Hamas had signaled its intent to escalate its attacks against Israel with the formation of the Izzedine al-Qassam Brigades, an armed wing named after a leader of the Arab revolt against British rule in Palestine during the late 1930s. The Qassam Brigades carried out its first car bombing on April 6, 1994, killing eight people in the Israeli city of Afula. Exactly one week later, the first suicide bomber sponsored by Hamas attacked Israeli civilians in Hadera, killing five people. Such high-profile suicide bombings, primarily targeting civilians, attracted international attention. Some Hamas officials called the suicide bomb the "Palestinian F-16," a reference to the U.S.-supplied warplane that had become a staple of Israel's military.

Although at the time primarily known in Israel and Western countries for its suicide bombings and other attacks against Israelis, much of Hamas's popularity in the territories, particularly in Gaza, flowed from its extensive network of schools, health clinics, and other social services. Funded by donations from Iran, some of the oil-rich Persian Gulf Arab states, and expatriate Palestinians, the Hamas network grew to offer tens of thousands of Palestinians the kinds of services that neither Israel through its occupation nor the PLO had been able or willing to provide. The popularity and necessity of these social services helped Hamas win numerous local elections in 2005 and Palestinian legislative elections in 2006 (The Hamas Government, p. 317).

Following are excerpts from the covenant of the Islamic Resistance Movement, or Hamas, adopted on August 18, 1988.

DOCUMENT

Hamas's Covenant

AUGUST 18, 1988

. . . This Covenant of the Islamic Resistance Movement (HAMAS), clarifies its picture, reveals its identity, outlines its stand, explains its aims, speaks about its hopes, and calls for its support, adoption and joining its ranks. Our struggle against the Jews is very great and very serious. It needs all sincere efforts. It is a step that inevitably should be followed by other steps. The Movement is but one squadron that should be supported by more and more squadrons from this vast Arab and Islamic world, until the enemy is vanquished and Allah's victory is realized. . . .

Definition of the Movement

Article One

The Islamic Resistance Movement: The Movement's programme is Islam. From it, it draws its ideas, ways of thinking and understanding of the universe, life and man. It resorts to it for judgment in all its conduct, and it is inspired by it for guidance of its steps. . . .

Article Two

The Islamic Resistance Movement is one of the wings of Moslem Brotherhood in Palestine. Moslem Brotherhood Movement is a universal organization which constitutes the largest Islamic movement in modern times. It is characterized by its deep understanding, accurate comprehension and its complete embrace of all Islamic concepts of all aspects of life, culture, creed, politics, economics, education, society, justice and judgment, the spreading of Islam, education, art, information, science of the occult and conversion to Islam. . . .

Article Three

The basic structure of the Islamic Resistance Movement consists of Moslems who have given their allegiance to Allah whom they truly worship,—"I have created the jinn and humans only for the purpose of worshipping"—who know their duty towards themselves, their families and country. In all that, they fear Allah and raise the banner of Jihad in the face of the oppressors, so that they would rid the land and the people of their uncleanliness, vileness and evils. . . .

Article Four

The Islamic Resistance Movement welcomes every Moslem who embraces its faith, ideology, follows its programme, keeps its secrets, and wants to belong to its ranks and carry out the duty. Allah will certainly reward such one. . . .

Article Five

Time extent of the Islamic Resistance Movement: By adopting Islam as its way of life, the Movement goes back to the time of the birth of the Islamic message, of the righteous ancestor, for Allah is its target, the Prophet is its example and the Koran is its constitution. Its extent in place is anywhere that there are Moslems who embrace Islam as their way of life everywhere in the globe. This being so, it extends to the depth of the earth and reaches out to the heaven. . . .

Article Six

The Islamic Resistance Movement is a distinguished Palestinian movement, whose allegiance is to Allah, and whose way of life is Islam. It strives to raise the banner of Allah over every inch of Palestine, for under the wing of Islam followers of all religions can coexist in security and safety where their lives, possessions and rights are concerned. In the absence of Islam, strife will be rife, oppression spreads, evil prevails and schisms and wars will break out. . . .

Article Seven

As a result of the fact that those Moslems who adhere to the ways of the Islamic Resistance Movement spread all over the world, rally support for it and its stands, strive towards enhancing its struggle, the Movement is a universal one. It is well-equipped for that because of the clarity of its ideology, the nobility of its aim and the loftiness of its objectives.

On this basis, the Movement should be viewed and evaluated, and its role be recognized. He who denies its right, evades supporting it and turns a blind eye to facts, whether intentionally or unintentionally, would awaken to see that events have overtaken him and with no logic to justify his attitude. One should certainly learn from past examples. . . .

The Islamic Resistance Movement is one of the links in the chain of the struggle against the Zionist invaders. It goes back to 1939, to the emergence of the martyr Izz al-Din al Kissam and his brethren the fighters, members of Moslem Brotherhood. It goes on to reach out and become one with another chain that includes the struggle of the Palestinians and Moslem Brotherhood in the 1948 war and the Jihad operations of the Moslem Brotherhood in 1968 and after.

Moreover, if the links have been distant from each other and if obstacles, placed by those who are the lackeys of Zionism in the way of the fighters obstructed the continuation of the struggle, the Islamic Resistance Movement aspires to the realization of Allah's promise, no matter how long that should take. The Prophet, Allah bless him and grant him salvation, has said:

"The Day of Judgment will not come about until Moslems fight the Jews (killing the Jews), when the Jew will hide behind stones and trees. The stones and trees will say O Moslems, O Abdulla, there is a Jew behind me, come and kill him. Only the Gharkad tree, [a thorny tree considered by some Arabs to be a "Jewish" tree] would not do that because it is one of the trees of the Jews." . . .

Article Eight
Allah is its target, the Prophet is its model, the Koran its constitution: Jihad is its path and death for the sake of Allah is the loftiest of its wishes. . . .

Article Nine
The Islamic Resistance Movement found itself at a time when Islam has disappeared from life. Thus rules shook, concepts were upset, values changed and evil people took control, oppression and darkness prevailed, cowards became like tigers: homelands were usurped, people were scattered and were caused to wander all over the world, the state of justice disappeared and the state of falsehood replaced it. Nothing remained in its right place. Thus, when Islam is absent from the arena, everything changes. From this state of affairs the incentives are drawn.

As for the objectives: They are the fighting against the false, defeating it and vanquishing it so that justice could prevail, homelands be retrieved and from its mosques would the voice of the mu'azen emerge declaring the establishment of the state of Islam, so that people and things would return each to their right places and Allah is our helper. . . .

Article Ten
As the Islamic Resistance Movement paves its way, it will back the oppressed and support the wronged with all its might. It will spare no effort to bring about justice and defeat injustice, in word and deed, in this place and everywhere it can reach and have influence therein. . . .

Article Eleven

The Islamic Resistance Movement believes that the land of Palestine is an Islamic Waqf [charity] consecrated for future Moslem generations until Judgment Day. It, or any part of it, should not be squandered: it, or any part of it, should not be given up. Neither a single Arab country nor all Arab countries, neither any king or president, nor all the kings and presidents, neither any organization nor all of them, be they Palestinian or Arab, possess the right to do that. Palestine is an Islamic Waqf land consecrated for Moslem generations until Judgment Day. This being so, who could claim to have the right to represent Moslem generations till Judgment Day?

This is the law governing the land of Palestine in the Islamic Shariah [law] and the same goes for any land the Moslems have conquered by force, because during the times of [Islamic] conquests, the Moslems consecrated these lands to Moslem generations till the Day of Judgment. . . .

Article Twelve

Nationalism, from the point of view of the Islamic Resistance Movement, is part of the religious creed. Nothing in nationalism is more significant or deeper than in the case when an enemy should tread Moslem land. Resisting and quelling the enemy become the individual duty of every Moslem, male or female. A woman can go out to fight the enemy without her husband's permission, and so does the slave: without his master's permission. . . .

Article Thirteen

Initiatives, and so-called peaceful solutions and international conferences, are in contradiction to the principles of the Islamic Resistance Movement. Abusing any part of Palestine is abuse directed against part of religion. Nationalism of the Islamic Resistance Movement is part of its religion. Its members have been fed on that. For the sake of hoisting the banner of Allah over their homeland they fight. "Allah will be prominent, but most people do not know."

Now and then the call goes out for the convening of an international conference to look for ways of solving the [Palestinian] question. Some accept, others reject the idea, for this or other reason, with one stipulation or more for consent to convening the conference and participating in it. Knowing the parties constituting the conference, their past and present attitudes towards Moslem problems, the Islamic Resistance Movement does not consider these conferences capable of realizing the demands, restoring the rights or doing justice to the oppressed. These conferences are only ways of setting the infidels in the land of the Moslems as arbitrators. When did the infidels do justice to the believers?

"But the Jews will not be pleased with thee, neither the Christians, until thou follow their religion; say, The direction of Allah is the true direction. And verily if thou follow their desires, after the knowledge which hath been given thee, thou shalt find no patron or protector against Allah." (The Cow—verse 120).

There is no solution for the Palestinian question except through Jihad. Initiatives, proposals and international conferences are all a waste of time and vain endeavors. The Palestinian people know better than to consent to having their future, rights and fate toyed with. . . .

Article Fourteen

The question of the liberation of Palestine is bound to three circles: the Palestinian circle, the Arab circle and the Islamic circle. Each of these circles has its role in the struggle against Zionism. Each has its duties, and it is a horrible mistake and a sign of deep ignorance to overlook any of these circles. Palestine is an Islamic land which has the first of the two kiblahs [which point Muslims toward Mecca for prayers], the third of the holy [Islamic] sanctuaries, and the point of departure [Jerusalem] for [the Prophet] Mohamed's midnight journey to the seven heavens. . . .

. . . . Since this is the case, liberation of Palestine is then an individual duty for [e]very Moslem wherever he may be. On this basis, the problem should be viewed. This should be realized by every Moslem.

The day the problem is dealt with on this basis, when the three circles mobilize their capabilities, the present state of affairs will change and the day of liberation will come nearer. . . .

Article Fifteen

The day that enemies usurp part of Moslem land, Jihad becomes the individual duty of every Moslem. In face of the Jews' usurpation of Palestine, it is compulsory that the banner of Jihad be raised. To do this requires the diffusion of Islamic conscious-ness among the masses, both on the regional, Arab and Islamic levels. It is necessary to instill the spirit of Jihad in the heart of the nation so that they would confront the enemies and join the ranks of the fighters. . . .

It is necessary to instill in the minds of the Moslem generations that the Palestin-ian problem is a religious problem, and should be dealt with on this basis. Palestine contains Islamic holy sites. In it there is al-Aqsa Mosque which is bound to the great Mosque in Mecca in an inseparable bond as long as heaven and earth speak of Isra` [Mohamed's midnight journey to the seven heavens] and Mi'raj [Mohamed's ascen-sion to the seven heavens from Jerusalem]. . . .

Article Twenty-Two

For a long time, the enemies have been planning, skillfully and with precision, for the achievement of what they have attained. They took into consideration the causes affect-ing the current of events. They strived to amass great and substantive material wealth which they devoted to the realization of their dream. With their money, they took con-trol of the world media, news agencies, the press, publishing houses, broadcasting sta-tions, and others. With their money they stirred revolutions in various parts of the world with the purpose of achieving their interests and reaping the fruit therein. They were behind the French Revolution, the Communist revolution and most of the revolutions we heard and hear about, here and there. With their money they formed secret societies, such as Freemasons, Rotary Clubs, the Lions and others in different parts of the world for the purpose of sabotaging societies and achieving Zionist interests. With their money they were able to control imperialistic countries and instigate them to colonize many countries in order to enable them to exploit their resources and spread corruption there.

You may speak as much as you want about regional and world wars. They were behind World War I, when they were able to destroy the Islamic Caliphate, making financial gains and controlling resources. They obtained the Balfour Declaration, formed the League of Nations through which they could rule the world. They were behind World War II, through which they made huge financial gains by trading in armaments, and paved the way for the establishment of their state. It was they who instigated the replacement of the League of Nations with the United Nations and the Security Council to enable them to rule the world through them. There is no war going on anywhere, without having their finger in it. . . .

The imperialistic forces in the Capitalist West and Communist East, support the enemy with all their might, in money and in men. These forces take turns in doing that. The day Islam appears, the forces of infidelity would unite to challenge it, for the infidels are of one nation. . . .

Our Attitudes Towards

A. Islamic Movements

Article Twenty-Three
The Islamic Resistance Movement views other Islamic movements with respect and appreciation. If it were at variance with them on one point or opinion, it is in agreement with them on other points and understandings. It considers these movements, if they reveal good intentions and dedication to Allah, that they fall into the category of those who are trying hard since they act within the Islamic circle. Each active person has his share.

The Islamic Resistance Movement considers all these movements as a fund for itself. It prays to Allah for guidance and directions for all and it spares no effort to keep the banner of unity raised, ever striving for its realization in accordance with the Koran and the Prophet's directives. . . .

B. Nationalist Movements in the Palestinian Arena

Article Twenty-Five
The Islamic Resistance Movement respects these movements and appreciates their circumstances and the conditions surrounding and affecting them. It encourages them as long as they do not give their allegiance to the Communist East or the Crusading West. It confirms to all those who are integrated in it, or sympathetic towards it, that the Islamic Resistance Movement is a fighting movement that has a moral and enlightened look of life and the way it should cooperate with the other (movements). It detests opportunism and desires only the good of people, individuals and groups alike. It does not seek material gains, personal fame, nor does it look for a reward from others. It works with its own resources and whatever is at its disposal "and prepare for them whatever force you can," for the fulfillment of the duty, and the earning of Allah's favor. It has no other desire than that.

The Movement assures all the nationalist trends operating in the Palestinian arena for the liberation of Palestine, that it is there for their support and assistance. It will never be more than that, both in words and deeds, now and in the future. It is there to bring together and not to divide, to preserve and not to squander, to unify and not to throw asunder. It evaluates every good word, sincere effort and good offices. It closes the door in the face of side disagreements and does not lend an ear to rumors and slanders, while at the same time fully realizing the right for self-defense.

Anything contrary or contradictory to these trends, is a lie disseminated by enemies or their lackeys for the purpose of sowing confusion, disrupting the ranks and occupy them with side issues. . . .

C. The Palestinian Liberation Organization

Article Twenty-Seven
The Palestinian Liberation Organization is the closest to the heart of the Islamic Resistance Movement. It contains the father and the brother, the next of kin and the friend. The Moslem does not estrange himself from his father, brother, next of kin or friend. Our homeland is one, our situation is one, our fate is one and the enemy is a joint enemy to all of us.

Because of the situations surrounding the formation of the Organization, of the ideological confusion prevailing in the Arab world as a result of the ideological invasion under whose influence the Arab world has fallen since the defeat of the Crusaders and which was, and still is, intensified through orientalists, missionaries and imperialists, the Organization adopted the idea of the secular state. And that it how we view it.

Secularism completely contradicts religious ideology. Attitudes, conduct and decisions stem from ideologies.

That is why, with all our appreciation for The Palestinian Liberation Organization—and what it can develop into—and without belittling its role in the Arab-Israeli conflict, we are unable to exchange the present or future Islamic Palestine with the secular idea. The Islamic nature of Palestine is part of our religion and whoever takes his religion lightly is a loser. . . .

The day The Palestinian Liberation Organization adopts Islam as its way of life, we will become its soldiers, and fuel for its fire that will burn the enemies.

Until such a day, and we pray to Allah that it will be soon, the Islamic Resistance Movement's stand towards the PLO is that of the son towards his father, the brother towards his brother, and the relative to relative, suffers his pain and supports him in confronting the enemies, wishing him to be wise and well-guided. . . .

D. Arab and Islamic Countries

Article Twenty-Eight
The Zionist invasion is a vicious invasion. It does not refrain from resorting to all methods, using all evil and contemptible ways to achieve its end. It relies greatly in its infiltration and espionage operations on the secret organizations it gave rise to, such as the Freemasons, The Rotary and Lions clubs, and other sabotage groups. All these organizations, whether secret or open, work in the interest of Zionism and according to its instructions. They aim at undermining societies, destroying values, corrupting consciences, deteriorating character and annihilating Islam. It is behind the drug trade and alcoholism in all its kinds so as to facilitate its control and expansion.

Arab countries surrounding Israel are asked to open their borders before the fighters from among the Arab and Islamic nations so that they could consolidate their efforts with those of their Moslem brethren in Palestine.

As for the other Arab and Islamic countries, they are asked to facilitate the movement of the fighters from and to it, and this is the least thing they could do.

We should not forget to remind every Moslem that when the Jews conquered the Holy City in 1967, they stood on the threshold of the Aqsa Mosque and proclaimed that "Mohammed is dead, and his descendants are all women." ...

SOURCE: Foundation for Middle East Peace, www.fmep.org/resources/official_documents/hamas_covenant_1988.html.

Oslo Accords

DOCUMENT IN CONTEXT

The Israeli elections held in June 1992 offered voters one of the starkest choices they had faced since the landmark election of 1977, when the rightist Likud Party stormed to power. In 1992 incumbent prime minister Yitzhak Shamir of Likud emphasized the importance of "Greater Israel"—in other words, holding on to all of the territories occupied in 1967 no matter the cost. Yitzhak Rabin, a former general who had served as defense minister in Shamir's unity government, assumed leadership of the Labor Party and campaigned on a platform of negotiating for peace with the Palestinians even if it meant relinquishing control of some of the territories.

Rabin won the elections with a broad enough margin to give him a mandate for his platform. After taking office on July 13, 1992, he called for new talks between Israel and a Jordanian-Palestinian delegation. In his first speech to the Knesset, Rabin also took the unusual step, for an Israeli prime minister, of addressing the Palestinians directly, telling them (in a reference to the first intifada, which was then fading) "you have failed in the war against us." Rabin appealed to the Palestinians to "give peace a chance—and to cease all violent and terrorist activity for the duration of the negotiations on autonomy."

Although demonstrating a new flexibility in negotiations with the Palestinians, Rabin continued to take an iron-fisted approach to Palestinian violence. In December 1992, after the murder of an Israeli policeman, he ordered the deportation to Lebanon of more than 400 Hamas activists, and in March 1993 he halted the entry into Israel of some 30,000 Palestinian workers after members of Hamas and other groups killed 13 Israelis. Meanwhile, bilateral talks between Israel and a Jordanian-Palestinian delegation continued into 1993 but made no progress (Madrid Conference, p. 138).

In December 1992, while the Madrid talks plodded along, two Israeli academics and a senior official from the Palestine Liberation Organization (PLO) began a series of informal sessions in Oslo, Norway, under the sponsorship of the Norwegian Foreign Ministry. Israeli foreign minister Shimon Peres and his deputy, Yossi Beilin, encouraged the secret talks, which at first were unofficial but became more serious when Israeli diplomats joined the discussions early in 1993. Of even more importance, the continuing strife of the Palestinian intifada had changed the political landscape, forcing both sides to accept the need for concessions. The PLO had begun losing public support to the more militant Hamas and Islamic Jihad factions, while Rabin felt pressure to show results from the negotiations he had promised during his election campaign.

The Oslo talks ultimately produced the Declaration of Principles on Interim Self-Government Arrangements, an agreement completed on August 24 by Peres and PLO negotiator Ahmed Qureia. The Israeli cabinet approved the accord on August 30 by a unanimous vote, with two abstentions—a remarkable degree of unity on the first formal agreement between Israel and the PLO.

Peres and Mahmoud Abbas, chief aide to PLO chairman Yasir Arafat, officially signed the Declaration of Principles on September 13, 1993, at a White House ceremony presided over by President Bill Clinton, with Rabin and Arafat looking on. In many ways, the substance of the agreement was overshadowed by the symbolism of the occasion, notably, the sight of old foes Rabin and Arafat shaking hands, an action that would have been inconceivable for either of them in times past. Four days earlier, the leaders had exchanged letters that amounted to formal recognition: Arafat recognized Israel's right to exist as a state, and Rabin acknowledged the PLO as the representative of the Palestinian people, but did not explicitly support the idea of a Palestinian state.

Better known as the Oslo Accord, the Declaration of Principles was simply that—a broad-brush of generalities intended to banish the long era of hostility between Israelis and Palestinians but not meant as a definitive answer to how that would be accomplished. The basic elements called for a gradual Israeli withdrawal from parts of the occupied territories, to be replaced by "self-government arrangements" for the Palestinians during a "transitional period" to last no more than five years. Specific details were to be negotiated under a rigid timetable, beginning with a two-month limit on talks leading to the withdrawal of the Israeli military from the Gaza Strip and the West Bank town of Jericho. The most controversial issues—the status of Jerusalem, the rights of Palestinian refugees, and the fate of Jewish settlements in the territories—were mentioned only as subjects to be addressed in future "permanent status" talks.

In essence, the intent of the Oslo agreement was to buy Israel peace with the Palestinians, to give Arafat and the PLO the right to immediately govern part of the territories and more later, and to give the Palestinian people the hope for self-governance and a brighter future that had been lacking for many years. Following a general concept outlined in the Framework for Peace in the Middle East negotiated by Israel and Egypt at Camp David fifteen years earlier, the Oslo Accords adopted a step-by-step approach: Palestinians would be given progressively greater authority in the territories as Israel withdrew, but each step would be subject to continuing negotiation and to events on the ground.

In a broader sense, the Oslo Accords represented an acknowledgment by each side that its long-time dream of controlling all of historic Palestine had died: Rabin reluctantly admitted that Israel would have to relinquish most of the Gaza Strip and at least some of the West Bank, and Arafat accepted the inevitability of governing a tiny Palestine overshadowed by a much more powerful Israel. The agreement also opened the way for Jordan's King Hussein to negotiate a peace agreement with Israel less than one year later (Jordanian-Israeli Peace, p. 142).

According to opinion polls, the accords had broad public support among Israelis, but the Knesset approved it only narrowly, with 61 votes in favor (a bare majority), 50 opposed, and 9 abstentions. The new leader of the Likud Party, Binyamin Netanyahu, bitterly denounced the agreement as "appeasement" and pledged to cancel it if he and his party took power in the next election. Palestinians also were divided, with radical factions denouncing what they called Arafat's lust for power and his willingness to accept something less than a genuine, independent Palestinian state. The PLO Executive Committee approved the agreement, but four members resigned in protest.

The next diplomatic task required the Israelis and Palestinians to negotiate a more substantive document setting the terms for how the Palestinians would govern themselves in the Gaza Strip and the town of Jericho in the Jordan Valley, on the West Bank—the first two areas from which Israel would withdraw. The negotiations took twice as long as the two months envisioned in the Oslo Accords, in part because Rabin assigned this task to military officers who demanded, and got, tough security conditions limiting Palestinian authority. The two sides initialed a preliminary accord in Cairo on February 4, 1994. Three weeks later, however, Baruch Goldstein, a U.S.-born Israeli settler, opened fire on worshipers at a mosque in the West Bank city of Hebron, killing twenty-five people before he was killed. The PLO angrily withdrew from further talks, and it took more than a month for the negotiating process to get back on track. With talks again under way, Hamas exploded a car bomb on April 6, killing eight people, and a suicide bomber a week later killed five people. In Cairo on May 4, 1994, Rabin and Arafat finally signed the agreement, referred to as the Cairo Agreement, setting the terms for the Palestinians to take control of Jericho and most of Gaza. It called for Israel to turn responsibility for governing those areas over to the Palestinians in three stages, culminating in elections in Gaza and the West Bank for a legislature and president, who together would constitute a quasi-government.

Israel immediately began redeploying its military forces in Gaza so they could concentrate on protecting Jewish settlements concentrated in the northern section of the strip. About a week after the signing of the Cairo Agreement, a small force of Palestinian police officers—who had been trained and equipped in Egypt—began manning outposts in Gaza; their presence represented the first visible sign of a transfer of responsibility from the Israelis to the Palestinians. On July 1, 1994, cheering Palestinians greeted Arafat, the long-exiled PLO leader, upon his arrival in Gaza. Meanwhile in Jerusalem, a right-wing Israeli rally against the peace agreements deteriorated into attacks on Palestinian residents of that city. In December, Arafat, Rabin, and Peres were awarded the Nobel Peace Prize for their work on the Oslo Accords.

Following the logic of the Oslo peace process, the Israelis and Palestinians next turned their attention to negotiating a detailed agreement incorporating and expanding on the preceding ones. Despite the complexity of the task—and continuing threats to the peace process in the form of violence by rejectionist on both sides—Israel and the PLO completed a comprehensive agreement in slightly more than a year. Rabin and Arafat signed it at the White House in Washington on September 28, 1995, with President Clinton, Egyptian president Hosni Mubarak, and Jordan's King Hussein acting as witnesses.

This agreement, formally the Interim Agreement on the West Bank and the Gaza Strip, was immediately dubbed Oslo II by diplomats and journalists. Including its annexes, maps, and amendments, known as "agreed minutes," the agreement consisted of nearly 350-typed pages and covered every aspect of the evolving Israeli-Palestinian relationship in minute detail. The heart of the agreement concerned the procedure for West Bank and Gaza Palestinians to elect an eighty-two-member legislature—the Palestinian Legislative Council—and a president of an administrative body—the Executive Authority—two elements of a new government called the Palestinian Interim Self-Government Authority, or Palestinian Authority for short. The Palestinian Authority was to serve for a five-year "interim" period, starting from the May 4, 1994, date of the earlier agreement on the Gaza Strip and Jericho.

Palestinian leaders would assume immediate responsibility for the Gaza Strip (except for the Jewish settlements, occupying about 35 percent of the land) and for the seven largest cities on the West Bank: Bethlehem, Jenin, Jericho (from which Israel already had withdrawn because of a previous agreement), Nablus, Qalqilya, Ramallah, and Tulkarm. Another city, Hebron, was treated as a separate case subject to later negotiations. The cities and their surrounding villages were designated as Area A, sections of the West Bank to be placed under full Palestinian control as soon as the Israeli military withdrew; their area constituted only about 4 percent of the West Bank, but included most of the Palestinian population. Several dozen other areas of the West Bank—some individual villages as well as large groupings of villages or lightly settled areas—were designated as Area B, where the new Palestinian government would control civil affairs but the Israeli military would remain in charge of security. The bulk of the West Bank, designated as Area C, would remain under Israeli control indefinitely and would include Jewish settlements and other lands that Israel had taken for roads and military installations. As had the previous agreements in the Oslo process, Oslo II gave the Palestinians something less than a fully independent state but substantially more than the total subservience to Israel that they had endured since June 1967.

Oslo II was another diplomatic triumph for the leaders who had started down the path to peace, but as with previous agreements, some elements on both sides bitterly opposed it, refusing to accept anything less than control for themselves of all of Palestine. The Knesset ratified the agreement by the slimmest possible margin, 61 in favor and 59 opposed. The debate was exceptionally contentious even by the raucous standards of that legislature, with Likud members accusing Rabin of appeasement.

The lengths to which some Israelis would go to block the peace process became clear in the wake of the Oslo II agreement. Extremist religious groups sponsored rallies in Jerusalem depicting Rabin as a Nazi and demanding that Israeli soldiers disobey government orders to withdraw from the West Bank. Although not as extreme, Likud leader Netanyahu joined in the chorus of denunciation, telling a large crowd that Rabin had brought about "national humiliation by accepting the dictates of the terrorist Arafat."

Countering this chorus of opposition, peace groups sponsored a giant rally in Tel Aviv on November 4, 1995. An ebullient Rabin attended and gave an emotional speech recalling his years as a soldier and affirming that the time had come for peace between Israel and its neighbors. "This rally must send a message to the Israeli public, to the Jews of the world, to the multitudes of Arab lands and in the world at large, that the nation of Israel wants peace, supports peace, and for this, I thank you." A few minutes later, three shots rang out, and Rabin fell to the ground. He died an hour later.

Rabin's assassination—the first of a high-level Israeli official—was doubly shocking because the assassin was an Israeli, Yigal Amir, a twenty-five-year-old student who shared the Messianic beliefs of many Jews that God intended every inch of Palestine for the Jews alone. For a moment, Amir's action forced Israelis to confront the fact that both societies in historic Palestine suffered from self-righteous extremism.

Peres, Rabin's long-time rival for Labor Party leadership, succeeded the assassinated prime minister. A decade earlier, Peres had served as prime minister for almost two years as part of a power-sharing deal with Yitzhak Shamir following the indecisive elections of 1984. This time, he was buoyed, temporarily, by a wave of public support and sympathy in the wake of Rabin's death. At the urging of President Clinton, Peres turned his attention to renewed negotiations with Syria, which dragged on for several inconclusive rounds through February 1996. In the meantime, Israel withdrew from several large and small West Bank towns, and the Palestinians held their first elections under the Oslo Accords on January 21, 1996. The elections produced overwhelming victories for Arafat, who was elected president of the Palestinian Authority, and his Fatah faction, which won most of the seats in the new Palestinian Legislative Council.

The promise of the Oslo peace process began to unravel in late February 1996 with a series of suicide bombings by Hamas and Islamic Jihad, which opposed any peace with Israel. Four bombings in nine days killed fifty-nine Israelis and quickly undermined public support in Israel for peace talks, as the bombers intended. With his public standing plummeting, Peres called for early elections in May. In April, fighting broke out on another front when the Lebanese-based Islamist group Hizballah launched rockets against villages in northern Israel for the first time in nearly three years. Israel responded with an attack on Hizballah bases in southern Lebanon; one of the attacks killed 107 Lebanese civilians in a refugee camp run by the United Nations in the town of Qana.

Renewed Palestinian suicide bombings—in defiance of a security crackdown by the Palestinian Authority—undermined Peres politically in the run-up to the May 29 elections, the first to be held under a new law providing for the direct election of the prime minister by the voters rather than by the Knesset. Peres lost narrowly to Netanyahu, who had played to public fears about the bombings.

Despite Netanyahu's earlier pledges to repeal the Oslo agreements if given the chance, upon entering office in July, Netanyahu bowed to what he called "the reality" of the agreements and said he would comply with them—but he also said he would "freeze" the negotiating process. The next step in that process proved to be one of the most difficult, involving Israel's military redeployment from Hebron, the location of shrines of historic and religious significance for Jews and Muslims (Hebron Protocol, p. 259).

Following are the texts of letters exchanged on September 9, 1993, by Palestine Liberation Organization (PLO) chairman Yasir Arafat and Israeli prime minister Yitzhak Rabin, plus a letter from Arafat to Norwegian foreign minister Johan Jorgen Holst; the text of the Declaration of Principles on Interim Self-Government Arrangements, or the Oslo Accord, signed in Washington, D.C., on September 13, 1993, by Israeli foreign minister Simon Peres and PLO negotiator Mahmoud Abbas; the text of an agreement between Israel and the PLO signed in Cairo on May 4, 1994, concerning Palestinian self-rule in the Gaza Strip and the West Bank city of Jericho; and the text of the main body of the Interim Agreement on the West Bank and the Gaza Strip between Israel and the PLO, or Oslo II, signed in Washington, D.C., on September 28, 1995.

DOCUMENT

Letter from Yasir Arafat to Yitzhak Rabin

SEPTEMBER 9, 1993

September 9, 1993

Yitzhak Rabin
Prime Minister of Israel

Mr. Prime Minister,

The signing of the Declaration of Principles marks a new era in the history of the Middle East. In firm conviction thereof, I would like to confirm the following PLO commitments:

The PLO recognizes the right of the State of Israel to exist in peace and security.

The PLO accepts United Nations Security Council Resolutions 242 and 338.

The PLO commits itself to the Middle East peace process, and to a peaceful resolution of the conflict between the two sides and declares that all outstanding issues relating to permanent status will be resolved through negotiations.

The PLO considers that the signing of the Declaration of Principles constitutes a historic event, inaugurating a new epoch of peaceful coexistence, free from violence and all other acts which endanger peace and stability. Accordingly, the PLO renounces the use of terrorism and other acts of violence and will assume responsibility over all PLO elements and personnel in order to assure their compliance, prevent violations and discipline violators.

In view of the promise of a new era and the signing of the Declaration of Principles and based on Palestinian acceptance of Security Council Resolutions 242 and 338, the PLO affirms that those articles of the Palestinian Covenant which deny Israel's right to exist, and the provisions of the Covenant which are inconsistent with the commitments of this letter are now inoperative and no longer valid. Consequently, the PLO undertakes to submit to the Palestinian National Council for formal approval the necessary changes in regard to the Palestinian Covenant.

Sincerely,
[signed] Yasir Arafat
Chairman
The Palestine Liberation Organization

SOURCE: U.S. Department of State, www.state.gov/p/nea/rls/22579.htm.

DOCUMENT

Letter from Yasir Arafat to Norwegian Foreign Minister Johan Jørgen Holst

SEPTEMBER 9, 1993

September 9, 1993

His Excellency
Johan Jorgen Holst
Foreign Minister of Norway

Dear Minister Holst,

I would like to confirm to you that, upon the signing of the Declaration of Principles, the PLO encourages and calls upon the Palestinian people in the West Bank and Gaza Strip to take part in the steps leading to the normalization of life, rejecting violence and terrorism, contributing to peace and stability and participating actively in shaping reconstruction, economic development and cooperation.

Sincerely,
[signed] Yasir Arafat
Chairman
The Palestine Liberation Organization

SOURCE: U.S. Department of State, www.state.gov/p/nea/rls/22579.htm.

DOCUMENT

Letter from Yitzhak Rabin to Yasir Arafat

SEPTEMBER 9, 1993

September 9, 1993

Yasir Arafat
Chairman
The Palestinian Liberation Organization

Mr. Chairman,

In response to your letter of September 9, 1993, I wish to confirm to you that, in light of the PLO commitments included in your letter, the Government of Israel has decided to recognize the PLO as the representative of the Palestinian people and commence negotiations with the PLO within the Middle East peace process.

[signed] Yitzhak Rabin
Prime Minister of Israel

SOURCE: U.S. Department of State, www.state.gov/p/nea/rls/22579.htm.

DOCUMENT

Oslo Accord: Declaration of Principles on Interim Self-Government Arrangements

SEPTEMBER 13, 1993

The Government of the State of Israel and the P.L.O. team (in the Jordanian-Palestinian delegation to the Middle East Peace Conference) (the "Palestinian Delegation"), representing the Palestinian people, agree that it is time to put an end to decades of confrontation and conflict, recognize their mutual legitimate and political rights, and strive to live in peaceful coexistence and mutual dignity and security and achieve a just, lasting and comprehensive peace settlement and historic reconciliation through the agreed political process. Accordingly, the two sides agree to the following principles:

Article I

AIM OF THE NEGOTIATIONS

The aim of the Israeli-Palestinian negotiations within the current Middle East peace process is, among other things, to establish a Palestinian Interim Self-Government Authority, the elected Council (the "Council"), for the Palestinian people in the West Bank and the Gaza Strip, for a transitional period not exceeding five years, leading to a permanent settlement based on Security Council Resolutions 242 (1967) and 338 (1973).

It is understood that the interim arrangements are an integral part of the whole peace process and that the negotiations on the permanent status will lead to the implementation of Security Council Resolutions 242 (1967) and 338 (1973).

Article II

FRAMEWORK FOR THE INTERIM PERIOD

The agreed framework for the interim period is set forth in this Declaration of Principles.

Article III

ELECTIONS

1. In order that the Palestinian people in the West Bank and Gaza Strip may govern themselves according to democratic principles, direct, free and general political elections will be held for the Council under agreed supervision and international observation, while the Palestinian police will ensure public order.
2. An agreement will be concluded on the exact mode and conditions of the elections in accordance with the protocol attached as Annex I, with the goal of holding the elections not later than nine months after the entry into force of this Declaration of Principles.
3. These elections will constitute a significant interim preparatory step toward the realization of the legitimate rights of the Palestinian people and their just requirements.

Article IV

JURISDICTION

Jurisdiction of the Council will cover West Bank and Gaza Strip territory, except for issues that will be negotiated in the permanent status negotiations. The two sides view the West Bank and the Gaza Strip as a single territorial unit, whose integrity will be preserved during the interim period.

Article V

TRANSITIONAL PERIOD AND PERMANENT STATUS NEGOTIATIONS

1. The five-year transitional period will begin upon the withdrawal from the Gaza Strip and Jericho area.
2. Permanent status negotiations will commence as soon as possible, but not later than the beginning of the third year of the interim period, between the Government of Israel and the Palestinian people['s] representatives.
3. It is understood that these negotiations shall cover remaining issues, including: Jerusalem, refugees, settlements, security arrangements, borders, relations and cooperation with other neighbors, and other issues of common interest.
4. The two parties agree that the outcome of the permanent status negotiations should not be prejudiced or preempted by agreements reached for the interim period.

Article VI

PREPARATORY TRANSFER OF POWERS AND RESPONSIBILITIES

1. Upon the entry into force of this Declaration of Principles and the withdrawal from the Gaza Strip and the Jericho area, a transfer of authority from

the Israeli military government and its Civil Administration to the authorized Palestinians for this task, as detailed herein, will commence. This transfer of authority will be of a preparatory nature until the inauguration of the
Council.

2. Immediately after the entry into force of this Declaration of Principles and the
   withdrawal from the Gaza Strip and Jericho area, with the view to promoting
   economic development in the West Bank and Gaza Strip, authority will be
   transferred to the Palestinians in the following spheres: education and culture,
   health, social welfare, direct taxation and tourism. The Palestinian side will
   commence in building the Palestinian police force, as agreed upon. Pending
   the inauguration of the Council, the two parties may negotiate the transfer of
   additional powers and responsibilities, as agreed upon.

Article VII

INTERIM AGREEMENT

1. The Israeli and Palestinian delegations will negotiate an agreement on the
   interim period (the "Interim Agreement").
2. The Interim Agreement shall specify, among other things, the structure of the
   Council, the number of its members, and the transfer of powers and responsibilities from the Israeli military government and its Civil Administration to
   the Council. The Interim Agreement shall also specify the Council's executive
   authority, legislative authority in accordance with Article IX below, and the
   independent Palestinian judicial organs.
3. The Interim Agreement shall include arrangements, to be implemented upon
   the inauguration of the Council, for the assumption by the Council of all of
   the powers and responsibilities transferred previously in accordance with Article
   VI above.
4. In order to enable the Council to promote economic growth, upon its inauguration, the Council will establish, among other things, a Palestinian Electricity Authority, a Gaza Sea Port Authority, a Palestinian Development Bank,
   a Palestinian Export Promotion Board, a Palestinian Environmental Authority,
   a Palestinian Land Authority and a Palestinian Water Administration Authority and any other Authorities agreed upon, in accordance with the Interim
   Agreement, that will specify their powers and responsibilities.
5. After the inauguration of the Council, the Civil Administration will be dissolved, and the Israeli military government will be withdrawn.

Article VIII

PUBLIC ORDER AND SECURITY

In order to guarantee public order and internal security for the Palestinians of the West
Bank and the Gaza Strip, the Council will establish a strong police force, while Israel
will continue to carry the responsibility for defending against external threats, as well
as the responsibility for overall security of Israelis for the purpose of safeguarding their
internal security and public order.

Article IX

LAWS AND MILITARY ORDERS

1. The Council will be empowered to legislate, in accordance with the Interim Agreement, within all authorities transferred to it.
2. Both parties will review jointly laws and military orders presently in force in remaining spheres.

Article X

JOINT ISRAELI-PALESTINIAN LIAISON COMMITTEE

In order to provide for a smooth implementation of this Declaration of Principles and any subsequent agreements pertaining to the interim period, upon the entry into force of this Declaration of Principles, a Joint Israeli-Palestinian Liaison Committee will be established in order to deal with issues requiring coordination, other issues of common interest and disputes.

Article XI

ISRAELI-PALESTINIAN COOPERATION IN ECONOMIC FIELDS

Recognizing the mutual benefit of cooperation in promoting the development of the West Bank, the Gaza Strip and Israel, upon the entry into force of this Declaration of Principles, an Israeli-Palestinian Economic Cooperation Committee will be established in order to develop and implement in a cooperative manner the programs identified in the protocols attached as Annex III and Annex IV.

Article XII

LIAISON AND COOPERATION WITH JORDAN AND EGYPT

The two parties will invite the Governments of Jordan and Egypt to participate in establishing further liaison and cooperation arrangements between the Government of Israel and the Palestinian representatives, on the one hand, and the Governments of Jordan and Egypt, on the other hand, to promote cooperation between them. These arrangements will include the constitution of a Continuing Committee that will decide by agreement on the modalities of admission of persons displaced from the West Bank and Gaza Strip in 1967, together with necessary measures to prevent disruption and disorder. Other matters of common concern will be dealt with by this Committee.

Article XIII

REDEPLOYMENT OF ISRAELI FORCES

1. After the entry into force of this Declaration of Principles, and not later than the eve of elections for the Council, a redeployment of Israeli military forces in the West Bank and the Gaza Strip will take place, in addition to withdrawal of Israeli forces carried out in accordance with Article XIV.

2. In redeploying its military forces, Israel will be guided by the principle that its military forces should be redeployed outside populated areas.
3. Further redeployments to specified locations will be gradually implemented commensurate with the assumption of responsibility for public order and internal security by the Palestinian police force pursuant to Article VIII above.

Article XIV

ISRAELI WITHDRAWAL FROM THE GAZA STRIP AND JERICHO AREA

Israel will withdraw from the Gaza Strip and Jericho area, as detailed in the protocol attached as Annex II.

Article XV

RESOLUTION OF DISPUTES

1. Disputes arising out of the application or interpretation of this Declaration of Principles, or any subsequent agreements pertaining to the interim period, shall be resolved by negotiations through the Joint Liaison Committee to be established pursuant to Article X above.
2. Disputes which cannot be settled by negotiations may be resolved by a mechanism of conciliation to be agreed upon by the parties.
3. The parties may agree to submit to arbitration disputes relating to the interim period, which cannot be settled through conciliation. To this end, upon the agreement of both parties, the parties will establish an Arbitration Committee.

Article XVI

ISRAELI-PALESTINIAN COOPERATION CONCERNING REGIONAL PROGRAMS

Both parties view the multilateral working groups as an appropriate instrument for promoting a "Marshall Plan," the regional programs and other programs, including special programs for the West Bank and Gaza Strip, as indicated in the protocol attached as Annex IV.

Article XVII

MISCELLANEOUS PROVISIONS

1. This Declaration of Principles will enter into force one month after its signing.
2. All protocols annexed to this Declaration of Principles and Agreed Minutes pertaining thereto shall be regarded as an integral part hereof.

Done at Washington, D.C., this thirteenth day of September, 1993.

For the Government of Israel:
(Signed) Shimon PERES

For the P.L.O.:
(Signed) Mahmoud ABBAS

Witnessed by:
The United States of America
(Signed) Warren CHRISTOPHER

The Russian Federation
(Signed) Andrei V. KOZYREV

ANNEX I

Protocol on the Mode and Conditions of Elections

1. Palestinians of Jerusalem who live there will have the right to participate in the election process, according to an agreement between the two sides.
2. In addition, the election agreement should cover, among other things, the following issues:
    a. The system of elections;
    b. The mode of the agreed supervision and international observation and their personal composition;
    c. Rules and regulations regarding election campaigns, including agreed arrangements for the organizing of mass media, and the possibility of licensing a broadcasting and television station.
3. The future status of displaced Palestinians who were registered on 4 June 1967 will not be prejudiced because they are unable to participate in the election process owing to practical reasons.

ANNEX II

Protocol on Withdrawal of Israeli Forces from the Gaza Strip and Jericho Area

1. The two sides will conclude and sign within two months from the date of entry into force of this Declaration of Principles an agreement on the withdrawal of Israeli military forces from the Gaza Strip and Jericho area. This agreement will include comprehensive arrangements to apply in the Gaza Strip and the Jericho area subsequent to the Israeli withdrawal.
2. Israel will implement an accelerated and scheduled withdrawal of Israeli military forces from the Gaza Strip and Jericho area, beginning immediately with the signing of the agreement on the Gaza Strip and Jericho area and to be completed within a period not exceeding four months after the signing of this agreement.
3. The above agreement will include, among other things:
    a. Arrangements for a smooth and peaceful transfer of authority from the Israeli military government and its Civil Administration to the Palestinian representatives;

b. Structure, powers and responsibilities of the Palestinian authority in these areas, except: external security, settlements, Israelis, foreign relations and other mutually agreed matters;

c. Arrangements for the assumption of internal security and public order by the Palestinian police force consisting of police officers recruited locally and from abroad (holding Jordanian passports and Palestinian documents issued by Egypt). Those who will participate in the Palestinian police force coming from abroad should be trained as police and police officers;

d. A temporary international or foreign presence, as agreed upon;

e. Establishment of a joint Palestinian-Israeli Coordination and Cooperation Committee for mutual security purposes;

f. An economic development and stabilization program including the establishment of an Emergency Fund, to encourage foreign investment and financial and economic support. Both sides will coordinate and cooperate jointly and unilaterally with regional and international parties to support these aims;

g. Arrangements for a safe passage for persons and transportation between the Gaza Strip and Jericho area.

4. The above agreement will include arrangements for coordination between both parties regarding passages:

a. Gaza–Egypt;

b. Jericho–Jordan.

5. The offices responsible for carrying out the powers and responsibilities of the Palestinian authority under this Annex II and Article VI of the Declaration of Principles will be located in the Gaza Strip and in the Jericho area pending the inauguration of the Council.

6. Other than these agreed arrangements, the status of the Gaza Strip and Jericho area will continue to be an integral part of the West Bank and Gaza Strip, and will not be changed in the interim period.

ANNEX III

Protocol on Israeli-Palestinian Cooperation in Economic and
Development Programs

The two sides agree to establish an Israeli-Palestinian Continuing Committee for Economic Cooperation, focusing, among other things, on the following:

1. Cooperation in the field of water, including a Water Development Program prepared by experts from both sides, which will also specify the mode of cooperation in the management of water resources in the West Bank and Gaza Strip, and will include proposals for studies and plans on water rights of each party, as well as on the equitable utilization of joint water resources for implementation in and beyond the interim period.

2. Cooperation in the field of electricity, including an Electricity Development Program, which will also specify the mode of cooperation for the production, maintenance, purchase and sale of electricity resources.

3. Cooperation in the field of energy, including an Energy Development Program, which will provide for the exploitation of oil and gas for industrial pur-

poses, particularly in the Gaza Strip and in the Negev, and will encourage further joint exploitation of other energy resources. This Program may also provide for the construction of a petrochemical industrial complex in the Gaza Strip and the construction of oil and gas pipelines.

4. Cooperation in the field of finance, including a Financial Development and Action Program for the encouragement of international investment in the West Bank and the Gaza Strip, and in Israel, as well as the establishment of a Palestinian Development Bank.

5. Cooperation in the field of transport and communications, including a Program, which will define guidelines for the establishment of a Gaza Sea Port Area, and will provide for the establishing of transport and communications lines to and from the West Bank and the Gaza Strip to Israel and to other countries. In addition, this Program will provide for carrying out the necessary construction of roads, railways, communications lines, etc.

6. Cooperation in the field of trade, including studies, and Trade Promotion Programs, which will encourage local, regional and interregional trade, as well as a feasibility study of creating free trade zones in the Gaza Strip and in Israel, mutual access to these zones and cooperation in other areas related to trade and commerce.

7. Cooperation in the field of industry, including Industrial Development Programs, which will provide for the establishment of joint Israeli-Palestinian Industrial Research and Development Centers, will promote Palestinian-Israeli joint ventures, and provide guidelines for cooperation in the textile, food, pharmaceutical, electronics, diamonds, computer and science-based industries.

8. A Program for cooperation in, and regulation of, labor relations and cooperation in social welfare issues.

9. A Human Resource Development and Cooperation Plan, providing for joint Israeli-Palestinian workshops and seminars, and for the establishment of joint vocational training centers, research institutes and data banks.

10. An Environmental Protection Plan, providing for joint and/or coordinated measures in this sphere.

11. A Program for developing coordination and cooperation in the field of communications and media.

12. Any other programmers of mutual interest.

ANNEX IV

Protocol on Israeli-Palestinian Cooperation Concerning Regional Development Programs

1. The two sides will cooperate in the context of the multilateral peace efforts in promoting a Development Program for the region, including the West Bank and the Gaza Strip, to be initiated by the Group of Seven. The parties will request the Group of Seven to seek the participation in this Program of other interested States, such as members of the Organisation for Economic Cooperation and Development, regional Arab states and institutions, as well as members of the private sector.

2. The Development Program will consist of two elements:
   a. An Economic Development Program for the West Bank and the Gaza Strip;
   b. A Regional Economic Development Program.
   c. The Economic Development Program for the West Bank and the Gaza Strip will consist of the following elements:
      1. A Social Rehabilitation Program, including a Housing and Construction Program;
      2. A Small and Medium Business Development Plan;
      3. An Infrastructure Development Program (water, electricity, transportation and communications, etc.);
      4. A Human Resources Plan;
      5. Other program.
   d. The Regional Economic Development Program may consist of the following elements:
      1. The establishment of a Middle East Development Fund, as a first step, and a Middle East Development Bank, as a second step;
      2. The development of a joint Israeli-Palestinian-Jordanian Plan for coordinated exploitation of the Dead Sea area;
      3. The Mediterranean Sea (Gaza) – Dead Sea Canal;
      4. Regional desalinization and other water development projects;
      5. A regional plan for agricultural development, including a coordinated regional effort for the prevention of desertification;
      6. Interconnection of electricity grids;
      7. Regional cooperation for the transfer, distribution and industrial exploitation of gas, oil and other energy resources;
      8. A Regional Tourism, Transportation and Telecommunications Development Plan;
      9. Regional cooperation in other spheres.
3. The two sides will encourage the multilateral working groups and will coordinate towards their success. The two parties will encourage intersessional activities, as well as pre-feasibility and feasibility studies, within the various multilateral working groups.

Agreed Minutes to the Declaration of Principles on Interim Self-Government Arrangements

A. General Understandings and Agreements

Any powers and responsibilities transferred to the Palestinians pursuant to the Declaration of Principles prior to the inauguration of the Council will be subject to the same principles pertaining to Article IV, as set out in these Agreed Minutes below.

B. Specific Understandings and Agreements

Article IV

It is understood that:

1. Jurisdiction of the Council will cover West Bank and Gaza Strip territory, except for issues that will be negotiated in the permanent status negotiations: Jerusalem, settlements, military locations and Israelis.
2. The Council's jurisdiction will apply with regard to the agreed powers, responsibilities, spheres and authorities transferred to it.

Article VI (2): It is agreed that the transfer of authority will be as follows:

1. The Palestinian side will inform the Israeli side of the names of the authorized Palestinians who will assume the powers, authorities and responsibilities that will be transferred to the Palestinians according to the Declaration of Principles in the following fields: education and culture, health, social welfare, direct taxation, tourism and any other authorities agreed upon.
2. It is understood that the rights and obligations of these offices will not be affected.
3. Each of the spheres described above will continue to enjoy existing budgetary allocations in accordance with arrangements to be mutually agreed upon. These arrangements also will provide for the necessary adjustments required in order to take into account the taxes collected by the direct taxation office.
4. Upon the execution of the Declaration of Principles, the Israeli and Palestinian delegations will immediately commence negotiations on a detailed plan for the transfer of authority on the above offices in accordance with the above understandings.

Article VII (2)
The Interim Agreement will also include arrangements for coordination and cooperation.

Article VII (5)
The withdrawal of the military government will not prevent Israel from exercising the powers and responsibilities not transferred to the Council.

Article VIII
It is understood that the Interim Agreement will include arrangements for cooperation and coordination between the two parties in this regard. It is also agreed that the transfer of powers and responsibilities to the Palestinian police will be accomplished in a phased manner, as agreed in the Interim Agreement.

Article X
It is agreed that, upon the entry into force of the Declaration of Principles, the Israeli and Palestinian delegations will exchange the names of the individuals designated by them as members of the Joint Israeli-Palestinian Liaison Committee. It is further agreed that each side will have an equal number of members in the Joint Committee. The Joint Committee will reach decisions by agreement. The Joint Committee may add other technicians and experts, as necessary. The Joint Committee will decide on the frequency and place or places of its meetings.

ANNEX II

It is understood that, subsequent to the Israeli withdrawal, Israel will continue to be responsible for external security, and for internal security and public order of settlements and Israelis. Israeli military forces and civilians may continue to use roads freely within the Gaza Strip and the Jericho area.

Done at Washington, D.C., this thirteenth day of September, 1993.

For the Government of Israel:
For the P.L.O:
(Signed) Shimon PERES
(Signed) Mahmoud ABBAS

Witnessed by:

The United States of America
The Russian Federation

(Signed) Warren CHRISTOPHER
(Signed) Andrei V. KOZYREV

SOURCE: U.S. Department of State, www.state.gov/p/nea/rls/22602.htm.

DOCUMENT

Cairo Agreement on Palestinian Self-Rule in Gaza and Jericho

MAY 4, 1994

The Government of the State of Israel and the Palestine Liberation Organization (hereinafter "the PLO"), the representative of the Palestinian people;

PREAMBLE

WITHIN the framework of the Middle East peace process initiated at Madrid in October 1991;

REAFFIRMING their determination to live in peaceful coexistence, mutual dignity and security, while recognizing their mutual legitimate and political rights;

REAFFIRMING their desire to achieve a just, lasting and comprehensive peace settlement through the agreed political process;

REAFFIRMING their adherence to the mutual recognition and commitments expressed in the letters dated September 9, 1993, signed by and exchanged between the Prime Minister of Israel and the Chairman of the PLO;

REAFFIRMING their understanding that the interim self-government arrangements, including the arrangements to apply in the Gaza Strip and the Jericho Area contained in this Agreement, are an integral part of the whole peace process and that the negotiations on the permanent status will lead to the implementation of Security Council Resolutions 242 and 338;

DESIROUS of putting into effect the Declaration of Principles on Interim Self-Government Arrangements signed at Washington, D.C. on September 13, 1993, and the Agreed Minutes thereto (hereinafter "the Declaration of Principles"), and in particular the Protocol on withdrawal of Israeli forces from the Gaza Strip and the Jericho Area;

HEREBY AGREE to the following arrangements regarding the Gaza Strip and the Jericho Area:

ARTICLE I

DEFINITIONS

For the purpose of this Agreement:

a. the Gaza Strip and the Jericho Area are delineated on map No. 1 and map No. 2 attached to this Agreement;
b. "the Settlements" means the Gush Katif and Erez settlement areas, as well as the other settlements in the Gaza Strip, as shown on attached map No. 1;
c. "the Military Installation Area" means the Israeli military installation area along the Egyptian border in the Gaza Strip, as shown on map No. 1; and
d. the term "Israelis" shall also include Israeli statutory agencies and corporations registered in Israel.

ARTICLE II

SCHEDULED WITHDRAWAL OF ISRAELI MILITARY FORCES

1. Israel shall implement an accelerated and scheduled withdrawal of Israeli military forces from the Gaza Strip and from the Jericho Area to begin immediately with the signing of this Agreement. Israel shall complete such withdrawal within three weeks from this date.
2. Subject to the arrangements included in the Protocol Concerning Withdrawal of Israeli Military Forces and Security Arrangements attached as Annex I, the Israeli withdrawal shall include evacuating all military bases and other fixed installations to be handed over to the Palestinian Police, to be established pursuant to Article IX below (hereinafter "the Palestinian Police").
3. In order to carry out Israel's responsibility for external security and for internal security and public order of Settlements and Israelis, Israel shall, concurrently with the withdrawal, redeploy its remaining military forces to the Settlements and the Military Installation Area, in accordance with the provisions of this Agreement. Subject to the provisions of this Agreement, this redeployment shall constitute full implementation of Article XIII of the Declaration of Principles with regard to the Gaza Strip and the Jericho Area only.

4. For the purposes of this Agreement, "Israeli military forces" may include Israel police and other Israeli security forces.

5. Israelis, including Israeli military forces, may continue to use roads freely within the Gaza Strip and the Jericho Area. Palestinians may use public roads crossing the Settlements freely, as provided for in Annex I.

6. The Palestinian Police shall be deployed and shall assume responsibility for public order and internal security of Palestinians in accordance with this Agreement and Annex I.

ARTICLE III
TRANSFER OF AUTHORITY

1. Israel shall transfer authority as specified in this Agreement from the Israeli military government and its Civil Administration to the Palestinian Authority, hereby established, in accordance with Article V of this Agreement, except for the authority that Israel shall continue to exercise as specified in this Agreement.

2. As regards the transfer and assumption of authority in civil spheres, powers and responsibilities shall be transferred and assumed as set out in the Protocol Concerning Civil Affairs attached as Annex II.

3. Arrangements for a smooth and peaceful transfer of the agreed powers and responsibilities are set out in Annex II.

4. Upon the completion of the Israeli withdrawal and the transfer of powers and responsibilities as detailed in paragraphs 1 and 2 above and in Annex II, the Civil Administration in the Gaza Strip and the Jericho Area will be dissolved and the Israeli military government will be withdrawn. The withdrawal of the military government shall not prevent it from continuing to exercise the powers and responsibilities specified in this Agreement.

5. A Joint Civil Affairs Coordination and Cooperation Committee (hereinafter "the CAC") and two Joint Regional Civil Affairs Subcommittees for the Gaza Strip and the Jericho Area respectively shall be established in order to provide for coordination and cooperation in civil affairs between the Palestinian Authority and Israel, as detailed in Annex II.

6. The offices of the Palestinian Authority shall be located in the Gaza Strip and the Jericho Area pending the inauguration of the Council to be elected pursuant to the Declaration of Principles.

ARTICLE IV
STRUCTURE AND COMPOSITION OF THE PALESTINIAN AUTHORITY

1. The Palestinian Authority will consist of one body of 24 members which shall carry out and be responsible for all the legislative and executive powers and responsibilities transferred to it under this Agreement, in accordance with this Article, and shall be responsible for the exercise of judicial functions in accordance with Article VI, subparagraph 1.b. of this Agreement.

2. The Palestinian Authority shall administer the departments transferred to it and may establish, within its jurisdiction, other departments and subordinate administrative units as necessary for the fulfillment of its responsibilities. It shall determine its own internal procedures.

3. The PLO shall inform the Government of Israel of the names of the members of the Palestinian Authority and any change of members. Changes in the membership of the Palestinian Authority will take effect upon an exchange of letters between the PLO and the Government of Israel.

4. Each member of the Palestinian Authority shall enter into office upon undertaking to act in accordance with this Agreement.

ARTICLE V

JURISDICTION

1. The authority of the Palestinian Authority encompasses all matters that fall within its territorial, functional and personal jurisdiction, as follows:
   a. The territorial jurisdiction covers the Gaza Strip and the Jericho Area territory, as defined in Article I, except for Settlements and the Military Installation Area.

Territorial jurisdiction shall include land, subsoil and territorial waters, in accordance with the provisions of this Agreement.

   b. The functional jurisdiction encompasses all powers and responsibilities as specified in this Agreement. This jurisdiction does not include foreign relations, internal security and public order of Settlements and the Military Installation Area and Israelis, and external security.
   c. The personal jurisdiction extends to all persons within the territorial jurisdiction referred to above, except for Israelis, unless otherwise provided in this Agreement.

2. The Palestinian Authority has, within its authority, legislative, executive and judicial powers and responsibilities, as provided for in this Agreement.

3.
   a. Israel has authority over the Settlements, the Military Installation Area, Israelis, external security, internal security and public order of Settlements, the Military Installation Area and Israelis, and those agreed powers and responsibilities specified in this Agreement.
   b. Israel shall exercise its authority through its military government, which, for that end, shall continue to have the necessary legislative, judicial and executive powers and responsibilities, in accordance with international law. This provision shall not derogate from Israel's applicable legislation over Israelis in person.

4. The exercise of authority with regard to the electromagnetic sphere and airspace shall be in accordance with the provisions of this Agreement.

5. The provisions of this Article are subject to the specific legal arrangements detailed in the Protocol Concerning Legal Matters attached as Annex III. Israel and the Palestinian Authority may negotiate further legal arrangements.

6. Israel and the Palestinian Authority shall cooperate on matters of legal assistance in criminal and civil matters through the legal subcommittee of the CAC.

ARTICLE VI

POWERS AND RESPONSIBILITIES OF
THE PALESTINIAN AUTHORITY

1. Subject to the provisions of this Agreement, the Palestinian Authority, within its jurisdiction:
   a. has legislative powers as set out in Article VII of this Agreement, as well as executive powers;
   b. will administer justice through an independent judiciary;
   c. will have, inter alia, power to formulate policies, supervise their implementation, employ staff, establish departments, authorities and institutions, sue and be sued and conclude contracts; and
   d. will have, inter alia, the power to keep and administer registers and records of the population, and issue certificates, licenses and documents.

2.
   a. In accordance with the Declaration of Principles, the Palestinian Authority will not have powers and responsibilities in the sphere of foreign relations, which sphere includes the establishment abroad of embassies, consulates or other types of foreign missions and posts or permitting their establishment in the Gaza Strip or the Jericho Area, the appointment of or admission of diplomatic and consular staff, and the exercise of diplomatic functions.
   b. Notwithstanding the provisions of this paragraph, the PLO may conduct negotiations and sign agreements with states or international organizations for the benefit of the Palestinian Authority in the following cases only:
      1. economic agreements, as specifically provided in Annex IV of this Agreement;
      2. agreements with donor countries for the purpose of implementing arrangements for the provision of assistance to the Palestinian Authority;
      3. agreements for the purpose of implementing the regional development plans detailed in Annex IV of the Declaration of Principles or in agreements entered into in the framework of the multilateral negotiations; and
      4. cultural, scientific and educational agreements.
   c. Dealings between the Palestinian Authority and representatives of foreign states and international organizations, as well as the establishment in the Gaza Strip and the Jericho Area of representative offices other than those described in subparagraph 2.a. above, for the purpose of implementing the agreements referred to in subparagraph 2.b. above, shall not be considered foreign relations.

ARTICLE VII

LEGISLATIVE POWERS OF THE PALESTINIAN AUTHORITY

1. The Palestinian Authority will have the power, within its jurisdiction, to promulgate legislation, including basic laws, laws, regulations and other legislative acts.
2. Legislation promulgated by the Palestinian Authority shall be consistent with the provisions of this Agreement.

3. Legislation promulgated by the Palestinian Authority shall be communicated to a legislation subcommittee to be established by the CAC (hereinafter "the Legislation Subcommittee"). During a period of 30 days from the communication of the legislation, Israel may request that the Legislation Subcommittee decide whether such legislation exceeds the jurisdiction of the Palestinian Authority or is otherwise inconsistent with the provisions of this Agreement.

4. Upon receipt of the Israeli request, the Legislation Subcommittee shall decide, as an initial matter, on the entry into force of the legislation pending its decision on the merits of the matter.

5. If the Legislation Subcommittee is unable to reach a decision with regard to the entry into force of the legislation within 15 days, this issue will be referred to a board of review. This board of review shall be comprised of two judges, retired judges or senior jurists (hereinafter "Judges"), one from each side, to be appointed from a compiled list of three Judges proposed by each.

In order to expedite the proceedings before this board of review, the two most senior Judges, one from each side, shall develop written informal rules of procedure.

6. Legislation referred to the board of review shall enter into force only if the board of review decides that it does not deal with a security issue which falls under Israel's responsibility, that it does not seriously threaten other significant Israeli interests protected by this Agreement and that the entry into force of the legislation could not cause irreparable damage or harm.

7. The Legislation Subcommittee shall attempt to reach a decision on the merits of the matter within 30 days from the date of the Israeli request. If this Subcommittee is unable to reach such a decision within this period of 30 days, the matter shall be referred to the Joint Israeli-Palestinian Liaison Committee referred to in Article XV below (hereinafter "the Liaison Committee"). This Liaison Committee will deal with the matter immediately and will attempt to settle it within 30 days.

8. Where the legislation has not entered into force pursuant to paragraphs 5 or 7 above, this situation shall be maintained pending the decision of the Liaison Committee on the merits of the matter, unless it has decided otherwise.

9. Laws and military orders in effect in the Gaza Strip or the Jericho Area prior to the signing of this Agreement shall remain in force, unless amended or abrogated in accordance with this Agreement.

ARTICLE VIII

ARRANGEMENTS FOR SECURITY AND PUBLIC ORDER

1. In order to guarantee public order and internal security for the Palestinians of the Gaza Strip and the Jericho Area, the Palestinian Authority shall establish a strong police force, as set out in Article IX below. Israel shall continue to carry the responsibility for defense against external threats, including the responsibility for protecting the Egyptian border and the Jordanian line, and for defense against external threats from the sea and from the air, as well as the responsi-

bility for overall security of Israelis and Settlements, for the purpose of safe-guarding their internal security and public order, and will have all the powers to take the steps necessary to meet this responsibility.

2. Agreed security arrangements and coordination mechanisms are specified in Annex I.

3. A joint Coordination and Cooperation Committee for mutual security purposes (hereinafter "the JSC"), as well as three joint District Coordination and Cooperation Offices for the Gaza district, the Khan Yunis district and the Jericho district respectively (hereinafter "the DCOs") are hereby established as provided for in Annex I.

4. The security arrangements provided for in this Agreement and in Annex I may be reviewed at the request of either Party and may be amended by mutual agreement of the Parties. Specific review arrangements are included in Annex I.

ARTICLE IX

THE PALESTINIAN DIRECTORATE OF POLICE FORCE

1. The Palestinian Authority shall establish a strong police force, the Palestinian Directorate of Police Force (hereinafter "the Palestinian Police"). The duties, functions, structure, deployment and composition of the Palestinian Police, together with provisions regarding its equipment and operation, are set out in Annex I, Article III. Rules of conduct governing the activities of the Palestinian Police are set out in Annex I, Article VIII.

2. Except for the Palestinian Police referred to in this Article and the Israeli military forces, no other armed forces shall be established or operate in the Gaza Strip or the Jericho Area.

3. Except for the arms, ammunition and equipment of the Palestinian Police described in Annex I, Article III, and those of the Israeli military forces, no organization or individual in the Gaza Strip and the Jericho Area shall manufacture, sell, acquire, possess, import or otherwise introduce into the Gaza Strip or the Jericho Area any firearms, ammunition, weapons, explosives, gunpowder or any related equipment, unless otherwise provided for in Annex I.

ARTICLE X

PASSAGES

Arrangements for coordination between Israel and the Palestinian Authority regarding the Gaza-Egypt and Jericho-Jordan passages, as well as any other agreed international crossings, are set out in Annex I, Article X.

ARTICLE XI

SAFE PASSAGE BETWEEN THE GAZA STRIP AND THE JERICHO AREA

Arrangements for safe passage of persons and transportation between the Gaza Strip and the Jericho Area are set out in Annex I, Article IX.

ARTICLE XII

RELATIONS BETWEEN ISRAEL AND THE PALESTINIAN AUTHORITY

1. Israel and the Palestinian Authority shall seek to foster mutual understanding and tolerance and shall accordingly abstain from incitement, including hostile propaganda, against each other and, without derogating from the principle of freedom of expression, shall take legal measures to prevent such incitement by any organizations, groups or individuals within their jurisdiction.
2. Without derogating from the other provisions of this Agreement, Israel and the Palestinian Authority shall cooperate in combatting criminal activity which may affect both sides, including offenses related to trafficking in illegal drugs and psychotropic substances, smuggling, and offenses against property, including offenses related to vehicles.

ARTICLE XIII

ECONOMIC RELATIONS

The economic relations between the two sides are set out in the Protocol on Economic Relations signed in Paris on April 29, 1994 and the Appendices thereto, certified copies of which are attached as Annex IV, and will be governed by the relevant provisions of this Agreement and its Annexes.

ARTICLE XIV

HUMAN RIGHTS AND THE RULE OF LAW

Israel and the Palestinian Authority shall exercise their powers and responsibilities pursuant to this Agreement with due regard to internationally-accepted norms and principles of human rights and the rule of law.

ARTICLE XV

THE JOINT ISRAELI-PALESTINIAN LIAISON COMMITTEE

1. The Liaison Committee established pursuant to Article X of the Declaration of Principles shall ensure the smooth implementation of this Agreement. It shall deal with issues requiring coordination, other issues of common interest and disputes.
2. The Liaison Committee shall be composed of an equal number of members from each Party. It may add other technicians and experts as necessary.
3. The Liaison Committee shall adopt its rules of procedure, including the frequency and place or places of its meetings.
4. The Liaison Committee shall reach its decisions by Agreement.

ARTICLE XVI

LIAISON AND COOPERATION WITH JORDAN AND EGYPT

1. Pursuant to Article XII of the Declaration of Principles, the two Parties shall invite the Governments of Jordan and Egypt to participate in establishing fur-

ther liaison and cooperation arrangements between the Government of Israel and the Palestinian representatives on the one hand, and the Governments of Jordan and Egypt on the other hand, to promote cooperation between them. These arrangements shall include the constitution of a Continuing Committee.

2. The Continuing Committee shall decide by agreement on the modalities of admission of persons displaced from the West Bank and the Gaza Strip in 1967, together with necessary measures to prevent disruption and disorder.

3. The Continuing Committee shall deal with other matters of common concern.

ARTICLE XVII

SETTLEMENT OF DIFFERENCES AND DISPUTES

Any difference relating to the application of this Agreement shall be referred to the appropriate coordination and cooperation mechanism established under this Agreement. The provisions of Article XV of the Declaration of Principles shall apply to any such difference which is not settled through the appropriate coordination and cooperation mechanism, namely:

1. Disputes arising out of the application or interpretation of this Agreement or any subsequent agreements pertaining to the interim period shall be settled by negotiations through the Liaison Committee.

2. Disputes which cannot be settled by negotiations may be settled by a mechanism of conciliation to be agreed between the Parties.

3. The Parties may agree to submit to arbitration disputes relating to the interim period, which cannot be settled through conciliation. To this end, upon the agreement of both Parties, the Parties will establish an Arbitration Committee.

ARTICLE XVIII

PREVENTION OF HOSTILE ACTS

Both sides shall take all measures necessary in order to prevent acts of terrorism, crime and hostilities directed against each other, against individuals falling under the other's authority and against their property, and shall take legal measures against offenders. In addition, the Palestinian side shall take all measures necessary to prevent such hostile acts directed against the Settlements, the infrastructure serving them and the Military Installation Area, and the Israeli side shall take all measures necessary to prevent such hostile acts emanating from the Settlements and directed against Palestinians.

ARTICLE XIX

MISSING PERSONS

The Palestinian Authority shall cooperate with Israel by providing all necessary assistance in the conduct of searches by Israel within the Gaza Strip and the Jericho Area for missing Israelis, as well as by providing information about missing Israelis. Israel shall cooperate with the Palestinian Authority in searching for, and providing necessary information about, missing Palestinians.

ARTICLE XX

CONFIDENCE BUILDING MEASURES

With a view to creating a positive and supportive public atmosphere to accompany the implementation of this Agreement, and to establish a solid basis of mutual trust and good faith, both Parties agree to carry out confidence building measures as detailed herewith:

1. Upon the signing of this Agreement, Israel will release, or turn over, to the Palestinian Authority within a period of 5 weeks, about 5,000 Palestinian detainees and prisoners, residents of the West Bank and the Gaza Strip. Those released will be free to return to their homes anywhere in the West Bank or the Gaza Strip. Prisoners turned over to the Palestinian Authority shall be obliged to remain in the Gaza Strip or the Jericho Area for the remainder of their sentence.
2. After the signing of this Agreement, the two Parties shall continue to negotiate the release of additional Palestinian prisoners and detainees, building on agreed principles.
3. The implementation of the above measures will be subject to the fulfillment of the procedures determined by Israeli law for the release and transfer of detainees and prisoners.
4. With the assumption of Palestinian authority, the Palestinian side commits itself to solving the problem of those Palestinians who were in contact with the Israeli authorities. Until an agreed solution is found, the Palestinian side undertakes not to prosecute these Palestinians or to harm them in any way.
5. Palestinians from abroad whose entry into the Gaza Strip and the Jericho Area is approved pursuant to this Agreement, and to whom the provisions of this Article are applicable, will not be prosecuted for offenses committed prior to September 13, 1993.

ARTICLE XXI

TEMPORARY INTERNATIONAL PRESENCE

1. The Parties agree to a temporary international or foreign presence in the Gaza Strip and the Jericho Area (hereinafter "the TIP"), in accordance with the provisions of this Article.
2. The TIP shall consist of 400 qualified personnel, including observers, instructors and other experts, from 5 or 6 of the donor countries.
3. The two Parties shall request the donor countries to establish a special fund to provide finance for the TIP.
4. The TIP will function for a period of 6 months. The TIP may extend this period, or change the scope of its operation, with the agreement of the two Parties.
5. The TIP shall be stationed and operate within the following cities and villages: Gaza, Khan Yunis, Rafah, Deir El Ballah, Jabaliya, Absan, Beit Hanun and Jericho.

6. Israel and the Palestinian Authority shall agree on a special Protocol to implement this Article, with the goal of concluding negotiations with the donor countries contributing personnel within two months.

ARTICLE XXII

RIGHTS, LIABILITIES AND OBLIGATIONS

1.
   a. The transfer of all powers and responsibilities to the Palestinian Authority, as detailed in Annex II, includes all related rights, liabilities and obligations arising with regard to acts or omissions which occurred prior to the transfer. Israel will cease to bear any financial responsibility regarding such acts or omissions and the Palestinian Authority will bear all financial responsibility for these and for its own functioning.
   b. Any financial claim made in this regard against Israel will be referred to the Palestinian Authority.
   c. Israel shall provide the Palestinian Authority with the information it has regarding pending and anticipated claims brought before any court or tribunal against Israel in this regard.
   d. Where legal proceedings are brought in respect of such a claim, Israel will notify the Palestinian Authority and enable it to participate in defending the claim and raise any arguments on its behalf.
   e. In the event that an award is made against Israel by any court or tribunal in respect of such a claim, the Palestinian Authority shall reimburse Israel the full amount of the award.
   f. Without prejudice to the above, where a court or tribunal hearing such a claim finds that liability rests solely with an employee or agent who acted beyond the scope of the powers assigned to him or her, unlawfully or with willful malfeasance, the Palestinian Authority shall not bear financial responsibility.
2. The transfer of authority in itself shall not affect rights, liabilities and obligations of any person or legal entity, in existence at the date of signing of this Agreement.

ARTICLE XXIII

FINAL CLAUSES

1. This Agreement shall enter into force on the date of its signing.
2. The arrangements established by this Agreement shall remain in force until and to the extent superseded by the Interim Agreement referred to in the Declaration of Principles or any other agreement between the Parties.
3. The five-year interim period referred to in the Declaration of Principles commences on the date of the signing of this Agreement.
4. The Parties agree that, as long as this Agreement is in force, the security fence erected by Israel around the Gaza Strip shall remain in place and that the line demarcated by the fence, as shown on attached map No. 1, shall be authoritative only for the purpose of this Agreement.

5. Nothing in this Agreement shall prejudice or preempt the outcome of the negotiations on the interim agreement or on the permanent status to be conducted pursuant to the Declaration of Principles. Neither Party shall be deemed, by virtue of having entered into this Agreement, to have renounced or waived any of its existing rights, claims or positions.

6. The two Parties view the West Bank and the Gaza Strip as a single territorial unit, the integrity of which will be preserved during the interim period.

7. The Gaza Strip and the Jericho Area shall continue to be an integral part of the West Bank and the Gaza Strip, and their status shall not be changed for the period of this Agreement. Nothing in this Agreement shall be considered to change this status.

8. The Preamble to this Agreement, and all Annexes, Appendices and maps attached hereto, shall constitute an integral part hereof.

SOURCE: U.S. Department of State, http://www.state.gov/p/nea/rls/22676.htm.

DOCUMENT

Oslo II: Interim Agreement on the West Bank and the Gaza Strip

SEPTEMBER 28, 1995

The Government of the State of Israel and the Palestine Liberation Organization (hereinafter "the PLO"), the representative of the Palestinian people;

PREAMBLE

WITHIN the framework of the Middle East peace process initiated at Madrid in October 1991;

REAFFIRMING their determination to put an end to decades of confrontation and to live in peaceful coexistence, mutual dignity and security, while recognizing their mutual legitimate and political rights;

REAFFIRMING their desire to achieve a just, lasting and comprehensive peace settlement and historic reconciliation through the agreed political process;

RECOGNIZING that the peace process and the new era that it has created, as well as the new relationship established between the two Parties as described above, are irreversible, and the determination of the two Parties to maintain, sustain and continue the peace process;

RECOGNIZING that the aim of the Israeli-Palestinian negotiations within the current Middle East peace process is, among other things, to establish a Palestinian

Interim Self-Government Authority, i.e. the elected Council (hereinafter "the Council" or "the Palestinian Council"), and the elected Ra'ees [*rais*] of the Executive Authority, for the Palestinian people in the West Bank and the Gaza Strip, for a transitional period not exceeding five years from the date of signing the Agreement on the Gaza Strip and the Jericho Area (hereinafter "the Gaza-Jericho Agreement") on May 4, 1994, leading to a permanent settlement based on Security Council Resolutions 242 and 338;

REAFFIRMING their understanding that the interim self-government arrangements contained in this Agreement are an integral part of the whole peace process, that the negotiations on the permanent status, that will start as soon as possible but not later than May 4, 1996, will lead to the implementation of Security Council Resolutions 242 and 338, and that the Interim Agreement shall settle all the issues of the interim period and that no such issues will be deferred to the agenda of the permanent status negotiations;

REAFFIRMING their adherence to the mutual recognition and commitments expressed in the letters dated September 9, 1993, signed by and exchanged between the Prime Minister of Israel and the Chairman of the PLO;

DESIROUS of putting into effect the Declaration of Principles on Interim Self-Government Arrangements signed at Washington, D.C. on September 13, 1993, and the Agreed Minutes thereto (hereinafter "the DOP") and in particular Article III and Annex I concerning the holding of direct, free and general political elections for the Council and the Ra'ees of the Executive Authority in order that the Palestinian people in the West Bank, Jerusalem and the Gaza Strip may democratically elect accountable representatives;

RECOGNIZING that these elections will constitute a significant interim preparatory step toward the realization of the legitimate rights of the Palestinian people and their just requirements and will provide a democratic basis for the establishment of Palestinian institutions;

REAFFIRMING their mutual commitment to act, in accordance with this Agreement, immediately, efficiently and effectively against acts or threats of terrorism, violence or incitement, whether committed by Palestinians or Israelis;

FOLLOWING the Gaza-Jericho Agreement; the Agreement on Preparatory Transfer of Powers and Responsibilities signed at Erez on August 29, 1994 (hereinafter "the Preparatory Transfer Agreement"); and the Protocol on Further Transfer of Powers and Responsibilities signed at Cairo on August 27, 1995 (hereinafter "the Further Transfer Protocol"); which three agreements will be superseded by this Agreement;

HEREBY AGREE as follows:

CHAPTER I—THE COUNCIL

ARTICLE I

TRANSFER OF AUTHORITY

1. Israel shall transfer powers and responsibilities as specified in this Agreement from the Israeli military government and its Civil Administration to the Council in accordance with this Agreement. Israel shall continue to exercise powers and responsibilities not so transferred.

2. Pending the inauguration of the Council, the powers and responsibilities transferred to the Council shall be exercised by the Palestinian Authority established in accordance with the Gaza-Jericho Agreement, which shall also have all the

rights, liabilities and obligations to be assumed by the Council in this regard. Accordingly, the term "Council" throughout this Agreement shall, pending the inauguration of the Council, be construed as meaning the Palestinian Authority.

3. The transfer of powers and responsibilities to the police force established by the Palestinian Council in accordance with Article XIV below (hereinafter "the Palestinian Police") shall be accomplished in a phased manner, as detailed in this Agreement and in the Protocol concerning Redeployment and Security Arrangements attached as Annex I to this Agreement (hereinafter "Annex I").

4. As regards the transfer and assumption of authority in civil spheres, powers and responsibilities shall be transferred and assumed as set out in the Protocol Concerning Civil Affairs attached as Annex III to this Agreement (hereinafter "Annex III").

5. After the inauguration of the Council, the Civil Administration in the West Bank will be dissolved, and the Israeli military government shall be withdrawn. The withdrawal of the military government shall not prevent it from exercising the powers and responsibilities not transferred to the Council.

6. A Joint Civil Affairs Coordination and Cooperation Committee (hereinafter "the CAC"), Joint Regional Civil Affairs Subcommittees, one for the Gaza Strip and the other for the West Bank, and District Civil Liaison Offices in the West Bank shall be established in order to provide for coordination and cooperation in civil affairs between the Council and Israel, as detailed in Annex III.

7. The offices of the Council, and the offices of its Ra'ees and its Executive Authority and other committees, shall be located in areas under Palestinian territorial jurisdiction in the West Bank and the Gaza Strip.

ARTICLE II

ELECTIONS

1. In order that the Palestinian people of the West Bank and the Gaza Strip may govern themselves according to democratic principles, direct, free and general political elections will be held for the Council and the Ra'ees of the Executive Authority of the Council in accordance with the provisions set out in the Protocol concerning Elections attached as Annex II to this Agreement (hereinafter "Annex II").

2. These elections will constitute a significant interim preparatory step towards the realization of the legitimate rights of the Palestinian people and their just requirements and will provide a democratic basis for the establishment of Palestinian institutions.

3. Palestinians of Jerusalem who live there may participate in the election process in accordance with the provisions contained in this Article and in Article VI of Annex II (Election Arrangements concerning Jerusalem).

4. The elections shall be called by the Chairman of the Palestinian Authority immediately following the signing of this Agreement to take place at the earliest practicable date following the redeployment of Israeli forces in accordance with Annex I, and consistent with the requirements of the election timetable as provided in Annex II, the Election Law and the Election Regulations, as defined in Article I of Annex II.

ARTICLE III

STRUCTURE OF THE PALESTINIAN COUNCIL

1. The Palestinian Council and the Ra'ees of the Executive Authority of the Council constitute the Palestinian Interim Self-Government Authority, which will be elected by the Palestinian people of the West Bank, Jerusalem and the Gaza Strip for the transitional period agreed in Article I of the DOP.
2. The Council shall possess both legislative power and executive power, in accordance with Articles VII and IX of the DOP. The Council shall carry out and be responsible for all the legislative and executive powers and responsibilities transferred to it under this Agreement. The exercise of legislative powers shall be in accordance with Article XVIII of this Agreement (Legislative Powers of the Council).
3. The Council and the Ra'ees of the Executive Authority of the Council shall be directly and simultaneously elected by the Palestinian people of the West Bank, Jerusalem and the Gaza Strip, in accordance with the provisions of this Agreement and the Election Law and Regulations, which shall not be contrary to the provisions of this Agreement.
4. The Council and the Ra'ees of the Executive Authority of the Council shall be elected for a transitional period not exceeding five years from the signing of the Gaza-Jericho Agreement on May 4, 1994.
5. Immediately upon its inauguration, the Council will elect from among its members a Speaker. The Speaker will preside over the meetings of the Council, administer the Council and its committees, decide on the agenda of each meeting, and lay before the Council proposals for voting and declare their results.
6. The jurisdiction of the Council shall be as determined in Article XVII of this Agreement (Jurisdiction).
7. The organization, structure and functioning of the Council shall be in accordance with this Agreement and the Basic Law for the Palestinian Interim Self-government Authority, which Law shall be adopted by the Council. The Basic Law and any regulations made under it shall not be contrary to the provisions of this Agreement.
8. The Council shall be responsible under its executive powers for the offices, services and departments transferred to it and may establish, within its jurisdiction, ministries and subordinate bodies, as necessary for the fulfillment of its responsibilities.
9. The Speaker will present for the Council's approval proposed internal procedures that will regulate, among other things, the decision-making processes of the Council.

ARTICLE IV

SIZE OF THE COUNCIL

The Palestinian Council shall be composed of 82 representatives and the Ra'ees of the Executive Authority, who will be directly and simultaneously elected by the Palestinian people of the West Bank, Jerusalem and the Gaza Strip.

ARTICLE V

THE EXECUTIVE AUTHORITY OF THE COUNCIL

1. The Council will have a committee that will exercise the executive authority of the Council, formed in accordance with paragraph 4 below (hereinafter "the Executive Authority").
2. The Executive Authority shall be bestowed with the executive authority of the Council and will exercise it on behalf of the Council. It shall determine its own internal procedures and decision making processes.
3. The Council will publish the names of the members of the Executive Authority immediately upon their initial appointment and subsequent to any changes.
4. a. The Ra'ees of the Executive Authority shall be an ex officio member of the Executive Authority.
   b. All of the other members of the Executive Authority, except as provided in subparagraph c. below, shall be members of the Council, chosen and proposed to the Council by the Ra'ees of the Executive Authority and approved by the Council.
   c. The Ra'ees of the Executive Authority shall have the right to appoint some persons, in number not exceeding twenty percent of the total membership of the Executive Authority, who are not members of the Council, to exercise executive authority and participate in government tasks. Such appointed members may not vote in meetings of the Council.
   d. Non-elected members of the Executive Authority must have a valid address in an area under the jurisdiction of the Council.

ARTICLE VI

OTHER COMMITTEES OF THE COUNCIL

1. The Council may form small committees to simplify the proceedings of the Council and to assist in controlling the activity of its Executive Authority.
2. Each committee shall establish its own decision-making processes within the general framework of the organization and structure of the Council.

ARTICLE VII

OPEN GOVERNMENT

1. All meetings of the Council and of its committees, other than the Executive Authority, shall be open to the public, except upon a resolution of the Council or the relevant committee on the grounds of security, or commercial or personal confidentiality.
2. Participation in the deliberations of the Council, its committees and the Executive Authority shall be limited to their respective members only. Experts may be invited to such meetings to address specific issues on an ad hoc basis.

ARTICLE VIII

JUDICIAL REVIEW

Any person or organization affected by any act or decision of the Ra'ees of the Executive Authority of the Council or of any member of the Executive Authority, who believes that such act or decision exceeds the authority of the Ra'ees or of such member, or is otherwise incorrect in law or procedure, may apply to the relevant Palestinian Court of Justice for a review of such activity or decision.

ARTICLE IX

POWERS AND RESPONSIBILITIES OF THE COUNCIL

1. Subject to the provisions of this Agreement, the Council will, within its jurisdiction, have legislative powers as set out in Article XVIII of this Agreement, as well as executive powers.
2. The executive power of the Palestinian Council shall extend to all matters within its jurisdiction under this Agreement or any future agreement that may be reached between the two Parties during the interim period. It shall include the power to formulate and conduct Palestinian policies and to supervise their implementation, to issue any rule or regulation under powers given in approved legislation and administrative decisions necessary for the realization of Palestinian self-government, the power to employ staff, sue and be sued and conclude contracts, and the power to keep and administer registers and records of the population, and issue certificates, licenses and documents.
3. The Palestinian Council's executive decisions and acts shall be consistent with the provisions of this Agreement.
4. The Palestinian Council may adopt all necessary measures in order to enforce the law and any of its decisions, and bring proceedings before the Palestinian courts and tribunals.
5. a. In accordance with the DOP, the Council will not have powers and responsibilities in the sphere of foreign relations, which sphere includes the establishment abroad of embassies, consulates or other types of foreign missions and posts or permitting their establishment in the West Bank or the Gaza Strip, the appointment of or admission of diplomatic and consular staff, and the exercise of diplomatic functions.
   b. Notwithstanding the provisions of this paragraph, the PLO may conduct negotiations and sign agreements with states or international organizations for the benefit of the Council in the following cases only:
      (1) economic agreements, as specifically provided in Annex V of this Agreement:
      (2) agreements with donor countries for the purpose of implementing arrangements for the provision of assistance to the Council,
      (3) agreements for the purpose of implementing the regional development plans detailed in Annex IV of the DOP or in agreements entered into in the framework of the multilateral negotiations, and

(4) cultural, scientific and educational agreements. Dealings between the Council and representatives of foreign states and international organizations, as well as the establishment in the West Bank and the Gaza Strip of representative offices other than those described in subparagraph 5.a above, for the purpose of implementing the agreements referred to in subparagraph 5.b above, shall not be considered foreign relations.

6. Subject to the provisions of this Agreement, the Council shall, within its jurisdiction, have an independent judicial system composed of independent Palestinian courts and tribunals.

CHAPTER 2—REDEPLOYMENT AND SECURITY ARRANGEMENTS

ARTICLE X

REDEPLOYMENT OF ISRAELI MILITARY FORCES

1. The first phase of the Israeli military forces redeployment will cover populated areas in the West Bank—cities, towns, villages, refugee camps and hamlets—as set out in Annex I, and will be completed prior to the eve of the Palestinian elections, i.e., 22 days before the day of the elections.

2. Further redeployments of Israeli military forces to specified military locations will commence after the inauguration of the Council and will be gradually implemented commensurate with the assumption of responsibility for public order and internal security by the Palestinian Police, to be completed within 18 months from the date of the inauguration of the Council as detailed in Articles XI (Land) and XIII (Security), below and in Annex I.

3. The Palestinian Police shall be deployed and shall assume responsibility for public order and internal security for Palestinians in a phased manner in accordance with XIII (Security) below and Annex I.

4. Israel shall continue to carry the responsibility for external security, as well as the responsibility for overall security of Israelis for the purpose of safeguarding their internal security and public order.

5. For the purpose of this Agreement, "Israeli military forces" includes Israel Police and other Israeli security forces.

ARTICLE XI

LAND

1. The two sides view the West Bank and the Gaza Strip as a single territorial unit, the integrity and status of which will be preserved during the interim period.

2. The two sides agree that West Bank and Gaza Strip territory, except for issues that will be negotiated in the permanent status negotiations, will come under the jurisdiction of the Palestinian Council in a phased manner, to be completed within 18 months from the date of the inauguration of the Council, as specified below:

a. Land in populated areas (Areas A and B), including government and Al Waqf land, will come under the jurisdiction of the Council during the first phase of redeployment.

b. All civil powers and responsibilities, including planning and zoning, in Areas A and B, set out in Annex III, will be transferred to and assumed by the Council during the first phase of redeployment.

c. In Area C, during the first phase of redeployment Israel will transfer to the Council civil powers and responsibilities not relating to territory, as set out in Annex III.

d. The further redeployments of Israeli military forces to specified military locations will be gradually implemented in accordance with the DOP in three phases, each to take place after an interval of six months, after the inauguration of the Council, to be completed within 18 months from the date of the inauguration of the Council.

e. During the further redeployment phases to be completed within 18 months from the date of the inauguration of the Council, powers and responsibilities relating to territory will be transferred gradually to Palestinian jurisdiction that will cover West Bank and Gaza Strip territory, except for the issues that will be negotiated in the permanent status negotiations.

f. The specified military locations referred to in Article X, paragraph 2 above will be determined in the further redeployment phases, within the specified timeframe ending not later than 18 months from the date of the inauguration of the Council, and will be negotiated in the permanent status negotiations.

3. For the purpose of this Agreement and until the completion of the first phase of the further redeployments:

a. "Area A" means the populated areas delineated by a red line and shaded in brown on attached map No. 1;

b. "Area B" means the populated areas delineated by a red line and shaded in yellow on attached map No. 1, and the built-up area of the hamlets listed in Appendix 6 to Annex I, and

c. "Area C" means areas of the West Bank outside Areas A and B, which, except for the issues that will be negotiated in the permanent status negotiations, will be gradually transferred to Palestinian jurisdiction in accordance with this Agreement.

ARTICLE XII

ARRANGEMENTS FOR SECURITY AND PUBLIC ORDER

1. In order to guarantee public order and internal security for the Palestinians of the West Bank and the Gaza Strip, the Council shall establish a strong police force as set out in Article XIV below. Israel shall continue to carry the responsibility for defense against external threats, including the responsibility for protecting the Egyptian and Jordanian borders, and for defense against external threats from the sea and from the air, as well as the responsibility for overall security of Israelis and Settlements, for the purpose of safeguarding their internal security and public order, and will have all the powers to take the steps necessary to meet this responsibility.

2. Agreed security arrangements and coordination mechanisms are specified in Annex I.

3. A Joint Coordination and Cooperation Committee for Mutual Security Purposes (hereinafter "the JSC"), as well as Joint Regional Security Committees (hereinafter "RSCs") and Joint District Coordination Offices (hereinafter "DCOs"), are hereby established as provided for in Annex I.

4. The security arrangements provided for in this Agreement and in Annex I may be reviewed at the request of either Party and may be amended by mutual agreement of the Parties. Specific review arrangements are included in Annex I.

5. For the purpose of this Agreement, "the Settlements" means, in the West Bank the settlements in Area C; and in the Gaza Strip—the Gush Katif and Erez settlement areas, as well as the other settlements in the Gaza Strip, as shown on attached map No. 2.

ARTICLE XIII

SECURITY

1. The Council will, upon completion of the redeployment of Israeli military forces in each district, as set out in Appendix 1 to Annex I, assume the powers and responsibilities for internal security and public order in Area A in that district.

2. a. There will be a complete redeployment of Israeli military forces from Area B. Israel will transfer to the Council and the Council will assume responsibility for public order for Palestinians. Israel shall have the overriding responsibility for security for the purpose of protecting Israelis and confronting the threat of terrorism.

   b. In Area B the Palestinian Police shall assume the responsibility for public order for Palestinians and shall be deployed in order to accommodate the Palestinian needs and requirements in the following manner:

     (1) The Palestinian Police shall establish 25 police stations and posts in towns, villages, and other places listed in Appendix 2 to Annex I and as delineated on map No. 3. The West Bank RSC may agree on the establishment of additional police stations and posts, if required.

     (2) The Palestinian Police shall be responsible for handling public order incidents in which only Palestinians are involved.

     (3) The Palestinian Police shall operate freely in populated places where police stations and posts are located, as set out in paragraph b(1) above.

     (4) While the movement of uniformed Palestinian policemen in Area B outside places where there is a Palestinian police station or post will be carried out after coordination and confirmation through the relevant DCO, three months after the completion of redeployment from Area B, the DCOs may decide that movement of Palestinian policemen from the police stations in Area B to Palestinian towns and villages in Area B on roads that are used only by Palestinian traffic will take place after notifying the DCO.

     (5) The coordination of such planned movement prior to confirmation through the relevant DCO shall include a scheduled plan, including the number of policemen, as well as the type and number of weapons and vehicles intended to take part. It shall also include details of arrangements

for ensuring continued coordination through appropriate communication links, the exact schedule of movement to the area of the planned operation, including the destination and routes thereto, its proposed duration and the schedule for returning to the police station or post.

The Israeli side of the DCO will provide the Palestinian side with its response, following a request for movement of policemen in accordance with this paragraph, in normal or routine cases within one day and in emergency cases no later than 2 hours.

(6) The Palestinian Police and the Israeli military forces will conduct joint security activities on the main roads as set out in Annex I.

(7) The Palestinian Police will notify the West Bank RSC of the names of the policemen, number plates of police vehicles and serial numbers of weapons, with respect to each police station and post in Area B.

(8) Further redeployments from Area C and transfer of internal security responsibility to the Palestinian Police in Areas B and C will be carried out in three phases, each to take place after an interval of six months, to be completed 18 months after the inauguration of the Council, except for the issues of permanent status negotiations and of Israel's overall responsibility for Israelis and borders.

(9) The procedures detailed in this paragraph will be reviewed within six months of the completion of the first phase of redeployment.

ARTICLE XIV

THE PALESTINIAN POLICE

1. The Council shall establish a strong police force. The duties, functions, structure, deployment and composition of the Palestinian Police, together with provisions regarding its equipment and operation, as well as rules of conduct, are set out in Annex I.

2. The Palestinian police force established under the Gaza-Jericho Agreement will be fully integrated into the Palestinian Police and will be subject to the provisions of this Agreement.

3. Except for the Palestinian Police and the Israeli military forces, no other armed forces shall be established or operate in the West Bank and the Gaza Strip.

4. Except for the arms, ammunition and equipment of the Palestinian Police described in Annex I, and those of the Israeli military forces, no organization, group or individual in the West Bank and the Gaza Strip shall manufacture, sell, acquire, possess, import or otherwise introduce into the West Bank or the Gaza Strip any firearms, ammunition, weapons, explosives, gunpowder or any related equipment, unless otherwise provided for in Annex I.

ARTICLE XV

PREVENTION OF HOSTILE ACTS

1. Both sides shall take all measures necessary in order to prevent acts of terrorism, crime and hostilities directed against each other, against individuals falling

under the other's authority and against their property and shall take legal measures against offenders.

2. Specific provisions for the implementation of this Article are set out in Annex I.

ARTICLE XVI

CONFIDENCE BUILDING MEASURES

With a view to fostering a positive and supportive public atmosphere to accompany the implementation of this Agreement, to establish a solid basis of mutual trust and good faith, and in order to facilitate the anticipated cooperation and new relations between the two peoples, both Parties agree to carry out confidence building measures as detailed herewith:

1. Israel will release or turn over to the Palestinian side, Palestinian detainees and prisoners, residents of the West Bank and the Gaza Strip. The first stage of release of these prisoners and detainees will take place on the signing of this Agreement and the second stage will take place prior to the date of the elections. There will be a third stage of release of detainees and prisoners. Detainees and prisoners will be released from among categories detailed in Annex VII (Release of Palestinian Prisoners and Detainees). Those released will be free to return to their homes in the West Bank and the Gaza Strip.

2. Palestinians who have maintained contact with the Israeli authorities will not be subjected to acts of harassment, violence, retribution or prosecution. Appropriate ongoing measures will be taken, in coordination with Israel, in order to ensure their protection.

3. Palestinians from abroad whose entry into the West Bank and the Gaza Strip is approved pursuant to this Agreement, and to whom the provisions of this Article are applicable, will not be prosecuted for offenses committed prior to September 13, 1993.

CHAPTER 3—LEGAL AFFAIRS

ARTICLE XVII

JURISDICTION

1. In accordance with the DOP, the jurisdiction of the Council will cover West Bank and Gaza Strip territory as a single territorial unit, except for:
   a. issues that will be negotiated in the permanent status negotiations: Jerusalem, settlements, specified military locations, Palestinian refugees, borders, foreign relations and Israelis; and
   b. powers and responsibilities not transferred to the Council.

2. Accordingly, the authority of the Council encompasses all matters that fall within its territorial, functional and personal jurisdiction, as follows:
   a. The territorial jurisdiction of the Council shall encompass Gaza Strip territory, except for the Settlements and the Military Installation Area shown on map No. 2, and West Bank territory, except for Area C which, except for the issues that will be negotiated in the permanent status negotiations, will

be gradually transferred to Palestinian jurisdiction in three phases, each to take place after an interval of six months, to be completed 18 months after the inauguration of the Council. At this time, the jurisdiction of the Council will cover West Bank and Gaza Strip territory, except for the issues that will be negotiated in the permanent status negotiations.

Territorial jurisdiction includes land, subsoil and territorial waters, in accordance with the provisions of this Agreement.

b. The functional jurisdiction of the Council extends to all powers and responsibilities transferred to the Council, as specified in this Agreement or in any future agreements that may be reached between the Parties during the interim period.

c. The territorial and functional jurisdiction of the Council will apply to all persons, except for Israelis, unless otherwise provided in this Agreement.

d. Notwithstanding subparagraph a. above, the Council shall have functional jurisdiction in Area C, as detailed in Article IV of Annex III.

3. The Council has, within its authority, legislative, executive and judicial powers and responsibilities, as provided for in this Agreement.

4. a. Israel, through its military government, has the authority over areas that are not under the territorial jurisdiction of the Council, powers and responsibilities not transferred to the Council and Israelis.

b. To this end, the Israeli military government shall retain the necessary legislative, judicial and executive powers and responsibilities, in accordance with international law. This provision shall not derogate from Israel's applicable legislation over Israelis in person.

5. The exercise of authority with regard to the electromagnetic sphere and air space shall be in accordance with the provisions of this Agreement.

6. Without derogating from the provisions of this Article, legal arrangements detailed in the Protocol Concerning Legal Matters attached as Annex IV to this Agreement (hereinafter "Annex IV") shall be observed. Israel and the Council may negotiate further legal arrangements.

7. Israel and the Council shall cooperate on matters of legal assistance in criminal and civil matters through a legal committee (hereinafter "the Legal Committee"), hereby established.

8. The Council's jurisdiction will extend gradually to cover West Bank and Gaza Strip territory, except for the issues to be negotiated in the permanent status negotiations, through a series of redeployments of the Israeli military forces. The first phase of the redeployment of Israeli military forces will cover populated areas in the West Bank—cities, towns, refugee camps and hamlets, as set out in Annex I—and will be completed prior to the eve of the Palestinian elections, i.e. 22 days before the day of the elections. Further redeployments of Israeli military forces to specified military locations will commence immediately upon the inauguration of the Council and will be effected in three phases, each to take place after an interval of six months, to be concluded no later than eighteen months from the date of the inauguration of the Council.

ARTICLE XVIII

LEGISLATIVE POWERS OF THE COUNCIL

1. For the purposes of this Article, legislation shall mean any primary and secondary legislation, including basic laws, laws, regulations and other legislative acts.
2. The Council has the power, within its jurisdiction as defined in Article XVII of this Agreement, to adopt legislation.
3. While the primary legislative power shall lie in the hands of the Council as a whole, the Ra'ees of the Executive Authority of the Council shall have the following legislative powers
   a. the power to initiate legislation or to present proposed legislation to the Council;
   b. the power to promulgate legislation adopted by the Council; and
   c. the power to issue secondary legislation, including regulations, relating to any matters specified and within the scope laid down in any primary legislation adopted by the Council.
4. a. Legislation, including legislation which amends or abrogates existing laws or military orders, which exceeds the jurisdiction of the Council or which is otherwise inconsistent with the provisions of the DOP, this Agreement, or of any other agreement that may be reached between the two sides during the interim period, shall have no effect and shall be void ab initio.
   b. The Ra'ees of the Executive Authority of the Council shall not promulgate legislation adopted by the Council if such legislation falls under the provisions of this paragraph.
5. All legislation shall be communicated to the Israeli side of the Legal Committee.
6. Without derogating from the provisions of paragraph 4 above, the Israeli side of the Legal Committee may refer for the attention of the Committee any legislation regarding which Israel considers the provisions of paragraph 4 apply, in order to discuss issues arising from such legislation. The Legal Committee will consider the legislation referred to it at the earliest opportunity.

ARTICLE XIX

HUMAN RIGHTS AND THE RULE OF LAW

Israel and the Council shall exercise their powers and responsibilities pursuant to this Agreement with due regard to internationally-accepted norms and principles of human rights and the rule of law.

ARTICLE XX

Rights, Liabilities and Obligations

1. a. The transfer of powers and responsibilities from the Israeli military government and its civil administration to the Council, as detailed in Annex III, includes all related rights, liabilities and obligations arising with regard to acts or omissions which occurred prior to such transfer. Israel will cease to bear

any financial responsibility regarding such acts or omissions and the Council will bear all financial responsibility for these and for its own functioning.

b. Any financial claim made in this regard against Israel will be referred to the Council.

c. Israel shall provide the Council with the information it has regarding pending and anticipated claims brought before any court or tribunal against Israel in this regard.

d. Where legal proceedings are brought in respect of such a claim, Israel will notify the Council and enable it to participate in defending the claim and raise any arguments on its behalf.

e. In the event that an award is made against Israel by any court or tribunal in respect of such a claim, the Council shall immediately reimburse Israel the full amount of the award.

f. Without prejudice to the above, where a court or tribunal hearing such a claim finds that liability rests solely with an employee or agent who acted beyond the scope of the powers assigned to him or her, unlawfully or with willful malfeasance, the Council shall not bear financial responsibility.

2. a. Notwithstanding the provisions of paragraphs 1.d through 1.f above, each side may take the necessary measures, including promulgation of legislation, in order to ensure that such claims by Palestinians including pending claims in which the hearing of evidence has not yet begun, are brought only before Palestinian courts or tribunals in the West Bank and the Gaza Strip, and are not brought before or heard by Israeli courts or tribunals.

b. Where a new claim has been brought before a Palestinian court or tribunal subsequent to the dismissal of the claim pursuant to subparagraph a. above, the Council shall defend it and, in accordance with subparagraph 1.a above, in the event that an award is made for the plaintiff, shall pay the amount of the award.

c. The Legal Committee shall agree on arrangements for the transfer of all materials and information needed to enable the Palestinian courts or tribunals to hear such claims as referred to in subparagraph b. above, and, when necessary, for the provision of legal assistance by Israel to the Council in defending such claims.

3. The transfer of authority in itself shall not affect rights, liabilities and obligations of any person or legal entity, in existence at the date of signing of this Agreement.

4. The Council, upon its inauguration, will assume all the rights, liabilities and obligations of the Palestinian Authority.

5. For the purpose of this Agreement, "Israelis" also includes Israeli statutory agencies and corporations registered in Israel.

ARTICLE XXI

SETTLEMENT OF DIFFERENCES AND DISPUTES

Any difference relating to the application of this Agreement shall be referred to the appropriate coordination and cooperation mechanism established under this Agreement.

The provisions of Article XV of the DOP shall apply to any such difference which is not settled through the appropriate coordination and cooperation mechanism, namely:

1. Disputes arising out of the application or interpretation of this Agreement or any related agreements pertaining to the interim period shall be settled through the Liaison Committee.
2. Disputes which cannot be settled by negotiations may be settled by a mechanism of conciliation to be agreed between the Parties.
3. The Parties may agree to submit to arbitration disputes relating to the interim period, which cannot be settled through conciliation. To this end, upon the agreement of both Parties, the Parties will establish an Arbitration Committee.

CHAPTER 4—COOPERATION

ARTICLE XXII

RELATIONS BETWEEN ISRAEL AND THE COUNCIL

1. Israel and the Council shall seek to foster mutual understanding and tolerance and shall accordingly abstain from incitement, including hostile propaganda, against each other and, without derogating from the principle of freedom of expression, shall take legal measures to prevent such incitement by any organizations, groups or individuals within their jurisdiction.
2. Israel and the Council will ensure that their respective educational systems contribute to the peace between the Israeli and Palestinian peoples and to peace in the entire region, and will refrain from the introduction of any motifs that could adversely affect the process of reconciliation.
3. Without derogating from the other provisions of this Agreement, Israel and the Council shall cooperate in combating criminal activity which may affect both sides, including offenses related to trafficking in illegal drugs and psychotropic substances, smuggling, and offenses against property, including offenses related to vehicles.

ARTICLE XXIII

COOPERATION WITH REGARD TO TRANSFER OF POWERS AND RESPONSIBILITIES

In order to ensure a smooth, peaceful and orderly transfer of powers and responsibilities, the two sides will cooperate with regard to the transfer of security powers and responsibilities in accordance with the provisions of Annex I, and the transfer of civil powers and responsibilities in accordance with the provisions of Annex III.

ARTICLE XXIV

ECONOMIC RELATIONS

The economic relations between the two sides are set out in the Protocol on Economic Relations signed in Paris on April 29, 1994, and the Appendices thereto, and the Supplement to the Protocol on Economic Relations all attached as Annex V, and will be governed by the relevant provisions of this Agreement and its Annexes.

ARTICLE XXV

COOPERATION PROGRAMS

1. The Parties agree to establish a mechanism to develop programs of cooperation between them. Details of such cooperation are set out in Annex VI.
2. A Standing Cooperation Committee to deal with issues arising in the context of this cooperation is hereby established as provided for in Annex VI.

ARTICLE XXVI

THE JOINT ISRAELI-PALESTINIAN LIAISON COMMITTEE

1. The Liaison Committee established pursuant to Article X of the DOP shall ensure the smooth implementation of this Agreement. It shall deal with issues requiring coordination, other issues of common interest and disputes.
2. The Liaison Committee shall be composed of an equal number of members from each Party. It may add other technicians and experts as necessary.
3. The Liaison Committee shall adopt its rules of procedures, including the frequency and place or places of its meetings.
4. The Liaison Committee shall reach its decisions by agreement.
5. The Liaison Committee shall establish a subcommittee that will monitor and steer the implementation of this Agreement (hereinafter "the Monitoring and Steering Committee"). It will function as follows:
   a. The Monitoring and Steering Committee will, on an ongoing basis, monitor the implementation of this Agreement, with a view to enhancing the cooperation and fostering the peaceful relations between the two sides.
   b. The Monitoring and Steering Committee will steer the activities of the various joint committees established in this Agreement (the JSC, the CAC, the Legal Committee, the Joint Economic Committee and the Standing Cooperation Committee) concerning the ongoing implementation of the Agreement, and will report to the Liaison Committee.
   c. The Monitoring and Steering Committee will be composed of the heads of the various committees mentioned above.
   d. The two heads of the Monitoring and Steering Committee will establish its rules of procedures, including the frequency and places of its meetings.

ARTICLE XXVII

LIAISON AND COOPERATION WITH JORDAN AND EGYPT

1. Pursuant to Article XII of the DOP, the two Parties have invited the Governments of Jordan and Egypt to participate in establishing further liaison and cooperation arrangements between the Government of Israel and the Palestinian representatives on the one hand, and the Governments of Jordan and Egypt

on the other hand, to promote cooperation between them. As part of these arrangements a Continuing Committee has been constituted and has commenced its deliberations.

2. The Continuing Committee shall decide by agreement on the modalities of admission of persons displaced from the West Bank and the Gaza Strip in 1967, together with necessary measures to prevent disruption and disorder.

3. The Continuing Committee shall also deal with other matters of common concern.

ARTICLE XXVIII

MISSING PERSONS

1. Israel and the Council shall cooperate by providing each other with all necessary assistance in the conduct of searches for missing persons and bodies of persons which have not been recovered, as well as by providing information about missing persons.

2. The PLO undertakes to cooperate with Israel and to assist it in its efforts to locate and to return to Israel Israeli soldiers who are missing in action and the bodies of soldiers which have not been recovered.

CHAPTER 5—MISCELLANEOUS PROVISIONS

ARTICLE XXIX

SAFE PASSAGE BETWEEN THE WEST BANK AND THE GAZA STRIP

Arrangements for safe passage of persons and transportation between the West Bank and the Gaza Strip are set out in Annex I.

ARTICLE XXX

PASSAGES

Arrangements for coordination between Israel and the Council regarding passage to and from Egypt and Jordan, as well as any other agreed international crossings, are set out in Annex I.

ARTICLE XXXI

FINAL CLAUSES

1. This Agreement shall enter into force on the date of its signing.

2. The Gaza-Jericho Agreement, except for Article XX (Confidence-Building Measures), the Preparatory Transfer Agreement and the Further Transfer Protocol will be superseded by this Agreement.

3. The Council, upon its inauguration, shall replace the Palestinian Authority and shall assume all the undertakings and obligations of the Palestinian

Authority under the Gaza-Jericho Agreement, the Preparatory Transfer Agreement, and the Further Transfer Protocol.

4. The two sides shall pass all necessary legislation to implement this Agreement.

5. Permanent status negotiations will commence as soon as possible, but not later than May 4, 1996, between the Parties. It is understood that these negotiations shall cover remaining issues, including: Jerusalem, refugees, settlements, security arrangements, borders, relations and cooperation with other neighbors, and other issues of common interest.

6. Nothing in this Agreement shall prejudice or preempt the outcome of the negotiations on the permanent status to be conducted pursuant to the DOP. Neither Party shall be deemed, by virtue of having entered into this Agreement, to have renounced or waived any of its existing rights, claims or positions.

7. Neither side shall initiate or take any step that will change the status of the West Bank and the Gaza Strip pending the outcome of the permanent status negotiations.

8. The two Parties view the West Bank and the Gaza Strip as a single territorial unit, the integrity and status of which will be preserved during the interim period.

9. The PLO undertakes that, within two months of the date of the inauguration of the Council, the Palestinian National Council will convene and formally approve the necessary changes in regard to the Palestinian Covenant, as undertaken in the letters signed by the Chairman of the PLO and addressed to the Prime Minister of Israel, dated September 9, 1993 and May 4, 1994.

10. Pursuant to Annex I, Article IX of this Agreement, Israel confirms that the permanent checkpoints on the roads leading to and from the Jericho Area (except those related to the access road leading from Mousa Alami to the Allenby Bridge) will be removed upon the completion of the first phase of redeployment.

11. Prisoners who, pursuant to the Gaza-Jericho Agreement, were turned over to the Palestinian Authority on the condition that they remain in the Jericho Area for the remainder of their sentence, will be free to return to their homes in the West Bank and the Gaza Strip upon the completion of the first phase of redeployment.

12. As regards relations between Israel and the PLO, and without derogating from the commitments contained in the letters signed by and exchanged between the Prime Minister of Israel and the Chairman of the PLO, dated September 9, 1993 and May 4, 1994, the two sides will apply between them the provisions contained in Article XXII, paragraph 1, with the necessary changes.

13. a. The Preamble to this Agreement, and all Annexes, Appendices and maps attached hereto, shall constitute an integral part hereof.

    b. The Parties agree that the maps attached to the Gaza-Jericho Agreement as:
        a. map No. 1 (The Gaza Strip), an exact copy of which is attached to this Agreement as map No. (in this Agreement "map No. 2");
        b. map No. 4 (Deployment of Palestinian Police in the Gaza Strip), an exact copy of which is attached to this Agreement as map No. 5 (in this Agreement "map No. 5"); and

c. map No. 6 (Maritime Activity Zones), an exact copy of which is attached to this Agreement as map No. 8 (in this Agreement "map No. 8"); are an integral part hereof and will remain in effect for the duration of this Agreement.

14. While the Jeftlik area will come under the functional and personal jurisdiction of the Council in the first phase of redeployment, the area's transfer to the territorial jurisdiction of the Council will be considered by the Israeli side in the first phase of the further redeployment phases.

Done at Washington DC, this 28th day of September, 1995.

SOURCE: U.S. Department of State, www.state.gov/p/nea/rls/22678.htm.

Hebron Protocol

DOCUMENT IN CONTEXT

The broad-ranging Interim Agreement on the West Bank and the Gaza Strip—signed by Israel and the Palestinians in September 1995 and popularly known as Oslo II—committed Israel to pulling its army out of the Gaza Strip and major Palestinian cities in the West Bank. The army had withdrawn from another major town, Jericho, under an earlier agreement. By early 1996, Israel had completed most of the required withdrawals, or in the language of diplomacy, "redeployments." Separate provisions of the Oslo II agreement allowed Israel to retain a military presence in parts of the West Bank city of Hebron, which holds special significance because of historical and religious sites revered by Jews and Muslims. These sites include the Tomb of the Patriarchs (the traditional burial place of Abraham and his family members), and the historic Ibrahimi Mosque. After Israel captured the West Bank from Jordan during the June 1967 War, the Orthodox Jewish group Gush Emunim (Block of the Faithful) established a settlement of about 400 people in the middle of Hebron's Old City, among some 120,000 Palestinian Arabs. Because of the presence of the Old City settlement, Oslo II divided Hebron into two zones—one controlled by Palestinians and consisting of about 80 percent of the city and the remaining 20 percent controlled by Israel. Israel was required to withdraw its army from the Palestinian zone by March 28, 1996 (Israeli Settlement of the Occupied Territories, p. 178; Oslo Accords, p. 213).

Prime Minister Shimon Peres, who had negotiated Oslo II while serving as foreign minister in the cabinet of Yitzhak Rabin, halted the Hebron withdrawal early in 1996 after a series of Palestinian suicide bombings. That temporary suspension turned into a prolonged interruption of the Oslo peace process after the rightist Likud Party, headed by Binyamin Netanyahu, won elections in May 1996. Netanyahu had opposed the Oslo accords and vowed to "freeze" Israel's compliance with them, including further withdrawals from West Bank territory. Netanyahu also said the Palestinians had not kept some of their promises, notably to halt violence against Israelis. Yet another blow to the peace process came on September 24, 1996, when Israeli authorities opened an exit from a tunnel running under much of the Western, or Wailing, Wall at the base of the hill in Jerusalem that Israelis call the Temple Mount and Muslims call the Haram al-Sharif. The government said the opening would improve tourists' access to Jewish holy sites, but Muslim authorities charged the Israelis with deliberately undermining the two mosques—the al-Aqsa Mosque and the Dome of the Rock—on the plateau. Palestinians protested the excavations in demonstrations that turned violent. Israel suppressed the disturbances after three days, but about seventy Palestinians and fifteen Israeli soldiers died in the violence. Hoping to calm the situation, in early October, U.S. president Bill Clinton summoned Netanyahu and Palestinian leader Yasir Arafat to a meeting in Washington, where the two, though angry, agreed to revive talks on the long-stalled Israeli withdrawal from Hebron.

From October through early January 1997, U.S. Middle East envoy Dennis Ross worked to bridge differences between the Israelis and the Palestinians on the Hebron withdrawal, which by that time had become the biggest stumbling block to the continuation of the Oslo peace process. As with every other step in the process, the negotiations became bogged down in minutiae; after nearly four years of direct negotiations, the Israelis and Palestinians still did not trust one another and wanted every aspect of any agreement nailed down Also on the negotiating table at this point was the date in 1998 on which Israel would complete its withdrawal from smaller towns and villages in the West Bank, with the Palestinians wanting it early in the year and the Israelis wanting it toward year's end. The negotiations concluded with an agreement on January 14, 1997, after Ross threatened to leave the region unless the two sides reached a deal and after Jordan's King Hussein flew to Gaza to intervene directly with Arafat.

The Israeli Knesset approved the agreement, the Protocol Concerning the Redeployment in Hebron, on January 16 with only a slim majority of Netanyahu's Likud voting in favor. Arafat easily won approval in his cabinet, though hard-line factions in the Palestine Liberation Organization (PLO) along with Hamas and Islamic Jihad opposed it. Saeb Erekat, the chief negotiator for the PLO, and Daniel Shomron, who headed the Israeli negotiating delegation, signed the protocol on January 17.

The Israeli army immediately withdrew from the sections of Hebron designated for Palestinian control. The withdrawal was the first pullback by a Likud-led government from any part of the so-called Land of Israel—the historic Palestine that Jews claimed had been given to them by God. Following another series of Palestinian suicide bombings in summer 1997, however, Netanyahu refused—even after direct pleas from Secretary of State Madeleine Albright and President Clinton—to carry out additional West Bank withdrawals that had been agreed to for 1997 and 1998. It would take another major diplomatic effort by the United States, during meetings in October 1998 at the Wye River Plantation in Maryland, before Netanyahu would agree grudgingly to follow through on his earlier commitments (Wye River Memorandum, p. 267).

Following is the text of the Protocol Concerning the Redeployment in Hebron, signed on January 17, 1997, by Daniel Shomron, representing Israel, and Saeb Erekat, representing the Palestine Liberation Organization.

DOCUMENT

Protocol Concerning the Redeployment in Hebron

JANUARY 17, 1997

In accordance with the provisions of the Interim Agreement and in particular of Article VII of Annex I to the Interim Agreement, both Parties have agreed on this Protocol for the implementation of the redeployment in Hebron.

Security Arrangements Regarding Redeployment in Hebron

1. Redeployment in Hebron
The redeployment of Israeli Military Forces in Hebron will be carried out in accordance with the Interim Agreement and this Protocol. This redeployment will be completed not later than ten days from the signing of this Protocol. During these ten days both sides will exert every possible effort to prevent friction and any action that would prevent the redeployment. This redeployment shall constitute full implementation of the provisions of the Interim Agreement with regard to the City of Hebron unless otherwise provided for in Article VII of Annex I to the Interim Agreement.

2. Security Powers and Responsibilities
   a.
   1. The Palestinian Police will assume responsibilities in Area H-1 similar to those in other cities in the West Bank; and
   2. Israel will retain all powers and responsibilities for internal security and public order in Area H-2. In addition, Israel will continue to carry the responsibility for overall security of Israelis.
   b. In this context—both sides reaffirm their commitment to honor the relevant security provisions of the Interim Agreement, including the provisions regarding— Arrangements for Security and Public Order (Article XII of the Interim Agreement); Prevention of Hostile Acts (Article XV of the Interim Agreement); Security Policy for the Prevention of Terrorism and Violence (Article II of Annex I to the Interim Agreement); Guidelines for Hebron (Article VII of Annex I to the Interim Agreement); and Rules of Conduct in Mutual Security Matters (Article XI of Annex I to the Interim Agreement).

3. Agreed Security Arrangements
   a. With a view to ensuring mutual security and stability in the City of Hebron, special security arrangements will apply adjacent to the areas under the security responsibility of Israel, in Area H-1, in the area between the Palestinian Police checkpoints delineated on the map attached to this Protocol as Appendix 1 (hereinafter referred to as "the attached map") and the areas under the security responsibility of Israel.

b. The purpose of the abovementioned checkpoints will be to enable the Palestinian Police, exercising their responsibilities under the Interim Agreement, to prevent entry of armed persons and demonstrators or other people threatening security and public order, into the abovementioned area.

4. Joint Security Measures

   a. The DCO will establish a sub-office in the City of Hebron as indicated on the attached map.

   b. JMU [Joint Mobile Units] will operate in Area H-2 to handle incidents that involve Palestinians only. The JMU movement will be detailed on the attached map. The DCO will coordinate the JMU movement and activity.

   c. As part of the security arrangements in the area adjacent to the areas under the security responsibility of Israel, as defined above, Joint Mobile Units will be operating in this area, with special focus on the following places:

     1. Abu Sneinah

     2. Harat A-Sheikh

     3. Sha'aba

     4. The high ground overlooking new Route No. 35.

   d. Two Joint Patrols will function in Area H-1:

     1. a Joint Patrol which will operate on the road from Ras e-Jura to the north of the Dura junction via E-Salaam Road, as indicated on the attached map; and

     2. a Joint Patrol which will operate on existing Route No. 35, including the eastern part of existing Route No. 35, as indicated on the attached map.

   e. The Palestinian and Israeli side of the Joint Mobile Units in the City of Hebron will be armed with equivalent types of weapons (Mini-[Ingram] submachine guns for the Palestinian side and short M16s for the Israeli side).

   f. With a view to dealing with the special security situation in the City of Hebron, a Joint Coordination Center (hereinafter the "JCC") headed by senior officers of both sides, will be established in the DCO at Har Manoah/Jabel Manoah. The purpose of the JCC will be to coordinate the joint security measures in the City of Hebron. The JCC will be guided by all the relevant provisions of the Interim Agreement, including Annex I and this Protocol. In this context, each side will notify the JCC of demonstrations and actions taken in respect of such demonstrations, and of any security activity, close to the areas under the responsibility of the other side, including in the area defined in Article 3(a) above. The JCC shall be informed of activities in accordance with Article 5(d)(3) of this Protocol.

5. The Palestinian Police

   a. Palestinian police stations or posts will be established in Area H-1, manned by a total of up to 400 policemen, equipped with 20 vehicles and armed with 200 pistols, and 100 rifles for the protection of the police stations.

   b. Four designated Rapid Response Teams (RRTs) will be established and stationed in Area H-1, one in each of the police stations, as delineated on the attached map. The main task of the RRTs will be to handle special security cases. Each RRT shall be comprised of up to 16 members.

   c. The above mentioned rifles will be designated for the exclusive use of the RRTs, to handle special cases.

   d.
      1. The Palestinian Police shall operate freely in Area H-1.
      2. Activities of the RRTs armed with rifles in the Agreed Adjacent Area, as defined in Appendix 2, shall require the agreement of the JCC.
      3. The RRTs will use the rifles in the rest of Area H-1 to fulfil their above mentioned tasks.

   e. The Palestinian Police will ensure that all Palestinian policemen, prior to their deployment in the City of Hebron, will pass a security check in order to verify their suitability for service, taking into account the sensitivity of the area.

6. Holy Sites
   a. Paragraphs 2 and 3(a) of Article 32 of Appendix 1 to Annex III of the Interim Agreement will be applicable to the following Holy Sites in Area H-1:
      1. The Cave of Othniel Ben Knaz/El-Khalil;
      2. Elonei Mamre/Haram Er-Rameh;
      3. Eshel Avraham/Balotat Ibrahim; and
      4. Maayan Sarah/Ein Sarah.

   b. The Palestinian Police will be responsible for the protection of the above Jewish Holy Sites. Without derogating from the above responsibility of the Palestinian Police, visits to the above Holy Sites by worshippers or other visitors shall be accompanied by a Joint Mobile Unit, which will ensure free, unimpeded and secure access to the Holy Sites, as well as their peaceful use.

7. Normalization of Life in the Old City
   a. Both sides reiterate their commitment to maintain normal life throughout the City of Hebron and to prevent any provocation or friction that may affect the normal life in the city.
   b. In this context, both sides are committed to take all steps and measures necessary for the normalization of life in Hebron, including:
      1. The wholesale market—Hasbahe—will be opened as a retail market in which goods will be sold directly to consumers from within the existing shops.
      2. The movement of vehicles on the Shuhada Road will be gradually returned, within 4 months, to the same situation which existed prior to February 1994.

8. The Imara

The Imara will be turned over to the Palestinian side upon the completion of the redeployment and will become the headquarters of the Palestinian Police in the City of Hebron.

9. City of Hebron

Both sides reiterate their commitment to the unity of the City of Hebron, and their understanding that the division of security responsibility will not divide the city. In this context, and without derogating from the security powers and responsibilities of either side, both sides share the mutual goal that movement of people, goods and vehicles within and in and out of the city will be smooth and normal, without obstacles or barriers.

Civil Arrangements Regarding the Redeployment in Hebron

10. Transfer of Civil Powers and Responsibilities
    a. The transfer of civil powers and responsibilities that have yet to be transferred to the Palestinian side in the city of Hebron (12 spheres) in accordance with Article VII of Annex I to the Interim Agreement shall be conducted concurrently with the beginning of the redeployment of Israeli military forces in Hebron.
    b. In Area H-2, the civil powers and responsibilities will be transferred to the Palestinian side, except for those relating to Israelis and their property, which shall continue to be exercised by the Israeli Military Government.

11. Planning, Zoning and Building
    a. The two parties are equally committed to preserve and protect the historic character of the city in a way which does not harm or change that character in any part of the city.
    b. The Palestinian side has informed the Israeli side that in exercising its powers and responsibilities, taking into account the existing municipal regulations, it has undertaken to implement the following provisions:
        1. Proposed construction of buildings above two floors (6 meters) within 50 meters of the external boundaries of the locations specified in the list attached to this Protocol as Appendix 3 (hereinafter referred to as "the attached list") will be coordinated through the DCL.
        2. Proposed construction of buildings above three floors (9 meters) between 50 and 100 meters of the external boundaries of the locations specified in the attached list will be coordinated through the DCL.
        3. Proposed construction of non-residential, non-commercial buildings within 100 meters of the external boundaries of the locations specified in the attached list that are designed for uses that may adversely affect the environment (such as industrial factories) or buildings and institutions in which more that 50 persons are expected to gather together will be coordinated through the DCL.
        4. Proposed construction of buildings above two floors (6 meters) within 50 meters from each side of the road specified in the attached list will be coordinated through the DCL.
        5. The necessary enforcement measures will be taken to ensure compliance on the ground with the preceding provisions.
        6. This Article does not apply to existing buildings or to new construction or renovation for which fully approved permits were issued by the Municipality prior to January 15th, 1997.

12. Infrastructure
    a. The Palestinian side shall inform the Israeli side, through the DCL, 48 hours in advance of any anticipated activity regarding infrastructure which may disturb the regular flow of traffic on roads in Area H-2 or which may affect

infrastructure (such as water, sewage, electricity and communications) serving Area H-2.

b. The Israeli side may request, through the DCL, that the Municipality carry out works regarding the roads or other infrastructure required for the well being of the Israelis in Area H-2. If the Israeli side offers to cover the costs of these works, the Palestinian side will ensure that these works are carried out as a top priority.

c. The above does not prejudice the provisions of the Interim Agreement regarding the access to infrastructure, facilities and installations located in the city of Hebron, such as the electricity grid.

13. Transportation

The Palestinian side shall have the power to determine bus stops, traffic arrangements and traffic signalization in the city of Hebron. Traffic signalization, traffic arrangements and the location of bus stops in Area H-2 will remain as they are on the date of the redeployment in Hebron. Any subsequent change in these arrangements in Area H-2 will be done in cooperation between the two sides in the transportation sub-committee.

14. Municipal Inspectors

a. In accordance with paragraph 4.c of Article VII of Annex I of the Interim Agreement, plainclothes unarmed municipal inspectors will operate in Area H-2. The number of these inspectors shall not exceed 50.

b. The inspectors shall carry official identification cards with a photograph issued by the Municipality.

c. The Palestinian side may request the assistance of the Israel Police, through the DCL of Hebron, in order to carry out its enforcement activities in Area H-2.

15. Location of Offices of the Palestinian Council

The Palestinian side, when operating new offices in Area H-2, will take into consideration the need to avoid provocation and friction. Where establishing such offices might affect public order or security the two sides will cooperate to find a suitable solution.

16. Municipal Services

In accordance with paragraph 5 of Article VII of Annex I of the Interim Agreement, municipal services shall be provided regularly and continuously to all parts of the city of Hebron, at the same quality and cost. The cost shall be determined by the Palestinian side with respect to work done and materials consumed, without discrimination.

Miscellaneous

17. Temporary International Presence

There will be a Temporary International Presence in Hebron (TIPH). Both sides will agree on the modalities of the TIPH, including the number of its members and its area of operation.

18. Annex I

Nothing in this Protocol will derogate from the security powers and responsibilities of either side in accordance with Annex I to the Interim Agreement.

19. Attached Appendices

The appendices attached to this Protocol shall constitute an integral part hereof.

Done at Jerusalem, this 17th day of January 1997.

D. Shomrom
For the Government of the State of Israel

S. Erakat
For the PLO

Appendix 1

Hebron Redeployment Map [Not shown here]

Appendix 2

(Article 5)
Agreed Adjacent Area

The Agreed Adjacent Area ("AAA") shall include the following:

1. An area defined by a line commencing from AAA Reference Point (RP) 100, proceeding along old Route No. 35 until RP 101, continuing by a straight line to RP 102, and from there connected by a straight line to RP 103.
2. An area defined by a line commencing at RP 104, following a straight line to RP 105, from there following a line immediately westward of checkpoints 4, 5, 6, 8, 9, 10, 11, 12 and 13, and from there connected by a straight line to RP 106.
3. An area defined by a line connecting RPs 107 and 108, passing immediately northward of checkpoint 15.

Appendix 3

(Article 12)

List of Locations

- The area of Al Haram Al Ibrahimi/the Tomb of the Patriarchs (including the military and police installations in its vicinity)
- Al Hisba/Abraham Avinu
- Osama School/Beit Romano (including the military location in its vicinity)
- Al Daboya/Beit Hadasseh

- Jabla Al Rahama/Tel Rumeida
- The Jewish Cemeteries
- Dir Al Arbein/the Tomb of Ruth and Yishai
- Tel Al Jaabra/Givaat Avot Neighborhood (including the police station in its vicinity)
- The Road connecting Al Haram Al Ibrahimi/the Tomb of the Patriarchs and Qiryat Arba

SOURCE: U.S. Department of State, www.state.gov/p/nea/rls/22680.htm.

Wye River Memorandum

DOCUMENT IN CONTEXT

The Oslo peace process between Israel and the Palestinians went on life support after the drawn-out negotiations that produced the January 1997 Hebron Protocol on Israel's partial withdrawal from the West Bank city of Hebron and other areas. Israeli prime minister Binyamin Netanyahu, facing pressure from his right-wing base not to make further concessions to the Palestinians, carried out few of his commitments to peace, and when he did, with each step he made additional demands on the Palestinians. Yasir Arafat, the Palestinian leader, also stalled on some of his commitments because he, too, faced pressure, from Hamas and Islamic Jihad, which used suicide bombings and other attacks to demonstrate their opposition to the peace process (Hebron Protocol, p. 259).

Citing security concerns, Israel missed deadlines in March and September 1997 for two withdrawals from West Bank areas. By fall 1997, Netanyahu had taken the position that Israel could give the Palestinians full or partial control of only about 40 percent of the West Bank, with Israel retaining responsibility for security in most of that territory. Negotiations between the Israelis and Palestinians, with U.S. mediation, fell into a stalemate that lasted well into 1998; even personal interventions by President Bill Clinton and Secretary of State Madeleine Albright failed to break the deadlock. Throughout 1998 Clinton was severely hobbled domestically by charges that he had tried to cover up his sexual relationship with a female White House intern; at year's end, the charges would lead to his impeachment by the House of Representatives.

In an attempt to break the impasse, Clinton summoned Netanyahu and Arafat to a summit at a conference center, the Wye River Plantation, in Maryland. The summit, which began on October 15, 1998, like all such negotiating sessions, quickly became ensnarled in mutual Israeli and Palestinian demands for more concessions from the other party. On the seventh day, the Israelis packed their bags and threatened to leave but then continued to negotiate under intense U.S. pressure. On the eighth day—which was to be Clinton's last day at the summit because he needed to campaign for midterm congressional elections—the ailing King Hussein of Jordan paid a visit and appealed to the leaders to reach agreement. Noting that each side had been emphasizing its own needs, he said, "These differences pale in comparison to what is at stake. After agreement both sides will look back and not even recall these issues. It is now time to finish, bearing in mind the responsibility that both leaders have to their people and especially the children." (The king had been undergoing treatment for cancer at the Mayo Clinic in Minnesota, and everyone at the summit knew he did not have much time to live; he died four months later). Hussein's dramatic plea did not, in itself, force the leaders to agree, but it put more pressure on Arafat and Netanyahu to negotiate compromises.

An all-night negotiating session ultimately produced an agreement, but not before one last crisis. After a deal had been reached, Netanyahu insisted that he could not accept it unless Clinton agreed to release Jonathon Pollard, a former U.S. Navy intelligence analyst serving a life sentence in prison following his conviction on charges of passing highly classified information to Israel. Pollard's case had become a major cause célèbre among right-wing Israelis, and Netanyahu wanted to secure his release to provide political cover for the modest concessions he had made to Arafat. Clinton rebuffed Netanyahu, promising only to "review" Pollard's case.

As signed at the White House on October 23—the conclusion of the ninth day of negotiations—the agreement required Israel to turn over to the Palestinians an additional 13 percent of the West Bank over a three-month period in three stages. All but 1 percent of this additional land was to remain under Israeli security control, however. Arafat promised a "work plan" to combat terrorism, including accepting assistance from the CIA in arresting Hamas and Islamic Jihad fighters. Arafat also pledged to call a session of the Palestine National Council to delete anti-Israel clauses from the 1968 national covenant. The two sides agreed to the immediate opening of negotiations on a permanent settlement of all outstanding issues, with the goal of achieving a final agreement by May 4, 1999.

Netanyahu delayed presenting the Wye River Memorandum to his cabinet for nearly three weeks, during which time right-wing opposition to the accord mounted and Netanyahu found himself on the defensive. The cabinet approved the agreement on November 11 by a narrow vote after an angry debate; the Knesset approved it by a much wider margin, representing broad support among the Israeli public for keeping the peace process intact. On November 20 Netanyahu carried out most of the first stage of the promises he had made at Wye River; his government turned over some 9 percent of the West Bank to full or partial Palestinian control, released about 250 Palestinian prisoners, and allowed the partial reopening of the airport in Gaza.

A month later, insisting that the Palestinians had not fulfilled their part of the agreement, Netanyahu's government announced the indefinite "suspension" of the Wye River Memorandum. This step amounted to Netanyahu's admission that he was hemmed in by a lack of public support for his policy of stalling on the Oslo peace process and stymied by the resistance of his right-wing supporters from moving forward with permanent peace talks. His government fell the next day; the Knesset called new elections for May 1999. Netanyahu lost the elections to the new Labor Party leader, Ehud Barak, an Israeli military hero who previously had served as army chief of staff and had since become a staunch advocate of securing peace with the Palestinians.

For his part, Arafat carried out several of the major provisions of the Wye agreement, including a limited crackdown on Hamas and Islamic Jihad. On December 14,

1998, he convened a meeting in Gaza of the Palestine National Council, which voted to delete the clauses in the national covenant that had called for Israel's destruction. President Clinton attended the session and thanked the Palestinian legislators with an emotional speech calling on Israelis and Palestinians to understand each other's need for peace (The Palestinian National Movement, p. 169).

Following is the text of the Wye River Memorandum, signed at the White House on October 23, 1998, by Yasir Arafat, chairman of the Palestine Liberation Organization, and Binyamin Netanyahu, prime minister of Israel. U.S. president Bill Clinton and Jordan's King Hussein signed as witnesses.

DOCUMENT

Wye River Memorandum

OCTOBER 23, 1998

The following are steps to facilitate implementation of the Interim Agreement on the West Bank and Gaza Strip of September 28, 1995 (the "Interim Agreement") and other related agreements including the Note for the Record of January 17, 1997 (hereinafter referred to as "the prior agreements") so that the Israeli and Palestinian sides can more effectively carry out their reciprocal responsibilities, including those relating to further redeployments and security respectively. These steps are to be carried out in a parallel phased approach in accordance with this Memorandum and the attached time line. They are subject to the relevant terms and conditions of the prior agreements and do not supersede their other requirements.

I. FURTHER REDEPLOYMENTS

A. Phase One and Two Further Redeployments

1. Pursuant to the Interim Agreement and subsequent agreements, the Israeli side's implementation of the first and second F.R.D. [further redeployments] will consist of the transfer to the Palestinian side of 13% from Area C as follows:

1% to Area (A)
12% to Area (B)

The Palestinian side has informed that it will allocate an area/areas amounting to 3% from the above Area (B) to be designated as Green Areas and/or Nature Reserves. The Palestinian side has further informed that they will act according to the established scientific standards, and that therefore there will be no changes in the status of these areas, without prejudice to the rights of the existing inhabitants in these areas including Bedouins; while these standards do not allow new construction in these areas, existing roads and buildings may be maintained.

The Israeli side will retain in these Green Areas/Nature Reserves the overriding security responsibility for the purpose of protecting Israelis and confronting the threat of ter-

rorism. Activities and movements of the Palestinian Police forces may be carried out after coordination and confirmation; the Israeli side will respond to such requests expeditiously.
2. As part of the foregoing implementation of the first and second F.R.D., 14.2% from Area (B) will become Area (A).

B. Third Phase of Further Redeployments

With regard to the terms of the Interim Agreement and of Secretary [Warren] Christopher's letters to the two sides of January 17, 1997 relating to the further redeployment process, there will be a committee to address this question. The United States will be briefed regularly.

II. SECURITY

In the provisions on security arrangements of the Interim Agreement, the Palestinian side agreed to take all measures necessary in order to prevent acts of terrorism, crime and hostilities directed against the Israeli side, against individuals falling under the Israeli side's authority and against their property, just as the Israeli side agreed to take all measures necessary in order to prevent acts of terrorism, crime and hostilities directed against the Palestinian side, against individuals falling under the Palestinian side's authority and against their property. The two sides also agreed to take legal measures against offenders within their jurisdiction and to prevent incitement against each other by any organizations, groups or individuals within their jurisdiction.

Both sides recognize that it is in their vital interests to combat terrorism and fight violence in accordance with Annex I of the Interim Agreement and the Note for the Record. They also recognize that the struggle against terror and violence must be comprehensive in that it deals with terrorists, the terror support structure, and the environment conducive to the support of terror. It must be continuous and constant over a long-term, in that there can be no pauses in the work against terrorists and their structure. It must be cooperative in that no effort can be fully effective without Israeli-Palestinian cooperation and the continuous exchange of information, concepts, and actions.

Pursuant to the prior agreements, the Palestinian side's implementation of its responsibilities for security, security cooperation, and other issues will be as detailed below during the time periods specified in the attached time line:

A. Security Actions

1. Outlawing and Combating Terrorist Organizations

The Palestinian side will make known its policy of zero tolerance for terror and violence against both sides.

A work plan developed by the Palestinian side will be shared with the U.S. and thereafter implementation will begin immediately to ensure the systematic and effective combat of terrorist organizations and their infrastructure.

In addition to the bilateral Israeli-Palestinian security cooperation, a U.S.-Palestinian committee will meet biweekly to review the steps being taken to eliminate terrorist cells and the support structure that plans, finances, supplies and abets terror.

In these meetings, the Palestinian side will inform the U.S. fully of the actions it has taken to outlaw all organizations (or wings of organizations, as appropriate) of a military, terrorist or violent character and their support structure and to prevent them from operating in areas under its jurisdiction.

The Palestinian side will apprehend the specific individuals suspected of perpetrating acts of violence and terror for the purpose of further investigation, and prosecution and punishment of all persons involved in acts of violence and terror.

A U.S.-Palestinian committee will meet to review and evaluate information pertinent to the decisions on prosecution, punishment or other legal measures which affect the status of individuals suspected of abetting or perpetrating acts of violence and terror.

2. Prohibiting Illegal Weapons

The Palestinian side will ensure an effective legal framework is in place to criminalize, in conformity with the prior agreements, any importation, manufacturing or unlicensed sale, acquisition or possession of firearms, ammunition or weapons in areas under Palestinian jurisdiction.

In addition, the Palestinian side will establish and vigorously and continuously implement a systematic program for the collection and appropriate handling of all such illegal items in accordance with the prior agreements. The U.S. has agreed to assist in carrying out this program.

A U.S.-Palestinian-Israeli committee will be established to assist and enhance cooperation in preventing the smuggling or other unauthorized introduction of weapons or explosive materials into areas under Palestinian jurisdiction.

3. Preventing Incitement

Drawing on relevant international practice and pursuant to Article XXII (1) of the Interim Agreement and the Note for the Record, the Palestinian side will issue a decree prohibiting all forms of incitement to violence or terror, and establishing mechanisms for acting systematically against all expressions or threats of violence or terror. This decree will be comparable to the existing Israeli legislation which deals with the same subject.

A U.S.-Palestinian-Israeli committee will meet on a regular basis to monitor cases of possible incitement to violence or terror and to make recommendations and reports on how to prevent such incitement. The Israeli, Palestinian and U.S. sides will each appoint a media specialist, a law enforcement representative, an educational specialist and a current or former elected official to the committee.

B. Security Cooperation

The two sides agree that their security cooperation will be based on a spirit of partnership and will include, among other things, the following steps:

1. Bilateral Cooperation

There will be full bilateral security cooperation between the two sides which will be continuous, intensive and comprehensive.

2. Forensic Cooperation

There will be an exchange of forensic expertise, training, and other assistance.

3. Trilateral Committee

In addition to the bilateral Israeli-Palestinian security cooperation, a high-ranking U.S.-Palestinian-Israeli committee will meet as required and not less than biweekly to assess current threats, deal with any impediments to effective security cooperation and coordination and address the steps being taken to combat terror and terrorist organizations. The committee will also serve as a forum to address the issue of external support for terror. In these meetings, the Palestinian side will fully inform the members of the committee of the results of its investigations concerning terrorist suspects already in custody and the participants will exchange additional relevant information. The committee will report regularly to the leaders of the two sides on the status of cooperation, the results of the meetings and its recommendations.

C. Other Issues

1. Palestinian Police Force

The Palestinian side will provide a list of its policemen to the Israeli side in conformity with the prior agreements.

Should the Palestinian side request technical assistance, the U.S. has indicated its willingness to help meet these needs in cooperation with other donors.

The Monitoring and Steering Committee will, as part of its functions, monitor the implementation of this provision and brief the U.S.

2. PLO Charter

The Executive Committee of the Palestine Liberation Organization and the Palestinian Central Council will reaffirm the letter of 22 January 1998 from PLO Chairman Yasir Arafat to President Clinton concerning the nullification of the Palestinian National Charter provisions that are inconsistent with the letters exchanged between the PLO and the Government of Israel on 9/10 September 1993. PLO Chairman Arafat, the Speaker of the Palestine National Council, and the Speaker of the Palestinian Council will invite the members of the PNC, as well as the members of the Central Council, the Council, and the Palestinian Heads of Ministries to a meeting to be addressed by President Clinton to reaffirm their support for the peace process and the aforementioned decisions of the Executive Committee and the Central Council.

3. Legal Assistance in Criminal Matters

Among other forms of legal assistance in criminal matters, the requests for arrest and transfer of suspects and defendants pursuant to Article II (7) of Annex IV of the Interim Agreement will be submitted (or resubmitted) through the mechanism of the Joint Israeli-Palestinian Legal Committee and will be responded to in conformity with Article

II (7) (f) of Annex IV of the Interim Agreement within the twelve week period. Requests submitted after the eighth week will be responded to in conformity with Article II (7) (f) within four weeks of their submission. The U.S. has been requested by the sides to report on a regular basis on the steps being taken to respond to the above requests.

4. Human Rights and the Rule of Law

Pursuant to Article XI (1) of Annex I of the Interim Agreement, and without derogating from the above, the Palestinian Police will exercise powers and responsibilities to implement this Memorandum with due regard to internationally accepted norms of human rights and the rule of law, and will be guided by the need to protect the public, respect human dignity, and avoid harassment.

III. INTERIM COMMITTEES AND ECONOMIC ISSUES

1. The Israeli and Palestinian sides reaffirm their commitment to enhancing their relationship and agree on the need actively to promote economic development in the West Bank and Gaza. In this regard, the parties agree to continue or to reactivate all standing committees established by the Interim Agreement, including the Monitoring and Steering Committee, the Joint Economic Committee (JEC), the Civil Affairs Committee (CAC), the Legal Committee, and the Standing Cooperation Committee.

2. The Israeli and Palestinian sides have agreed on arrangements which will permit the timely opening of the Gaza Industrial Estate. They also have concluded a "Protocol Regarding the Establishment and Operation of the International Airport in the Gaza Strip During the Interim Period."

3. Both sides will renew negotiations on Safe Passage immediately. As regards the southern route, the sides will make best efforts to conclude the agreement within a week of the entry into force of this Memorandum. Operation of the southern route will start as soon as possible thereafter. As regards the northern route, negotiations will continue with the goal of reaching agreement as soon as possible. Implementation will take place expeditiously thereafter.

4. The Israeli and Palestinian sides acknowledge the great importance of the Port of Gaza for the development of the Palestinian economy, and the expansion of Palestinian trade. They commit themselves to proceeding without delay to conclude an agreement to allow the construction and operation of the port in accordance with the prior agreements. The Israeli-Palestinian Committee will reactivate its work immediately with a goal of concluding the protocol within sixty days, which will allow commencement of the construction of the port.

5. The two sides recognize that unresolved legal issues adversely affect the relationship between the two peoples. They therefore will accelerate efforts through the Legal Committee to address outstanding legal issues and to implement solutions to these issues in the shortest possible period. The Palestinian side will provide to the Israeli side copies of all of its laws in effect.

6. The Israeli and Palestinian sides also will launch a strategic economic dialogue to enhance their economic relationship. They will establish within the framework of the JEC an Ad Hoc Committee for this purpose. The committee will review the following four issues: (1) Israeli purchase taxes; (2) cooperation in combating vehicle theft;

(3) dealing with unpaid Palestinian debts; and (4) the impact of Israeli standards as barriers to trade and the expansion of the A1 and A2 lists. The committee will submit an interim report within three weeks of the entry into force of this Memorandum, and within six weeks will submit its conclusions and recommendations to be implemented.

7. The two sides agree on the importance of continued international donor assistance to facilitate implementation by both sides of agreements reached. They also recognize the need for enhanced donor support for economic development in the West Bank and Gaza. They agree to jointly approach the donor community to organize a Ministerial Conference before the end of 1998 to seek pledges for enhanced levels of assistance.

IV. PERMANENT STATUS NEGOTIATIONS

The two sides will immediately resume permanent status negotiations on an accelerated basis and will make a determined effort to achieve the mutual goal of reaching an agreement by May 4, 1999. The negotiations will be continuous and without interruption. The U.S. has expressed its willingness to facilitate these negotiations.

V. UNILATERAL ACTIONS

Recognizing the necessity to create a positive environment for the negotiations, neither side shall initiate or take any step that will change the status of the West Bank and the Gaza Strip in accordance with the Interim Agreement.

ATTACHMENT: Time Line
This Memorandum will enter into force ten days from the date of signature.

Done at Washington, D.C. this 23d day of October 1998.

For the Government of the State of Israel:
Benjamin Netanyahu

For the PLO:
Yassir Arafat

Witnessed by:
William J. Clinton
The United States of America

TIME LINE
Note: Parenthetical references below are to paragraphs in "The Wye River Memorandum" to which this time line is an integral attachment. Topics not included in the time line follow the schedule provided for in the text of the Memorandum.

1. Upon Entry into Force of the Memorandum:
Third further redeployment committee starts (I (B))
Palestinian security work plan shared with the U.S. (II (A) (1) (b))

Full bilateral security cooperation (II (B) (1))
Trilateral security cooperation committee starts (II (B) (3))
Interim committees resume and continue; Ad Hoc Economic Committee starts (III)
Accelerated permanent status negotiations start (IV)

2. Entry into Force—Week 2:
Security work plan implementation begins (II (A) (1) (b)); (II (A) (1) (c)) committee starts
Illegal weapons framework in place (II (A) (2) (a)); Palestinian implementation report (II (A) (2) (b))
Anti-incitement committee starts (II (A) (3) (b)); decree issued (II (A) (3) (a))
PLO Executive Committee reaffirms Charter letter (II (C) (2))
Stage 1 of F.R.D. implementation: 2% C to B, 7.1% B to A. Israeli officials acquaint their Palestinian counterparts as required with areas; F.R.D. carried out; report on F.R.D. implementation (I(A))

3. Week 2–6:
Palestinian Central Council reaffirms Charter letter (weeks two to four) (II (C) (2))
PNC and other PLO organizations reaffirm Charter letter (weeks four to six) (II (C) (2))
Establishment of weapons collection program (II (A) (2) (b)) and collection stage (II (A) (2) (c)); committee starts and reports on activities.
Anti-incitement committee report (II (A) (3) (b))
Ad Hoc Economic Committee: interim report at week three; final report at week six (III)
Policemen list (II (C) (1) (a)); Monitoring and Steering Committee review starts (II (C) (1) (c)
Stage 2 of F.R.D. implementation: 5% C to B. Israeli officials acquaint their Palestinian counterparts as required with areas; F.R.D. carried out; report on F.R.D. implementation (I (A))

4. Week 6–12:
Weapons collection stage II (A) (2) (b); II (A) (2) (c) committee report on its activities.
Anti-incitement committee report (II (A) (3) (b))
Monitoring and Steering Committee briefs U.S. on policemen list (II (C) (1) (c))
Stage 3 of F.R.D. implementation: 5% C to B, 1% C to A, 7.1% B to A. Israeli officials acquaint Palestinian counterparts as required with areas; F.R.D. carried out; report on F.R.D. implementation (I (A))

5. After Week 12:
Activities described in the Memorandum continue as appropriate and if necessary, including:

Trilateral security cooperation committee (II (B)(3))
(II (A) (1) (c)) committee
(II (A) (1) (e)) committee
Anti-incitement committee (II (A) (3) (b))
Third Phase F.R.D. Committee (I (B))

Interim Committees (III)
Accelerated permanent status negotiations (IV)

SOURCE: U.S. Department of State, www.state.gov/p/nea/rls/22694.htm.

Camp David and the al-Aqsa Intifada

DOCUMENT IN CONTEXT

The election of former general Ehud Barak as Israel's prime minister in May 1999 appeared to herald an era of peacemaking similar to the 1993–1995 period, when Prime Minister Yitzhak Rabin negotiated peace agreements with the Palestinians and Jordan shortly before his assassination by an Israeli who opposed the idea of land for peace. Barak promised to revive the peace process that had made little progress since 1996 under Rabin's successor, Binyamin Netanyahu. In particular, he promised to carry out previous agreements with the Palestinians and to attempt to negotiate a final agreement with them; he also called for a revival of long-stalled peace talks with Syria (Olso Accords, p. 213; Hebron Protocol, p. 259; Wye River Memorandum, pp. 267).

Despite Barak's overwhelming personal mandate—Israelis gave him 56 percent of the vote in the direct election for prime minister—Barak headed an unstable coalition in the Knesset and could not count on automatic support for any peace agreements he might reach. Palestinian leader Yasir Arafat also faced domestic political pressure, in part because the long peace process had delivered only modest material gains for the average Palestinian and in part because of his inability or unwillingness to control Hamas and Islamic Jihad, which were opposed to any dealings with Israel.

The two sides got off to a relatively positive start during negotiations at the Egyptian resort of Sharm el-Sheikh. An agreement signed there by Arafat and Barak on September 4, 1999, provided for both sides to carry out the still-unfulfilled promises of the Wye River Memorandum, which Arafat and Netanyahu had approved eleven months earlier. Under this new agreement, Israel promised to withdraw from additional sections of the West Bank and to allow construction of a seaport in the Gaza Strip, along with other measures. Arafat agreed to step up his government's efforts to prevent attacks on Israelis by Hamas and Islamic Jihad. Moreover, both sides agreed to finish the "framework" for a final peace treaty by mid-February 2000. The two sides carried out little of the Sharm el-Sheikh agreement, however, because of renewed tensions arising from ongoing Palestinian attacks in Israel and the Barak government's expansion of Jewish settlements in the West Bank.

During the winter of 1999–2000, Israel focused instead on peace talks with Syria, centering around the question of Israel's return of the Golan Heights. These talks ultimately failed when Israel insisted on retaining control of the entire shoreline of the Sea of Galilee, and Syrian president Hafiz al-Assad refused.

Barak did manage to carry out one of the major promises of his campaign when in May 2000 he pulled Israeli troops from an area in southern Lebanon that they had occupied for more than eighteen years. Rather than inspiring confidence, however, the hurried manner of the withdrawal embarrassed Barak domestically by highlighting Israel's past failures in Lebanon. In the meantime, Barak's unwieldy coalition government continued to tear itself apart in disputes over domestic issues (Israeli Withdrawal from Lebanon, p. 354).

Hoping to reach a final agreement on the Israeli-Palestinian issue while Barak still retained some political capital, President Bill Clinton summoned Arafat and Barak to the presidential retreat at Camp David July 5, 2000, for a high-stakes summit. Barak, who had pressed for such a meeting, was eager to attend, but Arafat was reluctant, a sign that the Palestinians were not yet ready for a deal. On the Israeli side, a political crisis in the cabinet led some of Barak's key partners to desert his coalition, depriving him of a working majority in parliament.

The summit began at Camp David on July 11 and quickly focused on the three contentious issues long considered central to a final resolution of the Israeli-Palestinian dispute: the amount of West Bank land Israel would turn over to the Palestinians, the status of East Jerusalem (particularly the Old City, with its religious shrines) and its surrounding neighborhoods, and the rights of hundreds of thousands of Palestinians (and their descendants) who had fled Israel and the occupied territories during the 1948 and 1967 wars.

What at first appeared to be a breakthrough came on the eighth day of the negotiations when Barak—under U.S. pressure to offer compromises—verbally presented Clinton with the most forthcoming offer any Israeli leader had ever put forward in negotiations. According to a subsequent account by U.S. Middle East envoy Dennis Ross, Barak offered to turn over to the Palestinians 91 percent of the West Bank, with Israel retaining the major Jewish settlements (where the vast majority of settlers live) and a section of the border with Jordan along the Jordan River. The Palestinians would also receive a section of Israeli land adjacent to the Gaza Strip (comparable in size to 1 percent of the West Bank). In effect, according to Israeli figures, this meant the Palestinians would have the equivalent of 92 percent of the West Bank plus the Gaza Strip, for a new state. On Jerusalem, Barak offered to give the Palestinians sovereignty over the Muslim Quarter and the Christian Quarter in East Jerusalem's Old City as well as seven of the so-called outer neighborhoods. He proposed giving the Palestinians "custodianship," but not sovereignty, over the Haram al-Sharif (known to Jews as the Temple Mount), where sacred sites for Jews and Muslims are located. Without offering details, Barak also promised what he called a "satisfactory solution" for both sides on another central question, that of whether any Palestinian refugees could return to their former homes in Israel.

Clinton presented the offer to Arafat, who raised strong objections to each of the key points and ultimately rejected the offer. In the end, the main stumbling block, according to Ross's first-hand account of the summit, appears to have been the status of Jerusalem's Old City and the Haram al-Sharif/Temple Mount complex, with Arafat refusing to accept Barak's insistence on retaining at least some form of Israeli sovereignty over the complex. On the fourteenth day of negotiations, an angry Clinton, according to Ross, complained to Arafat that he had "said no to everything."

After a final attempt to bridge the differences on Jerusalem, Clinton held a meeting with Arafat and Barak—the only substantive direct meeting between the Israeli and Palestinian leaders during the two-week summit—and reached agreement on a face-saving "trilateral statement" calling for the negotiations to continue at a later date. The statement was released during a news conference at the White House on July 25. Clinton offered effusive praise for Barak, hoping to protect him domestically against the already mounting charges in Israel that he had conceded too much to Arafat and gotten nothing in return. Behind the scenes, U.S. officials and Israeli negotiators blamed Arafat for the lack of an agreement, saying he had refused to accept what they called the most "generous" offer any Israeli leader could make. Palestinians, in turn, played down the extent of Barak's offer, saying it did not provide for a viable Palestinian state because major Israeli settlements would remain on the West Bank, and Israel would still have effective control of the territory's airspace, borders, and public services. The Palestinians also noted that Barak offered only vague assurances to Arafat on the sensitive matter of the Palestinian refugees who had fled or been pushed from Israel during the 1948 Arab-Israeli war. Arafat's aides argued that Barak's offer was unacceptable to the broader Muslim world because of the insistence on Israeli sovereignty over the Haram al-Sharif. The debate over the extent of Barak's offer remains unresolved, adding to the long list of disputes, going back to the 1947 partition of Palestine, over which side spurned a chance for peace.

In the weeks after the Camp David summit, U.S. officials attempted again to bridge the differences between the two sides. Clinton met separately with Arafat and Barak early in September during a UN summit in New York, and Ross held a series of secret, high-level meetings with Israeli and Palestinian representatives in late September at a hotel near Washington. These sessions produced some progress.

Starting on September 28, events in the Middle East undermined the slim chances of reviving the peace process. Under heavy police protection, Ariel Sharon, the hard-line leader of Israel's Likud Party, led a large delegation of party officials to the Haram al-Sharif/Temple Mount complex. Sharon said his purpose was to demonstrate Israeli sovereignty over the area. His visit went without serious incident, though Palestinians and Israeli security forces clashed after Sharon had left the area. The following day, September 29, after Friday prayers, angry Palestinian men poured out of the mosques on the Haram al-Sharif, chanting anti-Israel slogans and throwing rocks down onto Jews worshipping at the historic Wailing Wall, located at the base of the plateau. Israeli police responded with live fire, killing five Palestinians. When news of the confrontation spread, thousands of enraged Palestinians began demonstrating throughout the West Bank and Gaza. These demonstrations quickly evolved into violence between rock-throwing Palestinians and armed Israeli police. In one week, more than fifty Palestinians were killed and several hundred others wounded; five Israeli civilians also died. The violence escalated into a self-perpetuating cycle, fueled by televised images showing one side or the other committing acts of violence.

Palestinians declared the start of a second uprising—the al-Aqsa intifada—named after the historic mosque on the Haram al-Sharif. Under intense U.S. pressure, Arafat insisted that he was trying to restrain the violence, but Israeli officials accused him instead of encouraging it in the hope of extracting diplomatic concessions from Israel. Regardless of what Arafat did or did not do in the early days of the intifada, it quickly became clear that he had lost much of his authority among Palestinians at large, especially among the more radical elements within his own Fatah party and among Hamas and Islamic Jihad. The Palestinian Authority under Arafat had proven to be a weak, unpopular government, riddled with corruption and unable to deliver basic services in the sections of the Gaza Strip and West Bank it controlled.

In an attempt to halt the violence and get peace talks back on track, senior U.S. officials met with Barak and Arafat in Paris on October 4. This meeting resulted in some progress on key issues but produced no written agreements. On October 12, Palestinians killed two Israeli reserve soldiers at a police station in the West Bank city of Ramallah, sending the violence spiraling further out of control. The Israeli military proceeded to destroy Palestinian Authority offices near Arafat's headquarters in Gaza City, close the new airport in Gaza, and blockade West Bank cities.

In this super-charged atmosphere, Egypt and the United States made yet another attempt at reaching an agreement to stop the violence. On October 16–17, Clinton and Egyptian president Hosni Mubarak hosted a summit at Sharm el-Sheikh attended by Arafat and Barak, along with UN secretary-general Kofi Annan, Jordan's King Abdallah II, and Javier Solana, the chief diplomat for the European Union. The summit produced an agreement for a cease-fire, to be backed by confidence-building steps by the Israelis and Palestinians. One element included a U.S.-led fact-finding mission to examine the causes of the intifada. Arafat issued a statement calling for an end to the violence, but neither he nor the Israelis followed through on the other steps they had promised to take to calm the situation.

Clinton held separate meetings at the White House with Arafat (on November 9) and with Barak (on November 12), hoping once again to craft the broad outlines of a potential final agreement. Arafat appeared willing to go along with proposals Clinton suggested. In another positive sign, there was a noticeable reduction in violence during most of November. Even more promising was a secret meeting between Ross, the U.S. negotiator, and Arafat in Rabat, Morocco, in November during which Arafat appeared to accept what Ross outlined as a bottom-line Israeli offer.

Another set of negotiations between senior Israeli and Palestinian diplomats (without Arafat and Barak) took place at Bolling Air Force Base outside Washington starting on December 19. When those talks bogged down on the same issues as before, and both sides asked for help, U.S. officials developed a final proposal, which Clinton presented to the negotiators on December 23. These ideas, which became known as the Clinton parameters, dealt with the fundamental issues that had separated the parties. Clinton insisted that the parameters were not his ideas, but instead represented his understanding of the bottom-line positions of each side.

On territory, Clinton called for a settlement in which Israel turned 94 to 96 percent of the West Bank over to the Palestinians, with the two sides swapping the equivalent of another 1 to 3 percent in the Gaza Strip area. On the issue of Jerusalem, Clinton proposed that "what is Arab in the city should be Palestinian and what is Jewish should be Israeli." With this concept, Clinton offered two alternatives for the sides to share forms of sovereignty over the Haram al-Sharif/Temple Mount. On the question of Palestinian refugees, Clinton said the Palestinians needed to understand that Israel would not allow for the unlimited right of refugees to return to Israeli territory, but that Israel should be willing to accept a small number of refugees, with priority given to those in Lebanon (some of whom had close relatives across the border in northern Israel). Other refugees could resettle in the new state of Palestine or be given international aid to settle where they were or in third countries. Addressing Israeli security concerns, Clinton suggested that Israel be permitted to keep three "early-warning stations" in the West Bank and be allowed to deploy troops to the Jordan River valley, along the border with Jordan, under specific "emergency" circumstances. Also, the new state of Palestine would be considered a "non-militarized state," meaning that it would have a security force and be able to patrol its borders, but would not have a conventional standing army.

Clinton said his ideas would provide for a "fair and lasting agreement," but also that they will "go with me when I leave office"—in other words, the two sides needed sign a peace agreement based on the parameters by the time Clinton's term ended the following January 20. Clinton said any agreement must represent a formal and final end to the conflict between the two sides, closing out their claims against one another. He asked the two sides to respond with a "yes" or "no" to his ideas within five days; a "maybe," he said, would be considered a "no."

On December 27, the deadline Clinton had set, the Israeli cabinet accepted Clinton's proposals, but with "reservations." Two days later, senior Palestinian diplomats said Arafat still had questions and was under pressure to reject Clinton's proposals. Clinton made another personal effort, meeting with Arafat at the White House on January 2, 2001, but got a series of reservations rather than a positive response.

At the request of Barak—who was facing an uphill battle in elections scheduled for early February—Clinton agreed to make one final effort by meeting again with Arafat and Barak in the Middle East. Arafat was unwilling to attend such a meeting (saying he had another engagement), so Clinton's peace-making came to an end.

On January 7, 2001, Clinton explained his proposals publicly for the first time during a speech in New York to the Israel Policy Forum, a liberal group that had long pushed for peace. The proposals, he said, would "entail real pain and sacrifices" for both sides but ultimately would be the only way to settle a conflict on terms that met the fundamental needs of both sides. Clinton also cautioned Israelis and Palestinians against continuing to use violence or military force to try to impose a settlement on the other side. "A peace viewed as imposed by one party upon the other, that puts one side up and the other down, rather than both ahead, contains the seeds of its own destruction," he said.

Another set of negotiations between Israeli and Palestinian officials took place during the last week of January 2001 at the Egyptian resort town of Taba. These talks made more progress on key issues, according to participants, but by then time had run out because of the impending Israeli elections and because Clinton already had left office. In the voting in Israel, on February 6, Ariel Sharon decisively defeated Barak, putting a final cap on the peace process Barak had embraced nearly two years earlier.

In the meantime, the intifada continued, punctuated by occasional atrocities committed by one side or the other. By the end of 2006, more than 4,000 Palestinians and 700 Israelis had been killed in violence between the two sides, according to figures compiled by B'Tselem, an Israeli human rights organization. The economy of the Palestinian territories, which had improved after the 1993 Oslo peace accords, went into a tailspin, costing the vast majority of Palestinians most of the benefits of a brief period of peace. As the violence continued, it became conventional wisdom that the Oslo peace process was dead and that some other, less ambitious formula would have to be tried. The first hesitant step down a new, uncertain, road would come in April 2001, when the U.S.-led committee reported its findings on the events that triggered the al-Aqsa intifada (The Mitchell Report, p. 287).

Following are the text of a statement issued by the White House under the names of President Bill Clinton, Israeli prime minister Ehud Barak, and Palestine Liberation Organization chairman Yasir Arafat on July 25, 2000, at the conclusion of their summit at Camp David, and excerpts from a speech by Clinton on January 7, 2001, in New York City to the Israel Policy Forum.

DOCUMENT

Trilateral Statement at the Conclusion of the Camp David Summit

JULY 25, 2000

Between July 11 and 24, under the auspices of President Clinton, Prime Minister Barak and Chairman Arafat met at Camp David in an effort to reach an agreement on permanent status. While they were not able to bridge the gaps and reach an agreement, their negotiations were unprecedented in both scope and detail. Building on the progress achieved at Camp David, the two leaders agreed on the following principles to guide their negotiations:

1) The two sides agreed that the aim of their negotiations is to put an end to decades of conflict and achieve a just and lasting peace.

2) The two sides commit themselves to continue their efforts to conclude an agreement on all permanent status issues as soon as possible.

3) Both sides agree that negotiations based on UN Security Council Resolutions 242 and 338 are the only way to achieve such an agreement and they undertake to create an environment for negotiations free from pressure, intimidation and threats of violence.

4) The two sides understand the importance of avoiding unilateral actions that prejudge the outcome of negotiations and that their differences will be resolved only by good faith negotiations.

5) Both sides agree that the United States remains a vital partner in the search for peace and will continue to consult closely with President Clinton and Secretary [Madeleine] Albright in the period ahead.

SOURCE: U.S. Department of State, www.state.gov/www/regions/nea/000725_trilateral_stmt.html.

DOCUMENT

Clinton Speech on Camp David to the Israel Policy Forum

JANUARY 7, 2001

... For over 3 months, we have lived through a tragic cycle of violence that has cost hundreds of lives. It has shattered the confidence in the peace process. It has raised questions in some people's minds about whether Palestinians and Israelis could ever really live and work together, support each other's peace and prosperity and security. It's been a heartbreaking time for me, too. But we have done our best to work with the parties to restore calm, to end the bloodshed, and to get back to working on an agreement to address the underlying causes that continuously erupt in conflicts.

Whatever happens in the next 2 weeks I've got to serve, I think it's appropriate for me tonight, before a group of Americans and friends from the Middle East who believe profoundly in the peace process and have put their time and heart and money where their words are, to reflect on the lessons I believe we've all learned over the last 8 years and how we can achieve the long-sought peace.

From my first day as President, we have worked to advance interests in the Middle East that are long standing and historically bipartisan. I was glad to hear of [Nebraska Republican senator Chuck] Hagel's recitation of President-elect Bush's commitment to peace in the Middle East. Those historic commitments include an ironclad commitment to Israel's security and a just, comprehensive, and lasting agreement between the Palestinians and the Israelis.

Along the way, since '93, through the positive agreements that have been reached between those two sides, through the peace between Israel and Jordan, through last summer's withdrawal from Lebanon in which Israel fulfilled its part of implementing U.N. Security Counsel Resolution 425—along this way we have learned some important lessons, not only because of the benchmarks of progress, because of the occasional eruption of terrorism, bombing, death, and then these months of conflict.

I think these lessons have to guide any effort, now or in the future, to reach a comprehensive peace. Here's what I think they are. Most of you probably believed in them, up to the last 3 months. I still do.

First, the Arab-Israeli conflict is not just a morality play between good and evil; it is a conflict with a complex history, whose resolution requires balancing the needs of both sides, including respect for their national identities and religious beliefs.

Second, there is no place for violence and no military solution to this conflict. The only path to a just and durable resolution is through negotiation.

Third, there will be no lasting peace or regional stability without a strong and secure Israel, secure enough to make peace, strong enough to deter the adversaries which will still be there, even if a peace is made in complete good faith. And clearly that is why the United States must maintain its commitment to preserving Israel's qualitative edge in military superiority.

Fourth, talks must be accompanied by acts—acts which show trust and partnership. For good will at the negotiating table cannot survive forever ill intent on the ground. And it is important that each side understands how the other reads actions. For example, on the one hand, the tolerance of violence and incitement of hatred in classrooms and the media in the Palestinian communities, or on the other hand, humiliating treatment on the streets or at checkpoints by Israelis, are real obstacles to even getting people to talk about building a genuine peace.

Fifth, in the resolution of remaining differences, whether they come today or after several years of heartbreak and bloodshed, the fundamental, painful, but necessary choices will almost certainly remain the same whenever the decision is made. The parties will face the same history, the same geography, the same neighbors, the same passions, the same hatreds. This is not a problem time will take care of. . . .

Now, what are we going to do now? The first priority, obviously, has got to be to drastically reduce the current cycle of violence. But beyond that, on the Palestinian side, there must be an end to the culture of violence and the culture of incitement that, since Oslo, has not gone unchecked. Young children still are being educated to believe in confrontation with Israel, and multiple militia-like groups carry and use weapons with impunity. Voices of reason in that kind of environment will be drowned out too often by voices of revenge.

Such conduct is inconsistent with the Palestinian leadership's commitment to Oslo's nonviolent path to peace, and its persistence sends the wrong message to the Israeli people and makes it much more difficult for them to support their leaders in making the compromises necessary to get a lasting agreement.

For their part, the Israeli people also must understand that they're creating a few problems, too; that the settlement enterprise and building bypass roads in the heart of what they already know will one day be part of a Palestinian state is inconsistent with the Oslo commitment that both sides negotiate a compromise.

And restoring confidence requires the Palestinians being able to lead a normal existence and not be subject to daily, often humiliating reminders that they lack basic freedom and control over their lives. These, too, make it harder for the Palestinians to believe the commitments made to them will be kept.

Can two peoples with this kind of present trouble and troubling history still conclude a genuine and lasting peace? I mean, if I gave you this as a soap opera, you would say they're going to divorce court. But they can't, because they share such a small piece of land with such a profound history of importance to more than a billion people around the world. So I believe with all my heart not only that they can, but that they must.

At Camp David I saw Israeli and Palestinian negotiators who knew how many children each other had, who knew how many grandchildren each other had, who knew how they met their spouses, who knew what their family tragedies were, who trusted each other in their word. It was almost shocking to see what could happen and how people still felt on the ground when I saw how their leaders felt about each other and the respect and the confidence they had in each other when they were talking.

The alternative to getting this peace done is being played out before our very eyes. But amidst the agony, I will say again, there are signs of hope. And let me try to put this into what I think is a realistic context.

Camp David was a transformative event, because the two sides faced the core issue of their dispute in a forum that was official for the first time. And they had to debate the tradeoffs required to resolve the issues. Just as Oslo forced Israelis and Palestinians to come to terms with each other's existence, the discussions of the past 6 months have forced them to come to terms with each other's needs and the contours of a peace that ultimately they will have to reach.

That's why Prime Minister [Ehud] Barak, I think, has demonstrated real courage and vision in moving toward peace in difficult circumstances while trying to find a way to continue to protect Israel's security and vital interests. So that's a fancy way of saying, we know what we have to do, and we've got a mess on our hands.

So where do we go from here? Given the impasse and the tragic deterioration on the ground a couple of weeks ago, both sides asked me to present my ideas. So I put forward parameters that I wanted to be a guide toward a comprehensive agreement, parameters based on 8 years of listening carefully to both sides and hearing them describe with increasing clarity their respective grievances and needs.

Both Prime Minister Barak and Chairman [Yasir] Arafat have now accepted these parameters as the basis for further efforts, though both have expressed some reservations. At their request, I am using my remaining time in office to narrow the differences between the parties to the greatest degree possible—[applause]—for which I deserve no applause. Believe me, it beats packing up all my old books. [Laughter]

The parameters I put forward contemplate a settlement in response to each side's essential needs, if not to their utmost desires; a settlement based on sovereign homelands, security, peace, and dignity for both Israelis and Palestinians. These parameters don't begin to answer every question; they just narrow the questions that have to be answered.

Here they are. First, I think there can be no genuine resolution to the conflict without a sovereign, viable, Palestinian state that accommodates Israeli's security requirements and the demographic realities. That suggests Palestinian sovereignty over Gaza, the vast majority of the West Bank; the incorporation into Israel of settlement blocks, with the goal of maximizing the number of settlers in Israel while minimizing the land annexed. For Palestine, to be viable, must be a geographically contiguous state. Now, the land annexed into Israel into settlement blocks should include as few Palestinians as possible, consistent with the logic of two separate homelands. And to make the agreement durable, I think there will have to be some territorial swaps and other arrangements.

Second, a solution will have to be found for the Palestinian refugees who have suffered a great deal—particularly some of them—a solution that allows them to return to a Palestinian state that will provide all Palestinians with a place they can safely and proudly call home. All Palestinian refugees who wish to live in this homeland should have the right to do so. All others who want to find new homes, whether in their current locations or in third countries, should be able to do so, consistent with those countries' sovereign decisions, and that includes Israel. All refugees should receive compensation from the international community for their losses and assistance in building new lives.

Now, you all know what the rub is. That was a lot of artful language for saying that you cannot expect Israel to acknowledge an unlimited right of return to present-day Israel and, at the same time, to give up Gaza and the West Bank and have the settlement blocks as compact as possible, because of where a lot of these refugees came from. We cannot expect Israel to make a decision that would threaten the very foundations of the state of Israel and would undermine the whole logic of peace. And it shouldn't be done.

But I have made it very clear that the refugees will be a high priority, and that the United States will take a lead in raising the money necessary to relocate them in the most appropriate manner, and that if the government of Israel, or a subsequent government of Israel ever there—will be in charge of their immigration policy, just as we and the Canadians and the Europeans and others who would offer Palestinians a home would be, they would be obviously free to do that, and I think they've indicated that they would do that, to some extent. But there cannot be an unlimited language in an agreement that would undermine the very foundations of the Israeli state or the whole reason for creating the Palestinian state. So that's what we're working on.

Third, there will be no peace and no peace agreement unless the Israeli people have lasting security guarantees. These need not and should not come at the expense of Palestinian sovereignty or interfere with Palestinian territorial integrity. So my parameters rely on an international presence in Palestine to provide border security along the Jordan Valley and to monitor implementation of the final agreement. They rely on a nonmilitarized Palestine, a phased Israeli withdrawal to address Israeli security needs in the Jordan Valley, and other essential arrangements to ensure Israel's ability to defend itself.

Fourth, I come to the issue of Jerusalem, perhaps the most emotional and sensitive of all. It is a historic, cultural, and political center for both Israelis and Palestinians, a unique city sacred to all three monotheistic religions. And I believe the parameters I have established flow from four fair and logical propositions.

First, Jerusalem should be an open and undivided city with assured freedom of access and worship for all. It should encompass the internationally recognized capitals of two states, Israel and Palestine. Second, what is Arab should be Palestinian, for why would Israel want to govern in perpetuity the lives of hundreds of thousands of Palestinians? Third, what is Jewish should be Israeli. That would give rise to a Jewish Jerusalem larger and more vibrant than any in history. Fourth, what is holy to both requires a special care to meet the needs of all. I was glad to hear what the Speaker said about that. No peace agreement will last if not premised on mutual respect for the religious beliefs and holy shrines of Jews, Muslims, and Christians.

I have offered formulations on the Haram al-Sharif and the area holy to the Jewish people, an area which for 2,000 years, as I said at Camp David, has been the focus of Jewish yearning, that I believed fairly addressed the concerns of both sides.

Fifth and finally, any agreement will have to mark the decision to end the conflict, for neither side can afford to make these painful compromises only to be subjected to further demands. They are both entitled to know that if they take the last drop of blood out of each other's turnip, that's it. It really will have to be the end of the struggle that has pitted Palestinians and Israelis against one another for too long. And the end of the conflict must manifest itself with concrete acts that demonstrate a new attitude and a new approach by Palestinians and Israelis toward each other, and by other states in the region toward Israel, and by the entire region toward Palestine, to help it get off to a good start.

The parties' experience with interim accords has not always been happy—too many deadlines missed, too many commitments unfulfilled on both sides. So for this to signify a real end of the conflict, there must be effective mechanisms to provide guarantees of implementation.

That's a lot of stuff, isn't it? It's what I think is the outline of a fair agreement.

Let me say this. I am well aware that it will entail real pain and sacrifices for both sides. I am well aware that I don't even have to run for reelection in the United States on the basis of these ideas. I have worked for 8 years without laying such ideas down. I did it only when both sides asked me to and when it was obvious that we had come to the end of the road, and somebody had to do something to break out of the impasse.

Now, I still think the benefits of the agreement, based on these parameters, far outweigh the burdens. For the people of Israel, they are an end to conflict, secure and defensible borders, the incorporation of most of the settlers into Israel, and the Jewish capital of Yerushalayim [Hebrew for Jerusalem], recognized by all, not just the United States, by everybody in the world. It's a big deal, and it needs to be done.

For the Palestinian people, it means the freedom to determine their own future on their own land, a new life for the refugees, an independent and sovereign state with Al-Quds [Arabic for Jerusalem] as its capital, recognized by all.

And for America, it means that we could have new flags flying over new Embassies in both these capitals.

Now that the sides have accepted the parameters with reservations, what's going to happen? Well, each side will try to do a little better than I did. [Laughter] You know, that's just natural. But a peace viewed as imposed by one party upon the other, that puts one side up and the other down, rather than both ahead, contains the seeds of its own destruction.

Let me say, those who believe that my ideas can be altered to one party's exclusive benefit are mistaken. I think to press for more will produce less. There can be no peace without compromise. Now, I don't ask Israelis or Palestinians to agree with everything I said. If they can come up with a completely different agreement, it would suit me just fine. But I doubt it.

I have said what I have out of a profound lifetime commitment to and love for the state of Israel; out of a conviction that the Palestinian people have been ignored or used as political footballs by others for long enough, and they ought to have a chance to make their own life with dignity; and out of a belief that in the homeland of the world's three great religions that believe we are all the creatures of one God, we ought to be able to prove that one person's win is not by definition another's loss, that one person's dignity is not by definition another's humiliation, that one person's worship of God is not by definition another's heresy.

There has to be a way for us to find a truth we can share. There has to be a way for us to reach those young Palestinian kids who, unlike the young people in this audience, don't imagine a future in which they would ever put on clothes like this and sit at a dinner like this. There has to be a way for us to say to them, struggle and pain and destruction and self-destruction are way overrated and not the only option.

There has to be a way for us to reach those people in Israel who have paid such a high price and believe, frankly, that people who embrace the ideas I just outlined are nuts, because Israel is a little country and this agreement would make it smaller; to understand that the world in which we live and the technology of modern weaponry no longer make defense primarily a matter of geography and of politics; and the human feeling and the interdependence and the cooperation and the shared values and the shared interests are more important and worth the considered risk, especially if the United States remains committed to the military capacity of the state of Israel.

So I say to the Palestinians: There will always be those who are sitting outside in the peanut gallery of the Middle East, urging you to hold out for more or to plant one more bomb. But all the people who do that, they're not the refugees languishing in those camps; you are. They're not the ones with children growing up in poverty, whose income is lower today than it was the day we had the signing on the White House Lawn in 1993; you are.

All the people that are saying to the Palestinian people, "Stay on the path of no," are people that have a vested interest in the failure of the peace process that has nothing to do with how those kids in Gaza and the West Bank are going to grow up and live and raise their own children.

To the citizens of Israel who have returned to an ancient homeland after 2,000 years, whose hopes and dreams almost vanished in the Holocaust, who have hardly had one day of peace and quiet since the state of Israel was created: I understand, I believe, something of the disillusionment, the anger, the frustration that so many feel when, just at the moment peace seemed within reach, all this violence broke out and raised the question of whether it is ever possible.

The fact is that the people of Israel dreamed of a homeland. The dream came through, but when they came home, the land was not all vacant. Your land is also their land. It is the homeland of two peoples. And therefore, there is no choice but to create two states and make the best of it.

If it happens today, it will be better than if it happens tomorrow, because fewer people will die. And after it happens, the motives of those who continue the violence will be clearer to all than they are today.

Today, Israel is closer than ever to ending a 100-year-long era of struggle. It could be Israel's finest hour. And I hope and pray that the people of Israel will not give up the hope of peace.

SOURCE: Presidential Documents Online via GPO Access, *Weekly Compilation of Presidential Documents,* http://frwebgate.access.gpo.gov/cgi-bin/getdoc.cgi?dbname=2001_presidential_documents&docid=pd15ja01_txt-8.

The Mitchell Report

DOCUMENT IN CONTEXT

The failure of U.S.-sponsored peace negotiations at Camp David in July 2000, the outbreak of a second Palestinian intifada two months later, the January 2001 inauguration in the United States of a new administration leery of getting involved in the Middle East, and the election in February 2001 of hard-line former general Ariel Sharon as Israel's prime minister combined to bring an end to nearly eight years of diplomacy aimed at settling the conflict between Israelis and Palestinians. Instead, during the early months of 2001 the Middle East reverted to the violence and political intransigence that had shaped the conflict for decades before the Oslo peace process began in 1993.

One tiny ray of hope for a revival of the peace process came with the publication on May 21, 2001, of a report by an international commission that investigated the causes of the violence that started in 2000. President Bill Clinton had appointed the commission following a summit in Sharm el-Sheikh, Egypt, in mid-October 2000 that had attempted to impose a cease-fire in the violence and restart Israeli-Palestinian peace talks. The investigation had been requested by Palestinian leaders, apparently in the expectation that it would pin blame for the violence on Sharon, who on September 28, 2000, had paid a provocative visit to a holy site in Jerusalem called Haram al-Sharif by Muslims and the Temple Mount by Jews. Sharon had said he wanted to demonstrate Jewish sovereignty over the site of historic Jewish and Muslim religious shrines. A Palestinian demonstration at Haram al-Sharif the day after Sharon's visit turned violent and sparked an escalating series of attacks against one another by Israelis and Palestinians.

Former U.S. senator George Mitchell chaired the Sharm el-Sheikh Fact-Finding Committee in charge of investigating the situation. After visiting the region and interviewing officials and ordinary people on both sides of the conflict, the committee asserted that Israelis as well as Palestinians shared blame for the immediate outbreak of violence and for the underlying causes of it. The panel recommended a series of "confidence-building" measures to break the ongoing cycle of violence and to establish conditions for a resumption of long-term peace negotiations.

On the immediate causes of violence, Mitchell's committee cited Sharon's visit to the holy site as provocative under the circumstances and said that it should have been blocked by Israeli authorities. The visit, however, was not the sole cause of the violence, it said, charging officials on both sides with taking irresponsible actions that led to the violence during the subsequent Palestinian demonstrations. "Amid rising anger, fear, and mistrust, each side assumed the worst about the other and acted accordingly," the report said. Over the longer term, the panel reported, each side blamed the other for the failure of the peace process to produce genuine peace with tangible benefits for Israelis and Palestinians alike.

Looking to the future, the Mitchell committee called on the Israelis and Palestinians to take actions to restore each other's confidence in the peace process. It suggested that the Palestinian Authority crack down on those Palestinians attacking Israelis and prevent others from doing so and that the Israelis freeze construction of Jewish settlements in the West Bank and Gaza Strip.

The Bush administration and other governments endorsed the panel's findings, and Israeli and Palestinian officials said the report had positive elements. Sharon announced a unilateral cease-fire the day after the report's publication, but he rejected the recommendation for a settlement freeze, saying that it would "reward" Palestinian terrorism.

Any optimism sparked by the Mitchell commission report was short-lived, however, in the face of repeated Palestinian suicide bombings and aggressive Israeli actions.

Sharon sent the army into West Bank cities and barred thousands of Palestinians from traveling to their jobs in Israel. In December, the army surrounded the Palestinian Authority compound in the West Bank city of Ramallah, effectively imprisoning Palestinian leader Yasir Arafat.

The Bush administration took two modest steps to bring the situation under control, but both proved to be short-term and ineffective. In mid-June, CIA director George Tenet negotiated a cease-fire that calmed the violence for a few days, but it never went fully into effect. On November 26, retired marine general Anthony C. Zinni—the former head of the U.S. Central Command, covering the Middle East—visited the region as the envoy of Secretary of State Colin Powell. Upon Zinni's arrival, fresh violence broke out, and the envoy was called home for "consultations" after fewer than three weeks on the ground.

President Bush in June 2002 called on Palestinians to elect a "new leadership" in place of Arafat, and he officially endorsed, for the first time, the creation of a Palestinian state. Further international moves to encourage resumption of an Israeli-Palestinian peace process were delayed until after the U.S.-led invasion of Iraq in 2003 (The Roadmap, p. 298).

Following are excerpts from the final report of the Sharm el-Sheikh Fact-Finding Committee, chaired by former U.S. senator George Mitchell. The panel submitted its report to President George W. Bush on April 30, 2001, and it was released publicly on May 21, 2001. The panel's other members consisted of former U.S. senator Warren B. Rudman, former Turkish prime minister Suleyman Demirel, Norwegian foreign minister Thorbjoern Jagland, and Javier Solana, the high representative for the Common Foreign and Security Policy of the European Union.

DOCUMENT

Sharm el-Sheikh Fact-Finding Committee Final Report

MAY 21, 2001

INTRODUCTION

. . . After our first meeting, held before we visited the region, we urged an end to all violence. Our meetings and our observations during our subsequent visits to the region have intensified our convictions in this regard. Whatever the source, violence will not solve the problems of the region. It will only make them worse. Death and destruction will not bring peace, but will deepen the hatred and harden the resolve on both sides. There is only one way to peace, justice, and security in the Middle East, and that is through negotiation.

Despite their long history and close proximity, some Israelis and Palestinians seem not to fully appreciate each other's problems and concerns. Some Israelis appear not to comprehend the humiliation and frustration that Palestinians must endure every day as a result of living with the continuing effects of occupation, sustained by the presence of Israeli military forces and settlements in their midst, or the determination of the Palestinians to achieve independence and genuine self-determination. Some Palestinians appear not to comprehend the extent to which terrorism creates fear among the Israeli people and undermines their belief in the possibility of co-existence, or the determination of the GOI [Government of Israel] to do whatever is necessary to protect its people.

Fear, hate, anger, and frustration have risen on both sides. The greatest danger of all is that the culture of peace, nurtured over the previous decade, is being shattered. In its place there is a growing sense of futility and despair, and a growing resort to violence.

Political leaders on both sides must act and speak decisively to reverse these dangerous trends; they must rekindle the desire and the drive for peace. That will be difficult. But it can be done and it must be done, for the alternative is unacceptable and should be unthinkable.

Two proud peoples share a land and a destiny. Their competing claims and religious differences have led to a grinding, demoralizing, dehumanizing conflict. They can continue in conflict or they can negotiate to find a way to live side-by-side in peace.

There is a record of achievement. In 1991 the first peace conference with Israelis and Palestinians took place in Madrid to achieve peace based on UN Security Council Resolutions 242 and 338. In 1993, the Palestine Liberation Organization (PLO) and Israel met in Oslo for the first face-to-face negotiations; they led to mutual recognition and the Declaration of Principles (signed by the parties in Washington, D.C., on September 13, 1993), which provided a road map to reach the destination agreed in Madrid. Since then, important steps have been taken in Cairo, in Washington, and elsewhere. Last year the parties came very close to a permanent settlement.

So much has been achieved. So much is at risk. If the parties are to succeed in completing their journey to their common destination, agreed commitments must be implemented, international law respected, and human rights protected. We encourage them to return to negotiations, however difficult. It is the only path to peace, justice and security.

DISCUSSION

It is clear from their statements that the participants in the summit of last October hoped and intended that the outbreak of violence, then less than a month old, would soon end. The U.S. President's letters to us, asking that we make recommendations on how to prevent a recurrence of violence, reflect that intention.

Yet the violence has not ended. It has worsened. Thus the overriding concern of those in the region with whom we spoke is to end the violence and to return to the process of shaping a sustainable peace. That is what we were told, and were asked to address, by Israelis and Palestinians alike. It was the message conveyed to us as well by President [Hosni] Mubarak of Egypt, King Abdullah [II] of Jordan, and UN Secretary General [Kofi] Annan.

Their concern must be ours. If our report is to have effect, it must deal with the situation that exists, which is different from that envisaged by the summit participants.

In this report, we will try to answer the questions assigned to us by the Sharm el-Sheikh summit: What happened? Why did it happen? . . .

WHAT HAPPENED?

We are not a tribunal. We complied with the request that we not determine the guilt or innocence of individuals or of the parties. We did not have the power to compel the testimony of witnesses or the production of documents. Most of the information we received came from the parties and, understandably, it largely tended to support their arguments.

In this part of our report, we do not attempt to chronicle all of the events from late September 2000 onward. Rather, we discuss only those that shed light on the underlying causes of violence.

In late September 2000, Israeli, Palestinian, and other officials received reports that Member of the Knesset (now Prime Minister) Ariel Sharon was planning a visit to the Haram al-Sharif/Temple Mount in Jerusalem. Palestinian and U.S. officials urged then Prime Minister Ehud Barak to prohibit the visit. Mr. Barak told us that he believed the visit was intended to be an internal political act directed against him by a political opponent, and he declined to prohibit it.

Mr. Sharon made the visit on September 28 accompanied by over 1,000 Israeli police officers. Although Israelis viewed the visit in an internal political context, Palestinians saw it as highly provocative to them. On the following day, in the same place, a large number of unarmed Palestinian demonstrators and a large Israeli police contingent confronted each other. According to the U.S. Department of State, "Palestinians held large demonstrations and threw stones at police in the vicinity of the Western Wall. Police used rubber-coated metal bullets and live ammunition to disperse the demonstrators, killing 4 persons and injuring about 200." According to the GOI, 14 Israeli policemen were injured.

Similar demonstrations took place over the following several days. Thus began what has become known as the "Al-Aqsa Intifada" (Al-Aqsa being a mosque at the Haram al-Sharif/Temple Mount).

The GOI asserts that the immediate catalyst for the violence was the breakdown of the Camp David negotiations on July 25, 2000, and the "widespread appreciation in the international community of Palestinian responsibility for the impasse." In this view, Palestinian violence was planned by the PA leadership, and was aimed at "provoking and incurring Palestinian casualties as a means of regaining the diplomatic initiative."

The Palestine Liberation Organization (PLO) denies the allegation that the intifada was planned. It claims, however, that "Camp David represented nothing less than an attempt by Israel to extend the force it exercises on the ground to negotiations," and that "the failure of the summit, and the attempts to allocate blame on the Palestinian side only added to the tension on the ground." . . .

From the perspective of the PLO, Israel responded to the disturbances with excessive and illegal use of deadly force against demonstrators; behavior which, in the PLO's view, reflected Israel's contempt for the lives and safety of Palestinians. For Palestinians, the widely seen images of the killing of 12-year-old Muhammad al Durra in Gaza on September 30, shot as he huddled behind his father, reinforced that perception.

From the perspective of the GOI, the demonstrations were organized and directed by the Palestinian leadership to create sympathy for their cause around the world by provoking Israeli security forces to fire upon demonstrators, especially young people. For Israelis, the lynching of two military reservists, First Sgt. Vadim Novesche and First Cpl. Yosef Avrahami, in Ramallah on October 12, reflected a deep-seated Palestinian hatred of Israel and Jews.

What began as a series of confrontations between Palestinian demonstrators and Israeli security forces, which resulted in the GOI's initial restrictions on the movement of people and goods in the West Bank and Gaza Strip (closures), has since evolved into a wider array of violent actions and responses. There have been exchanges of fire between built-up areas, sniping incidents and clashes between Israeli settlers and Palestinians. There have also been terrorist acts and Israeli reactions thereto (characterized by the GOI as counter-terrorism), including killings, further destruction of property and economic measures. Most recently, there have been mortar attacks on Israeli locations and IDF [Israeli Defense Forces] ground incursions into Palestinian areas.

From the Palestinian perspective, the decision of Israel to characterize the current crisis as "an armed conflict short of war" is simply a means "to justify its assassination policy, its collective punishment policy, and its use of lethal force." From the Israeli perspective, "The Palestinian leadership have instigated, orchestrated and directed the violence. It has used, and continues to use, terror and attrition as strategic tools."

In their submissions, the parties traded allegations about the motivation and degree of control exercised by the other. However, we were provided with no persuasive evidence that the Sharon visit was anything other than an internal political act; neither were we provided with persuasive evidence that the PA [Palestinian Authority] planned the uprising.

Accordingly, we have no basis on which to conclude that there was a deliberate plan by the PA to initiate a campaign of violence at the first opportunity; or to conclude that there was a deliberate plan by the GOI to respond with lethal force.

However, there is also no evidence on which to conclude that the PA made a consistent effort to contain the demonstrations and control the violence once it began; or that the GOI made a consistent effort to use non-lethal means to control demonstrations of unarmed Palestinians. Amid rising anger, fear, and mistrust, each side assumed the worst about the other and acted accordingly.

The Sharon visit did not cause the "Al-Aqsa Intifada." But it was poorly timed and the provocative effect should have been foreseen; indeed it was foreseen by those who urged that the visit be prohibited. More significant were the events that followed: the decision of the Israeli police on September 29 to use lethal means against the Palestinian demonstrators; and the subsequent failure, as noted above, of either party to exercise restraint.

WHY DID IT HAPPEN?

The roots of the current violence extend much deeper than an inconclusive summit conference. Both sides have made clear a profound disillusionment with the behavior of the other in failing to meet the expectations arising from the peace process launched in Madrid in 1991 and then in Oslo in 1993. Each side has accused the other of violating specific undertakings and undermining the spirit of their commitment to resolving their political differences peacefully.

Divergent Expectations

We are struck by the divergent expectations expressed by the parties relating to the implementation of the Oslo process. Results achieved from this process were unthinkable less than 10 years ago. During the latest round of negotiations, the parties were closer to a permanent settlement than ever before.

Nonetheless, Palestinians and Israelis alike told us that the premise on which the Oslo process is based—that tackling the hard "permanent status" issues be deferred to the end of the process—has gradually come under serious pressure. The step-by-step process agreed to by the parties was based on the assumption that each step in the negotiating process would lead to enhanced trust and confidence. To achieve this, each party would have to implement agreed upon commitments and abstain from actions that would be seen by the other as attempts to abuse the process in order to predetermine the shape of the final outcome. If this requirement is not met, the Oslo road map cannot successfully lead to its agreed destination. Today, each side blames the other for having ignored this fundamental aspect, resulting in a crisis in confidence. This problem became even more pressing with the opening of permanent status talks.

The GOI has placed primacy on moving toward a Permanent Status Agreement in a nonviolent atmosphere, consistent with commitments contained in the agreements between the parties. "Even if slower than was initially envisaged, there has, since the start of the peace process in Madrid in 1991, been steady progress towards the goal of a Permanent Status Agreement without the resort to violence on a scale that has characterized recent weeks." The "goal" is the Permanent Status Agreement, the terms of which must be negotiated by the parties.

The PLO view is that delays in the process have been the result of an Israeli attempt to prolong and solidify the occupation. Palestinians "believed that the Oslo process would yield an end to Israeli occupation in five years," the timeframe for the transitional period specified in the Declaration of Principles. Instead there have been, in the PLO's view, repeated Israeli delays culminating in the Camp David summit, where, "Israel proposed to annex about 11.2% of the West Bank (excluding Jerusalem) . . ." and offered unacceptable proposals concerning Jerusalem, security and refugees. "In sum, Israel's proposals at Camp David provided for Israel's annexation of the best Palestinian lands, the perpetuation of Israeli control over East Jerusalem, a continued Israeli military presence on Palestinian territory, Israeli control over Palestinian natural resources, airspace and borders, and the return of fewer than 1% of refugees to their homes."

Both sides see the lack of full compliance with agreements reached since the opening of the peace process as evidence of a lack of good faith. This conclusion led to an erosion of trust even before the permanent status negotiations began.

Divergent Perspectives

During the last seven months, these views have hardened into divergent realities. Each side views the other as having acted in bad faith; as having turned the optimism of Oslo into the suffering and grief of victims and their loved ones. In their statements and actions, each side demonstrates a perspective that fails to recognize any truth in the perspective of the other.

The Palestinian Perspective

For the Palestinian side, "Madrid" and "Oslo" heralded the prospect of a State, and guaranteed an end to the occupation and a resolution of outstanding matters within an agreed time frame. Palestinians are genuinely angry at the continued growth of settlements and at their daily experiences of humiliation and disruption as a result of Israel's presence in the Palestinian territories. Palestinians see settlers and settlements in their midst not only as violating the spirit of the Oslo process, but also as an application of force in the form of Israel's overwhelming military superiority, which sustains and protects the settlements.

The Interim Agreement provides that "the two parties view the West Bank and Gaza as a single territorial unit, the integrity and status of which will be preserved during the interim period." Coupled with this, the Interim Agreement's prohibition on taking steps which may prejudice permanent status negotiations denies Israel the right to continue its illegal expansionist settlement policy. In addition to the Interim Agreement, customary international law, including the Fourth Geneva Convention, prohibits Israel (as an occupying power) from establishing settlements in occupied territory pending an end to the conflict.

The PLO alleges that Israeli political leaders "have made no secret of the fact that the Israeli interpretation of Oslo was designed to segregate the Palestinians in noncontiguous enclaves, surrounded by Israeli military-controlled borders, with settlements and settlement roads violating the territories' integrity."

According to the PLO, "In the seven years since the [Declaration of Principles], the settler population in the West Bank, excluding East Jerusalem and the Gaza Strip, has doubled to 200,000, and the settler population in East Jerusalem has risen to 170,000. Israel has constructed approximately 30 new settlements, and expanded a number of existing ones to house these new settlers."

The PLO also claims that the GOI has failed to comply with other commitments such as the further withdrawal from the West Bank and the release of Palestinian prisoners. In addition, Palestinians expressed frustration with the impasse over refugees and the deteriorating economic circumstances in the West Bank and Gaza Strip.

The Israeli Perspective

From the GOI perspective, the expansion of settlement activity and the taking of measures to facilitate the convenience and safety of settlers do not prejudice the outcome of permanent status negotiations.

Israel understands that the Palestinian side objects to the settlements in the West Bank and the Gaza Strip. Without prejudice to the formal status of the settlements, Israel accepts that the settlements are an outstanding issue on which there will have to be agreement as part of any permanent status resolution between the sides. This point was acknowledged and agreed upon in the Declaration of Principles of 13 September 1993 as well as in other agreements between the two sides. There has in fact been a good deal of discussion on the question of settlements between the two sides in the various negotiations toward a permanent status agreement.

Indeed, Israelis point out that at the Camp David summit and during subsequent talks the GOI offered to make significant concessions with respect to settlements in the context of an overall agreement.

Security, however, is the key GOI concern. The GOI maintains that the PLO has breached its solemn commitments by continuing the use of violence in the pursuit of political objectives. "Israel's principal concern in the peace process has been security. This issue is of overriding importance . . . [S]ecurity is not something on which Israel will bargain or compromise. The failure of the Palestinian side to comply with both the letter and spirit of the security provisions in the various agreements has long been a source of disturbance in Israel."

According to the GOI, the Palestinian failure takes several forms: institutionalized anti-Israel, anti-Jewish incitement; the release from detention of terrorists; the failure to control illegal weapons; and the actual conduct of violent operations, ranging from the insertion of riflemen into demonstrations to terrorist attacks on Israeli civilians. The GOI maintains that the PLO has explicitly violated its renunciation of terrorism and other acts of violence, thereby significantly eroding trust between the parties. The GOI perceives "a thread, implied but nonetheless clear, that runs throughout the Palestinian submissions. It is that Palestinian violence against Israel and Israelis is somehow explicable, understandable, legitimate." . . .

RECOMMENDATIONS

The GOI and the PA must act swiftly and decisively to halt the violence. Their immediate objectives then should be to rebuild confidence and resume negotiations. What we are asking is not easy. Palestinians and Israelis—not just their leaders, but two publics at large—have lost confidence in one another. We are asking political leaders to do, for the sake of their people, the politically difficult: to lead without knowing how many will follow.

During this mission our aim has been to fulfill the mandate agreed at Sharm el-Sheikh. We value the support given our work by the participants at the summit, and we commend the parties for their cooperation. Our principal recommendation is that they recommit themselves to the Sharm el-Sheikh spirit, and that they implement the decisions made there in 1999 and 2000. We believe that the summit participants will support bold action by the parties to achieve these objectives.

END THE VIOLENCE

The GOI and the PA should reaffirm their commitment to existing agreements and undertakings and should immediately implement an unconditional cessation of violence. Anything less than a complete effort by both parties to end the violence will render the effort itself ineffective, and will likely be interpreted by the other side as evidence of hostile intent.

The GOI and PA should immediately resume security cooperation. Effective bilateral cooperation aimed at preventing violence will encourage the resumption of negotiations. We are particularly concerned that, absent effective, transparent security cooperation, terrorism and other acts of violence will continue and may be seen as officially sanctioned whether they are or not. The parties should consider widening the scope of security cooperation to reflect the priorities of both communities and to seek acceptance for these efforts from those communities.

We acknowledge the PA's position that security cooperation presents a political difficulty absent a suitable political context, i.e., the relaxation of stringent Israeli security measures combined with ongoing, fruitful negotiations. We also acknowl-edge the PA's fear that, with security cooperation in hand, the GOI may not be dis-posed to deal forthrightly with Palestinian political concerns. We believe that secu-rity cooperation cannot long be sustained if meaningful negotiations are unreasonably deferred, if security measures "on the ground" are seen as hostile, or if steps are taken that are perceived as provocative or as prejudicing the outcome of negotiations.

REBUILD CONFIDENCE

The PA and GOI should work together to establish a meaningful "cooling off period" and implement additional confidence building measures, some of which were proposed in the October 2000 Sharm el-Sheikh Statement and some of which were offered by the U.S. on January 7, 2001 in Cairo.

The PA and GOI should resume their efforts to identify, condemn and discour-age incitement in all its forms.

The PA should make clear through concrete action to Palestinians and Israelis alike that terrorism is reprehensible and unacceptable, and that the PA will make a 100 per-cent effort to prevent terrorist operations and to punish perpetrators. This effort should include immediate steps to apprehend and incarcerate terrorists operating within the PA's jurisdiction.

The GOI should freeze all settlement activity, including the "natural growth" of existing settlements.

The kind of security cooperation desired by the GOI cannot for long co-exist with settlement activity described very recently by the European Union as causing "great concern" and by the U.S. as "provocative."

The GOI should give careful consideration to whether settlements which are focal points for substantial friction are valuable bargaining chips for future negotiations or provocations likely to preclude the onset of productive talks.

The GOI may wish to make it clear to the PA that a future peace would pose no threat to the territorial contiguity of a Palestinian State to be established in the West Bank and the Gaza Strip.

The IDF should consider withdrawing to positions held before September 28, 2000 which will reduce the number of friction points and the potential for violent confrontations.

The GOI should ensure that the IDF adopt and enforce policies and procedures encouraging non-lethal responses to unarmed demonstrators, with a view to minimiz-ing casualties and friction between the two communities. The IDF should:

Re-institute, as a matter of course, military police investigations into Palestinian deaths resulting from IDF actions in the Palestinian territories in incidents not involv-ing terrorism. The IDF should abandon the blanket characterization of the current uprising as "an armed conflict short of war," which fails to discriminate between ter-rorism and protest.

Adopt tactics of crowd-control that minimize the potential for deaths and casual-ties, including the withdrawal of metal-cored rubber rounds from general use.

Ensure that experienced, seasoned personnel are present for duty at all times at known friction points.

Ensure that the stated values and standard operating procedures of the IDF effectively instill the duty of caring for Palestinians in the West Bank and Gaza Strip as well as Israelis living there, consistent with *The Ethical Code of The IDF.*

The GOI should lift closures, transfer to the PA all tax revenues owed, and permit Palestinians who had been employed in Israel to return to their jobs; and should ensure that security forces and settlers refrain from the destruction of homes and roads, as well as trees and other agricultural property in Palestinian areas. We acknowledge the GOI's position that actions of this nature have been taken for security reasons. Nevertheless, their economic effects will persist for years.

The PA should renew cooperation with Israeli security agencies to ensure, to the maximum extent possible, that Palestinian workers employed within Israel are fully vetted and free of connections to organizations and individuals engaged in terrorism.

The PA should prevent gunmen from using Palestinian populated areas to fire upon Israeli populated areas and IDF positions. This tactic places civilians on both sides at unnecessary risk.

The GOI and IDF should adopt and enforce policies and procedures designed to ensure that the response to any gunfire emanating from Palestinian populated areas minimizes the danger to the lives and property of Palestinian civilians, bearing in mind that it is probably the objective of gunmen to elicit an excessive IDF response.

The GOI should take all necessary steps to prevent acts of violence by settlers.

The parties should abide by the provisions of the Wye River Agreement prohibiting illegal weapons.

The PA should take all necessary steps to establish a clear and unchallenged chain of command for armed personnel operating under its authority.

The PA should institute and enforce effective standards of conduct and accountability, both within the uniformed ranks and between the police and the civilian political leadership to which it reports.

The PA and GOI should consider a joint undertaking to preserve and protect holy places sacred to the traditions of Muslims, Jews, and Christians. An initiative of this nature might help to reverse a disturbing trend: the increasing use of religious themes to encourage and justify violence.

The GOI and PA should jointly endorse and support the work of Palestinian and Israeli non-governmental organizations (NGOs) involved in cross-community initiatives linking the two peoples. It is important that these activities, including the provision of humanitarian aid to Palestinian villages by Israeli NGOs, receive the full backing of both parties.

RESUME NEGOTIATIONS

We reiterate our belief that a 100 percent effort to stop the violence, an immediate resumption of security cooperation and an exchange of confidence building measures are all important for the resumption of negotiations. Yet none of these steps will long be sustained absent a return to serious negotiations.

It is not within our mandate to prescribe the venue, the basis or the agenda of negotiations. However, in order to provide an effective political context for practical cooperation between the parties, negotiations must not be unreasonably deferred and they must, in our view, manifest a spirit of compromise, reconciliation and partnership, notwithstanding the events of the past seven months.

In the spirit of the Sharm el-Sheikh agreements and understandings of 1999 and 2000, we recommend that the parties meet to reaffirm their commitment to signed agreements and mutual understandings, and take corresponding action. This should be the basis for resuming full and meaningful negotiations.

The parties are at a crossroads. If they do not return to the negotiating table, they face the prospect of fighting it out for years on end, with many of their citizens leaving for distant shores to live their lives and raise their children. We pray they make the right choice. That means stopping the violence now. Israelis and Palestinians have to live, work, and prosper together. History and geography have destined them to be neighbors. That cannot be changed. Only when their actions are guided by this awareness will they be able to develop the vision and reality of peace and shared prosperity. . . .

SOURCE: U.S. Department of State, www.state.gov/p/nea/rls/rpt/3060.htm

The Road Map

DOCUMENT IN CONTEXT

After watching the cycle of violence between Israelis and Palestinians spiral out of control for two years, the international community in late 2002 and early 2003 tried to revive the peace process that had collapsed in 2000. This new effort failed, in part because the violence had become so entrenched, because neither side was fully ready for another effort at compromise, and because the United States and other international players were too distracted by the war in Iraq and its aftermath to follow through on what had become a lesser priority.

The attempt to revive international diplomacy on the Israeli-Palestinian conflict began with a series of steps in 2002. First, on March 28, the Arab League adopted a plan calling for peace with and recognition of Israel. Although unsatisfactory to the Israelis, this plan, sponsored by Saudi Arabia's crown prince Abdallah, came closer to acknowledging Israel's legitimacy than any previous statement by Arab leaders. Even so, it was undone in part by the ongoing violence between Palestinians and Israel (see Arab League Beirut Summit, p. 156).

On June 24, 2002, President George W. Bush presented a carrot and a stick to the Palestinians: the carrot—an explicit call for the creation of a Palestinian state; the stick—a demand that the Palestinians elect new leaders "not compromised by terror," or in other words, replace long-time leader Yasir Arafat. Also in mid-2002, diplomats from the European Union, Russia, the United Nations, and the United States formed a group, the so-called Quartet, to push for an international solution to the Israeli-

Palestinian conflict. The Quartet developed a step-by-step "performance-based roadmap for peace." At the request of Israeli prime minister Ariel Sharon, however, Bush agreed in December 2002 to withhold official publication of the plan until after Israeli elections scheduled for late January 2003. Regardless, copies of the document circulated widely.

Sharon won reelection, but two other developments brought yet another postponement in publication of the road map peace plan. First, under strong international pressure, Arafat agreed in February to appoint a prime minister to manage the day-to-day affairs of the Palestinian Authority. His long-time aide, Mahmoud Abbas (also known as Abu Mazen) ultimately accepted the job after extracting from Arafat what were supposed to be broad powers. Abbas formally accepted the position on March 19 a few hours before the other major event: the invasion of Iraq by the United States and a handful of allies. Within three weeks, that invasion had pushed Iraq's leader, Saddam Hussein, from power (Iraq War, p. 504).

On April 30, a day after Abbas formed a new government, diplomats formally handed copies of the document to Abbas and Sharon, and the White House issued a statement heralding the event and calling on both sides to carry out the responsibilities outlined for them in it. Abbas accepted the road map without any conditions, but the Israeli cabinet lodged fourteen reservations, some of them serious, when it narrowly approved the document on May 25.

The road map presented a three-phase timeline leading to establishment of a Palestinian state by a deadline vaguely defined as "2004–2005." Because of the delay in publication, little time remained for the first phase, scheduled for completion by June 2003. In that phase, the Palestinian Authority was to act to halt terrorism against Israel, including negotiating a cease-fire with factions, among them Hamas and Islamic Jihad, that had carried out most of the suicide bombings and other attacks against Israelis. For its part, Israel was supposed to withdraw most of the troops that had reoccupied the West Bank and Gaza Strip since the eruption of violence in late 2000 and to dismantle so-called outposts, which had been built in the West Bank by religious groups without official government authorization (though often with government collusion).

The road map process began on a modestly hopeful note when on May 17 and May 29 Abbas and Sharon held their first meetings and agreed on several steps, including a limited withdrawal of Israeli troops from parts of the Palestinian territories. In June, Bush made his first personal foray into the region since becoming president more than two years earlier. On June 3, he met in the Egyptian resort city of Sharm el-Sheikh with key Arab leaders, who pledged to support the road map process. The next day, Bush met with Abbas and Sharon at the Jordanian port city of Aqaba for a sunny, outdoor summit session. Abbas, who had long been opposed to the use of violence, promised to try to rein in the groups launching attacks on Israelis, and Sharon pledged to dismantle unauthorized settlements. For his part, Bush said he was "committed" to the peace process, and he later told reporters that he had warned Abbas and Sharon that he would "ride herd" on them to fulfill their road map responsibilities.

The first few months of the road map were relatively positive. Aided by a U.S. diplomatic push, Abbas successfully convinced Palestinian factions to agree to a three-month cease-fire, starting on June 29. Sharon withdrew the Israeli army from the northern part of the Gaza Strip and ordered the dismantling of several unauthorized settlements, most of which were uninhabited (and some of which were quietly rebuilt later).

The road map went off track on August 19, when a Palestinian suicide bomber attacked a bus in Jerusalem, killing twenty Israelis and wounding several dozen others. An angry Sharon called a halt to the peace process and sent the army deeper into the West Bank, including into the cities of Jenin and Nablus. The Israelis also resumed a tactic of "targeted killings" of senior officials and other members of the Palestinian groups involved in attacks on Israelis. The initial target, Abu Shanab, a leader of Hamas, had been one of that group's leading advocates of the cease-fire. Hamas responded by withdrawing from the cease-fire, and the cycle of violence resumed. The Bush administration, which had entered the Middle East peace process with much fanfare just four months earlier, quietly backed away, not to return for more than a year, after Arafat's sudden death in November 2004.

Following is the text of the Performance-Based Roadmap to a Permanent Two-State Solution to the Israeli-Palestinian Conflict, published on April 30, 2003, by the Quartet—the European Union, Russia, the United Nations, and the United States.

D O C U M E N T

Performance-Based Roadmap to a Permanent Two-State Solution to the Israeli-Palestinian Conflict

APRIL 30, 2003

The following is a performance-based and goal-driven roadmap, with clear phases, timelines, target dates, and benchmarks aiming at progress through reciprocal steps by the two parties in the political, security, economic, humanitarian, and institution-building fields, under the auspices of the Quartet [the United States, European Union, United Nations, and Russia]. The destination is a final and comprehensive settlement of the Israel-Palestinian conflict by 2005, as presented in President [George W.] Bush's speech of 24 June, and welcomed by the EU, Russia and the UN in the 16 July and 17 September Quartet Ministerial statements.

A two-state solution to the Israeli-Palestinian conflict will only be achieved through an end to violence and terrorism, when the Palestinian people have a leadership acting decisively against terror and willing and able to build a practicing democracy based on tolerance and liberty, and through Israel's readiness to do what is necessary for a democratic Palestinian state to be established, and a clear, unambiguous acceptance by both parties of the goal of a negotiated settlement as described below. The Quartet will assist and facilitate implementation of the plan, starting in Phase I, including direct discussions between the parties as required. The plan establishes a realistic timeline for implementation. However, as a performance-based plan, progress will require and depend upon the good faith efforts of the parties, and their compliance with each of the obligations outlined below. Should the parties perform their obligations rapidly, progress within and through the phases may come sooner than indicated in the plan. Non-compliance with obligations will impede progress.

A settlement, negotiated between the parties, will result in the emergence of an independent, democratic, and viable Palestinian state living side by side in peace and security with Israel and its other neighbors. The settlement will resolve the Israel-Palestinian conflict, and end the occupation that began in 1967, based on the foundations of the Madrid Conference, the principle of land for peace, UNSCRs [United Nations Security Council Resolutions] 242, 338 and 1397, agreements previously reached by the parties, and the initiative of Saudi Crown Prince Abdullah—endorsed by the Beirut Arab League Summit—calling for acceptance of Israel as a neighbor living in peace and security, in the context of a comprehensive settlement. This initiative is a vital element of international efforts to promote a comprehensive peace on all tracks, including the Syrian-Israeli and Lebanese-Israeli tracks.

The Quartet will meet regularly at senior levels to evaluate the parties' performance on implementation of the plan. In each phase, the parties are expected to perform their obligations in parallel, unless otherwise indicated.

Phase I: Ending Terror and Violence, Normalizing Palestinian Life, and Building Palestinian Institutions— Present to May 2003

In Phase I, the Palestinians immediately undertake an unconditional cessation of violence according to the steps outlined below; such action should be accompanied by supportive measures undertaken by Israel. Palestinians and Israelis resume security cooperation based on the Tenet work plan to end violence, terrorism, and incitement through restructured and effective Palestinian security services. Palestinians undertake comprehensive political reform in preparation for statehood, including drafting a Palestinian constitution, and free, fair and open elections upon the basis of those measures. Israel takes all necessary steps to help normalize Palestinian life. Israel withdraws from Palestinian areas occupied from September 28, 2000 and the two sides restore the status quo that existed at that time, as security performance and cooperation progress. Israel also freezes all settlement activity, consistent with the Mitchell report.

At the outset of Phase I:

- Palestinian leadership issues unequivocal statement reiterating Israel's right to exist in peace and security and calling for an immediate and unconditional ceasefire to end armed activity and all acts of violence against Israelis anywhere. All official Palestinian institutions end incitement against Israel.
- Israeli leadership issues unequivocal statement affirming its commitment to the two-state vision of an independent, viable, sovereign Palestinian state living in peace and security alongside Israel, as expressed by President Bush, and calling for an immediate end to violence against Palestinians everywhere. All official Israeli institutions end incitement against Palestinians.

Security

- Palestinians declare an unequivocal end to violence and terrorism and undertake visible efforts on the ground to arrest, disrupt, and restrain individuals and groups conducting and planning violent attacks on Israelis anywhere.

- Rebuilt and refocused Palestinian Authority security apparatus begins sustained, targeted, and effective operations aimed at confronting all those engaged in terror and dismantlement of terrorist capabilities and infrastructure. This includes commencing confiscation of illegal weapons and consolidation of security authority, free of association with terror and corruption.
- GOI [Government of Israel] takes no actions undermining trust, including deportations, attacks on civilians; confiscation and/or demolition of Palestinian homes and property, as a punitive measure or to facilitate Israeli construction; destruction of Palestinian institutions and infrastructure; and other measures specified in the Tenet work plan.
- Relying on existing mechanisms and on-the-ground resources, Quartet representatives begin informal monitoring and consult with the parties on establishment of a formal monitoring mechanism and its implementation.
- Implementation, as previously agreed, of U.S. rebuilding, training and resumed security cooperation plan in collaboration with outside oversight board (U.S.–Egypt–Jordan). Quartet support for efforts to achieve a lasting, comprehensive cease-fire.
  - All Palestinian security organizations are consolidated into three services reporting to an empowered Interior Minister.
  - Restructured/retrained Palestinian security forces and IDF [Israel Defense Forces] counterparts progressively resume security cooperation and other undertakings in implementation of the Tenet work plan, including regular senior-level meetings, with the participation of U.S. security officials.
  - Arab states cut off public and private funding and all other forms of support for groups supporting and engaging in violence and terror.
  - All donors providing budgetary support for the Palestinians channel these funds through the Palestinian Ministry of Finance's Single Treasury Account.
  - As comprehensive security performance moves forward, IDF withdraws progressively from areas occupied since September 28, 2000 and the two sides restore the status quo that existed prior to September 28, 2000. Palestinian security forces redeploy to areas vacated by IDF.

Palestinian Institution-Building

- Immediate action on credible process to produce draft constitution for Palestinian statehood. As rapidly as possible, constitutional committee circulates draft Palestinian constitution, based on strong parliamentary democracy and cabinet with empowered prime minister, for public comment/debate. Constitutional committee proposes draft document for submission after elections for approval by appropriate Palestinian institutions.
- Appointment of interim prime minister or cabinet with empowered executive authority/decision-making body.
- GOI fully facilitates travel of Palestinian officials for PLC [Palestinian Legislative Council] and Cabinet sessions, internationally supervised security retraining, electoral and other reform activity, and other supportive measures related to the reform efforts.
- Continued appointment of Palestinian ministers empowered to undertake fundamental reform. Completion of further steps to achieve genuine separation of powers, including any necessary Palestinian legal reforms for this purpose.

- Establishment of independent Palestinian election commission. PLC reviews and revises election law.
- Palestinian performance on judicial, administrative, and economic benchmarks, as established by the International Task Force on Palestinian Reform.
- As early as possible, and based upon the above measures and in the context of open debate and transparent candidate selection/electoral campaign based on a free, multi-party process, Palestinians hold free, open, and fair elections.
- GOI facilitates Task Force election assistance, registration of voters, movement of candidates and voting officials. Support for NGOs [non-governmental organizations] involved in the election process.
- GOI reopens Palestinian Chamber of Commerce and other closed Palestinian institutions in East Jerusalem based on a commitment that these institutions operate strictly in accordance with prior agreements between the parties.

Humanitarian Response

- Israel takes measures to improve the humanitarian situation. Israel and Palestinians implement in full all recommendations of the Bertini report to improve humanitarian conditions, lifting curfews and easing restrictions on movement of persons and goods, and allowing full, safe, and unfettered access of international and humanitarian personnel.
- AHLC [Ad-Hoc Liaison Committee] reviews the humanitarian situation and prospects for economic development in the West Bank and Gaza and launches a major donor assistance effort, including to the reform effort.
- GOI and PA [Palestinian Authority] continue revenue clearance process and transfer of funds, including arrears, in accordance with agreed, transparent monitoring mechanism.

Civil Society

- Continued donor support, including increased funding through PVOs/NGOs, for people to people programs, private sector development and civil society initiatives.

Settlements

- GOI immediately dismantles settlement outposts erected since March 2001.
- Consistent with the Mitchell Report, GOI freezes all settlement activity (including natural growth of settlements).

Phase II: Transition—June 2003–December 2003

In the second phase, efforts are focused on the option of creating an independent Palestinian state with provisional borders and attributes of sovereignty, based on the new constitution, as a way station to a permanent status settlement. As has been noted, this goal can be achieved when the Palestinian people have a leadership acting decisively against terror, willing and able to build a practicing democracy based on tolerance and liberty. With such a leadership, reformed civil institutions and security structures, the Palestinians will have the active support of the Quartet and the broader international community in establishing an independent, viable, state.

Progress into Phase II will be based upon the consensus judgment of the Quartet of whether conditions are appropriate to proceed, taking into account performance of both parties. Furthering and sustaining efforts to normalize Palestinian lives and build Palestinian institutions, Phase II starts after Palestinian elections and ends with possible creation of an independent Palestinian state with provisional borders in 2003. Its primary goals are continued comprehensive security performance and effective security cooperation, continued normalization of Palestinian life and institution-building, further building on and sustaining of the goals outlined in Phase I, ratification of a democratic Palestinian constitution, formal establishment of office of prime minister, consolidation of political reform, and the creation of a Palestinian state with provisional borders.

- International Conference: Convened by the Quartet, in consultation with the parties, immediately after the successful conclusion of Palestinian elections, to support Palestinian economic recovery and launch a process, leading to establishment of an independent Palestinian state with provisional borders.
    - Such a meeting would be inclusive, based on the goal of a comprehensive Middle East peace (including between Israel and Syria, and Israel and Lebanon), and based on the principles described in the preamble to this document.
    - Arab states restore pre-intifada links to Israel (trade offices, etc.).
    - Revival of multilateral engagement on issues including regional water resources, environment, economic development, refugees, and arms control issues.
- New constitution for democratic, independent Palestinian state is finalized and approved by appropriate Palestinian institutions. Further elections, if required, should follow approval of the new constitution.
- Empowered reform cabinet with office of prime minister formally established, consistent with draft constitution.
- Continued comprehensive security performance, including effective security cooperation on the basis laid out in Phase I.
- Creation of an independent Palestinian state with provisional borders through a process of Israeli-Palestinian engagement, launched by the international conference. As part of this process, implementation of prior agreements, to enhance maximum territorial contiguity, including further action on settlements in conjunction with establishment of a Palestinian state with provisional borders.
- Enhanced international role in monitoring transition, with the active, sustained, and operational support of the Quartet.
- Quartet members promote international recognition of Palestinian state, including possible UN membership.

Phase III: Permanent Status Agreement and End of the Israeli-Palestinian Conflict—2004–2005

Progress into Phase III, based on consensus judgment of Quartet, and taking into account actions of both parties and Quartet monitoring. Phase III objectives are consolidation of reform and stabilization of Palestinian institutions, sustained, effective Palestinian security performance, and Israeli-Palestinian negotiations aimed at a permanent status agreement in 2005.

- Second International Conference: Convened by Quartet, in consultation with the parties, at beginning of 2004 to endorse agreement reached on an independent Palestinian state with provisional borders and formally to launch a process with the active, sustained, and operational support of the Quartet, leading to a final, permanent status resolution in 2005, including on borders, Jerusalem, refugees, settlements; and, to support progress toward a comprehensive Middle East settlement between Israel and Lebanon and Israel and Syria, to be achieved as soon as possible.
- Continued comprehensive, effective progress on the reform agenda laid out by the Task Force in preparation for final status agreement.
- Continued sustained and effective security performance, and sustained, effective security cooperation on the basis laid out in Phase I.
- International efforts to facilitate reform and stabilize Palestinian institutions and the Palestinian economy, in preparation for final status agreement.
- Parties reach final and comprehensive permanent status agreement that ends the Israel-Palestinian conflict in 2005, through a settlement negotiated between the parties based on UNSCR 242, 338, and 1397, that ends the occupation that began in 1967, and includes an agreed, just, fair, and realistic solution to the refugee issue, and a negotiated resolution on the status of Jerusalem that takes into account the political and religious concerns of both sides, and protects the religious interests of Jews, Christians, and Muslims worldwide, and fulfills the vision of two states, Israel and sovereign, independent, democratic and viable Palestine, living side-by-side in peace and security.
- Arab state acceptance of full normal relations with Israel and security for all the states of the region in the context of a comprehensive Arab-Israeli peace.

SOURCE: U.S. Department of State, Office of the Spokesman, www.state.gov/r/pa/prs/ps/2003/20062.htm.

Abbas Succeeds Arafat

DOCUMENT IN CONTEXT

Few figures were as ubiquitous on the world stage during the last decades of the twentieth century as Yasir Arafat, the long-time chairman of the Palestine Liberation Organization (PLO). With his trademark checkered headdress, or *kaffiyah,* Arafat symbolized the Palestinian people and almost single-handedly guaranteed that their struggle for national identity remained high on the international agenda for four decades. Arafat was able to bring his people close to nationhood, but he never made it. He died of unexplained causes in November 2004.

In the last decade of Arafat's life, the Palestinians experienced both the euphoria of peace and the tragedy of violence and accompanying economic stagnation. From 1993 to 1995, Arafat negotiated a series of agreements with Israel that offered Palestinians their first taste of self-governance, albeit with heavy dependence on Israel. For the rest of the 1990s, Arafat presided over the Palestinian Authority, a quasi-government whose writ covered only parts of the Gaza Strip and the major cities of the West Bank. During 2000, PLO and Israeli leaders, with U.S. mediation, worked toward a final peace, but the two sides ultimately failed to reach an agreement. In the wake of that diplomatic failure—with Palestinians having experienced no real improvement in their daily lives and with Israel continuing to expand settlements in the occupied territories—Palestinians rebelled in late September, marking the start of the al-Aqsa intifada. The situation quickly spun out of control, settling into a cycle of Palestinian attacks on Israelis and Israeli military suppression of the Palestinians. By the time Arafat died, he had been confined for more than two years by Israel to the ruins of the Palestinian Authority's once-sparkling compound in Ramallah, and Arafat's dream of a Palestinian state seemed as distant from reality as ever (Oslo Accords, p. 213; Hebron Protocol, p. 259; Wye River Memorandum, p. 267; Camp David and the al-Aqsa Intifada, p. 276; The Mitchell Report, p. 287).

With Arafat gone, leaders of his power base, the Fatah faction and the PLO, turned to his most logical successor: Mahmoud Abbas (also known as Abu Mazen). Abbas had been an aide to Arafat for nearly forty years and had served briefly in 2003 as the Palestinians' first prime minister. A man who had shunned the limelight as much as Arafat sought it, Abbas was little-known to Palestinians, and as a consequence, had no personal base of public support. He served as acting president of the Palestinian Authority for about six weeks, until elections on January 9, 2005. A host of minor candidates entered the race to succeed Arafat, but aside from Abbas only one—Mustafa Barghouti—had any name recognition. Barghouti, a medical doctor, actively campaigned for reform of the corruption-riddled Palestinian Authority. Barghouti was a distant relative, but not a political ally, of Marwan Barghouti, the leader of the so-called young guard of Fatah and probably the one man who could have seriously challenged Abbas. Marwan Barghouti, however, was serving five life terms in an Israeli prison for his alleged role in planning the murders of five Israelis. Despite his imprisonment, for a time he considered running for the presidency. Abbas won the election with 62.3 percent of the vote, giving him a dose of political support.

In the context of Arafat's death and the ongoing violence between Israelis and Palestinians during the al-Aqsa intifada, the inauguration of Abbas on January 15 gave hope to many for the resumption of the quest for peace. Abbas asserted that he wanted to seize the opportunity, saying his first priority would be to "calm" the violence. "Our hand is extended toward an Israeli partner for making peace," he said in his inaugural speech to the Palestinian Legislative Council. Two days later, Abbas stationed several hundred Palestinian security personnel along the border between the Gaza Strip and Israel, with orders to prevent the launching of mortars and rockets against nearby Israeli towns.

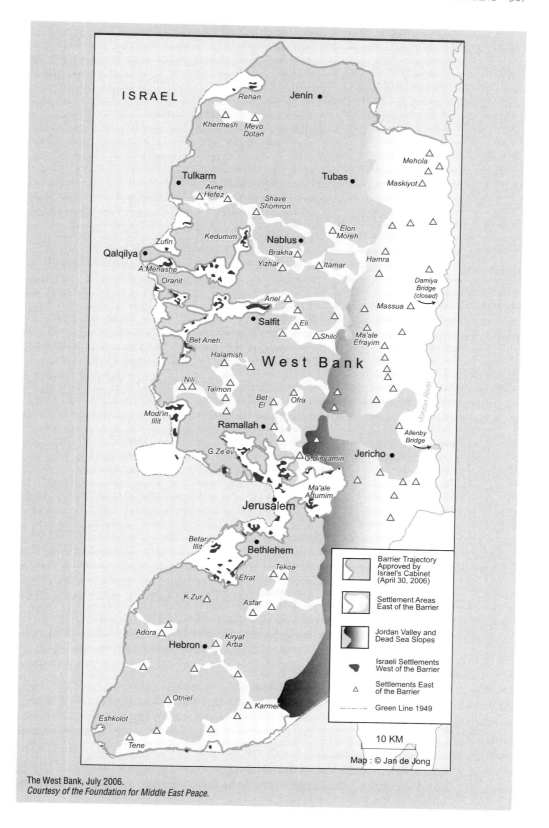

ISRAEL

Rehan

Jenin •

Khermesh   Mevo
               Dotan

Mehola

Maskiyot

Tulkarm •

Avne
Hefez

Shave
Shomron

Tubas •

Kedumim

Nablus •

Elon
Moreh

Zufin

Brakha

Hamra

Qalqilya •

A.Menashe

Yizhar

Itamar

Oranit

Damiya
Bridge
(closed)

Ariel

Massua

Salfit •

Eli

Bet Arieh

Shilo

Ma'ale
Efrayim

Halamish

West Bank

Nili

Talmon

Modi'in
Illit

Bet
El

Ofra

Ramallah •

Allenby
Bridge

G.Ze'ev

G.Binyamin

Jericho •

Jerusalem

Ma'ale
Adumim

Betar
Illit

Bethlehem •

Tekoa

Efrat

K.Zur

Asfar

Adora

Kiryat
Arba

Hebron •

Otniel

Karmel

Eshkolot

Tene

Jordan River

**Barrier Trajectory
Approved by
Israel's Cabinet
(April 30, 2006)**

Settlement Areas
East of the Barrier

Jordan Valley and
Dead Sea Slopes

Israeli Settlements
West of the Barrier

Settlements East
of the Barrier

Green Line 1949

10 KM

Map : © Jan de Jong

The West Bank, July 2006.
Courtesy of the Foundation for Middle East Peace.

A more important step came a week later when Abbas secured acceptance of a short-term cease-fire by Hamas and other groups engaged in violence against Israelis. With that agreement in hand, Abbas met with Israeli prime minister Ariel Sharon on February 8, and the two announced mutual cease-fires of an uncertain duration. The Palestinian groups agreed in mid-March to extend the cease-fire for the rest of the year, a pledge that Hamas generally honored but Islamic Jihad and some others did not.

Despite this accomplishment and relative calm, Abbas was unable to use the crucial first year of his presidency to build a broad base of support for his government and his declared nonviolent approach to dealing with Israel. Abbas did, however, succeed in convincing Hamas's leaders to enter elective politics, based on the theory that facing the voters might force Hamas to moderate its positions. Hamas candidates did unexpectedly well in local elections held throughout 2005, sweeping them in some areas by capitalizing on public disgust with the corruption and ineffectiveness of Arafat's old cronies.

Abbas also failed to prepare adequately for the Palestinian takeover of large portions of the Gaza Strip that for three decades had been held by Israeli settlements or were the site of Israeli military installations. Sharon had decided in 2004 to evacuate all Israeli settlers and soldiers from the Gaza Strip. Sections of Gaza erupted in chaos after the last Israeli soldiers left on September 12, 2005, as armed gangs from the various factions battled for control of the former Israeli settlement areas. In the eyes of many Palestinians, they had succeeded in forcing Israel out of Gaza, and they gave much of the credit to Hamas. Incidents of violence among Palestinian factions took place in the West Bank as well, serving as an unsettling prelude to the parliamentary elections scheduled for the following January 2006 that would bring Hamas to power (Israeli Disengagement, p. 313; Hamas Government, p. 317).

Following are excerpts from the speech delivered to the Palestinian Legislative Council by Prime Minister Mahmoud Abbas on January 15, 2005, following his election as president of the Palestinian Authority to succeed the late Yasir Arafat.

DOCUMENT

Abbas's First Address as President of the Palestinian Authority

JANUARY 15, 2005

As I address you today, I am full of pride over the Palestinian people's exceptional democratic achievement. Our people have stood in the face of the [Israeli] occupation to say "first and foremost to our selves but also to the whole world" that no matter how great the challenges may be, we will not give up on our national project. That no matter how many obstacles may stand in our way; we will not be deterred from advancing our democratic process. The winner in these elections is the great Palestinian people who have created this democratic epic and who will safeguard it.

I dedicate this victory in the name of our whole people to the soul and memory of our eternal leader, the symbol of our cause, Yasir Arafat. It was he who planted the first seed of this democratic process, it was he who held its banner high, and it was he who consolidated its traditions. Our respect and gratitude go to your noble soul, Abu Ammar [Arafat's nom de guerre], on this day of Palestinian democracy.

This is [an] historic day in our national process, and I say to all our people who voted: you have kept the flame of democracy alive; and all my thanks and gratitude go to you. I pledge to exert all of my efforts to implement the program according to which I was elected, and to continue on the path towards achieving our national goals.

My thanks and appreciation also go to all those who worked to make the election campaign a success, my brothers in the Fatah movement [the ruling political party] all over Palestine, and to all political forces, organizations, institutions, movements and individuals who spared no effort to defend our national democratic program. This program now has the widest public support.

To all the other candidates, I say: we highly appreciate your efforts in making the democratic process a success. You have my pledge to encourage and guarantee the active role of all of our political forces and strands, and to protect the freedom of expression in accordance with the law.

For even if our opinions may differ, we share one national cause; and even if our judgments may diverge, we defend one goal. We will make sure that we work together to achieve the national goals to which we all aspire.

Today, the results of the elections are final, and our great people have passed this important test. I stand before you as the President and representative of the whole Palestinian people to say: we will continue consolidating national unity. We will deepen dialogue with all the active forces in our nation, and we will remain devoted to strengthening the unity of our society and institutions. We will also continue on the path of Yasir Arafat to achieve just peace "the peace of the brave" for which he had always worked, and to which he dedicated all his life and effort. . . .

And I salute all of our people, particularly the residents of Jerusalem "the capital of our independent state." You have proven to the whole world your national commitment, determination to move forward, and commitment to our national goals and democratic choice. Your turnout exceeded all expectations, and you overcame difficulties, obstacles, and hardships.

The people have spoken for the end of occupation and the democratic choice, for the continuation and consolidation of development and reform,

The people have voted for the rule of law, order, pluralism, the peaceful transfer of authority, and equality for all,

The people have chosen just peace, ending the occupation, and coexistence based on equality and international legitimacy.

Ladies and Gentlemen,

This year is the year of Palestinian elections presidential, legislative, and municipal elections. Let us muster our national efforts to further extend the election process to civil organizations, trade unions, and political forces and factions so as to rejuvenate our domestic political life.

The greatest challenge before us, and the fundamental task facing us is national liberation. The task of ending the occupation, establishing the Palestinian state on the

1967 borders, with Jerusalem as its capital, and reaching a just and agreed solution to the refugee problem on the basis of international resolutions, first and foremost [United Nations] resolution 194 and the Beirut Arab Summit Resolution.

To achieve these national goals, we will remain committed to the PLO's [Palestine Liberation Organization] strategic choice: the choice of achieving just peace and our national goals through negotiations. The path to these goals is what we and the world have agreed upon in the Road Map [a peace plan drafted by the European Union, Russia, the United Nations, and the United States in 2003]. We have repeatedly stated that we are committed to our responsibilities in the Road Map. We will implement our obligations as a matter of Palestinian national interest. In return, Israel has to implement its obligations.

In the last few days, a number of incidents took place [a reference to violent attacks]. We condemn these actions, whether by the Israeli occupation forces or the reactions of some Palestinian factions. This does not help bring about the calm needed to enable a credible, serious peace process. We are seeking a mutual ceasefire to end this vicious circle.

Our hand is extended towards an Israeli partner for making peace. But partnership is not through words but rather deeds. It is through ending assassinations, the siege on our towns, arrests, land confiscations, settlement activity and the separation wall. Partnership cannot be achieved by dictation, and peace cannot be reached by partial or interim solutions. Peace can only be achieved by working together to reach a permanent status solution that deals with all of the outstanding issues, and which turns a new page on the basis of two neighboring states.

I would like to stress here that we are fully prepared to resume permanent status negotiations, and that we are politically ready to reach a comprehensive agreement over all of the issues.

From this forum, and on this day, I say to the Israeli leadership and to the Israeli people: we are two peoples destined to live side by side, and to share this land between us. The only alternative to peace is the continuation of the occupation and the conflict. Let us start implementing the Road Map, and "in parallel" let us start discussing the permanent status issues so that we can end, once and for all, the historic conflict between us.

From this forum, I call upon all concerned international actors, particularly the Quartet, to play a direct role in guaranteeing the implementation of the Road Map. You must ensure that we do not re-enter the labyrinth of preconditions that preclude progress in implementation. You must ensure that we do not get stuck in the maze of long-term partial or interim solutions designed to delay reaching a full and comprehensive solution.

As we at the Palestinian Authority express our readiness to implement all of our Road Map obligations, we expect all other parties to implement theirs. It is not reasonable that only we are required to take action while settlements continue; or while the Wall expands within Palestinian land to separate Palestinian from Palestinian, and to destroy the livelihoods of hundreds of thousands of our people; or while closures, the siege, arrests, and other violations continue against our people, spreading despair, frustration, and loss of hope.

Today, it is up to the world to give our people hope, and it is up to the world not to repeat the same mistakes that sabotaged many initiatives and positive efforts in the past. In particular, I direct this call to all of the leaders of the Quartet members, and to all those committed to re-launching the peace process, and particularly to the US as the main player in this context.

Welcoming Palestinian democracy and supporting it is important, but this support will remain deficient if it is not shored up with efforts to end all aspects of the occupation so that this democracy may continue and thrive.

I also call upon the international community to take the necessary measures to implement the decision of the International Court of Justice, this decision that condemned the racist separation wall as illegal and called for its removal.

Brothers and Sisters,
Palestinians at the Homeland and in the Diaspora,

Ending the occupation was and will remain at the top of our national Palestinian agenda, but it is not the only priority. I can find no justification for ignoring the rest of our national issues under the pretext that we are an occupied people. The same proud Palestinian spirit that has struggled to ensure recognition of our just cause must guide us in dealing with our domestic agenda.

For decades, Palestinians have been a beacon of creativity and achievement; a light that has shone with talent and skill over the whole world. It is our duty to continue faithfully working in the same spirit and with the same determination to build an enlightened, civilized society that will be "both in its official and civil parts" a democratic example to be followed, and a basis for a bright outlook for our future generations.

I believe that we all agree that the first step towards building our society lies in establishing the rule of law. Only then will our people enjoy safety and security; only then will we be able to truly develop our institutions of governance and our political system; and only then will we achieve development and economic prosperity and make progress in social, cultural, and other fields.

The rule of law is embodied in one authority and one legal weapon in the hands of this authority, within the framework of political pluralism and the peaceful periodic transfer of authority. We all have the right to differ, and we all have the right to present our case to the people through the ballot box, but no-one has the right to bypass the will of the people or to take law into their own hand in the service of their own agenda. Let law and democracy remain the only method of dealing with all aspects of our domestic concerns.

We have started the process of reform, and we will "God willing" continue. Reforming and developing the judiciary, security and government agencies, and continuing the development of our financial and economic system, and establishing a new mechanism for cooperation between the public and private sectors are prerequisites for enabling the National Authority to play its role in serving the Palestinian people. But more than that, they are also a national duty so as to establish the foundations of the Palestinian state to which we aspire. It is our duty, whether in the Authority, opposition, or civil society not to allow the occupation to derail us from this path, or internal chaos to sabotage this process.

We will work to establish close cooperation between the various institutions of the Palestinian Authority "the legislative, judicial and executive authorities" while respecting their separation and distinct role in accordance with the Basic Law. This should become the solid foundation and the established tradition of our political life, so as to develop our political system and to preserve its vitality.

We will exert all of our efforts to revitalize the PLO institutions and to activate its national role as the sole legitimate representative of our people. This will intensify our efforts to serve our people in the Diaspora. The PLO must assume its leading role in supporting the National Authority, in emphasizing the unity of Palestinian decision, and in protecting the National Program of 1988 and the Palestinian Declaration of Independence.

Ladies and Gentlemen,

The way forward will not be easy. Our goals will not be achieved with dreams or miracles, but with constant tireless work. The challenges ahead are grave: the occupation is still strangling us, and there are those who wish the failure of our experience. But those who hope for it to succeed and flourish, both among our people and our friends throughout the world, are the overwhelming majority. The road ahead is long, but it is a road that we will take and a challenge that we will accept. The alternative is stagnation and regression, and this is an alternative that we will never accept.

It was a great opportunity that women used their right to participate in local and presidential elections. This is an important step on the path of ensuring full equality for women, including the right to assume leading positions in the Authority and in society.

The late Abu Ammar has left us a legacy that lights our path and shows us the way. His legacy will always be present to remind us that no matter how great the challenges may [be], or how intricate the conspiracies may become, the will of the people, unwavering determination, and tireless work will lead to our goals. In the midst of our struggle for liberation and state-building, there is no place for despair or lethargy.

Today, I address the families of our revered martyrs [Palestinians who died in violence against Israel or were killed by Israel] to assure you that we will remain faithful to their memory and committed to protecting the future of their children. We will continue to care for the injured and the handicapped, and all of those affected by the violations of the occupation, whether home demolitions, the destruction of agricultural facilities, and all other forms of collective punishment.

I also address my brothers the prisoners and detainees [Palestinians jailed by Israel] to assure them that their cause will remain at the forefront of our efforts and will figure high on all levels. Opening the path of freedom before them is a noble purpose that we will do our utmost to achieve. We will also protect our fugitives and deportees, and we will absorb them and guarantee their future.

I have been throughout my field visits to the refugee camps here in the homeland and in Syria, Lebanon, and the Arab world. I have met our people who have entrusted us with their national aspirations and daily concerns. These will remain a central part of our own concerns. While we reject involuntary settlement outside the homeland, we must guarantee that our people wherever they are enjoy the best standards of living, through cooperation with our brothers in the host countries.

In this path, and in the face of every hurdle and difficulty, I will remain strong in the knowledge of the trust that you have bestowed upon me, steadfast in my unshakable belief in the maturity of the Palestinian people, in all of its sectors and segments, and with all of its diverse opinions and positions. I will draw my strength first and foremost from my faith in God, and from my belief in the justice of cause and the unwavering dedication of our historic leader Yasir Arafat second, and from your trust. I pledge today to do all that I can, and to exert all of my efforts and energies to put an end to the suffering of our great people.

I would like to express my gratitude to the Arab states and their leaders who have assured us of their continued support for our people and National Authority at this time where their brotherly help is most needed.

I would also like to express my gratitude for the support for the world leaders, leaders of European states, the United States, Russia, China, Japan, and Islamic, Asian, African, Latin American and Non-Aligned states, as well as to the Secretary General of the UN and the various Arab, Islamic and international organizations.

It is the time for work, so let us start it strong and unified for the sake of our people, our youth and future generations, and for the sake of freedom, independence, reform, and democratic development.

In the Name of Allah, Most Gracious, Most Merciful
Lord! (they says) Let not our hearts deviate now after Thou hast guided us, but grant us mercy from Thee: For Thou art the Grantor

SOURCE: Jerusalem Media and Communication Center, "First Speech of Palestinian National Authority President Mr. Mahmoud Abbas (Abu Mazen)," www.jmcc.org/documents/abumazen1stspeech05.htm.

Israeli Disengagement

DOCUMENT IN CONTEXT

At the beginning of the twenty-first century, the Gaza Strip—a 140-square-mile section of land along the Mediterranean Sea at the boundary of Israel and Egypt—was home to more than 1 million Palestinians, many of them long-term refugees (and their descendants) from the 1948 Arab-Israeli war. It was also where Israel had established or allowed more than twenty Jewish settlements to develop, with a total population of approximately 8,000. To protect the Jewish settlers, the Israeli government stationed thousands of troops in Gaza, many of them assigned to escort the settlers as they traveled to and from work and school. As with settlements on the Golan Heights and the West Bank, affordable housing attracted most settlers to Gaza, as did in some cases the chance to live by the sea. A minority of settlers were in Gaza because they believed that God intended Jews—not Arabs—to occupy all the land of Palestine between the Mediterranean and the Jordan River.

To the surprise of many, in December 2003 Israeli prime minister Ariel Sharon began speaking of Israel "disengaging" from the Palestinians—in other words, setting

itself apart as much as possible from the Palestinians, their internal strife, and the suicide bombers and others opposed to Israel or the military occupation. Sharon transformed his thoughts into a plan, approved by his cabinet in April 2004 and again in
June 2004, for withdrawal from the Gaza Strip. According to the plan, all twenty-one
civilian settlements and all Israeli military installations would be evacuated in Gaza,
and new housing would be provided for the settlers in Israel or in the West Bank.
Four small isolated settlements in the West Bank also would be closed because their
exposed location had made them difficult to defend. The Knesset approved Sharon's
plan during an exceptionally raucous debate in October 2004, and the cabinet gave
its final approval on February 20, 2005.

Sharon's decision to close down the settlements had been surprising because he,
more than any other figure, long had been considered the father of settling Jews on
lands captured from Arab states in the June 1967 War. A former general who had
held several cabinet posts since the late 1970s, Sharon had used his influence and his
government positions to promote the settlements and to advance the idea that Israel
had legitimate historic and strategic reasons for occupying all of what he and others
called "Greater Israel" (Israeli Settlement of the Occupied Territories, p. 178).

Sharon decided on disengagement after concluding that practical reasons made an
evacuation of Gaza necessary. One reason was the sizable cost, in blood and money,
of protecting a tiny number of settlers in the midst of so many Palestinians. Demographic forces proved to be equally compelling, he said. Israel had about 5 million
Jewish and 1 million Arab citizens, while about 3 million Palestinian Arabs lived under
Israel's ultimate control in Gaza and the West Bank. Because the birth rate was so
much higher among Palestinians than among Jews, the Jewish state of Israel faced the
prospect, in a few years, of ruling over more Palestinians than Jews. Leaving Gaza
would subtract 1 million Arabs from the equation.

Regardless, many in the settler movement, particularly conservative religious leaders, bitterly opposed Sharon's decision. Settler groups fought the government on legal
grounds, ultimately losing their case in the High Court of Justice. Several leading rab-
bis openly encouraged Israeli police officers and soldiers to disobey orders to evacuate
the settlers by force, if necessary, and settler groups staged several mass demonstrations
protesting the withdrawal.

On August 15, 2005, the day set by the government for the beginning of the pull-
out from Gaza, Sharon went on national television with an emotional defense of disengagement and a plea for calm. He used this speech to emphasize the demographic
imperative of ending Israel's occupation of Gaza. "Over 1 million Palestinians live
there, and they double their numbers with every generation," he said. "They live in
incredibly cramped refugee camps, in poverty and squalor, in hotbeds of ever-increasing hatred, with no hope whatsoever on the horizon." Leaving Gaza "is the Israeli
answer to this reality," he said.

Despite the tense atmosphere leading up to the event and the presence in the settlements of several thousand outside protesters, the evacuation of Gaza went remarkably smoothly. Most settlers left the area before the August 15 deadline. The only serious confrontations occurred on August 17 in the largest settlement, Neve Dekalim,
where protesters threw eggs and paint at police, and the following day in the Kfar
Darom, where about 100 protesters gathered on the roof of a synagogue and clashed
with police. Under an agreement with the Palestinians, the Israeli army demolished all

the buildings in the settlements, except for the synagogues, which the cabinet decided to leave intact for religious reasons. The four small West Bank settlements closed as part of Sharon's plan also were evacuated without incident, despite fears that religious settlers in one of them would resist violently. The army completed its withdrawal from Gaza on September 12, after which throngs of Palestinians surged into the settlements and picked through the rubble the Israelis had left behind. The ensuing chaos undermined the Abbas government's hopes of transforming the former Jewish settlements into new zones of economic opportunity for Palestinians.

Two months after the withdrawal, Sharon announced that he was leaving the rightist Likud Party, his political home of many years, and forming Kadima ("forward," in Hebrew), a new, more centrist party. He cited the opposition of many Likud leaders to his Gaza disengagement as influencing his decision to found Kadima. Prominent figures joining Sharon in the new party included the center-left Labor Party's Shimon Peres, who had served twice as prime minister and had been a political rival of Sharon and a close personal friend. Sharon's leadership of the new party was to be short-lived, however. The prime minister suffered a mild stroke on December 18, 2005, and then on January 4, 2006, suffered a much more serious stroke that put him in a long-term coma.

Deputy Prime Minister Ehud Olmert assumed Sharon's office and led Kadima to a narrow victory in elections in March 2006, running on a platform of carrying out what he said would have been Sharon's next step concerning the Palestinians—disengaging on the West Bank by closing most of the settlements and consolidating the Jewish population there into communities around and near Jerusalem. Olmert's base of support would, however, prove to be uncomfortably thin, depriving him of the political momentum he would need to move forward on this plan. The January 2006 victory by Hamas in legislative elections for the Palestinian Legislative Council complicated matters even more and further undermined support among Israelis for a large-scale withdrawal from the West Bank (The Hamas Government, p. 317).

The following is an address to the Israeli public by Prime Minister Ariel Sharon on August 15, 2005, the day Israeli forces began evacuating settlers and withdrawing from Gaza under Sharon's disengagement plan.

DOCUMENT

Sharon Statement on Gaza Disengagement

AUGUST 15, 2005

Citizens of Israel,
The day has arrived. We are beginning the most difficult and painful step of all—evacuating our communities from the Gaza Strip and Northern Samaria [the northern section of the West Bank].

This step is very difficult for me personally. It was with a heavy heart that the Government of Israel made the decision regarding Disengagement, and the Knesset did not lightly approve it.

It is no secret that I, like many others, believed and hoped that we could forever hold on to Netzarim and Kfar Darom [two settlements in Gaza]. However, the changing reality in this country, in this region, and in the world, required another reassessment and changing of positions.

Gaza cannot be held onto forever. Over one million Palestinians live there, and they double their numbers with every generation. They live in incredibly cramped refugee camps, in poverty and squalor, in hotbeds of ever-increasing hatred, with no hope whatsoever on the horizon.

It is out of strength and not weakness that we are taking this step. We tried to reach agreements with the Palestinians which would move the two peoples towards the path of peace. These were crushed against a wall of hatred and fanaticism.

The unilateral Disengagement Plan, which I announced approximately two years ago, is the Israeli answer to this reality. This Plan is good for Israel in any future scenario. We are reducing the day-to-day friction and its victims on both sides. The IDF will redeploy on defensive lines behind the Security Fence. Those who continue to fight us will meet the full force of the IDF [Israeli Defense Forces] and the security forces.

Now the Palestinians bear the burden of proof. They must fight terror organizations, dismantle its infrastructure and show sincere intentions of peace in order to sit with us at the negotiating table.

The world awaits the Palestinian response—a hand offered in peace or continued terrorist fire. To a hand offered in peace, we will respond with an olive branch. But if they chose fire, we will respond with fire, more severe than ever.

The Disengagement will allow us to look inward. Our national agenda will change. In our economic policy we will be free to turn to closing the social gaps and engaging in a genuine struggle against poverty. We will advance education and increase the personal security of every citizen in the country.

The disagreement over the Disengagement Plan has caused severe wounds, bitter hatred between brothers and severe statements and actions. I understand the feelings, the pain and the cries of those who object. However, we are one nation even when fighting and arguing.

Residents of the Gaza Strip, today marks the end of a glorious chapter in the story of Israel, and a central chapter in the story of your lives as pioneers, as realizers of a dream and as those who bore the security and settlement burden for all of us. Your pain and your tears are an inseparable part of the history of this country. Whatever disagreements we have, we will not abandon you, and following the evacuation, we will do everything in our power to rebuild your lives and communities.

I wish to tell the soldiers of the IDF, the police officers of the Israel Police and Border Police: you face a difficult mission—it's not an enemy you face, rather your brothers and sisters. Sensitivity and patience are the order of the hour. I am certain that this is how you will behave. I want you to know: the entire nation stands behind you and is proud of you.

Citizens of Israel,

The responsibility for the future of Israel rests on my shoulders. I initiated the Plan because I concluded that this action is vital for Israel. Believe me, the extent of pain that I feel at this act is equal only to the measure of resolved recognition that it was something that had to be done.

We are embarking on a new path which has many risks, but also a ray of hope for all of us.

With the help of God, may this path be one of unity and not division, of mutual respect, and not animosity between brothers, of unconditional love, and not baseless hatred.

I will do my utmost to ensure that it will be so.

SOURCE: State of Israel, Prime Minister's Office, "PM Sharon's Statement on the Day of the Implementation of the Disengagement Plan," www.pmo.gov.il/PMOEng/Archive/Speeches/2005/08/speech150805.htm.

The Hamas Government

DOCUMENT IN CONTEXT

The death of long-time Palestinian leader Yasir Arafat in November 2004 unleashed powerful centrifugal forces that within thirty months brought chaos to the Gaza Strip and threatened a similar result in the West Bank. Rampant violence, political infighting, and economic decline transformed hopes of a viable Palestinian state into a potential nightmare.

Palestinian society's increasing polarization—between the secular nationalism that Arafat had championed and an increasingly popular Islamist approach symbolized by Hamas—emerged as one of the most visible causes of strife in the territories. Until the first intifada, or uprising, against Israeli occupation in the late 1980s, the vast majority of Palestinians appeared to accept Arafat's view that creating a national state represented the paramount Palestinian goal. By the early 1990s Arafat came to embrace a two-state solution that acknowledged Israel's existence. Hamas, however, along with a handful of smaller groups, such as Islamic Jihad, argued that Islam should be the fundamental ideology of any Palestinian state. These groups also rejected any form of legitimacy for Israel (Hamas's Covenant, p. 206). In 1994, the year after Arafat, as chairman of the Palestine Liberation Organization (PLO), signed the Palestinians first peace agreement with Israel and officially recognized the Israeli government, Hamas signaled its disapproval of that course by launching its first suicide bomb attacks against Israel (Oslo Accords, p. 213).

Hamas had over the years built up an extensive network of schools, medical clinics, and other social services in the Gaza Strip, where its support was greatest. Financed largely by Iran, these services undermined public support for Arafat's quasi-governmental Palestinian Authority, which failed to deliver important public services and developed a reputation for corruption and inefficiency.

The second uprising, the al-Aqsa intifada in late 2000—after the failure of peace talks with Israel, little improvement in the lives of Palestinians, and a near doubling of Jewish settlers since 1994—placed additional stresses on Palestinian society. Arafat's political base, Fatah, fractured along generational and ideological lines. By contrast, Hamas used suicide bombings and shrill anti-Israel rhetoric to build public support among Palestinians increasingly frustrated by the failure of the peace process launched in the 1990s to produce positive results in their daily lives. These stresses became increasingly obvious after the death of Arafat, the only leader most Palestinians had ever known. His successor, Mahmoud Abbas, attempted with little success to negotiate compromises with Hamas and other groups.

Abbas encouraged Hamas to enter the political process, hoping that the need to face voters would lead the group to moderate its positions. Hamas did surprisingly well in 2005 local elections, in several cases sweeping entrenched Fatah leaders from power. This success led Hamas to put forth candidates for the Palestinian Legislative Council in January 2006 elections, the first parliamentary elections in a decade. As election day, January 25, approached, opinion polls showed strong support for Hamas candidates, running on a platform with the appealing slogan "Change and Renewal." In addition, Fatah in many cases ran two candidates for a single seat, splitting whatever support existed for it. Hamas won a stunning victory, taking 74 of the 132 seats—more than enough to give it effective control of the government. Fatah ran a distant second, winning only 45 seats, and several smaller parties (including factions that had broken away from Fatah) took the remaining 13 seats.

The prospect of a Palestinian government run by Hamas alarmed the Israeli government, which had worked with Fatah because the party and its leadership had recognized the Jewish state in 1993. Israel's acting prime minister, Ehud Olmert—who had taken office three weeks earlier after Prime Minister Ariel Sharon suffered a massive stroke—immediately refused to negotiate with the Palestinian government "if its members include an armed terrorist organization that calls for the destruction of the State of Israel," a reference to Hamas.

On January 30, UN secretary-general Kofi Annan, U.S. secretary of state Condoleezza Rice, and the European and Russian representatives of the diplomatic grouping called the Quartet met in London to discuss a united approach to a Hamas-led government. While congratulating the Palestinians on holding successful elections, the Quartet issued a statement essentially demanding that Hamas abandon much of its core ideology. All members of the new Palestinian government "must be committed to nonviolence, recognition of Israel, and acceptance of previous agreements and obligations, including the Roadmap," the Quartet insisted. The so-called road map was the phased plan for Israeli-Palestinian peace outlined by the Quartet in 2003 (The Road Map, p. 298).

Implicit in the Quartet's statement was a threat by the United States and the European Union to suspend tens of millions of dollars in aid to the Palestinian Authority unless Hamas met the three conditions. The Israeli government also announced that it would cease transferring to the Palestinian Authority some $50 million a month that it collected, on the authority's behalf, from various taxes on imports to the Gaza Strip and West Bank. These taxes and international aid provided most of the Palestinian government's income, which in turn underpinned the economy of the territories.

Hamas's leaders rejected the Quartet's demands and on March 20 published their official program for the new government. Although milder in language than traditional Hamas statements, the twelve-point document made none of the concessions demanded by the Quartet. The fourth point of the program explicitly rejected the Quartet's demand for nonviolence, stating that "resistance in its various forms is a legitimate right of the Palestinian people to end the occupation and regain the national rights."

The new Hamas-led government took office on March 29, but because of travel restrictions imposed by Israel, some legislators gathered at the Palestinian Authority headquarters in Ramallah, on the West Bank, while others convened at the authority's office in Gaza City; they communicated by video link. Hamas had chosen Ismail Haniyeh, considered one of the group's moderate leaders, as prime minister.

The Quartet issued a statement the next day, March 30, expressing "grave concern" that the Hamas government had not met the conditions of its January 30 declaration and warning that "there inevitably will be an effect on direct assistance" to the Palestinian government. Responding to this statement, and even stronger warnings from Washington, the new Palestinian foreign minister, long-time Hamas official Mahmoud Zahar, on April 4 sent UN secretary-general Kofi Annan a mildly worded letter appealing for international support of the new government. Noting that Hamas had won internationally recognized elections, Zahar wrote, "We also hope that certain States will re-examine the premature stands and hasty decisions they have taken, especially with regard to withholding assistance and adopting a language of threats rather than dialogue." Despite this appeal, the European Union and the United States in subsequent weeks announced the suspension of their direct aid to the Palestinian government, but continued deliveries of food, medicine, and other forms of humanitarian aid that bypassed the government.

The installation of the Hamas-led government made the Palestinian Authority a two-headed institution: Abbas continued as president, with little direct administrative control but authority over several of the security services established under Arafat, while Haniyeh and other Hamas-appointed cabinet officials headed the executive agencies charged with carrying out the daily affairs of the government. Despite pledges of cooperation by both sides, the inherent conflicts in the arrangement soon came to the fore, exacerbated by economic deterioration because of the loss of most of the government's international aid. The Palestinian Authority, by far the biggest employer in the territories, paid the salaries of tens of thousands of teachers, administrators, and policemen with guns who suddenly faced the loss of their paychecks.

Over the next several months, leaders from Fatah and Hamas worked to devise a formula for a "national unity" government that would preserve the Hamas electoral victory but also meet the Quartet's conditions for resumption of international aid. For a few weeks, the most promising of these efforts appeared to be a "national conciliation document" composed by leading Fatah and Hamas members in Israeli prisons. Negotiations between the factions based on this prisoners' document ultimately failed, however. Subsequent negotiations produced another agreement in September that also called for a national unity government. A key point of that accord called on the Palestinian Authority to respect the peace agreements that the PLO had signed with Israel; this provision might have met one of the demands of the Quartet. Hamas leaders later backed away from the document, and several additional attempts to negotiate an accord between Fatah and Hamas also failed.

The intra-Palestinian political stalemate was damaging enough, but during the summer of 2006, the situation worsened. On June 25, guerrillas from Hamas and Islamic Jihad crossed into Israel and attacked an army installation. Two soldiers and two guerrillas died in the ensuing firefight, but the guerrillas managed to capture an Israeli soldier and take him into Gaza. After demanding the release of the soldier but failing to secure it, the Israeli government unleashed a military assault on Gaza; troops moved into several parts of the territory, and the air force destroyed key installations, including a power plant that provided most of its electricity. Israel stopped short of reoccupying all of Gaza, from which it had withdrawn ten months earlier, but the assault wreaked even more havoc on a territory with an economy already in a nose-dive (Israeli Disengagement, p. 313).

Violence among Palestinian factions, which had been an increasing problem for several years, worsened and by mid-December 2006 threatened to erupt into a full-scale civil war. This crisis began when gunmen shot and killed three children of a Fatah security official in Gaza; three days later, Fatah gunmen attacked a convoy carrying Prime Minister Haniyeh, who was returning to Gaza from a trip during which he had collected millions of dollars in cash from Arab governments. One of Haniyeh's bodyguards died in the attack, and the next day thousands of people turned out in Gaza City for a demonstration that included threats against Fatah in general and Abbas in particular.

On December 16, in this tense atmosphere, Abbas played his one trump card, announcing that he planned to call early presidential and parliamentary elections for 2007. That threat led to a series of negotiations between Fatah and Hamas resulting in the formation of a "national unity" government in mid-March 2007. Hamas's Haniyeh continued to head the government, which by agreement now included several senior officials from Fatah and technocrats independent of both factions.

The Palestinians' newfound harmony did not last long. By early June in Gaza, armed supporters of Fatah and Hamas engaged each other in renewed violence. Hamas—which by 2007 had a much broader base of support in Gaza than did Fatah—prevailed in this battle, defeating Fatah security forces and taking outright control of Gaza on June 13. Thousands of Fatah supporters fled into Egypt or Israel or went into hiding. Abbas, based in the West Bank, responded by dissolving the Hamas-led government and appointing a new government of Fatah members and technocrats whose writ by this point extended only to the West Bank. Thus, in mid-2007, the Palestinians had two competing centers of power: Hamas in Gaza and Fatah on the West Bank. Israel and Western powers, notably the United States, moved quickly to bolster Abbas and his Fatah faction with money and weapons in hopes that improving the quality of life for Palestinians on the West Bank might undermine the position of Hamas in Gaza.

Following are two documents: the English-language text of a statement released by the Palestinian Authority's Palestine Information Center on March 20, 2006, outlining the main points of the new Hamas-led government's agenda and the text of a letter from Mahmoud Zahar, the foreign minister of the Palestinian Authority, to United Nations Secretary General Kofi Annan, dated April 4, 2006, and appealing for international support for the new Palestinian government.

DOCUMENT

Hamas Government Platform

MARCH 20, 2006

[The following translation is reproduced verbatim as it appears on the Web site of the Palestine Information Center, a department of the Palestinian Authority's State Information Service.]

1. Removing Occupation and building the Independent Palestinian state with whole sovereignty with Jerusalem its capital.

2. Keeping on the Palestinian refugees' right of return to their homes and their properties as the individuals and a public right could not be abandoned.

3. Working on releasing all the prisoners, facing the occupation's procedures on earth, especially; Judaizing Jerusalem, annexing the valleys, expanding settlements, tearing down the West Bank, apartheid separation wall and the practices resulted, facing the collective sanctions, rejecting blackmailing and rapping the Authority' merits.

4. Resistance with all its forms is a legal right for the Palestinian people to end the occupation and regaining the people's national rights that legally could not be abandoned.

5. Holding comprehensive reforms for the internal situation, building the people and society's institutions on democratic basics that guarantee justice, equality and partnership, practicing political variety, acting the jurisdiction of law, separating between authorities, enabling that the judiciary is independent as well as protecting it, guaranteeing the private and public freedoms.

6. Building our different national institutions on national and professional bases far away from appropriation and factionalism.

7. The government confirmed adherence to implement Cairo understandings and talks held on March 2005 between the Palestinian national and Islamic factions over the issue of PLO and its institutions.

8. Dealing with all previous agreements assigned between PNA and Israelis, the government has the right for reconsidering depending on respecting the international law, and applying its texts in respecting Palestinian people's rights and interests.

Among other points of the agenda, the government will deal with the international resolutions that save and protect the Palestinian people and their interests.

Cooperating with the international community in order to remove the Israeli occupation from the 1967-occupied territories including east Jerusalem, as a proposal to accomplish stability and calm in the region, particularly, in this period.

SOURCE: Palestine Information Center of the Palestinian National Authority, www.ipc.gov.ps/ipc_new/english/details.asp?name=14573.

DOCUMENT

Letter from Palestinian Foreign Minister Mahmoud Zahar to the UN Secretary-General

APRIL 4, 2006

His Excellency Mr. Kofi Annan
Secretary-General of the United Nations

Sir,

I have the pleasure, at the outset of this, my first letter to you, to express to you our appreciation for your continuing efforts and tireless work towards firmly establishing the values of justice, equality and development and the preservation of international peace and security. It is also a pleasure for me to express, through you, our appreciation of the role of the United Nations, its bodies and its specialized agencies in offering the necessary support to the Palestinian people and the Palestinian National Authority. In this context, I wish to stress the importance of the role of the United Nations and its ongoing historical responsibility towards the Palestinian cause until a just and comprehensive solution is reached on all the issues, as well as your important and constructive role within the Quartet, aimed at putting an end to the Israeli occupation and the state of conflict and bringing about a just and comprehensive peace. Through this letter I appeal to you to seek within the Quartet the start of an earnest, constructive dialogue with the Palestinian National Authority and its new Government.

The new Palestinian Government has received its assignments, beginning its work on 30 March 2006, and I myself have been appointed to the post of Minister for Foreign Affairs. This Government came into being as a result of the exercise by the Palestinian people of their right to choose their Government by means of free and fair democratic elections, as witnessed by the United Nations and the entire world. We look to the international community to respect the democratic choice of the Palestinian people and to work with this Government towards strengthening that democratic trend and safeguarding political pluralism as we move towards peace and stability in the region.

We trust that you will work with the international community and within the Quartet to ensure that support for the Palestinian people and their institutions continues and that they are enabled to obtain their legitimate rights, including the right to establish an independent, fully sovereign State with Jerusalem as its capital and the rights of return and compensation of Palestinian refugees. We also hope that certain States will re-examine the premature stands and hasty decisions they have taken, especially with regard to withholding assistance and adopting a language of threats rather than dialogue. Here I wish to assure you that our Government is ready to engage in earnest, constructive dialogue and to work together with the United Nations and the various countries of the world towards strengthening international peace and security and achieving peace and stability in our own region, based on a just and comprehensive solution.

Mr. Secretary-General,

Israel, the occupying power, still continues to move forward with its illegal settlement policies, seizing land, attempting to annex it de facto, expanding settlements and even starting the implementation of what is known as the E1 plan, the purpose of which is the total expropriation of East Jerusalem and the division of the West Bank into bantustans isolated from one another. All this, together with recent Israeli steps to cut off the Palestinian Aghwar (Jordan valley area) and prevent its inhabitants from gaining access to their fields and the destruction of their homes in order to force them to leave, so as to be able to impose de facto annexation of the area, will definitively rule out any hope of achieving a settlement and peace based on a two-state solution.

Furthermore, the Israeli occupying forces continue their unremitting aggression against our people oppressed by the occupation, making excessive use of military force, as in the operations, during the past few days, of bombing and destruction of infrastructures and civilian and sports facilities, in which they twice targeted a football field in the Gaza Strip, employing warplanes and heavy artillery against areas with dense civilian populations. They also continue to pursue their policy of extrajudicial killing, imposing sieges and closures on many parts of the occupied Palestinian territory, refusing to pay moneys owing to us that are in their possession and turning military checkpoints at the entrances to towns in the West Bank into something more akin to international border-crossings. The blockade and closure of the Gaza Strip has created a tragic humanitarian situation that has led numerous international and humanitarian institutions to warn of a deterioration of the humanitarian situation owing to the blocking by the occupation authorities of the entry into the Gaza Strip of basic humanitarian supplies such as medicines and basic foodstuffs, including flour and milk for infants. Israel carries out these illegal measures before the eyes and ears of the world, with little concern for the grave violations of international law and international humanitarian law that they entail, as if it were a State above the law.

The international community is called on today to take urgent, tangible steps to put an end to these grave Israeli violations of international law; to exert pressure on Israel to abide by international law and, in particular, international humanitarian law; and to comply with international agreements and the advisory legal opinion of the International Court of Justice. We further call on the international community to reject unilateral measures and solutions, live up to its commitments and fulfill its duties, especially with regard to respect for, and the ensuring of respect for, international humanitarian law in the occupied Palestinian territory, including East Jerusalem, as stressed by the Security Council in numerous resolutions.

Mr. Secretary-General,

We believe ours is a just cause. We have faith in the ability of our people to hold out and to stand up to the military occupation of our land and the occupier's illegal measures. We also believe that the solution must be founded on justice and law, the only basis for security and stability in the region. The logic of using force and of attempting to impose faits accomplis is an unsound logic that is doomed to failure. It can only lead to more destruction and instability. We, like all the other peoples of the world, look forward to a life of peace and security, a life of dignity in which our people enjoy freedom and independence side by side with the rest of our neighbours in this sacred corner of the world.

Lebanon and Syria

CHAPTER 4 DOCUMENTS

Overview

Of the countries in the Middle East, Lebanon is one of the smallest, weakest, and arguably the most fraught with trouble, as sectarian divisions have been at the core of its existence since France created it after World War I. Lebanon's difficulties beginning in the 1970s were especially painful because the country once was seen, and liked to portray itself, as the most progressive and westward-looking country in the Arab Middle East. Indeed, many Lebanese thought of themselves not as Middle Eastern Arabs but as Lebanese—a superior group of people in an otherwise backward region. Their capital, Beirut, was the "Paris of the Middle East" and the region's banking and business center. From the Lebanese perspective, it surely must have been the work of outside powers, not themselves, that led Lebanon into fifteen years of civil war, decades of domination by Syria, and repeated invasions by Israel.

Nearly every country in the Middle East has a multiethnic society, but in most of them, historical forces and strong central governments have kept in check the inherent conflicts among people of different backgrounds. Until the recent conflict in Iraq, Lebanon had been the most striking exception. France took control of Greater Syria—which included the territory of Lebanon—after World War I and the collapse of the Ottoman Empire. It then created Lebanon in 1920 as a distinct entity primarily for the benefit of one ethnic group: the Maronite Christians living in the hilly region known as Mount Lebanon. France essentially put the Maronites in charge while discounting the presence of Shiite and Sunni Muslims, along with Armenians, Greek Orthodox Christians, and others of non-Maronite heritage.

For years after France split Lebanon from Syria, Lebanon was considered one of the world's foremost bastions of ethnic harmony. The Lebanese peacefully resolved most conflicts among groups, usually through agreements among the leaders of the clans that held much of the country's economic and political power. One such agreement, the National Covenant (or National Pact) of 1943, appeared at the time to resolve competing claims for power, but in the long run planted the seeds for civil strife decades later. The covenant guaranteed Christians the largest share of political power, matching their dominance of the economy. Under the agreement, Lebanon's president would be a Christian, the prime minister a Sunni Muslim, and the Speaker of the parliament a Shiite Muslim. Moreover, Christians would hold a six-to-five majority in the parliament. Of the three top officers, the president held the most power because of the position's authority to appoint the prime minister, select the cabinet in consultation with the prime minister and legislators, and command the army.

A 1932 census identifying Christians as a slight majority of Lebanon's population formed the basis of the National Covenant. To this day, that count stands as the last census taken in Lebanon. By the time the Lebanese reached agreement on the covenant, however, Muslims almost certainly had become the majority. The extent of their majority continued to grow in subsequent decades.

For years Muslims generally tolerated the division of political power although it put them at a disadvantage. Nonetheless, conflict seemed all but inevitable. The first significant period of trouble came in 1958, when President Camille Chamoun called on the United States to help him suppress a revolt that he accused Syria of fomenting. On that occasion, the presence of nearly 15,000 U.S. marines brought short-term stability and allowed the negotiation of a compromise that kept Lebanon relatively quiet for more than a decade.

Lebanon's later descent into civil war stems in large part from the presence of Palestinian guerrillas, who after the June 1967 Arab-Israeli war became increasingly active in and around refugee camps in southern Lebanon that housed some 300,000 Palestinians. Fighters from the Palestine Liberation Organization (PLO) and more radical groups staged repeated raids and launched rockets across the border into Israel, provoking Israeli strikes against Palestinian leaders and bombings of villages and refugee camps on Lebanese territory. Tens of thousands of Shiite Muslims fled their homes in southern Lebanon and moved to ever-expanding slums outside Beirut. The miserable conditions in these areas bred resentment against a government that seemed indifferent to the plight of Shiite Lebanese, who also felt victimized by Israel and the Palestinians.

Yet another agreement papered over Lebanon's latent conflicts for a time. Meeting with Arab leaders in Cairo in 1969, Lebanese and Palestinian officials worked out an arrangement under which the PLO could continue to operate in southern Lebanon but would need government permission to strike across the border into Israel. The Palestinians used the Cairo agreement as broad authority to do what they wanted from their bases in southern Lebanon.

Battles in April 1975 between Palestinians and the Phalange militia—part of a group affiliated with the Gemayels, one of Lebanon's most powerful Christian families—sparked a civil war that lasted, with intervals of relative quiet, until 1990. In its various forms, the war involved all of Lebanon's ethnic and political factions and resulted in the deaths of more than 100,000 people—an exact number has never been determined—the dislocation of hundreds of thousands more, and the destruction of what had been one of the most vibrant economies in the Middle East.

The intervention of outside powers, notably Israel and Syria, became a constant feature of the war. Israeli raids against Palestinian guerrillas had also helped create the conditions for the war. In 1978 Israel launched a limited incursion into Lebanon and in 1982 a full-scale invasion that eventually devolved into a long-term occupation of southern Lebanon. Syria's intervention proved to be even more long-lasting and pervasive than that of Israel. Damascus sent its army into Lebanon in 1976 to help quell the violence. Later that year, Syria's presence gained a semblance of international legitimacy when the Arab League endorsed the creation of a "deterrent force" to end the civil war. Syria led that force and eventually became the sole contributor to it. Damascus also claimed historic justification for its role in Lebanon based on the fact that Lebanon was considered part of "Greater Syria' before France split them into separate countries in the 1920s.

Another political compromise—reached by Lebanese leaders in October 1989 under pressure from Saudi Arabia and other countries—redressed some of the political imbalances that had fueled the civil war and helped bring the conflict to an end in 1990. Even so, the agreement signed in Taif, Saudi Arabia, essentially ratified the sectarian basis for the division of political power in Lebanon. Under the agreement, Christians no longer had the greatest share of power, but they still held more power than their proportion of the population would seem to warrant, and key government posts, including representation in the parliament, continued to be assigned on the basis of religious belief.

The war's end generated a mild flurry of international interest in ending the Israeli and Syrian occupations, but to little effect until 2000, when Israel withdrew its forces. In 2001 Syrian president Bashar al-Assad redeployed troops from Beirut to the Bekaa Valley (adjacent to the Lebanon-Syria border), but this symbolic gesture did nothing to diminish Syria's ultimate veto power over its neighbor. Once again, violence proved to be the driving force in Lebanon: in February 2005 a massive bomb killed former prime minister Rafiq Hariri, the most successful politician in the country's recent history who was credited with the reconstruction of the country after the civil war. Hariri's murder shocked even the Lebanese—no strangers to political assassinations and civil violence—ushering in a new era of national awareness. Huge demonstrations against Syria, coupled with a new round of international diplomacy, finally forced Damascus to withdraw its army and its omnipresent intelligence agency from Lebanon in April 2005.

Parliamentary elections the following month produced Lebanon's first government in more than three decades not born of civil war or strictly beholden to a foreign power. As always in Lebanon, however, there was a catch, as voters again cast their ballots along sectarian lines: The historical power-sharing agreements left Shiite Muslims—the country's largest group—with fewer parliamentary seats (and thus less power) than their numbers might otherwise have dictated. Moreover, by 2005 the single most powerful military entity in Lebanon was a Shiite militia, Hizballah (Party of God), which had formed largely in reaction to Israel's 1982 invasion. With money and arms from Iran, Hizballah set about building a disciplined fighting force and developing a network of schools, health clinics, and other social services for Shiites, who rarely had received government services. Hizballah had created its own state-within-a-state in southern Lebanon, but with the potential to influence events in the entire country.

That potential developed into a painful reality in mid-2006, when Hizballah conducted a cross-border raid into Israel that triggered another brief but severely damaging war. Israel, responding more aggressively to this provocation than Hizballah's leadership assumed it would, began what would become a month-long bombing campaign coupled with a short ground invasion intended to destroy Hizballah as a fighting force.

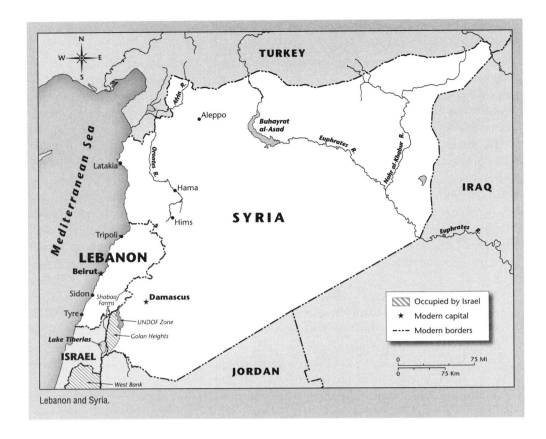

Lebanon and Syria.

Israeli missiles and bombs killed at least 200 Hizballah fighters and destroyed numerous Hizballah military positions, but the attacks also flattened civilian neighborhoods of Beirut and led some 900,000 Lebanese to flee their homes. The Israeli bombing also destroyed much of the infrastructure only recently restored after the long civil war. The reputation of the United States also suffered damage because during crucial moments in the war the Bush administration appeared less eager to end the fighting than to give Israel more time to inflict damage on Hizballah.

Lebanon's weak government once again showed itself incapable of protecting its citizens. The outside world eventually intervened in the form of UN mediation and an expanded UN peacekeeping force that along with Lebanese Army troops deployed to south Lebanon to replace Hizballah as the area's security force. A resolution of Lebanon's underlying economic and political imbalances that might guarantee stability remained elusive, however.

Lebanese Civil War

DOCUMENT IN CONTEXT

Two developments in the late 1960s set in motion a series of events that led to the unraveling of Lebanon's political and social fabric: an increasing desire by Muslims for a fair share of the nation's wealth and political power and the presence of guerrillas from the Palestine Liberation Organization (PLO) and other groups fighting on behalf of Palestinian Arabs.

Lebanon's society was highly polarized economically. The Lebanese population consisted of Shiite Muslims, most of whom lived in slums outside Beirut or in impoverished rural areas in the south, and wealthier Christians and Sunni Muslims. In 1969 Kamal Jumblatt, a leader of the Druze—Arabs whose religious beliefs mixed elements of Christianity and Islam—joined with several Muslim leaders to form the Lebanese National Movement, a loose coalition demanding economic and political reforms. The Maronites, the dominate community of Christians, opposed their demands. Some prominent Maronites had their own militias, notably, Pierre Gemayel, the head of the Phalange Party, whose militia ranked as one of the largest.

After Israel captured the Gaza Strip and the West Bank in the June 1967 Arab-Israeli war, the PLO and similar groups moved into neighboring Arab nations, especially Jordan and Lebanon. From their bases in these countries, Palestinian guerrillas launched repeated attacks against Israel, which retaliated with cross-border strikes. In December 1968 Israeli commandos destroyed thirteen Lebanese planes at the Beirut airport. The following year, Arab leaders meeting in Cairo worked out an agreement under which the Lebanese government accepted the presence of the Palestinian guerrillas, who in turn were supposed to (but rarely did) seek permission from the government before launching operations against Israel.

The incident that triggered Lebanon's descent into civil war occurred on April 13, 1975, when unknown gunmen assassinated Pierre Gemayel along with four Phalangist militiamen. Later that same day, Phalange militia members, acting on the assumption that the assassins were Palestinians, attacked a bus full of Palestinians, killing more than twenty passengers. These actions sparked fierce confrontations between the Phalange and Palestinians that lasted until July 1, when a cease-fire led the Palestinians to withdraw from fighting for the rest of the year. Reflecting the underlying disputes among the various Lebanese communities, a new and broader round of fighting erupted in August between militia supporting Jumblatt's Lebanese National Movement and Christian militias, including the Phalange. Much of this fighting took place in downtown Beirut, destroying many of the city's famed office towers and luxury hotels.

In December, the Phalange began expelling Muslims from predominantly Christian areas of Beirut, heightening the conflict. The following month, January 1976, the Lebanese Forces, a group of Christian militias, attacked a Palestinian refugee camp in southern Beirut, reportedly killing upwards of 3,000 people. The PLO, joined by Jumblatt's militia, responded with attacks against the Christians. Meanwhile, the ineffectual Lebanese Army disintegrated, and its soldiers and officers sided with the opposing militias.

Apparently fearing that Israel would invade Lebanon to prevent a takeover of the country by Muslim groups aligned with the PLO, Syria intervened, at the request of the Maronites, in May 1976 to prevent the defeat of the Christian militias and restore order. This intervention marked the beginning of what would turn into four decades of Syrian hegemony in Lebanon.

A cease-fire negotiated by Arab diplomats in Riyadh, Saudi Arabia, on October 18, 1976, brought the worst of the fighting to a halt, for the time being. The agreement, ratified at an Arab League summit one week later, called for the deployment of a 30,000-man Arab peacekeeping force—the Arab Deterrent Force—in the end composed primarily of Syrian troops. The Riyadh agreement also affirmed the 1969 Cairo agreement blessing the presence of the PLO in southern Lebanon. For the next six years, Lebanon became a patchwork of sectarian enclaves ruled by partisan militias, with Syrian troops maintaining a semblance of overall peace and a national Lebanese government lacking any effective role.

In this first phase of Lebanon's civil war, tens of thousands of people were killed, with more than 100,000 wounded. Tens of thousands of people—many of them Christians who had been prominent business leaders—left the country, never to return. The economy collapsed. The once-vibrant city of Beirut lie in ruins, divided into Christian and Muslim quarters separated by a virtual barrier known as the Green Line.

Kamal Jumblatt was assassinated in 1977, prompting another spate of sectarian fighting. Israeli invasions in 1978 and 1982 forced the PLO to leave Lebanon but left the country even more devastated. Another round of sectarian violence in the late 1980s proved to be just as murderous as the first phase. The war came to an end after Arab leaders, led by Saudi Arabia, negotiated another compromise, the Taif Accord, in 1989 (Israeli Invasion of Lebanon, p. 334; Taif Accord, p. 344).

Following are excerpts from the resolution adopted by the leaders of Egypt, Kuwait, Lebanon, the Palestine Liberation Organization, Saudi Arabia, and Syria, on October 18, 1976, following a conference held in Riyadh, Saudi Arabia, on the civil war in Lebanon.

DOCUMENT

Riyadh Conference Statement on the Lebanese Civil War

OCTOBER 18, 1976

The limited Arab summit conference which met in Riyadh, October 16–18, 1976, at the initiative of His Majesty King Khalidi ibn 'Abd al-Aziz al-Saud, King of Saudi Arabia, and H. E. Sheikh Sabah al-Salim al Sabah, Ruler of the State of Kuwait, having reviewed the resolution of the Arab League Council during the extraordinary sessions it held between June 8–10, June 23, July 1, and September 4, 1976 . . . the conference resolves the following:

1. A ceasefire and an end to all hostilities throughout Lebanese territory and by all parties in a final manner, as from 6:00 a.m. on October 21, 1976. All parties must abide by this in every respect.

2. To reinforce the present Arab peace forces so as to become a deterrent force acting inside Lebanon and under the personal command of the President of the Republic, provided their numbers are about 30,000 soldiers. Among the basic functions of this force will be the following:

a) To improve adherence to the cease-fire and the cessation of hostilities, to separate the combatants and deter all violators.

b) To implement the Cairo Agreement and its appendices. [The 1969 Cairo agreement provided for the presence of Palestinian security forces in southern Lebanon for the stated purpose of protecting Palestinian refugees in camps there.]

c) To maintain internal security.

d) To supervise the withdrawal of armed elements to the places they occupied before April 13, 1975, and to remove all armed manifestations in accordance with the schedule set forth in the appendix [not shown].

e) To supervise the gathering of all heavy arms such as artillery, mortars, rocket launchers, armored vehicles, etc., with the various parties being responsible for this.

f) To assist the Lebanese authorities when necessary to take over public institutions and utilities prior to reactivating them, and to protect public institutions, both civil and military.

3. To restore normal life to Lebanon to where it was before the beginning of those events, that is before April 13, 1975, as a first step and in accordance with the time schedule set forth in the appendix.

4. To implement the Cairo Agreement and its appendices and adherence to their text, in both letter and spirit, with the participating Arab states acting as guarantors. A committee shall be formed of representatives of the Kingdom of Saudi Arabia, the Arab Republic of Egypt, the Syrian Arab Republic, and the State of Kuwait, which shall undertake to coordinate its work with the President of Lebanon in all that concerns the implementation of the Cairo Agreement and its appendices. It shall function for 90 days starting from the date of the announcement of the cease-fire.

5. The Palestine Liberation Organization affirms its respect for Lebanon's sovereignty and well-being and its non-interference in its domestic affairs, all of which is based upon its total adherence to the national objectives of the Palestinian question. Lebanon's legitimate authorities, in return, guarantee the security and activities of the PLO in Lebanon within the framework of the Cairo Agreement and its appendices.

6. The participant Arab states undertake to respect Lebanon's sovereignty, security and unity, both of its people and of its territory.

7. The participant Arab states affirm their adherence to the resolutions of the Arab summits in Algeria and Rabat and their support for Palestinian resistance represented by the PLO as well as their respect for the rights of the Palestinian people in all ways to recover its national rights.

8. Information media:

a) All media campaigns and negative psychological mobilization by all parties are to cease.

b) The media are to be directed towards the consolidation of the cease-fire, the establishment of peace and the propagation of a spirit of cooperation and fraternity among all parties.

c) The governmental media must be reunified. . . .

SOURCE: Library of Congress, Congressional Research Service, Foreign Affairs and National Defense Division, *The Search for Peace in the Middle East: Documents and Statements, 1967–1979.* Report Prepared for the Subcommittee on Europe and the Middle East of the Committee on Foreign Affairs, U.S. House of Representatives (Washington, D.C.: Government Printing Office, 1979), 336–337.

Israeli Invasion of Lebanon

DOCUMENT IN CONTEXT

Palestinian guerrillas remained in southern Lebanon following the first round of the Lebanese civil war during 1975–1976. The next round of the war can be divided into two phases driven in large part by Israeli actions: a limited Israeli invasion in March 1978 followed by a much broader and longer-lasting Israeli invasion starting in June 1982. The 1982 invasion resulted in consequences whose effects would be felt throughout the region for more than two decades.

In the 1978 invasion, Israel attempted to shore up a "security zone" that it had tried to create along its border inside Lebanon at the end of the fighting in 1976. Israel at that time had equipped a predominantly Christian militia led by Saad Haddad, a renegade major in the Lebanese Army. Israel had hoped that the zone would prevent Palestinian guerrillas from using the border area as a base for launching attacks against it. Haddad's militia, however, was unable to control the territory, so on March 14, 1978, Israel sent its army into Lebanon to clear a zone some six miles deep.

At about the same time, the United Nations deployed the UN Interim Force in Lebanon (UNIFIL) in a multinational peacekeeping operation. This 6,000-man force operated in the area just north of the zone established by Israel but was unable to stop Palestinians from launching mid-range rockets and other operations against Israel. A series of cross-border clashes between Israeli troops and Palestinian guerrillas in mid-1981 ended in a U.S.-brokered cease-fire that had the distinction of being the first diplomatic arrangement between Israel and the Palestine Liberation Organization (PLO).

Although the Israeli-Palestinian cease-fire was relatively successful in halting further cross-border violence, the Israeli government of Prime Minister Menachem Begin decided late in 1981 on another invasion of Lebanon, to be launched when appropriate circumstances arose. As a pretext, the Begin government cited the June 3, 1982, attempted assassination of its ambassador to Great Britain by the Palestinian group headed by Abu Nidal. The declared intent of the invasion—Operation Peace for the Galilee, launched on June 6—was to establish in southern Lebanon a twenty-five-mile-deep security zone, which would put northern Israel (the Galilee) out of range of Palestinian artillery and rocket fire. Begin and Defense Minister Ariel Sharon had several additional purposes in mind for the invasion, including pushing the PLO out of Lebanon (thus weakening the organization) and supporting Bashir Gemayel, a candidate for president of Lebanon.

Gemayel was the son of Pierre Gemayel, a long-time leader of Lebanon's Maronite Christians and founder of the right-wing Phalange Party and militia. Israeli officials expected that Bashir Gemayel, once in office, would negotiate a formal peace treaty between Israel and Lebanon. Some historians also have cited evidence that Sharon envisioned an even broader and more dramatic outcome from the invasion: pushing the PLO back into Jordan and thereby causing the collapse of King Hussein's government and the transformation of Jordan into a Palestinian state. Israel would then be free to "transfer" to that state the Palestinians living in the West Bank, thus giving Israel free rein over that territory (Jordan Relinquishes the West Bank, p. 200).

In a June 8 speech to the Knesset justifying the invasion, Begin omitted reference to any broader goals, saying only that Israel sought to establish the zone in southern Lebanon free of Palestinian guerrillas and their rockets. "We want only one thing: That no one harm our settlements in the Galilee any more, that our citizens in the Galilee settlements will not have to choke in shelters day and night, that they will not have to live under the threat of sudden death from the missile called a Katyusha," he said.

Although Begin presented Israel's invasion merely as a response to the events of the previous few days, the extent of military operations made clear the extensive, months-long planning of it. Ground forces moved through southern Lebanon in three directions. In western and central Lebanon, the Israeli army quickly pushed Palestinian guerrillas north of the twenty-five-mile zone and into Beirut. In the east, the army attacked Syrian troops that had been stationed in Lebanon as Arab League peacekeepers since 1976, and Israeli warplanes destroyed antiaircraft missiles that Syria had installed in the Bekaa Valley. By the time a U.S.-negotiated cease-fire took effect on June 11, Israeli forces had taken control of most of southern and central Lebanon and had surrounded Beirut.

On June 14 Israel began a siege of the Lebanese capital, demanding the surrender of PLO forces in the western suburbs. It took nearly two months of fighting—including nearly constant Israeli bombardment of the city—before U.S. special envoy Philip Habib could secure another cease-fire. Under the terms of that agreement, PLO leaders, including Chairman Yasir Arafat, and thousands of fighters left Lebanon, most of them aboard ships bound for other Arab countries. Arafat and a core of the leadership eventually headed to Tunis, where they would remain for more than a decade. A short-term multinational force composed of troops from the United States, France, and other countries supervised the evacuation.

The last contingent of PLO members left Lebanon on September 2, thus securing for Israel one of the prime objectives of its invasion. (Israel later claimed that approximately 2,000 PLO fighters remained in Lebanon.) The exile of Arafat and his top aides to Tunisia hampered the PLO for years by weakening their ties to the Palestinians in Gaza and the West Bank. Israel also achieved its objective of a security zone by stationing troops south of the Litani River alongside the Israeli-financed South

Lebanon Army. Israel's occupation of southern Lebanon would last for nearly eighteen years, until 2000 (Israeli Withdrawal from Lebanon, p. 354).

Israel's third objective, the peace treaty with Lebanon, proved more elusive. As Israel had hoped, Bashir Gemayel was elected president on August 23. Before he could take office, however, he was assassinated, on September 14. His killers were never identified, but most evidence pointed toward Syrian military intelligence. Amin Gemayel, Bashir's younger brother, was then elected president, and on May 17, 1983, he signed an agreement with Israel. Under intense Syrian pressure, however, Gemayel later abrogated it.

The assassination of Bashir Gemayel led, at least indirectly, to another defining event of the invasion. Under orders from Sharon, Israeli troops on the evening of September 16 allowed Phalange militia members to enter Sabra and Shatilla, two adjacent Palestinian refugee camps in southern Beirut. The stated purpose of the operation was to find Palestinian guerrillas supposedly hiding there. Instead, the Phalange fighters—apparently seeking revenge for the killing of Gemayel—indiscriminately killed Palestinians in the camps, including children and women. A subsequent Israeli investigation concluded that it was impossible to determine the exact number of people killed over the course of nearly two days in the camp. The Lebanese Red Cross counted more than 300 bodies, Israeli military intelligence estimated the dead at 700 to 800, and Palestinian authorities in the camps claimed at least 2,000 killed.

The massacre of the Palestinians caused an international uproar, during which Israel generally was blamed for allowing the Phalange into the camps, making much worse an image already damaged by the invasion in general. Hoping to calm the situation, the United States, France, and other countries sent another peacekeeping force into Lebanon. These troops began arriving in late September, but their stay was cut short after suicide bombings in October 1983 killed approximately 300 U.S. and French servicemen (U.S. Involvement in Lebanon, p. 339).

The Israeli government appointed a commission to investigate the Sabra and Shatilla massacres. The report it issued in February 1983 faulted senior Israeli officials for not having prevented the killings. The commission laid particular blame on Sharon "for having disregarded the danger of acts of vengeance and bloodshed by the Phalangists against the population of the refugee camps, and having failed to take this danger into account when he decided to have the Phalangists enter the camps." Sharon, though forced to resign as defense minister, remained in the cabinet as minister without portfolio.

No accurate count exists of the casualties from Israel's invasion, but most estimates put the number of Lebanese civilians in the low thousands. Another 1,000 or so PLO fighters probably were killed, along with at least 500 Syrian troops. Israel had lost 650 soldiers by the time it withdrew the bulk of its forces in 1985. The physical damage to Lebanon was immense, adding to the toll of destruction from the civil war that started in 1975. Beirut neighborhoods that had escaped damage during earlier rounds of fighting were turned to rubble, and thousands of acres of cropland in southern Lebanon were destroyed.

Israeli gains from the invasion proved to be only temporary. With the departure of the Palestinians, Shiite Muslims in Lebanon became more assertive politically and militarily. With support from Iran, a Shiite faction formed Hizballah, an organization with a militia that starting in 1983 began carrying out guerrilla attacks against Israel.

Its members likely were responsible for the October 1983 bombings that drove U.S. and French peacekeepers from Lebanon. During the next two decades, Hizballah would become a major influence in Lebanese life, establishing schools, health clinics, and other social services that the government failed to provide. After Israeli forces withdrew from southern Lebanon in 2000—for which Hizballah claimed credit—the group launched the same kinds of rocket attacks against northern Israel as had the Palestinians in the early 1980s. Its actions along the border would lead to a brief but deadly war with Israel in summer 2006 (Hizballah-Israeli War, pp. 365–368).

The Israeli invasion of Lebanon also failed to achieve an unstated goal of Begin's and Sharon's: the ouster of Syria from Lebanon. Instead, Syria's grip on Lebanon tightened, while Israel held only the southern strip of the country. Syria emerged by far as the dominant power in Lebanon, until it was forced to withdraw under intense international pressure in 2005 (Syrian Withdrawal from Lebanon, pp. 359–361).

Overall, most historians have argued that Israel's 1982 invasion of Lebanon proved to be a huge miscalculation. Disillusioned by public criticism of the operation and disheartened by the loss of Israeli lives in combat, Begin abruptly resigned as prime minister in August 1983 and disappeared from public life until his death in 1992.

Following are excerpts from a speech by Prime Minister Menachem Begin to the Knesset on June 8, 1982, following Israel's invasion of Lebanon.

DOCUMENT

Begin Speech to the Knesset on Invading Lebanon

JUNE 8, 1982

[Note: The first part of Begin's speech recounted the events leading up to Israel's invasion of Lebanon on June 6, including an attempted assassination of the Israeli ambassador to Great Britain by a Palestinian group, followed by Israel's aerial bombardment of Palestinian bases in southern Lebanon, and Palestinian artillery and rocket attacks on the Galilee, in northern Israel.]

I want to declare to all nations: The children of Israel will happily go to school and joyfully return home, just like the children in Washington, in Moscow and in Peking; in Paris and in Rome; in Oslo, in Stockholm and in Copenhagen. The fate of a million and half a million Jewish children has been different from all the children of the world throughout the generations. No more. We will defend our children. If the hand of any two-footed animal is raised against them, that hand will be cut off, and our children will grow up in joy in the homes of their parents.

But, here there are Katyushas [rockets], missiles and artillery shells day and night, with the sole intention of murdering our women and children. There are military targets in the Galilee. What a characteristic phenomenon, they are protected, completely immune to these terrorists. Only at the civilian population, only to shed our blood, just to kill our children, our wives, our sisters, our elderly. Such a method, so despicable, terroristic. Despicable. There has been none so despicable since the days of the S.A., the S.S. and the Gestapo [security forces in Nazi Germany].

There was never an armed organization so low, so despicable as this terrorist organization, which aims its unclean weapons against men, women and children [a reference to the Palestine Liberation Organization]. Therefore we have implemented our right to national self-defense.

In reply to U.S. President Reagan's letter, a very friendly letter, I explained to him: Here the U.S. supports Britain's actions in the Falkland Islands, or the Malvinas as the Argentinians call them. How does Mrs. Thatcher justify it? On the basis of Article 51 of the United Nations Charter, which speaks of "The inherent right of self defense." [Eight thousand] miles from that country, this is a right of national self-defense? Whereas one mile, two miles, three miles, on our doorstep, our threshold, we are attacked and have no right to national self-defense? We have to sit by and watch the shells falling on our brothers and sisters? It is clear that we had to implement our right of national self-defense, and we did so. We continue to do so.

Once more, I would like to tell all peoples—for a long time, too long, the Jew was excluded from all the laws which applied to all nations. No more. The laws which apply to other nations will apply to our nation—to the Jewish people. The right of self-defense accorded to all other nations is also accorded to us. No more and no less.

Since I am still on the subject of Britain, I want to return to the important and famous newspaper, "Times," which today published a leader attacking Israel and me, personally, for what we have done in the north in order to protect our people in the Galilee and in Lebanon. That is its right—we believe in freedom of the press—however, if someone attacks he has to expect a response. I wish to say:

A newspaper which supported the treachery of the Munich Agreement must be very careful about moralizing to a small nation fighting for its life. Were we to listen to it, we would no longer be in existence. Czechoslovakia vanished because of the famous line of the "Times" in 1938, and the famous, or infamous lead article at the time of Runciman's visit to Prague. But we learned the lesson. Therefore, we are also not taking the latest advice of the "Times," just as we did not take its advice at the time of Munich. It should take stock of its deeds and articles.

Mr. Speaker, I announce once again: We do not want war with Syria. From this rostrum, I call on President [Hafiz al-] Assad to instruct the Syrian army not to harm Israeli soldiers, and then nothing will happen to them. We actually do not want to harm anyone. We want only one thing: That no one harm our settlements in the Galilee any more, that our citizens in the Galilee settlements will not have to choke in shelters day and night, that they will not have to live under the threat of sudden death from the missile called a Katyusha. That is what we want. We do not want any clash with the Syrian army. If we achieve the 40 kilometer line from our northern border, the job is done, all fighting will cease.

I make this appeal to the Syrian President. He knows how to keep an agreement. He signed a cease-fire agreement with us and kept it. He did not let Syria and the terrorists take action. Let him act in this spirit now in Lebanon and no Syrian soldier will be harmed by our forces.

Mr. Speaker, from time to time our nation has an encounter with history. And so, our soldiers are now in Tyre. We recall Ezekiel, chapter 27, verse 8: "Thy wise men, O Tyre, were in thee, they were thy pilots." We are standing today in Sidon and we recall Isaiah, chapter 23, verse 12: "Thou shalt no more rejoice, O thou oppressed virgin daughter of Sidon." We also recall the two chapters in the Book of Kings on the friendship between Hiram, King of Tyre, and our King David, and on the alliance our King Solomon formed with the King of Tyre at the time of the construction of the First Temple. We will not be able to give Tyre what Solomon gave it, but we can give it security, peace and tranquility. And only on condition that there be peace and tranquility in Nahariya, which was shelled from Tyre for many years, with Katyusha shells. No longer. All will be tranquil—both we and they.

The day will dawn, the day is coming soon, when we will renew negotiations with the legitimate government of Lebanon and propose a peace treaty based on absolute territorial integrity for Lebanon. I hereby announce—with the concurrence of all the Zionist factions—that we do not want even one square millimeter of Lebanese territory. We ask for only one thing: That our border be renewed—peaceful, green, quiet and beautiful—between Lebanon and Israel. As it existed 19 whole years. Because this pastoral, beautiful, quiet was completely destroyed by these murderers.

That is our goal. There is a basis for believing that we will achieve it, God willing. There will be peace for the Galilee, peace for Israel, peace for the Middle East, peace for all nations.

SOURCE: Israel Ministry of Foreign Affairs, www.mfa.gov.il/MFA/Foreign%20Relations/Israels%20 Foreign%20Relations%20since%201947/1982-1984/7%20Statement%20in%20the%20Knesset%20by%20 Prime%20Minister%20Begin.

U.S. Involvement in Lebanon

DOCUMENT IN CONTEXT

In September 1982, Lebanon appeared to be on the verge of even greater chaos than it had suffered at anytime since the outbreak of civil war in 1975. The armies of Israel and Syria controlled most of the country, while renegade militias wreaked havoc almost everywhere. Following the assassination of President-elect Bashir Gemayel and the subsequent massacre of Palestinians the at Shabra and Shatila refugee camps by Phalange militiamen, Western leaders concluded that only a large-scale international presence could bring some stability to the country (Israel Invasion of Lebanon, p. 334).

On September 20, 1982, President Ronald Reagan announced that the United States, France, and Italy had agreed to send a multinational force "to assist the Government of Lebanon in reasserting authority over all its territory." Acknowledging the near-impossibility of achieving that goal in the immediate future, Reagan said the international troops would begin by deploying to Beirut, with the goal of "enabling the Lebanese Government to resume full sovereignty over its capital, the essential precondition for extending its control over the entire country." The first U.S. troops arrived in Lebanon one week after Reagan's announcement. By the end of 1982 nearly 1,600 marines had taken up positions at the Beirut airport, along with an equivalent number of soldiers from France, Italy, and Great Britain.

Some Muslim leaders denounced the presence of U.S. and European troops, which they viewed as an extension of Israel's invasion earlier in the year. The first sign of verbal opposition being turned into action appeared in March 1983, when apparently coordinated attacks left five U.S. marines and six Italian soldiers wounded. A more ominous sign arrived on April 18, when a suicide bomber blew up the U.S. embassy in Beirut, killing sixty-three people, among them seventeen U.S. citizens, including CIA station chief Robert Ames. More than 100 others were wounded.

Opponents of the deployment struck double blows to the international peace-keeping effort on the morning of October 23, 1983. First, a suicide bomber drove a van laden with several tons of explosives into the barracks at the Beirut airport housing U.S. Marines: 220 marines, 18 sailors, and 3 soldiers were killed, and some 60 were wounded. Seconds later, a truck bomb destroyed the nearby French military compound nearby, killing 59 soldiers. A group calling itself Islamic Jihad claimed responsibility for both attacks, but some U.S. officials subsequently charged that Hizballah, at the time a new Shiite militia, had carried out the attacks. Less than two weeks later, a similar suicide truck bomb destroyed a building housing Israeli intelligence headquarters in Tyre, on the coast south of Beirut, killing 28 Israelis, along with 32 Arabs jailed there.

The bombing of the marine barracks represented at the time the biggest and boldest attack against a U.S. target in the Middle East. It appeared initially that the bombers had failed to achieve their goal of driving the multinational force from Lebanon. Reagan vowed to keep the marines there, and both houses of Congress rejected attempts to force the president to bring the troops home. Even so, uncertainty about the value of the international presence in Lebanon continued to grow. Slightly more than three months later, on February 7, 1984, Reagan announced that he had ordered U.S. troops redeployed to warships on the Lebanese coast, adding that they would return if needed. Britain, France, and Italy withdrew their forces in subsequent weeks. Sectarian violence continued in Lebanon at a relatively modest level until the next big explosion, in 1988 (Taif Accord, p. 344).

Following are two speeches that President Ronald Reagan made to the nation on September 20, 1982, and February 7, 1984, concerning the situation in Lebanon.

DOCUMENT

Reagan on the Multinational Force for Lebanon

SEPTEMBER 20, 1982

My fellow Americans:

The scenes that the whole world witnessed this past weekend were among the most heart-rending in the long nightmare of Lebanon's agony. Millions of us have seen pictures of the Palestinian victims of this tragedy [the massacre at Shabra and Shatila refugee camps]. There is little that words can add, but there are actions we can and must take to bring that nightmare to an end.

It's not enough for us to view this as some remote event in which we, ourselves, are not involved. For our friends in Lebanon and Israel, for our friends in Europe and elsewhere in the Middle East, and for us as Americans, this tragedy, horrible as it is, reminds us of the absolute imperative of bringing peace to that troubled country and region. By working for peace in the Middle East, we serve the cause of world peace and the future of mankind.

For the criminals who did this deed, no punishment is enough to remove the blot of their crime. But for the rest of us, there are things that we can learn and things that we must do. The people of Lebanon must have learned that the cycle of massacre upon massacre must end. Children are not avenged by the murder of other children. Israel must have learned that there is no way it can impose its own solutions on hatreds as deep and bitter as those that produced this tragedy. If it seeks to do so, it will only sink more deeply into the quagmire that looms before it. Those outsiders who have fed the flames of civil war in Lebanon for so many years need to learn that the fire will consume them, too, if it is not put out. And we must all rededicate ourselves to the cause of peace. I reemphasize my call for early progress to solve the Palestinian issue and repeat the U.S. proposals which are now even more urgent.

For now is not the time for talk alone; now is a time for action—to act together to restore peace to Beirut, to help a stable government emerge that can restore peace and independence to all of Lebanon, and to bring a just and lasting resolution to the conflict between Israel and its Arab neighbors, one that satisfies the legitimate rights of the Palestinians, who are all too often its victims.

Our basic objectives in Lebanon have not changed, for they're the objectives of the Government and the people of Lebanon themselves. First and foremost, we seek the restoration of a strong and stable central government in that country, brought into being by orderly constitutional processes. Lebanon elected a new President two short weeks ago, only to see him murdered even before he could assume his office. This week a distressed Lebanon will again be electing a new President. May God grant him safety as well as the wisdom and courage to lead his country into a new and happier era.

The international community has an obligation to assist the Government of Lebanon in reasserting authority over all its territory. Foreign forces and armed factions have too long obstructed the legitimate role of the Government of Lebanon's security forces. We must pave the way for withdrawal of foreign forces.

The place to begin this task is in Beirut. The Lebanese Government must be permitted to restore internal security in its capital. It cannot do this if foreign forces remain in or near Beirut. With this goal in mind, I have consulted with our French and Italian allies. We have agreed to form a new multinational force, similar to the one which served so well last month, with the mission of enabling the Lebanese Government to resume full sovereignty over its capital, the essential precondition for extending its control over the entire country.

The Lebanese Government, with the support of its people, requested this help. For this multinational force to succeed, it is essential that Israel withdraw from Beirut. With the expected cooperation of all parties, the multinational force will return to Beirut for a limited period of time. Its purpose is not to act as a police force, but to make it possible for the lawful authorities of Lebanon to discharge those duties for themselves.

Secretary [George] Shultz, on my behalf, has also reiterated our views to the Government of Israel through its Ambassador in Washington. Unless Israel moves quickly and courageously to withdraw, it will find itself ever more deeply involved in problems that are not its own and which it cannot solve.

The participation of American forces in Beirut will again be for a limited period. But I've concluded there is no alternative to their returning to Lebanon if that country is to have a chance to stand on its own feet.

Peace in Beirut is only a first step. Together with the people of Lebanon, we seek the removal of all foreign military forces from that country. The departure of all foreign forces at the request of the Lebanese authorities has been widely endorsed by Arab as well as other states. Israel and Syria have both indicated that they have no territorial ambitions in Lebanon and are prepared to withdraw. It is now urgent that specific arrangements for withdrawal of all foreign forces be agreed upon. This must happen very soon. The legitimate security concerns of neighboring states, including, particularly, the safety of Israel's northern population, must be provided for. But this is not a difficult task, if the political will is there. The Lebanese people must be allowed to chart their own future. They must rely solely on Lebanese Armed Forces who are willing and able to bring security to their country. They must be allowed to do so, and the sooner the better.

Ambassador [Morris] Draper, who's been in close consultation with the parties concerned in Lebanon, will remain in the area to work for the full implementation of our proposal. Ambassador [Philip] Habib will join him, will represent me at the inauguration of the new President of Lebanon, and will consult with the leaders in the area. He will return promptly to Washington to report to me.

Early in the summer, our government met its responsibility to help resolve a severe crisis and to relieve the Lebanese people of a crushing burden. We succeeded. Recent events have produced new problems, and we must again assume our responsibility.

I am especially anxious to end the agony of Lebanon because it is both right and in our national interest. But I am also determined to press ahead on the broader effort to achieve peace between Israel and its Arab neighbors. The events in Beirut of last week have served only to reinforce my conviction that such a peace is desperately needed and that the initiative we undertook on September 1st is the right way to proceed. We will not be discouraged or deterred in our efforts to seek peace in Lebanon and a just and lasting peace throughout the Middle East.

All of us must learn the appropriate lessons from this tragedy and assume the responsibilities that it imposes upon us. We owe it to ourselves and to our children. The whole world will be a safer place when this region which has known so much trouble can begin to know peace instead. Both our purpose and our actions are peaceful, and we're taking them in a spirit of international cooperation.

So, tonight, I ask for your prayers and your support as our country continues its vital role as a leader for world peace, a role that all of us as Americans can be proud of.

Thank you, and God bless you.

SOURCE: Ronald Reagan Presidential Archives, University of Texas, www.reagan.utexas.edu/archives/speeches/1982/92082f.htm.

DOCUMENT

Reagan Statement on the Situation in Lebanon

FEBRUARY 7, 1984

The bloodshed we have witnessed in Lebanon over the last several days only demonstrates once again the lengths to which the forces of violence and intimidation are prepared to go to prevent a peaceful reconciliation process from taking place. If a moderate government is overthrown because it had the courage to turn in the direction of peace, what hope can there be that other moderates in the region will risk committing themselves to a similar course? Yielding to violence and terrorism today may seem to provide temporary relief, but such a course is sure to lead to a more dangerous and less manageable future crisis.

Even before the latest outbreak of violence, we had been considering ways of reconcentrating our forces and the nature of our support in order to take the initiative away from the terrorists. Far from deterring us from this course, recent events only confirm the importance of the decisive new steps I want to outline for you now. Thus, after consultation with our MNF [Multinational Force] partners and President [Amin] Gemayel, and at his request, we are prepared to do the following:

First, to enhance the safety of American and other MNF personnel in Lebanon, I have authorized U.S. naval forces, under the existing mandate of the MNF, to provide naval gunfire and air support against any units firing into greater Beirut from parts of Lebanon controlled by Syria, as well as against any units directly attacking American or MNF personnel and facilities. Those who conduct these attacks will no longer have sanctuary from which to bombard Beirut at will. We will stand firm to deter those who seek to influence Lebanon's future by intimidation.

Second, when the Government of Lebanon is able to reconstitute itself into a broadly based representative government, we will vigorously accelerate the training, equipping, and support of the Lebanese Armed Forces, on whom the primary responsibility rests for maintaining stability in Lebanon. We will speed up delivery of equipment; we will improve the flow of information to help counter hostile bombardments; and we will intensify training in counter-terrorism to help the Lebanese confront the terrorist threat that poses such a danger to Lebanon, to Americans in Lebanon, and indeed to peace in the Middle East.

Third, in conjunction with these steps, I have asked Secretary of Defense [Casper] Weinberger to present to me a plan for redeployment of the marines from Beirut Airport to their ships offshore. This redeployment will begin shortly and will proceed in stages. U.S. military personnel will remain on the ground in Lebanon for training and equipping the Lebanese Army and protecting the remaining personnel. These are traditional functions that U.S. personnel perform in many friendly countries. Our naval and marine forces offshore will stand ready, as before, to provide support for the protection of American and other MNF personnel in Lebanon and thereby help ensure security in the Beirut area as I have described.

These measures, I believe, will strengthen our ability to do the job we set out to do and to sustain our efforts over the long term. They are consistent with the compromise joint resolution worked out last October with the Congress with respect to our participation in the multinational force.

SOURCE: Ronald Reagan Presidential Archives, University of Texas, www.reagan.utexas.edu/archives/speeches/1984/20784d.htm.

The Taif Accord

DOCUMENT IN CONTEXT

In December 1985, Syria arranged negotiations among key sectarian factions that resulted in the Tripartite Agreement, an attempt to resolve Lebanon's conflicts by giving increased authority to their various militias and political organizations at the expense of the already weak central government. Signing the agreement were Elie Hobeika, leader of the Lebanese Forces, a Phalangist-controlled Christian militia; Walid Jumblatt, leader of the Druze community and head of the most powerful Druze militia; and Nabih Berri, head of the Shiite group Amal. That agreement never took full effect, and then it completely collapsed in 1986 when Phalangist leader Amin Gemayel, also Lebanon's president, ousted Hobeika from his post with the Lebanese Forces. The collapse of the Tripartite Agreement led to renewed conflict, most of it intramural in nature, with various elements of Christian and Shiite militias battling each other for dominance. Syria attempted to impose a degree of order by expanding its military presence in Lebanon, thus increasing its overall control of it.

Another crisis erupted in September 1988, when the parliament, or Chamber of Deputies, failed to agree on a successor to President Gemayel before the mandated end of his second term on September 23. The parliament consisted of the same legislators who had been elected in 1972 because there had been no elections during the civil war. The stalemate resulting from the parliament's failure to act led to two governments competing for leadership of the country—one headed by the sitting prime minister, Selim al-Hoss, and the other led by Michel Aoun, the commander of the Lebanese Army who declared himself president and moved into the presidential palace outside Beirut.

This situation erupted into another round of fighting early in 1989, when Aoun declared a "war of liberation" against Syrian occupation and also attempted to assert control over all of Lebanon's sectarian militias. Syria intervened on behalf of the Druze and Muslim militias. A summer of artillery duels and ground battles almost matched the worst of the 1975–1976 civil war violence and that of the 1982 Israeli invasion.

Hoping to mediate an end to the dispute, Saudi Arabia convened a peace conference in the Saudi resort town of Taif at the end of September 1989. Most members of the Lebanese legislature attended. Working from a draft document prepared by the Arab League, the delegates spent three weeks debating the political issues at the heart of Lebanon's civil war. On October 22, they reached agreement on a document formally called the National Reconciliation Charter, popularly known as the Taif Accord. The document, also approved by Syria, quickly won international endorsements, including by the UN Security Council.

In essence, the Taif Accord adjusted (while preserving the basic character of) the sectarian division of power in effect since adoption of the National Pact in 1943. The most important change involved increasing the size of the Chamber of Deputies from ninety-nine to one hundred eight seats, with the membership split equally between Christian and Muslim representatives. The previous ratio had been six Christians to five Muslims. The sectarian division of top government posts—a Christian president, Sunni prime minister, and Shiite Speaker of parliament—remained in effect, though some of the president's powers shifted to the prime minister. The accord also promised a review, at an unspecified time, of the entire system of assigning government posts according to religious sect.

Another key element of the accord dealt with Syrian military involvement in Lebanon. In a compromise, the accord gave Syria the role of helping the army "of the legitimate Lebanese government" to broaden its authority over the entire country during a two-year period. At that point, the Lebanese and Syrian governments were to negotiate the terms for Syria to withdraw its military. The provision gave Damascus even more legitimacy for its presence in Lebanon, although with an explicit promise that it would, in fact, withdraw its army when asked to do so.

After returning to Lebanon, members of the parliament formally endorsed the Taif Accord on November 5, 1989, and elected a new president, Rene Muawwad. Aoun, however, refused to step aside and to recognize Muawwad or accept the agreement. Muawwad was assassinated in a car bombing on November 22, and the parliament promptly chose Elias Hrawi to succeed him. In mid-August 1990, the parliament formally incorporated the Taif Accord provisions into a revised constitution. President Hrawi signed the changes into law on September 21, brushing aside a threat by Aoun to use military force against him. About three weeks later, on October 13, the Syrian army and elements of the Lebanese Army loyal to Hrawi attacked Aoun's forces, which still claimed to be the legitimate army. With defeat imminent, Aoun surrendered command of his troops and took refuge in the French embassy. He later went into exile in France, where he remained for nearly fifteen years.

The defeat of Aoun essentially ended the civil war that had wracked Lebanon since 1975. By early 1991, the Lebanese government, still dominated by Syria, had disarmed most of the sectarian militias and asserted at least some degree of control over most of the countryside. Two significant limits on the government's control, however, remained: the Shiite organization Hizballah refused to disarm and instead grew stronger, building a state within a state (much as the Palestinians had done previously) in southern and central Lebanon and in the southern suburbs of Beirut; and Israel continued to control a self-declared "security zone" in the south inside the Lebanese border. Clashes between Hizballah and Israel (and its proxy force, the South Lebanon Army) continued for years. Israel finally and hastily withdrew from the area in 2000. In summer 2006, an all-out war would erupt between Israel and Hizballah (Hizballah-Israeli War, p. 365).

In political terms, the government's decision in 1992 to hold elections, the first in twenty years, stood as the most significant indicator of the end of civil war. The balloting, held in stages in August, September, and October, brought to office a new government headed by Prime Minister Rafiq Hariri, a billionaire contractor who used his personal wealth to help rebuild the country. Nabih Berri, whose Amal militia had participated in the civil war, became Speaker. Despite the modest reforms mandated by the Taif Accord and subsequent elections, the central government possessed only limited powers and remained vulnerable to the sectarian conflicts built into the political system. Moreover, Syria would retain ultimate veto power until its withdrawal in 2005, and Hizballah would remain the dominant force in southern Lebanon.

Following is the text of the National Reconciliation Charter as approved by members of the Lebanese parliament on October 22, 1989, during a conference in Taif, Saudi Arabia.

DOCUMENT

Lebanese National Reconciliation Charter

OCTOBER 22, 1989

First. General Principles and Reforms

I. General Principles

A. The Identity of Lebanon: Lebanon is a sovereign and independent homeland, united in territory, people, and institutions within its border, which is stipulated in the

Lebanese Constitution and recognized internationally. Lebanon is Arab by belonging and identity. It is a working member of the Arab League and is committed to all its charters. It is a founding and active member of the United Nations and committed to its charter, and it is also a member of the Nonaligned Movement. The Lebanese state embodies all these principles in all fields and spheres without exception.

B. Political System: Lebanon is a democratic parliamentary republic based on respect for public liberties, at the forefront of which are the freedom of opinion and belief; the principle of separating the authorities and their balance and cooperation; social justice; and equality of duties and rights among all citizens without prejudice or favoritism;

C. The economic system is a liberal one which guarantees individual initiative and private property.

D. The balanced cultural, social, and economic development of the region is an essential element for the state's unity and the stability of the political system.

E. Work must be done to achieve comprehensive social justice through financial, economic, and social reforms.

F. Lebanon is one land for all Lebanese. Every Lebanese has the right to settle on any part of this land and enjoy it under the shadow of the rule of law. There will be no discrimination among the people on the basis of any affiliation. Neither will there be any partition, division, or incorporation.

G. No legitimacy will be given to any authority which opposes the charter of coexistence.

II. The Political Reforms

A. The Chamber of Deputies

The Chamber of Deputies is the legislative power which exercises full supervision of the government's policy and its actions.

1. The speaker and his deputy are elected for a period equal to the life of the legislature.

2. Two years after the election of its speaker and his deputy and at its first session, the legislature can withdraw its confidence in its speaker or his deputy once and with a majority of two-thirds of the total number of its members on the basis of a petition signed by at least 10 deputies. In such a case the legislature must immediately hold a session to fill the vacant post.

3. Any draft bill referred by the Council of Ministers to the legislature urgently cannot be issued until it is included in the agenda of a plenary session and then discussed. No decision can be made on it before the period of time stipulated in the Constitution has lapsed and before the approval of the Council of Ministers.

4. The electoral constituency is the governorate.

5. Until the parliament has laid down an electoral bill which is free from sectarian restraints, the parliamentary seats will be distributed along the following lines:

   a. equal numbers for Christians and Muslims.

   b. proportionally among the sects of the two groups.

   c. proportionally among the regions.

6. The number of the deputies will be increased to 108 equally divided between Christians and Muslims. The new posts created on the basis of this document and the

posts which became vacant before it was proclaimed will be filled exceptionally and once only by appointment decided by the would-be government of national accord.

7. With the election of the first legislature on a national and not a sectarian basis a senate will be created and it will represent all the spiritual families. Its prerogatives will be restricted to fateful issues.

B. The President of the Republic

The president is the head of state and symbol of national unity. He ensures respect for the Constitution and protection of the independence of Lebanon and its territorial integrity and safety. He is the supreme commander of the armed forces which are under the authority of the Council of Ministers. The president has the following powers:

1. He presides over the Council of Ministers when he wishes and without voting.

2. He presides over the Supreme Defense Council.

3. He issues decrees and requests their publication. He has the right to ask the Council of Ministers to reconsider any decision it makes within 15 days of his installation [as heard] as president of the republic. If the Council of Ministers insists on the decision made or if the deadline has lapsed without the publication or reconsideration of the decree the decree or the decision is considered legally valid and must be published.

4. He issues laws according to the deadlines defined in the Constitution and requests their publication after they are ratified by the legislature. He is also entitled—after informing the Council of Ministers—to request that laws be reconsidered within the deadlines defined in the Constitution and in accordance with its provisions. If the deadlines have expired and these laws have not been published or reconsidered, the laws become legally valid and must be published.

5. He refers draft bills which are submitted to him by the Council of Ministers to the legislature.

6. He nominates the prime minister after consulting the speaker of the legislature on the basis of binding parliamentary consultations whose results are formally conveyed to him by the speaker.

7. He issues a separate decree nominating the prime minister.

8. He issues—with the agreement of the prime minister—the decree for the formation of the government.

9. He issues the decrees on accepting the resignation of the government or the resignation of ministers or their dismissal.

10. He accredits ambassadors and accepts their credentials and awards state medals by decree.

11. He is in charge of negotiations on the signing of international treaties and signs these treaties with the agreement of the prime minister. These treaties will only be in force after approval by the Council of Ministers. The government informs the legislature about these treaties when the country's interest and the state's safety allow it. The treaties which concern state finances, commercial treaties, and other treaties which cannot be abrogated year after year cannot be signed until they are approved by the legislature.

12. When needed, the president sends letters to the legislature.

13. He calls on the legislature—with the agreement of the prime minister—to hold extraordinary sessions by decree.

14. The president of the republic has the right to submit any urgent matter to the Council of Ministers through its agenda. [as heard]

15. He calls for an extraordinary meeting of the Council of Ministers whenever he deems it necessary with the agreement of the prime minister.

16. He grants private pardons by decree.

17. The president of the republic cannot be prevented from carrying out his function except when he violates the Constitution or in the case of high treason.

C. The Chairman of the Council of Ministers

The chairman of the Council of Ministers is the head of government and represents the latter, speaks on its behalf, and is considered to be responsible for the execution of the general policy adopted by the Council of Ministers. He exercises the following powers:

1. He presides over the Council of Ministers.

2. He holds legislative consultations to form the government and signs with the president of the republic the decree of its formation. The government has to present to the parliament its ministerial statement [as heard] in order to win its confidence within a deadline of 30 days. The government cannot exercise its powers before winning confidence nor after its resignation. It will also be considered dissolved only in the strict sense to enable it to expedite remaining business.

3. He submits the government's general policy before the legislature.

4. He signs all decrees except the decree nominating the head of government and the decree accepting the resignation of the government, which dissolves it.

5. He signs decrees requesting the opening of an extraordinary session, decrees on the publication of laws, and requests for their reconsideration.

6. He calls for a meeting of the Council of Ministers and draws up its agenda and informs the president of the republic in advance about the topics included in the agenda and the urgent topics which will be discussed. He also signs the usual minutes of the sittings.

7. He follows the activities of the public administration and public enterprises and coordinates between the ministries. He also gives general directives to ensure the good functioning of the work.

8. He holds working sessions with the state's competent authorities in the presence of the competent minister.

9. He is by law deputy to the chairman of the Supreme Defense Council.

D. The Council of Ministers

Procedural powers are entrusted to the Council of Ministers. Among the powers exercised by the Council of Ministers are the following:

1. Lay down the general policy of the state in all domains, draw up draft laws and decrees, and make the decisions necessary for their implementation.

2. Attend to the execution of the laws and official ordinances and supervise the activity of all the state's apparatuses, including the administrations, the civil, military, and security institutions without exception.

3. The Council of Ministers is the authority which the armed forces obey.

4. Appoint the civil servants, dismiss them, and accept their resignations in accordance with the law.

5. Has the right to dissolve the legislature at the request of the president of the republic if the legislature refrains from meeting during an ordinary or extraordinary session for at least 1 month despite two successive calls or if it rejects the whole schedule with a view to paralyzing the work of the government. This right cannot be exercised for the same reasons which led to the dissolution of the legislature the first time.

6. When the president of the republic is present he chairs the sessions of the Council of Ministers. The meetings of the Council of Ministers are to be held at a venue designated by the Council of Ministers. The legal quorum of its meetings is two-thirds of its members. It adopts its decisions by consent, and if this is not possible, by voting. Decisions require the majority of those present except in fundamental issues where they require a two-thirds majority of the members of the Council of Ministers. The following are considered as fundamental issues:

Declaring and ending the state of emergency, war and peace, and general mobilization; concluding international agreements and treaties the general budget of the state and the comprehensive and long-term development plans; the appointment of officials of the first grade or its equivalent; the administrative redistribution of governorates; the dissolution of the legislature; election law, the law of personal status, the law of nationality; and the dismissal of ministers.

E. The Minister

The powers of the minister should be consolidated in a way compatible with the general policy of the government and the collective responsibility. The minister should not be removed except by a decision by the Council of Ministers or by a vote of no confidence in him by the Chamber of Deputies.

F. The Resignation of the Government, Considering It Resigned, and Firing of Ministers

1. The government is considered as resigned in the following situation:
    a. if the prime minister resigns.
    b. if it loses more than one-third of the members specified in its formation decree.
    c. if the prime minister dies.
    d. at the beginning of the term of the president.
    e. at the beginning of the term of the legislature.
    f. by a vote of no confidence by the legislature whether at the chamber's initiative or at the government's initiative.

2. The minister is fired by a decree signed by the president and the prime minister after the approval of the Council of Ministers.

3. When the government resigns or is considered resigned, the legislature is considered as a ruler in an extraordinary session until the formation of a new government and its obtaining a vote of confidence.

G. Abolition of Political Sectarianism

The abolition of political sectarianism is a basic national aim toward which work should be carried out according to a step-by-step plan. The legislature, elected on the basis of half Muslims and half Christians, should adopt the necessary measures to achieve this aim. A national organization, headed by the president, should be formed. It should include, in addition to the speaker of the legislature and the prime minister, political, intellectual and social personalities. The duty of the organization is to study and propose the necessary means to abolish sectarianism, to present these proposals to the Council of Ministers and the legislature, and to follow up the implementation of the step-by-step plan. During the transitional stage, the following should be done:

1. The abolition of the principle of sectarian representation and adopting proficiency and personal qualities in appointment, in civil service, judiciary, military and security establishments, public and mixed institutions, and independent organizations according to the requirements of national reconciliation, with the exception of the first rank positions and their equivalent, which should be divided equally between Muslims and Christians without allocating any specific job to any sect.

2. The abolition of any mention of religion or sect in identity cards.

III. Other Reforms

A. Administrative Decentralization

1. The Lebanese state is a single united state with strong centralized authority.

2. Extending the powers of governors and mayors and representing all state departments in the greatest possible form in the administrative regions to facilitate the services for the citizens and to respond to their needs locally.

3. Revising the administrative division to secure national cohesion and to preserve the joint coexistence and the unity of the people, land, and institutions.

4. Establishing extended administrative decentralization at the level of the minor administrative units—constituency and smaller—by electing a council for every constituency chaired by the mayor to secure the local participation.

5. Approving a comprehensive united development plan for the whole country, which should be able to develop Lebanese regions economically and socially, and supporting the resources of the municipalities, united municipalities, and municipal unions with the necessary financial resources.

B. The Courts

1. To secure that all officials and citizens are subject to the law and to secure the harmony of the work of both the legislative and executive authorities with the requirements of coexistence and the basic rights of the Lebanese specified by the Constitution:

    a. The supreme council specified by the Constitution, whose job is the trial of presidents and ministers, should be formed, and a law for the principles of trials by it should be adopted.

    b. A constitutional council for interpreting the Constitution, monitoring the constitutional status of laws, and deciding the contests and disputes stemming from the presidential and legislative elections should be formed.

    c. The following sides have the right to consult the constitutional council about the interpretation of the Constitution and the monitoring of the constitutional status of law:

      aa. The president,
      bb. The speaker of the legislature,
      cc. The prime minister, and
      dd. A certain percentage of deputies.
    d. To secure the principle of harmony between religion and state, the heads of Lebanese sects have the right to consult the constitutional council concerning:
      aa. Personal statutes,
      bb. The freedom of belief and to practice religious rites,
      cc. Freedom of religious education.
    e. To consolidate the independence of the judiciary, a certain number of the members of the Supreme Judicial Council should be elected from the Judiciary.
    2. The law on legislative elections:

Legislative elections should be conducted according to a new elections law on the basis of provinces which takes into consideration the bases which secure coexistence for the Lebanese and secure the correctness of effectiveness of the political representation for all sectors and generations of the people. This is after reviewing the administrative divisions within the framework of the unity of the land, people, and institutions.

    3. Formation of the Economic and Social Council for Development:

An economic and social council should be formed to secure the participation of the representatives of the various sectors in drafting the economic and social policy of the state through consultations and submitting proposals.

    4. Education:
    a. Providing education for everyone, and making it compulsory, at the primary age at least.
    b. Stressing the freedom of education according to public laws and regulations.
    c. Protecting private education and consolidating the state supervision of private schools and school textbooks.
    d. Reforming official, vocational, and technical education and consolidating and developing them to achieve cohesion and spiritual and cultural development and growth. Standardizing the books in the subjects of history and national education.
    5. The Media:

Reorganizing the media under the law and within the framework of responsible freedom to serve reconciliation tendencies and ending the state of war.

Second. Extending the Sovereignty of the Lebanese State over All Lebanese Territory

In view of the fact that agreement has been reached among the Lebanese parties on the establishment of a strong and capable state based on the principle of national accord, the national accord government will lay down a security plan for 1 year, the objective of which will be to extend the authority of the Lebanese state gradually over all Lebanese territory with the aid of its internal forces, the broad outlines of which are as follows:

    1. Declaration of the dissolution of Lebanese and non-Lebanese militia, and their weapons to be handed to the Lebanese state within 6 months, starting after the endorsement of the National Accord document, the election of a president, and the formation of a national accord government, and constitutional endorsement of political reforms.

2. Consolidation of internal security forces by:

a. Opening the door of voluntary conscription to all Lebanese without exception, beginning their training centrally, and then allocating them to unity in the governorates. They should also be attached to periodic and regular training courses.

b. Strengthening the security apparatus in a way that would conform to controlling the entry and exit of people across the border by land, sea, and air.

3. Consolidating the Armed Forces:

a. The basic duty of the armed forces is to defend the homeland, and when necessary protect public order when the danger exceeds the abilities of the internal security forces to deal with it on their own.

b. The armed forces are used to support the internal security forces in preserving security in circumstances decided by the Council of Ministers.

c. The armed forces should be united, prepared, and trained to be able to shoulder their national responsibilities in confronting Israeli aggression.

d. When the internal security forces are ready to shoulder their security duties, the armed forces should return to their barracks.

e. Military intelligence should be reorganized to serve military purposes and nothing else.

4. The problem of the Lebanese evacuees should be radically solved and the right of every Lebanese evacuee since 1975 to return to the place from which he was evacuated should be guaranteed. Legislation to secure this right and to secure the necessary means for reconstruction of destroyed places should be issued.

Since the goal of the Lebanese state is to extend its authority over the entire Lebanese territory by means of its own forces represented primarily in the forces of internal security, and owing to the fraternal relations existing between Syria and Lebanon, the Syrian troops will graciously assist legitimate Lebanese forces to extend the authority of the Lebanese state within a limited period of time not exceeding 2 years after the ratification of the national accord document, the election of the president of the republic, the formation of a national accord government, and the confirmation of political reforms in the Constitution.

At the end of this period, the Syrian Government and the Lebanese Government of national accord will decide on the redeployment of Syrian troops in the al-Biqa' region and the entry to the western al-Biqa' at Dahr al-Baydar to the line al-Mudayrij–'Ayn Darah, or if need be at other points to be determined by a joint Lebanese-Syrian military committee. The two governments will also agree to determine the number of Syrian troops to be deployed in the aforementioned areas and to define the nature of the relationship between these troops and the authorities of the Lebanese state in the areas where they will be deployed. In this respect, the higher Arab tripartite committee is prepared to assist the two states to reach such an agreement if they so wish.

Third. Liberating Lebanon from the Israeli Occupation

Restoring state sovereignty up to the international borders with Israel requires the following:

1. Working toward the implementation of Resolution No. 425 and all the UN Security Council's resolutions specifying the complete removal of the Israeli occupation.

2. Insisting on the truce treaty signed on 23 March 1949.

3. Adopting all the necessary measures for liberating all Lebanese territories from Israeli occupation and spreading state authority on all of these territories, deploying the Lebanese Army to the borders with Israel, and working toward consolidating the international peacekeeping forces in southern Lebanon to secure the Israeli withdrawal and to secure the opportunity for restoring security and stability to the border regions.

Fourth. Lebanese-Syrian Relations

Lebanon, which is of Arab identity and belonging, is linked by sincere fraternal relations with all Arab countries. There are distinguished relations, which draw their strength from the roots of neighborhood, history, and joint strategic interests, between Lebanon and Syria. This concept is the base of coordination and cooperation between the two countries, and it will be manifested by joint treaties in all fields, which will serve the interests of the two sister countries within the framework of mutual independence and sovereignty. Because of this, and because consolidating the bases of security provides the required atmosphere for developing these distinguished links, it is imperative that Lebanon not become a threat to Syrian security and Syria not become a threat to Lebanon's security, whatever the situation may be. Therefore Lebanon does not allow itself to be a passage for or a residence for any force, state, or organization which aims at violating Lebanese or Syrian security; and Syria, which is committed to the security, stability, and unity of Lebanon and the reconciliation of the Lebanese, does not allow any action which threatens the Lebanese security, independence, or sovereignty.

SOURCE: Foreign Broadcast Information Service, Near East and South Asia, October 24, 1989, pp. NES 1–6.

Israeli Withdrawal from Lebanon

DOCUMENT IN CONTEXT

In May 2000, twenty-two years after launching its first invasion of Lebanon and establishing a "security zone" in the south of that country, Israel finally withdrew its military forces. Israel's occupation of parts of Lebanon had brought short-term peace to the residents of northern Israel, but at the cost of hardening anti-Israel sentiment in what had been a relatively moderate Arab state.

Israel had invaded Lebanon twice: in March 1978 to clear a zone north of its border to prevent Palestinian guerrillas from launching artillery and rocket attacks across the border into northern Israel, and again in June 1982 for the same purpose as well as to broaden its assault on the guerrillas. During the 1978 invasion, Israel established a six-mile-deep zone inside Lebanon along the border, using its military power to eject Palestinian fighters from the border area. Despite a demand by the UN Security Council, in Resolution 425 adopted in March 1978, that it withdraw completely from Lebanon, Israel maintained the zone and then temporarily expanded it to a depth of twenty-five miles during the 1982 invasion. The latter invasion resulted in the forced evacuation of Palestinian leaders and most of their fighters from Lebanon, but it also allowed Syria to tighten its grip on most of Lebanon (Israeli Invasion of Lebanon, pp. 334–337).

Israel had delegated to the South Lebanon Army (SLA), a proxy militia primarily of Christian and Druze fighters, most of the work of patrolling the border area inside Lebanon. Israeli troops manned the key positions in southern Lebanon, and Israel retained overall control of the territory. Through the rest of the 1980s and into the 1990s, Israel's occupation of southern Lebanon became increasingly unpopular in both countries. In Lebanon, the Israeli presence fueled support among Shiite Muslims for the Iranian-backed Hizballah (Party of God), created in response to the 1982 invasion to fight the Israelis. Many Israelis referred to Lebanon as their "Vietnam," using words such as "quagmire" to describe how their country had become bogged down in the long-term occupation of a neighboring state.

In a successful campaign for Israeli prime minister in May 1999, retired general Ehud Barak pledged to pull Israeli troops from Lebanon within a year. Once in office, Barak first turned his attention to negotiating a peace agreement with Syria, reportedly hoping that such an accord would lead Damascus to act as a stabilizing force in southern Lebanon.

As the final stages of Israeli-Syrian negotiations got under way, Barak asked and won his cabinet's approval, on March 5, 2000, to withdraw from Lebanon. The withdrawal was to be completed by that July, and the Israelis hoped that it would be carried out "in the framework of an agreement" with Syria. Three weeks later, however, all prospects of an agreement collapsed when Syrian president Hafiz al-Assad rejected as inadequate Barak's offer on the central issue dividing the two countries: the scope of Israel's withdrawal from the Golan Heights, the strategic plateau Israel had captured from Syria in 1967. Barak wanted Israel to retain control of the shores of the Sea of Galilee, while Assad insisted on the return of all territory he regarded as belonging to Syria.

When it became clear that the withdrawal would be unilateral, Israel began shifting more responsibility to the SLA. Israel also asked the United Nations to beef up its peacekeeping force—the United Nations Interim Force in Lebanon (UNIFIL)—which had been monitoring the situation in southern Lebanon since 1978. UN member countries, however, refused to provide more troops for a mission that would likely bring peacekeepers into conflict with Hizballah.

Israel's plans for an orderly withdrawal began to fall apart on May 21, when several hundred Lebanese civilians surged into the security zone. In the next two days, thousands more civilians, in some cases accompanied by Hizballah guerrillas, moved into the area. The SLA fell away, and thousands of its troops and their family members crossed the border into Israel along with the Israeli army. By May 24, the last Israeli soldiers had withdrawn from Lebanon, weeks earlier than had been planned. Hizballah leaders immediately proclaimed a great "victory" over Israel, asserting that Israel had retreated from Lebanon because of its long-running military operations.

To determine Israeli compliance with UN Security Council Resolution 425 of 1978 demanding its withdrawal from Lebanon, Secretary-General Kofi Annan sent a delegation headed by his special Middle East envoy, Terje Roed-Larsen. UN officials determined that no Israeli soldiers remained in Lebanon, and they mapped out a "blue line" to serve as a temporary border between Israel and Lebanon. In part because the two countries had never reached a peace agreement following the 1948 Arab-Israeli war, the exact border remained unclear, and the two sides disputed several locations.

The most serious dispute concerned the status of the Shabaa Farms, a small, agricultural area at the intersection of Israel, Lebanon, and Syria. Israel had held most of this area since June 1967, when it captured the neighboring Golan Heights from Syria. Lebanon claimed Shabaa Farms, but Israel insisted that the land belonged to Syria and stated that it would not return it until reaching a peace agreement with Syria resolving the fate of the Golan Heights. This dispute's significance stretched beyond the demarcations on a map, as Hizballah made known that it would retain its militia, and the option to strike against Israel, as long as Israel occupied any Lebanese territory (Map, p. 330).

Despite these lingering border disputes, Roed-Larsen reported to Annan on June 7 that Israel had withdrawn from Lebanon, and Annan officially informed the Security Council on June 16. Speaking to reporters after meeting with the council, Annan said, "This is a happy day for Lebanon—but also for Israel. It is a day of hope for the Middle East as a whole, and it is a day of pride for the United Nations" because its resolutions finally had been respected.

Five years later, Syria—the other occupying power in Lebanon—would withdraw its army and intelligence services under international pressure. Any hope that the removal of foreign forces would end Lebanon's painful agony was short-lived, however, as a cross-border raid by Hizballah in July 2006 led to a month-long war that destroyed much of what had been rebuilt in Lebanon since the civil war ended in 1990 (Lebanese Civil War, p. 331; Syrian Withdrawal from Lebanon, p. 359; Hizballah-Israeli War, p. 365).

Following are three documents relating to Israel's withdrawal from Lebanon in 2000: the text of the resolution adopted by the Israeli cabinet on March 5, 2000, approving the withdrawal of forces; an excerpt from the report on the withdrawal to the UN Security Council by Secretary-General Kofi Annan on June 16, 2000; the text of Annan's statement to the media following his meeting with the Security Council on June 16, 2000, informing it of a complete Israeli withdrawal.

DOCUMENT

Israeli and Cabinet Approval of Israel's Withdrawal from Lebanon

MARCH 5, 2000

In accordance with the government's commitment on the basis of its guidelines and the announcement by the Prime Minister and Minister of Defense:

    a. The Israel Defense Forces will deploy on the border with Lebanon by July 2000, and from there will secure the safety of the northern towns and villages.

    b. The government will act to ensure that this deployment will be carried out in the framework of an agreement.

    c. In the event that conditions will not be conducive to IDF deployment in the framework of an agreement, the government will convene, at an appropriate time, to discuss the method of implementation of the above-mentioned decision.

    d. Israel will honor its commitment toward the South Lebanese Army and the civil aid forces in Southern Lebanon.

    e. The government will act to strengthen the frontline towns and villages in both the security and the socio-economic aspects.

SOURCE: Israel Ministry of Foreign Affairs, www.mfa.gov.il/MFA/Foreign%20Relations/Israels%20Foreign %20Relations%20since%201947/1999-2001/94%20Government%20Resolution%20regarding%20the %20redeploymen.

DOCUMENT

UN Secretary-General's Report on Security Council Resolutions 425 (1978) and 426 (1978)

JUNE 16, 2000

. . . Conclusion

37. Israel has met the requirements for the implementation of Security Council resolution 425 (1978) as set forth in my report to the [Security] Council of 22 May 2000. Namely, Israel has completed its withdrawal in conformity with the line identified by the United Nations, SLA [South Lebanon Army] has been dismantled; accordingly

there are no more supply lines; its heavy weapons have been removed or destroyed by Israel or are now in the hands of the Government of Lebanon; and there are no more detainees at Al-Khiam prison.

38. The Government of Lebanon cooperated with the United Nations in the implementation of the report of 22 May and has moved quickly to re-establish its effective authority in the area through the deployment of security forces in the area. On 12 June, the Government informed the United Nations that it would send a composite force composed of army and internal security personnel to be based in Marjayoun. Although the Government has not yet deployed the armed forces throughout southern Lebanon, it has stated that it will consider doing so as soon as I have confirmed Israel's withdrawal in compliance with Security Council resolution 425 (1978) and my report of 22 May 2000.

39. The Government of the Syrian Arab Republic was very cooperative throughout the latest mission of my Special Envoy, as were other interested Member States in the region and elsewhere.

40. On the basis of these developments, I can report to the Security Council that Israel has withdrawn its forces from Lebanon in accordance with resolution 425 (1978) and met the requirements defined in my report of 22 May 2000.

SOURCE: United Nations Information System on the Question of Palestine, http://domino.un.org/unispal.nsf/ 9a798adbf322aff38525617b006d88d7/736411af9bc6369585256903004f90c1!OpenDocument.

DOCUMENT

UN Secretary-General's Press Statement on the Israeli Withdrawal from Lebanon

JUNE 16, 2000

I am delighted to tell you that the United Nations force in Lebanon today reported to me that Israel has withdrawn from the country in full compliance with Security Council resolution 425 (1978). I have just conveyed this information to the Security Council.

The people of Lebanon have waited more than 22 years for this moment. We must all admire the fortitude with which they have borne this long ordeal. This is a happy day for Lebanon—but also for Israel. It is a day of hope for the Middle East as a whole, and it is a day of pride for the United Nations. It shows that United Nations resolutions, when fully implemented by all parties working together, can be the building blocks of peace. Lebanon is now closer to peace than it has been in decades.

The main task of UNIFIL will be to help the Lebanese Government and armed forces assume their responsibilities along the border and throughout the area from which Israel has withdrawn. I trust the international community will also be quick to assist Lebanon with the task of reconstructing the economy in the south, and rebuilding its links with the rest of the country. This will help move the whole country to peace and stability.

I also hope that the implementation of Security Council resolution 425 (1978) will be seen by all the peoples in the region, especially Syrians, Palestinians and Israelis, as well as Lebanese, as an encouragement to move ahead faster in negotiating peace treaties based on earlier Security Council resolutions 242 (1967) and 338 (1973).

Those resolutions, enshrining the formula of land for peace, form the bedrock on which the 1991 Madrid formula for achieving a just, lasting and comprehensive peace in the Middle East was built. I, myself, shall be leaving immediately after this press conference for the region to meet the leaders there and to see what the United Nations can do to consolidate and build on today's achievement.

Finally, let me thank the leaders of Lebanon, Israel and Syria—here I am referring to President [Emile] Lahoud, Prime Minister [Ehud] Barak and, of course, the late President Hafez Al-Assad—for the cooperation they have extended to the United Nations in the past few weeks.

I would also like to thank the Governments of Egypt, Iran, Jordan and Saudi Arabia for their support, as well as members of the Security Council and, last but not least, my own special envoy, Terje Roed-Larsen, for all they have done to make this day possible.

This is not the end of the long road towards peace in the region, but I hope it will be seen as the beginning of the end.

SOURCE: United Nations Information System on the Question of Palestine, http://domino.un.org/unispal.nsf/ 9a798adbf322aff38525617b006d88d7/d04f161eae550bdd85256903004ec856!OpenDocument.

Syrian Withdrawal from Lebanon

DOCUMENT IN CONTEXT

Intense international pressure and massive protests in Lebanon following the assassination of a former prime minister forced Syria to withdraw its army and legions of intelligence agents from Lebanon in 2005. Syria had first occupied much of Lebanon in 1976 and for years afterward had seemed prepared to stay indefinitely. Lebanon had been part of Syria during the centuries of rule by the Ottoman Empire, a history that constituted part of the Syrian government's justification for its continuing role there (Lebanese Civil War, p. 331).

Syria's occupation of Lebanon did not rise to major international concern until 2003–2005, when a series of events focused attention on it. One event was the U.S. overthrow of Iraqi president Saddam Hussein in 2003. By 2004 the administration of President George W. Bush was threatening sanctions and even military action against

Syria because of its alleged aid to Hussein loyalists and others battling the U.S. occupation of Iraq. Another event was Syria's decision during summer 2004 to press the Lebanese parliament for a three-year extension of the term of President Emile Lahoud, widely viewed as pro-Syrian. Prime Minister Rafiq Hariri initially opposed the extension, which would require amendment of the constitution's mandate of a single, six-year presidential term. Hariri backed down, however, after an August 27 meeting in Damascus with the head of the Syrian intelligence service (The Iraq War, p. 504).

Seeking to somehow head off the reappointment of Lahoud, the United States and France decided in late August to press for adoption of a long-discussed UN Security Council resolution demanding Syrian withdrawal from Lebanon. The Security Council adopted Resolution 1559 on September 2, 2004, but with the bare minimum of support: nine members voted for it, and six abstained, including China and Russia, two of the council's permanent members with veto power. The resolution called for the withdrawal of "all remaining foreign forces," a clear reference to Syria, which according to UN secretary-general Kofi Annan was the only country with armed forces—14,000, according to his estimate—in Lebanon. The resolution also demanded international respect for the sovereignty and "political independence" of Lebanon and called for the disarming of all militias there, a reference primarily to the armed wing of the Shiite organization Hizballah (Party of God).

This unusual attempt by the Security Council to influence the political process in a member country failed to accomplish its goal. The next day, September 3, the Lebanese parliament voted overwhelmingly to amend the constitution to allow Lahoud to serve three additional years. Hariri and his parliamentary supporters voted for the amendment, and then he and his entire cabinet resigned on October 20, citing differences with Damascus among the reasons. It was speculated that Hariri would contest the next parliamentary elections, in May 2005, and if successful use a popular mandate to challenge Syrian hegemony. On February 14, 2005, however, a massive bomb exploded as Hariri passed through central Beirut in a motorcade. The dead included Hariri, six bodyguards, and fourteen others, including bystanders. Another 200 people were injured.

For more than a decade, Hariri, a billionaire contractor, had been the only Lebanese political figure who had seemed capable of dragging the country out of its violent, sectarian-driven past. The bomb that killed him ignited an explosion of domestic and international protests. The burial of Hariri on February 16 sparked a series of public demonstrations over the next month, most of them aimed against Syria, which was widely assumed to have sponsored, if not directly carried out, the assassination. Hizballah, which received support from Syria and Iran, countered these protests by organizing explicitly pro-Syrian rallies. The largest single protest took place on March 14, when nearly 1 million people gathered in central Beirut to denounce Syria. One of Hariri's sons, Saad, later created the March 14 Coalition, an anti-Syrian political alliance named after that event.

In February 15, the UN Security Council again demanded that Syrian forces leave Lebanon. In addition, international pressure came down on Syria from other Arab countries, notably Saudi Arabia, which early in March bluntly rejected Syrian president Bashar al-Assad's request for support. Assad then began signaling a willingness to withdraw from Lebanon on a vague timetable. This prompted new international pressure for an immediate withdrawal, resulting in more specific pledges by Assad. On March 16, Syrian intelligence closed its Beirut seafront office, which Lebanese long had considered their country's de facto government. During the remainder of March, and well into April, convoys of trucks took Syrian soldiers and equipment eastward across the Lebanon-Syria border. On April 26, Syria reported to the United Nations that it had completed its withdrawal from Lebanon of all military and intelligence units.

The Security Council issued a statement on May 4 praising the "significant and noticeable progress" toward compliance with Resolution 1559 while awaiting confirmation from UN officials on the ground of an actual withdrawal. The council also renewed its call for the disarming of all militias in Lebanon, the other step demanded by Resolution 1559. On May 23, Annan reported that UN observers had verified that Syria had indeed withdrawn all its military and intelligence forces from Lebanon, "and so, in principle, Lebanon should be free of all foreign forces today."

The Lebanese then held parliamentary elections—the first in more than three decades not overshadowed by civil war or military occupation by neighboring countries. The elections took place on four successive Sundays beginning on May 29, rotating around areas of the country. Among the more noteworthy participants was Hizballah. The Shiite organization had for several years been reconstituting itself as a political party and social service agency. Also of note was the faction of Maronite Christians headed by Michel Aoun, a former army commander who had declared himself president in 1988 and then fled to France after Syria moved against him. In one of the many odd twists of Lebanese politics, Aoun made a dramatic return to Lebanon early in May and aligned himself with parties that supported Syria, his former enemy.

Voters gave a majority of 72 seats in the 128-member parliament to the March 14 Coalition of parties headed by Saad Hariri that had united principally around the demand for Syrian withdrawal. Even so, the elections demonstrated that Lebanese voters still clung to the sectarian lines that had always defined the country's politics. One of the most notable such results was in southern Lebanon—dominated by Shiite Muslims—where Hizballah and the long-standing Shiite party Amal captured 23 seats. Their showing gave the Shiite parties an effective veto over major government actions requiring a two-thirds majority. After weeks of intense jockeying for power, Fouad Siniora, a banker who had served as Rafiq Hariri's finance minister, emerged as the new prime minister, with five representatives from Hizballah and Amal serving in his cabinet. Amal leader Nabih Berri remained Speaker of parliament, a post he had held since 1992.

Despite Lebanon's successful elections, violence remained a potent force in Lebanese public life. During 2005, car bombs took the lives of three other leading anti-Syrian figures: Samir Kassir and Gibran Tueni, columnists for the influential al-Nahar, and George Hawi, the former head of Lebanon's Communist Party. Tueni was killed on December 12, the same day that Detlev Mehlis, a UN-appointed German investigator, submitted the second of two reports to Secretary-General Annan strongly implying that top-level Syrian officials had ordered the assassination of Rafiq Hariri. Hizballah later blocked an attempt by the United Nations to obtain the Lebanese government's official cooperation for prosecution of those responsible for Hariri's murder. More violence visited Lebanon in 2006, when a Hizballah attack on an Israeli military post sparked a month-long war and another leading anti-Syrian figure, Pierre Gemayal, namesake and grandson of the long-time Phalange leader, was assassinated (Hizballah-Israeli War, pp. 365–368).

Following are the text of UN Security Council Resolution 1559, adopted on September 2, 2004, demanding the withdrawal of Syrian intelligence and military forces from Lebanon, along with the disarmament of all militias in that country, and a statement by the president of the Security Council on May 4, 2005, following the Syrian withdrawal from Lebanon.

DOCUMENT

UN Security Council Resolution 1559 (2004)

SEPTEMBER 2, 2004

The Security Council,

Recalling all its previous resolutions on Lebanon, in particular resolutions 425 (1978) and 426 (1978) of 19 March 1978, resolution 520 (1982) of 17 September 1982, and resolution 1553 (2004) of 29 July 2004 as well as the statements of its President on the situation in Lebanon, in particular the statement of 18 June 2000,

Reiterating its strong support for the territorial integrity, sovereignty and political independence of Lebanon within its internationally recognized borders,

Noting the determination of Lebanon to ensure the withdrawal of all non-Lebanese forces from Lebanon,

Gravely concerned at the continued presence of armed militias in Lebanon, which prevent the Lebanese Government from exercising its full sovereignty over all Lebanese territory,

Reaffirming the importance of the extension of the control of the Government of Lebanon over all Lebanese territory,

Mindful of the upcoming Lebanese presidential elections and *underlining* the importance of free and fair elections according to Lebanese constitutional rules devised without foreign interference or influence,

1. *Reaffirms* its call for the strict respect of the sovereignty, territorial integrity, unity, and political independence of Lebanon under the sole and exclusive authority of the Government of Lebanon throughout Lebanon;
2. *Calls upon* all remaining foreign forces to withdraw from Lebanon;
3. *Calls for* the disbanding and disarmament of all Lebanese and non-Lebanese militias;
4. *Supports* the extension of the control of the Government of Lebanon over all Lebanese territory;
5. *Declares* its support for a free and fair electoral process in Lebanon's upcoming presidential election conducted according to Lebanese constitutional rules devised without foreign interference or influence;

6. *Calls upon* all parties concerned to cooperate fully and urgently with the Security Council for the full implementation of this and all relevant resolutions concerning the restoration of the territorial integrity, full sovereignty, and political independence of Lebanon;

7. *Requests* that the Secretary-General report to the Security Council within thirty days on the implementation by the parties of this resolution and *decides* to remain actively seized of the matter.

SOURCE: United Nations, http://www.un.org/Docs/sc/unsc_resolutions04.html

DOCUMENT

Statement by the UN Security Council on Syrian Withdrawal from Lebanon

MAY 4, 2005

At the 5175th meeting of the Security Council, held on 4 May 2005, in connection with the Council's consideration of the item entitled "The situation in the Middle East," the President of the Security Council made the following statement on behalf of the Council:

"The Security Council recalls all its previous resolutions on Lebanon, in particular resolutions 1559 (2004), 425 (1978) and 426 (1978), resolution 520 (1982) and resolution 1583 (2005) of 28 January 2005 as well as the statements of its President on the situation in Lebanon, in particular the statement of 18 June 2000 (S/PRST/2000/21) and of 19 October 2004 (S/PRST/2004/36).

"The Security Council reiterates its strong support for the territorial integrity, sovereignty and political independence of Lebanon within its internationally recognized borders and under the sole and exclusive authority of the Government of Lebanon.

"The Security Council welcomes the First semi-annual Report of the Secretary-General to the Security Council of 26 April 2005 (S/2005/272) on the implementation of Security Council resolution 1559 (2004).

"The Security Council welcomes also that the parties concerned have made significant and noticeable progress towards implementing some of the provisions contained in resolution 1559 (2004), while expressing concern at the determination of the Secretary-General that there has been no progress on the implementation of other provisions of the resolution, in particular the disarmament of Lebanese and non-Lebanese militia and the extension of the control of the Government of Lebanon over all Lebanese territory, and that the requirements of the resolution have not yet been met.

"The Security Council reiterates its call for the full implementation of all requirements of resolution 1559 (2004), and calls upon all concerned parties to cooperate fully with the Security Council and the Secretary-General to achieve this goal.

"The Security Council acknowledges the letter of 26 April 2005 from the Minister for Foreign Affairs of the Syrian Arab Republic to the Secretary-General stating that Syria has completed the full withdrawal of its forces, military assets and the intelligence apparatus from Lebanon.

"The Security Council calls upon the Government of Syria and the Government of Lebanon to extend their full cooperation to the United Nations verification team dispatched by the Secretary-General with their agreement to verify whether there has been full and complete withdrawal, and looks forward to his report.

"The Security Council acknowledges that the full and complete Syrian withdrawal would represent a significant and important step towards Lebanon's full political independence and full exercise of its sovereignty that is the ultimate goal of resolution 1559 (2004), thus opening a new chapter in Lebanese history.

"The Security Council welcomes the deployment of Lebanese Armed Forces to positions vacated by Syrian forces and the Government of Lebanon's assumption of responsibility for these areas and calls for the deployment of additional Lebanese Armed Forces throughout the south of the country.

"The Security Council urges all concerned parties to do their utmost to safeguard Lebanon's stability and national unity and underlines the importance of national dialogue among all Lebanese political forces in this regard.

"The Security Council commends the Lebanese people for the dignified manner in which they have expressed their views and for their commitment to a peaceful and democratic process, and stresses that the Lebanese people must be allowed to decide the future of their country free of violence and intimidation. It condemns in this context the recent terrorist acts in Lebanon that have resulted in several deaths and injuries, and calls for their perpetrators to be brought to justice.

"The Security Council welcomes the decision of the Lebanese Government to conduct elections beginning on 29 May 2005, and underlines the importance that such elections be held according to schedule. The Security Council shares the opinion of the Secretary-General that a delay in holding the parliamentary elections would contribute to exacerbating further the political divisions in Lebanon and threaten the security, stability and prosperity of the country. The Council underlines that free and credible elections held without foreign interference or influence would be another central indication of the political independence and sovereignty of Lebanon.

"The Security Council encourages the Secretary-General and the Lebanese Government to reach arrangements for international assistance, including United Nations assistance, to ensure that such elections are conducted in a free and credible manner, in particular through inviting international governmental and/or non-governmental electoral observers to monitor the electoral process. The Council urges Member States to extend assistance accordingly.

"The Security Council commends the Secretary-General and his Special Envoy for their relentless efforts and dedication to facilitate and assist the parties in the implementation of all provisions of resolution 1559 (2004), and requests that they continue their work in this regard.

"The Security Council shares the view that the full implementation of resolution 1559 (2004) would contribute positively to the situation in the Middle East in general."

SOURCE: United Nations Information System on the Question of Palestine, http://unispal.un.org/unispal.nsf/ 9a798adbf322aff38525617b006d88d7/ee059592a598f41285256ff80051dacc!OpenDocument.

The Hizballah-Israeli War

DOCUMENT IN CONTEXT

A relatively minor incident along the Israel-Lebanon border in July 2006 developed into a month-long war causing severe damage in Lebanon, undermining the political leaderships of Israel and Lebanon, and eroding the already sagging prestige of the United States in the Middle East. The self-proclaimed winner, the Islamist group Hizballah, provoked the war and scored at least a partial victory by not losing against the overwhelming military force of Israel.

The war began on July 12, when Hizballah launched rockets into Israel and in a cross-border raid captured two Israeli soldiers and took them back into Lebanon. Eight other Israeli soldiers were killed in subsequent skirmishes that day. Hizballah had planned to use the captured soldiers as bargaining chips to bolster its demand that Israel release several Lebanese prisoners, some of them Hizballah members. Calling the attack an "act of war," Israel responded not with bargaining but with a military assault of aerial bombing runs and artillery strikes against Hizballah military positions in southern Lebanon and, eventually, its command post and other targets in the Beirut suburbs. Although Israel insisted that it was attacking only military or "terrorist" targets, thousands of bombs landed in civilian areas, destroying houses and apartment buildings and killing noncombatants. The United Nations estimated that, within one week, about 400,000 people had been left homeless or had fled their homes to avoid the bombardments. Also according to the United Nations, by the time the war ended three weeks later, about 900,000 people, one-fourth of Lebanon's population, had fled their homes at least temporarily.

Israel relied initially almost entirely on aerial bombing and artillery strikes to achieve its stated goal of destroying Hizballah's military infrastructure in Lebanon. Hizballah responded with flurries of rocket attacks against cities and towns in northern Israel. Some of the rockets reached as far as Haifa, a coastal city twenty-five miles south of the border. Several dozen Israeli civilians died in the attacks, and thousands of Israelis spent much of the war in underground bomb shelters. Israel launched a large-scale ground invasion of Lebanon on August 2, after its aerial campaign had failed to halt the Hizballah rocket launches—which at times exceeded 200 a day—much less destroy Hizballah militarily.

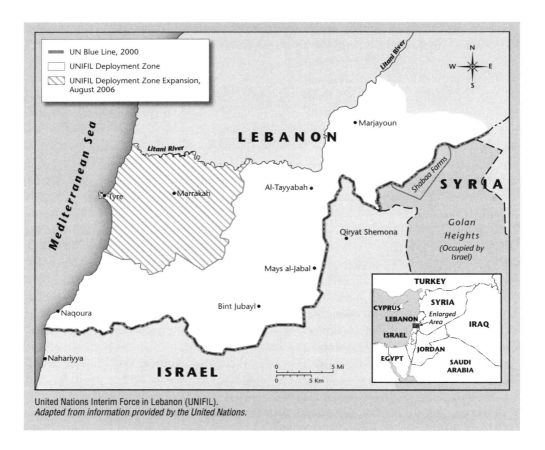

United Nations Interim Force in Lebanon (UNIFIL).
Adapted from information provided by the United Nations.

The war appeared to catch everyone off guard. Hizballah leader Hassan Nasrallah later said he would not have authorized the cross-border raid if he had known how Israel would respond. A subsequent investigation by an Israeli commission found that the government was ill-prepared for such a war and had rushed into decision making. Outside powers—notably the United States—also were caught unaware. Washington struggled to find the right approach. For more than two weeks, the administration of President George W. Bush blocked moves at the United Nations to impose a cease-fire, saying that only a "sustainable" cease-fire would really end the fighting. Many in the Middle East and elsewhere interpreted this position as a "green light" for Israel to continue its bombardment of Lebanon. On July 21, at the height of the fighting, U.S. secretary of state Condoleezza Rice described the situation in Lebanon as the "birth pangs of a new Middle East," a comment that many Arabs felt reflected a cynical, one-sided U.S. policy favoring Israel. U.S. officials also joined Israel in rejecting widespread international criticism that Israel's attacks in Lebanon were "disproportionate" to the original Hizballah provocation.

The Lebanese government was powerless to intervene. Its army had no air force to defend Lebanese territory, nor did it have any soldiers in the southern part of the country, which Hizballah's militia essentially controlled. Frantic to halt the bombing, on July 26 the government of Prime Minister Fouad Siniora articulated a seven-point plan centering around a cease-fire and an expansion of the United Nations Interim Force in

Lebanon (UNIFIL), the small peacekeeping force that had been in place since 1978. These points eventually became the basis of UN negotiations to end the conflict.

After several inconclusive attempts to bring about a cease-fire, the United States and France agreed on the essence of a resolution on August 5, but objections from Lebanon and other Arab nations held up final agreement on language until August 11. Adopted unanimously by the Security Council, Resolution 1701 called for a "full cessation of hostilities" by all sides in Lebanon. Although welcoming the resolution, Secretary-General Kofi Annan expressed frustration at the lengthy diplomacy, telling the council that its "inability to act sooner has badly shaken the world's faith in its authority and integrity."

The heart of the resolution consisted of a plan for the rapid expansion of UNIFIL, at the time comprised of a staff of about 2,000 monitors and over the years unable to prevent any of the numerous outbreaks of hostilities in Lebanon. Resolution 1701 called for a new force, subsequently named UNIFIL II, with 15,000 troops and a mandate to enforce peace in southern Lebanon. Meanwhile, Lebanon's army would station an equivalent number of troops in the region. Between them, these two forces were to fill the security vacuum that Hizballah had claimed necessitated its armed presence.

The UN-mandated cease-fire went into effect, and the fighting finally ended, early on August 14, which meant the war lasted either 33 or 34 days, depending on which days are counted. The Lebanese government announced that 1,191 people, most of them civilians, had been killed. Hizballah acknowledged the loss of 200 of its fighters, although Israel insisted that it had killed more than 500 Hizballah members. Government and UN figures also tallied some 15,000 homes and 900 commercial buildings as being destroyed. On the Israeli side, the government announced a death toll of 116 soldiers and 43 civilians. Few buildings in Israel were destroyed, but the Israeli economy suffered serious damage.

In late August, the Lebanese Army began moving into the area south of the Litani River as part of the mandate under Resolution 1701 for the Beirut government to establish its authority over all of Lebanon's territory. The army had not had a presence in the south for decades. Members of the new UN force began arriving in mid-September and by the end of October had about half of its 15,000-man contingent in place. Although Resolution 1701 called for the disarmament of all "armed groups" in Lebanon other than the official army, it became clear that neither the Lebanese Army nor the new UN force would force Hizballah to give up its weapons. Even so, the presence of the army and UNIFIL II had the potential to weaken Hizballah's military grip on the region, at least for a while.

During the conflict, respected voices in Israel had already begun bemoaning the results. The liberal *Ha'aretz,* in an August 9 editorial, characterized the war as "a stinging defeat" for Israel and demanded that the country's political leaders be held accountable. Returning soldiers told stories of bungled military operations and surprising shortages of such necessities as fuel and water, a deeply embarrassing situation for a country proud of having the most powerful and efficient military in the Middle East. The government of Prime Minister Ehud Olmert, which had won elections in March, promised an official inquiry into management of the war, but refused to name a completely independent investigation as had been done on some occasions.

The government's management of the war raised serious questions about Olmert's leadership that were echoed when the official inquiry, headed by former High Court justice Eliyahu Winograd, submitted its preliminary report on April 30, 2007. The report faulted Olmert, Defense Minister Amir Peretz, and the military chief of staff,

Lt. Gen. Dan Halutz, for "very serious failings" in prosecuting the war. Halutz resigned shortly after the war, and Peretz was forced from office in June 2007. Olmert survived in office as of mid-2007, but his political career appeared to be damaged beyond repair.

In Lebanon, Hizballah moved quickly on two fronts to blunt criticism that it had rashly provoked a war and brought destruction upon Lebanon. As early as August 18, Hizballah operatives began handing out cash payments of more than $10,000 each to Beirut residents whose apartments had been destroyed by Israeli bombing. The money reportedly came from Iran, Hizballah's prime backer. Hizballah leader Nasrallah, in a speech to a crowd of several hundred thousand people in Beirut on September 22, declared that his group had won a "divine victory" over Israel. Two months later, Nasrallah stepped up pressure on the still-weak Lebanese government: the five Shiite cabinet ministers and a Christian ally withdrew from the government, after which Nasrallah demanded elections for a new "national unity" government that would give Hizballah an effective veto power. Prime Minister Siniora rejected the demand. In December, Hizballah began the first of a promised series of escalating public protests and demonstrations that continued into 2007 and further undermined the Siniora government's already eroded authority. Thus, despite agreement on a UN settlement intended to strengthen the Lebanese central government, the prospects for long-term success appeared little better than previous UN efforts to bring stability to Lebanon.

Following is the text of UN Security Council Resolution 1701, adopted on August 11, 2006.

DOCUMENT

UN Security Council Resolution 1701 (2006)

AUGUST 11, 2006

The Security Council,

Recalling all its previous resolutions on Lebanon, in particular resolutions 425 (1978), 426 (1978), 520 (1982), 1559 (2004), 1655 (2006), 1680 (2006) and 1697 (2006), as well as the statements of its President on the situation in Lebanon, in particular the statements of 18 June 2000 (S/PRST/2000/21), of 19 October 2004 (S/PRST/2004/36), of 4 May 2005 (S/PRST/2005/17), of 23 January 2006 (S/PRST/2006/3) and of 30 July 2006 (S/PRST/2006/35),

Expressing its utmost concern at the continuing escalation of hostilities in Lebanon and in Israel since Hizbollah's attack on Israel on 12 July 2006, which has already caused hundreds of deaths and injuries on both sides, extensive damage to civilian infrastructure and hundreds of thousands of internally displaced persons,

Emphasizing the need for an end of violence, but at the same time *emphasizing* the need to address urgently the causes that have given rise to the current crisis, including by the unconditional release of the abducted Israeli soldiers,

Mindful of the sensitivity of the issue of prisoners and *encouraging* the efforts aimed at urgently settling the issue of the Lebanese prisoners detained in Israel,

Welcoming the efforts of the Lebanese Prime Minister and the commitment of the Government of Lebanon, in its seven-point plan, to extend its authority over its territory, through its own legitimate armed forces, such that there will be no weapons without the consent of the Government of Lebanon and no authority other than that of the Government of Lebanon, *welcoming also* its commitment to a United Nations force that is supplemented and enhanced in numbers, equipment, mandate and scope of operation, and *bearing in mind* its request in this plan for an immediate withdrawal of the Israeli forces from southern Lebanon,

Determined to act for this withdrawal to happen at the earliest,

Taking due note of the proposals made in the seven-point plan regarding the Shebaa farms area,

Welcoming the unanimous decision by the Government of Lebanon on 7 August 2006 to deploy a Lebanese armed force of 15,000 troops in South Lebanon as the Israeli army withdraws behind the Blue Line [the interim border between Israel and Lebanon, as demarcated by the UN in 2000] and to request the assistance of additional forces from the United Nations Interim Force in Lebanon (UNIFIL) as needed, to facilitate the entry of the Lebanese armed forces into the region and to restate its intention to strengthen the Lebanese armed forces with material as needed to enable it to perform its duties,

Aware of its responsibilities to help secure a permanent ceasefire and a longterm solution to the conflict,

Determining that the situation in Lebanon constitutes a threat to international peace and security,

1. *Calls for* a full cessation of hostilities based upon, in particular, the immediate cessation by Hizbollah of all attacks and the immediate cessation by Israel of all offensive military operations;

2. Upon full cessation of hostilities, *calls upon* the Government of Lebanon and UNIFIL as authorized by paragraph 11 to deploy their forces together throughout the South and *calls upon* the Government of Israel, as that deployment begins, to withdraw all of its forces from southern Lebanon in parallel;

3. *Emphasizes* the importance of the extension of the control of the Government of Lebanon over all Lebanese territory in accordance with the provisions of resolution 1559 (2004) and resolution 1680 (2006), and of the relevant provisions of the Taif Accords, for it to exercise its full sovereignty, so that there will be no weapons without the consent of the Government of Lebanon and no authority other than that of the Government of Lebanon;

4. *Reiterates* its strong support for full respect for the Blue Line;

5. *Also reiterates* its strong support, as recalled in all its previous relevant resolutions, for the territorial integrity, sovereignty and political independence of Lebanon within its internationally recognized borders, as contemplated by the Israeli-Lebanese General Armistice Agreement of 23 March 1949;

6. *Calls on* the international community to take immediate steps to extend its financial and humanitarian assistance to the Lebanese people, including through facilitating the safe return of displaced persons and, under the authority of the Government of Lebanon, reopening airports and harbours, consistent with paragraphs 14 and

15, and *calls on* it also to consider further assistance in the future to contribute to the reconstruction and development of Lebanon;

7. *Affirms* that all parties are responsible for ensuring that no action is taken contrary to paragraph 1 that might adversely affect the search for a long-term solution, humanitarian access to civilian populations, including safe passage for humanitarian convoys, or the voluntary and safe return of displaced persons, and *calls on* all parties to comply with this responsibility and to cooperate with the Security Council;

8. *Calls for* Israel and Lebanon to support a permanent ceasefire and a long-term solution based on the following principles and elements:

—full respect for the Blue Line by both parties;

—security arrangements to prevent the resumption of hostilities, including the establishment between the Blue Line and the Litani river of an area free of any armed personnel, assets and weapons other than those of the Government of Lebanon and of UNIFIL as authorized in paragraph 11, deployed in this area;

—full implementation of the relevant provisions of the Taif Accords, and of resolutions 1559 (2004) and 1680 (2006), that require the disarmament of all armed groups in Lebanon, so that, pursuant to the Lebanese cabinet decision of 27 July 2006, there will be no weapons or authority in Lebanon other than that of the Lebanese State;

—no foreign forces in Lebanon without the consent of its Government;

—no sales or supply of arms and related materiel to Lebanon except as authorized by its Government;

—provision to the United Nations of all remaining maps of landmines in Lebanon in Israel's possession;

9. *Invites* the Secretary-General to support efforts to secure as soon as possible agreements in principle from the Government of Lebanon and the Government of Israel to the principles and elements for a long-term solution as set forth in paragraph 8, and *expresses* its intention to be actively involved;

10. *Requests* the Secretary-General to develop, in liaison with relevant international actors and the concerned parties, proposals to implement the relevant provisions of the Taif Accords, and resolutions 1559 (2004) and 1680 (2006), including disarmament, and for delineation of the international borders of Lebanon, especially in those areas where the border is disputed or uncertain, including by dealing with the Shebaa farms area, and to present to the Security Council those proposals within thirty days;

11. *Decides,* in order to supplement and enhance the force in numbers, equipment, mandate and scope of operations, to authorize an increase in the force strength of UNIFIL to a maximum of 15,000 troops, and that the force shall, in addition to carrying out its mandate under resolutions 425 and 426 (1978):

(a) Monitor the cessation of hostilities;

(b) Accompany and support the Lebanese armed forces as they deploy throughout the South, including along the Blue Line, as Israel withdraws its armed forces from Lebanon as provided in paragraph 2;

(c) Coordinate its activities related to paragraph 11 (b) with the Government of Lebanon and the Government of Israel;

(d) Extend its assistance to help ensure humanitarian access to civilian populations and the voluntary and safe return of displaced persons;

(e) Assist the Lebanese armed forces in taking steps towards the establishment of the area as referred to in paragraph 8;

(f) Assist the Government of Lebanon, at its request, to implement paragraph 14;

12. Acting in support of a request from the Government of Lebanon to deploy an international force to assist it to exercise its authority throughout the territory, *authorizes* UNIFIL to take all necessary action in areas of deployment of its forces and as it deems within its capabilities, to ensure that its area of operations is not utilized for hostile activities of any kind, to resist attempts by forceful means to prevent it from discharging its duties under the mandate of the Security Council, and to protect United Nations personnel, facilities, installations and equipment, ensure the security and freedom of movement of United Nations personnel, humanitarian workers and, without prejudice to the responsibility of the Government of Lebanon, to protect civilians under imminent threat of physical violence;

13. *Requests* the Secretary-General urgently to put in place measures to ensure UNIFIL is able to carry out the functions envisaged in this resolution, *urges* Member States to consider making appropriate contributions to UNIFIL and to respond positively to requests for assistance from the Force, and *expresses* its strong appreciation to those who have contributed to UNIFIL in the past;

14. *Calls upon* the Government of Lebanon to secure its borders and other entry points to prevent the entry in Lebanon without its consent of arms or related materiel and *requests* UNIFIL as authorized in paragraph 11 to assist the Government of Lebanon at its request;

15. *Decides* further that all States shall take the necessary measures to prevent, by their nationals or from their territories or using their flag vessels or aircraft:

(a) The sale or supply to any entity or individual in Lebanon of arms and related materiel of all types, including weapons and ammunition, military vehicles and equipment, paramilitary equipment, and spare parts for the aforementioned, whether or not originating in their territories; and

(b) The provision to any entity or individual in Lebanon of any technical training or assistance related to the provision, manufacture, maintenance or use of the items listed in subparagraph (a) above; except that these prohibitions shall not apply to arms, related material, training or assistance authorized by the Government of Lebanon or by UNIFIL as authorized in paragraph 11;

16. *Decides* to extend the mandate of UNIFIL until 31 August 2007, and *expresses its intention* to consider in a later resolution further enhancements to the mandate and other steps to contribute to the implementation of a permanent ceasefire and a long-term solution;

17. *Requests* the Secretary-General to report to the Council within one week on the implementation of this resolution and subsequently on a regular basis;

18. *Stresses* the importance of, and the need to achieve, a comprehensive, just and lasting peace in the Middle East, based on all its relevant resolutions including its resolutions 242 (1967) of 22 November 1967, 338 (1973) of 22 October 1973 and 1515 (2003) of 19 November 2003;

19. *Decides* to remain actively seized of the matter.

SOURCE: United Nations, http://www.un.org/Docs/sc/unsc_resolutions06.htm

CHAPTER 5 DOCUMENTS

Overview

I n a region beset by almost constant turmoil over the past century, few Middle Eastern countries have faced as many dramatic changes as Iran. Whether in economics, politics, or social affairs, the Iran of the early twenty-first century bears little resemblance to the Persia of a century ago after experiencing domestic changes that also broadly affected the region as a whole. During much of the twentieth century, Iran often stood at the mercy of foreign powers. Since the Islamic revolution of 1978–1979, Iran has shaped or helped shape major events and trends in the region, charting its own course in the face of equally determined opposition by its neighbors and great powers halfway around the world.

The past influence of foreigners continues to be a major factor driving Iranian behavior. Contemporary political rhetoric in Iran focuses almost as much on the past, particularly past injustices allegedly foisted on Iran by outside powers, as on the important issues of the day. The resentment felt by many Iranians is compounded when it appears to them that policymakers in Western capitals, particularly in Washington, have a disdain or ignorance of that history.

The Pahlavi Dynasty

The contemporary history of Iran can be charted from the post–World War I years, when the long-running Qajar dynasty began to crumble at the hands of a strong leader who insisted on dragging Persia into the modern world. Reza Khan, an army colonel, gained substantial political and military power in Iran in 1921, and within five years had succeeded in pushing from power Ahmad Shah, the last Qajar ruler. Reza Khan took the title of shah for himself in 1925, establishing the Pahlavi family as a new dynasty that would rule Iran for nearly fifty-three years.

Reza Shah permitted some of the institutional trappings of a democracy—notably a parliament, or Majlis, and a prime minister—but refused to allow any serious political opposition, retaining all governing authority for himself and for the military leaders who formed the core of support for his autocratic regime. The shah put much of his energy into modernizing Iran, which by his definition included suppressing tribal leaders in rural areas and reducing the influence of Islam on state institutions and some aspects of daily life, such as prohibiting women from wearing the veil. Reza Shah also changed the country's name from Persia to Iran, as a way of emphasizing its origins as an Aryan nation. Reza Shah's transformation of his country was similar to, and in some respects modeled on, the contemporaneous modernization of Turkey by Mustafa Kemal Ataturk (Turkey Emerges from World War I, p. 631).

In August 1941, with World War II under way, Britain and the Soviet Union invaded Iran to ensure the British transport of military supplies across Iran to the Soviet Union, its beleaguered war-time ally. Reza Shah, accused by London of having pro-German sympathies, surrendered his throne and fled the country. His twenty-two-year-old son, Mohammad Reza, succeeded to the throne, while London and Moscow essentially divided Iran into spheres of influence for the remainder of the war. Britain was particularly keen to control Iran's oil-producing region in the province of Khuzestan, neighboring Iraq. The London-based Anglo-Iranian Oil Company obtained an exclusive contract to pump Iran's oil under provisions highly favorable to the company.

After World War II, Britain withdrew its military forces from Iran, but the Soviet Union kept its armies in the north for several years. The decade after the war saw almost unending turmoil as the young shah struggled to gain his footing, a handful of civilian political leaders emerged to challenge him, and foreign powers intervened repeatedly to protect their interests.

Aside from the shah, Mohammad Mosaddeq, a longtime government official, emerged as a key figure during this period. Mosaddeq had spent several years under house arrest in the late 1930s because of his opposition to Reza Shah's authoritarianism. He won election to the Majlis in 1943 and quickly rose as the leader of the National Front, a nationalist movement opposed to foreign influence in Iran.

In the late 1940s, Mosaddeq and the National Front became concerned about the Anglo-Iranian Oil Company acting as a virtual state within a state. This issue came to the fore in 1950, when the shah's government submitted to the Majlis a revision of the agreement under which the oil company operated in Iran. Mosaddeq and his allies used this opportunity to launch public demonstrations against the presence of a foreign-owned and -operated oil company on Iranian soil. The Majlis responded in 1951 by adopting legislation nationalizing the oil industry and by installing Mosaddeq as prime minister. The Anglo-Iranian Oil Company initiated an international boycott of Iranian oil to force the Majlis to back down. The British navy enforced the boycott, and the United States joined it in 1952, effectively freezing Iran out of the international oil market and plunging the Iranian economy into a deep recession.

In the face of such pressure, Mosaddeq sought to strengthen his position by requesting that the Majlis grant him sweeping emergency powers, which he then used to try to undermine the shah's authority. By 1953, however, Mosaddeq's position had weakened, as key allies defected from his coalition and as the leftist Tudeh (Masses) Party gained strength at the expense of the National Front.

In summer 1953, pro-shah military officers collaborating with the British government and the U.S. Central Intelligence Agency set in motion a plot to overthrow Mosaddeq and return full political authority to the shah. Their first two attempts failed, and the shah fled to Rome. The third attempt succeeded, on August 19, 1953. A military force under the command of Gen. Fazlollan Zahedi captured Mosaddeq as he tried

Iran.

to flee his home, suppressed the Tudeh Party and the National Front, and restored the shah to the throne. Mosaddeq was held under house arrest until his death in 1967.

The extent of CIA involvement in this coup has been the subject of much speculation but remains shrouded in some mystery. Washington refused to acknowledge any role in the coup until May 2000, when Secretary of State Madeleine Albright told a group of Iranian-Americans that "the United States played a significant role in orchestrating the overthrow" of Mosaddeq for "strategic reasons"—a reference to the Dwight D. Eisenhower administration's concern that the Iranian prime minister was falling under the sway of communists (Albright Remarks before the American-Iranian Council, p. 401).

After Mosaddeq's ouster, the shah's government negotiated a new oil contract, and the United States advanced a large loan to Tehran to restore the economy. The shah ruled with an autocratic hand for another quarter-century, until his overthrow in the 1978–1979 revolution that created the first theocratic state in modern times. Washington's role in ousting Mosaddeq and restoring the shah has not been forgotten in Iran, where leaders frequently cite it as an example of U.S. interference in the country's internal affairs (The Iranian Revolution, p. 379).

New Role in Region

Nearly three decades after the revolution, Iran's position in the region is in some ways stronger but in other ways weaker than it had been at the outset of the Islamic republic. During the 1980s and 1990s, Iran suffered from isolation. Most neighboring Arab leaders scorned it for fear that the Islamist message of Iran's mullahs would inspire their own populations to rise up against them, and Western nations, particularly the United States, considered it a pariah. Revolutionary leader Ayatollah Ruhollah Khomeini and his successors also faced endless domestic stresses during these decades, including the ravages of an eight-year war with Iraq, constant dissension over how far to take the Islamic revolution, and the failure of Khomeini's theocratic system to provide all the answers for managing a state in modern times.

The 2003 U.S.-led invasion and subsequent occupation of Iraq handed Iran an opportunity to strengthen its position in the region. Washington's removal of long-time Iraqi leader Saddam Hussein eliminated any lingering security threat that Iraq posed to Iran. The subsequent rise to power of the majority Shiites in Iraq—many of whose leaders had spent years in exile in Iran—provided Tehran natural allies in the country that long had been its enemy. Moreover, stumbles by the George W. Bush administration in Iraq after the 2003 invasion undermined the broader U.S. position in the region, and thus, in the zero-sum game of Middle Eastern politics, Iran benefited through an increase in its own influence.

The Iranian Revolution

DOCUMENT IN CONTEXT

As with most revolutions, in the case of Iran, any one of a number of dates or episodes can be cited as the start of the upheaval that swept Mohammad Reza, the shah, from power in 1979 in favor of an Islamic theocracy headed by Ayatollah Ruhollah Khomeini. According to Khomeini, the revolution began more than fifteen years earlier. In June 1963, a coalition of Shiite clergy and landowners provoked demonstrations against the so-called White Revolution, a modernization program set in motion by the shah. The central feature of this program was a land "reform" scheme that entailed breaking many large landholdings, including those owned by Islamic institutions, into smaller plots for peasant farmers to work. The shah's security services brutally suppressed these demonstrations, but at the price of radicalizing the clergy and other elements of society and undercutting the shah's political legitimacy. In suppressing the rebellion, in 1964 the regime exiled Khomeini, the cleric who had fomented opposition to the White Revolution. He went first to Turkey, but later took up residence in the Shiite holy city of Najaf, Iraq.

Iran experienced unprecedented modernization and economic prosperity during the late 1960s and the early years of the 1970s. The shah brought in Western experts to upgrade the oil industry and create the infrastructure of a modern state. When world oil prices soared after the October 1973 Arab-Israeli war, he spent billions of dollars buying the latest warplanes and other weapons from the United States, which began to view Iran, along with Saudi Arabia, as one of two pillars supporting its twin policies of safeguarding Persian Gulf oil and keeping the Soviet Union out of the region.

The shah failed, however, to couple his program for modernization with an opening of the political system. In 1975 he abolished all political parties except for one, which he controlled. This quelling of dissent inspired not only fear but widespread anger across a broad range of Iranian society. The shah's overspending on weapons and other imports from the West resulted in high inflation and economic decline during the mid-1970s just as oil revenues began to decline. Public anger at the shah and his policies boiled over into a series of protests beginning in 1976 and continuing throughout 1977. Despite such discontent, U.S. president Jimmy Carter, during a visit to Tehran in December 1977, referred to Iran as "an island of tranquility in a sea of turbulence." The shah took Carter's visit and statement as a sign of U.S. support for his regime.

In January 1978, a pro-government newspaper published a harsh attack against Khomeini, prompting large protests in Qom, a center of Shiite scholarship southwest of Tehran. Security forces fired on the protesters, killing several dozen students. This episode spawned more protests throughout the year. An imposition of economic austerity measures by the shah added fuel to the fire. The government then compounded popular anger with a violent effort to break up a large demonstration in Tehran on September 8, 1978, and an attempted use of force to quell a strike by oil workers at the end of October. Khomeini, who had been exiled to Paris by a nervous Iraqi government on October 6, encouraged the oil workers' strike and other protests, which escalated in the last two months of 1978. During this period, President Carter continued to express backing for the shah. His statements of support reportedly were encouraged, at least in part, by CIA assessments that the shah ultimately would weather the challenges to his authority.

After the initial crackdown on demonstrations failed, the shah turned increasingly to appeasement to quell the protests, even granting amnesty to Khomeini. In a final desperate move to calm the situation, on December 29, 1978, the shah turned to a leading opposition politician, Shapour Bakhtiar, as prime minister. The Carter administration also attempted to intervene, sending a senior U.S. general, Robert Huyser, to Tehran in early January 1979 with the hope of mobilizing the Iranian military into a takeover of the government. This effort failed, as the military began to abandon its allegiance to the crown. The shah left Iran on January 16, 1979, and headed to Egypt, announcing that he was on "vacation." He never returned, but a triumphant Khomeini did, on February 1, and promptly declared Bakhtiar's government "illegal." Ten days later, the government fell, and Bakhtiar went into exile. Khomeini appointed a "provisional" government that on March 30–31 sponsored a referendum on a Khomeini plan to establish an Islamic republic. More than 97 percent of Iranians voted in favor, the only option offered on the ballot. Even before all the votes were counted, Khomeini proclaimed the establishment of the Islamic Republic of Iran on April 1, 1979. He described the republic in almost utopian terms, asserting that it would provide "a government under which all the nation's strata enjoy equality and the light of God's justice shines equally on everyone. . . ."

The Islamic republic was based, and continues to be based, on a novel concept outlined by Khomeini in a 1971 collection of sermons, *Velayat-e-Faqih: Hukumat-e Islami* (loosely translated, "government of the Islamic jurist"). The basic element is that all government must derive from the teachings of Islam as interpreted by learned members of the clergy. Since the days of the Prophet Muhammad, there had existed a close relationship between religion and state in most Islamic lands. Khomeini took this a step further, however, by arguing that all aspects of national as well as personal life should be governed by the teachings of the Quran. A senior religious figure, or perhaps a group of them, would guide the nation according to those teachings.

At Khomeini's behest, the provisional government drafted a new constitution, but it omitted key provisions establishing the preeminent role of the *faqih,* the Islamic jurist who would serve as the country's supreme leader, the first of whom would be Khomeini. As a result, Khomeini arranged for the popular election of the Assembly of Experts—clergy members with the authority to amend the constitution to make it conform to Khomeini's vision of Islamic government. The assembly did so, for example, giving the *faqih* the power to decide all important matters of state, including declaring war and appointing military commanders and leading judges. Voters approved the constitution in a plebiscite in December 1979 during the early stages of the long standoff between Iran and the United States resulting from the occupation of the U.S. embassy in Tehran by young militants. Khomeini and his allies used the embassy takeover and hostage crisis to maintain public support for the new regime (Iranian Hostage Crisis, p. 383).

In 1985, Khomeini selected Ayatollah Hossein Ali Montazeri as his eventual successor, establishing a process of succession left uncertain by the constitution. Montazeri later proved to be a controversial choice, however, because he questioned the status of the faqih as the all-powerful leader free to make decisions without consulting fellow clergy members. In addition, other religious leaders—notably Ayatollah Ali Khamenei, then serving as president—considered Montazeri a threat because he held a higher status as a student of Islam than they did. (Khamenei was a lower-ranking cleric.)

At the urging of Khamenei and others, an ailing Khomeini in March 1989 dismissed Montazeri as his successor and appointed a committee to revise the constitution. That committee's revisions gave the supreme leader even more power than before and at the same time reduced the degree of stature a religious figure would require to become faqih. While the new constitution was being debated, Khomeini died, on June 3, 1989. His funeral three days later was a dramatic event, memorable for its frantic mourners and a chaotic scene during which thousands of them upended the litter carrying Khomeini's corpse, forcing soldiers to deliver it to the burial site on a helicopter.

Under the provisions of the new constitution, which had not yet been adopted, the Assembly of Experts immediately appointed Khamenei as the new supreme leader. Voters ratified the constitution in a plebiscite on July 29, 1989. A month later, voters elected Ali Akbar Hashemi Rafsanjani as president to succeed Khamenei; Rafsanjani had been Speaker of the parliament. The constitution had eliminated the post of prime minister to oversee the day-to-day affairs of the government. This change gave more power to the president, who was responsible to and could be dismissed by the supreme leader despite being elected by the citizenry.

Rafsanjani served two terms as president and was succeeded in 1997 by Mohammad Khatami, a moderate cleric who also served two terms and made modest changes in social policy (for example, allowing somewhat greater freedom for women). Khatami's program of more serious economic and political reform was blocked, however, by Khamenei and the clerical establishment, particularly after the police violently put down a student revolt at Tehran University in July 1999. Among other things, this event demonstrated the president's inability to control the security services, which in theory were under his authority (U.S.-Iranian Relations, p. 395).

In 2005 Mahmoud Ahmadinejad, a former mayor of Tehran, succeeded Khatami in a surprising electoral victory based on a platform of reinvigorating Khomeini's revolutionary ideals. Once in office, Ahmadinejad traveled the country promising every region more jobs and social services, but a sluggish economy made it difficult for him to keep these promises. The new president also heightened tensions with Europe and the United States—and ultimately with the UN Security Council—by rejecting efforts to bring Iran's nuclear energy program into compliance with international protocols and allay concerns about the government's ambitions to build nuclear weapons (Iranian Nuclear Ambitions, p. 404).

Following is a speech delivered by Ayatollah Ruhollah Khomeini on April 1, 1979,
in which he proclaims the establishment of an Islamic republic in Iran.

DOCUMENT

Proclamation of an Islamic Republic in Iran

APRIL 1, 1979

Attention please: Here is a message by the leader of the Iranian Islamic revolution on the proclamation of an Islamic republic in Iran, read by the Interior Ministry's political undersecretary:

Praise be to Almighty God [word indistinct]. I sincerely congratulate the great Iranian nation, which has throughout the imperial history [words indistinct]. God Almighty bestowed grace upon us and toppled the despotic regime with a powerful hand, which is the power of the oppressed people, and rendered our great nation the [word indistinct] forerunner of oppressed nations, and conferred upon them the rightful heritage with the establishment of an Islamic republic.

I declare the Islamic republic of Iran on this auspicious day, the day of the nation's leadership and the day of triumph and victory for the nation. I declare to the world that a referendum such as this is unprecedented in the history of Iran, which witnessed the entire nation rushing to the ballot box with enthusiasm and fervor, casting its [?affirmative vote], and burying the satanic regime in the annals of history forever. I admire this peerless solidarity which comprised all but a handful of adventure-seeking individuals who are unmindful of God and [words indistinct], and cast affirmative votes nearly unanimously for the Islamic republic, and thus proved their political and social maturity to the East and West.

I congratulate you on this day when you toppled the devilish enemy of [word indistinct] time thanks to the sacrifice of the illustrious martyred youth who left their mothers and fathers and [word indistinct] in a state of bereavement, and proclaimed the government of Islamic justice with your decisive vote for the Islamic republic; a government under which all the nation's strata enjoy equality and the light of God's justice shines equally on everyone, and the mercy of the Quran and the Sunnah showers equally on everyone. I congratulate you on this government under which there is no racial discrimination or difference on the basis of color between the white, black, red and [words indistinct] and Lors and Baluchi [two of Iran's ethnic minorities], all of whom are equal and fraternal. Only piety, superior morality and good deeds can count as the basis of preference. I congratulate you on the day in which all the nation's strata realize their just rights. There is no difference in the implementation of justice between the male and female, religious minorities or anyone else. Satan is being drowned, and mutiny and rebellion are to follow suit. The country is rescued from the claws of the internal and foreign enemies, plunderers and professional looters.

Now, you brave people are the guardians of the Islamic republic. Now it is up to you to safeguard this divine [word indistinct] with strength and decisiveness, and not allow the remnants of the previous stinking regime who are sitting in hiding, and the supporters of the international robbers and greedy oil devourers to penetrate your concentrated ranks. Now you should hold your destiny in your own hands and not give any opportunity to those who are waiting for an excuse. With the power of God, which is manifested in the people, take the next steps. Send the [word indistinct] class and your leaders to the constituent assembly to approve the constitution of the Islamic republic and, in the same way that with love and joy, you voted for the Islamic republic, vote for the trusted ones of the nation so that there is no room left for those who have evil designs. The [word indistinct] of 1 April, which is the first day of the government of God, is one of our greatest religious and national feasts.

Our nation should celebrate this day and keep it alive. This is the day when the parapets of a 2,500-year-old palace of an idolatrous government were torn down, and the satanic dominance was destroyed forever. The government of the lowly people, the government of God, has taken its place. Now, dear nation, you who have achieved your right with the blood of your youth, regard this right as precious and defend it. Under the banner of Islam and the flag of the Quran, establish divine justice by your support of it. I will use your service, which is service to Islam, and I expect the nation to guard Islam and the Islamic republic with all its might. I expect the governments to cleanse the country of the remnants of the idolatrous regime, whose effects are still evident in all aspects of the nation's life, without fear of either the West or the East and with independence, thoughtfulness and decision; to transform education and justice and all other ministries and departments which are built upon Western forms and are inspired from the West, to their Islamic forms; and to demonstrate to the world their social justice and their cultural, economic and political independence. I beseech the Almighty God for the greatness and independence of the country and the Islamic nation. Greetings be upon you and God's grace. Ruhollah Mosavi Khomeini. 1 April 1979.

SOURCE: Foreign Broadcast Information Service, Daily Report: Middle East and North Africa, April 2, 1979, pp. R7–R8 (Iran).

Iranian Hostage Crisis

DOCUMENT IN CONTEXT

The seizure of the U.S. embassy in Tehran by a group of Iranian students in late 1979 developed into a major diplomatic and political crisis that attracted world attention for fifteen months, contributed to the electoral defeat of a sitting U.S. president, and continued to poison relations between Iran and the United States for decades afterward. The Iranian hostage crisis, as the incident came to be known in the United States, also illustrated the limits to U.S. military power in the Middle East, a lesson still being learned in Washington in the early twenty-first century.

The crisis began on November 4, 1979, when several hundred students participating in a demonstration stormed the U.S. embassy in Tehran and took hostage all sixty-six U.S. citizens there, most of them diplomats. A Marxist group had overrun the embassy on February 14, only to be forced out by supporters of Ayatollah Ruhollah Khomeini, who had just returned to Iran from years in exile.

It was unclear initially whether the November embassy takeover had the explicit approval of Iran's revolutionary government, which had been in power since the ouster of Shah Mohammad Reza Pahlavi at the beginning of the year. Regardless, Khomeini, who had become the country's dominant leader, quickly endorsed the embassy seizure, thus escalating the diplomatic conflict and the danger of the episode developing into a military clash between Iran and the United States. It soon became clear that Khomeini saw the situation as an opportunity to bolster domestic support for the Islamic revolution, which had faced a backlash of opposition in previous months. Relatively moderate prime minister Mehdi Bazargan resigned two days after the embassy seizure, giving Khomeini's faction total control of the new government (The Iranian Revolution, p. 379).

President Jimmy Carter responded by demanding the release of all the hostages and making the issue a central focus of his foreign policy, inadvertently giving the hostage takers additional leverage. On November 12, Carter ordered a ban on the importation into the United States of oil from Iran; he also sought, and quickly received, nearly universal diplomatic support from world capitals for his demand that Iran release the hostages immediately. Khomeini ordered the release of thirteen of the captives on November 17. All were black or female employees at the embassy and thus, he said, probably were not spies, as he insisted the other embassy employees were.

The hostage crisis quickly settled into a stalemate, with each side accusing the other of acting in bad faith. Carter and Khomeini personified the crisis, each playing to a domestic constituency while trying to generate support and sympathy from a broader international audience.

On November 20 on Tehran radio, Khomeini portrayed the embassy seizure as justified recompense for U.S. "oppression and mischief" in Iran. He specifically cited Washington's long-term support for the shah and Carter's decision the previous month to allow the deposed shah into the United States for emergency medical treatment. Khomeini accused Carter of apparently being unaware or choosing to ignore that the shah "is guilty, was oppressive, was a criminal and committed many crimes in this country, caused much deprivation to this nation and imprisoned, exiled and killed its citizens."

Carter made his first extended statements on the matter during a November 28 White House news conference, stating that "we will persist in our efforts, through every means available, until every single American has been freed." He also warned that the Iranian government would suffer "grave consequences" if the hostages were harmed, and he rejected Khomeini's assertion that Iran's historical grievances against the United States justified the hostage taking.

For Khomeini and many Iranians, those grievances stood at the heart of the matter, but most Americans probably were only dimly aware, if knowledgeable at all, of that history. For the students who occupied the embassy, the central event was U.S. support for the military coup in August 1953 that ousted the government of Mohammad Mosaddeq, the prime minister who in 1951 had orchestrated the nationalization of Iran's oil industry and who the Dwight D. Eisenhower administration feared had aligned himself too closely with Iran's communist party. The coup restored power to the shah, who had fled Iran after an earlier attempt to dismiss Mosaddeq.

Since 1953, Iranian nationalists had nursed grievances against the United States because of its role in the coup and support for the shah. Some of the students at the embassy reportedly brandished copies of an autobiography by Kermit Roosevelt, Jr., a CIA official (and grandson of former president Theodore Roosevelt) who had said that he had engineered the 1953 coup. Khomeini's government also cited the coup as its central claim against the United States in a December 10 letter to the International Court of Justice (the World Court), which was considering a U.S. petition against the hostage taking. (The court later sided with the United States.)

The Iranians' sense of grievance and the Americans' feeling of impotence to resolve the crisis grew after April 1980, when a U.S. commando team flew into Iran on a secret mission to rescue the hostages. Equipment failures forced the military to abort the mission, and eight U.S. servicemembers died when a helicopter and a transport plane crashed as the commandos were leaving the desert base of the rescue mission. The attempted U.S. resort to military force stiffened the determination of Khomeini and his allies to hold on to the hostages. In the United States, the failure of the operation ultimately hardened a public perception of Carter as too weak to bring the hostages home.

Subsequent attempts to negotiate a diplomatic solution stalled, particularly after the outbreak of war between Iran and Iraq in September 1980 distracted Tehran's attention. It also became evident that the Iranians were using the crisis to weaken Carter, who faced a tough reelection battle against a formidable Republican opponent, Ronald Reagan. The Iranians released one of the fifty-three remaining hostages for medical reasons in July 1980, but the others remained imprisoned as Americans went to the polls in November and voted Carter out of office. Some observers argue that Khomeini wanted to demonstrate that he could push a U.S. president from power, just as the United States had dumped an Iranian leader twenty-seven years earlier (Iran-Iraq War and Diplomacy, p. 430).

Khomeini and his government had one last humiliation for Carter. An agreement for the release of the hostages, mediated by Algerian diplomats, was signed on January 19, 1981—one day before Carter's departure from office. Iran held up the actual release until minutes after Reagan took the oath of office on January 20. The fifty-two Americans had been held hostage for 444 days.

The agreement for the hostages' freedom satisfied only a small part of the numerous demands Khomeini had made the previous September as the price for releasing them. Of note, the agreement provided for the United States to release most of the $12 billion in Iranian government assets that Carter had ordered frozen after the embassy seizure; most of these funds were deposited in an escrow fund, however, and Iran received only about $2.3 billion. In partial satisfaction of Iran's historical grievances, the United States also pledged "that it is and from now on will be the policy of the United States not to intervene, directly or indirectly, politically or militarily, in Iran's internal affairs." The Reagan administration later announced that it would observe the terms of the hostage-release agreement.

Despite the peaceful settlement of the hostage crisis, the wounds it caused remained raw for decades in the United States, just as earlier U.S. interventions in Iran festered in that country. Until Iran elected Mohammad Khatami, a moderate, as president in 1997, it was virtually impossible for an American politician to suggest improving the relations between the United States and Iran. The administration of President Bill Clinton took tentative steps in that direction between 1998 and 2000, only to be rebuffed by Khomeini's successor, Ayatollah Ali Khamenei (U.S.-Iranian Relations, p. 395).

Following are three documents relating to the Iranian hostage crisis: excerpts from a speech by Ayatollah Ruhollah Khomeini, supreme leader of Iran, carried on Tehran Radio on November 20, 1979; excerpts of remarks by President Jimmy Carter at a White House news conference on November 28, 1979; and the text of the agreement between the governments of Iran and the United States, dated January 19, 1981, providing for the release of U.S. hostages held in Iran.

DOCUMENT

Khomeini Denounces Carter

NOVEMBER 20, 1979

Mr. Carter himself, and other people like him around the world who number less than 50,000 out of the three billion inhabitants of the world—it is these leaders of countries who encourage others to indulge in oppression and mischief. The outlook of people like him is that all the nations are worth nothing. Those people are part of the world and make up a small number of people like Carter and his clique, and some people in other places have, unfortunately, joined his clique, too.

This is what they think the whole world consists of. This is the outlook of the oppressors. They do not see the other great strata of various societies which are an ocean, compared to which Carter and the people like him are only drops. It means that this disease of self-glorification has caused them not to see the people.

This is why, when on the throne of his Presidency and looking through his sick outlook and seeing few ministers and others who belong to assemblies or are his lackeys in other places, and seeing that they get angry, he regards them as the whole world and says that if you do anything to these diplomats—he regards them as diplomats, those who acts of espionage have been proved on the basis of evidence, he regards them as diplomats, and he regards the world in terms of himself and these people.

Mohammed Reza [the deposed Iranian shah] also had this illness to some extent, and the same illness led to his destruction—the illness only to see himself and a few flatterers and a number of clowns around him, to see only these people and not to have any consideration for the nation, to understand that in every country the nation counts.

No matter how much Mr. Carter tried to keep Mohammed Reza in power—he repeatedly sent people to us saying that the shah should stay; then he wanted to keep Bakhtiar—he was not able to, and was defeated. Although it was a defeat, a major defeat, compared to the second defeat that he shall face, it was small.

The second defeat was to give asylum to a person who is guilty and who has been guilty for 30-odd years, and the 35 million people of our country can testify to his guilt. It is possible that a number of people may know of his guilt and not testify. But 35 million people know, and hundreds of millions of people in other countries of the world know, that this man is guilty, was oppressive, was a criminal and committed many crimes in this country, caused much deprivation to this nation and imprisoned, exiled and killed its citizens. To give asylum to such a person is a political defeat in the world. But due to the illness that Mr. Carter is suffering from, he is not able to understand this. To leave these people who are spies and who are in this den of espionage behind, and not to return this guilty man to this country, is in itself another defeat which is greater than the second defeat because if Carter does not send the shah, it is possible that the hostages may be tried, and if they are tried, Carter knows what will happen.

At times, Carter intimidates us with military threats, and at times with economic threats, but he himself knows that he is beating an empty drum.

Carter does not have the guts to engage in a military operation, and they [unspecified whom] do not listen to him. This mistake is due to that same illness from which these superpowers suffer, and this in itself is a mistake, as he thinks that all countries are like a ring on his finger; that if he says, "Do not sell wheat to Iran," all countries will fold their arms upon their chests, bow and obey.

And what need do we have of America's wheat? We have oil. We have that substance of which Churchill, that great British statesman during the war—when confronting the Germans and frightened that he might lose, speaking to the British House of Commons about all their problems, saying that we have suffered this and that and have been defeated—said: however, victory belongs to those who are sitting on a wave of oil. We are sitting on a wave of oil.

You plundered us and took away our oil, and gave us guns and rifles. But these weapons were for your sake and not for ours. We have oil. The world needs oil. The world does not need America. The world does not need Carter. The world needs oil. Other countries will turn to those of us who have oil and not to you, who sighs to be made president but do not know what to do. All Carter's efforts and endeavors are aimed at his being reelected president when his term comes to an end. But he is barking up the wrong tree. He thought that if he were to frighten Iran, and if he were to say that we shall impose an economic embargo on Iran and shall damage Iran's economy, his nation would applaud him and later he would be made president. . . .

SOURCE: "American Hostages in Iran," *Historic Documents of 1979* (Washington, D.C.: CQ Press, 1980), pp. 873–875.

DOCUMENT

Carter News Conference on Iran

NOVEMBER 28, 1979

The President: For the last 24 days our Nation's concern has been focused on our fellow Americans being held hostage in Iran. We have welcomed some of them home to their families and their friends. But we will not rest, nor deviate from our efforts, until all have been freed from their imprisonment and their abuse.

We hold the Government of Iran fully responsible for the well-being and the safe return of every single person.

I want the American people to understand the situation as much as possible, but there may be some questions tonight which I cannot answer fully, because of my concern for the well-being of the hostages.

First of all, I would like to say that I am proud of this great Nation, and I want to thank all Americans for their prayers, their courage, their persistence, their strong support and patience.

During these past days our national will, our courage, and our maturity have all been severely tested, and history will show that the people of the United States have met every test.

In the days to come our determination may be even more sorely tried but we will continue to defend the security, the honor and the freedom of Americans everywhere. This Nation will never yield to blackmail.

For all Americans, our constant concern is the well-being and the safety of our fellow citizens who are being held illegally and irresponsibly hostage in Iran. The actions of Iran have shocked the civilized world.

For a government to applaud mob violence and terrorism, for a government actually to support and, in effect, participate in the taking and the holding of hostages is unprecedented in human history. This violates not only the most fundamental precepts of international law but the common ethical and religious heritage of humanity. There is no recognized religious faith on Earth which condones kidnapping. There is no recognized religious faith on Earth which condones blackmail. There is certainly no religious faith on Earth which condones the sustained abuse of innocent people.

We are deeply concerned about the inhuman and degrading conditions imposed on the hostages. From every corner of the world, nations and people have voiced their strong revulsion and condemnation of Iran and have joined us in calling for the release of the hostages.

Last night, a statement of support was released and was issued by the President of the United Nations General Assembly, the Security Council, on behalf of all its members. We expect a further Security Council meeting on Saturday night, at which more firm and official action may be taken to help in obtaining the release of the American hostages.

Any claims raised by government officials of Iran will ring hollow while they keep innocent people bound and abused and threatened. We hope that this exercise of diplomacy and international law will bring a peaceful solution, because a peaceful solution is preferable to the other remedies available to the United States. At the same time we pursue such a solution with grim determination. The Government of Iran must recognize the gravity of the situation which it has itself created, and the grave consequences which will result if harm comes to any of the hostages.

I want the American people to know and I want the world to know that we will persist in our efforts, through every means available, until every single American has been freed. We must also recognize now, as we never have before, that it is our entire Nation which is vulnerable, because of our overwhelming and excessive dependence on oil from foreign countries. We have got to accept the fact that this dependence is a direct physical threat to our national security, and we must join together to fight for our Nation's energy freedom.

We know the ways to win this war: more American energy and the more efficient use of what we have. The United States Congress is now struggling with this extremely important decision. The way to victory is long and difficult, but we have the will, and we have the human and the natural resources of our great Nation.

However hard it might be to see into the future, one thing tonight is clear: We stand together. We stand as a Nation unified, a people determined to protect the life and the honor of every American. And we are determined to make America an energy-secure Nation once again. It is unthinkable that we will allow ourselves to be dominated by any form of overdependence at home or any brand of terrorism abroad. We are determined that the freest Nation on Earth shall protect and enhance its freedom.

I'll be glad to answer questions.

Q: Mr. President, the Ayatollah Khomeini said the other day—and I'm using his words—that he doesn't believe you have the guts to use military force. He puts no credibility in our military deterrent. I'm wondering, how do we get out of this mess in Iran and still retain credibility with our allies and with our adversaries overseas?

The President: We have the full support of our allies, and in this particular instance we have no adversaries overseas. There is no civilized country on Earth which has not condemned the seizure and the holding of the hostages by Iran.

It would not be advisable for me to explore publicly all of the options open to our country. As I said earlier, I'm determined to do the best I can through diplomatic means and through peaceful means to ensure the safety of our hostages and their release. Other actions which I might decide to take would come in the future after those peaceful means have been exhausted.

But I believe that the growing condemnation of the world community on Iran will have a beneficial effect.

Q: Mr. President, why did you reverse your policy and permit the Shah to come into this country when, one, medical treatment was available elsewhere; two, you had been warned by our Chargé that the Americans might be endangered in Teheran, and three, the [Mehdi] Bazargan government was so shaky that it was questionable whether he could deliver on the promise to protect our embassy? And last of all, in view of the consequences, do you regret the decision?

The President: No. The decision that I made, personally and without pressure from anyone, to carry out the principles of our country, to provide for the means of giving the Shah necessary medical assistance to save his life, was proper. At the same time we notified the Government of Iran. We were assured by the Prime Minister and the Foreign Minister that our embassy would be protected, and it was protected for several days, in spite of threats from outside.

Then peremptorily, after Khomeini made an aggravating speech to the crowds in the streets and withdrew protection from the Embassy, it was attacked successfully. The Embassy was protected by our people for the length of time possible without help from the host government. No embassy on Earth is a fortress that can withstand constant attacks by a mob, unless a host government comes to the rescue of the people within the embassy.

But I took the right decision. I have no regrets about it nor apologies to make, because it did help to save a man's life, and it was compatible with the principles of our country.

SOURCE: "The President's News Conference of November 28th, 1979: Situation in Iran," from John Woolley and Gerhard Peters, The American Presidency Project, University of California, Santa Barbara, www.presidency. ucsb.edu/ws/index.php?pid=31752#.

DOCUMENT

Agreement to Release Hostages

JANUARY 19, 1981

The Government of the Democratic and Popular Republic of Algeria, having been requested by the Governments of the Islamic Republic of Iran and the United States of America to serve as an intermediary in seeking a mutually acceptable resolution of the crisis in their relations arising out of the detention of the 52 United States nationals in Iran, has consulted extensively with the two governments as to the commitments which each is willing to make in order to resolve the crisis within the framework of the four points stated in the resolution of November 2, 1980, of the Islamic Consultative Assembly of Iran.

On the basis of formal adherences received from Iran and the United States, the Government of Algeria now declares that the following interdependent commitments have been made by the two governments:

General Principles

The undertakings reflected in this Declaration are based on the following general principles:

A. Within the framework of and pursuant to the provisions of the two Declarations of the Government of the Democratic and Popular Republic of Algeria, the United States will restore the financial position of Iran, in so far as possible, to that which existed prior to November 14, 1979. In this context, the United States commits itself to ensure the mobility and free transfer of all Iranian assets within its jurisdiction, as set forth in Paragraphs 4–9.

B. It is the purpose of both parties, within the framework of and pursuant to the provisions of the two Declarations of the Government of the Democratic and Popular Republic of Algeria, to terminate all litigation as between the Government of each party and the nationals of the other, and to bring about the settlement and termination of all such claims through binding arbitration. Through the procedures provided in the Declaration, relating to the Claims Settlement Agreement, the United States agrees to terminate all legal proceedings in United States courts involving claims of United States persons and institutions against Iran and its state enterprises, to nullify all attachments and judgments obtained therein, to prohibit all further litigation based on such claims, and to bring about the termination of such claims through binding arbitration.

Point I: Non-Intervention in Iranian Affairs

1. The United States pledges that it is and from now on will be the policy of the United States not to intervene, directly or indirectly, politically or militarily, in Iran's internal affairs.

Points II and III: Return of Iranian Assets and Settlement of U.S. Claims

2. Iran and the United States (hereinafter "the parties") will immediately select a mutually agreeable central bank (hereinafter "the Central Bank") to act, under the instructions of the Government of Algeria and the Central Bank of Algeria (hereinafter "The Algerian Central Bank") as depositary of the escrow and security funds hereinafter prescribed and will promptly enter into depositary arrangements with the Central Bank in accordance with the terms of this declaration. All funds placed in escrow with the Central Bank pursuant to this declaration shall be held in an account in the name of the Algerian Central Bank. Certain procedures for implementing the obligations set forth in this Declaration and in the Declaration of the Democratic and Popular Republic of Algeria concerning the settlement of claims by the government of the United States and the government of the Islamic Republic of Iran (hereinafter "the Claims Settlement Agreement") are separately set forth in certain Undertakings of the Government of the United States of America and the Government of the Islamic Republic of Iran with respect to the Declaration of the Democratic and Popular Republic of Algeria.

   3. The depository arrangement shall provide that, in the event that the Government of Algeria certifies to the Algerian Central Bank that the 52 U.S. nationals have safely departed from Iran, the Algerian Central Bank will thereupon instruct the Central Bank to transfer immediately all monies or other assets in escrow with the Central Bank pursuant to this declaration, provided that at any time prior to the making of such certification by the Government of Algeria, each of the two parties, Iran and the United States, shall have the right on seventy-two hours notice to terminate its commitments under this declaration.

   If such notice is given by the United States and the foregoing certification is made by the Government of Algeria within the seventy-two hour period of notice, the Algerian Central Bank will thereupon instruct the Central Bank to transfer such monies and assets. If the seventy-two hour period of notice by the United States expires without such a certification having been made, or if the notice of termination is delivered by Iran, the Algerian Central Bank will thereupon instruct the Central Bank to return all such monies and assets to the United States, and thereafter the commitments reflected in this declaration shall be of no further force and effect.

Assets in the Federal Reserve Bank

4. Commencing upon completion of the requisite escrow arrangements with the Central Bank, the United States will bring about the transfer to the Central Bank of all gold

bullion which is owned by Iran and which is in the custody of the Federal Reserve Bank of New York, together with all other Iranian assets (or the cash equivalent thereof) in the custody of the Federal Reserve Bank of New York, to be held by the Central Bank in escrow until such time as their transfer or return is required by Paragraph 3 above.

Assets in Foreign Branches of U.S. Banks

5. Commencing upon the completion of the requisite escrow arrangements with the Central Bank, the United States will bring about the transfer to the Central Bank, to the account of the Algerian Central Bank, of all Iranian deposits and securities which on or after November 14, 1979, stood upon the books of overseas banking offices of U.S. banks, together with interest thereon through December 31, 1980, to be held by the Central Bank, to the account of the Algerian Central Bank, in escrow until such time as their transfer or return is required in accordance with Paragraph 3 of this Declaration.

Assets in U.S. Branches of U.S. Banks

6. Commencing with the adherence by Iran and the United States to this declaration and the claims settlement agreement attached hereto, and following the conclusion of arrangements with the Central Bank for the establishment of the interest-bearing security account specified in that agreement and Paragraph 7 below, which arrangements will be concluded within 30 days from the date of this Declaration, the United States will act to bring about the transfer to the Central Bank, within six months from such date, of all Iranian deposits and securities in U.S. banking institutions in the United States, together with interest thereon, to be held by the Central Bank in escrow until such time as their transfer or return is required by Paragraph 3.

7. As funds are received by the Central Bank pursuant to Paragraph 6 above, the Algerian Central Bank shall direct the Central Bank to (1) transfer one-half of each such receipt to Iran and (2) place the other half in a special interest-bearing security account in the Central Bank, until the balance in the security account has reached the level of $1 billion. After the $1 billion balance has been achieved, the Algerian Central Bank shall direct all funds received pursuant to Paragraph 6 to be transferred to Iran. All funds in the security account are to be used for the sole purpose of securing the payment of, and paying, claims against Iran in accordance with the claims settlement agreement. Whenever the Central Bank shall thereafter notify Iran that the balance in the security account has fallen below $500 million, Iran shall promptly make new deposits sufficient to maintain a minimum balance of $500 million in the account. The account shall be so maintained until the President of the Arbitral Tribunal established pursuant to the claims settlement agreement has certified to the Central Bank of Algeria that all arbitral awards against Iran have been satisfied in accordance with the claims settlement agreement, at which point any amount remaining in the security account shall be transferred to Iran.

Other Assets in the U.S. and Abroad

8. Commencing with the adherence of Iran and the United States to this declaration and the attached claims settlement agreement and the conclusion of arrangements for

the establishment of the security account, which arrangements will be concluded within 30 days from the date of this Declaration, the United States will act to bring about the transfer to the Central Bank of all Iranian financial assets (meaning funds or securities) which are located in the United States and abroad, apart from those assets referred to in Paragraph 5 and 6 above, to be held by the Central Bank in escrow until their transfer or return is required by Paragraph 3 above.

9. Commencing with the adherence by Iran and the United States to this declaration and the attached claims settlement agreement and the making by the Government of Algeria of the certification described in Paragraph 3 above, the United States will arrange, subject to the provisions of U.S. law applicable prior to November 14, 1979, for the transfer to Iran of all Iranian properties which are located in the United States and abroad and which are not within the scope of the preceding paragraphs.

Nullification of Sanctions and Claims

10. Upon the making by the Government of Algeria of the certification described in Paragraph 3 above, the United States will revoke all trade sanctions which were directed against Iran in the period November 4, 1979, to date.

11. Upon the making by the Government of Algeria of the certification described in Paragraph 3 above, the United States will promptly withdraw all claims now pending against Iran before the International Court of Justice and will thereafter bar and preclude the prosecution against Iran of any pending or future claim of the United States or a United States national arising out of events occurring before the date of this declaration related to (A) the seizure of the 52 United States nationals on November 4, 1979, (B) their subsequent detention, (C) injury to United States property or property of the United States nationals within the United States Embassy compound in Tehran after November 3, 1979, and (D) injury to the United States nationals or their property as a result of popular movements in the course of the Islamic Revolution in Iran which were not an act of the Government of Iran. The United States will also bar and preclude the prosecution against Iran in the courts of the United States of any pending or future claim asserted by persons other than the United States nationals arising out of the events specified in the preceding sentence.

Point IV: Return of the Assets of the Family of the Former Shah

12. Upon the making by the Government of Algeria of the certification described in Paragraph 3 above, the United States will freeze, and prohibit any transfer of, property and assets in the United States within the control of the estate of the former Shah or of any close relative of the former Shah served as a defendant in U.S. litigation brought by Iran to recover such property and assets as belonging to Iran. As to any such defendant, including the estate of the former Shah, the freeze order will remain in effect until such litigation is finally terminated. Violation of the freeze order shall be subject to the civil and criminal penalties prescribed by U.S. law.

13. Upon the making by the Government of Algeria of the certification described in Paragraph 3 above, the United States will order all persons within U.S. jurisdiction to report to the U.S. Treasury within 30 days, for transmission to Iran, all informa-

tion known to them, as of November 3, 1979, and as of the date of the order, with respect to the property and assets referred to in Paragraph 12. Violation of the requirement will be subject to the civil and criminal penalties prescribed by U.S. law.

14. Upon the making by the Government of Algeria of the certification described in Paragraph 3 above, the United States will make known, to all appropriate U.S. courts, that in any litigation of the kind described in Paragraph 12 above the claims of Iran should not be considered legally barred either by sovereign immunity principles or by the act of state doctrine and that Iranian decrees and judgments relating to such assets should be enforced by such courts in accordance with United States law.

15. As to any judgment of a U.S. court which calls for the transfer of any property or assets to Iran, the United States hereby guarantees the enforcement of the final judgment to the extent that the property or assets exist within the United States.

16. If any dispute arises between the parties as to whether the United States has fulfilled any obligation imposed upon it by Paragraphs 12–15, inclusive, Iran may submit the dispute to binding arbitration by the tribunal established by, and in accordance with the provisions of, the claims settlement agreement. If the tribunal determines that Iran has suffered a loss as a result of a failure by the United States to fulfill such obligation, it shall make an appropriate award in favor of Iran which may be enforced by Iran in the courts of any nation in accordance with its laws.

Settlement of Disputes

17. If any other dispute arises between the parties as to the interpretation of performance of any provision of this declaration, either party may submit the dispute to binding arbitration by the tribunal established by, and in accordance with the provisions of, the claims settlement agreement. Any decision of the tribunal with respect to such dispute, including any award of damages to compensate for a loss resulting from a breach of this declaration or the claims settlement agreement, may be enforced by the prevailing party in the courts of any nation in accordance with its laws.

Initialed on January 19, 1981
by Warren M. Christopher
Deputy Secretary of State
of the Government of the United States
By virtue of the powers vested in him by his
Government as deposited with the government of Algeria

Source: "Iranian Release of U.S. Hostages," *Historic Documents of 1981* (Washington, D.C.: CQ Press, 1982).

U.S.-Iranian Relations

During the last years of President Bill Clinton's second term, some leaders in Iran and the United States appeared anxious to set aside nearly two decades of mutual hostility and put relations on a more normal footing. Each side made gestures clearly intended to be received positively by the other side, but domestic politics restrained each side from moving quickly to reach a substantive rapprochement before time ran out.

A series of hesitant diplomatic moves began after the surprise election, in May 1997, of Mohammad Khatami as president of Iran. A mid-level cleric known as a relative moderate in the Iranian political context, Khatami campaigned on a platform of domestic reform and won a landslide victory against a more hard-line Muslim cleric who had the backing of the country's conservative rulers. Khatami focused primarily on a domestic agenda that included easing some of the restrictions on daily life and political discourse imposed after the 1979 revolution.

Once he had strengthened his domestic position by gaining control (temporarily) over the powerful security services, Khatami turned his attention to foreign affairs—specifically to Iran's relations, or lack thereof, with the United States. In a news conference six days after his election, Khatami criticized the United States for its harsh and "domineering" foreign policy toward Iran. Any hope of renewed relations between the two nations, he said, would first require the United States to alter this approach. Khatami then expressed skepticism that such change would be forthcoming. Some seven months later, however, during a news conference on December 14, 1997, Khatami sent an important signal to the Clinton administration, stating, "I would hope for a thoughtful dialogue with the American people and through this thoughtful dialogue we could get closer to peace and security and tranquility." Khatami's words were by themselves innocuous, but in the context of the rocky history of U.S.-Iranian relations, they appeared to herald a dramatic new attitude in Tehran.

Khatami was even more forthcoming in an interview with correspondent Christiane Amanpour, aired on January 7, 1998, by the Cable News Network (CNN). Khatami began with a long discourse paying tribute to the "great American people" and explaining some of Iran's historical grievances against the United States. "There is a bulky wall of mistrust between us and the U.S. administration, a mistrust rooted in improper behaviors of the American governments," he said, citing in particular U.S. participation in the coup against Prime Minister Mohammad Mosaddeq in 1953, a subsequent U.S. loan to bolster the shah's government, and Washington's demand that Iran exempt U.S. officials from prosecution under local laws.

Despite these grievances, Khatami called in that interview for a "dialogue between civilizations and cultures" that he said would start with exchanges of scholars, artists, journalists, and tourists. "We are looking for a world in which misunderstandings can be overcome, nations can understand one another and mutual respect and logic govern relations among states," he said. Political relations between Iran and the United

States would be possible only when Washington dropped its hostile attitude toward Iran, Khatami added. He also acted on his words, reportedly dispatching numerous academics, businessmen, and other supporters of his government to the United States for informal meetings that explored the possibility of improved relations.

The Clinton administration moved cautiously in response to Khatami's outreach, starting with the authorization for an American wrestling team to participate in a tournament in Tehran in February 1998. Administration officials compared this move to the exchange of table tennis teams between the United States and China—an exchange referred to as "ping-pong diplomacy"—that preceded President Richard M. Nixon's historic visit to China in 1972.

On June 17, 1998, Secretary of State Madeleine Albright gave a speech to the Asia Society proposing that Washington and Tehran work together on a "road map leading to normal relations." At an April 12, 1999, White House dinner celebrating the impending change of millennium, President Clinton, apparently eager to set aside past grievances, in an off-the-cuff talk acknowledged that Iran "has been the subject of quite a lot of abuse from various Western nations." He added that Americans should set aside their "total denial" about Iran's grievances. This was the closest any president had come to acknowledging that Iran had legitimate complaints about past U.S. activities there. The Clinton administration followed with limited moves, lifting some sanctions against trade with Iran that had been in place since the 1979–1980 hostage crisis, including easing the sale of humanitarian goods and safety-related spare parts for U.S.-made aircraft.

In the meantime, however, Khatami had begun losing internal power struggles with the more hard-line factions in Tehran. In July 1999, Iranian police violently suppressed a student revolt at Tehran University, indicating that Khatami ultimately had lost his battle to control the security services.

The Clinton administration's final, and most important, opening to Iran came on March 17, 2000, when Albright delivered a speech in Washington to the American-Iranian Council, a group promoting better relations between Iran and the United States. Surveying the broad scope of U.S.-Iranian relations in recent years, Albright became the first high-level U.S. official to recognize explicitly one of Tehran's major grievances: "In 1953 the United States played a significant role in orchestrating the overthrow of Iran's popular Prime Minister, Mohammed Massadegh," she said. "The Eisenhower Administration believed its actions were justified for strategic reasons; but the coup was clearly a setback for Iran's political development. And it is easy to see now why many Iranians continue to resent this intervention by America in their internal affairs." Albright also acknowledged that the shah's government, which was backed by the United States, "brutally repressed political dissent."

Albright also recited long-standing U.S. complaints about Iran, notably its support for groups that used terror in the Middle East, but the broad thrust of her speech was positive and included an announcement of the administration's plan to ease an embargo on the importation of some Iranian consumer goods, among them carpets, nuts, dried fruit, and caviar. "I call upon Iran to join us in writing a new chapter in our shared history," she said. "Let us be open about our differences and strive to overcome them. Let us acknowledge our common interests and strive to advance them."

Any hopes were quickly dashed in Washington that Albright's speech—notably its extraordinary admission of U.S. involvement in the 1953 coup—would lead to a rapid warming of relations. On March 25, Iran's supreme leader, Ayatollah Ali Khamenei, gave a speech in Mashhad, in northeast Iran, directly replying to—and rejecting—Albright's initiative. Kenneth M. Pollack, in *The Persian Puzzle,* quotes Khamenei as saying, "What good does this admission—that you acted in that way then—do us now?" he asked. "Any admission years after the crime was committed, while they might be committing similar crimes now, will not do the Iranian nation any good."

In subsequent months, the judiciary and elements of the Iranian security services under Khamenei's control stepped up their repression of students and others who had been pushing for more reform, signaling that President Khatami had lost much of his last remaining political clout. Khatami won a second term as president in 2001, but by this time much of Iran's youth, who had hoped he would ease religious restrictions on all aspects of daily life, had become disillusioned and stayed away from the polls. In 2004 the Council of Guardians blocked key reformers aligned with Khatami from running in parliamentary elections, and most other reformers withdrew in protest; this resulted in the election of a parliament consisting almost entirely of hard-liners. When it became clear that the parliament would fall under the control of hard-liners, Khatami withdrew his two main legislative proposals that sought to curb the power of institutions that carried out Ayatollah Khamenei's wishes. "I withdraw the bills and declare that I have met with defeat," he said in March 2004 to reporters.

The final blow to Khatami's reform movement came in 2005 when Tehran's conservative mayor, Mahmoud Ahmadinejad, won a close election as president. Ahmadinejad quickly made clear that he had no intention of pursuing the liberalized political and social policies that had been at the heart of Khatami's stalled initiatives. Moreover, Ahmadinejad reverted to the tough anti-U.S. rhetoric of Iran's conservative religious leaders. That rhetoric was mirrored by U.S. president George W. Bush and his aides, who accused Iran of attempting to develop nuclear weapons and of supporting Islamist groups in Lebanon and elsewhere in the Middle East labeled as terrorist by the United States. Bush had signaled a confrontational approach in his January 2002 State of the Union speech, when he referred to Iran, Iraq, and North Korea as an "axis of evil" that cooperated with terrorists and sought to build weapons of mass destruction to threaten the rest of the world.

A few months earlier, after the al-Qaida attacks of September 11, 2001, the Iranians had cooperated extensively with Washington in its pursuit of al-Qaida, allowing the United States use of its territory and airspace, and in forming a post-Taliban government in Afghanistan. The tone of the relationship changed in January 2002 after Israel intercepted a shipment of arms from Iran bound for the Palestinian territories. What some observers view as a missed opportunity by the Bush administration to improve relations occurred in May 2003, shortly after the U.S.-led invasion of Iraq, when Iran apparently passed a two-page message to the United States through the Swiss embassy in which the Iranians expressed a desire to enter into bilateral talks. Controversy surrounded the document and the Bush administration's handling of the overture, with some high-ranking official claiming never to have seen the document and others acknowledging its existence.

Ahmadinejad reached out to the United States in 2006 with two letters, one addressed to Bush and the other to the American people. Each letter appeared, however, to be more of an affirmation of Ahmadinejad's positions on international affairs than a genuine call for dialogue. The Bush administration rebuffed both letters, accusing Ahmadinejad of attempting to undermine Western resolve to oppose Iran's alleged plans to build nuclear weapons (Iranian Nuclear Ambitions, p. 404).

In 2007 a slight thaw of sorts appeared to develop in U.S.-Iranian relations. In March, the U.S. ambassador to Iraq met with a group of Iranians at a gathering of countries neighboring Iraq. In early May, U.S. and Iranian ambassadors held face-to-face meetings in Egypt at the UN-sponsored conference for the International Compact with Iraq to try to find a way forward in Iraq. The ambassador held two more rounds of talks in Baghdad in July and August, but no results were announced as of mid-August 2007.

> *Following are excerpts from three documents: a news conference by Iranian president Mohammad Khatami on March 27, 1997, as translated, six days after his election as president of Iran; remarks on U.S.-Iranian relations by President Bill Clinton at a White House dinner on April 12, 1999; and a speech by Secretary of State Madeleine Albright to the American-Iranian Council in Washington, D.C., on March 17, 2000.*

DOCUMENT

Khatami on U.S.-Iranian Relations

MAY 27, 1997

In the name of God, the compassionate and merciful, at the outset I would like to extend my greetings to the journalists that are representatives of the mass media, external and internal, from our country that are the ear, the tongue and the eye—the reliable ear, eye and tongue of the people. . . .

And also I would like to welcome all the foreign journalists and the media representatives who have come to our country to witness one of the glorious stages of our determination of the destiny of our nation by themselves to witness the stability and the strength of our nation and also their active, happy presence in this stage of our country. . . .

Whatever that has occurred is a unique opportunity for all of us. Our nation has been able to regain its . . . identity in the light of the revolution. And has established a system of the cultural religious values [based] upon its religion, that people do have a major role in. And an example of that could be seen in the recent elections.

All these grandeurs of the presence of the people is definitely in the palm of the late Iman Khomeini and also the understanding and the awakened conscience of our people at this stage. And this great outcome which has been incarnated in the form of the Islamic Republic of Iran shall continue its way under the leadership of His Imminence Ayatollah Khamenei for years to come.

I am ready to answer to the questions of the journalists and the media. . . .

Question: Mr. President, 20 million people cast a vote for a change of course of direction in their revolution. You have spoken about civil liberties, civil rights and the rule of law.

What specifically do you plan to do to meet those demands? Are you surprised by the 20 million vote[s] and what they said?

And one last question. Do you think the atmosphere will exist for better relations between Iran and the United States?

Khatami: Prior to being surprised from the number of the votes, I should say that I am—it is a matter of honor to me. And of course, to the same extent, I do feel a heavy-duty burden. And as I mentioned at the beginning, this vote has been [cast] as a [vote of] confidence towards the system, the leadership and the revolution. And it is an indication of the presence of our people with vigilance at the stage of determining their destiny and the future.

And they are all living within a system that has been quite—it is quite dear to them and has been quite costly for them. And they would not easily get parted from [it]. And of course, fortunately there is freedom and the right of choice in our system. And also one of the reasons for having the exciting stages of the revolution has been the right to compete.

That means the people interested in the system have been able to make a choice within the framework of the system. And naturally what they have chosen would be a matter of respect to everybody. While we do have due respect for the programs and the ideas of the other competitors or the rivals, and also there shall be chances of having debates and discussions between different points of view existing as well in [the] future.

It would be quite natural that I would be committed to the programs that I have introduced and I do hope that I would be able to materialize them through the legal channels in coordination with the other organizations. And what I could say in one sentence was that all election was participation and the right of choice for the people and no opposition to the system. And God willing, that the grounds of the participation and the power of the choice of the people shall remain in place and it would be strengthened as well.

In regards to the relations with the United States . . . , I should say that the America is the source or the [spring] of this problem.

We are sorry to say that the U.S. policies [have] always been directed or [have] been hostile toward our revolution, our system. The great outcome of our revolution is independence and we are not willing to give up on this valuable outcome that we have gained. The basis of our relation[s] with the other countries is reliance upon the independence and the national interests of our country.

[As long as] the Americans are willing to bring any harm to this independence and the national interests of our country, there would be no ground for any relations. We cannot accept the domineering or [injunctive] policies in general.

Any change in the relation with the United States is dependent upon the changes of the policies of . . . America towards the revolution and Iran. And unfortunately, we do not see any sign of such change in the Americans' policy. . . .

SOURCE: "Khatami on his Election as President of Iran." *Historic Documents of 1997* (Washington, D.C.: CQ Press, 1998), 286–289. Editorial insertions and deletions by CQ Press, 2007.

DOCUMENT

Clinton Remarks on Iran at the White House Millennium Dinner

APRIL 12, 1999

. . . I would like to make one more point which I think is very important in the dealings between the West and the Islamic countries, generally, and I will use Iran as an example.

It may be that the Iranian people have been taught to hate or distrust the United States or the West on the grounds that we are infidels and outside the faith. And therefore, it is easy for us to be angry and to respond in kind. I think it is important to recognize, however, that Iran, because of its enormous geopolitical importance over time, has been the subject of quite a lot of abuse from various Western nations. And I think sometimes it's quite important to tell people, "Look, you have a right to be angry at something my country or my culture or others that are generally allied with us today did to you 50 or 60 or 100 or 150 years ago. But that is different from saying that I am outside the faith, and you are God's chosen."

So sometimes people will listen to you if you tell them, "You're right, but your underlying reason is wrong." So we have to find some way to get dialog, and going into total denial when you're in a conversation with somebody who's been your adversary, in a country like Iran that is often worried about its independence and its integrity, is not exactly the way to begin.

So I think while we speak out against religious intolerance, we have to listen for possible ways we can give people the legitimacy of some of their fears or some of their angers or some of their historic grievances, and then say they rest on other grounds; now, can we build a common future? I think that's very important.

Sometimes I think we in the United States, and Western culture generally, we hate to do that. But we're going to have to if we want to have an ultimate accommodation.

SOURCE: "Remarks at the Seventh Millennium Evening at the White House," April 12, 1999, *Public Papers of the Presidents of the United States: William J. Clinton*, p. 545, http://frwebgate.access.gpo.gov/cgi-bin/ getpage.cgi?position=all&page=545&dbname=1999_public_papers_vol1_misc.

DOCUMENT

Albright Remarks before the American-Iranian Council

MARCH 17, 2000

. . . The democratic winds in Iran are so refreshing, and many of the ideas espoused by its leaders so encouraging. There is a risk we will assume too much. In truth, it is too early to know precisely where the democratic trends will lead. Certainly the primary impetus for change is not ideology but pragmatism. Iranians want a better life. They want broader social freedom, greater government accountability and wider prosperity. Despite reviving oil prices, Iran's economy remains hobbled by inefficiency, corruption and excessive state control. Due in part to demographic factors, unemployment is higher and per capita income lower than 20 years ago.

The bottom line is that Iran is evolving on its own terms and will continue to do so. Iranian democracy, if it blossoms further, is sure to have its own distinctive features consistent with the country's traditions and culture. And like any dramatic and political and social evolution, it will go forward at its own speed on a timetable Iranians set for themselves.

The question we face is how to respond to all this. On the people-to-people level, the answer is not hard to discern. Americans should continue to reach out. We have much to learn from Iranians and Iranians from us. We should work to expand and broaden our exchanges. We should engage Iranian academics and leaders in civil society on issues of mutual interest. And, of course, we should strive even more energetically to develop our soccer skills. (Laughter.)

The challenge of how to respond to Iran on the official [level] is more complex, and it requires a discussion not only of our present perception and future hopes but also of the somewhat tumultuous past. . . .

But that common ground has sometimes been shaken by other factors. In 1953 the United States played a significant role in orchestrating the overthrow of Iran's popular Prime Minister, Mohammed Massadegh. The Eisenhower Administration believed its actions were justified for strategic reasons; but the coup was clearly a setback for Iran's political development. And it is easy to see now why many Iranians continue to resent this intervention by America in their internal affairs.

Moreover, during the next quarter century, the United States and the West gave sustained backing to the Shah's regime. Although it did much to develop the country economically, the Shah's government also brutally repressed political dissent.

As President Clinton has said, the United States must bear its fair share of responsibility for the problems that have arisen in U.S.-Iranian relations. Even in more recent years, aspects of U.S. policy towards Iraq, during its conflict with Iran appear now to have been regrettably shortsighted, especially in light of our subsequent experiences with Saddam Hussein.

However, we have our own list of grievances, and they are serious.

The embassy takeover was a disgraceful breach of Iran's international responsibility and the trauma for the hostages and their families and for all of us. And innocent Americans and friends of America have been murdered by terrorist groups that are supported by the Iranian Government.

In fact, Congress is now considering legislation that would mandate the attachment of Iranian diplomatic and other assets as compensation for acts of terrorism committed against American citizens.

We are working with Congress to find a solution that will satisfy the demands of justice without setting a precedent that could endanger vital U.S. interests in the treatment of diplomatic or other property, or that would destroy prospects for a successful dialog with Iran.

Indeed, we believe that the best hope for avoiding similar tragedies in the future is to encourage change in Iran's policies, and to work in a mutual and balanced way to narrow differences between our two countries.

Neither Iran, nor we, can forget the past. It has scarred us both.

But the question both countries now face is whether to allow the past to freeze the future or to find a way to plant the seeds of a new relationship that will enable us to harvest shared advantages in years to come, not more tragedies. Certainly, in our view, there are no obstacles that wise and competent leadership cannot remove.

As some Iranians have pointed out, the United States has cordial relations with a number of countries that are less democratic than Iran. Moreover, we have no intention or desire to interfere in the country's internal affairs. We recognize that Islam is central to Iran's cultural heritage and perceive no inherent conflict between Islam and the United States.

Moreover, we see a growing number of areas of common interest. For example, we both have a stake in the future stability and peace in the Gulf. Iran lives in a dangerous neighborhood. We welcome efforts to make it less dangerous and would encourage regional discussions aimed at reducing tensions and building trust. . . .

The United States recognizes Iran's importance in the Gulf, and we've worked hard in the past to improve difficult relationships with many other countries—whether the approach used has been called detente or principle engagements or constructive dialogue or something else.

We are open to such a policy now. We want to work together with Iran to bring down what President Khatami refers to as "the wall of mistrust."

For that to happen, we must be willing to deal directly with each other as two proud and independent nations and address on a mutual basis the issues that have been keeping us apart.

As a step towards bringing down that wall of mistrust, I want today to discuss the question of economic sanctions. The United States imposed sanctions against Iran because of our concerns about proliferation, and because the authorities exercising control in Tehran financed and supported terrorist groups, including those violently opposed to the Middle East peace process.

To date, the political developments in Iran have not caused its military to cease its determined effort to acquire technology, materials and assistance needed to develop nuclear weapons, nor have those developments caused Iran's Revolutionary Guard Corps or its Ministry of Intelligence and Security to get out of the terrorism business.

Until these policies change, fully normal ties between our governments will not be possible, and our principle sanctions will remain.

The purpose of our sanctions, however, is to spur changes in policy. They are not an end in themselves, nor do they seek to target innocent civilians.

And so for this reason, last year I authorized the sale of spare parts needed to ensure the safety of civilian passenger aircraft previously sold to Iran, aircraft often used by Iranian-Americans transiting to or from that country. And President Clinton eased restrictions on the export of food, medicine and medical equipment to sanctioned countries including Iran. This means that Iran can purchase products such as corn and wheat from America.

And today, I am announcing a step that will enable Americans to purchase and import carpets and food products such as dried fruits, nuts and caviar from Iran.

This step is a logical extension of the adjustments we made last year. It also [is] designed to show the millions of Iranian craftsmen, farmers and fisherman who work in these industries, and the Iranian people as a whole, that the United States bears them no ill will.

Second, the United States will explore ways to remove unnecessary impediments to increase contact between American and Iranian scholars, professional artists, athletes, and non-governmental organizations. We believe this will serve to deepen bonds of mutual understanding and trust.

Third, the United States is prepared to increase efforts with Iran aimed at eventually concluding a global settlement of outstanding legal claims between our two countries.

This is not simply a matter of unfreezing assets. After the fall of the Shah the United States and Iran agreed on a process to resolve existing claims through an arbitral tribunal in The Hague. In 1981, the vast majority of Iranian assets seized during the hostage crisis were returned to Iran. Since then, nearly all of the private claims have been resolved through The Hague Tribunal process.

Our goal now is to settle the relatively few but very substantial claims that are still outstanding between our two governments at The Hague. And by so doing, to put this issue behind us once and for all.

The points I've made and the concrete measures I have announced today reflect our desire to advance our common interests through improved relations with Iran. They respond to the broader perspective merited by the democratic trends in that country, and our hope that these internal changes will gradually produce external effects. And that as Iranians grow more free, they will express their freedom through actions and support of international law and on behalf of stability and peace.

I must emphasize, however, that in adopting a broader view of events in Iran, we are not losing sight of the issues that have long troubled us. We looked toward Iran truly fulfilling its promises to serve as an "anchor of stability," and to live up, indeed as well as were [sic], to the pledges its leaders have made in such areas as proliferation and opposition to terrorism.

We have no illusions that the United States and Iran will be able to overcome decades of estrangement overnight. We can't build a mature relationship on carpets and grain alone. But the direction of our relations is more important than the pace. The United States is willing either to proceed patiently, on step-by-step basis, or to move very rapidly if Iran indicates a desire and commitment to do so.

Next Tuesday will mark the beginning of a new year for Iran and the start of spring for us all. And it is true that for everything under Heaven there is a season. Surely the time has come for America and Iran to enter a new season in which mutual trust may grow and a quality of warmth supplant the long, cold winter of our mutual discontent.

For we must recognize that around the world today the great divide is no longer between East and West or North and South; nor is it between one civilization and another.

The great divide today is between people anywhere who are still ensnared by the perceptions and prejudices of the past, and those everywhere who have freed themselves to embrace the promise of the future.

This morning on behalf of the government and the people of the United States, I call upon Iran to join us in writing a new chapter in our shared history. Let us be open about our differences and strive to overcome them. Let us acknowledge our common interests and strive to advance them. Let us think boldly about future possibilities and strive to achieve them, and thereby, turn this new year and season of hope into the reality of a safer and better life for our two peoples.

To that mission I pledge my own best efforts this morning. And I respectfully solicit the counsel and understanding and support of all.

SOURCE: U.S. Department of State, Office of the Spokesman, "American-Iranian Relations," Remarks by Madeleine Albright before the American-Iranian Council, Washington, D.C., March 17, 2000, http://secretary. state.gov/www/statements/2000/000317.html.

Iranian Nuclear Ambitions

DOCUMENT IN CONTEXT

Suspicions of Iranian efforts to develop nuclear weapons have led to several recent years of inconclusive diplomacy involving these concerns. In 2007 Iran continued to insist that it sought not to develop nuclear weapons, but only to exercise its right to develop key aspects of a civilian nuclear energy program. Such a civilian program would also enable it to possibly build nuclear weapons. The United States has emerged as the most adamant country in disputing Iranian assertions about the peacefulness of its nuclear program and arguing that Tehran must be stopped before it acquires the technology to build nuclear weapons and thus become a threat to world peace.

Israel is the only country in the Middle East known to have nuclear weapons, although no Israeli government has ever officially acknowledged possessing them. According to most reports, the Jewish state first acquired a nuclear capability in the late 1970s. Though Israel's neighbors routinely denounce these weapons, no action has been taken against Israel because of them. Iran, however, has been a different story.

Leaders in neighboring states are anxious about the prospect of a nuclear-armed Iran because they remain suspicious of its theocratic leaders, whom they view as extreme and unpredictable. Israeli leaders consider an Iran with nuclear weapons a threat to their country's existence and have openly discussed possible military action to thwart any Iranian nuclear weapons program, thus validating from Iran's perspective its own interest in having such weapons in the first place.

Iran had begun building a civilian nuclear energy program in the mid-1970s, but Ayatollah Ruhollah Khomeini and his fellow clerics halted it after coming to power in the 1978–1979 revolution. Concerns that Iran had secretly built facilities intended to produce nuclear weapons arose in late 2002, just as the United States accused Iraq— Iran's long-time enemy—of doing the same. President George W. Bush justified his decision to launch an invasion of Iraq in March 2003 largely on intelligence claiming that Iraq had built up massive arsenals of biological and chemical weapons and was moving rapidly toward a nuclear weapons capability. After the invasion, a thorough search of Iraq by U.S. intelligence agencies proved this assumption to be wrong (The Missing WMD, p. 516).

The controversy over Iran's weapons program flowed from claims by a banned leftist opposition group, the National Council of Resistance of Iran, that the Tehran government had built secret facilities to enrich uranium, used as a fuel for nuclear weapons, and to produce heavy water, a necessary element in producing plutonium, another fuel for weapons. Iranian president Mohammad Khatami acknowledged that Iran had built nuclear facilities but insisted that they were part of a program to produce electrical power, not weapons. The International Atomic Energy Agency (IAEA), the UN body that monitors nuclear programs, conducted inspections of Iranian facilities in 2003 that raised questions about the truthfulness of Khatami's contention that Iran had no intention of building nuclear weapons. As a signatory of the Nuclear Nonproliferation Treaty (NPT), Iran was required to report its nuclear activities to the IAEA.

After numerous negotiations between Iranian officials and European diplomats, who had taken the lead on the issue, the IAEA's Board of Governors on November 26, 2003, announced that it "strongly deplores Iran's past failures" to disclose all its nuclear activities and warned that "any further serious Iranian failures" would lead the IAEA to consider "all options at its disposal." This latter statement hinted at the prospect of sending the matter to the UN Security Council for possible sanctions against Iran.

Under European pressure, Iran agreed in late 2003 to suspend some of its nuclear activities. During the subsequent three years, Iran's refusal to uphold that suspension became the central focus of international negotiations that pitted Iran against a good-cop, bad-cop team of European negotiators trying to use friendly persuasion in direct negotiations and the United States threatening international sanctions in the background.

Iran resumed its uranium enrichment efforts in stages between late 2005 and early 2006. This raised the diplomatic stakes because it appeared to confirm the Bush administration's assertions of Iran's determination to proceed with a weapons program and a policy of playing for time by engaging in seemingly endless rounds of negotiations with the Europeans. The issue finally reached the UN Security Council in late March 2006. The council issued a statement pressing Iran to stop its weapons work within thirty days, but Tehran missed that deadline and two others later in the year.

By the end of 2006, the international community's patience with Iran was close to running out. On December 23, the Security Council adopted Resolution 1737, which stepped up its demand that Iran stop its weapons work "without delay" and imposed financial sanctions targeting the assets of ten Iranian government agencies and companies and those of twelve officials and businessmen involved in the nuclear and missile programs. Iran again refused to comply, so the Security Council toughened its position on March 24, 2007, with Resolution 1747, prohibiting all weapons exports to some of Iran's elite military units and tightening the sanctions against individuals and companies associated with the nuclear programs. This resolution had the solid backing from China and Russia, the two Security Council members that previously had been most reluctant to punish Iran. In May 2007, Iran missed another UN-imposed deadline for halting its nuclear work, but in mid-July reached an agreement with the IAEA to inspect a heavy-water reactor and to respond to questions about past testing. Ahmadinejad was quoted on July 11, 2007, as saying that Iran might adjust the pace of its nuclear work "but no one should expect us to give up our rights and stop its process."

Following is the text of UN Security Council Resolution 1737, adopted on December 23, 2006, calling on Iran to stop work on programs thought to be aimed at developing nuclear weapons.

DOCUMENT

UN Security Council Resolution 1737 (2006)

DECEMBER 23, 2006

The Security Council,

Recalling the Statement of its President, of 29 March 2006, and its resolution 1696 (2006) of 31 July 2006,

Reaffirming its commitment to the Treaty on the Non-Proliferation of Nuclear Weapons, and recalling the right of States Party, in conformity with Articles I and II of that Treaty, to develop research, production and use of nuclear energy for peaceful purposes without discrimination,

Reiterating its serious concern over the many reports of the IAEA [International Atomic Energy Agency] Director General and resolutions of the IAEA Board of Governors related to Iran's nuclear program, reported to it by the IAEA Director General, including IAEA Board resolution,

Reiterating its serious concern that the IAEA Director General's report of 27 February 2006 lists a number of outstanding issues and concerns on Iran's nuclear program, including topics which could have a military nuclear dimension, and that the IAEA is unable to conclude that there are no undeclared nuclear materials or activities in Iran,

Reiterating its serious concern over the IAEA Director General's report of 28 April 2006 and its findings, including that, after more than three years of Agency efforts to seek clarity about all aspects of Iran's nuclear program, the existing gaps in knowledge continue to be a matter of concern, and that the IAEA is unable to make progress in its efforts to provide assurances about the absence of undeclared nuclear material and activities in Iran,

Noting with serious concern that, as confirmed by the IAEA Director General's reports of 8 June 2006, 31 August 2006, and 14 November 2006, Iran has not established full and sustained suspension of all enrichment-related and reprocessing activities as set out in resolution 1696 (2006), nor resumed its cooperation with the IAEA under the Additional Protocol, nor taken the other steps required of it by the IAEA Board of Governors, nor complied with the provisions of Security Council resolution 1696 (2006) and which are essential to build confidence, and *deploring* Iran's refusal to take these steps,

Emphasizing the importance of political and diplomatic efforts to find a negotiated solution guaranteeing that Iran's nuclear program is exclusively for peaceful purposes, and *noting* that such a solution would benefit nuclear nonproliferation elsewhere, and *welcoming* the continuing commitment of China, France, Germany, the Russian Federation, the United Kingdom and the United States, with the support of the European Union's High Representative to seek a negotiated solution,

Determined to give effect to its decisions by adopting appropriate measures to persuade Iran to comply with resolution 1696 (2006) and with the requirements of the IAEA, and also to constrain Iran's development of sensitive technologies in support of its nuclear and missile programs, until such time as the Security Council determines that the objectives of this resolution have been met,

Concerned by the proliferation risks presented by the Iranian nuclear program and, in this context, by Iran's continuing failure to meet the requirements of the IAEA Board of Governors and to comply with the provisions of Security Council resolution 1696 (2006), *mindful* of its primary responsibility under the Charter of the United Nations for the maintenance of international peace and security,

Acting under Article 41 of Chapter VII of the Charter of the United Nations,

1. *Affirms* that Iran shall without further delay take the steps required by the IAEA Board of Governors in its resolution, which are essential to build confidence in the exclusively peaceful purpose of its nuclear program and to resolve outstanding questions;

2. *Decides,* in this context, that Iran shall without further delay suspend the following proliferation sensitive nuclear activities:
   (a) all enrichment-related and reprocessing activities, including research and development, to be verified by the IAEA; and
   (b) work on all heavy water–related projects, including the construction of a research reactor moderated by heavy water, also to be verified by the IAEA;

3. *Decides* that all States shall take the necessary measures to prevent the supply, sale or transfer directly or indirectly from their territories, or by their nationals or using their flag vessels or aircraft to, or for the use in or benefit of, Iran, and whether or not originating in their territories, of all items, materials, equipment, goods and technology which could contribute to Iran's enrichment-related, reprocessing or heavy water–related activities, or to the development of nuclear weapon delivery systems, namely:

(a) those set out in sections B.2, B.3, B.4, B.5, B.6 and B.7 of INFCIRC/254/Rev.8/Part 1 in document S/2006/814;

(b) those set out in sections A.1 and B.1 of INFCIRC/254/Rev.8/Part 1 in document S/2006/814, except the supply, sale or transfer of:

    (i) equipment covered by B.1 when such equipment is for light water reactors;

    (ii) low-enriched uranium covered by A.1.2 when it is incorporated in assembled nuclear fuel elements for such reactors;

(c) those set out in document S/2006/815, except the supply, sale or transfer of items covered by 19.A.3 of Category II;

(d) any additional items, materials, equipment, goods and technology, determined as necessary by the Security Council or the Committee established by paragraph 18 below (herein "the Committee"), which could contribute to enrichment-related, or reprocessing, or heavy water–related activities, or to the development of nuclear weapon delivery systems;

4. *Decides* that all States shall take the necessary measures to prevent the supply, sale or transfer directly or indirectly from their territories, or by their nationals or using their flag vessels or aircraft to, or for the use in or benefit of, Iran, and whether or not originating in their territories, of the following items, materials, equipment, goods and technology:

(a) those set out in INFCIRC/254/Rev.7/Part 2 of document S/2006/814 if the State determines that they would contribute to enrichment-related, reprocessing or heavy water–related activities;

(b) any other items not listed in documents S/2006/814 or S/2006/815 if the State determines that they would contribute to enrichment-related, reprocessing or heavy water–related activities, or to the development of nuclear weapon delivery systems;

(c) any further items if the State determines that they would contribute to the pursuit of activities related to other topics about which the IAEA has expressed concerns or identified as outstanding;

5. *Decides* that, for the supply, sale or transfer of all items, materials, equipment, goods and technology covered by documents S/2006/814 and S/2006/815 the export of which to Iran is not prohibited by subparagraphs 3 (b), 3 (c) or 4 (a) above, States shall ensure that:

(a) the requirements, as appropriate, of the Guidelines as set out in documents S/2006/814 and S/2006/985 have been met; and

(b) they have obtained and are in a position to exercise effectively a right to verify the end-use and end-use location of any supplied item; and

(c) they notify the Committee within ten days of the supply, sale or transfer; and

(d) in the case of items, materials, equipment, goods and technology contained in document S/2006/814, they also notify the IAEA within ten days of the supply, sale or transfer;

6. *Decides* that all States shall also take the necessary measures to prevent the provision to Iran of any technical assistance or training, financial assistance, investment, brokering or other services, and the transfer of financial resources or services, related to the supply, sale, transfer, manufacture or use of the pro-

hibited items, materials, equipment, goods and technology specified in paragraphs 3 and 4 above;

7. *Decides* that Iran shall not export any of the items in documents S/2006/814 and S/2006/815 and that all Member States shall prohibit the procurement of such items from Iran by their nationals, or using their flag vessels or aircraft, and whether or not originating in the territory of Iran;

8. *Decides* that Iran shall provide such access and cooperation as the IAEA requests to be able to verify the suspension outlined in paragraph 2 and to resolve all outstanding issues, as identified in IAEA reports, and *calls upon* Iran to ratify promptly the Additional Protocol;

9. *Decides* that the measures imposed by paragraphs 3, 4 and 6 above shall not apply where the Committee determines in advance and on a case-by-case basis that such supply, sale, transfer or provision of such items or assistance would clearly not contribute to the development of Iran's technologies in support of its proliferation sensitive nuclear activities and of development of nuclear weapon delivery systems, including where such items or assistance are for food, agricultural, medical or other humanitarian purposes, provided that:

   (a) contracts for delivery of such items or assistance include appropriate end-user guarantees; and

   (b) Iran has committed not to use such items in proliferation sensitive nuclear activities or for development of nuclear weapon delivery systems;

10. *Calls upon* all States to exercise vigilance regarding the entry into or transit through their territories of individuals who are engaged in, directly associated with or providing support for Iran's proliferation sensitive nuclear activities or for the development of nuclear weapon delivery systems, and *decides* in this regard that all States shall notify the Committee of the entry into or transit through their territories of the persons designated in the Annex to this resolution (herein "the Annex"), as well as of additional persons designated by the Security Council or the Committee as being engaged in, directly associated with or providing support for Iran's proliferation sensitive nuclear activities and for the development of nuclear weapon delivery systems, including through the involvement in procurement of the prohibited items, goods, equipment, materials and technology specified by and under the measures in paragraphs 3 and 4 above, except where such travel is for activities directly related to the items in subparagraphs 3 (b) (i) and (ii) above;

11. *Underlines* that nothing in the above paragraph requires a State to refuse its own nationals entry into its territory, and that all States shall, in the implementation of the above paragraph, take into account humanitarian considerations as well as the necessity to meet the objectives of this resolution, including where Article XV of the IAEA Statute is engaged;

12. *Decides* that all States shall freeze the funds, other financial assets and economic resources which are on their territories at the date of adoption of this resolution or at any time thereafter, that are owned or controlled by the persons or entities designated in the Annex, as well as those of additional persons or entities designated by the Security Council or by the Committee as being engaged in, directly associated with or providing support for Iran's proliferation sensitive nuclear activities or the development of nuclear weapon

delivery systems, or by persons or entities acting on their behalf or at their direction, or by entities owned or controlled by them, including through illicit means, and that the measures in this paragraph shall cease to apply in respect of such persons or entities if, and at such time as, the Security Council or the Committee removes them from the Annex, and *decides further* that all States shall ensure that any funds, financial assets or economic resources are prevented from being made available by their nationals or by any persons or entities within their territories, to or for the benefit of these persons and entities;

13. *Decides* that the measures imposed by paragraph 12 above do not apply to funds, other financial assets or economic resources that have been determined by relevant States:

    (a) to be necessary for basic expenses, including payment for foodstuffs, rent or mortgage, medicines and medical treatment, taxes, insurance premiums, and public utility charges or exclusively for payment of reasonable professional fees and reimbursement of incurred expenses associated with the provision of legal services, or fees or service charges, in accordance with national laws, for routine holding or maintenance of frozen funds, other financial assets and economic resources, after notification by the relevant States to the Committee of the intention to authorize, where appropriate, access to such funds, other financial assets or economic resources and in the absence of a negative decision by the Committee within five working days of such notification;

    (b) to be necessary for extraordinary expenses, provided that such determination has been notified by the relevant States to the Committee and has been approved by the Committee;

    (c) to be the subject of a judicial, administrative or arbitral lien or judgment, in which case the funds, other financial assets and economic resources may be used to satisfy that lien or judgment provided that the lien or judgment was entered into prior to the date of the present resolution, is not for the benefit of a person or entity designated pursuant to paragraphs 10 and 12 above, and has been notified by the relevant States to the Committee;

    (d) to be necessary for activities directly related to the items specified in subparagraphs 3 (b) (i) and (ii) and have been notified by the relevant States to the Committee;

14. *Decides* that States may permit the addition to the accounts frozen pursuant to the provisions of paragraph 12 above of interests or other earnings due on those accounts or payments due under contracts, agreements or obligations that arose prior to the date on which those accounts became subject to the provisions of this resolution, provided that any such interest, other earnings and payments continue to be subject to these provisions and are frozen;

15. *Decides* that the measures in paragraph 12 above shall not prevent a designated person or entity from making payment due under a contract entered into prior to the listing of such a person or entity, provided that the relevant States have determined that:

    (a) the contract is not related to any of the prohibited items, materials, equipment, goods, technologies, assistance, training, financial assistance, investment, brokering or services referred to in paragraphs 3, 4 and 6 above;

(b) the payment is not directly or indirectly received by a person or entity designated pursuant to paragraph 12 above; and after notification by the relevant States to the Committee of the intention to make or receive such payments or to authorize, where appropriate, the unfreezing of funds, other financial assets or economic resources for this purpose, ten working days prior to such authorization;

16. *Decides* that technical cooperation provided to Iran by the IAEA or under its auspices shall only be for food, agricultural, medical, safety or other humanitarian purposes, or where it is necessary for projects directly related to the items specified in subparagraphs 3 (b) (i) and (ii) above, but that no such technical cooperation shall be provided that relates to the proliferation sensitive nuclear activities set out in paragraph 2 above;

17. *Calls upon* all States to exercise vigilance and prevent specialized teaching or training of Iranian nationals, within their territories or by their nationals, of disciplines which would contribute to Iran's proliferation sensitive nuclear activities and development of nuclear weapon delivery systems;

18. *Decides* to establish, in accordance with rule 28 of its provisional rules of procedure, a Committee of the Security Council consisting of all the members of the Council, to undertake the following tasks:

(a) to seek from all States, in particular those in the region and those producing the items, materials, equipment, goods and technology referred to in paragraphs 3 and 4 above, information regarding the actions taken by them to implement effectively the measures imposed by paragraphs 3, 4, 5, 6, 7, 8, 10 and 12 of this resolution and whatever further information it may consider useful in this regard;

(b) to seek from the secretariat of the IAEA information regarding the actions taken by the IAEA to implement effectively the measures imposed by paragraph 16 of this resolution and whatever further information it may consider useful in this regard;

(c) to examine and take appropriate action on information regarding alleged violations of measures imposed by paragraphs 3, 4, 5, 6, 7, 8, 10 and 12 of this resolution;

(d) to consider and decide upon requests for exemptions set out in paragraphs 9, 13 and 15 above;

(e) to determine as may be necessary additional items, materials, equipment, goods and technology to be specified for the purpose of paragraph 3 above;

(f) to designate as may be necessary additional individuals and entities subject to the measures imposed by paragraphs 10 and 12 above;

(g) to promulgate guidelines as may be necessary to facilitate the implementation of the measures imposed by this resolution and include in such guidelines a requirement on States to provide information where possible as to why any individuals and/or entities meet the criteria set out in paragraphs 10 and 12 and any relevant identifying information;

(h) to report at least every 90 days to the Security Council on its work and on the implementation of this resolution, with its observations and recommendations, in particular on ways to strengthen the effectiveness of the measures imposed by paragraphs 3, 4, 5, 6, 7, 8, 10 and 12 above;

19. *Decides* that all States shall report to the Committee within 60 days of the adoption of this resolution on the steps they have taken with a view to implementing effectively paragraphs 3, 4, 5, 6, 7, 8, 10, 12 and 17 above;

20. *Expresses* the conviction that the suspension set out in paragraph 2 above as well as full, verified Iranian compliance with the requirements set out by the IAEA Board of Governors, would contribute to a diplomatic, negotiated solution that guarantees Iran's nuclear program is for exclusively peaceful purposes, *underlines* the willingness of the international community to work positively for such a solution, *encourages* Iran, in conforming to the above provisions, to re-engage with the international community and with the IAEA, and *stresses* that such engagement will be beneficial to Iran;

21. *Welcomes* the commitment of China, France, Germany, the Russian Federation, the United Kingdom and the United States, with the support of the European Union's High Representative, to a negotiated solution to this issue and encourages Iran to engage with their June 2006 proposals (S/2006/521), which were endorsed by the Security Council in resolution 1696 (2006), for a long-term comprehensive agreement which would allow for the development of relations and cooperation with Iran based on mutual respect and the establishment of international confidence in the exclusively peaceful nature of Iran's nuclear program;

22. *Reiterates* its determination to reinforce the authority of the IAEA, strongly supports the role of the IAEA Board of Governors, *commends* and *encourages* the Director General of the IAEA and its secretariat for their ongoing professional and impartial efforts to resolve all remaining outstanding issues in Iran within the framework of the IAEA, *underlines* the necessity of the IAEA continuing its work to clarify all outstanding issues relating to Iran's nuclear program;

23. *Requests* within 60 days a report from the Director General of the IAEA on whether Iran has established full and sustained suspension of all activities mentioned in this resolution, as well as on the process of Iranian compliance with all the steps required by the IAEA Board and with the other provisions of this resolution, to the IAEA Board of Governors and in parallel to the Security Council for its consideration;

24. *Affirms* that it shall review Iran's actions in the light of the report referred to in paragraph 23 above, to be submitted within 60 days, and:

(a) that it shall suspend the implementation of measures if and for so long as Iran suspends all enrichment-related and reprocessing activities, including research and development, as verified by the IAEA, to allow for negotiations;

(b) that it shall terminate the measures specified in paragraphs 3, 4, 5, 6, 7, 10 and 12 of this resolution as soon as it determines that Iran has fully complied with its obligations under the relevant resolutions of the Security Council and met the requirements of the IAEA Board of Governors, as confirmed by the IAEA Board;

(c) that it shall, in the event that the report in paragraph 23 above shows that Iran has not complied with this resolution, adopt further appropriate measures under Article 41 of Chapter VII of the Charter of the United Nations to persuade Iran to comply with this resolution and the requirements of the IAEA, and underlines that further decisions will be required should such additional measures be necessary;

25. *Decides* to remain seized of the matter.

Annex

A. Entities involved in the nuclear program
1. Atomic Energy Organization of Iran
2. Mesbah Energy Company (provider for A40 research reactor—Arak)
3. Kala-Electric (aka Kalaye Electric) (provider for PFEP—Natanz)
4. Pars Trash Company (involved in centrifuge program, identified in IAEA reports)
5. Farayand Technique (involved in centrifuge program, identified in IAEA reports)
6. Defense Industries Organization (overarching MODAFL-controlled entity, some of whose subordinates have been involved in the centrifuge program making components, and in the missile program)
7. 7th of Tir (subordinate of DIO, widely recognized as being directly involved in the nuclear program)

B. Entities involved in the ballistic missile program
1. Shahid Hemmat Industrial Group (SHIG) (subordinate entity of AIO)
2. Shahid Bagheri Industrial Group (SBIG) (subordinate entity of AIO)
3. Fajr Industrial Group (formerly Instrumentation Factory Plant, subordinate entity of AIO)

C. Persons involved in the nuclear program
1. Mohammad Qannadi, AEOI Vice President for Research & Development
2. Behman Asgarpour, Operational Manager (Arak)
3. Dawood Agha-Jani, Head of the PFEP (Natanz)
4. Ehsan Monajemi, Construction Project Manager, Natanz
5. Jafar Mohammadi, Technical Adviser to the AEOI (in charge of managing the production of valves for centrifuges)
6. Ali Hajinia Leilabadi, Director General of Mesbah Energy Company
7. Lt Gen Mohammad Mehdi Nejad Nouri, Rector of Malek Ashtar University of Defense Technology (chemistry dept, affiliated to MODALF, has conducted experiments on beryllium)

D. Persons involved in the ballistic missile program
1. Gen Hosein Salimi, Commander of the Air Force, IRGC (Pasdaran)
2. Ahmad Vahid Dastjerdi, Head of the AIO
3. Reza-Gholi Esmaeli, Head of Trade & International Affairs Dept, AIO
4. Bahmanyar Morteza Bahmanyar, Head of Finance & Budget Dept, AIO

E. Persons involved in both the nuclear and ballistic missile programs
1. Maj Gen Yahya Rahim Safavi, Commander, IRGC (Pasdaran)

SOURCE: United Nations, "UN Security Council Resolutions, 2006: S/RES/1737 (2006), Non-Proliferation," www.un.org/Docs/sc/unsc_resolutions06.htm.

Iraq and the Gulf Wars

CHAPTER 6 DOCUMENTS

Overview

Iraq is one of the many Middle Eastern countries artificially created by European colonial powers in the years after World War I. Because of its history, ethnic composition, oil reserves, and strategic location, Iraq has been one of the most troubled, and troublesome, of the region's neocolonial creations. From its ancient origins to its central role in major conflicts during the last three decades, Iraq's influence on the world has far exceeded its population and land mass. As the British discovered in the 1920s and the Americans have learned in the early 2000s, it can be a quagmire for outside powers.

Mesopotamia—the lush "cradle of civilization" between the Tigris and Euphrates rivers in southern and central Iraq—formed the seat of some of the great civilizations of ancient times, including those of the Sumerians and the Amorites, the latter of whom built the great capital of Babylon on the Euphrates. The Abbasids, the first Arab dynasty, ruled from Baghdad for five hundred years beginning in 750 A.D. In the sixteenth century, all of present-day Iraq fell under the control of the Turkish Ottoman Empire.

Iraq's entry onto the world stage as a separate country began in World War I, when Britain gradually invaded and took over the three Ottoman provinces of Basra, Baghdad, and Mosul as part of a broader campaign of pressure against the Ottomans, who had sided with Germany in the war. The British also sought to protect trade routes with India, the crown jewel of their empire. Arabs hoped that after the war, Iraq would become part of an independent Arab state, but the British already had decided to hold on to that territory as part of the secret Sykes-Picot agreement of 1916 with France for dividing up much of the Middle East. In 1919 the British created Iraq by combining the three formerly autonomous provinces—Basra in the south, Baghdad in the center, and Mosul in the north.

Iraq's Shiite and Sunni Muslims joined in a brief but bloody revolt against the British during the summer of 1920 after it became clear that London would rule Iraq under a League of Nations mandate rather than grant it independence. Although the revolt failed, it was an important event in the country's history because it marked the first time that Shiites and Sunnis of differing backgrounds and tribal loyalties cooperated in any kind of organized way in Iraq. In response to this revolt, the British created a provisional government that gave limited authority to local representatives—most of them Sunnis—under overall British supervision. This step marked the beginning of a trend in which the minority Sunnis would hold power at the expense of the majority Shiites and the other large minority, the Kurds of northern Iraq. This pattern would continue until the U.S. invasion of Iraq in 2003, when the United States would hand progressively greater authority to local Shiite leaders.

The British in 1921 selected Faisal ibn Hussein as the country's first king. The son of Sharif Hussein, then-leader of the Hijaz (which would later become part of Saudi Arabia), Faisal had portrayed himself as representing Arabs during the postwar peace conference in Paris and had served briefly in 1920 as king of Syria before being removed by France. Faisal was not an Iraqi—and apparently had never even been there before he became king of it—but he was an Arab the British could trust and could use to put an Arab face on the British government in Baghdad. In an effort to give legitimacy to Faisal's rule, the British arranged for a plebiscite that produced a 96 percent vote in favor of the new king. A subsequent election resulted in the creation of a Constituent Assembly with only modest powers. Despite the elections and the strong backing of the British, Faisal never was able to establish himself as a legitimate ruler in the eyes of many Iraqis, nor would his son, Ghazi, who succeeded to the throne in 1933 when Faisal died unexpectedly. Ghazi died six years later in an automobile accident, a new phenomenon in the Middle East.

Under a treaty signed in 1930, Iraq formally became a sovereign state in 1932 and was admitted to the League of Nations. The country remained, however, under British influence. A series of governments in Baghdad proved unable to quell conflicts among the numerous ethnic and tribal groups that the British had forced together in the Iraqi nation-state.

In 1936 the first of several military coups took place, this one carried out by army officers opposed to British influence in Iraq. This coup lead to a string of unstable governments, one of which tried to align Iraq with the Axis powers at the outset of World War II, provoking another British intervention in 1941. In 1955 the government signed a British-engineered mutual defense agreement, the Baghdad Pact, with Iran, Pakistan, and Turkey, marking another turning point in Iraqi history. The primary reason for the agreement was to establish a regional counterbalance to Egypt's Gamal Abdel Nasser, who was provoking British ire by threatening Britain's control of the Suez Canal and by claiming to be the leader of a pan-Arab movement. A contingent of Iraqi army officers opposed to the Baghdad Pact and calling themselves the Free Officers staged a coup on July 14, 1958, that overthrew the monarchy as well as the government. The conspirators killed King Faisal II, the young grandson of King Faisal, withdrew from the Baghdad Pact, and established a military dictatorship under Brig. Gen. Abd al-Karim al-Qasim.

Qasim's regime lasted slightly less than five years before being overthrown on February 9, 1963, in a coup sponsored by members of the Baath Party, a pan-Arab socialist party founded in Syria. This new regime was then ousted in another coup nine months later, but the Baath Party returned to power in July 1968. Saddam Hussein, a Baath Party political operative, quickly rose to become number two in the party hierarchy and thus in the government. Eleven years later, in July 1979, Hussein took all power into his hands, where it would remain until his ouster by the U.S. military in 2003.

Hussein's rule evolved into nearly twenty-five years of almost endless conflict and economic disaster for Iraq. Less than a year after taking sole control of the government, he launched a long and ultimately fruitless war with Iran. Two years after the end of that war, Iraqi forces invaded Kuwait, only to be defeated by an international military coalition headed by the United States. A dozen years of UN-sponsored economic sanctions followed, depriving Iraq of most of its oil export revenue and leaving the country an economic basket case. The United States, with the invasion of 2003, promised to bring democracy and economic stability to Iraq, and a democracy did emerge in the form of an elected government that gave political power to the majority Shiites for the first time. Four years after the invasion, however, Iraq remained an extremely violent place headed by new leaders trying, with only modest success, to salvage the national unity that the British had imposed eight decades earlier.

Saddam Hussein Takes Power

DOCUMENT IN CONTEXT

Saddam Hussein dominated Iraq for more than one-third of the period between the establishment of Iraq as an independent country following World War I and the first decade of the twenty-first century. He built a power structure based on loyalty to him rather than to the state of Iraq and anchored in security services, the Baath Party, and family allegiances from his home region around Tikrit. All these splintered after the United States forced Hussein from power in 2003.

Hussein's rise to unrivaled power began with a 1968 coup by leaders of the Baath Party, which had briefly governed Iraq five years earlier. Maj. Gen. Ahmad Hasan al-Bakr, the central figure in the coup, ultimately emerged as president of Iraq and chairman of the Revolutionary Command Council, which ran the government. Within a year, however, Bakr's tribal relative and fellow native of Tikrit, Saddam Hussein, assumed much of the real power as vice chairman of the council. Unlike Bakr and most other senior leaders, Hussein did not have a military background, but as a Baath Party organizer he possessed valuable political experience, which he used to maneuver past his rivals.

During the 1970s, Iraq improved its often-strained relations with other Arab countries and its economic performance, largely because of the increase in world oil prices after the October 1973 Arab-Israeli war. Troubled by ill health, Bakr increasingly yielded power to Hussein until July 16, 1979, when Bakr resigned suddenly. Hussein immediately succeeded to all the top positions, becoming president of the country, commander in chief of the military, chairman of the Revolutionary Command Council, and head of the Baath Party. In a speech on July 17—the eleventh anniversary of the Baath Party's return to power—Hussein asserted that the passage of leadership from Bakr to himself had been a "moral and normal constitutional" event for Iraq. In an example of the grandiose rhetoric that was to become one of his trademarks, Hussein also characterized this peaceful leadership change as "unique among all the experiments in the ancient and contemporary worlds."

Despite his supposed admiration for constitutional processes, Hussein immediately demonstrated just how ruthless his rule would be by purging the government and Baath Party of those he suspected of not being sufficiently loyal to him. Much of this took place in public at a special Baath Party meeting shortly after he seized power. As Hussein smoked a cigar and pretended to be shocked by the presentation of evidence of disloyalty, dozens of party members were led from the room, one by one, never to be seen again.

Little more than a year after taking power, Hussein led Iraq into a war with Iran, apparently expecting an easy victory over his neighbor's army, which had been decimated in the fallout of the Islamic revolution. The war proved to be a disaster for Iran and for Iraq, lasting eight years, ending in defeat for both countries, and serving as a prelude to future wars (Iran-Iraq War and Diplomacy, p. 430).

Following are excerpts from a speech by Saddam Hussein as the new president of Iraq on July 17, 1979.

DOCUMENT

Hussein's First Presidential Address to the Nation

JULY 17, 1979

In the name of God, the merciful, the compassionate. Citizens, masses of our great people: On this blessed occasion—the anniversary of our people's revolution, the revolution of honest strugglers—I greet you from the depths of my heart. My speech to you today will not be official or traditional. I will not deal with political or general affairs as is customary. It is a special speech from the heart to the great people in great Iraq and to the great Arab nation.

Yesterday you listened to the speech of the father and great comrade, Abu Haytham [Ahmad Hasan al-Bakr]. What his speech described is a unique example among all the experiments in the world. Today I will clarify to you other basic aspects, dimensions and facts of this 15-year experiment.

The transfer of power from leader to leader in the moral and constitutional manner that took place in our country, party and revolution is unique among all the experiments in the ancient and contemporary worlds. It is unique but not strange because it emanates from the Arab nation's nobility, the greatness of the message of Islam and the principles of the Arab Socialist Ba'ath Party—the standard bearer of the nation's resurgence in the current age. It is a phenomenon that is compatible with the nature of the 17 July revolution's march in all its details and dimensions.

During the revolution's march, we dealt with the issue of authority as Ba'athists and as the grandsons of those great men who propagated the most brilliant humanitarian messages to the farthest corners of the world and who were glorious models of good breeding, courage and chivalry. In our opinion, authority is not power, dominance and self-satisfaction. It is a burden that we carry to apply practical principles in the service of the people, in support of the nation and in order to end injustice. This concept, brothers, is the result of our party's rich experiment in Iraq, particularly the [1963] Ramadan revolution experiment and our party's experiment in the pan-Arab arena. These experiments helped us safeguard this concept and played a major role in fortifying us against error. . . .

[In the next section of his speech, Hussein asserts that he had requested that he not be given a formal position in the government once the Baath Party took power. His party colleagues rejected his request, however, and made him vice chairman of the Revolution Command Council in July 1968.]

. . . We feel that never in history—including the history of our nation, despite its radiance—has it been possible for two leaders within one leadership to remain in power without the occurrence of a serious schism in the moral aspects of the march, without one leader deposing the other, or without losing heavenly values and the radiant and honorable values of history.

Throughout this march we have preserved the values of manliness and honor and have accorded our great and beloved Comrade Abu Haytham all the love and respect that he duly deserves as a man who is sincere to his homeland and nation, and to his party, principles, and values. He offered great services to the party, homeland and nation. These services will be recorded in history with appreciation and admiration.

All the intervention and base attempts by hostile forces and all temptations of power and life failed to make us covet the advanced position of authority. If we had done this, we would have alienated ourselves from the principles and values by which we were raised, thus depriving ourselves of the principles of chivalry, Arab ethics and eternal spiritual values.

Brothers, Comrade Abu Haytham has explained to you about his reported requests to step down because of his health. I always took the initiative with our comrades to prevent fulfilling Abu Haytham's desire.

I used to repeat that we must insure that Comrade Abu Haytham stays with us until his last breath because he is a great symbol of struggle. Even when, God forbid, he becomes unable to walk, I said we should raise him on our shoulders so he might stand as a symbol of our principles and so he might remain a living example for us to present to our party, people and coming generations. However, Comrade Abu Haytham persisted this time and his health conditions made us unable to dissuade him from his request to resign from all official posts. Thus, we are losing an opportunity that would help us complete the duty to which we have devoted ourselves—the duty to further deepen the concepts that will enrich the revolution's march with noble humanitarian and ethical values. . . .

. . . In assuming the honor and responsibility of leading the country from the present position, I say to you, honorable Iraqi citizens, that I pledge as a struggle that I will not ask my comrades in the leadership and party and my brothers the sons of the people to carry out any act which I would not want to do by myself.

I will also not make them abstain from doing something I myself would not abstain from doing. I will act inspired by the creed of the party and the Arab nation's heritage and the spirit of heavenly messages.

Our duty is to stand for justice and combat injustice, we will not allow any struggler in the party or any citizen to be humiliated. We will punish the oppressor and come to the aid of right.

I will struggle to be one of the banners, but not only banner; I will seek to be one of the swords, but not only the sword; I will seek to be one of the leaders, but not the only leader; and I will struggle to be one of the knights among the strugglers of the party and the people, but not the only knight. I will not hesitate to take the initiative and shoulder the responsibility of leading the revolution and country forward and facing the pan-Arab tasks along the road of unity, freedom and socialism. I will take on what is required of the revolutionary initiative from a leader within the framework of collective leadership which gives each struggler his role and dictates his duty to him.

Brother citizens, strugglers in the Arab Socialist Ba'ath Party. This is a pledge before you, the pledge of men and strugglers, a pledge given for today and tomorrow.

We ask God to help us fulfill it and to preserve for us the beloved father, leader Ahmad Hasan al-Bakr, and give him long life. I also ask almighty God to preserve you, take care of you and grant you victory. May the peace and blessings of God be upon you.

SOURCE: Foreign Broadcast Information Service, *Daily Report: Middle East and North Africa,* July 18, 1979, E-1–E-5.

Iran and Iraq: Prelude to War

DOCUMENT IN CONTEXT

The longest and deadliest war in recent Middle Eastern history is among the major wars of modern times rarely discussed in the West, particularly in the United States. For eight years during the 1980s, Iran and Iraq fought to a virtual standstill in a war over territory, regime preservation, and bragging rights to regional supremacy. Iraq started the war against its much-larger neighbor in September 1980, but failed to achieve any of its objectives. Iran suffered major military defeats late in the war, but was the more reluctant party to end the fighting in 1988; its only significant achievement was proving that a revolutionary government ruled by Islamic clerics could mobilize sufficient public support to sustain itself in power.

By most estimates, at least 500,000, and possibly as many as 1.5 million, people died during the Iran-Iraq War, most of them Iranians. The war severely damaged cities, oil installations, military bases, and other infrastructure and weakened the economies in both countries. The war also served as a precursor to the Persian Gulf War of 1991 that resulted from Iraq's invasion of another neighbor, Kuwait (Persian Gulf War, p. 455).

The roots of the Iran-Iraq War grow from a centuries-old rivalry between Iraq—a predominantly Arab nation long ruled by Sunni Muslims—and Iran—most of whose residents are Persians adhering to the Shiite branch of Islam. Historical mutual grievances deepened in the early 1970s, when Baghdad and Tehran each began providing aid to insurgent groups in the other's country. Iran supported a drive for independence by Iraqi Kurds, who mounted a brief but bloody war beginning in summer 1974. Iraq retaliated by supporting several ethnic and political groups opposed to the shah's rule in Iran. An age-old dispute over control of the Shatt al-Arab waterway also helped bring Iran and Iraq to the verge of war by early 1975. This channel—the confluence of the Euphrates and Tigris rivers—demarcates part of the border between the two countries and is an essential transit route for oil exports by Iraq.

The prospect of war between Iran and Iraq was temporarily avoided through the mediation of Algeria, which helped the shah and Saddam Hussein (at the time, Iraq's vice president) to negotiate a peace agreement in Algiers in March 1975. Incorporated into a formal treaty signed on June 13, 1975, the agreement had two key elements. First, Iran and Iraq essentially agreed to split the Shatt al-Arab down the middle by recognizing the thalweg line as the boundary between them; a thalweg is the center of any navigable channel that is the border between two countries. This compromise represented a significant concession by Iraq because the previously disputed border was along the eastern, or Iranian, side of the waterway, which meant Iraq had controlled the entire channel. Second, the treaty had general provisions for good relations between Iran and Iraq, including a pledge by each side not to aid insurgent groups in the other country. This part of the agreement ended Iranian support for the Iraqi Kurdish rebels, whose revolt against Baghdad collapsed as a consequence.

Less than four years after the Algiers treaty, the Iranian Revolution brought to power a regime in Tehran with nationalist aspirations and a religious zeal that leaders in Arab countries perceived as threatening. The mullahs in Iran asserted a claim to Bahrain—a Persian Gulf island-nation with a majority Shiite population off the coast of Saudi Arabia—and called on Shiites to rise up against the Sunni-led regimes in the Gulf region. These regimes included Iraq, where Saddam Hussein had taken full control of the government in July 1979 after several years of serving as vice president and the power behind the scenes. As a Sunni leader of a country with a Shiite majority, Hussein had reason to fear a revolt inspired by the radical Shiite leaders in Tehran. Iraq suspended diplomatic relations with Iran in October 1979 (Iranian Revolution, p. 379; Saddam Hussein Takes Power, p. 420).

The prospect of outright conflict between Iran and Iraq grew with several incidents in April 1980: Baghdad blamed Iran for an unsuccessful assassination attempt against Iraqi deputy prime minister Tariq Aziz; Iraq demanded that Iran withdraw from three disputed islands; Iraq executed a respected Shiite cleric, Ayatollah Muhammad Bakr al-Sadr, an event that led Iran's new leader, Ayatollah Ruhollah Khomeini, to call for Iraqis to topple the "corrupt regime" in Baghdad, which in turn drew a heated response from Hussein; and suspected Iraqi agents attacked the Iranian embassy in London.

By late summer, Hussein apparently had concluded that the political and military weaknesses of the new Iranian regime afforded him an opportunity to assert Iraqi dominance over its neighbor and to reverse the territorial concession involving the Shatt al-Arab that Iraq had made five years earlier. On the political front, Khomeini's new government was beset by disagreement between radicals and moderates over how far to push the revolution. In terms of the military, Iran's army had suffered greatly because of the revolution. Khomeini's government purged it of thousands of officers suspected of remaining loyal to the ousted shah, leaving the military divided and in chaos. Moreover, the United States, which had been the shah's major supplier of weapons, had halted the flow of armaments and vital spare parts after Iranian students took U.S. diplomats hostage in Tehran in November 1979. With the Iranian army weakened and the government distracted by revolutionary infighting, Hussein reportedly believed an attack would give him significant leverage over Iraq's old enemy and would preempt any attempt by the mullahs in Tehran to oust him from power.

Within this context, Hussein appeared before the National Assembly on September 17, 1980, to announce his government's abrogation of the 1975 Algiers treaty and to claim all of the Shatt al-Arab. "This Shatt shall again be, as it has been throughout history, Iraqi and Arab in name and reality, with all rights of full sovereignty over it," he said. Hussein placed full blame for abrogation of the treaty on Iran, claiming that the shah and the new revolutionary government had failed to carry out their legal commitments.

The war began five days later, on September 22, when nine divisions of the Iraqi army surged into the oil-producing province of Khuzestan on the Iranian side of the Shatt al-Arab. The Iraqi air force bombed Iranian air bases and oil fields, causing only modest damage. Iraq also threatened to block the Strait of Hormuz, the strategic point through which all Persian Gulf oil shipments (including those from Iraq) passed.

The prospect of a full-scale war in the Gulf caused widespread alarm internationally. On September 23, the United States and the Soviet Union each pledged neutrality in the conflict, and on September 28 the UN Security Council adopted a resolution demanding that both Iran and Iraq "refrain immediately from the further use of force." Iraq quickly accepted the resolution—with reservations—but Iran flatly rejected it on October 1.

The Iraqi offensive caught Iran off guard and succeeded in capturing a large chunk of territory in western Iran, notably in Khuzestan. Iraq claimed rights to the province because most of its residents were Sunni Arabs, rather than Persians or Shiites. Iraq's advances came at a high price, however. Its army captured the city of Khorramshahr early in November, but only after weeks of shelling and an intense urban battle that cost thousands of lives.

Iranian resistance demonstrated serious flaws in Hussein's assumptions about the weakness of Iran's military and the fragility of the revolutionary government in Tehran. Khomeini's regime had little difficulty marshaling public support for a massive show of defense against the Iraqi invasion. Urged on by rhetoric proclaiming the virtues of "martyrdom," tens of thousands of Iranians flocked to volunteer militias that the army threw against the Iraqi advance. Hussein quickly replaced the ousted shah as the chief villain in Iranian rhetoric.

According to some military experts, Iran's most important weapon in the early stages of the war may have been the incompetence of the Iraqi army. Beset by technical failures and flawed leadership, Iraq's army quickly proved that it was not the powerhouse that the Iraqi leader had claimed it to be. By the end of November 1980—two months into the war—Iraq's offensive had stalled and expectations of an easy victory over Iran had proven to be wishful thinking.

Iran exhibited its own military problems in a failed counteroffensive near the town of Susangerd (just east of the Iran-Iraq border) in January 1981. The failure of this ill-planned operation undermined the standing of Iranian president Abolhassan Bani-Sadr, the leading moderate in Khomeini's government who also served as commander in chief of the military. Bani-Sadr fled Iran six months later, and Tehran then became engulfed in a new wave of political infighting, including assassinations of senior officials by leftist opposition groups.

The first phase of the war lasted a year and was followed in late 1981 by a dramatic Iranian counteroffensive, which recovered most of the territory Iraq had gained at the war's outset. The war then settled into a stalemate that persisted from mid-1982 until Iran reluctantly accepted a UN-brokered cease-fire in 1988 (Iran-Iraq War and Diplomacy, p. 430; Conclusion of the Iran-Iraq War, p. 437).

Following is a speech delivered by Iraqi president Saddam Hussein to the National Assembly on September 17, 1980.

DOCUMENT

Hussein Speech to the National Assembly before War with Iran

SEPTEMBER 17, 1980

. . .We considered it a good opportunity to save the security and national unity of Iraq as well as the security of the valiant Iraqi Army. Thus, the party and government leadership made a decision to negotiate with Iran on the basis that the Thalweg line would be the border line in Shatt al-Arab. In exchange, Iran would return the Iraqi territories it retained under previous administrations contrary to the 1913 Constantinople protocol, including the areas of Zayn al-Qaws and Sayf Sa'd liberated by our forces a few days ago, and would also refrain from giving military aid and any other kind of aid to the mercenary renegade gang in the northern part of the homeland.

Negotiations were held with Iran on this basis and the 6 March 1975 agreement was signed. It was a big event at the time. As soon as the agreement was proclaimed, the forces of the mercenary mutiny collapsed and the mutineers surrendered. The weapons seized by the Iraqi Army amounted to 50,000 pieces, not counting the many other Iranian weapons which were withdrawn during the 2-week respite given them. Even after the end of the 2 weeks, the Iranians had to leave behind large quantities of arms and equipment, which were seized by our brave army.

Brothers, the March 1975 agreement was a courageous and serious decision. It was a national and pan-Arab decision. Courage is not only expressed by the skillful use of the rifle and sword on the frontline with the enemy and in attack or defense, but also by the ability of the leadership to make a courageous decision in defense of the people and the nation to safeguard sovereignty when the rifle and sword alone cannot achieve the objective.

The decision, made under those circumstances, saved Iraq from real dangers, which were threatening its unity, security and future. That decision enabled our people to continue with their revolution and the process of reconstruction and development and so attain a high level of strength, progress and prosperity, preserving the dignity and sovereignty of the Iraqis and enabling strong Iraq to serve the Arab nation and its great mission.

The decision was not a surrender to a bitter reality—although the reality was bitter and grave—but was an understanding of the reality through sensible and balanced thinking, which took all circumstances and capabilities into consideration. The March agreement was the result of circumstances. Our people understood it and considered it, under the circumstances, a great victory. They welcomed it with great rejoicing.

Although our army was courageously fighting the renegades and was not aware of the facts we mentioned earlier—that is, the shortage in vital ammunition—and was dealing punishing blows to the traitor renegades, it, too, welcomed the agreement with great joy because it understood the significance of that agreement to the homeland's unity and future. It appreciated the objective reasons for concluding the agreement.

Brothers, after the signing of the March [1975] agreement, many negotiations and contacts were held to implement its provisions, especially those on the demarcation of the borders, the setting up of border markers and other matters. The three major protocols attached to the agreement were signed. These were: the protocol on determining the river borders, the protocol on redemarcating the land borders and the protocol on border security.

The Iranian side benefited from the protocol on determining the river borders in Shatt al-Arab. But more time was needed to apply the protocol on the land borders. It was as if this was normal. The handing over of the land was disrupted by the circumstances resulting from the overthrow of the former Iranian regime in 1978 and 1979.

The new Iranian authorities came. However, our lands remained under the control of the other side. We realized that the new regime needed time to carry out its obligations under the agreement. However, the group ruling Iran showed hostility toward us right from the first day. It violated the relations of good neighborliness. We began hearing continuous statements from them that they were not bound by the March agreement.

The ruling group in Iran violated a basic provision in the agreement when it recalled the leader of the mercenary mutiny from the United States. Agent Barzani and some of his sons were getting ready to return to Iran to resume their aggressive activities against Iraq. But Barzani died among his American benefactors. His sons and the heads of the mercenary mutiny returned to Iran to use it as a springboard to threaten Iraq's unity and national security with the support of the ruling authorities.

Since their assumption of power to date, the conduct of the rulers of Iran has demonstrated their violation of the relations of good neighborliness and their non-commitment to the provisions of the March agreement. Therefore, they are legally totally and actually responsible for the abrogation of this agreement.

Despite the difficult circumstances which Iraq was experiencing at the time it was signed, this agreement was based on balanced elements. Upsetting any of these elements meant upsetting the spirit of the agreement.

Since the rulers of Iran have violated this agreement as of the beginning of their reign by blatantly and deliberately intervening in Iraq's domestic affairs by backing and financing, as did the shah before them, the leaders of the mutiny, which is backed by America and Zionism, and by refusing to return the Iraqi territories, which we were compelled to liberate by force, I announce before you that we consider the 6 March 1975 agreement as abrogated from our side also. The RCC [Revolutionary Command Council] has made a decision to this effect.

Thus, the legal relationship concerning Shatt al-Arab [river] should return to what it was before 6 March 1975. This Shatt shall again be, as it has been throughout history, Iraqi and Arab in name and reality, with all rights of full sovereignty over it.

Brothers, in its relations with the entire world, Iraq has demonstrated that it honorably respects all its pledges. It has also demonstrated that it cannot accept any form of threats, aggression and violation of its sovereignty and dignity. The Iraqi people and army are fully prepared to wage all valiant battles, no matter what the sacrifices, to safeguard their honor and sovereignty. We have taken our historic decision to restore our total sovereignty over our soil and waters. We will act strongly and efficiently against anyone who defiles this legitimate decision.

We assure you, brothers, as well as the entire world, as we did in the past, that we aspire to establishing good relations of neighborliness with the neighboring states, particularly Iran, and Iraq has no ambitions on the Iranian territories; we did not at all intend to launch war against Iran or expand the circle of struggle with it beyond the limits of defending our rights and sovereignty. We tell those blinded by vanity in Iran, and those who were driven by their suspicious motives, and those moving them in public or secretly from the imperialist, Zionist and opportunists [sic] powers that they must benefit from the past days' lessons when our valiant army restored Zayn al-Qaws, Sayf Sa'd and our border posts as brave and faithful men.

We call on them to respond to the voice of right and justice, which calls for maintaining relations of good neighborliness with Iraq and the Arab nation and relinquishing every inch they usurped from the territories of Iraq and the Arab nation. Only in this way can they serve their people, if they are really faithful to them. Only in this way can they prove that they are real revolutionaries and not agents for the colonialist and Zionist powers, that they are not racist, backward usurpers who harbor hatred and hostility for the Arab nation and that they are not trying to instigate sedition among the Arab ranks in order to divide and weaken this nation in accordance with or in implementation of the Zionist design.

We say before you, before the Arab nation and before the entire world, that we have unmasked the false face by which the ruling clique in Iran came to power. This clique has used the face of religion falsely to expand at the expense of the Arab sovereignty and the nobler Arab interests. This clique has used the face of religion to foment sedition and division among the nation's ranks despite the difficult circumstances through which the Arab nation is passing and despite the Arab nation's struggle against the Zionist aggression and the imperialist powers.

This face of religion is only a mask to cover the Persian racism and a buried resentment for the Arabs. The clique in Iran is using this face of religion to flame fanaticism, resentment and division among the peoples of this area to serve the designs of world Zionism, whether this clique realizes it or not.

Some of the circles that are moved by this clique have different motives—and this is now not the time to discuss these motives—these circles say that Khomeini differs from the shah. They ask: Why do you deal with Khomeini in this way? We answer them: We honestly hoped that Khomeini would be different from the shah in his positions on our national and pan-Arab causes, particularly the cause of the occupied Arab territories. We gave him enough time to prove whether he was really different from the shah or not. Yet he and those ruling with him in Iran these days have proved that they are no different from the shah in their expansionist ambitions and in their racist stands toward the Arabs. They have unjustly maintained all the Iraqi territories which the shah occupied and maintained—the three Arab islands of Greater Tunb, Lesser Tunb and Abu Musa. They have even renewed the expansionist calls which the shah relinquished under the pressure of the Arab will. As for Iraq, they refused even to return the territories which the shah agreed to return according to the 1975 agreement.

Brothers, when we speak with pain of the Iranian regime's racism and of its aggressive stands, we cannot forget to highlight with great appreciation the stands of good men among the Iranian peoples, the Persian in particular, for we harbor amity towards them. We also have bonds of friendship with these peoples and hope that they will survive the ordeal they are now enduring.

We warmly greet our brothers, the Arabs of Ahvaz who are suffering from suppression and tyranny under the Khomeini regime more than they suffered during the shah's reign. We also greet the honorable Kurdish militants and all the other friendly Iranian peoples. We assure them that we do not have any ambitions on any inch of their territories and that we harbor toward them nothing but feelings of amity and affection. We hope that neighbor Iran will be free and independent, making a positive contribution to the region, the nonaligned movement and to the peoples' struggle for liberty, independence and progress.

Brothers, we affirm to the world that Iraq, which was administering navigational affairs in Shatt al-Arab prior to March 1975, in accordance with the rights of total sovereignty, has shown genuine ability and effectiveness as well as high responsibility in this respect. Today's Iraq is more capable of carrying out its tasks in this regard. We hope that all the sides concerned, including the Iranian side, will respect Iraq's sovereignty over Shatt al-Arab and deal in accordance with these new facts.

Brothers, at a certain party meeting, a comrade asked me: What is the guaranteed reserve which you have to confront the suspect racist enemy in the new regime in Iran?

I told this comrade: The leadership has accustomed the Iraqi people to always have a guaranteed reserve to be used at historic moments to confront enemies. However, I would like to tell you and tell all the Iraqi people and all the honest sons of the Arab nation that the basic, known and guaranteed reserve with which we will confront the machinations of the suspect agents in Iran—who have rancorous and backward mentalities and racist motives, and the hostile colonialist, Zionist and racist machinations—is the great Iraqi people. The known and guaranteed reserve is the great Iraqi people with their spirit of seriousness, their unlimited readiness to give and make sacrifices and their strong adherence to their legitimate rights, guided and inspired by their great historical heritage—the great legacy of Islam, the history of the glorious Arab nation and the glories of great Iraq. This reserve is our valiant Iraqi Army which has sprung from this spirit and which adheres to the principles of the revolution, epitomizing in its life and battles the glittering history of its nation and the glorious history of Iraq.

Brothers, you are the known and guaranteed reserve. The guaranteed reserve is all the valiant and honest officers and soldiers of our Iraqi Army and the sons of our people, men and women, young and old. This reserve is the honest spirit of Arabs everywhere who are struggling against aggression, usurpation, exploitation and subservience and who refuse to bow down to the odious Persian occupation just as they are struggling fiercely and bravely against the treacherous Zionist occupation in Palestine and other Arab areas.

Brothers, I give you greetings of honor and pledge [as heard] and thank you for attending this extraordinary session. I am confident that our great people, who have shouldered their national and pan-Arab responsibilities throughout history effectively and courageously, will proceed along this course. God willing, these people will strengthen their positive and effective role in this area and on the international level. Iraq will continue to be a steadfast bastion of steel against all aggressors and usurpers. It will always be a center of support for liberty, progress and good in the world. Iraq will always be a bastion for the Arab nation and for glory.

May God's blessings and peace be upon you.

SOURCE: Foreign Broadcast Information Service, *Daily Report: Middle East and North Africa,* September 18, 1980, E–1–E–7.

Iran-Iraq War and Diplomacy

DOCUMENT IN CONTEXT

For more than six years, between late 1981 and early 1988, the Iran-Iraq War ground on as a military stalemate punctuated by a series of attacks and counterattacks. Small amounts of territory changed hands, but without either of the combatants able to inflict defeat on the other. Hundreds of thousands of people, including civilians, regular army soldiers, and volunteers in militias, died during this period of inconclusive fighting. Diplomats finally entered the fray in 1987, setting the stage for a settlement that would eventually be reached the following year.

In September 1981—one year after Iraq began the war by capturing chunks of Iranian territory near the Persian Gulf—Iran launched a counteroffensive that gave it the strategic initiative, at least temporarily. A key Iranian tactic involved the use of well-coordinated "waves" of volunteers, most of whom had little military training or weapons but were fervent supporters of the religious leaders in Tehran. Volunteer units known as the Pasdaran (Revolutionary Guards) and Basij (Peoples Army) would attack in large numbers, effectively overwhelming Iraqi positions. By April 1982, Iran had retaken Khorramshahr, the largest city that had been captured by Iraq early in the war, and had pushed nearly all Iraqi forces out of Iran.

Iraqi president Saddam Hussein announced in June 1982 that he was withdrawing the Iraqi army from Iran. He characterized the withdrawal as a tactical measure that would enable Iraq to come to the aid of Lebanon, which had just been invaded by Israel in its pursuit of Palestinian guerrillas operating there. This claim represented little more than a cover for the failure of the Iraqi invasion of Iran. Hussein proceeded to fire the generals who had failed him and replace them with more capable leaders, spend hundreds of millions of dollars buying upgraded military equipment, and order the construction of massive defensive positions in southern Iraq in anticipation of an expected counterinvasion by the Iranians.

Iran began its invasion in July 1982, when it sent wave after wave of volunteer soldiers—many armed only with copies of the Quran—across the border in an attempt to capture the holy city of Karbala. Iran's supreme leader, Ayatollah Ruhollah Khomeini, asserted that the offensive eventually would "liberate" Baghdad and then sweep westward to take Jerusalem from the Israelis. In the face of fierce Iraqi defenses, however, the first attack quickly withered, as did several subsequent attacks along the Iran-Iraq border in the following months. Tens of thousands of Iranian volunteers lost their lives in these futile offensives. Regardless, leaders in Tehran refused to give up, in part because of their expectation that the Shiites of southern Iraq—long oppressed by successive governments in Baghdad—would rise up to support their Shiite brethren from Iran.

Another front, the so-called tanker war, opened in August 1983, when Iraq stepped up attacks in the Persian Gulf against ocean-going oil tankers, most of which were from neutral countries. Most of these attacks failed, largely because the Iraqis relied on French-supplied Exocet missiles unable to penetrate the hulls of the large supertankers. Iran proved to be more successful in curtailing Iraqi oil exports, because the main oil-export terminals lie just across the border from Iran. They fell victim to Iranian attacks early in the war.

In an attempt to break the stalemate, Iraq in February 1984 began attacking Iranian cities using warplanes, short-range rockets, and medium-range missiles. Iran responded with its own attacks against Iraqi cities. These tit-for-tat raids came to be known as the "war of the cities." Iraq had the advantage of air superiority because the Iranian air force had deteriorated without access to spare parts for its U.S.-supplied fleet. Iran, however, had a bigger advantage: Its main cities had developed well eastward of the border and thus stood out of range of most Iraqi attacks, but most of Iraq's principal cities are located near the border and thus made easy targets for Iranian missiles. Bombardment of the cities continued at various stages for the remaining four years of the war. By 1988 Iraq had developed a longer-range missile capable of hitting key Iranian cities. These attacks caused widespread panic among civilians just as Iran's military forces began suffering major defeats on the battlefield.

U.S. Intervention

At the outset of the Iran-Iraq War, the United States had declared its neutrality while hoping that both countries would lose the war. The administrations of Jimmy Carter and Ronald Reagan were particularly hostile toward Iran because of the crisis in which fifty-two U.S. diplomats were held hostage between November 1979 and January 1981 in Tehran. The Reagan administration initially also had no sympathy for Iraq, which Washington believed to be a client of the Soviet Union.

The U.S. attitude began to shift in 1982 after the successful Iranian counteroffensive and Khomeini's call for an Islamic holy war against U.S. allies in the region. In February 1982, the Reagan administration removed Iraq from a list of countries designated as having supported or facilitated terrorism. Iraq's presence on that list had made any kind of military cooperation between the United States and Iraq illegal; removing the designation signaled the administration's "tilt" toward Iraq in its war with Iran. The first real U.S. support for Iraq took the form of a secret supply of data from satellites and other intelligence information that helped Baghdad bolster its defenses against Iranian offensives.

The Reagan administration followed up in 1983 with the approval of loan guarantees enabling Iraq to buy U.S. agricultural products. These guarantees started at the level of $400 million in 1983 and rose to more than $600 million four years later, allowing Iraq to spend its increasingly scarce cash on weapons. By 1985 the administration was permitting Iraq to buy military-related equipment and supplies directly from the United States (including material that Iraq would use to develop the chemical weapons that it would use against Iraqi Kurds as well as Iranian soldiers).

In 1985 the Reagan administration began tilting not only toward Iraq but also toward Iran. This came about because of President Reagan's concern about the fate of seven Americans held hostage in Lebanon by guerrilla groups backed by Iran. Robert C. McFarlane, Reagan's national security advisor, believed a claim by an Iranian businessman that he could secure the release of the hostages if the United States sold missiles and military spare parts to Iran. With Reagan's approval, the United States supplied 2,000 antitank missiles, 18 high-tech antiaircraft missiles, and numerous shipments of spare parts to Iran between May 1985 and October 1986. White House officials used the money that Iran paid for these weapons to support the contras, guerrillas battling the leftist Sandinista government of Nicaragua. Congress had halted U.S. aid to the contras, so Reagan's aides devised this illegal means of helping them. The arms sales secured the release of three of the hostages in Lebanon, but three more Americans were kidnapped in late 1986.

The administration's secret dealings with Iran began to come to light in November 1986, when a Lebanese newsmagazine revealed that McFarlane had traveled to Tehran for negotiations with the government. That disclosure led to public revelations about the link between the Iranian arms sales and aid to the contras. The Iran-contra affair developed into a scandal that severely damaged the credibility of the Reagan administration in its last years.

Major Battles in 1986

On February 11, 1986, Iran launched one of its largest and most important offensives of the war. Crossing over the Shatt al-Arab at the extreme southeastern tip of Iraq, Iran's army easily overran weak Iraqi defenses on the Faw Peninsula and marched north toward Basra, Iraq's second largest city. The initial success of this offensive owed much to intelligence information and the missiles the Reagan administration had provided. Iran's army and its volunteer militias were incapable of overcoming Iraq's defenses around Basra, however, and the situation evolved into another stalemate, lasting throughout 1986. Iranian units occupied the Faw Peninsula while Iraq furiously strengthened its defenses of Basra. Iran attempted one last major assault on Basra in January 1987, but fell short at the cost of tens of thousands of lives, in part because of Iraq's heavy use of chemical weapons against the invading Iranians.

In another important development at this stage of the war, the U.S. military intervened on behalf of Kuwait, a major oil exporter with tankers being targeted by Iran. In late 1986, Kuwait asked the United States to protect its shipping in the Gulf. The Reagan administration at first hesitated, leading Kuwait to turn for help to the Soviet Union. This got the attention of the White House, which then agreed to Kuwait's request. Starting in July 1987, eleven Kuwaiti oil tankers were reflagged as American ships and escorted in the Gulf by the U.S. Navy. An Iranian antiship missile hit one of the tankers in Kuwaiti territorial waters in October, leading the United States to retaliate by bombing an oil platform from which Iran had launched attacks against ships in the Gulf.

UN Resolution

Lasting eight years, the Iran-Iraq War took place in the context of many other major international developments, including the final stages of the cold war between the

United States (and its allies) and the Soviet Union (and its allies). During the first years of the 1980s, tensions between Washington and Moscow in part prevented the United Nations from taking any effective diplomatic action to bring the Iran-Iraq War to a conclusion. Competition between the two superpowers for influence in the Persian Gulf even contributed to some aspects of the war, such as the U.S. decision to reflag Kuwaiti oil tankers in 1987 rather than allow Moscow to do so.

By mid-1987, however, several elements had come together to allow the UN Security Council to take its first decisive stand on the war. One element concerned the increasing threat to world oil supplies because of attacks on shipping in the Persian Gulf. Another involved the overall easing of tension between Washington and Moscow following reformist Mikhail Gorbachev's rise to power as Soviet leader. It had also become clear by 1987 that neither Iran nor Iraq would be able to muster a complete victory in the war.

After months of negotiations, the Security Council in mid-July finally produced a comprehensive diplomatic initiative that included elements encouraging Iran and Iraq to end their fighting. The council adopted Resolution 598 on a unanimous vote on July 20. It was the first time in UN history that the five permanent members of the Security Council had voted to demand an end to an ongoing war although the combatants had not accepted a peace agreement. Key elements of the resolution demanded an immediate cease-fire, the withdrawal "without delay" of military forces to international boundaries, the exchange of prisoners of war, and the cooperation of both parties in the negotiation of a "comprehensive, just and honorable settlement" of the underlying issues. The resolution did not provide for any kind of enforcement; for example, it did not authorize an outside party to intervene to ensure that Iran and Iraq comply with the council's demands. The council did, however, adopt the resolution under the chapters of the UN Charter, giving it the power to impose sanctions against member countries, thus creating the prospect that either Iran or Iraq or both could be subjected to an arms embargo. U.S. secretary of state George P. Shultz suggested the possibility of such sanctions, stating on July 20 that Washington would back "the decisive application of enforcement measures" if either Iran or Iraq rejected the call for a cease-fire.

Iraq immediately accepted the UN resolution—providing that Iran do likewise. Tehran refused, however, with its chief representative at the UN calling the measure a "vicious American diplomatic maneuver." UN secretary-general Javier Pérez de Cúellar embarked on a series of diplomatic missions lasting through the remainder of 1987 that created modest hope but no end to the war. Even as de Cúellar negotiated with the two sides, the Reagan administration pushed the Security Council to impose an arms embargo against Iran because of its refusal to accept Resolution 598. China and Russia blocked the effort.

Arab Summit

One other diplomatic initiative on the war came in late 1987 from the Arab League, which previously had avoided taking a strong position on the conflict although one of the combatants—Iraq—was a member of the league. After a four-day summit in Amman, Arab leaders on November 11 took a surprisingly strong position condemning Iran for its "procrastination" in accepting Resolution 598.

The Arab League's earlier hesitation to take sides had resulted, in large part, from a feud between Iraqi leader Saddam Hussein and Syrian leader Hafiz al-Assad. The two men led competing branches of the Baath Party and long had been at odds, in this case to the point that Assad openly supported Iran during much of the war. Brought together by their fellow Arab leaders, however, Hussein and Assad appeared to resolve enough of their differences to reach agreement on a common approach to the war—placing blame on Iran for refusing to accept the UN resolution.

The Iran-Iraq War finally came to an end in July 1988, but not because of international diplomatic pressure. Rather, Iran relented and accepted a peace agreement after a string of military losses that made the price of continuing the fight too steep, even for a government that insisted it was doing God's will (Conclusion of the Iran-Iraq War, p. 437).

Following are excerpts from the text of UN Security Council Resolution 598 adopted July 20, 1987, calling for a cease-fire in the Iran-Iraq War, and the final communiqué of the Arab League meeting in Amman, Jordan, issued November 11, 1987.

DOCUMENT

UN Security Council Resolution 598 (1987)

JULY 20, 1987

The Security Council,

Reaffirming its resolution 582 (1986),

Deeply concerned that, despite its calls for a cease-fire, the conflict between the Islamic Republic of Iran and Iraq continues unabated, with further heavy loss of human life and material destruction,

Deploring the initiation and continuation of the conflict,

Deploring also the bombing of purely civilian population centers, attacks on neutral shipping or civilian aircraft, the violation of international humanitarian law and other laws of armed conflict, and, in particular, the use of chemical weapons contrary to obligations under the 1925 Geneva Protocol,

Deeply concerned that further escalation and widening of the conflict may take place,

Determined to bring to an end all military actions between Iran and Iraq,

Convinced that a comprehensive, just, honorable and durable settlement should be achieved between Iran and Iraq,

Recalling the provisions of the Charter of the United Nations, and in particular the obligation of all Member States to settle their international disputes by peaceful means in such a manner that international peace and security and justice are not endangered,

Determining that there exists a breach of the peace as regards the conflict between Iran and Iraq,

Acting under Articles 39 and 40 of the Charter,

1. *Demands* that, as a first step towards a negotiated settlement, the Islamic Republic of Iran and Iraq observe an immediate cease-fire, discontinue all military actions on land, at sea and in the air, and withdraw all forces to the internationally recognized boundaries without delay;

2. *Requests* the Secretary-General to dispatch a team of United Nations observers to verify, confirm and supervise the cease-fire and withdrawal and further requests the Secretary-General to make the necessary arrangements in consultation with the Parties and to submit a report thereon to the Security Council;

3. *Urges* that prisoners-of-war be released and repatriated without delay after the cessation of active hostilities in accordance with the Third Geneva Convention of 12 August 1949;

4. *Calls upon* Iran and Iraq to co-operate with the Secretary-General in implementing this resolution and in mediation efforts to achieve a comprehensive, just and honorable settlement, acceptable to both sides, of all outstanding issues, in accordance with the principles contained in the Charter of the United Nations;

5. *Calls upon* all other States to exercise the utmost restraint and to refrain from any act which may lead to further escalation and widening of the conflict, and thus to facilitate the implementation of the present resolution;

6. *Requests* the Secretary-General to explore, in consultation with Iran and Iraq, the question of entrusting an impartial body with inquiring into responsibility for the conflict and to report to the Council as soon as possible;

7. *Recognizes* the magnitude of the damage inflicted during the conflict and the need for reconstruction efforts, with appropriate international assistance, once the conflict is ended and, in this regard, requests the Secretary-General to assign a team of experts to study the question of reconstruction and to report to the Council;

8. *Further requests* the Secretary-General to examine, in consultation with Iran and Iraq and with other States of the region, measures to enhance the security and stability of the region;

9. *Requests* the Secretary-General to keep the Council informed on the implementation of this resolution;

10. *Decides* to meet again as necessary to consider further steps to ensure compliance with this resolution.

Adopted unanimously at the 2750th meeting.

SOURCE: United Nations, www.un.org/docs/scres/1987/scres87.htm.

DOCUMENT

Arab League Summit Communiqué on Ending the Iran-Iraq War

NOVEMBER 11, 1987

. . . From the premise of our historical responsibility and pan-Arab principles; based on the relations of brotherhood and the interconnection of security, political, and economic interests and the interconnection of history and civilization; out of an awareness of the sensitive and difficult stage the Arab homeland is experiencing and of the challenges against the Arab homeland's present and future which pose a threat to its existence; and realizing that the state of division and fragmentation causes a weakness that dissipates the Arab nation's resources and exhausts its potentialities, the issue of Arab solidarity has been the focus of the Arab leaders' attention. They discussed its various aspects, and pinpointed its weak and strong points. They stressed the need to support and enhance it, and allotted it priority. Their viewpoints were in agreement on this issue, and they agreed that Arab solidarity is the only means to achieve the Arab nation's dignity and pride and to ward off danger and harm from it. The leaders unanimously agreed to overcome differences and to eliminate the causes of weakness and the factors of dismemberment and division. From the premise of their loyalty to their homeland and their genuine affiliation to their nationalism, they decided to adopt Arab solidarity as a basis for a joint Arab action whose objective is to embody the unity of their stand, build the capabilities of the Arab nation, and provide it with factors of strength and impregnability.

After listening to His Majesty King Hussein's speech at the first closed session of the summit, the leaders decided to consider the speech in which His Majesty launched the slogan of reconciliation and accord as the title of the summit and an official document of the summit. They reiterated their abidance by the need to support Arab-African cooperation. They condemned the terrorism and racial discrimination which the racist regime in South Africa is carrying out. They also reiterated their support for the struggle of the people in South Africa and Namibia.

In adherence to the Arab League Charter, the Collective Arab Defense Pact, and the Arab Solidarity Charter; to emphasize the determination to protect pan-Arab security and to safeguard the Arab territory; and in an atmosphere filled with the spirit of fraternity and love which prevailed at the Amman summit, the Iraq-Iran war and the situation in the gulf region topped the summit agenda. The leaders expressed their concern over the continuation of the war and expressed their dissatisfaction with the Iranian regime's insistence on continuing it and on going too far in provoking and threatening the Arabian Gulf states. The conference condemned Iran for occupying part of the Iraqi territory and its procrastination in accepting UN Security Council Resolution Number 598. The conferees called on Iran to accept and fully implement this resolution in accordance with the sequence of its clauses. They appealed to the international community to assume its responsibilities, exert effective efforts, and adopt the necessary measures to make the Iranian regime respond to the peace calls. The conference also announced its solidarity with Iraq and its appreciation for its acceptance of Security Council Resolution Number 598 and its response to all peace initiatives. It also stressed its solidarity with and support for Iraq in protecting its territory and waters, and in defending its legitimate rights.

The leaders reviewed the developments in the gulf area and the serious consequences resulting from Iranian threats, provocations and aggressions. The conference announced its solidarity with Kuwait in confronting the Iranian regime's aggression. It also denounced the bloody criminal incidents perpetrated by Iranians in the Holy Mosque of Mecca. The conference affirmed its support for Kuwait in all of the measures it has taken to protect its territory and waters, and to guarantee its security and stability. The conference announced its support for Kuwait in confronting the Iranian regime's threats and aggressions. . . .

[The remainder of the communiqué deals with the Arab-Israeli conflict and other regional matters.]

SOURCE: *Historic Documents of 1987* (Washington, D.C.: CQ Press, 1988), 872–874.

Conclusion of the Iran-Iraq War

DOCUMENT IN CONTEXT

The Iran-Iraq War sputtered to an end in July 1988, nearly eight years after it had begun, when top Iranian officials concluded that they had no other choice but to agree to the cease-fire. Iraq had begun the war in 1980, and Iran had prolonged it for years in a futile attempt to procure an historic victory for its Islamic revolution. In the end, both sides lost the war, but Iraq emerged in a stronger position militarily. Iran suffered heavier losses in terms of human casualties, economic decline, and damage to its international reputation. The war served as a direct precursor to the much shorter Persian Gulf War of 1991. The latter resulted from Iraq's invasion of Kuwait, an action prompted by Iraqi president Saddam Hussein's illusions of greatness and a need for Kuwaiti oil and wealth following what he perceived to be victory over Iran (Iran-Iraq War and Diplomacy, p. 430; Persian Gulf War, p. 455).

The first significant diplomatic move toward ending the Iran-Iraq War began in July 1987 with the adoption of UN Security Council Resolution 598, calling for an immediate cease-fire. Iraq accepted the resolution, but Iran did not, apparently believing that it held the upper hand militarily because its forces still occupied small bits of southern Iraq.

If Tehran had a strategic edge as of mid-1987, it quickly disappeared in the early months of 1988. In late February, Iraq began using the al-Hussein, an improved version of a Scud missile. Over the course of several weeks, Iraq launched more than two hundred of them against Iranian cities, primarily Tehran and the religious center of Qom. Hundreds of thousands of terrified residents fled, many of them after rumors spread of an Iraqi plan to equip the missiles with chemical weapons.

Having demoralized much of Iran's civilian population with attacks from the air, Iraq proceeded to launch its most successful ground operations of the war. On April 17, 1988, the Iraqi army began an offensive that quickly recaptured the Faw Peninsula (in extreme southeastern Iraq), which Iran had occupied for more than two years. Iraq carried out four more large-scale military operations from late May through mid-July that drove all remaining Iranian forces from Iraqi territory and succeeded in capturing several strategic points inside Iran. As in other stages of the war, Iraq used chemical weapons against Iranian troops. In contrast to earlier in the war, the Iraqi army in 1988 was well led and its units carefully coordinated. By mid-July, the Iraqi forces had their Iranian counterparts on the run and threatened to press deep into Iran.

As these military battles unfolded on the ground, on July 3 an Iranian civilian airliner operating as Iran Air Flight 655, took off from Bandar Abbas airfield, in southern Iran, en route to Dubai. The plane's flight path tracked over U.S. naval ships deployed to protect international shipping in the Gulf. The cruiser USS *Vincennes,* mistaking the airliner for an Iranian warplane, fired two antiaircraft missiles at it, forcing it to crash and killing all 290 passengers and crew members. U.S. officials apologized, but the Iranian government insisted that the downing of the plane had been a deliberate act of war. Many Iranians also interpreted the incident as signaling the determination of the Reagan administration to topple their government, by military force if necessary.

These developments laid the groundwork for a heated debate among top Iranian officials about ending the war. According to most historical accounts, the majority of senior government leaders argued that the war was lost and should be stopped before Iran's big enemies—Iraq and the United States—destroyed what remained of Iran's army. Ayatollah Ruhollah Khomeini, Iran's supreme leader, reportedly was deeply reluctant to accept this advice but ultimately relented.

On July 18, Ali Khamenei, Iran's new president (and future successor to Khomeini), sent a letter to UN secretary-general Javier Pérez de Cúellar announcing his government's acceptance of the cease-fire called for in Security Council Resolution 598 almost exactly one year earlier. His letter cited the downing of Iran Air Flight 655 as evidence that "other countries" (meaning the United States) were engaged in aggression against Iran.

Two days later, on July 20, Ayatollah Khomeini published a lengthy message to the Iranian people defending the actions of his government and bitterly denouncing Iraq, the United States, the Soviet Union, and other enemies determined, he said, to destroy the Islamic revolution. Khomeini acknowledged only indirectly that he had agreed to accept the UN resolution to end the war. In the most memorable and direct reference to the war's outcome, he stated, "I repeat that the acceptance of this issue is more lethal for me than poison; but I surrender to God's satisfaction. I have drunk this for the sake of God's satisfaction."

Iraqi officials at first insisted that Iran's acceptance of the cease-fire was a ruse, but under pressure from Moscow and Washington, Baghdad reaffirmed its own willingness to stop the fighting. A formal cease-fire went into effect on August 20. Subsequent attempts by UN diplomats to negotiate a formal peace agreement failed, however. As with many other conflicts, the Iran-Iraq War simply stopped: no immediate effort followed to reach a military or diplomatic resolution of underlying issues. The two countries in September 1990 finally restored diplomatic relations and resolved border disputes that Saddam Hussein had cited in launching the war; this step coincided with Iraq's invasion of Kuwait, itself another outgrowth of the war.

Eight years of war caused massive destruction and misery in both countries, particularly in the border areas, where most of the fighting took place. Neither Iran nor Iraq has published a reliable accounting of its dead and wounded, but unofficial estimates by historians and others range from a low of about 500,000 to a high of more than 1.5 million. Whatever the total, the consensus among experts is that many more Iranians died than did Iraqis, largely because of Iran's widespread use of volunteers in its "human wave" attacks. The war was an economic disaster for both countries, particularly Iraq, which saw its oil exports plummet because of Iranian destruction and occupation of its oil terminals along the Shatt al-Arab.

In the war's aftermath, Iran and Iraq embarked on a new arms race in the expectation that the fighting would resume one day. That never happened, but two years later, in August 1990, Hussein sent the Iraqi army into Kuwait, apparently with the expectation of seizing Kuwait's flourishing oil industry to subsidize the Iraqi economy. The invasion led early in 1991 to the second major, late twentieth-century war in the Persian Gulf. This brief conflict would end with Iraqi troops being forced from Kuwait and the stage set for a much more far reaching conflict a dozen years later, with the United States invading Iraq to oust Hussein from power (Persian Gulf War, p. 455; Iraq War, p. 504).

Following are the text of Iranian president Ali Khamenei's letter of July 18, 1988, to UN secretary-general Javier Perez de Cuéllar accepting Security Council Resolution 598, declaring a cease-fire in the war between Iran and Iraq, and excerpts from a message to the people of Iran delivered over Tehran Radio on July 20, 1988, in which Ayatollah Ruhollah Khomeini explains the decision to accept Resolution 598.

DOCUMENT

Khamenei's Letter Accepting UN Security Council Resolution 598

JULY 18, 1988

Excellency, please accept my warm greetings with best wishes for your excellency's success in efforts to establish peace and justice.

As you are well-aware, the fire of the wars which was started by the Iraqi regime on 22 September 1980 through and [as received] aggression against the territorial integrity of the Islamic Republic of Iran has now gained unprecedented dimensions, bringing other countries into the war and even engulfing innocent civilians.

The killing of 290 innocent human beings, caused by the shooting down of an Airbus aircraft of the Islamic Republic of Iran by one of [the] American warships in the Persian Gulf is a clear manifestation of this contention.

Under these circumstances, Your Excellency's efforts for the implementation of Resolution 598 is of particular importance. The Islamic Republic of Iran has always provided you with its assistance and support to achieve this objective. In this context, we have decided to officially declare, that the Islamic Republic of Iran—because of the importance it attaches to saving the lives of human beings and the establishment of justice and regional and international peace and security—accepts Security Council Resolution 598 [as received].

We hope that the official declaration of this position by the Islamic Republic of Iran would assist you in continuing your efforts which has always received our support and appreciation.

SOURCE: Foreign Broadcast Information Service, *Daily Report: Near East and South Asia,* July 18, 1988, 44–45.

DOCUMENT

Khomeini Statement on the Cease-Fire with Iraq

JULY 20, 1988

. . .The acceptance of the resolution [598] was truly a very bitter and tragic issue for everyone, particularly for me. Up to a few days ago I believed in the methods of defense and the stances announced in the war. I saw in its implementation the interest of the system, the country, and the revolution. However, due to some incidents and factors which, for the time being I will refrain from elaborating on and which—God willing—will be made clear in the future, and in view of the opinion of all the high-ranking political and military experts of the country, whose commitment, sympathy and sincerity I trust, I agreed with the acceptance of the resolution and the cease-fire. At this juncture I regard it to be in the interest of the revolution and of the system. God knows that had it not been for the motive whereby all of us, our honor and credibility, should be sacrificed in the interests of Islam and the Muslims, I would never have agreed to this issue. Death and martyrdom would have been more bearable to me. What is to be done? We should all submit ourselves to the pleasure of Almighty God. Certainly the valiant and heroic Iranian nation has been and will remain this way.

I hereby express my thanks and appreciation to all my beloved children on the fronts of fire and blood, who, from the start of the war until now, have in some way endeavored and labored in connection with the war.

I call upon the entire Iranian nation to remain vigilant, patient, and steadfast. It is possible that in the future certain individuals may knowingly, or through ignorance, raise the question among the people as to what was the fruit of all the blood, martyrdom, and self-sacrifice. These people are surely unaware of the unseen worlds and of the philosophy of martyrdom. They do not know that for a person who has engaged in jihad for the sake of God's satisfaction, and who has surrendered himself to submission and devotion, events will in no way harm this person's eternal, everlasting, and exalted position.

To understand fully the value and the path of our martyrs we must cover a long distance. We must look for it in the passage of time and the history of the current revolution and of those to come.

The blood of the martyrs has definitely ensured the revolution and Islam. The blood of the martyrs has taught a permanent lesson of resistance to the people of the world. God knows that the way of martyrdom cannot be hidden. The nations and those to come will be the ones to follow in the footsteps of the martyrs. The immaculate dust of the martyrs will provide the resting place of those in love, the mystics, and will also provide the healing place for the free people. Happy are those who departed through martyrdom. Happy are those who lost their lives in this convoy of light. Happy are the mothers who raised these gems. O God, keep this book of martyrdom open to those who are willing; and do not deprive us of reaching it.

O God, our country and our nation are still at the beginning of the path of struggle; they need the torch of martyrdom. Please be the guardian of this shining lamp. Happy are you, the nation. Happy are you, women and men. Happy are the disabled, the prisoners of war and those missing in action and the great families of the martyrs. And how unhappy I am because I have survived and drunk the poisonous chalice of accepting the resolution, and feel ashamed in front of the greatness and sacrifices of this great nation. Unhappy are those who were not in this convoy. Unhappy are those who have so far passed by this great event of martyrdom and war, and the great divine examination—those who have remained silent and indifferent, who have criticized or verbally attacked it.

Yes, yesterday was the day of divine trial. And tomorrow there will be another trial which is to come our way. And all of us have a day of yet greater accountability.

Those who during the past few years of struggle and war avoided performing this great duty of theirs—no matter what their reasons—and kept themselves, their lives and property and children and others from the fire of events must know for sure that they have avoided their divine duty. And they have suffered a great loss. They will feel sorry on the day of judgment. I once again tell all the people and the responsible authorities that they must keep the account of such people separate from the account of those who have crusaded on the path of God. They must not let these undeserved claimants of today and those shortsighted leaders of yesterday return to the scenes.

Whether I am in your midst or not, I bequeath and recommend to all of you not to allow the revolution to fall into the hands of those who are unqualified and alien. Do not let the torch-bearers of martyrdom and blood be forgotten in the course of your daily lives.

I strongly recommend you, the dear Iranian nation, to be on your guard. The acceptance of the resolution by the Islamic Republic of Iran does not mean that the war has been resolved. The propaganda weapon of the world devourers against us has been blunted through announcements of this decision. But one cannot foresee future events in definite and serious ways. The enemy has not yet abandoned his tricks. He may well continue the same aggressive ways by resorting to excuses. We must be prepared to repel possible aggression by the enemy. Our nation must not yet regard the issue as closed. Of course, we officially announce that our objective is not a new tactic in continuation of the war. It is not impossible that the enemy will follow up its attacks through these excuses. Our military forces must never be ignorant of the deception and tricks of the enemies.

Under any conditions the defensive strength of the country must be in the best positions. Our people, who during the long years of struggle have felt the dimensions of the hatred and ruthlessness and animosity of the enemies of God, must regard the danger of the invasion of the world devourers in different forms as more serious. Now, as in the past, all the military personnel, whether belonging to the Army, the IRGC [Iranian Revolutionary Guard Corps], or the mobilization corps must continue their missions at the fronts to defend against the tricks of arrogance and Iraq.

Once we leave this stage of the revolution behind us by the same special way and regulations which are special to us, I will have recommendations for the next phase and construction of the country and the general policy of the regime and the revolution, which I shall talk about at an opportune time. But at this stage I demand most seriously of all speakers, authorities, and responsible people of the country and media and press directors to forego adventures and the creation of adventures. They must be on guard not to serve inadvertently as the tool of extreme thoughts and beliefs. They must rely on their common sense to stand alongside each other to watch the enemies.

During these days it is possible that many individuals may raise questions with why's and should-be's and should-not-be's; they may be motivated by their feelings. While in itself this is a beautiful thing, now is not the right time to attend to these queries. It is possible that those who until yesterday were taking positions against this regime, who used to talk of peace with the motive only of seeing the Iranian regime and government fall, today too many raise other deceptive words harboring the same objective. The lackeys of arrogance—those who until yesterday under the fake cover of peace stabbed the heart of the nation—also may well support the war. And the nationalists who lack culture may well begin their poisonous propaganda in order to waste the blood of the dear martyrs and to destroy the glory and honor of the people.

God willing, our dear nation, relying on farsightedness and intelligence, will rebuff all seditions.

I repeat that the acceptance of this issue is more lethal for me than poison; but I surrender to God's satisfaction. I have drunk this for the sake of God's satisfaction. . . .

SOURCE: Foreign Broadcast Information Service, *Daily Report: Near East and South Asia,* July 21, 1988, 49–50.

Iraqi Invasion of Kuwait

D O C U M E N T   I N   C O N T E X T

The second of the two wars in the Persian Gulf during the last decades of the twenti-eth century began unexpectedly on August 2, 1990, when Iraq sent its army across the border into neighboring Kuwait. Iraq quickly announced that it had annexed Kuwait as its nineteenth province, citing as justification disputed claims arising from the pre-World War I era, when the Ottoman Empire ruled much of the Middle East, and Brit-ain's subsequent creation of Iraq as an independent nation. The invasion caused great alarm worldwide because of the potential threat to Persian Gulf oil supplies.

The Iraqi invasion of Kuwait grew directly from the eight-year-long Iran-Iraq War, which ended in 1988 after the combatants had blooded each other into mutual sub-mission. The earlier war severely damaged the economies of both countries, particu-larly Iraq, which lost most of its ability to export oil because of Iranian military actions. Iraqi president Saddam Hussein saw Kuwait's oil production as a quick economic fix, making it a primary motivation for invading Kuwait. He also appeared to believe that by adding Kuwait's oil production to that of Iraq, he would control enough of the world's oil output to enable him to dictate a rise in world oil prices, which had tum-bled at the conclusion of the Iran-Iraq War. Another factor involved the financing of the war against Iran. During that conflict, Kuwait (along with Saudi Arabia) had loaned Iraq billions of dollars and afterward had refused Hussein's request that the loans be forgiven; by taking control of Kuwait, Hussein apparently believed that he could eliminate these debts. Hussein also accused Kuwait of stealing Iraqi oil from the Rumaila oilfield along the border between the two countries.

Iraq first threatened Kuwait in July 1990, when it began massing troops along the lightly defended border. The United States responded quickly, first by announcing "joint maneuvers" in the Persian Gulf with the United Arab Emirates and then dis-patching Ambassador April Glaspie to meet with Hussein on July 25. The signals con-veyed at that meeting later became the subject of dispute: The Iraqis claimed that Glaspie had given them a green light for the invasion, but Glaspie staunchly denied that she said anything to encourage Iraq's territorial ambitions.

Iraq's invasion of Kuwait on August 2 was a one-sided affair. An enormous Iraqi force easily rolled past Kuwait's weak defenses and by the end of the day had gained control of almost the entire country. Kuwait's ruler, Amir Jabir al-Ahmad al-Sabah, fled to Saudi Arabia, along with tens of thousands of compatriots and foreign work-ers who had been living in Kuwait. In subsequent days and weeks, Iraqi forces com-mitted numerous atrocities against Kuwaiti citizens, particularly business and political leaders.

Hussein offered his most extensive explanation of the invasion in a statement broadcast on August 12, in which he stated that Iraq had provided "assistance" to the people of Kuwait, "who have saved themselves from the al Sabah rule." The Iraqi leader also sought to link his occupation of Kuwait with Israel's occupation of Palestinian territories and other Arab lands, arguing that the United Nations should impose the same sanctions against Israel that were being planned against Iraq.

International reaction to the Iraqi occupation was swift. Hours after the invasion had begun, the UN Security Council on August 2 adopted Resolution 660 condemning the invasion and threatening punitive action against Iraq. The United States, France, and Great Britain moved to freeze Iraqi and Kuwaiti financial assets, and the Soviet Union canceled planned weapons deliveries to Iraq. The Security Council on August 6 followed its earlier resolution with another, Resolution 661, imposing mandatory economic sanctions against Iraq, including a ban on international purchases of Iraqi oil. (These sanctions would remain in effect, with some changes, until after Hussein's ouster in 2003.) The Security Council put teeth into its sanctions on August 25 when it adopted Resolution 665, authorizing countries (such as the United States) with naval ships in the Persian Gulf to enforce the ban on Iraq's trade. The U.S. Navy had been doing this unilaterally since August 16.

UN sanctions and international denunciations of immediate symbolic effect began within a few weeks to affect the Iraqi economy. The most important response at this point, however, was an intense diplomatic effort by the United States to assemble a coalition of countries willing to contribute troops to an international effort to force Iraq from Kuwait, if necessary. Secretary of State James A. Baker III flew to capitals around the world, and President George H. W. Bush telephoned dozens of fellow leaders in one of the most successful U.S. diplomatic campaigns of the late twentieth century.

A unified position by the United States and the Soviet Union—countries in the past fiercely at odds on many Middle Eastern issues—emerged as a result of this diplomacy and the simultaneous improvement in relations between the two superpowers in the final years before the Soviet Union collapsed. In a joint statement issued during a meeting in Helsinki on September 9, Bush and Soviet president Mikhail Gorbachev pledged to take whatever actions were necessary to demonstrate "beyond any doubt that aggression cannot and will not pay." (This would be one of the last major international initiatives by Gorbachev, whose country would disintegrate a year later.)

All the diplomatic work paid off. On November 29, the Security Council adopted Resolution 678, authorizing the U.S.-led coalition to use "all necessary means" to force Iraq out of Kuwait if it had not left voluntarily by January 15, 1991. This was the first UN authorization of war against a member nation since 1950, when the Security Council authorized the United States and other countries to defend South Korea against an invasion by North Korea. By the time the council adopted Resolution 678, the United States had positioned more than 200,000 troops in Saudi Arabia and other Persian Gulf countries, joining tens of thousands of troops from Britain, several other European countries, and a handful of Arab states. The Pentagon called this massive military presence Operation Desert Shield, signifying Washington's determination to protect Saudi Arabia from Iraq.

Another significant element of the international response to Iraq's invasion of Kuwait involved financial support for the planned operations. At U.S. urging, Germany, Japan, Saudi Arabia, and other countries pledged billions of dollars to Middle Eastern countries, such as Egypt, that provided troops to the U.S.-led coalition. They also agreed to subsidize the U.S. military build-up in the Persian Gulf. (By the time the war had ended, in February 1991, U.S. allies had pledged $54 billion, all of which they eventually contributed.)

Arab Reactions

Iraq's invasion of an Arab neighbor put great stress on Arab leaders, all of whom liked to talk about Arab unity but most of whom perceived the invasion of one Arab country by another as threatening their own interests. Aside from Kuwait, Saudi Arabia was the country most directly threatened by Iraq's actions. Saudi leaders believed that they might be next on Hussein's list of targets in part because their army was much weaker than his.

Arab leaders also felt threatened by Hussein's claim that the invasion of Kuwait sought to rectify an injustice created by British colonialism after World War I. Similar colonial-era decision making had determined the borders of nearly every Arab state, so Iraq's unilateral redrawing of boundaries could be seen as a precedent, putting at risk numerous other borders in the region. In addition, many of Hussein's counterparts did not trust the Iraqi leader, viewing him as rash, unstable, and likely to cause problems for the broader Arab world. Despite such concerns, some Arab leaders remained reluctant to denounce the invasion of Kuwait. Some wanted to maintain the fiction of Arab unity, while others did not want to be seen as siding with the United States and the other Western powers that had taken the lead in opposing Iraq's action.

Saudi Arabia, on the front line of possible confrontation with Iraq, was among the first Arab countries to denounce the invasion, and of more importance, to take action. On August 6, U.S. secretary of defense Dick Cheney visited Riyadh to provide intelligence showing that Iraqi military positions threatened Saudi Arabia. King Fahd immediately agreed to allow the U.S. military onto Saudi soil, a decision that led to the largest presence of U.S. forces in the Middle East to date. Fahd explained his decision in a speech to the nation on August 9, declaring the presence of foreign forces "merely and purely for defensive purposes" and "of a temporary nature." Fahd also said that they would leave "immediately" when requested to do so.

Fahd's decision to allow U.S. troops into Saudi Arabia held special significance for religious reasons: Saudi Arabia, the birthplace of Islam, is also the home to its most important shrines, and the king is the official protector of these places. A large contingent of U.S. forces remained in Saudi Arabia long after the Persian Gulf War, provoking widespread Muslim criticism of the Saudi regime and the United States. The last U.S. service personnel left the country in 2003 after the invasion of Iraq (Iraq War, p. 504).

An effort to achieve an Arab consensus took place in Cairo on August 10 at the initiative of Egyptian president Hosni Mubarak. Responding to Mubarak's call for an "Arab solution," leaders from most Arab countries met in a heated session that instead brought out old grievances. Twelve of the twenty-one members of the Arab League voted to support Saudi Arabia's request for troops to help defend it against Iraq. In addition to Saudi Arabia, Bahrain, Djibouti, Egypt, Kuwait (through its exiled leaders), Lebanon, Morocco, Oman, Qatar, Somalia, Syria, and the United Arab Emirates supported the call. Jordan, Mauritania, and Sudan voted to support the Saudi request but with "reservations." Algeria and Yemen abstained. Jordan's King Hussein, whose country depended heavily on Iraq for trade, including oil, later sided with Iraq, but provided no military support for his neighbor. Libya and the Palestine Liberation Organization (PLO) backed Iraq in opposing the Saudi request. The vote was one of the most contentious ever taken by the Arab League, which under its charter is supposed to operate by consensus (The Charter of the Arab League, p. 50).

Following are seven documents pertaining to Iraq's invasion of Kuwait on August 2, 1990: UN Security Resolution 660, condemning the invasion, adopted on August 2 (with Yemen abstaining); Resolution 661, imposing economic sanctions against Iraq, adopted on August 6 (with Cuba and Yemen abstaining); an address to the people of Saudi Arabia by King Fahd, on August 9, 1990, on the deployment of foreign troops to the kingdom; UN Security Council Resolution 665, authorizing enforcement of sanctions against Iraq, adopted on August 25 (with Cuba and Yemen abstaining); excerpts from a speech by Iraqi president Saddam Hussein on August 12, 1990, in which he defends Iraq's invasion; a joint statement issued in Helsinki by U.S. president George H. W. Bush and Soviet president Mikhail Gorbachev on September 9, 1990, pledging to take action to reverse the Iraqi invasion; and UN Security Council Resolution 678, authorizing the use of military force against Iraq, adopted on November 29 (with Cuba and Yemen voting no and China abstaining).

DOCUMENT

UN Security Council Resolution 660 (1990)

AUGUST 2, 1990

The Security Council,

Alarmed by the invasion of Kuwait on 2 August 1990 by the military forces of Iraq,

Determining that there exists a breach of international peace and security as regards the Iraqi invasion of Kuwait,

Acting under Articles 39 and 40 of the Charter of the United Nations,

1. *Condemns* the Iraqi invasion of Kuwait;

2. *Demands* that Iraq withdraw immediately and unconditionally all its forces to the positions in which they were located on 1 August 1990;

3. *Calls upon* Iraq and Kuwait to begin immediately intensive negotiations for the resolution of their differences and supports all efforts in this regard, and especially those of the League of Arab States;

4. *Decides* to meet again as necessary to consider further steps to ensure compliance with the present resolution.

Adopted at the 2932nd meeting by 14 votes to none. One member (Yemen) did not participate in the vote.

DOCUMENT

UN Security Council Resolution 661 (1990)

AUGUST 6, 1990

The Security Council,

Reaffirming its resolution 660 (1990) of 2 August 1990,

Deeply concerned that the resolution has not been implemented and that the invasion by Iraq of Kuwait continues with further loss of human life and material destruction,

Determined to bring the invasion and occupation of Kuwait by Iraq to an end and to restore the sovereignty, independence and territorial integrity of Kuwait,

Noting that the legitimate Government of Kuwait has expressed its readiness to comply with resolution 660 (1990),

Mindful of its responsibilities under the Charter of the United Nations for the maintenance of international peace and security,

Affirming the inherent right of individual or collective self-defence, in response to the armed attack by Iraq against Kuwait, in accordance with Article 51 of the Charter,

Acting under Chapter VII of the Charter,

1. *Determines* that Iraq so far has failed to comply with paragraph 2 of resolution 660 (1990) and has usurped the authority of the legitimate Government of Kuwait;
2. *Decides*, as a consequence, to take the following measures to secure compliance of Iraq with paragraph 2 of resolution 660 (1990) and to restore the authority of the legitimate Government of Kuwait;
3. *Decides* that all States shall prevent:
   (a) The import into their territories of all commodities and products originating in Iraq or Kuwait exported therefrom after the date of the present resolution;
   (b) Any activities by their nationals or in their territories which would promote or are calculated to promote the export or trans-shipment of any commodities or products from Iraq or Kuwait; and any dealings by their nationals or their flag vessels or in their territories in any commodities or products originating in Iraq or Kuwait and exported therefrom after the date of the present resolution, including in particular any transfer of funds to Iraq or Kuwait for the purposes of such activities or dealings;
   (c) The sale or supply by their nationals or from their territories or using their flag

vessels of any commodities or products, including weapons or any other military equipment, whether or not originating in their territories but not including supplies intended strictly for medical purposes, and, in humanitarian circumstances, foodstuffs, to any person or body in Iraq or Kuwait or to any person or body for the purposes of any business carried on in or operated from Iraq or Kuwait, and any activities by their nationals or in their territories which promote or are calculated to promote such sale or supply of such commodities or products;

4. *Decides* that all States shall not make available to the Government of Iraq or to any commercial, industrial or public utility undertaking in Iraq or Kuwait, any funds or any other financial or economic resources and shall prevent their nationals and any persons within their territories from removing from their territories or otherwise making available to that Government or to any such undertaking any such funds or resources and from remitting any other funds to persons or bodies within Iraq or Kuwait, except payments exclusively for strictly medical or humanitarian purposes and, in humanitarian circumstances, foodstuffs;

5. *Calls upon* all States, including States non-members of the United Nations, to act strictly in accordance with the provisions of the present resolution notwithstanding any contract entered into or license granted before the date of the present resolution;

6. *Decides* to establish, in accordance with rule 28 of the provisional rules of procedure, a Committee of the Security Council consisting of all the members of the Council, to undertake the following tasks and to report on its work to the Council with its observations and recommendations:

(a) To examine the reports on the progress of the implementation of the present resolution which will be submitted by the Secretary-General;

(b) To seek from all States further information regarding the action taken by them concerning the effective implementation of the provisions laid down in the present resolution;

7. *Calls upon* all States to co-operate fully with the Committee in the fulfillment of its task, including supplying such information as may be sought by the Committee in pursuance of the present resolution;

8. *Requests* the Secretary-General to provide all necessary assistance to the Committee and to make the necessary arrangements in the Secretariat for the purpose;

9. *Decides* that, notwithstanding paragraphs 4 to 8 above, nothing in the present resolution shall prohibit assistance to the legitimate Government of Kuwait, and calls upon all States;

(a) To take appropriate measures to protect assets of the legitimate Government of Kuwait and its agencies;

(b) Not to recognize any regime set up by the occupying Power;

10. *Requests* the Secretary-General to report to the Security Council on the progress made in the implementation of the present resolution, the first report to be submitted within thirty days;

11. *Decides* to keep this item on its agenda and to continue its efforts to put an early end to the invasion by Iraq.

Adopted at the 2933rd meeting by 13 votes to none, with 2 abstentions (Cuba and Yemen).

SOURCE: United Nations, www.un.org/Docs/scres/1990/scres90.htm.

DOCUMENT

King Fahd Statement on the Iraqi Invasion of Kuwait and Foreign Troop Deployments to Saudi Arabia

AUGUST 9, 1990

In the name of God, the Merciful, the Compassionate. Thanks be to God, Master of the Universe and Prayers of Peace be upon the last of Prophets Mohamad and all his kinfolk and companions.

Dear brother citizens, May God's peace and mercy be upon you.

You realize, no doubt, through following up the course of the regrettable events in the Arab Gulf region during the last few days the gravity of the situation the Arab nation faces in the current circumstances. You undoubtedly know that the government of the Kingdom of Saudi Arabia has exerted all possible efforts with the governments of the Iraqi Republic and the State of Kuwait to contain the dispute between the two countries.

In this context, I made numerous telephone calls and held fraternal talks with the brothers. As a result, a bilateral meeting was held between the Iraqi and Kuwaiti delegations in Saudi Arabia with the aim of bridging the gap and narrowing differences to avert any further escalation.

A number of brotherly Arab kings and presidents contributed, thankfully, in these efforts based on their belief in the unity of the Arab nation and the cohesion of its solidarity and cooperation to achieve success in serving its fateful causes.

However, regrettably enough, events took an adverse course, to our endeavors and the aspirations of the Peoples of the Islamic and Arab nation, as well as all peace-loving countries.

Nevertheless, these painful and regrettable events started in the predawn hours of Thursday 11 Muharram 1411H., corresponding to 2nd August A.D. 1990. They took the whole world by surprise when the Iraqi forces stormed the brotherly state of Kuwait in the most sinister aggression witnessed by the Arab nation in its modern history. Such an invasion inflicted painful suffering on the Kuwaitis and rendered them homeless.

While expressing its deep displeasure at this aggression on the brotherly neighbor Kuwait, the Kingdom of Saudi Arabia declares its categorical rejection of all ensuing measures and declarations that followed that aggression, which were rejected by all the statements issued by Arab leaderships, the Arab League, the Islamic Conference Organization, and the Gulf Cooperation Council, as well as all Arab and international bodies and organizations.

The Kingdom of Saudi Arabia reaffirms its demand to restore the situation in the brotherly state of Kuwait to its original status before the Iraqi storming as well as the return of the ruling family headed by H.H. [His Highness] Sheik Jaber al-Ahmed al-Sabah, the Emir of Kuwait and his government.

We hope that the emergency Arab summit called by H.E. [His Excellency] President Mohamad Hosni Mubarak of sisterly Egypt will lead to the achievement of the results that realize the aspirations of the Arab nation and bolster its march towards solidarity and unity of opinion.

In the aftermath of this regrettable event, Iraq massed huge forces on the borders of the Kingdom of Saudi Arabia. In view of these bitter realities and out of the eagerness of the Kingdom to safeguard its territory and protect its vital and economic potentials, and its wish to bolster its defensive capabilities and to raise the level of training of its armed forces—in addition to the keenness of the government of the Kingdom to resort to peace and non-recourse to force to solve disputes—the Kingdom of Saudi Arabia expressed its wish for the participation of fraternal Arab forces and other friendly forces.

Thus, the governments of the United States, Britain and other nations took the initiative, based on the friendly relations that link the Kingdom of Saudi Arabia and these countries, to dispatch air and land forces to sustain the Saudi armed forces in performing their duty to defend the homeland and the citizens against any aggression with the full emphasis that this measure is not addressed to anybody. It is merely and purely for defensive purposes, imposed by the current circumstances faced by the Kingdom of Saudi Arabia.

It is worth mentioning in this context that the forces which will participate in the joint training exercises with the Saudi armed forces are of a temporary nature. They will leave the Saudi territory immediately at the request of the Kingdom.

We pray to Almighty God to culminate our steps towards everything in which lie the good of our religion and safety of our homeland, and to guide us on the right path.

May God's peace and blessing be upon you.

SOURCE: *Historic Documents of 1990* (Washington, D.C.: CQ Press, 1991), 559–560.

DOCUMENT

UN Security Council Resolution 665 (1990)

AUGUST 25, 1990

The Security Council,

Recalling its Resolutions 660 (1990) of 2 August 1990, 661 (1990) of 6 August 1990, 662 (1990) of 9 August 1990 and 664 (1990) of 18 August 1990 and demanding their full and immediate implementation;

Having decided in resolution 661 (1990) to impose economic sanctions under Chapter VII of the Charter of the United Nations;

Determined to bring to an end the occupation of Kuwait by Iraq which imperils the existence of a Member State, and to restore the legitimate authority and the sovereignty, independence and territorial integrity of Kuwait, which requires the speedy implementation of the above resolutions;

Deploring the loss of innocent life stemming from the Iraqi invasion of Kuwait and determined to prevent further such losses:

Gravely alarmed that Iraq continues to refuse to comply with Resolutions 660 (1990), 661 (1990), 662 (1990) and 664 (1990) and in particular at the conduct of the Government of Iraq in using Iraqi flag vessels to export oil;

1. *Calls upon* those member states cooperating with the Government of Kuwait which are deploying maritime forces to the area to use such measures commensurate to the specific circumstances as may be necessary under the authority of the Security Council to halt all inward and outward maritime shipping, in order to inspect and verify their cargoes and destinations and to ensure strict implementation of the provisions related to such shipping laid down in Resolution 661 (1990);

2. *Invites* member states accordingly to co-operate as may be necessary to ensure compliance with the provisions of Resolution 661 (1990) with maximum use of political and diplomatic measures, in accordance with paragraph 1 above;

3. *Requests* all States to provide, in accordance with the Charter of the United Nations, such assistance as may be required by the states referred to in paragraph 1 above.

4. *Also requests* the States concerned to co-ordinate their actions in pursuit of the above paragraphs of the present resolution using, as appropriate, mechanisms of the Military Staff Committee and, after consultation with the Secretary-General, to submit reports to the Security Council and the Security Council Committee established by resolution 661 (1990) concerning the situation between Iraq and Kuwait, in order to facilitate the monitoring of the implementation of the present resolution;

5. *Decides* to remain actively seized of the matter.

Adopted at the 2938th meeting by 13 votes to none, with 2 abstentions (Cuba and Yemen).

SOURCE: United Nations, www.un.org/Docs/scres/1990/scres90.htm.

DOCUMENT

Hussein Message on the Invasion of Kuwait and the International Response

AUGUST 12, 1990

In the name of God the merciful, the compassionate. So as to contribute to creating an atmosphere of true peace in the region, to facilitate placing the region in a state of stability, to expose the falsehood of America and its deformed midget ally, Israel, to expose its small agents and their crimes against the nation, and to reaffirm right from a position of strength with faith in God, the people, and the nation, we have decided to propose the following initiative:

The United States has tried to cover its moves, which are hostile to humanity and the region's peoples, on the pretext that the decisions of the economic boycott of Iraq constitute a protest against Iraq's assistance to the people of Kuwait, who have saved themselves from the al-Sabah rule. Then it lost its mind when the Kuwaitis and the Iraqis decided to reconnect what British colonialism severed between Iraq and Kuwait, when Kuwait had been part of Iraq until World War I. Iraq had not recognized the crime perpetrated by colonialism until the present time. Later, the United States began to mass war fleets and aircraft squadrons, and to beat the drums of war against Iraq on the pretext of confronting Iraqi threats to Saudi Arabia. Because the spark of war, if it begins, will burn many people and inflict many catastrophes on those who are in its field; and in order to state facts as they are to world public opinion in general, and Western public opinion in particular, and to expose the falsehood of the assertions of the United States that it supports people's causes and rights, and that it seeks to maintain security and the West's interests only, I propose that all issues of occupation, or the issues that have been depicted as occupation in the entire region, be resolved in accordance with the same bases, principles, and premises to be set by the UN Security Council, as follows:

First, the preparation of withdrawal arrangements in accordance with the same principals for the immediate and unconditional withdrawal of Israel from the occupied Arab territories in Palestine, Syria, and Lebanon, Syria's withdrawal from Lebanon, a withdrawal between Iraq and Iran, the formulation of arrangements for the situation in Kuwait, and that the timing of the military arrangements and related political arrangements which must apply to all cases and in accordance with the same bases, principles, and premises, taking into consideration the historic rights of Iraq in its territory and the Kuwaiti people's choice, provided the implementation of the program begins with the oldest occupation, or what was called occupation, beginning with the enforcement of all applicable UN Security Council and UN resolutions, until we get to the most recent occupation, and on condition that the same measures passed by the UN Security Council against Iraq be adopted against any party that fails to obligate itself or comply with this arrangement.

Second, with the purpose of displaying the facts to world public opinion to judge in accordance with objective conditions apart from U.S. wishes and pressure, we propose the immediate withdrawal from Saudi Arabia of U.S. Forces and the other forces that responded to its conspiracy—they will be replaced by Arab forces whose number, nationality, duties, and location will be defined by the UN Security Council, assisted by the UN secretary-general. The nationality of the military forces between Iraq and Saudi Arabia will also be agreed upon, on the condition that the forces of the Government of Egypt, which the United States used in carrying out its plot against the Arab nation, be excluded.

Third, all boycott and siege decisions against Iraq shall be frozen immediately. Matters should return to normal in the economic, political, and scientific dealings between Iraq and the rest of the world. These resolutions should not be discussed and implemented again except when they are violated in light of what is stated above in items one, two, and three.

However, if America and its small agents do not respond to our initiative we, the good sons of the Arab nation and the great Iraqi people, will strongly resist its evil intentions and aggressive schemes. We will triumph, with God's help, and the evildoers will regret their actions after they leave the region defeated, cursed, and humiliated. God is great. Cursed be the lowly.

[Signed] Saddam Husayn, on 12 August 1990, corresponding to 21 Muharram 1411 hegira.

SOURCE: Foreign Broadcast Information Service, *Daily Report: Near East and South Asia,* August 13, 1990, Iraq 48–49.

DOCUMENT

U.S.-Soviet Statement on the Iraqi Invasion of Kuwait

SEPTEMBER 9, 1990

With regard to Iraq's invasion and continued military occupation of Kuwait, President Bush and President Gorbachev issue the following joint statement:

We are united in the belief that Iraq's aggression must not be tolerated. No peaceful international order is possible if larger states can devour their smaller neighbors.

We reaffirm the joint statement of our Foreign Ministers of August 3, 1990 and our support for United Nations Security Council Resolutions 660, 661, 662, 664 and 665.

Today, we once again call upon the Government of Iraq to withdraw unconditionally from Kuwait, to allow the restoration of Kuwait's legitimate government, and to free all hostages now held in Iraq and Kuwait.

Nothing short of the complete implementation of the United Nations Security Council Resolutions is acceptable.

Nothing short of a return to the pre-August 2 status of Kuwait can end Iraq's isolation.

We call upon the entire world community to adhere to the sanctions mandated by the United Nations, and we pledge to work, individually and in concert, to ensure full compliance with the sanctions. At the same time, the United States and the Soviet Union recognize that UN Security Council Resolution 661 permits, in humanitarian circumstances, the importation into Iraq and Kuwait of food. The Sanctions Committee will make recommendations to the Security Council on what would constitute humanitarian circumstances. The United States and the Soviet Union further agree that any such imports must be strictly monitored by the appropriate international agencies to ensure that food reaches only those for whom it is intended, with special priority being given to meeting the needs of children.

Our preference is to resolve the crisis peacefully, and we will be united against Iraq's aggression as long as the crisis exists. However, we are determined to see this aggression end, and if the current steps fail to end it, we are prepared to consider additional ones consistent with the UN Charter. We must demonstrate beyond any doubt that aggression cannot and will not pay.

As soon as the objectives mandated by the UN Security Council resolutions mentioned above have been achieved, and we have demonstrated that aggression does not pay, the Presidents direct their Foreign Ministers to work with countries in the region and outside it to develop regional security structures and measures to promote peace and stability. It is essential to work actively to resolve all remaining conflicts in the Middle East and Persian Gulf. Both sides will continue to consult each other and initiate measures to pursue these broader objectives at the proper time.

SOURCE: George Bush Presidential Library and Museum, http://bushlibrary.tamu.edu/research/papers/1990/90090900.html.

DOCUMENT

UN Security Council Resolution 678 (1990)

NOVEMBER 29, 1990

The Security Council,

Recalling and reaffirming its resolutions 660 (1990) of 2 August 1990, 661 (1990) of 6 August 1990, 662 (1990) of 9 August 1990, 664 (1990) of 18 August 1990, 665 (1990) of 25 August 1990, 666 (1990) of 13 September 1990, 667 (1990) of 16 September 1990, 669 (1990) of 24 September 1990, 670 (1990) of 25 September 1990, 674 (1990) of 29 October 1990, and 677 (1990) of 28 November 1990,

Noting that, despite all efforts by the United Nations, Iraq refuses to comply with its obligation to implement resolution 660 (1990) and the above-mentioned subsequent relevant resolutions, in flagrant contempt of the Security Council,

Mindful of its duties and responsibilities under the Charter of the United Nations for the maintenance and preservation of international peace and security,

Determined to secure full compliance with its decisions,

Acting under Chapter VII of the Charter,

1. *Demands* that Iraq comply fully with resolution 660 (1990) and all subsequent relevant resolutions and decides, while maintaining all its decisions, to allow Iraq one final opportunity, as a pause of goodwill, to do so;

2. *Authorizes* Member States cooperating with the Government of Kuwait, unless Iraq on or before 15 January 1991 fully implements, as set forth in paragraph 1 above, the above-mentioned resolutions, to use all necessary means to uphold and implement Security Council resolution 660 (1990) and all subsequent relevant resolutions and to restore international peace and security in the area;

3. *Requests* all States to provide appropriate support for the actions undertaken in pursuance of paragraph 2 above;

4. *Requests* the States concerned to keep the Security Council regularly informed on the progress of actions undertaken pursuant to paragraphs 2 and 3 above;

5. *Decides* to remain seized of the matter.

Adopted at the 2963rd meeting by 12 votes to 2 (China and Yemen), with one abstention (China).

SOURCE: United Nations, www.un.org/Docs/scres/1990/scres90.htm.

Persian Gulf War

DOCUMENT IN CONTEXT

In the months after Iraq's invasion of Kuwait on August 2, 1990, the international strategy (devised primarily in Washington) for dealing with the situation called for exerting so much economic and political pressure on Iraq that its leader, Saddam Hussein, would find an excuse to withdraw Iraqi troops. In the meantime, the United States would assemble a military coalition to drive Iraqi forces out of Kuwait if necessary (Iraqi Invasion of Kuwait, p. 443).

The first part of this strategy failed: With the approval of the UN Security Council, the international community isolated Iraq diplomatically and economically, but Hussein remained defiant. The second part of the strategy succeeded: The United States and its allies bombed Iraq and its military positions in Kuwait for thirty-eight days in January and February 1991 before launching a ground invasion that drove the Iraqi army from Kuwait in 100 hours. Pentagon officials called the military campaign Operation Desert Storm.

There never was any question that the coalition that went to war against Iraq in January and February 1991 was primarily a U.S. endeavor. The United States contributed by far the largest number of military personnel—more than 400,000 from all four military branches—and the bulk of equipment and supplies for the air war and the ground invasion. Britain made the second-largest contribution—with 35,000 troops—and it coordinated most closely with the U.S. military. France sent 17,000 troops, and several other Western nations provided ships, warplanes, and other support services.

In addition to Saudi Arabia, several Arab nations—among them Egypt (about 30,000 troops) and Syria (19,000 troops)—contributed soldiers to the coalition. This Arab presence offered the United States significant diplomatic backing and cover for its intervention in an Arab nation. Twelve years later, President George W. Bush would attempt but fail to obtain such backing in assembling what would be a much smaller coalition for a much more controversial invasion of Iraq.

In its November 29, 1990, resolution authorizing military action against Iraq, the UN Security Council had set January 15, 1991, as the deadline for Iraq to withdraw its forces from Kuwait. Last-minute diplomatic efforts to avert war included an unproductive meeting on January 9 in Geneva between U.S. secretary of state James A. Baker III and Iraqi foreign minister Tariq Aziz and a similarly unproductive meeting on January 13 in Baghdad between UN secretary-general Javier Pérez de Cuéllar and Hussein.

On January 15, having secured authorization from Congress to go to war, Bush ordered an air campaign to weaken Iraqi military positions and to convince Hussein, again, that he had no choice but to withdraw Iraqi troops from Kuwait. The air campaign began early in the morning of January 17 (local time), with hundreds of warplanes, along with missiles fired from warships in the Persian Gulf, striking military and economic infrastructure targets in Iraq and Kuwait. The U.S.-led coalition operated virtually unhindered, losing a minimal number of planes to Iraqi antiaircraft fire.

Coalition leaders said they targeted only military installations and facilities supporting Iraq's military operations. One tragedy brought this claim into question, however, when on February 13 a U.S. cruise missile hit a civilian bomb shelter in Baghdad, killing about 1,000 people. Iraq accused the United States of deliberately targeting civilians, a charge the Pentagon denied in claiming that the facility actually was a military command center and that Iraq had deliberately put the civilians at risk.

Iraq's most potent response to the bombardment was the firing of medium-range Scud missiles at coalition forces in Saudi Arabia and at Israel. Iraq chose Israel as a target in hopes that it would retaliate, thus enabling Baghdad to proclaim itself the victim of Israeli "aggression" and thereby undermining the position of Egypt and other

Arab countries participating in the U.S.-led coalition. The Iraqi strategy failed, however, because Israeli leaders gave in to pressure by the United States to stay out of the conflict. Washington also sent Patriot air defense missiles to Israel, along with the troops to operate them, in the first deployment of U.S. forces to Israel during wartime. In any event, Iraqi missile attacks caused widespread panic in Israel but little damage and few deaths.

The Ground War

Expectations in Washington and other capitals that the massive bombardment of Iraq would force a retreat from Kuwait proved overly optimistic. A daily average of about 2,000 bombing runs by warplanes, plus hundreds of precision-guided cruise missile strikes, destroyed much of Iraq's military-related infrastructure, including electrical stations, bridges, antiaircraft positions, and government offices. In the two years after the end of the Iran-Iraq War, Hussein had spent hundreds of millions of dollars rebuilding the Iraqi military; thirty-eight days of coalition bombing destroyed much of that effort.

Iraq offered on February 15 to withdraw from Kuwait but with conditions that the U.S.-led coalition found unacceptable. On February 22, Bush announced a deadline of noon Eastern Standard Time on the following day for Iraq to begin withdrawing. When that deadline passed, he ordered a ground invasion, saying he had done so "only after extensive consultations within our coalition partnership."

The invasion began on the morning of February 24 (local time), when coalition ground units—backed by air and naval forces operating primarily from the Persian Gulf—began moving from Saudi Arabia in two directions. From the south, two U.S. Marine Corps divisions and an army brigade, along with army units from several Arab countries, surged across the border into Kuwait, headed for Kuwait City. From the west, U.S. British, and French units swept into southern Iraq to cut off the line of retreat of Iraqi forces in Kuwait.

The enormous coalition force outmatched defending Iraqi forces by every measurement. A few Iraqi units resisted, but most retreated or surrendered in the face of overwhelming force. The border area of Iraq and Kuwait quickly became gripped by massive gridlock, with Iraqi tanks and personnel carriers blocked from retreating northward into Iraq and pushed from the south by advancing coalition forces. Washington had expressed concerns that Iraq might use chemical weapons against invading troops, but such an attack never materialized.

On February 26, after little more than two days of fighting, Hussein announced by radio that he had ordered the Iraqi army in Kuwait to withdraw, something Iraqi soldiers had been desperately trying to do already. Hussein remained defiant, declaring that Iraq had achieved a victory in what he called the "mother of all battles." He said Iraq had withdrawn because of "certain circumstances," but continued to insist that Kuwait remained part of Iraq.

Arab armies, along with U.S. marines, entered Kuwait City on February 27. Later that day, Bush announced in a televised speech that "Kuwait is liberated" and that Iraq had been defeated. "Seven months ago, America and the world drew a line in the sand," he said. "We declared that the aggression against Kuwait would not stand. And tonight, America and the world have kept their word." The fighting stopped at 8 A.M. (local time) on February 28—100 hours after the ground invasion had begun.

Bush by this point had made one of the most fateful decisions of the entire war: to halt the U.S. advance into Iraq and leave Hussein in power. Later in the 1990s, many conservative Republicans would harshly criticize this decision, arguing that the United States had lost an opportunity to rid Iraq of a dangerous dictator. Some of these same Republicans would also play a key role in advising George W. Bush to launch the 2003 invasion that accomplished that goal (Iraq War, p. 504).

Iraq and Kuwait suffered heavy damage during the seven-month period from Iraq's invasion in August 1990 until its retreat at the end of February 1991. The Iraqis turned much of Kuwait into a disaster area, brutalizing the population, setting fire to more than 600 oil wells, dumping thousands of barrels of oil into the Persian Gulf, and carting off valuables worth millions of dollars. A UN survey team visited Iraq in March and reported that coalition bombing had reduced the country to the "preindustrial age." More than 70,000 Iraqis had lost their homes, and the country's electrical system was destroyed, the UN team reported. No reliable estimates of Iraqi military and civilian casualties during the war have been published, but some Western observers estimate that as many as 50,000 Iraqis died during the air and ground campaigns.

The single most significant damage to coalition forces occurred on February 25, when an Iraqi Scud hit a U.S. barracks in Dhahran, Saudi Arabia, killing 28 U.S. soldiers. During the entire war, U.S. military personnel suffered 125 deaths, fewer than had occurred in accidents during the run-up to war.

Following are excerpts from a televised speech by President George H. W. Bush on January 16, 1991, announcing the beginning of an air war campaign against Iraq; a televised address by Bush on February 23, 1991, setting a deadline for Iraq to withdraw from Kuwait or face a major ground invasion; a radio address by Iraqi president Saddam Hussein on February 26, 1991, announcing that he had ordered the withdrawal of military forces from Kuwait; and a televised address by Bush on February 27, 1991, announcing that "Kuwait is liberated."

DOCUMENT

Bush Announces the Start of the Air War against Iraq

JANUARY 16, 1991

Just 2 hours ago, allied air forces began an attack on military targets in Iraq and Kuwait. These attacks continue as I speak. Ground forces are not engaged.

This conflict started August 2d when the dictator of Iraq invaded a small and helpless neighbor. Kuwait—a member of the Arab League and a member of the United Nations—was crushed; its people, brutalized. Five months ago, Saddam Hussein started this cruel war against Kuwait. Tonight, the battle has been joined.

This military action, taken in accord with United Nations resolutions and with the consent of the United States Congress, follows months of constant and virtually endless diplomatic activity on the part of the United Nations, the United States, and many, many other countries. Arab leaders sought what became known as an Arab solution, only to conclude that Saddam Hussein was unwilling to leave Kuwait. Others traveled to Baghdad in a variety of efforts to restore peace and justice. Our Secretary of State, James Baker, held an historic meeting in Geneva, only to be totally rebuffed. This past weekend, in a last-ditch effort, the Secretary-General of the United Nations went to the Middle East with peace in his heart—his second such mission. And he came back from Baghdad with no progress at all in getting Saddam Hussein to withdraw from Kuwait.

Now the 28 countries with forces in the Gulf area have exhausted all reasonable efforts to reach a peaceful resolution—have no choice but to drive Saddam from Kuwait by force. We will not fail.

As I report to you, air attacks are underway against military targets in Iraq. We are determined to knock out Saddam Hussein's nuclear bomb potential. We will also destroy his chemical weapons facilities. Much of Saddam's artillery and tanks will be destroyed. Our operations are designed to best protect the lives of all the coalition forces by targeting Saddam's vast military arsenal. Initial reports from General [Norman] Schwarzkopf are that our operations are proceeding according to plan.

Our objectives are clear: Saddam Hussein's forces will leave Kuwait. The legitimate government of Kuwait will be restored to its rightful place, and Kuwait will once again be free. Iraq will eventually comply with all relevant United Nations resolutions, and then, when peace is restored, it is our hope that Iraq will live as a peaceful and cooperative member of the family of nations, thus enhancing the security and stability of the Gulf.

Some may ask: Why act now? Why not wait? The answer is clear: The world could wait no longer. Sanctions, though having some effect, showed no signs of accomplishing their objective. Sanctions were tried for well over 5 months, and we and our allies concluded that sanctions alone would not force Saddam from Kuwait.

While the world waited, Saddam Hussein systematically raped, pillaged, and plundered a tiny nation, no threat to his own. He subjected the people of Kuwait to unspeakable atrocities—and among those maimed and murdered, innocent children.

While the world waited, Saddam sought to add to the chemical weapons arsenal he now possesses, an infinitely more dangerous weapon of mass destruction—a nuclear weapon. And while the world waited, while the world talked peace and withdrawal, Saddam Hussein dug in and moved massive forces into Kuwait.

While the world waited, while Saddam stalled, more damage was being done to the fragile economies of the Third World, emerging democracies of Eastern Europe, to the entire world, including to our own economy.

The United States, together with the United Nations, exhausted every means at our disposal to bring this crisis to a peaceful end. However, Saddam clearly felt that by stalling and threatening and defying the United Nations, he could weaken the forces arrayed against him.

While the world waited, Saddam Hussein met every overture of peace with open contempt. While the world prayed for peace, Saddam prepared for war.

I had hoped that when the United States Congress, in historic debate, took its resolute action, Saddam would realize he could not prevail and would move out of Kuwait in accord with the United Nation[s] resolutions. He did not do that. Instead, he remained intransigent, certain that time was on his side.

Saddam was warned over and over again to comply with the will of the United Nations: Leave Kuwait, or be driven out. Saddam has arrogantly rejected all warnings. Instead, he tried to make this a dispute between Iraq and the United States of America.

Well, he failed. Tonight, 28 nations—countries from 5 continents, Europe and Asia, Africa, and the Arab League—have forces in the Gulf area standing shoulder to shoulder against Saddam Hussein. These countries had hoped the use of force could be avoided. Regrettably, we now believe that only force will make him leave.

Prior to ordering our forces into battle, I instructed our military commanders to take every necessary step to prevail as quickly as possible, and with the greatest degree of protection possible for American and allied service men and women. I've told the American people before that this will not be another Vietnam, and I repeat this here tonight. Our troops will have the best possible support in the entire world, and they will not be asked to fight with one hand tied behind their back. I'm hopeful that this fighting will not go on for long and that casualties will be held to an absolute minimum.

This is an historic moment. We have in this past year made great progress in ending the long era of conflict and cold war. We have before us the opportunity to forge for ourselves and for future generations a new world order—a world where the rule of law, not the law of the jungle, governs the conduct of nations. When we are successful—and we will be—we have a real chance at this new world order, an order in which a credible United Nations can use its peacekeeping role to fulfill the promise and vision of the U.N.'s founders.

We have no argument with the people of Iraq. Indeed, for the innocents caught in this conflict, I pray for their safety. Our goal is not the conquest of Iraq. It is the liberation of Kuwait. It is my hope that somehow the Iraqi people can, even now, convince their dictator that he must lay down his arms, leave Kuwait and let Iraq itself rejoin the family of peace-loving nations.

Thomas Paine wrote many years ago: "These are the times that try men's souls." Those well-known words are so very true today. But even as planes of the multinational forces attack Iraq, I prefer to think of peace, not war. I am convinced not only that we will prevail but that out of the horror of combat will come the recognition that no nation can stand against a world united. No nation will be permitted to brutally assault its neighbor.

No President can easily commit our sons and daughters to war. They are the Nation's finest. Ours is an all-volunteer force, magnificently trained, highly motivated. The troops know why they're there. And listen to what they say, for they've said it better than any President or Prime Minister ever could.

Listen to Hollywood Huddleston, Marine lance corporal. He says, "Let's free these people, so we can go home and be free again." And he's right. The terrible crimes and tortures committed by Saddam's henchmen against the innocent people of Kuwait are an affront to mankind and a challenge to the freedom of all.

Listen to one of our great officers out there, Marine Lieutenant General Walter Boomer. He said: "There are things worth fighting for. A world in which brutality and lawlessness are allowed to go unchecked isn't the kind of world we're going to want to live in."

Listen to Master Sergeant J. P. Kendall of the 82d Airborne: "We're here for more than just the price of a gallon of gas. What we're doing is going to chart the future of the world for the next 100 years. It's better to deal with this guy now than 5 years from now."

And finally, we should all sit up and listen to Jackie Jones, an Army lieutenant, when she says, "If we let him get away with this, who knows what's going to be next?"

I have called upon Hollywood and Walter and J. P. and Jackie and all their courageous comrades-in-arms to do what must be done. Tonight, America and the world are deeply grateful to them and to their families. And let me say to everyone listening or watching tonight: When the troops we've sent in finish their work, I am determined to bring them home as soon as possible.

Tonight, as our forces fight, they and their families are in our prayers. May God bless each and every one of them, and the coalition forces at our side in the Gulf, and may He continue to bless our nation, the United States of America.

SOURCE: George Bush Presidential Library, http://bushlibrary.tamu.edu/research/papers/1991/91011602. html.

DOCUMENT

Bush Announces the Start of the Ground War against Iraq

FEBRUARY 23, 1991

Good evening. Yesterday, after conferring with my senior national security advisers, and following extensive consultations with our coalition partners, Saddam Hussein was given one last chance—set forth in very explicit terms—to do what he should have done more than 6 months ago: withdraw from Kuwait without condition or further delay, and comply fully with the resolutions passed by the United Nations Security Council.

Regrettably, the noon deadline passed without the agreement of the Government of Iraq to meet demands of United Nations Security Council Resolution 660, as set forth in the specific terms spelled out by the coalition to withdraw unconditionally from Kuwait. To the contrary, what we have seen is a redoubling of Saddam Hussein's efforts to destroy completely Kuwait and its people.

I have, therefore, directed General Norman Schwarzkopf, in conjunction with coalition forces, to use all forces available, including ground forces, to eject the Iraqi army from Kuwait. Once again, this was a decision made only after extensive consultations within our coalition partnership.

The liberation of Kuwait has now entered a final phase. I have complete confidence in the ability of the coalition forces swiftly and decisively to accomplish their mission.

Tonight, as this coalition of countries seeks to do that which is right and just, I ask only that all of you stop what you are doing and say a prayer for all the coalition forces, and especially for our men and women in uniform who this very moment are risking their lives for their country and for all of us.

May God bless and protect each and every one of them. And may God bless the United States of America. Thank you very much.

SOURCE: George Bush Presidential Library, http://bushlibrary.tamu.edu/research/papers/1991/91022302. html.

DOCUMENT

Hussein Announces the Withdrawal of Iraqi Forces from Kuwait

FEBRUARY 26, 1991

In the name of God, the merciful, the compassionate. O great people; O stalwart men in the forces of holy war and faith, glorious men of the mother of battles; O zealous, faithful and sincere people in our glorious nations, and among all Muslims and all virtuous people in the world; O glorious Iraqi women:

... We start by saying that on this day, our valiant armed forces will complete their withdrawal from Kuwait.... It was an epic duel which lasted for two months, which came to clearly confirm a lesson that God has wanted as a prelude of faith, impregnability and capability for the faithful, and a prelude of an [abyss], weakness and humiliation which God Almighty has wanted for the infidels, the criminals, the traitors, the corrupt and the deviators.

To be added to this time is the time of the military and nonmilitary duel, including the military and the economic blockade, which was imposed on Iraq and which lasted throughout 1990 until today, and until the time God Almighty wishes it to last.

Before that, the duel lasted, in other forms, for years before this period of time. It was an epic struggle between right and wrong; we have talked about this in detail on previous occasions.

It gave depth to the age of the showdown for the year 1990, and the already elapsed part of the year 1991.

Hence, we do not forget, because we will not forget this great struggling spirit, by which men of great faith stormed the fortifications and the weapons of deception and the Croesus [Kuwaiti rulers] treachery on the honorable day of the call. They did what they did within the context of legitimate deterrence and great principled action.

All that we have gone through or decided within its circumstances, obeying God's will and choosing a position of faith and chivalry, is a record of honor, the significance of which will not be missed by the people and nation and the values of Islam and humanity.

Their days will continue to be glorious and their past and future will continue to relate the story of a faithful, jealous and patient people, who believed in the will of God and in the values and stands accepted by the Almighty for the Arab nation in its leading role and for the Islamic nation in the essentials of its true faith and how they should be.

These values—which had their effect in all those situations, offered the sacrifices they had offered in the struggle, and symbolized the depth of the faithful character in Iraq—will continue to leave their effects on the souls. . . .

The harvest in the mother of battles has succeeded. After we have harvested what we have harvested, the greater harvest and its yield will be in the time to come, and it will be much greater than what we have at present, in spite of what we have at present in terms of the victory, dignity and glory that was based on the sacrifices of a deep faith which is generous without any hesitation or fear.

It is by virtue of this faith that God has bestowed dignity upon the Iraqi mujahedeen, and upon all the depth of this course of holy war at the level of the Arab homeland and at the level of all those men whom God has chosen to be given the honor of allegiance, guidance and honorable position, until He declares that the conflict has stopped, or amends its directions and course and the positions in a manner which would please the faithful and increase their dignity.

O valiant Iraqi men, O glorious Iraqi women. Kuwait is part of your country and was carved from it in the past.

Circumstances today have willed that it remain in the state in which it will remain after the withdrawal of our struggling forces from it. It hurts you that this should happen.

We rejoiced on the day of the call when it was decided that Kuwait should be one of the main gates for deterring the plot and for defending all Iraq from the plotters. We say that we will remember Kuwait on the great day of the call, on the days that followed it, and in documents and events, some of which date back 70 years.

The Iraqis will remember and will not forget that on 8 August, 1990, Kuwait became part of Iraq legally, constitutionally and actually. They remember and will not forget that it remained throughout this period from 8 August 1990 and until last night, when withdrawal began, and today we will complete withdrawal of our forces, God willing.

Today certain circumstances made the Iraqi Army withdraw as a result of the ramifications which we mentioned, including the combined aggression by 30 countries. Their repugnant siege has been led in evil and aggression by the machine and the criminal entity of America and its major allies.

. . . Everyone will remember that the gates of Constantinople were not opened before the Muslims in the first struggling attempt. . . . The confidence of the nationalists and the faithful mujahedeen and the Muslims has grown bigger than before, and great hope more and more.

Slogans have come out of their stores to strongly occupy the facades of the pan-Arab and human holy war and struggle. Therefore, victory is [great] now and in the future, God willing. . . .

O you valiant men; you have fought the armies of 30 states and the capabilities of an even greater number of states which supplied them with the means of aggression and support. Faith, belief, hope and determination continue to fill your chests, souls and hearts.

They have even become deeper, stronger, brighter and more deeply rooted. God is great; God is great; may the lowly be defeated.

Victory is sweet with the help of God.

SOURCE: *Historic Documents of 1991* (Washington, D.C.: CQ Press, 1992), 102–104.

DOCUMENT

Bush Announces the Suspension of Combat against Iraq

FEBRUARY 27, 1991

Kuwait is liberated. Iraq's army is defeated. Our military objectives are met. Kuwait is once more in the hands of Kuwaitis, in control of their own destiny. We share in their joy, a joy tempered only by our compassion for their ordeal.

Tonight the Kuwaiti flag once again flies above the capital of a free and sovereign nation. And the American flag flies above our Embassy.

Seven months ago, America and the world drew a line in the sand. We declared that the aggression against Kuwait would not stand. And tonight, America and the world have kept their word.

This is not a time of euphoria, certainly not a time to gloat. But it is a time of pride: pride in our troops; pride in the friends who stood with us in the crisis; pride in our nation and the people whose strength and resolve made victory quick, decisive, and just. And soon we will open wide our arms to welcome back home to America our magnificent fighting forces.

No one country can claim this victory as its own. It was not only a victory for Kuwait but a victory for all the coalition partners. This is a victory for the United Nations, for all mankind, for the rule of law, and for what is right.

After consulting with Secretary of Defense [Dick] Cheney, the Chairman of the Joint Chiefs of Staff, General [Colin] Powell, and our coalition partners, I am pleased to announce that at midnight tonight eastern standard time, exactly 100 hours since ground operations commenced and 6 weeks since the start of Desert Storm, all United States and coalition forces will suspend offensive combat operations. It is up to Iraq whether this suspension on the part of the coalition becomes a permanent cease-fire.

Coalition political and military terms for a formal cease-fire include the following requirements:

Iraq must release immediately all coalition prisoners of war, third country nationals, and the remains of all who have fallen. Iraq must release all Kuwaiti detainees. Iraq also must inform Kuwaiti authorities of the location and nature of all land and sea mines. Iraq must comply fully with all relevant United Nations Security Council resolutions. This includes a rescinding of Iraq's August decision to annex Kuwait, and acceptance in principle of Iraq's responsibility to pay compensation for the loss, damage, and injury its aggression has caused.

The coalition calls upon the Iraqi Government to designate military commanders to meet within 48 hours with their coalition counterparts at a place in the theater of operations to be specified, to arrange for military aspects of the cease-fire. Further, I have asked Secretary of State [James] Baker to request that the United Nations Security Council meet to formulate the necessary arrangements for this war to be ended.

This suspension of offensive combat operations is contingent upon Iraq's not firing upon any coalition forces and not launching Scud missiles against any other country. If Iraq violates these terms, coalition forces will be free to resume military operations.

At every opportunity, I have said to the people of Iraq that our quarrel was not with them but instead with their leadership and, above all, with Saddam Hussein. This remains the case. You, the people of Iraq, are not our enemy. We do not seek your destruction. We have treated your POW's with kindness. Coalition forces fought this war only as a last resort and look forward to the day when Iraq is led by people prepared to live in peace with their neighbors.

We must now begin to look beyond victory and war. We must meet the challenge of securing the peace. In the future, as before, we will consult with our coalition partners. We've already done a good deal of thinking and planning for the postwar period, and Secretary Baker has already begun to consult with our coalition partners on the region's challenges. There can be, and will be, no solely American answer to all these challenges. But we can assist and support the countries of the region and be a catalyst for peace. In this spirit, Secretary Baker will go to the region next week to begin a new round of consultations.

This war is now behind us. Ahead of us is the difficult task of securing a potentially historic peace. Tonight though, let us be proud of what we have accomplished. Let us give thanks to those who risked their lives. Let us never forget those who gave their lives. May God bless our valiant military forces and their families, and let us all remember them in our prayers.

Good night, and may God bless the United States of America.

SOURCE: George Bush Presidential Library, http://bushlibrary.tamu.edu/research/papers/1991/91022702.html.

Persian Gulf War's Aftermath

DOCUMENT IN CONTEXT

After the quick and easy military victory of the U.S.-led coalition against Iraq in February 1991, many people—especially in Western countries—appeared to believe that the Middle East finally might be ripe for a era of peace and harmony. With Saddam Hussein defeated, and the United States having emerged as the chief power in the region, President George H. W. Bush had no reluctance in describing to Congress on March 6, 1991, the "very real prospect of a new world order."

Even before Bush spoke these words, however, aspects of the old order already had re-emerged in the Middle East. On March 1, reports began circulating of a widespread uprising of Shiites in Basra, the largest city in southern Iraq. The spontaneous rebellion quickly spread to other cities in the majority-Shiite south, spawned in part by a revolt by a number of Shiite soldiers in Iraq's defeated army. Under orders from Baghdad, however, remnants of the army attacked the Shiite rebels in what, for a time, appeared to be the opening stages of a major civil war. Sensing an opportunity to achieve the independence they had long sought, Kurds in the north of Iraq also rebelled, announcing on March 6 that they had seized control of much of their home provinces, which they called Kurdistan. The Kurdish rebellion crested on March 19 with the capture of Kirkuk, the capital of Iraq's northern oil-producing region.

Although most of Iraq's regular army lay in ruins, Hussein still had command of some reserve forces, primarily the Republican Guard, which he had held back from the fighting in Kuwait. These units suppressed the Shiite rebellion within two weeks and then turned their attention to the Kurdish north. Hundreds of thousands of Kurds fled the attacking Iraqi troops, most of them heading across the mountainous border areas into Turkey and Iran, where they faced the ravages of a lingering winter. On March 16, with fighting still under way in the north, Hussein delivered a televised speech promising political reforms, including a multiparty democracy. He subsequently failed to fulfill these promises.

The Shiite and Kurdish rebellions resulted in thousands of deaths and failed to achieve their stated goals—the overthrow of Hussein's regime and the establishment of an independent Kurdistan—but they succeeded in forcing the rest of the world to pay attention to the postwar internal dynamics of Iraq. In particular, the plight of the Kurds who had fled into Turkey momentarily captured the world's concern and brought an outpouring of humanitarian aid, most of it delivered by the U.S. military. The Shiites in southern Iraq were left to fend for themselves because they remained within Hussein's grasp. The UN Security Council on April 5 adopted Resolution 688 demanding that Iraq "immediately end this repression" of Kurds and Shiites. The United States and Britain later cited that resolution as authority for their establishment in Iraq of "no-fly" zones—the areas south of the 32nd parallel and north of the 36th parallel to be patrolled by NATO warplanes to prevent aerial attacks on the civilian population by Iraq's military. The NATO flights would continue until the U.S.-led invasion of Iraq in 2003.

Resolution 687

The Iraqi government's suppression of the Kurdish and Shiite rebellions coincided with the lengthy diplomatic process at the United Nations of drafting a postwar resolution dealing with Iraq. The war had ended on February 28, and generals on the ground had signed a cease-fire on March 3, but the Bush administration and its allies wanted a more permanent truce imposing conditions that would prevent Iraq from attempting renewed aggression against its neighbors.

Over the course of March, diplomats at the United Nations negotiated the terms of what would become the longest, most detailed, and most complex resolution to emerge from the Security Council. On April 3 by a vote of 12-1 (Cuba voted no, Ecuador and Yemen abstained), the council adopted Resolution 687, effectively putting Iraq at the mercy of the United Nations.

The economic sanctions imposed against Iraq following its invasion of Kuwait were to continue but could be lifted gradually as Iraq met certain conditions. Chief among these were requirements that Iraq recognize the sovereignty of Kuwait; pay reparations to Kuwait for damages caused during the seven-month occupation; provide an accounting of the thousands of Kuwaitis who had disappeared during the occupation; end the repression of Iraqi citizens; and cease to threaten the security and stability of its other neighbors.

Some of the most important provisions of the resolution generated little controversy at the time but would play a major role in Middle Eastern affairs for the next dozen years. Among them, the resolution required that Iraq eliminate all of its so-called weapons of mass destruction, including biological and chemical weapons, and programs to build them. The resolution also ordered Iraq to comply with the Nuclear Nonproliferation Treaty (NPT)—which bars Iraq's development of nuclear weapons— and it prohibited Iraq from possessing ballistic missiles with a range of ninety miles or greater. These requirements marked the first time the Security Council had ordered an individual country to divest itself of specific types of weapons.

Iraqi compliance regarding biological and chemical weapons and missiles was to be monitored by the United Nations Special Commission (UNSCOM). Responsibility for monitoring its compliance with the NPT continued to rest with the UN's International Atomic Energy Agency (IAEA).

The UN agencies began their work on Iraq almost immediately but faced restrictions on their access to sensitive Iraqi weapons facilities despite the UN resolution's demand for full cooperation by Baghdad. Even so, UNSCOM chief Rolf Ekeus reported on July 3 that his inspectors had found four times as many chemical weapons as the Iraqi government had acknowledged. Under international pressure, the government also acknowledged the existence of nuclear weapons programs suggesting that its work in this area had been further along than Western experts believed. The combination of the weapons inspections and continued economic sanctions provided the United Nations leverage over Iraq and would be the dominant factor in the international community's relationship—or lack thereof—with Iraq for the next dozen years (UN Weapons Inspections, p. 473).

Following are excerpts from UN Security Council Resolution 687, adopted on April 3, 1991, imposing postwar conditions and sanctions on Iraq.

DOCUMENT

UN Security Council Resolution 687 (1991)

APRIL 3, 1991

The Security Council,

Recalling its resolutions 660 (1990) of 2 August 1990, 661 (1990) of 6 August 1990, 662 (1990) of 9 August 1990, 664 (1990) of 18 August 1990, 665 (1990) of 25 August 1990, 666 (1990) of 13 September 1990, 667 (1990) of 16 September 1990, 669 (1990) of 24 September 1990, 670 (1990) of 25 September 1990, 674 (1990) of 29 October 1990, 677 (1990) of 28 November 1990, 678 (1990) of 29 November 1990 and 686 (1991) of 2 March 1991, . . .

1. *Affirms* all thirteen resolutions noted above, except as expressly changed below to achieve the goals of the present resolution, including a formal cease-fire;

A

2. *Demands* that Iraq and Kuwait respect the inviolability of the international boundary and the allocation of islands set out in the "Agreed Minutes Between the State of Kuwait and the Republic of Iraq Regarding the Restoration of Friendly Relations, Recognition and Related Matters," signed by them in the exercise of their sovereignty at Baghdad on 4 October 1963 and registered with the United Nations;

3. *Calls upon* the Secretary-General to lend his assistance to make arrangements with Iraq and Kuwait to demarcate the boundary between Iraq and Kuwait.

4. *Decides* to guarantee the inviolability of the above-mentioned international boundary and to take, as appropriate, all necessary measures to that end in accordance with the Charter of the United Nations;

B

5. *Requests* the Secretary-General, after consulting with Iraq and Kuwait, to submit within three days to the Council for its approval a plan for the immediate deployment of a United Nations observer unit to monitor the Khawr 'Abd Allah and a demilitarized zone, which is hereby established, extending ten kilometres into Iraq and five kilometres into Kuwait from the boundary.

6. *Notes* that as soon as the Secretary-General notifies the Council of the completion of the deployment of the United Nations observer unit, the conditions will be established for the Member States cooperating with Kuwait in accordance with resolution 678 (1990) to bring their military presence in Iraq to an end consistent with resolution 686 (1991);

C

7. *Invites* Iraq to reaffirm unconditionally its obligations under the [Geneva] Protocol for the Prohibition of the Use in War of Asphyxiating, Poisonous or Other Gases, and of Bacteriological Methods of Warfare, signed at Geneva on 17 June 1925, and to ratify the Convention on the Prohibition of the Development, Production and Stockpiling of Bacteriological (Biological) and Toxin Weapons and on Their Destruction, of 10 April 1972;

8. *Decides* that Iraq shall unconditionally accept the destruction, removal, or rendering harmless, under international supervision, of:

(a) All chemical and biological weapons and all stocks of agents and all related subsystems and components and all research, development, support and manufacturing facilities related thereto;

(b) All ballistic missiles with a range greater than 150 kilometres, and related major parts, and repair and production facilities;

9. *Decides* also, for the implementation of paragraph 8, the following:

(a) Iraq shall submit to the Secretary-General, within fifteen days of the adoption of the present resolution, a declaration on the locations, amounts and types of all items specified in paragraph 8 and agree to urgent, on-site inspection as specified below;

(b) The Secretary-General, in consultation with the appropriate Governments and, where appropriate, with the Director-General of the World Health Organization, within forty-five days of the passage of the present resolution shall develop and submit to the Council for approval a plan calling for the completion of the following acts within forty-five days of such approval:

(i) The forming of a special commission which shall carry out immediate on-site inspection of Iraq's biological, chemical and missile capabilities.

(ii) The yielding by Iraq of possession to the Special Commission for destruction, removal or rendering harmless of all items specified under paragraph 8 (a) and the destruction by Iraq, under the supervision of the Special Commission, of all its missile capabilities, including launchers, as specified under paragraph 8 (b);

(iii) The provision by the Special Commission to the Director General of the International Atomic Energy Agency required of the assistance and cooperation in paragraphs 12 and 13;

10. *Decides further* that Iraq shall unconditionally undertake not to use, develop, construct or acquire any of the items specified in paragraphs 8 and 9, and requests the Secretary-General, in consultation with the Special Commission, to develop a plan for the future ongoing monitoring and verification of Iraq's compliance with the present paragraph, to be submitted to the Council for approval within one hundred and twenty days of the passage of the present resolution;

11. *Invites* Iraq to reaffirm unconditionally its obligations under the Treaty on the Non-Proliferation of Nuclear Weapons, of 1 July 1968;

12. *Decides* that Iraq shall unconditionally agree not to acquire or develop nuclear weapons or nuclear-weapons-usable material or any subsystems or components or any research, development, support or manufacturing facilities related to the above; to submit to the Secretary-General and the Director General of the International Atomic Energy

Agency within fifteen days of the adoption of the present resolution a declaration of the locations, amounts and types of all items specified above; to place all of its nuclear-weapons-usable materials under the exclusive control, for custody and removal, of the [International Atomic Energy] Agency, with the assistance and cooperation of the Special Commission as provided for in the plan of the Secretary-General discussed in paragraph 9 (b); to accept, in accordance with the arrangements provided for in paragraph 13, urgent on-site inspection and the destruction, removal or rendering harmless as appropriate of all items specified above; and to accept the plan discussed in paragraph 13 for the future ongoing monitoring and verification of its compliance with these undertakings;

13. *Requests* the Director General of the International Atomic Energy Agency, through the Secretary-General and with the assistance and cooperation of the Special Commission as provided for in the plan of the Secretary-General referred to in paragraph 9 (*b*), to carry out immediate on-site inspection of Iraq's nuclear capabilities based on Iraq's declarations and the designation of any additional locations by the Special Commission; to develop a plan for submission to the Council within forty-five days calling for the destruction, removal, or rendering harmless as appropriate of all items listed in paragraph 12; to carry out the plan within forty-five days following approval by the Council and to develop a plan for the future ongoing monitoring and verification of Iraq's compliance with paragraph 12, including an inventory of all nuclear material in Iraq subject to the Agency's verification and inspections to confirm that Agency safeguards cover all relevant nuclear activities in Iraq, to be submitted to the Council for approval within one hundred and twenty days of the adoption of the present resolution;

14. *Notes* that the actions to be taken by Iraq in paragraphs 8 to 13 represent steps towards the goal of establishing in the Middle East a zone free from weapons of mass destruction and all missiles for their delivery and the objective of a global ban on chemical weapons;

D

15. *Requests* the Secretary-General to report to the Council on the steps taken to facilitate the return of all Kuwaiti property seized by Iraq, including a list of any property that Kuwait claims has not been returned or which has not been returned intact;

E

16. *Reaffirms* that Iraq is liable under international law for any direct loss, damage—including environmental damage and the depletion of natural resources—or injury to foreign Governments, nationals and corporations as a result of its unlawful invasion and occupation of Kuwait;

17. *Decides* that all Iraqi statements made since 2 August 1990 repudiating its foreign debt are null and void, and demands that Iraq adhere scrupulously to all of its obligations concerning servicing and repayment of its foreign debt;

18. *Decides also* to create a fund to pay compensation for claims that fall within paragraph 16 and to establish a commission that will administer the fund;

19. *Directs* the Secretary-General to develop and present to the Council for decision, no later than thirty days following the adoption of the present resolution, rec-

ommendations for the Fund to be established in accordance with paragraph 18 and for a program to implement the decisions in paragraphs 16 to 18, including the following: administration of the fund; mechanisms for determining the appropriate level of Iraq's contribution to the Fund, based on a percentage of the value of its exports of petroleum and petroleum products, not to exceed a figure to be suggested to the Council by the Secretary-General, taking into account the requirements of the people of Iraq, Iraq's payment capacity as assessed in conjunction with the international financial institutions taking into consideration external debt service, and the needs of the Iraqi economy; arrangements for ensuring that payments are made to the Fund; the process by which funds will be allocated and claims paid; appropriate procedures for evaluating losses, listing claims and verifying their validity, and resolving disputed claims in respect of Iraq's liability as specified in paragraph 16; and the composition of the Commission designated above;

F

20. *Decides,* effective immediately, that the prohibitions against the sale or supply to Iraq of commodities or products other than medicine and health supplies, and prohibitions against financial transactions related thereto contained in resolution 661 (1990), shall not apply to foodstuffs notified to the Security Council Committee established by resolution 661 (1990) concerning the situation between Iraq and Kuwait or, with the approval of that Committee, under the simplified and accelerated "no-objection" procedure, to materials and supplies for essential civilian needs as identified in the report to the Secretary-General dated 20 March 1991, and in any further findings of humanitarian need by the Committee;

21. *Decides* to review the provisions of paragraph 20 every sixty days in the light of the policies and practices of the Government of Iraq, including the implementation of all relevant resolutions of the Council, for the purpose of determining whether to reduce or lift the prohibitions referred to therein;

22. *Decides also* that upon the approval by the Council of the program called for in paragraph 19 above and upon Council agreement that Iraq has completed all actions contemplated in paragraphs 8 to 13, the prohibitions against the import of commodities and products originating in Iraq and the prohibitions against financial transactions related thereto contained in resolution 661 (1990) shall have no further force or effect;

23. *Decides further* that, pending action by the Council under paragraph 22, the Security Council Committee established by resolution 661 (1990) shall be empowered to approve, when required to assure adequate financial resources on the part of Iraq to carry out the activities under paragraph 20, exceptions to the prohibition against the import of commodities and products originating in Iraq;

24. *Decides* that, in accordance with resolution 661 (1990) and subsequent related resolutions and until it takes a further decision, all States shall continue to prevent the sale or supply to Iraq, or the promotion or facilitation of such sale or supply, by their nationals or from their territories or using their flag vessels or aircraft, of:

(a) Arms and related *matériel* of all types, specifically including the sale or transfer through other means of all forms of conventional military equipment, including for paramilitary forces, and spare parts and components and their means of production for such equipment;

(b) Items specified and defined in paragraphs 8 and 12 not otherwise covered above;

(c) Technology under licensing or other transfer arrangements used in the production, utilization or stockpiling of items specified in paragraphs (a) and (b);

(d) Personnel or materials for training or technical support services relating to the design, development, manufacture, use, maintenance or support of items specified in paragraphs (a) and (b);

25. *Calls upon* all States and international organizations to act strictly in accordance with paragraph 24, notwithstanding the existence of any contracts, agreements, licenses or any other arrangements;

26. *Requests* the Secretary-General, in consultation with appropriate Governments, to develop within sixty days, for the approval of the Council, guidelines to facilitate full international implementation of paragraphs 24, 25, and 27, and to make them available to all States and to establish a procedure for updating these guidelines periodically;

27. *Calls upon* all States to maintain such national controls and procedures and to take such other actions consistent with the guidelines to be established by the Council under paragraph 26 as may be necessary to ensure compliance with the terms of paragraph 24, and calls upon international organizations to take all appropriate steps to assist in ensuring such full compliance;

28. *Agrees* to review its decisions in paragraphs 22 to 25, except for the items specified and defined in paragraphs 8 and 12, on a regular basis and in any case one hundred and twenty days following adoption of the present resolution, taking into account Iraq's compliance with the resolution and general progress towards the control of armaments in the region;

29. *Decides* that all States, including Iraq, shall take the necessary measures to ensure that no claim shall lie at the instance of the Government of Iraq, or of any person or body in Iraq, or of any person claiming through or for the benefit of any such person or body, in connection with any contract or other transaction where its performance was affected by reason of the measures taken by the Council in resolution 661 (1990) and related resolutions;

G

30. *Decides* that, in furtherance of its commitment to facilitate the repatriation of all Kuwaiti and third-State nationals, Iraq shall extend all necessary cooperation to the International Committee of the Red Cross by providing lists of such persons, facilitating the access of the International Committee to all such persons wherever located or detained and facilitating the search by the International Committee for those Kuwaiti and third-State nationals still unaccounted for;

31. *Invites* the International Committee of the Red Cross to keep the Secretary-General apprised, as appropriate, of all activities undertaken in connection with facilitating the repatriation or return of all Kuwaiti and third-State nationals or their remains present in Iraq on or after 2 August 1990;

H

32. *Requires* Iraq to inform the Council that it will not commit or support any act of international terrorism or allow any organization directed towards commission

of such acts to operate within its territory and to condemn unequivocally and renounce all acts, methods and practices of terrorism;

I

33. *Declares* that, upon official notification by Iraq to the Secretary-General and to the Security Council of its acceptance of the above provisions, a formal cease-fire is effective between Iraq and Kuwait and the Member States cooperating with Kuwait in accordance with resolution 678 (1990);

34. *Decides* to remain seized of the matter and to take such further steps as may be required for the implementation of the present resolution and to secure peace and security in the region.

SOURCE: United Nations, www.un.org/Docs/scres/1991/scres91.htm.

UN Weapons Inspections

DOCUMENT IN CONTEXT

At the end of the Persian Gulf War in 1991, the UN Security Council adopted Resolution 687, imposing tough punishment on Iraq for its invasion of Kuwait the previous August. The most important and lasting of these penalties was the continuation of most of the economic sanctions that the council had mandated because of the invasion and a requirement that Iraq eliminate all of its weapons of mass destruction, including biological and chemical weapons, along with any work it had done to acquire nuclear weapons and any ballistic missiles with a range of ninety miles or more. The Security Council suggested at the time that the sanctions would be lifted progressively as Iraq demonstrated its compliance with the weapons mandates and other requirements (Persian Gulf War, p. 455; Persian Gulf War's Aftermath, p. 465).

Iraq officially accepted these UN mandates and, as later discovered, disposed of its weapons in 1991. It cooperated only grudging, however, and often not at all, with UN inspectors assigned the task of ensuring the elimination of Iraqi weapons programs. Baghdad's resistance to the UN mandates led many to believe for the next dozen years that it still had banned weapons and was working rapidly to build more.

The drama over Iraq's weapons lasted from April 1991, when the Security Council first acted on the issue, until the fall of 2003, months after the United States invaded Iraq and ousted Iraqi leader Saddam Hussein from power. As with any drama, there were high points and low points, but much of the action took place behind the scenes when the world's attention was focused elsewhere.

The UN inspectors who began arriving in Iraq in May 1991 worked for two agencies. The United Nations Special Commission (UNSCOM) had the task of locating and destroying Iraq's presumably large arsenal of chemical weapons (some of which Iraq had used during the 1980–1988 war with Iran), biological weapons, and missiles that exceeded a ninety-mile range. Inspectors from the International Atomic Energy Agency (IAEA) were responsible for monitoring compliance with the Nuclear Nonproliferation Treaty (NPT), which barred Iraq from possessing nuclear weapons.

Initial inspections in 1991 quickly uncovered evidence that Iraq's arsenal of chemical weapons was much larger than UN officials and Western intelligence experts had believed. More startling was evidence that Iraq's work to build nuclear weapons had advanced much further than was generally assumed; some experts later suggested that in 1991 Iraq had been only a few years short of completing work on a rudimentary nuclear bomb. These findings—that the Iraqi government had successfully concealed its weapons work from U.S. spy satellites and other espionage—would color international perceptions for years and lead the United States to claim that Iraq continued to build banned weapons.

Despite successes in documenting Iraqi weapons and programs, the UN inspectors repeatedly reported to the Security Council on refusals by the Iraqi government to cooperate with them in their work. The Security Council responded to these complaints by passing additional resolutions, beginning with Resolution 715, adopted on October 11, 1991, demanding that Iraq cooperate with the inspectors "unconditionally." The United States twice bombed Iraqi targets in 1993 in part because of Baghdad's refusal to cooperate with the inspectors but for other reasons as well. The first bombing occurred on January 13, 1993, by order of President George H. W. Bush, when Iraq appeared to threaten Kuwait. Five months later, on June 26, President Bill Clinton, Bush's successor, ordered missile attacks against Iraqi intelligence services in Baghdad to retaliate for a failed assassination attempt—attributed to Iraq—against former president Bush during a visit to Kuwait that April. In both cases, the presidents also cited complaints by UNSCOM that Iraq had blocked its inspection work.

On November 26, 1993, Iraq finally accepted Resolution 715, demanding that it cooperate with the weapons inspectors. The decision appeared to be part of a campaign, futile at the time, to win international support for weakening economic sanctions against it. Instead, Iraqi acceptance of the resolution cleared the way for more intrusive inspections than Baghdad had previously allowed.

On July 11, 1994, UNSCOM chairman Rolf Ekeus reported to the Security Council that all of the prohibited weapons acknowledged by Iraq had been destroyed and that a long-term system for monitoring its weapons programs was being put in place. Even so, Ekeus said he could not be certain that Iraq was not still hiding weapons or facilities to make them. The report by Ekeus marked a turning point in the struggle over Iraq's weapons because it appeared that Iraq finally was complying with UN resolutions. Even so, Baghdad quickly reverted to its policy of resisting UN inspections, thus hardening international skepticism about its claims. Another confrontation took place in October 1994, when Iraq again appeared to threaten Kuwait by moving army units to the border. President Clinton responded by sending some 36,000 troops to the Persian Gulf, forcing Iraq to back down and formally recognize the international border with Kuwait.

The UN weapons inspections came to an abrupt end in 1998 after two years of Iraqi refusals to cooperate. This period began in June 1996, when Iraq blocked inspectors from sites that UNSCOM had identified as weapons-storage locations. The confrontation arose as Iraq and the United Nations negotiated the terms under which Iraq could sell oil on the international market to raise money for purchases of food and humanitarian goods. The standoff continued throughout 1997 and into 1998, with Iraq defying repeated Security Council resolutions demanding that it allow the inspectors total access to suspect sites. In particular, Iraq for several months barred the inspectors from entering any of eight presidential palaces, giant buildings scattered around the country that the United Nations suspected of housing some weapons programs. Iraq also sought to delay and undermine the inspections by accusing the United States of putting intelligence agents on the inspection teams. (It was later revealed that U.S. agents were indeed posted on the UN teams.)

In August 1998 Iraq announced that it was ending all cooperation with UNSCOM. After more confrontations and attempts to negotiate an arrangement, the United Nations withdrew its inspectors on December 15, 1998. The next day, the United States and Britain began a four-day bombing campaign, Operation Desert Fox, targeting suspected weapons plants and intelligence and military installations in Iraq. These bombings were the most extensive attacks against Iraq since the Persian Gulf War nearly eight years earlier.

Political developments in the United States made the bombing campaign somewhat controversial. In October, Congress had passed, and President Bill Clinton had signed, the Iraq Liberation Act (PL 105-338), a resolution explicitly calling for the removal of Saddam Hussein's regime from power. This elicited protests from UN secretary-general Kofi Annan and others that the United States was undermining UN diplomacy toward Iraq. Also at the time of the bombings, Clinton faced impeachment proceedings in the House of Representatives resulting from his extramarital affair with a White House intern. Some Republicans in Congress accused Clinton of ordering the bombings of Iraq to distract attention from the impeachment.

On January 25, 1999, UNSCOM sent what turned out to be its final substantive report to the Security Council reviewing the status of its inspections and Iraq's weapons programs. Written by Australian diplomat Richard Butler, the last head of UNSCOM, the report confirmed that Iraq had eliminated many of the weapons and weapons programs banned by the Security Council. Butler wrote, however, that many questions remained concerning whether Iraq continued to conceal large quantities of these weapons. In particular, Butler suggested that Iraq might not have destroyed all of two major types of chemical weapons—mustard gas and the VX nerve gas—and appeared still to be hiding elements of its ballistic missile and biological weapons programs. Butler's report hardened suspicions, particularly in the United States, that Iraq was still producing banned weapons. These suspicions, bolstered by the reports of U.S. intelligence agencies, helped form the basis of the allegations by President George W. Bush in 2002–2003 that Iraq still had weapons of mass destruction (Iraq War Prelude, p. 486).

Oil for Food

The economic sanctions that the United Nations imposed against Iraq after its invasion of Kuwait in August 1990 prohibited nearly all international trade with Iraq. The most important result was the halt of oil exports, which had been Iraq's main source of revenue. In 1992 the Security Council indicated its willingness to consider a revision of the sanctions to allow Iraq to sell enough oil on world markets to subsidize its purchase of food, medicine, and other humanitarian supplies. By this point, Iraq's economy was in a severe depression resulting from the sanctions as well as the effects of the 1980–1988 Iran-Iraq War and the 1990–1991 Persian Gulf crisis and war (Iran-Iraq War and Diplomacy, p. 430; Persian Gulf War, p. 455).

Iraq rejected the Security Council offer, apparently hoping that its economic troubles would generate enough international sympathy to force the council to scrap the sanctions altogether. The council renewed its offer in April 1995, passing Resolution 986, allowing Iraq to sell $2 billion worth of oil every six months, provided the money went toward the purchase of food and medicine. Iraq again rejected the proposal, leading to lengthy negotiations during which Iraq demanded increased flexibility in its oil sales and use of the proceeds. In May 1996, Iraq finally accepted the UN offer, which required nearly half of the oil proceeds to be used to pay reparations to Kuwait, to provide aid to Iraq's Kurdish minority, and to fund UN operations in Iraq; the remainder was to purchase food and medicine for the Iraqi people. The United Nations, however, suspended this so-called oil-for-food program after a few months, when the Iraqi army invaded Kurdish territory and sided with one party in an intra-Kurdish political dispute. It revived the program early in 1997 and in February 1998 increased to $5.2 billion the amount of oil Iraq could sell every six months.

The oil-for-food program continued until shortly after the U.S.-led invasion of Iraq in 2003, but it created constant controversy, in part because Iraq sold some of its oil on the black market (to evade UN restrictions) and because member nations of the Security Council fought among themselves over whether and when to lift some of the restrictions. France and Russia—both with extensive business interests in Iraq—lobbied to ease the sanctions, while the United States insisted on upholding them.

The oil-for-food controversy developed into a full-scale scandal after the 2003 invasion. In 2004 U.S. investigators discovered that the Iraqi government had bribed dozens of international companies and individuals—including several UN officials—to help it evade the UN limitations on oil sales. This controversy besmirched the reputation even of UN secretary-general Kofi Annan, whose son worked for a Swiss company hired by the United Nations to monitor Iraq's use of the oil-for-food money. A high-level investigation commissioned by the United Nations found extensive problems in the management of the oil-for-food program that appeared to reflect broader systemic failures in management of the world body.

Following are excerpts from a letter dated July 11, 1994, from Rolf Ekeus, chairman of the United Nations Special Commission (UNSCOM), to the president of the UN Security Council on the status of the commission's inspection and destruction of Iraqi weapons of mass destruction; the text of UN Security Council Resolution 986, adopted on April 14, 1995, outlining the oil-for-food program for Iraq; the Iraq Liberation Act (HR 4655), passed by Congress and signed into law (PL 105-338) by President Bill Clinton on October 31, 1998, calling for the removal of Saddam Hussein in Iraq; and a letter, dated January 25, 1999, to the UN secretary-general from Richard Butler, UNSCOM executive chairman, discussing the progress made by UN weapons inspectors withdrawn from Iraq in December 1998.

DOCUMENT

Ekeus Letter on UNSCOM's Progress in Destroying Iraqi WMD and Related Programs

JULY 11, 1994

As regards the first responsibility of the Special Commission, to identify and to destroy or otherwise to dispose of Iraq's weapons of mass destruction and the capabilities for their destruction, as defined in paragraph 8 of resolution 687 (1991), the situation, in the absence of new and unexpected disclosures, is as follows:

(a) declared or otherwise identified chemical weapons, precursors and means for their production have been destroyed;

(b) declared biological research facilities have been eliminated and biological strains of concern to the Commission have been disposed of;

(c) the Commission now believes that it has a credible accounting for all of Iraq's missiles with a range greater than 150 kilometers and that such missiles remaining in Iraq after the termination of hostilities have been destroyed. Iraq's program to develop a two-stage, long-range ballistic missile has been terminated.

A full understanding of all aspects of Iraq's past programs in the above areas should, with the assistance of member states [of the UN], be mapped out in the near future. Had Iraq placed the relevant documentation on its past programs at the disposal of the Commission this could already have been the case. However, in light of Iraq's insistence that such documentation has been destroyed, it has been necessary to resort to other and more time-consuming procedures to verify Iraq's accounts of its past programs. The Special Commission hopes to be able to report to the Council shortly that the full accounting of Iraq's past programs, which the Council requires, has been arrived at.

The second of the responsibilities of the Special Commission and of the IAEA [International Atomic Energy Agency] is to undertake ongoing monitoring and verification of Iraq's compliance with its undertaking not to use, develop, construct or acquire any of the items proscribed by paragraphs 8, 9 and 12 of resolution 687 (1991) [these were the paragraphs banning Iraq's possession of biological, chemical, or nuclear weapons, and long-range ballistic missiles].

[Since July of 1993, when it reversed its stance of refusing to cooperate] . . . Iraq has extended its full cooperation in putting ongoing monitoring and verification in place in the areas coming within the responsibilities of the Special Commission. In January 1994, Iraq provided its first formal declarations under the monitoring plan, thus permitting the Commission to commence arrangements for monitoring each facility in the manner deemed most appropriate by the Commission. . . .

SOURCE: United Nations, http://documents.un.org/advance.asp (advanced search: symbol S/1994/860; publication date 20/7/1994).

DOCUMENT

UN Security Council Resolution 986 (1995)

APRIL 14, 1995

The Security Council,

Recalling its previous relevant resolutions,

Concerned by the serious nutritional and health situation of the Iraqi population, and by the risk of further deterioration in this situation,

Convinced of the need as a temporary measure to provide for the humanitarian needs of the Iraqi people until the fulfillment by Iraq of the relevant Security Council resolutions, including notably resolution 687 (1991) of April 3, 1991, allows the Council to take further action with regard to the prohibitions referred to in resolution 661 (1990) of August 6, 1990, in accordance with the provisions of those resolutions,

Convinced also of the need for equitable distribution of humanitarian relief to all segments of the Iraqi population throughout the country,

Reaffirming the commitment of all Member States to the sovereignty and territorial integrity of Iraq,

Acting under Chapter VII of the Charter of the United Nations,

1. *Authorizes* States, notwithstanding the provision of paragraphs 3(a), 3(b) and 4 of resolution 661 (1990) and subsequent relevant resolutions, to permit the import of petroleum and petroleum products originating in Iraq, including financial and other essential transactions directly relating thereto, sufficient to produce a sum not exceeding a total of one billion United States dollars every 90 days for the purposes set out in this resolution and subject to the following conditions:
   (a) Approval by the [Security Council] Committee established by resolution 661 (1990), in order to ensure the transparency of each transaction and its conformity with the other provisions of this resolution, after submission of an application by the State concerned, endorsed by the Government of Iraq, for each proposed purchase of Iraqi petroleum and petroleum products, including details of the purchase price at fair market value, the export route, the opening of a letter of credit payable to the escrow account to be established by the Secretary-General for the purposes of this resolution, and of any other directly related financial or other essential transaction;
   (b) Payment of the full amount of each purpose of Iraqi petroleum and petroleum products directly by the purchaser in the State concerned into the escrow

account to be established by the Secretary-General for the purposes of this resolution; . . .

SOURCE: United Nations, www.un.org/Docs/scres/1995/scres95.htm.

D O C U M E N T

Iraq Liberation Act of 1998

OCTOBER 31, 1988

SEC. 3. SENSE OF THE CONGRESS REGARDING UNITED STATES POLICY TOWARD IRAQ.

It should be the policy of the United States to support efforts to remove the regime headed by Saddam Hussein from power in Iraq and to promote the emergence of a democratic government to replace that regime.

SEC. 7. ASSISTANCE FOR IRAQ UPON REPLACEMENT OF SADDAM HUSSEIN REGIME.

It is the sense of the Congress that once the Saddam Hussein regime is removed from power in Iraq, the United States should support Iraq's transition to democracy by providing immediate and substantial humanitarian assistance to the Iraqi people, by providing democracy transition assistance to Iraqi parties and movements with democratic goals, and by convening Iraq's foreign creditors to develop a multilateral response to Iraq's foreign debt incurred by Saddam Hussein's regime.

SOURCE: Iraq Liberation Act of 1998, Public Law 105–338, 105th Cong., 2d sess. (October 31, 1998). GPO Access, http://frwebgate.access.gpo.gov/cgi-bin/getdoc.cgi?dbname=105_cong_public_laws&docid=f:publ338.105.

DOCUMENT

Butler Letter on UNSCOM's Work in Iraq

January 25, 1999

REPORT: DISARMAMENT

. . . 7. The Commission's work has taken five main forms:
- evaluation and analysis of Iraq's declarations;
- inspections of relevant sites in Iraq;
- interviews of Iraqi personnel connected to proscribed weapons programs;
- seeking access to and study of relevant Iraqi documentation;
- seeking assistance from Member States, particularly through the provision of relevant information, as required of them by the Security Council.

8. As has been reported to the Council, over the years, and as has been widely recognized, notwithstanding the very considerable obstacles placed by Iraq in the way of the Commission's work, a great deal has been achieved in: verifying Iraq's frequently revised declarations; accounting for its proscribed weapons capabilities; and in destroying, removing or rendering harmless substantial portions of that capability. . . .

12. Three basic points about this disarmament record need to be made. First, the overall period of the Commission's disarmament work must be divided into two parts, separated by the events following the departure from Iraq, in August 1995, of Lt. General Hussein Kamal. This which resulted in the provision to the Commission of an extensive cache of documents on Iraq's prohibited programs. These documents and subsequent disclosures by Iraq indicated that, during the first four years of its activities, the Commission had been very substantially misled by Iraq both in terms of its understanding of Iraq's proscribed weapons programs and the continuation of prohibited activities, even under the Commission's monitoring. Positive conclusions on Iraq's compliance reported to the Council previously by the Commission had to be revised. They were conclusions generally based on accepting Iraq's declarations at face value. Analysis of the new material shaped the direction of the Commission's subsequent work including the emphasis on: obtaining verifiable evidence including physical materials or documents; investigation of the successful concealment activities by Iraq; and, the thorough verification of the unilateral destruction events.

13. Secondly, the Commission has been obliged to undertake a degree of forensic work which was never intended to be the case. This was derived, virtually exclusively, from Iraq's inadequate disclosures, unilateral destruction and concealment activities. These actions, all of which were contrary to the resolutions, made the Commission's work more difficult and, in many cases, continued even after 1995. Had this behavior not occurred, a far less searching inquiry by the Commission would have been necessary. The work of verification of Iraq's declarations would have and should have been far easier and should have been able to be undertaken far more quickly than

has proven to be the case. Such concerted obstructions naturally raise the question of why Iraq has carried out these activities.

14. Thirdly, these overall circumstances have meant that, in spite of the years that have passed and the extensive work that has been undertaken, it has not been possible to verify, fully, Iraq's statements with respect to the nature and magnitude of its proscribed weapons programs and their current disposition.

15. With respect to this latter point, two comments are apposite. First, Iraq's current claims that; it has fulfilled all of its disarmament obligations in each weapons area; ceased concealment policies and actions; and, that it has neither proscribed weapons nor the ability to make them are not able to be verified.

16. Secondly, documents or records available in Iraq in which relevant details of its proscribed programs and actions are set out: production and acquisition records; records of disposition of weapons; and, records of claimed destruction, relevant policy decisions and decisions on termination of concealment, would be invaluable in helping to close remaining gaps and achieve acceptable confidence in Iraq's declarations. The Security Council recognized these two aspects in resolution 707 (1991) when it demanded Iraq provide immediate and unconditional access to, *inter alia*, records, and, demanded that Iraq cease attempts to conceal prohibited materials.

17. In response to the Commission's requests for relevant documents, Iraq has repeatedly claimed that they no longer exist or cannot be located, a claim which often has been shown to be false, either because inspection activities have in fact located precisely such documents or because Iraq has reversed its stated position and then produced relevant documents. The Commission briefed the Council on its assessment of the existence and importance of documents in June 1998. The Commission has assessed that the documents provided in August 1995 were only selected categories of documents provided and that other categories were retained by Iraq. It remains the Commission's strong view that, under the present circumstances, relevant documentation exists in Iraq and that provision of such documentation is the best hope for revealing the full picture, as required by the relevant resolutions.

18. On certain other occasions, Iraq has not claimed that documents sought by the Commission do not exist but has stated instead that they are not relevant to the Commission. The judgment of relevance of any given document is for the Commission, not Iraq, to make, as has been recognized by the Security Council.

19. In August 1998, Iraq declared that unless the Commission could demonstrate that Iraq retained prohibited items, then it must declare that Iraq had fully implemented its obligations under section C of resolution 687. This is contrary to the system established by the Council which imposed upon Iraq the obligation of full disclosure and upon the Commission the duty to verify those disclosures. Were a reversal of these obligations to be accepted, the possibility of serious error would be high as it is Iraq which controls access to the most fundamental information. The Commission remains convinced that Iraq has the capacity to provide credible information thus allowing the Commission to have confidence in an accurate declaration, when it is provided.

20. Notwithstanding the fundamental sources of difficulty described above, and building on both its past achievements and the substantial body of knowledge of Iraq's proscribed programs the Commission assembled, in June of 1998, and indicated, first to the Security Council and then to Iraq, what it believed to be the remaining

priority issues in disarmament, in particular as regards proscribed weapons. This reflected the Commission's understanding of the desire of the Council to focus on selected important parts of the requirements of its resolutions. The methodology used in drawing up this list was to focus on unaccounted proscribed weapons and to set aside other aspects such as fully verifying production capacities, research activities, etc. Satisfactory resolution of the specific "priority issues" would make it easier to conclude that other unverified elements were of lesser substantive importance. Conversely, the inability of Iraq to satisfy these issues would point to more ominous explanations for other unverified parts of Iraq's declarations. Whether these other parts will ultimately be addressed is an open question, but one which has a direct bearing upon confidence in future monitoring.

PRIORITY ISSUES

21. In the view of the Commission, a correct understanding of the nature of the list of priority issues is essential. It should rest on the following considerations.

22. First, these remaining issues must be resolved as they are the necessary conditions for an acceptable material balance in each of the three weapons areas for which the Commission is responsible.

23. Secondly, it should be noted that, even if full resolution was able to be made of these priority issues, this would not mean that there had been a full accounting of all of the proscribed materials and activities listed in paragraphs 8 and 9 of section C of resolution 687 (1991), as summarized in paragraph 2 of this report. However, their full accounting would considerably increase the level of confidence of the Commission's overall verification.

24. Thirdly, if the priority issues are not able to be satisfactorily resolved, then it is likely that the settlement of so-called non-priority outstanding issues will assume a greater importance in achieving confident verification.

25. Finally, the implications of not achieving a credible resolution of the priority disarmament issues needs to be considered, both with respect to the assessment of Iraq's compliance, as well as its implications for the system of ongoing monitoring and verification.

Priority Issues in the Missile Area

Proscribed Missile Warheads

Special warheads

26. Analysis at the laboratories designated by the Commission has detected the presence of degradation products of nerve agents, in particular VX, on a number of warhead remnants which had been excavated at the sites of the unilateral destruction. The October 1998 meeting of international experts convened by the Commission concluded that "the existence of VX degradation products conflicts with Iraq's declarations that the unilaterally destroyed special warheads had never been filled with any chemical warfare agents. The findings by all three laboratories of chemicals known to be degradation products of decontamination compounds also do not support Iraq's declarations that those warhead containers had only been in contact with alcohols." Clarification by Iraq of these issues as recommended by the meeting would allow the Commission to make a determination

whether or not the current assessment of the quantity of special warheads identified amongst the remnants excavated, accounts for all special warheads declared to have been produced by Iraq and provides for the verification of their unilateral destruction.

27. The Commission found that Iraq's explanations on procedures and methods of unilateral destruction of the special warheads were, in general, plausible. In one aspect related to the destruction of BW warheads, the Commission, after consulting a group of international experts, assessed that Iraq's declaration that 15 warheads had been destroyed simultaneously conflicted with physical evidence collected at the declared location of their unilateral destruction. This finding indicated that not all BW warheads had been destroyed at the same time as claimed by Iraq and that Iraq had retained some BW warheads after the date of the declared July 1991 unilateral destruction. Obviously, any retained warheads after the declared destruction date would be an indication that not all proscribed missiles for such warheads were destroyed as claimed by Iraq. The discrepancies between Iraq's declarations and the physical evidence collected need to be resolved. In addition, the Commission's investigations showed that, despite repeated attempts, Iraq had not provided the true locations of the hiding, immediately prior to the declared unilateral destruction, of at least half of the special warheads including abovementioned 15 BW warheads. Iraq's continuous inability to disclose hide sites of the special warheads has also prevented the Commission from verification of the declared unilateral destruction of the special warheads.

Conventional warheads

28. The full and verifiable accounting for proscribed missile conventional warheads remains outstanding in the verification of the premise that Iraq has not retained any holding of proscribed missiles and that all proscribed missiles and their warheads indeed had been destroyed. Issues related to remnants of warheads that have not been recovered, but which have been declared by Iraq as unilaterally destroyed (some 25 imported warheads and some 25 Iraqi manufactured warheads), remain unresolved in the accounting of proscribed warheads that Iraq claimed to have destroyed unilaterally. Iraq has not provided a definite explanatory statement for the Commission to be able to determine the reasons why no remnants to account for some 50 warheads declared as unilaterally destroyed, were recovered.

Proscribed Single-Use Liquid Missile Propellant

29. The full accounting for imported proscribed missile propellants is outstanding. Any retention of such propellants would be an indication that not all proscribed missiles were destroyed as claimed by Iraq. The propellants at issue are used exclusively for such proscribed missiles only. Documents, including an inventory list on their declared unilateral destruction, requested by the Commission, have not been made available by Iraq to support its declaration on the quantities (over 500 tons) of proscribed propellants it claims to have destroyed unilaterally.

Proscribed Indigenous Missile Production

Complete missiles

30. An inventory of proscribed missiles that Iraq declared as destroyed unilaterally contained a reference to seven indigenously produced missiles which were in pos-

session of the Army in 1991. No remnants which could prove such destruction, have been recovered. The Commission has not been able to verify the nature and destruction of these missiles and repeatedly requested Iraq to confirm, through physical evidence, the declared unilateral destruction of these seven missiles. The verification in this area is considered essential as it might involve operational missiles produced indigenously by Iraq. The November 1997 Emergency Session of the Commission determined that the accounting for these seven missiles was one of the priority requirements.

Major components
31. It should be noted that due to the methods used by Iraq for the declared unilateral destruction and lack of supporting documentation made available by Iraq, the verifiable material balance of major proscribed components for indigenous missile production could not be established, or that this work would take a prolonged period of time. Iraq is required to provide, *inter alia*, unambiguous physical evidence of the unilateral destruction of combustion chamber/nozzle assemblies for indigenously produced missiles and documentary evidence sufficient for complete accounting of all indigenously produced major missile parts and for verification of their unilateral destruction.

Priority Issues in the Chemical Weapons Area

Material Balance of Chemical Munitions

Expenditure of chemical munitions in the 1980s
32. In July 1998 during an inspection the Commission found a document which detailed the consumption of special munitions by Iraq in the 1980s. Iraq took the document from the Chief Inspector and did not return it to the Commission despite demands by Security Council that it do so. The figures in this document indicate serious discrepancies with Iraq's declarations on the expenditure of CW-munitions in the 1980s. According to this document, Iraq consumed about 6,000 chemical aerial bombs less than it is stated in its declarations. This invalidates the starting point of the Commission's accounting for chemical weapons which remained in 1991. The provision by Iraq of this document together with clarifications of the discrepancies is required to increase the degree of confidence with respect to Iraq's declarations of chemical weapons which remained in Iraq in 1991 and their disposition.

550 artillery shells filled with mustard
33. Iraq declared that 550 shells filled with mustard had been "lost" shortly after the Gulf War. To date, no evidence of the missing munitions has been found. Iraq claimed that the chemical warfare agents filled into these weapons would be degraded a long time ago and, therefore, there would be no need for their accounting. However, a dozen mustard-filled shells were recovered at a former CW storage facility in the period 1997–1998. The chemical sampling of these munitions, in April 1998, revealed that the mustard was still of the highest quality. After seven years, the purity of mustard ranged between 94 and 97%. Thus, Iraq has to account for these munitions which would be ready for combat use. The resolution of this specific issue would also increase

confidence in accepting Iraq's other declarations on losses of chemical weapons which it has not been possible to verify.

R–400 aerial bombs
34. Among 1,550 R–400 bombs produced by Iraq, more than 1,000 bombs were declared as destroyed unilaterally by Iraq, including 157 bombs stated as having been filled with biological warfare agents. The accounting for about 500 bombs unilaterally destroyed has not been possible due to the state and extent of their destruction. In order to bridge the gap, the Commission asked Iraq to provide documentation on the disposition of the parachute tail sections of R–400 bombs. The accounting for these components would enable the Commission to verify the maximum number of R–400 bombs, which Iraq could have produced. Though this would not solve the specific issue of the quantity and composition of BW bombs, including allocation of BW agents, it may facilitate the final accounting for the chemical R–400 bombs. Iraq presented the information sought on the disposition of tail sections but field inspection activities are still required to verify the full accounting for these weapons.

Accounting for the Production of the Chemical Warfare Agent VX

35. The degree of verification achieved is not satisfactory. Iraq declared that it had produced a total of 3.9 tons of VX. Iraq provided documents on production in 1988, but failed to provide verifiable evidence for its activities in 1990. Iraq also denies that it weaponized VX. Sampling by the Commission of special warheads has thrown significant doubt upon this claim. Iraq needs to provide verifiable evidence and clarifications to support its declarations on the production and weaponization of VX. Technical meetings with the Iraqi specialists and field verification are required.

Material Balance of CW-Production Equipment

36. One hundred and ninety-seven pieces of glass CW production equipment were removed by Iraq from its prime CW facility prior to the Commission's arrival in 1991 and were repeatedly moved in shipping containers between several facilities throughout Baghdad until 1996. This production equipment from two of 20 shipping containers was destroyed under the Commission's supervision in 1997. To ensure that all CW production equipment removed from the CW facility has been accounted for, the Commission requested Iraq to provide its clarifications on their movement. Iraq presented such clarifications in July 1998. Field verification is still required to increase the degree of confidence that all equipment has been accounted for.

Priority Issues in the Biological Weapons Area

37. Since the adoption of Security Council resolution 687 (1991) in April 1991 and until July 1995, Iraq denied that it had had any proscribed biological warfare (BW) activities. Based on the results of its inspection and verification activities, the Commission assessed and reported to the Council in its report of April 1995, that Iraq had not provided an account of its proscribed biological program nor accounted for materials and items that may have been used or acquired for such a program. The

Commission stated that with Iraq's failure to account for the use of these items and materials for legitimate purposes, the only conclusion that can be drawn is that there is a high risk that they had been purchased and used for a proscribed purpose—acquisition of biological warfare agent. Iraq was provided with evidence collected by the Commission. On 1 July 1995, Iraq, for the first time, acknowledged that it had had an offensive BW program but still denied any weaponization. Subsequently, in August 1995, after the departure from Iraq of Lt. Gen. Hussein Kamel Hassan, Iraq admitted that it had weaponized BW agents and deployed biological weapons for combat use.

38. Since August 1995, Iraq has submitted a number of "Full, Final and Complete Disclosures" (FFCD) of its declared BW program. These declarations have been assessed by the Commission and by international experts as incomplete, inadequate and containing substantial deficiencies. They were not accepted as a full account of the scale and the scope of Iraq's BW program. This refers in particular to weaponization of produced BW agents, bulk BW agent production and acquisitions for the BW program.

39. In the Commission's view, Iraq has not complied with requirements of the relevant Security Council resolutions on the disclosure of its biological warfare program. A full, complete and verifiable disclosure of all its biological weapons activities needs to be presented by Iraq.

40. Because Iraq has failed to disclose fully, the scope and nature of its BW program, the priority issue in this weapons area involves the whole scope of the BW program. This means that Iraq must furnish a complete and verifiable disclosure as a matter of absolute first priority. The Commission would then need to assess and verify that disclosure.

41. Finally, it needs to be recognized that Iraq possesses an industrial capability and knowledge base, through which biological warfare agents could be produced quickly and in volume, if the Government of Iraq decided to do so.

SOURCE: United Nations, www.un.org/Depts/unscom/s99-94.htm.

Iraq War Prelude

DOCUMENT IN CONTEXT

The long road to the U.S.-led invasion of Iraq in 2003 had many twists and turns. It can be argued that Iraq's invasion of Kuwait in 1990 set in motion a series of events that ultimately led to the war of 2003. The conclusion of the Persian Gulf War in February 1991 with Iraqi leader Saddam Hussein weakened but still in power is another important point along this road. Some people insist that President George W. Bush launched the 2003 invasion to retaliate for Iraq's alleged attempt to assassinate his father, former president George H. W. Bush, during a visit to Kuwait in April 1993, three months after leaving office. Others point to 1998, when a diverse group of out-of-office Republican politicians, neoconservative intellectuals, and Iraqi exiles persuaded Congress to adopt—and President Bill Clinton to sign—legislation putting the United States on record as favoring the removal of Hussein from office.

The September 11, 2001, al-Qaida attacks against the United States created a sense of crisis that was necessary before any president could order American troops to invade another country. Within days following the September 11 attacks, senior officials of the Bush administration began talking in private about options for retaliating against Iraq although no evidence existed, then or later, that Iraq had any involvement in the attacks or those who launched them.

Bush signaled his focus on Iraq with two high-profile statements. At the White House on November 26, 2001, the president warned that Iraq possessed weapons of mass destruction and might hand them over to terrorists. Then, in his January 29, 2002, State of the Union Address, Bush declared that Iran, Iraq, and North Korea, along with "their terrorist allies," constituted an "axis of evil . . . arming to threaten the peace of the world." Bush focused particularly on Iraq, stating that it had "plotted to develop anthrax, and nerve gas, and nuclear weapons for over a decade" and was "a regime that has something to hide from the civilized world." The Bush administration spent much of 2002 making the case publicly for an invasion of Iraq that had been put on course following the September 11 attacks. By spring 2002, Pentagon officials had begun formulating detailed plans for an invasion, and one key international ally, British prime minister Tony Blair, had signaled his support.

Administration officials offered two rationales for targeting Baghdad. First, the departure of UN weapons inspectors from Iraq in 1998 had given Iraqi leader Saddam Hussein free rein to step up its production of weapons of mass destruction—biological and chemical weapons and perhaps nuclear weapons as well—all of which Hussein could in theory turn over to terrorists. Second, proposals to send UN inspectors back to Iraq were misguided because the Iraqis had succeeded in misleading the previous inspectors during the 1990s and would do so again (UN Weapons Inspections, p. 473).

Vice President Dick Cheney was the first senior administration official to go public with these arguments, telling a convention of the Veterans of Foreign Wars in Nashville on August 26, 2002, that UN inspections offered the world "false comfort" while Iraq, behind the scenes, continued to build dangerous weapons. "Simply stated, there is no doubt that Saddam Hussein now has weapons of mass destruction," Cheney told the veterans. "There is no doubt he is amassing them to use against our friends, against our allies, and against us. And there is no doubt that his aggressive regional ambitions will lead him into future confrontations with his neighbors—confrontations that will involve both the weapons he has today, and the ones he will continue to develop with his oil wealth."

Some two weeks later, during his annual speech to the opening session of the UN General Assembly on September 12, President Bush made a similarly broad case against Hussein. Reciting the history of Iraq's refusal to cooperate with UN weapons inspections during the 1990s, Bush argued that Iraq posed "exactly the kind of aggressive threat the United Nations was born to confront." Bush challenged the Security Council to take stronger action against Iraq than it had in the past, but he also made clear that the United States would act even if the Security Council did not. "The Security Council resolutions will be enforced—the just demands of peace and security will be met—or action will be unavoidable," he said. "And a regime that has lost its legitimacy will also lose its power."

At this same time, Bush began pushing Congress to enact a resolution giving him explicit authority to go to war against Iraq. He insisted that he did not need such authorization because under the Constitution he already had it as commander in chief of the armed forces. Even so, he wanted political support for such a momentous undertaking. In pressuring Congress, Bush gave a nationally televised speech from Cincinnati on October 8 laying out the potential threat from Iraq in stark terms. Citing past reports from UN weapons inspectors and other, unspecified sources, the president stated categorically that Iraq possessed large quantities of biological and chemical weapons and was "reconstituting its nuclear weapons program." Bush acknowledged that "we don't know exactly" how far Iraq's nuclear weapons program had advanced, but he gave this ominous warning: "Facing clear evidence of peril, we cannot wait for the final proof—the smoking gun—that could come in the form of a mushroom cloud."

Congress responded quickly to Bush's grave warnings of the need for immediate action. Two days later, on October 10, the House of Representatives overwhelmingly approved a resolution (H J Res 114) giving the president authority to use force against Iraq, and the Senate acted the following day, again by a broad bipartisan majority. Bush signed the measure into law (PL 107-243) on October 16.

With congressional support in hand, Bush insisted on action by the United Nations. There, U.S. diplomats, led by Secretary of State Colin Powell, had been negotiating for several weeks on the wording of a resolution demanding that Iraq allow the return of weapons inspectors or face the consequences. The key question concerned whether the resolution should specify what those consequences might be. The United States wanted a resolution explicitly warning Iraq that it would be punished if it refused to cooperate with the UN weapons inspections. France, which since the late 1990s had been sympathetic to Iraqi appeals to lift economic sanctions, wanted a two-step process in which the Security Council would demand that Iraq allow the return of the inspectors and would decide only later on what punishment Iraq would face if it refused.

These diplomatic negotiations produced a compromise early in November that recited a long list of grievances against Iraq, demanded the return of the weapons inspectors, and warned Iraq of "serious consequences" should it balk. Although it served as a warning to Iraq, the language of the resolution was vague on two main counts: it did not set benchmarks for measuring Iraqi cooperation or lack thereof, and its warning of consequences did not provide the explicit authorization for war that the Bush administration had sought in the event Iraq failed to cooperate. Even so, Bush hailed the measure as posing the "final test" for Iraq. The council adopted Resolution 1441 on November 8 by a unanimous vote, which meant that it had garnered support even from the three nations that had been most reluctant: France, Russia, and Syria (the only Arab nation then serving on the council).

In a blustery letter delivered to the United Nations on November 13, Iraq reluctantly agreed to the resolution but insisted that the U.S. allegations about its weapons were "fabrications." UN inspectors began arriving in Iraq on November 18, and on

December 7—one day ahead of a deadline set by the Security Council—Iraq handed boxes of documents to them. Iraqi officials said they proved that the country no longer had any banned weapons.

The next few months, until mid-March 2003, brought the interplay of diplomacy in the world's capitals, drama on the ground in Iraq, and the inexorable buildup to war. The diplomacy involved frantic efforts by the Bush administration to rally support for war against Iraq over widespread international objections, including from some of its most important allies. European nations were divided, with some (notably, Britain, Spain, and several formerly communist countries in Eastern Europe) supporting the U.S. position, while others (notably, France, Germany, and Russia) were adamantly opposed. U.S. secretary of defense Donald H. Rumsfeld sarcastically called this a division between "New Europe" (the supporters) and "Old Europe" (the dissenters).

In Iraq, weapons inspectors made halting progress, winning limited cooperation with government officials but still facing some of the same obstacles placed in their way during most of the 1990s. On January 27, 2003, Hans Blix, the Swedish diplomat who headed the UN inspectors, told the Security Council that Iraq "appears not to have come to a genuine acceptance, even today, of the disarmament which was demanded of it."

In a central event of this period, Secretary of State Powell delivered a ninety-minute presentation to the Security Council on February 5 citing intelligence information—including photographs of alleged weapons installations and tape recordings of Iraqi officials—that he insisted amounted to irrefutable evidence of Iraq's biological, chemical, and nuclear weapons programs. Powell also sought to link the Iraqi government to the al-Qaida network. Most of the evidence Powell presented to the Security Council later proved to be false or misleading. For example, only two days after Powell made the administration's claims at the United Nations, Mohamed El Baradei, head of the International Atomic Energy Agency, disputed those about nuclear weapons. U.S. officials brushed aside his statements.

Powell's dramatic presentation garnered headlines around the world, but it failed to convince wavering countries to support another Security Council resolution expressly endorsing a war against Iraq. British prime minister Blair had sought such a resolution to help him overcome domestic opposition to British participation in a war. France and Russia, among other countries, made clear that they were not prepared to give a U.S.-led war the legal blessing of the United Nations. The Security Council thus took no further action.

The military buildup to war proceeded while inspectors worked in Iraq and diplomats debated next steps at the United Nations. During the second half of 2002 and the first two months of 2003, the United States, Britain, and a handful of their allies positioned troops in Kuwait and Qatar and on board ships in the Persian Gulf. In February, Turkey caused a hitch in plans when its parliament refused to allow the U.S. Army to invade Iraq from Turkish territory. Regardless, by mid-March all the elements stood in place for the invasion of Iraq that anxious U.S. officials said would complete the job that should have been done in the Persian Gulf War twelve years earlier (Persian Gulf War's Aftermath, p. 465).

Following are excerpts from the speech by President George W. Bush to the UN General Assembly on September 12, 2002, demanding that the United States enforce

*its numerous resolutions requiring Iraq to relinquish weapons of mass destruction;
a speech by Bush, delivered in Cincinnati, Ohio, on October 7, 2002, warning that
Iraq's campaign to build weapons of mass destruction directly threatened the United
States and its interests in the Middle East; and UN Security Council Resolution
1441, adopted on November 8, 2002, demanding that Iraq comply with previous
resolutions regarding its weapons of mass destruction and submit to renewed inspections of its weapons programs by UN experts or face "serious consequences."*

DOCUMENT

Bush's Annual Speech to the UN General Assembly

SEPTEMBER 12, 2002

. . . Our common security is challenged by regional conflicts—ethnic and religious strife that is ancient, but not inevitable. In the Middle East, there can be no peace for either side without freedom for both sides. America stands committed to an independent and democratic Palestine, living side by side with Israel in peace and security. Like all other people, Palestinians deserve a government that serves their interests and listens to their voices. My nation will continue to encourage all parties to step up to their responsibilities as we seek a just and comprehensive settlement to the conflict.

Above all, our principles and our security are challenged today by outlaw groups and regimes that accept no law of morality and have no limit to their violent ambitions. In the attacks on America a year ago, we saw the destructive intentions of our enemies. This threat hides within many nations, including my own. In cells and camps, terrorists are plotting further destruction, and building new bases for their war against civilization. And our greatest fear is that terrorists will find a shortcut to their mad ambitions when an outlaw regime supplies them with the technologies to kill on a massive scale.

In one place—in one regime—we find all these dangers, in their most lethal and aggressive forms, exactly the kind of aggressive threat the United Nations was born to confront.

Twelve years ago, Iraq invaded Kuwait without provocation. And the regime's forces were poised to continue their march to seize other countries and their resources. Had Saddam Hussein been appeased instead of stopped, he would have endangered the peace and stability of the world. Yet this aggression was stopped—by the might of coalition forces and the will of the United Nations.

To suspend hostilities, to spare himself, Iraq's dictator accepted a series of commitments. The terms were clear, to him and to all. And he agreed to prove he is complying with every one of those obligations.

He has proven instead only his contempt for the United Nations, and for all his pledges. By breaking every pledge—by his deceptions, and by his cruelties—Saddam Hussein has made the case against himself.

In 1991, Security Council Resolution 688 demanded that the Iraqi regime cease at once the repression of its own people, including the systematic repression of minorities—which the Council said, threatened international peace and security in the region. This demand goes ignored.

Last year, the U.N. Commission on Human Rights found that Iraq continues to commit extremely grave violations of human rights, and that the regime's repression is all pervasive. Tens of thousands of political opponents and ordinary citizens have been subjected to arbitrary arrest and imprisonment, summary execution, and torture by beating and burning, electric shock, starvation, mutilation, and rape. Wives are tortured in front of their husbands, children in the presence of their parents—and all of these horrors concealed from the world by the apparatus of a totalitarian state.

In 1991, the U.N. Security Council, through Resolutions 686 and 687, demanded that Iraq return all prisoners from Kuwait and other lands. Iraq's regime agreed. It broke its promise. Last year the Secretary-General's high-level coordinator for this issue reported that Kuwait, Saudi, Indian, Syrian, Lebanese, Iranian, Egyptian, Bahraini, and Omani nationals remain unaccounted for—more than 600 people. One American pilot is among them.

In 1991, the U.N. Security Council, through Resolution 687, demanded that Iraq renounce all involvement with terrorism, and permit no terrorist organizations to operate in Iraq. Iraq's regime agreed. It broke this promise. In violation of Security Council Resolution 1373, Iraq continues to shelter and support terrorist organizations that direct violence against Iran, Israel, and Western governments. Iraqi dissidents abroad are targeted for murder. In 1993, Iraq attempted to assassinate the Emir of Kuwait and a former American President. Iraq's government openly praised the attacks of September the 11th. And al Qaeda terrorists escaped from Afghanistan and are known to be in Iraq.

In 1991, the Iraqi regime agreed to destroy and stop developing all weapons of mass destruction and long-range missiles, and to prove to the world it has done so by complying with rigorous inspections. Iraq has broken every aspect of this fundamental pledge.

From 1991 to 1995, the Iraqi regime said it had no biological weapons. After a senior official in its weapons program defected and exposed this lie, the regime admitted to producing tens of thousands of liters of anthrax and other deadly biological agents for use with Scud warheads, aerial bombs, and aircraft spray tanks. U.N. inspectors believe Iraq has produced two to four times the amount of biological agents it declared, and has failed to account for more than three metric tons of material that could be used to produce biological weapons. Right now, Iraq is expanding and improving facilities that were used for the production of biological weapons.

United Nations' inspections also revealed that Iraq likely maintains stockpiles of VX, mustard and other chemical agents, and that the regime is rebuilding and expanding facilities capable of producing chemical weapons.

And in 1995, after four years of deception, Iraq finally admitted it had a crash nuclear weapons program prior to the Gulf War. We know now, were it not for that war, the regime in Iraq would likely have possessed a nuclear weapon no later than 1993.

Today, Iraq continues to withhold important information about its nuclear program—weapons design, procurement logs, experiment data, an accounting of nuclear materials and documentation of foreign assistance. Iraq employs capable nuclear scientists and technicians. It retains physical infrastructure needed to build a nuclear weapon. Iraq has made several attempts to buy high-strength aluminum tubes used to enrich uranium for a nuclear weapon. Should Iraq acquire fissile material, it would be able to build a nuclear weapon within a year. And Iraq's state-controlled media has reported numerous meetings between Saddam Hussein and his nuclear scientists, leaving little doubt about his continued appetite for these weapons.

Iraq also possesses a force of Scud-type missiles with ranges beyond the 150 kilometers permitted by the U.N. Work at testing and production facilities shows that Iraq is building more long-range missiles that it can inflict mass death [on] throughout the region.

In 1990, after Iraq's invasion of Kuwait, the world imposed economic sanctions on Iraq. Those sanctions were maintained after the war to compel the regime's compliance with Security Council resolutions. In time, Iraq was allowed to use oil revenues to buy food. Saddam Hussein has subverted this program, working around the sanctions to buy missile technology and military materials. He blames the suffering of Iraq's people on the United Nations, even as he uses his oil wealth to build lavish palaces for himself, and to buy arms for his country. By refusing to comply with his own agreements, he bears full guilt for the hunger and misery of innocent Iraqi citizens.

In 1991, Iraq promised U.N. inspectors immediate and unrestricted access to verify Iraq's commitment to rid itself of weapons of mass destruction and long-range missiles. Iraq broke this promise, spending seven years deceiving, evading, and harassing U.N. inspectors before ceasing cooperation entirely. Just months after the 1991 ceasefire, the Security Council twice renewed its demand that the Iraqi regime cooperate fully with inspectors, condemning Iraq's serious violations of its obligations. The Security Council again renewed that demand in 1994, and twice more in 1996, deploring Iraq's clear violations of its obligations. The Security Council renewed its demand three more times in 1997, citing flagrant violations; and three more times in 1998, calling Iraq's behavior totally unacceptable. And in 1999, the demand was renewed yet again.

As we meet today, it's been almost four years since the last U.N. inspectors set foot in Iraq, four years for the Iraqi regime to plan, and to build, and to test behind the cloak of secrecy.

We know that Saddam Hussein pursued weapons of mass murder even when inspectors were in his country. Are we to assume that he stopped when they left? The history, the logic, and the facts lead to one conclusion: Saddam Hussein's regime is a grave and gathering danger. To suggest otherwise is to hope against the evidence. To assume this regime's good faith is to bet the lives of millions and the peace of the world in a reckless gamble. And this is a risk we must not take.

Delegates to the General Assembly, we have been more than patient. We've tried sanctions. We've tried the carrot of oil for food, and the stick of coalition military strikes. But Saddam Hussein has defied all these efforts and continues to develop weapons of mass destruction. The first time we may be completely certain he has a— nuclear weapons is when, God forbid, he uses one. We owe it to all our citizens to do everything in our power to prevent that day from coming.

The conduct of the Iraqi regime is a threat to the authority of the United Nations, and a threat to peace. Iraq has answered a decade of U.N. demands with a decade of defiance. All the world now faces a test, and the United Nations a difficult and defining moment. Are Security Council resolutions to be honored and enforced, or cast aside without consequence? Will the United Nations serve the purpose of its founding, or will it be irrelevant?

The United States helped found the United Nations. We want the United Nations to be effective, and respectful, and successful. We want the resolutions of the world's most important multilateral body to be enforced. And right now those resolutions are being unilaterally subverted by the Iraqi regime. Our partnership of nations can meet the test before us, by making clear what we now expect of the Iraqi regime.

If the Iraqi regime wishes peace, it will immediately and unconditionally forswear, disclose, and remove or destroy all weapons of mass destruction, long-range missiles, and all related material.

If the Iraqi regime wishes peace, it will immediately end all support for terrorism and act to suppress it, as all states are required to do by U.N. Security Council resolutions.

If the Iraqi regime wishes peace, it will cease persecution of its civilian population, including Shi'a, Sunnis, Kurds, Turkomans, and others, again as required by Security Council resolutions.

If the Iraqi regime wishes peace, it will release or account for all Gulf War personnel whose fate is still unknown. It will return the remains of any who are deceased, return stolen property, accept liability for losses resulting from the invasion of Kuwait, and fully cooperate with international efforts to resolve these issues, as required by Security Council resolutions.

If the Iraqi regime wishes peace, it will immediately end all illicit trade outside the oil-for-food program. It will accept U.N. administration of funds from that program, to ensure that the money is used fairly and promptly for the benefit of the Iraqi people.

If all these steps are taken, it will signal a new openness and accountability in Iraq. And it could open the prospect of the United Nations helping to build a government that represents all Iraqis—a government based on respect for human rights, economic liberty, and internationally supervised elections.

The United States has no quarrel with the Iraqi people; they've suffered too long in silent captivity. Liberty for the Iraqi people is a great moral cause, and a great strategic goal. The people of Iraq deserve it; the security of all nations requires it. Free societies do not intimidate through cruelty and conquest, and open societies do not threaten the world with mass murder. The United States supports political and economic liberty in a unified Iraq.

We can harbor no illusions—and that's important today to remember. Saddam Hussein attacked Iran in 1980 and Kuwait in 1990. He's fired ballistic missiles at Iran and Saudi Arabia, Bahrain, and Israel. His regime once ordered the killing of every person between the ages of 15 and 70 in certain Kurdish villages in northern Iraq. He has gassed many Iranians, and 40 Iraqi villages.

My nation will work with the U.N. Security Council to meet our common challenge. If Iraq's regime defies us again, the world must move deliberately, decisively to hold Iraq to account. We will work with the U.N. Security Council for the necessary resolutions. But the purposes of the United States should not be doubted. The Security Council resolutions will be enforced—the just demands of peace and security will be met—or action will be unavoidable. And a regime that has lost its legitimacy will also lose its power.

Events can turn in one of two ways: If we fail to act in the face of danger, the people of Iraq will continue to live in brutal submission. The regime will have new power to bully and dominate and conquer its neighbors, condemning the Middle East to more years of bloodshed and fear. The regime will remain unstable—the region will remain unstable, with little hope of freedom, and isolated from the progress of our times. With every step the Iraqi regime takes toward gaining and deploying the most terrible weapons, our own options to confront that regime will narrow. And if an emboldened regime were to supply these weapons to terrorist allies, then the attacks of September the 11th would be a prelude to far greater horrors.

If we meet our responsibilities, if we overcome this danger, we can arrive at a very different future. The people of Iraq can shake off their captivity. They can one day join a democratic Afghanistan and a democratic Palestine, inspiring reforms throughout the Muslim world. These nations can show by their example that honest government, and respect for women, and the great Islamic tradition of learning can triumph in the Middle East and beyond. And we will show that the promise of the United Nations can be fulfilled in our time.

Neither of these outcomes is certain. Both have been set before us. We must choose between a world of fear and a world of progress. We cannot stand by and do nothing while dangers gather. We must stand up for our security, and for the permanent rights and the hopes of mankind. By heritage and by choice, the United States of America will make that stand. And, delegates to the United Nations, you have the power to make that stand, as well.

SOURCE: The White House, Office of the Press Secretary, www.whitehouse.gov/news/releases/2002/ 09/20020912-1.html.

DOCUMENT

Bush Speech Warning of Iraqi WMD

OCTOBER 7, 2002

Tonight I want to take a few minutes to discuss a grave threat to peace, and America's determination to lead the world in confronting that threat.

The threat comes from Iraq. It arises directly from the Iraqi regime's own actions—its history of aggression, and its drive toward an arsenal of terror. Eleven years ago, as a condition for ending the Persian Gulf War, the Iraqi regime was required to destroy its weapons of mass destruction, to cease all development of such weapons, and to stop all support for terrorist groups. The Iraqi regime has violated all of those obligations. It possesses and produces chemical and biological weapons. It is seeking nuclear weapons. It has given shelter and support to terrorism, and practices terror against its own people. The entire world has witnessed Iraq's eleven-year history of defiance, deception and bad faith.

We also must never forget the most vivid events of recent history. On September the 11th, 2001, America felt its vulnerability—even to threats that gather on the other side of the earth. We resolved then, and we are resolved today, to confront every threat, from any source, that could bring sudden terror and suffering to America.

Members of the Congress of both political parties, and members of the United Nations Security Council, agree that Saddam Hussein is a threat to peace and must disarm. We agree that the Iraqi dictator must not be permitted to threaten America and the world with horrible poisons and diseases and gases and atomic weapons. Since we all agree on this goal, the issue is: how can we best achieve it?

Many Americans have raised legitimate questions: about the nature of the threat; about the urgency of action—why be concerned now; about the link between Iraq developing weapons of terror, and the wider war on terror. These are all issues we've discussed broadly and fully within my administration. And tonight, I want to share those discussions with you.

First, some ask why Iraq is different from other countries or regimes that also have terrible weapons. While there are many dangers in the world, the threat from Iraq stands alone—because it gathers the most serious dangers of our age in one place. Iraq's weapons of mass destruction are controlled by a murderous tyrant who has already used chemical weapons to kill thousands of people. This same tyrant has tried to dominate the Middle East, has invaded and brutally occupied a small neighbor, has struck other nations without warning, and holds an unrelenting hostility toward the United States.

By its past and present actions, by its technological capabilities, by the merciless nature of its regime, Iraq is unique. As a former chief weapons inspector of the U.N. has said, "The fundamental problem with Iraq remains the nature of the regime, itself. Saddam Hussein is a homicidal dictator who is addicted to weapons of mass destruction."

Some ask how urgent this danger is to America and the world. The danger is already significant, and it only grows worse with time. If we know Saddam Hussein has dangerous weapons today—and we do—does it make any sense for the world to wait to confront him as he grows even stronger and develops even more dangerous weapons?

In 1995, after several years of deceit by the Iraqi regime, the head of Iraq's military industries defected. It was then that the regime was forced to admit that it had produced more than 30,000 liters of anthrax and other deadly biological agents. The inspectors, however, concluded that Iraq had likely produced two to four times that amount. This is a massive stockpile of biological weapons that has never been accounted for, and capable of killing millions.

We know that the regime has produced thousands of tons of chemical agents, including mustard gas, sarin nerve gas, VX nerve gas. Saddam Hussein also has experience in using chemical weapons. He has ordered chemical attacks on Iran, and on more than forty villages in his own country. These actions killed or injured at least 20,000 people, more than six times the number of people who died in the attacks of September the 11th.

And surveillance photos reveal that the regime is rebuilding facilities that it had used to produce chemical and biological weapons. Every chemical and biological weapon that Iraq has or makes is a direct violation of the truce that ended the Persian Gulf War in 1991. Yet, Saddam Hussein has chosen to build and keep these weapons despite international sanctions, U.N. demands, and isolation from the civilized world.

Iraq possesses ballistic missiles with a likely range of hundreds of miles—far enough to strike Saudi Arabia, Israel, Turkey, and other nations—in a region where more than 135,000 American civilians and service members live and work. We've also discovered through intelligence that Iraq has a growing fleet of manned and unmanned aerial vehicles that could be used to disperse chemical or biological weapons across broad areas. We're concerned that Iraq is exploring ways of using these UAVs for missions targeting the United States. And, of course, sophisticated delivery systems aren't required for a chemical or biological attack; all that might be required are a small container and one terrorist or Iraqi intelligence operative to deliver it.

And that is the source of our urgent concern about Saddam Hussein's links to international terrorist groups. Over the years, Iraq has provided safe haven to terrorists such as Abu Nidal, whose terror organization carried out more than 90 terrorist attacks in 20 countries that killed or injured nearly 900 people, including 12 Americans. Iraq has also provided safe haven to Abu Abbas, who was responsible for seizing the *Achille Lauro* and killing an American passenger. And we know that Iraq is continuing to finance terror and gives assistance to groups that use terrorism to undermine Middle East peace.

We know that Iraq and the al Qaeda terrorist network share a common enemy— the United States of America. We know that Iraq and al Qaeda have had high-level contacts that go back a decade. Some al Qaeda leaders who fled Afghanistan went to Iraq. These include one very senior al Qaeda leader who received medical treatment in Baghdad this year, and who has been associated with planning for chemical and biological attacks. We've learned that Iraq has trained al Qaeda members in bomb-making and poisons and deadly gases. And we know that after September the 11th, Saddam Hussein's regime gleefully celebrated the terrorist attacks on America.

Iraq could decide on any given day to provide a biological or chemical weapon to a terrorist group or individual terrorists. Alliance with terrorists could allow the Iraqi regime to attack America without leaving any fingerprints.

Some have argued that confronting the threat from Iraq could detract from the war against terror. To the contrary; confronting the threat posed by Iraq is crucial to winning the war on terror. When I spoke to Congress more than a year ago, I said that those who harbor terrorists are as guilty as the terrorists themselves. Saddam Hussein is harboring terrorists and the instruments of terror, the instruments of mass death and destruction. And he cannot be trusted. The risk is simply too great that he will use them, or provide them to a terror network.

Terror cells and outlaw regimes building weapons of mass destruction are different faces of the same evil. Our security requires that we confront both. And the United States military is capable of confronting both.

Many people have asked how close Saddam Hussein is to developing a nuclear weapon. Well, we don't know exactly, and that's the problem. Before the Gulf War, the best intelligence indicated that Iraq was eight to ten years away from developing a nuclear weapon. After the war, international inspectors learned that the regime has been much closer—the regime in Iraq would likely have possessed a nuclear weapon no later than 1993. The inspectors discovered that Iraq had an advanced nuclear weapons development program, had a design for a workable nuclear weapon, and was pursuing several different methods of enriching uranium for a bomb.

Before being barred from Iraq in 1998, the International Atomic Energy Agency dismantled extensive nuclear weapons–related facilities, including three uranium enrichment sites. That same year, information from a high-ranking Iraqi nuclear engineer who had defected revealed that despite his public promises, Saddam Hussein had ordered his nuclear program to continue.

The evidence indicates that Iraq is reconstituting its nuclear weapons program. Saddam Hussein has held numerous meetings with Iraqi nuclear scientists, a group he calls his "nuclear mujahideen"—his nuclear holy warriors. Satellite photographs reveal that Iraq is rebuilding facilities at sites that have been part of its nuclear program in the past. Iraq has attempted to purchase high-strength aluminum tubes and other equipment needed for gas centrifuges, which are used to enrich uranium for nuclear weapons.

If the Iraqi regime is able to produce, buy, or steal an amount of highly enriched uranium a little larger than a single softball, it could have a nuclear weapon in less than a year. And if we allow that to happen, a terrible line would be crossed. Saddam Hussein would be in a position to blackmail anyone who opposes his aggression. He would be in a position to dominate the Middle East. He would be in a position to threaten America. And Saddam Hussein would be in a position to pass nuclear technology to terrorists.

Some citizens wonder, after 11 years of living with this problem, why do we need to confront it now? And there's a reason. We've experienced the horror of September the 11th. We have seen that those who hate America are willing to crash airplanes into buildings full of innocent people. Our enemies would be no less willing, in fact, they would be eager, to use biological or chemical, or a nuclear weapon.

Knowing these realities, America must not ignore the threat gathering against us. Facing clear evidence of peril, we cannot wait for the final proof—the smoking gun—that could come in the form of a mushroom cloud. As President Kennedy said in October of 1962, "Neither the United States of America, nor the world community of nations can tolerate deliberate deception and offensive threats on the part of any nation, large or small. We no longer live in a world," he said, "where only the actual firing of weapons represents a sufficient challenge to a nations security to constitute maximum peril."

Understanding the threats of our time, knowing the designs and deceptions of the Iraqi regime, we have every reason to assume the worst, and we have an urgent duty to prevent the worst from occurring.

Some believe we can address this danger by simply resuming the old approach to inspections, and applying diplomatic and economic pressure. Yet this is precisely what the world has tried to do since 1991. The U.N. inspections program was met with systematic deception. The Iraqi regime bugged hotel rooms and offices of inspectors to find where they were going next; they forged documents, destroyed evidence, and developed mobile weapons facilities to keep a step ahead of inspectors. Eight so-called presidential palaces were declared off-limits to unfettered inspections. These sites actually encompass twelve square miles, with hundreds of structures, both above and below the ground, where sensitive materials could be hidden.

The world has also tried economic sanctions—and watched Iraq use billions of dollars in illegal oil revenues to fund more weapons purchases, rather than providing for the needs of the Iraqi people.

The world has tried limited military strikes to destroy Iraq's weapons of mass destruction capabilities—only to see them openly rebuilt, while the regime again denies they even exist.

The world has tried no-fly zones to keep Saddam from terrorizing his own people—and in the last year alone, the Iraqi military has fired upon American and British pilots more than 750 times.

After eleven years during which we have tried containment, sanctions, inspections, even selected military action, the end result is that Saddam Hussein still has chemical and biological weapons and is increasing his capabilities to make more. And he is moving ever closer to developing a nuclear weapon.

Clearly, to actually work, any new inspections, sanctions or enforcement mechanisms will have to be very different. America wants the U.N. to be an effective organization that helps keep the peace. And that is why we are urging the Security Council to adopt a new resolution setting out tough, immediate requirements. Among those requirements: the Iraqi regime must reveal and destroy, under U.N. supervision, all existing weapons of mass destruction. To ensure that we learn the truth, the regime must allow witnesses to its illegal activities to be interviewed outside the country— and these witnesses must be free to bring their families with them so they all [are] beyond the reach of Saddam Hussein's terror and murder. And inspectors must have access to any site, at any time, without pre-clearance, without delay, without exceptions.

The time for denying, deceiving, and delaying has come to an end. Saddam Hussein must disarm himself—or, for the sake of peace, we will lead a coalition to disarm him.

Many nations are joining us in insisting that Saddam Hussein's regime be held accountable. They are committed to defending the international security that protects the lives of both our citizens and theirs. And that's why America is challenging all nations to take the resolutions of the U.N. Security Council seriously.

And these resolutions are clear. In addition to declaring and destroying all of its weapons of mass destruction, Iraq must end its support for terrorism. It must cease the persecution of its civilian population. It must stop all illicit trade outside the Oil for Food program. It must release or account for all Gulf War personnel, including an American pilot, whose fate is still unknown.

By taking these steps, and by only taking these steps, the Iraqi regime has an opportunity to avoid conflict. Taking these steps would also change the nature of the Iraqi regime itself. America hopes the regime will make that choice. Unfortunately, at least so far, we have little reason to expect it. And that's why two administrations— mine and President Clinton's—have stated that regime change in Iraq is the only certain means of removing a great danger to our nation.

I hope this will not require military action, but it may. And military conflict could be difficult. An Iraqi regime faced with its own demise may attempt cruel and desperate measures. If Saddam Hussein orders such measures, his generals would be well advised to refuse those orders. If they do not refuse, they must understand that all war criminals will be pursued and punished. If we have to act, we will take every precaution that is possible. We will plan carefully; we will act with the full power of the United States military; we will act with allies at our side, and we will prevail.

There is no easy or risk-free course of action. Some have argued we should wait— and that's an option. In my view, it's the riskiest of all options, because the longer we wait, the stronger and bolder Saddam Hussein will become. We could wait and hope that Saddam does not give weapons to terrorists, or develop a nuclear weapon to blackmail the world. But I'm convinced that is a hope against all evidence. As Americans, we want peace—we work and sacrifice for peace. But there can be no peace if our security depends on the will and whims of a ruthless and aggressive dictator. I'm not willing to stake one American life on trusting Saddam Hussein.

Failure to act would embolden other tyrants, allow terrorists access to new weapons and new resources, and make blackmail a permanent feature of world events. The United Nations would betray the purpose of its founding, and prove irrelevant to the problems of our time. And through its inaction, the United States would resign itself to a future of fear.

That is not the America I know. That is not the America I serve. We refuse to live in fear. This nation, in world war and in Cold War, has never permitted the brutal and lawless to set history's course. Now, as before, we will secure our nation, protect our freedom, and help others to find freedom of their own.

Some worry that a change of leadership in Iraq could create instability and make the situation worse. The situation could hardly get worse, for world security and for the people of Iraq. The lives of Iraqi citizens would improve dramatically if Saddam Hussein were no longer in power, just as the lives of Afghanistan's citizens improved after the Taliban. The dictator of Iraq is a student of Stalin, using murder as a tool of terror and control, within his own cabinet, within his own army, and even within his own family.

On Saddam Hussein's orders, opponents have been decapitated, wives and mothers of political opponents have been systematically raped as a method of intimidation, and political prisoners have been forced to watch their own children being tortured.

America believes that all people are entitled to hope and human rights, to the nonnegotiable demands of human dignity. People everywhere prefer freedom to slavery; prosperity to squalor; self-government to the rule of terror and torture. America is a friend to the people of Iraq. Our demands are directed only at the regime that enslaves them and threatens us. When these demands are met, the first and greatest benefit will come to Iraqi men, women and children. The oppression of Kurds, Assyrians, Turkomans, Shi'a, Sunnis and others will be lifted. The long captivity of Iraq will end, and an era of new hope will begin.

Iraq is a land rich in culture, resources, and talent. Freed from the weight of oppression, Iraq's people will be able to share in the progress and prosperity of our time. If military action is necessary, the United States and our allies will help the Iraqi people rebuild their economy, and create the institutions of liberty in a unified Iraq at peace with its neighbors.

Later this week, the United States Congress will vote on this matter. I have asked Congress to authorize the use of America's military, if it proves necessary, to enforce U.N. Security Council demands. Approving this resolution does not mean that military action is imminent or unavoidable. The resolution will tell the United Nations, and all nations, that America speaks with one voice and is determined to make the demands of the civilized world mean something. Congress will also be sending a message to the dictator in Iraq: that his only chance—his only choice is full compliance, and the time remaining for that choice is limited.

Members of Congress are nearing an historic vote. I'm confident they will fully consider the facts, and their duties.

The attacks of September the 11th showed our country that vast oceans no longer protect us from danger. Before that tragic date, we had only hints of al Qaeda's plans and designs. Today in Iraq, we see a threat whose outlines are far more clearly defined, and whose consequences could be far more deadly. Saddam Hussein's actions have put us on notice, and there is no refuge from our responsibilities.

We did not ask for this present challenge, but we accept it. Like other generations of Americans, we will meet the responsibility of defending human liberty against violence and aggression. By our resolve, we will give strength to others. By our courage, we will give hope to others. And by our actions, we will secure the peace, and lead the world to a better day.

SOURCE: The White House, Office of the Press Secretary, www.whitehouse.gov/news/releases/2002/10/20021007-8.html.

DOCUMENT

UN Security Council Resolution 1441 (2002)

NOVEMBER 8, 2002

The Security Council,

Recalling all its previous relevant resolutions, in particular its resolutions 661 (1990) of 6 August 1990, 678 (1990) of 29 November 1990, 686 (1991) of 2 March 1991, 687 (1991) of 3 April 1991, 688 (1991) of 5 April 1991, 707 (1991) of 15 August 1991, 715 (1991) of 11 October 1991, 986 (1995) of 14 April 1995, and 1284 (1999) of 17 December 1999, and all the relevant statements of its President,

Recalling also its resolution 1382 (2001) of 29 November 2001 and its intention to implement it fully,

Recognizing the threat Iraq's noncompliance with Council resolutions and proliferation of weapons of mass destruction and long-range missiles poses to international peace and security,

Recalling that its resolution 678 (1990) authorized Member States to use all necessary means to uphold and implement its resolution 660 (1990) of 2 August 1990 and all relevant resolutions subsequent to Resolution 660 (1990) and to restore international peace and security in the area,

Further recalling that its resolution 687 (1991) imposed obligations on Iraq as a necessary step for achievement of its stated objective of restoring international peace and security in the area,

Deploring the fact that Iraq has not provided an accurate, full, final, and complete disclosure, as required by resolution 687 (1991), of all aspects of its programs to develop weapons of mass destruction and ballistic missiles with a range greater than one hundred and fifty kilometers, and of all holdings of such weapons, their components and production facilities and locations, as well as all other nuclear programs, including any which it claims are for purposes not related to nuclear-weapons-usable material,

Deploring further that Iraq repeatedly obstructed immediate, unconditional, and unrestricted access to sites designated by the United Nations Special Commission (UNSCOM) and the International Atomic Energy Agency (IAEA), failed to cooperate fully and unconditionally with UNSCOM and IAEA weapons inspectors, as required by resolution 687 (1991), and ultimately ceased all cooperation with UNSCOM and the IAEA in 1998,

Deploring the absence, since December 1998, in Iraq of international monitoring, inspection, and verification, as required by relevant resolutions, of weapons of mass destruction and ballistic missiles, in spite of the Council's repeated demands that Iraq provide immediate, unconditional, and unrestricted access to the United Nations Monitoring, Verification and Inspection Commission (UNMOVIC), established in resolution 1284 (1999) as the successor organization to UNSCOM, and the IAEA, and regretting the consequent prolonging of the crisis in the region and the suffering of the Iraqi people,

Deploring also that the Government of Iraq has failed to comply with its commitments pursuant to resolution 687 (1991) with regard to terrorism, pursuant to resolution 688 (1991) to end repression of its civilian population and to provide access by international humanitarian organizations to all those in need of assistance in Iraq, and pursuant to resolutions 686 (1991), 687 (1991), and 1284 (1999) to return or cooperate in accounting for Kuwaiti and third country nationals wrongfully detained by Iraq, or to return Kuwaiti property wrongfully seized by Iraq,

Recalling that in its resolution 687 (1991) the Council declared that a ceasefire would be based on acceptance by Iraq of the provisions of that resolution, including the obligations on Iraq contained therein,

Determined to ensure full and immediate compliance by Iraq without conditions or restrictions with its obligations under resolution 687 (1991) and other relevant resolutions and recalling that the resolutions of the Council constitute the governing standard of Iraqi compliance,

Recalling that the effective operation of UNMOVIC, as the successor organization to the Special Commission, and the IAEA is essential for the implementation of resolution 687 (1991) and other relevant resolutions,

Noting the letter dated 16 September 2002 from the Minister for Foreign Affairs of Iraq addressed to the Secretary-General is a necessary first step toward rectifying Iraq's continued failure to comply with relevant Council resolutions,

Noting further the letter dated 8 October 2002 from the Executive Chairman of UNMOVIC and the Director General of the IAEA to General Al-Saadi of the Government of Iraq laying out the practical arrangements, as a follow-up to their meeting in Vienna, that are prerequisites for the resumption of inspections in Iraq by UNMOVIC and the IAEA, and expressing the gravest concern at the continued failure by the Government of Iraq to provide confirmation of the arrangements as laid out in that letter,

Reaffirming the commitment of all Member States to the sovereignty and territorial integrity of Iraq, Kuwait, and the neighboring States,

Commending the Secretary-General and members of the League of Arab States and its Secretary-General for their efforts in this regard,

Determined to secure full compliance with its decisions,

Acting under Chapter VII of the Charter of the United Nations,

1. *Decides* that Iraq has been and remains in material breach of its obligations under relevant resolutions, including resolution 687 (1991), in particular through Iraq's failure to cooperate with United Nations inspectors and the IAEA, and to complete the actions required under paragraphs 8 to 13 of resolution 687 (1991);

2. *Decides,* while acknowledging paragraph 1 above, to afford Iraq, by this resolution, a final opportunity to comply with its disarmament obligations under relevant resolutions of the Council; and accordingly decides to set up an enhanced inspection regime with the aim of bringing to full and verified completion the disarmament process established by resolution 687 (1991) and subsequent resolutions of the Council;

3. *Decides* that, in order to begin to comply with its disarmament obligations, in addition to submitting the required biannual declarations, the Government of Iraq shall provide to UNMOVIC, the IAEA, and the Council, not later than 30 days from the date of this resolution, a currently accurate, full, and complete declaration of all aspects of its programmes to develop chemical, biological, and nuclear weapons, ballistic missiles, and other delivery systems such as unmanned aerial vehicles and dispersal systems designed for use on aircraft, including any holdings and precise locations of such weapons, components, sub-components, stocks of agents, and related material and equipment, the locations and work of its research, development and production facilities, as well as all other chemical, biological, and nuclear programmes, including any which it claims are for purposes not related to weapon production or material;

4. *Decides* that false statements or omissions in the declarations submitted by Iraq pursuant to this resolution and failure by Iraq at any time to comply with, and cooperate fully in the implementation of, this resolution shall constitute a further material breach of Iraq's obligations and will be reported to the Council for assessment in accordance with paragraphs 11 and 12 below;

5. *Decides* that Iraq shall provide UNMOVIC and the IAEA immediate, unimpeded, unconditional, and unrestricted access to any and all, including underground, areas, facilities, buildings, equipment, records, and means of transport which they wish to inspect, as well as immediate, unimpeded, unrestricted, and private access to all officials and other persons whom UNMOVIC or the IAEA wish to interview in the mode or location of UNMOVIC's or the IAEA's choice pursuant to any aspect of their mandates; further decides that UNMOVIC and the IAEA may at their discretion conduct

interviews inside or outside of Iraq, may facilitate the travel of those interviewed and family members outside of Iraq, and that, at the sole discretion of UNMOVIC and the IAEA, such interviews may occur without the presence of observers from the Iraqi government; and instructs UNMOVIC and requests the IAEA to resume inspections no later than 45 days following adoption of this resolution and to update the Council 60 days thereafter;

6. *Endorses* the 8 October 2002 letter from the Executive Chairman of UNMOVIC and the Director General of the IAEA to General Al-Saadi of the Government of Iraq, which is annexed hereto, and decides that the contents of the letter shall be binding upon Iraq;

7. *Decides* further that, in view of the prolonged interruption by Iraq of the presence of UNMOVIC and the IAEA and in order for them to accomplish the tasks set forth in this resolution and all previous relevant resolutions and notwithstanding prior understandings, the Council hereby establishes the following revised or additional authorities, which shall be binding upon Iraq, to facilitate their work in Iraq:

- UNMOVIC and the IAEA shall determine the composition of their inspection teams and ensure that these teams are composed of the most qualified and experienced experts available;
- All UNMOVIC and IAEA personnel shall enjoy the privileges and immunities, corresponding to those of experts on mission, provided in the Convention on Privileges and Immunities of the United Nations and the Agreement on the Privileges and Immunities of the IAEA;
- UNMOVIC and the IAEA shall have unrestricted rights of entry into and out of Iraq, the right to free, unrestricted, and immediate movement to and from inspection sites, and the right to inspect any sites and buildings, including immediate, unimpeded, unconditional, and unrestricted access to Presidential Sites equal to that at other sites, notwithstanding the provisions of resolution 1154 (1998);
- UNMOVIC and the IAEA shall have the right to be provided by Iraq the names of all personnel currently and formerly associated with Iraq's chemical, biological, nuclear, and ballistic missile programs and the associated research, development, and production facilities;
- Security of UNMOVIC and IAEA facilities shall be ensured by sufficient UN security guards;
- UNMOVIC and the IAEA shall have the right to declare, for the purposes of freezing a site to be inspected, exclusion zones, including surrounding areas and transit corridors, in which Iraq will suspend ground and aerial movement so that nothing is changed in or taken out of a site being inspected;
- UNMOVIC and the IAEA shall have the free and unrestricted use and landing of fixed- and rotary-winged aircraft, including manned and unmanned reconnaissance vehicles;
- UNMOVIC and the IAEA shall have the right at their sole discretion verifiably to remove, destroy, or render harmless all prohibited weapons, subsystems, components, records, materials, and other related items, and the right to impound or close any facilities or equipment for the production thereof; and
- UNMOVIC and the IAEA shall have the right to free import and use of equipment or materials for inspections and to seize and export any equipment, mate-

rials, or documents taken during inspections, without search of UNMOVIC or IAEA personnel or official or personal baggage;

8. *Decides* further that Iraq shall not take or threaten hostile acts directed against any representative or personnel of the United Nations or the IAEA or of any Member State taking action to uphold any Council resolution;

9. *Requests* the Secretary-General immediately to notify Iraq of this resolution, which is binding on Iraq; demands that Iraq confirm within seven days of that notification its intention to comply fully with this resolution; and demands further that Iraq cooperate immediately, unconditionally, and actively with UNMOVIC and the IAEA;

10. *Requests* all Member States to give full support to UNMOVIC and the IAEA in the discharge of their mandates, including by providing any information related to prohibited programs or other aspects of their mandates, including on Iraqi attempts since 1998 to acquire prohibited items, and by recommending sites to be inspected, persons to be interviewed, conditions of such interviews, and data to be collected, the results of which shall be reported to the Council by UNMOVIC and the IAEA;

11. *Directs* the Executive Chairman of UNMOVIC and the Director General of the IAEA to report immediately to the Council any interference by Iraq with inspection activities, as well as any failure by Iraq to comply with its disarmament obligations, including its obligations regarding inspections under this resolution;

12. *Decides* to convene immediately upon receipt of a report in accordance with paragraphs 4 or 11 above, in order to consider the situation and the need for full compliance with all of the relevant Council resolutions in order to secure international peace and security;

13. *Recalls,* in that context, that the Council has repeatedly warned Iraq that it will face serious consequences as a result of its continued violations of its obligations;

14. *Decides* to remain seized of the matter.

SOURCE: United Nations, www.un.org/Docs/scres/2002/sc2002.htm.

The Iraq War

DOCUMENT IN CONTEXT

With help from Britain and a handful of other allies, the United States invaded Iraq in March 2003 and quickly overthrew the government of Saddam Hussein, who had ruled the country with an iron fist for nearly a quarter-century. The relative ease of this military victory proved illusory, however. Remnants of Hussein's regime, along with Islamist extremists and others opposed to the U.S. occupation, launched an insurgency that threw much of the country into chaos. A subsequent U.S. effort to implant a Western-style democracy in Iraq produced an elected government, but four years after the invasion, Baghdad and many other parts of Iraq continued to be wracked by widespread violence—much of it sectarian in nature—that made the ultimate success of Washington's endeavors in Iraq appear problematic at best.

Rationales for the War

In speeches and other presentations leading up to the war, President George W. Bush and his aides offered a two-part justification for the decision to invade Iraq: Hussein's government had built, and continued to develop, weapons of mass destruction, which could be passed on to terrorists, some of whom were determined to attack the United States and its allies. Bush cited this rationale in his most important speech explaining the war, on March 17, 2003, two days before the war began. "Intelligence gathered by this and other governments leaves no doubt that the Iraq regime continues to possess and conceal some of the most lethal weapons ever devised," Bush said, adding that the Hussein regime had a history of "reckless aggression" in the Middle East. "The danger is clear: Using chemical, biological or, one day, nuclear weapons obtained with the help of Iraq, the terrorists could fulfill their stated ambitions and kill thousands or hundreds of thousands of innocent people in our country or any other."

Bush offered no evidence—then or later—to support his claim that Iraq would give weapons to terrorist groups, such as the al-Qaida network that had sponsored the September 11, 2001, attacks against the United States. Numerous subsequent investigations and accounts of decision making by administration officials indicate that no such evidence ever existed, although this argument formed the central basis for Bush's justification of the war to the American people and the world at large.

At various points Bush offered other explanations for his decision to go to war, all centering around the goal of replacing a dangerous dictatorship in Iraq with a democratically elected government that would live in peace with its neighbors. The president referred briefly to this rationale in his March 17 speech, telling Iraqis that "we will tear down the apparatus of terror, and we will help you to build a new Iraq that is prosperous and free." Bush also suggested, with increasing passion after Hussein had been ousted, that a newly democratic Iraq would serve as a model for the rest of the Middle East, thus reducing tensions regionwide and even making possible a final settlement of the Israeli-Palestinian conflict.

A Three-Week War

There never was much question that the United States, with the most powerful and technologically advanced military in the world, could overwhelm Iraq's army, which had not been fully rebuilt after more than a decade of war followed by a decade of international sanctions. Pentagon war planners did worry, however, about the prospect of Iraq using biological or chemical weapons against the invading armies, and for this reason U.S soldiers and marines went into battle wearing hot and bulky protective clothing in the Iraqi desert. This precaution proved to be unnecessary. The Iraqi military did not use weapons of mass destruction simply because it no longer had any.

On Bush's orders, the assault against Iraq began early in the morning of March 20 (local time), with a bombing attack against a house in Baghdad where Hussein was believed to be meeting with aides. A full-scale invasion from Kuwait followed. Approximately 150,000 U.S. troops, along with 44,000 British personnel and a few thousand soldiers from other countries, moved quickly into southern Iraq. The invasion slowed for a few days, starting on March 24, because of desert sandstorms and then because of fierce hit-and-run resistance from Iraqi volunteer units called *fedayeen*. U.S. units reached the Baghdad airport on April 3 and then stormed into the city. By April 9, the U.S. Army and marines had gained overall control of most of Baghdad, with the fall of Hussein's government symbolized by the toppling of a monumental statue of the Iraqi leader in the city center. Widespread looting, which the U.S. military made little effort to control, offered a hint of the chaos to come.

Hussein and his top aides disappeared. In the months after the invasion, coalition forces captured most senior Iraqi officials, and U.S. forces captured Hussein in December as he hid in a hole in the ground at a farmhouse along the Tigris River north of Baghdad. The new Iraqi government put him on trial for ordering the murders of innocent civilians earlier in his rule following an assassination attempt against him. He was hanged in late December 2006 after his conviction.

With the collapse of the Iraqi military, Pentagon officials on April 14, 2003 announced the end of most fighting in Iraq. U.S. warships based in the Persian Gulf began returning to their bases, and the Pentagon sent home units that had done some of the heaviest fighting, replacing them with fresh units held in reserve.

"Mission Accomplished"

One of the most controversial elements of the Iraq War was the extravaganza the Bush White House staged to celebrate the coalition victory. On May 1, Bush flew in a Navy jet to the aircraft carrier *Abraham Lincoln* as it steamed toward San Diego harbor; he stepped onto the ship's deck wearing a pilot's flight suit. With a large banner in the background proclaiming "Mission Accomplished," Bush gave a triumphant speech, announcing that "major combat operations in Iraq have ended."

Without a doubt, White House officials hoped to use footage from this event in the president's election campaign the following year. Instead, the president's claim of success proved to be premature and later came back to haunt him. In retrospect, May 1, 2003, marked the divide between two phases of the war in Iraq: the rapid overthrow of the Hussein government and the years of chaos that would follow. To the administration's embarrassment, news organizations also used May 1 to gauge U.S. casualties in the war. As of that date in 2003, 115 U.S. service personnel had died in combat. Four years later, U.S. deaths in Iraq from all causes exceeded 3,300.

President Bush had drummed up strong domestic support for the war when he launched it, but the descent of Iraq into chaos under U.S. stewardship and rising casualty figures greatly undercut that support. In 2006 voters defeated Bush's Republican allies and put control of Congress in the hands of Democrats who vowed to end the U.S. military occupation of Iraq (Postwar Iraq, p. 510).

> *Following is the text of a nationally televised speech by President George W. Bush, on May 17, 2003, demanding that Iraqi leader Saddam Hussein and his two sons leave Iraq within forty-eight hours or face a major invasion of Iraq by the United States and its allies.*

DOCUMENT

Bush Ultimatum to Hussein to Leave Iraq

MARCH 17, 2003

My fellow citizens, events in Iraq have now reached the final days of decision. For more than a decade, the United States and other nations have pursued patient and honorable efforts to disarm the Iraqi regime without war. That regime pledged to reveal and destroy all its weapons of mass destruction as a condition for ending the Persian Gulf war in 1991.

Since then, the world has engaged in 12 years of diplomacy. We have passed more than a dozen resolutions in the United Nations Security Council. We have sent hundreds of weapons inspectors to oversee the disarmament of Iraq. Our good faith has not been returned.

The Iraqi regime has used diplomacy as a ploy to gain time and advantage. It has uniformly defied Security Council resolutions demanding full disarmament. Over the years, U.N. weapon inspectors have been threatened by Iraqi officials, electronically bugged, and systematically deceived. Peaceful efforts to disarm the Iraqi regime have failed again and again because we are not dealing with peaceful men.

Intelligence gathered by this and other governments leaves no doubt that the Iraq regime continues to possess and conceal some of the most lethal weapons ever devised. This regime has already used weapons of mass destruction against Iraq's neighbors and against Iraq's people.

The regime has a history of reckless aggression in the Middle East. It has a deep hatred of America and our friends. And it has aided, trained, and harbored terrorists, including operatives of Al Qaida.

The danger is clear: Using chemical, biological or, one day, nuclear weapons obtained with the help of Iraq, the terrorists could fulfill their stated ambitions and kill thousands or hundreds of thousands of innocent people in our country or any other.

The United States and other nations did nothing to deserve or invite this threat. But we will do everything to defeat it. Instead of drifting along toward tragedy, we will set a course toward safety. Before the day of horror can come, before it is too late to act, this danger will be removed.

The United States of America has the sovereign authority to use force in assuring its own national security. That duty falls to me as Commander in Chief, by the oath I have sworn, by the oath I will keep.

Recognizing the threat to our country, the United States Congress voted overwhelmingly last year to support the use of force against Iraq. America tried to work with the United Nations to address this threat because we wanted to resolve the issue peacefully. We believe in the mission of the United Nations. One reason the U.N. was founded after the Second World War was to confront aggressive dictators actively and early, before they can attack the innocent and destroy the peace.

In the case of Iraq, the Security Council did act in the early 1990s. Under Resolutions 678 and 687, both still in effect, the United States and our allies are authorized to use force in ridding Iraq of weapons of mass destruction. This is not a question of authority. It is a question of will.

Last September, I went to the U.N. General Assembly and urged the nations of the world to unite and bring an end to this danger. On November 8th, the Security Council unanimously passed Resolution 1441, finding Iraq in material breach of its obligations and vowing serious consequences if Iraq did not fully and immediately disarm.

Today, no nation can possibly claim that Iraq has disarmed, and it will not disarm so long as Saddam Hussein holds power. For the last 4 1/2 months, the United States and our allies have worked within the Security Council to enforce that Council's longstanding demands. Yet, some permanent members of the Security Council have publicly announced they will veto any resolution that compels the disarmament of Iraq. These governments share our assessment of the danger but not our resolve to meet it.

Many nations, however, do have the resolve and fortitude to act against this threat to peace, and a broad coalition is now gathering to enforce the just demands of the world. The United Nations Security Council has not lived up to its responsibilities, so we will rise to ours.

In recent days, some governments in the Middle East have been doing their part. They have delivered public and private messages urging the dictator to leave Iraq, so that disarmament can proceed peacefully. He has thus far refused.

All the decades of deceit and cruelty have now reached an end. Saddam Hussein and his sons must leave Iraq within 48 hours. Their refusal to do so will result in military conflict, commenced at a time of our choosing. For their own safety, all foreign nationals, including journalists and inspectors, should leave Iraq immediately.

Many Iraqis can hear me tonight in a translated radio broadcast, and I have a message for them: If we must begin a military campaign, it will be directed against the lawless men who rule your country and not against you. As our coalition takes away their power, we will deliver the food and medicine you need. We will tear down the apparatus of terror, and we will help you to build a new Iraq that is prosperous and free. In a free Iraq, there will be no more wars of aggression against your neighbors, no more poison factories, no more executions of dissidents, no more torture chambers and rape rooms. The tyrant will soon be gone. The day of your liberation is near.

It is too late for Saddam Hussein to remain in power. It is not too late for the Iraqi military to act with honor and protect your country by permitting the peaceful entry of coalition forces to eliminate weapons of mass destruction. Our forces will give Iraqi military units clear instructions on actions they can take to avoid being attacked and destroyed. I urge every member of the Iraqi military and intelligence services: If war comes, do not fight for a dying regime that is not worth your own life.

And all Iraqi military and civilian personnel should listen carefully to this warning: In any conflict, your fate will depend on your actions. Do not destroy oil wells, a source of wealth that belongs to the Iraqi people. Do not obey any command to use weapons of mass destruction against anyone, including the Iraqi people. War crimes will be prosecuted. War criminals will be punished. And it will be no defense to say, "I was just following orders."

Should Saddam Hussein choose confrontation, the American people can know that every measure has been taken to avoid war and every measure will be taken to win it. Americans understand the costs of conflict because we have paid them in the past. War has no certainty, except the certainty of sacrifice. Yet, the only way to reduce the harm and duration of war is to apply the full force and might of our military, and we are prepared to do so.

If Saddam Hussein attempts to cling to power, he will remain a deadly foe until the end. In desperation, he and terrorist groups might try to conduct terrorist operations against the American people and our friends. These attacks are not inevitable. They are, however, possible. And this very fact underscores the reason we cannot live under the threat of blackmail. The terrorist threat to America and the world will be diminished the moment that Saddam Hussein is disarmed.

Our Government is on heightened watch against these dangers. Just as we are preparing to ensure victory in Iraq, we are taking further actions to protect our homeland. In recent days, American authorities have expelled from the country certain individuals with ties to Iraqi intelligence services. Among other measures, I have directed additional security of our airports and increased Coast Guard patrols of major seaports. The Department of Homeland Security is working closely with the Nation's Governors to increase armed security at critical facilities across America.

Should enemies strike our country, they would be attempting to shift our attention with panic and weaken our morale with fear. In this, they would fail. No act of theirs can alter the course or shake the resolve of this country. We are a peaceful people. Yet we're not a fragile people, and we will not be intimidated by thugs and killers. If our enemies dare to strike us, they and all who have aided them will face fearful consequences.

We are now acting because the risks of inaction would be far greater. In 1 year, or 5 years, the power of Iraq to inflict harm on all free nations would be multiplied many times over. With these capabilities, Saddam Hussein and his terrorist allies could choose the moment of deadly conflict when they are strongest. We choose to meet that threat now, where it arises, before it can appear suddenly in our skies and cities.

The cause of peace requires all free nations to recognize new and undeniable realities. In the 20th century, some chose to appease murderous dictators, whose threats were allowed to grow into genocide and global war. In this century, when evil men plot chemical, biological, and nuclear terror, a policy of appeasement could bring destruction of a kind never before seen on this Earth.

Terrorists and terror states do not reveal these threats with fair notice, in formal declarations, and responding to such enemies only after they have struck first is not self-defense; it is suicide. The security of the world requires disarming Saddam Hussein now.

As we enforce the just demands of the world, we will also honor the deepest commitments of our country. Unlike Saddam Hussein, we believe the Iraqi people are deserving and capable of human liberty. And when the dictator has departed, they can set an example to all the Middle East of a vital and peaceful and self-governing nation.

The United States, with other countries, will work to advance liberty and peace in that region. Our goal will not be achieved overnight, but it can come over time. The power and appeal of human liberty is felt in every life and every land. And the greatest power of freedom is to overcome hatred and violence and turn the creative gifts of men and women to the pursuits of peace.

That is the future we choose. Free nations have a duty to defend our people by uniting against the violent. And tonight, as we have done before, America and our allies accept that responsibility.

Good night, and may God continue to bless America.

SOURCE: *Weekly Compilation of Presidential Documents 39,* no. 12 (March 24, 2003): 338–341. National Archives and Records Administration, Washington, D.C., http://frwebgate.access.gpo.gov/cgi-bin/getdoc.cgi?dbname=2003_presidential_documents&docid=pd24mr03_txt-9.

Postwar Iraq

DOCUMENT IN CONTEXT

In its limited planning for postwar Iraq, the Bush administration had worked from the assumption that Iraq would be pacified quickly after Saddam Hussein's ouster, that a new government installed under U.S. tutelage would gain broad public support, and that U.S. soldiers and marines could be withdrawn rapidly. All of these and other similarly optimistic assumptions proved to be false. Rather than stabilizing, Iraq rapidly descended into increasingly worse chaos. The Bush administration found itself frantically attempting to develop one plan after another to deal with changing circumstances. Each plan succumbed, however, to stubborn realities on the ground, the foremost being violence driven by Iraqis opposed to the continued U.S. presence and those determined to assert their sectarian interests above the interests of others. By 2006 Iraq had a democratically elected government that survived only with U.S. military protection and was itself in thrall to the sectarian interests of the majority Shiite population (The Iraq War, p. 504).

That the situation in Iraq would calm shortly after the overthrow of Hussein became the first of the Bush administration's assumptions to prove false. Instead, violence grew, first in the form of sporadic attacks on occupation forces, then in bombings of high-profile targets, and then in a generalized pattern of shootings, roadside bombings, suicide bombings, assassinations, and other forms of violence intended to drive out the occupiers and frighten Iraqis.

In August 2003 a series of major bombings set the pattern for later years. In the first of these attacks, on August 7, a truck bomb exploded outside the Jordanian embassy in Baghdad, killing seventeen Iraqis and wounding more than forty others. Twelve days later, a cement mixer filled with almost a ton of explosives blew up outside UN headquarters in Baghdad. Twenty-three people were killed, including nineteen UN staffers, the most prominent being Sergio Vieira de Mello, the chief UN representative in Iraq who had been a key intermediary between U.S. occupation authorities and Iraqi politicians. The killing of Vieira de Mello and his colleagues dispirited the United Nations, which subsequently pulled most of its staff from Iraq. The incident is widely viewed as a turning point in Iraq's descent into chaos. Another step in that direction occurred ten days later, when the bombing of a mosque in the southern city of Najaf killed more than eighty people, including Ayatollah Muhammad Bakir al-Hakim. One of Iraq's leading Shiite clerics, with ties to Iran, Hakim had expressed a willingness to work with the U.S. occupation to achieve greater rights for Iraq's Shiite majority. His death removed an important moderating influence at a crucial moment.

Back to the United Nations

Shaken by the August bombings and similar events, the Bush administration returned to the United Nations with the hope of obtaining more military and political support from the international community for its occupation of Iraq. It made the appeal a few months after President George W. Bush had scorned the Security Council, which he had accused of not having "lived up to its responsibilities" because of its failure to endorse the U.S.-led invasion.

After several weeks of negotiations in September and early October 2003, the administration won agreement on a resolution that endorsed the U.S. occupation of Iraq, committed the United Nations to helping with Iraq's political transition, and called on other countries to contribute financial and military assistance to Iraq. The Security Council endorsed this measure, Resolution 1151, on October 16, 2003, by a unanimous vote.

Although this resolution served as the model for subsequent ones authorizing a continued international presence in Iraq, it did not inspire other countries to send soldiers to ease the U.S. military burden there, as the Bush administration had hoped. U.S. officials asked India, Pakistan, Turkey, and other countries with large Muslim populations to contribute troops to the new UN-endorsed coalition in Iraq, but all refused. Over the course of later years, other countries that had provided small contingents of troops for the invasion and occupation of Iraq decided to pull out. By 2007, only the United States and Britain maintained sizable military forces there, but even the British government was planning to withdraw most of its remaining 7,000 troops in the near future.

Governing Iraq

The U.S. assumption that governing Iraq would be a straightforward matter also failed the test of reality. To the extent the Bush administration had a governance plan, it involved stationing a small group of American advisors in Baghdad who would work with Iraqi exiles and known moderates from the various domestic constituencies to establish a new government that would call elections, thereby implanting democracy. This plan survived only a few weeks before being superseded in May 2003 by another one, in which a full-scale occupation authority—the Coalition Provisional Authority (CPA)—would run Iraq and help select a new Iraqi government. Former U.S. diplomat L. Paul Bremer III headed the CPA and had almost unlimited powers to govern Iraq as he saw fit. An advisory body, the Iraqi Governing Council, served alongside

Bremer but had no power and little domestic political legitimacy as a body appointed by the United States.

Bremer governed Iraq for about thirteen months, until June 28, 2004, when he handed political power, and sovereignty, to a new "interim" government. This government was headed by Ayad Allawi, a prominent Shiite politician who had lived many years in exile and had survived an assassination attempt by agents of Saddam Hussein's government. Allawi's chief tasks were to keep Iraq from disintegrating and to oversee (with technical assistance from the United Nations) Iraq's first free election, held on January 30, 2005. This election generally was successful despite ongoing violence in much of the country and a boycott by Sunni Muslims, who believed that the new political system was rigged against them. The election brought to office yet another temporary government—a "transitional" national assembly that served through 2005 and into the first part of 2006. This assembly selected a cabinet led by Ibrahim al-Jaafari, head of the Shiite party known as al-Dawa (Iraq's New Government, p. 526).

> *Following is the text of UN Security Council Resolution 1511, adopted on October 16, 2003, endorsing the creation of an Iraqi Governing Council as a representative body to advise the U.S.-led occupation authority in Iraq and authorizing a multinational force led by the United States "to take all necessary measures to contribute to the maintenance of security and stability in Iraq."*

DOCUMENT

UN Security Council Resolution 1511 (2003)

OCTOBER 16, 2003

The Security Council,

Reaffirming its previous resolutions on Iraq, including resolution 1483 (2003) of 22 May 2003 and 1500 (2003) of 14 August 2003, and on threats to peace and security caused by terrorist acts, including resolution 1373 (2001) of 28 September 2001, and other relevant resolutions,

Underscoring that the sovereignty of Iraq resides in the State of Iraq, *reaffirming* the right of the Iraqi people freely to determine their own political future and control their own natural resources, *reiterating* its resolve that the day when Iraqis govern themselves must come quickly, and *recognizing* the importance of international support, particularly that of countries in the region, Iraq's neighbors, and regional organizations, in taking forward this process expeditiously,

Recognizing that international support for restoration of conditions of stability and security is essential to the well-being of the people of Iraq as well as to the ability of all concerned to carry out their work on behalf of the people of Iraq, and *welcoming* Member State contributions in this regard under resolution 1483 (2003),

Welcoming the decision of the Governing Council of Iraq to form a preparatory constitutional committee to prepare for a constitutional conference that will draft a constitution to embody the aspirations of the Iraqi people, and *urging* it to complete this process quickly,

Affirming that the terrorist bombings of the Embassy of Jordan on 7 August 2003, of the United Nations headquarters in Baghdad on 19 August 2003, of the Imam Ali Mosque in Najaf on 29 August 2003, and of the Embassy of Turkey on 14 October 2003, and the murder of a Spanish diplomat on 9 October 2003 are attacks on the people of Iraq, the United Nations, and the international community, and *deploring* the assassination of Dr. Akila al-Hashimi, who died on 25 September 2003, as an attack directed against the future of Iraq,

In that context, *recalling* and *reaffirming* the statement of its President of 20 August 2003 and resolution 1502 (2003) of 26 August 2003,

Determining that the situation in Iraq, although improved, continues to constitute a threat to international peace and security,

Acting under Chapter VII of the Charter of the United Nations,

1. *Reaffirms* the sovereignty and territorial integrity of Iraq, and *underscores,* in that context, the temporary nature of the exercise by the Coalition Provisional Authority (Authority) of the specific responsibilities, authorities, and obligations under applicable international law recognized and set forth in resolution 1483 (2003), which will cease when an internationally recognized, representative government established by the people of Iraq is sworn in and assumes the responsibilities of the Authority, inter alia through steps envisaged in paragraphs 4 through 7 and 10 below;

2. *Welcomes* the positive response of the international community, in fora such as the Arab League, the Organization of the Islamic Conference, the United Nations General Assembly, and the United Nations Educational, Scientific and Cultural Organization, to the establishment of the broadly representative Governing Council as an important step towards an internationally recognized, representative government;

3. *Supports* the Governing Council's efforts to mobilize the people of Iraq, including by the appointment of a cabinet of ministers and a preparatory constitutional committee to lead a process in which the Iraqi people will progressively take control of their own affairs;

4. *Determines* that the Governing Council and its ministers are the principal bodies of the Iraqi interim administration, which, without prejudice to its further evolution, embodies the sovereignty of the State of Iraq during the transitional period until an internationally recognized, representative government is established and assumes the responsibilities of the Authority;

5. *Affirms* that the administration of Iraq will be progressively undertaken by the evolving structures of the Iraqi interim administration;

6. *Calls upon* the Authority, in this context, to return governing responsibilities and authorities to the people of Iraq as soon as practicable and *requests* the Authority, in cooperation as appropriate with the Governing Council and the Secretary-General, to report to the Council on the progress being made;

7. *Invites* the Governing Council to provide to the Security Council, for its review, no later than 15 December 2003, in cooperation with the Authority and, as circumstances

permit, the Special Representative of the Secretary-General, a timetable and a program for the drafting of a new constitution for Iraq and for the holding of democratic elections under that constitution;

8. *Resolves* that the United Nations, acting through the Secretary-General, his Special Representative, and the United Nations Assistance Mission in Iraq, should strengthen its vital role in Iraq, including by providing humanitarian relief, promoting the economic reconstruction of and conditions for sustainable development in Iraq, and advancing efforts to restore and establish national and local institutions for representative government;

9. *Requests* that, as circumstances permit, the Secretary-General pursue the course of action outlined in paragraphs 98 and 99 of the report of the Secretary-General of 17 July 2003;

10. *Takes note* of the intention of the Governing Council to hold a constitutional conference and, recognizing that the convening of the conference will be a milestone in the movement to the full exercise of sovereignty, *calls for* its preparation through national dialogue and consensus-building as soon as practicable and *requests* the Special Representative of the Secretary-General, at the time of the convening of the conference or, as circumstances permit, to lend the unique expertise of the United Nations to the Iraqi people in this process of political transition, including the establishment of electoral processes;

11. *Requests* the Secretary-General to ensure that the resources of the United Nations and associated organizations are available, if requested by the Iraqi Governing Council and, as circumstances permit, to assist in furtherance of the program provided by the Governing Council in paragraph 7 above, and encourages other organizations with expertise in this area to support the Iraqi Governing Council, if requested;

12. *Requests* the Secretary-General to report to the Security Council on his responsibilities under this resolution and the development and implementation of a timetable and program under paragraph 7 above;

13. *Determines* that the provision of security and stability is essential to the successful completion of the political process as outlined in paragraph 7 above and to the ability of the United Nations to contribute effectively to that process and the implementation of resolution 1483 (2003), and *authorizes* a multinational force under unified command to take all necessary measures to contribute to the maintenance of security and stability in Iraq, including for the purpose of ensuring necessary conditions for the implementation of the timetable and program as well as to contribute to the security of the United Nations Assistance Mission for Iraq, the Governing Council of Iraq and other institutions of the Iraqi interim administration, and key humanitarian and economic infrastructure;

14. *Urges* Member States to contribute assistance under this United Nations mandate, including military forces, to the multinational force referred to in paragraph 13 above;

15. *Decides* that the Council shall review the requirements and mission of the multinational force referred to in paragraph 13 above not later than one year from the date of this resolution, and that in any case the mandate of the force shall expire upon the completion of the political process as described in paragraphs 4 through 7 and 10 above, and *expresses* readiness to consider on that occasion any future need for the continuation of the multinational force, taking into account the views of an internationally recognized, representative government of Iraq;

16. *Emphasizes* the importance of establishing effective Iraqi police and security forces in maintaining law, order, and security and combating terrorism consistent with paragraph 4 of resolution 1483 (2003), and *calls upon* Member States and international and regional organizations to contribute to the training and equipping of Iraqi police and security forces;

17. *Expresses* deep sympathy and condolences for the personal losses suffered by the Iraqi people and by the United Nations and the families of those United Nations personnel and other innocent victims who were killed or injured in these tragic attacks;

18. *Unequivocally condemns* the terrorist bombings of the Embassy of Jordan on 7 August 2003, of the United Nations headquarters in Baghdad on 19 August 2003, and of the Imam Ali Mosque in Najaf on 29 August 2003, and of the Embassy of Turkey on 14 October 2003, the murder of a Spanish diplomat on 9 October 2003, and the assassination of Dr. Avila al-Hashimi, who died on 25 September 2003, and *emphasizes* that those responsible must be brought to justice;

19. *Calls upon* Member States to prevent the transit of terrorists to Iraq, arms for terrorists, and financing that would support terrorists, and *emphasizes* the importance of strengthening the cooperation of the countries of the region, particularly neighbors of Iraq, in this regard;

20. *Appeals* to Member States and the international financial institutions to strengthen their efforts to assist the people of Iraq in the reconstruction and development of their economy, and *urges* those institutions to take immediate steps to provide their full range of loans and other financial assistance to Iraq, working with the Governing Council and appropriate Iraqi ministries;

21. *Urges* Member States and international and regional organizations to support the Iraq reconstruction effort initiated at the 24 June 2003 United Nations Technical Consultations, including through substantial pledges at the 23–24 October 2003 International Donors Conference in Madrid;

22. *Calls upon* Member States and concerned organizations to help meet the needs of the Iraqi people by providing resources necessary for the rehabilitation and reconstruction of Iraq's economic infrastructure;

23. *Emphasizes* that the International Advisory and Monitoring Board (IAMB) referred to in paragraph 12 of resolution 1483 (2003) should be established as a priority, and *reiterates* that the Development Fund for Iraq shall be used in a transparent manner as set out in paragraph 14 of resolution 1483 (2003);

24. *Reminds* all Member States of their obligations under paragraphs 19 and 23 of resolution 1483 (2003) in particular the obligation to immediately cause the transfer of funds, other financial assets and economic resources to the Development Fund for Iraq for the benefit of the Iraqi people;

25. *Requests* that the United States, on behalf of the multinational force as outlined in paragraph 13 above, report to the Security Council on the efforts and progress of this force as appropriate and not less than every six months;

26. *Decides* to remain seized of the matter.

SOURCE: United Nations, www.un.org/Docs/sc/unsc_resolutions03.html.

The Missing WMD

DOCUMENT IN CONTEXT

President George W. Bush said in March 2003 that he had decided to order the invasion of Iraq because Iraqi leader Saddam Hussein posed a "growing danger" to the Middle East and even to the United States. The danger, according to Bush, came from Iraq's arsenal of biological and chemical weapons, its feverish work to develop nuclear weapons, and—most importantly—the likelihood that Iraq would give these weapons to international terrorists. The president and his aides claimed to have irrefutable evidence for their statements about the threats posed by Iraq (Iraq War Prelude, p. 486).

Weeks after the U.S. military overthrew Hussein in April 2003, Bush's charges about Iraq's weapons—and thus the primary rationale he had offered for the invasion of Iraq—began to crumble. U.S. intelligence and military officials searched frantically for the caches of weapons they believed Iraq had hidden for years from UN inspectors. U.S. officials also dug into civilian and military installations where the Iraqi government was believed to have produced weapons. They found nothing remotely resembling the giant arsenal about which President Bush, Vice President Dick Cheney, and other top officials in Washington had warned.

David Kay, assigned by the Central Intelligence Agency to find Iraq's weapons, acknowledged to Congress in October 2003 that his efforts had been unsuccessful. In what he called an "interim" report—investigations remained ongoing—Kay said that Iraq had intended to build biological, chemical, and possibly even nuclear weapons, but the U.S. searches so far had not found any.

In a more definitive report a year later, Charles A. Duelfer, Kay's successor, submitted what he called a "comprehensive" review of the U.S. search for Iraq's weapons. Duelfer's 1,000-page report stated that Iraq had destroyed its stocks of biological and chemical weapons shortly after the Persian Gulf War in 1991 and had never made a serious effort to restart its program to build nuclear weapons, which had been destroyed during and after the Gulf war. "We were almost all wrong" about Iraq's weapons, Duelfer told a Senate committee on October 6, 2004, the day his report became public.

These findings raised serious questions about U.S. intelligence-gathering capabilities, because Bush's allegations about Iraq's weapons had been based largely on assessments by the CIA and other intelligence agencies. Congressional committees launched investigations that revealed that the intelligence agencies had failed to question conventional wisdom and had relied on Iraqi exiles and other sources whose information was outdated or false.

Duelfer also addressed in his report the question of why the Baghdad government had refused during most of the 1990s to cooperate with the UN agencies looking for weapons. The chief answer, Duelfer suggested, was that Saddam Hussein saw deterrent value in having the rest of the world believe that he still had such weapons.

Following are excerpts from the executive summary of the "Comprehensive Report of the Special Advisor to the DCI [Director of Central Intelligence] on Iraq's WMD [weapons of mass destruction]," submitted to the Central Intelligence Agency on September 30, 2004, by Charles A. Duelfer and made public on October 6, 2004.

DOCUMENT

Executive Summary of the Duelfer Report on the Search for Iraqi WMD

OCTOBER 6, 2004

REGIME STRATEGIC INTENT

Key Findings

Saddam Husayn so dominated the Iraqi Regime that its strategic intent was his alone. He wanted to end sanctions while preserving the capability to reconstitute his weapons of mass destruction (WMD) when sanctions were lifted.

- *Saddam totally dominated the Regime's strategic decision making.* He initiated most of the strategic thinking upon which decisions were made, whether in matters of war and peace (such as invading Kuwait), maintaining WMD as a national strategic goal, or on how Iraq was to position itself in the international community. Loyal dissent was discouraged and constructive variations to the implementation of his wishes on strategic issues were rare. Saddam was the Regime in a strategic sense and his intent became Iraq's strategic policy.
- *Saddam's primary goal from 1991 to 2003 was to have UN sanctions lifted, while maintaining the security of the Regime.* He sought to balance the need to cooperate with UN inspections—to gain support for lifting sanctions—with his intention to preserve Iraq's intellectual capital for WMD with a minimum of foreign intrusiveness and loss of face. Indeed, this remained the goal to the end of the Regime, as the starting of any WMD program, conspicuous or otherwise, risked undoing the progress achieved in eroding sanctions and jeopardizing a political end to the embargo and international monitoring.
- *The introduction of the Oil-For-Food program (OFF) in late 1996 was a key turning point for the Regime.* OFF rescued Baghdad's economy from a terminal decline created by sanctions. The Regime quickly came to see that OFF could be corrupted to acquire foreign exchange both to further undermine sanctions and to provide the means to enhance dual-use infrastructure and potential WMD-related development.
- By 2000–2001, Saddam had managed to mitigate many of the effects of sanctions and undermine their international support. Iraq was within striking distance

of a de facto end to the sanctions regime, both in terms of oil exports and the trade embargo, by the end of 1999.

Saddam wanted to re-create Iraq's WMD capability—which was essentially destroyed in 1991—after sanctions were removed and Iraq's economy stabilized, but probably with a different mix of capabilities to that which previously existed. Saddam aspired to develop a nuclear capability—in an incremental fashion, irrespective of international pressure and the resulting economic risks—but he intended to focus on ballistic missile and tactical chemical warfare (CW) capabilities.

- *Iran was the pre-eminent motivator of this policy.* All senior level Iraqi officials considered Iran to be Iraq's principal enemy in the region. The wish to balance Israel and acquire status and influence in the Arab world were also considerations, but secondary.
- *Iraq Survey Group (ISG) judges that events in the 1980s and early 1990s shaped Saddam's belief in the value of WMD.* In Saddam's view, WMD helped to save the Regime multiple times. He believed that during the Iran-Iraq war chemical weapons had halted Iranian ground offensives and that ballistic missile attacks on Tehran had broken its political will. Similarly, during Desert Storm, Saddam believed WMD had deterred Coalition Forces from pressing their attack beyond the goal of freeing Kuwait. WMD had even played a role in crushing the Shi'a revolt in the south following the 1991 cease-fire.
- *The former Regime had no formal written strategy or plan for the revival of WMD after sanctions.* Neither was there an identifiable group of WMD policy makers or planners separate from Saddam. Instead, his lieutenants understood WMD revival was his goal from their long association with Saddam and his infrequent, but firm, verbal comments and directions to them. . . .

[The Executive Summary at this point includes an explanation that many of the findings were based, in part, on the statements of former Iraqi officials (including Saddam Hussein) who had been captured following the 2003 war and had been interviewed by U.S. intelligence agents.]

NUCLEAR

Key Findings

Iraq Survey Group (ISG) discovered further evidence of the maturity and significance of the pre-1991 Iraqi Nuclear Program but found that Iraq's ability to reconstitute a nuclear weapons program progressively decayed after that date.

- Saddam Husayn ended the nuclear program in 1991 following the Gulf war. ISG found no evidence to suggest concerted efforts to restart the program.
- Although Saddam clearly assigned a high value to the nuclear progress and talent that had been developed up to the 1991 war, the program ended and the intellectual capital decayed in the succeeding years.

Nevertheless, after 1991, Saddam did express his intent to retain the intellectual capital developed during the Iraqi Nuclear Program. Senior Iraqis—several of them from the Regime's inner circle—told ISG they assumed Saddam would restart a nuclear program once UN sanctions ended.

- Saddam indicated that he would develop the weapons necessary to counter any Iranian threat.

Initially, Saddam chose to conceal his nuclear program in its entirety, as he did with Iraq's BW program. Aggressive UN inspections after Desert Storm forced Saddam to admit the existence of the program and destroy or surrender components of the program.

In the wake of Desert Storm, Iraq took steps to conceal key elements of its program and to preserve what it could of the professional capabilities of its nuclear scientific community.

- Baghdad undertook a variety of measures to conceal key elements of its nuclear program from successive UN inspectors, including specific direction by Saddam Husayn to hide and preserve documentation associated with Iraq's nuclear program.
- ISG, for example, uncovered two specific instances in which scientists involved in uranium enrichment kept documents and technology. Although apparently acting on their own, they did so with the belief and anticipation of resuming uranium enrichment efforts in the future.
- Starting around 1992, in a bid to retain the intellectual core of the former weapons program, Baghdad transferred many nuclear scientists to related jobs in the Military Industrial Commission (MIC). The work undertaken by these scientists at the MIC helped them maintain their weapons knowledge base.

As with other WMD areas, Saddam's ambitions in the nuclear area were secondary to his prime objective of ending UN sanctions.

- Iraq, especially after the defection of Husayn Kamil in 1995, sought to persuade the IAEA that Iraq had met the UN's disarmament requirements so sanctions would be lifted.

ISG found a limited number of post-1995 activities that would have aided the reconstitution of the nuclear weapons program once sanctions were lifted.

- The activities of the Iraqi Atomic Energy Commission sustained some talent and limited research with potential relevance to a reconstituted nuclear program.
- Specific projects, with significant development, such as the efforts to build a rail gun and a copper vapor laser could have been useful in a future effort to restart a nuclear weapons program, but ISG found no indications of such purpose. As funding for the MIC and the IAEC increased after the introduction of the Oil-for-Food program, there was some growth in programs that involved former nuclear weapons scientists and engineers.
- The Regime prevented scientists from the former nuclear weapons program from leaving either their jobs or Iraq. Moreover, in the late 1990s, personnel from both MIC and the IAEC received significant pay raises in a bid to retain them, and the Regime undertook new investments in university research in a bid to ensure that Iraq retained technical knowledge.

CHEMICAL

Key Findings

Saddam never abandoned his intentions to resume a CW effort when sanctions were lifted and conditions were judged favorable:

- Saddam and many Iraqis regarded CW as a proven weapon against an enemy's superior numerical strength, a weapon that had saved the nation at least once already—during the Iran-Iraq war—and contributed to deterring the Coalition in 1991 from advancing to Baghdad.

While a small number of old, abandoned chemical munitions have been discovered, ISG judges that Iraq unilaterally destroyed its undeclared chemical weapons stockpile in 1991. There are no credible indications that Baghdad resumed production of chemical munitions thereafter, a policy ISG attributes to Baghdad's desire to see sanctions lifted, or rendered ineffectual, or its fear of force against it should WMD be discovered.

- The scale of the Iraqi conventional munitions stockpile, among other factors, precluded an examination of the entire stockpile; however, ISG inspected sites judged most likely associated with possible storage or deployment of chemical weapons.

Iraq's CW program was crippled by the Gulf war and the legitimate chemical industry, which suffered under sanctions, only began to recover in the mid-1990s. Subsequent changes in the management of key military and civilian organizations, followed by an influx of funding and resources, provided Iraq with the ability to reinvigorate its industrial base.

- Poor policies and management in the early 1990s left the Military Industrial Commission (MIC) financially unsound and in a state of almost complete disarray.
- Saddam implemented a number of changes to the Regime's organizational and programmatic structures after the departure of Husayn Kamil.
- Iraq's acceptance of the Oil-for-Food (OFF) program was the foundation of Iraq's economic recovery and sparked a flow of illicitly diverted funds that could be applied to projects for Iraq's chemical industry.

The way Iraq organized its chemical industry after the mid-1990s allowed it to conserve the knowledge-base needed to restart a CW program, conduct a modest amount of dual-use research, and partially recover from the decline of its production capability caused by the effects of the Gulf war and UN-sponsored destruction and sanctions. Iraq implemented a rigorous and formalized system of nationwide research and production of chemicals, but ISG will not be able to resolve whether Iraq intended the system to underpin any CW-related efforts.

- The Regime employed a cadre of trained and experienced researchers, production managers, and weaponization experts from the former CW program.
- Iraq began implementing a range of indigenous chemical production projects in 1995 and 1996. Many of these projects, while not weapons-related, were designed

to improve Iraq's infrastructure, which would have enhanced Iraq's ability to produce CW agents if the scaled-up production processes were implemented.

- Iraq had an effective system for the procurement of items that Iraq was not allowed to acquire due to sanctions. ISG found no evidence that this system was used to acquire precursor chemicals in bulk; however documents indicate that dual-use laboratory equipment and chemicals were acquired through this system.

Iraq constructed a number of new plants starting in the mid-1990s that enhanced its chemical infrastructure, although its overall industry had not fully recovered from the effects of sanctions, and had not regained pre-1991 technical sophistication or production capabilities prior to Operation Iraqi Freedom (OIF).

- ISG did not discover chemical process or production units configured to produce key precursors or CW agents. However, site visits and debriefs revealed that Iraq maintained its ability for reconfiguring and "making-do" with available equipment as substitutes for sanctioned items.
- ISG judges, based on available chemicals, infrastructure, and scientist debriefings, that Iraq at OIF probably had a capability to produce large quantities of sulfur mustard within three to six months.
- A former nerve agent expert indicated that Iraq retained the capability to produce nerve agent in significant quantities within two years, given the import of required phosphorous precursors. However, we have no credible indications that Iraq acquired or attempted to acquire large quantities of these chemicals through its existing procurement networks for sanctioned items.

In addition to new investment in its industry, Iraq was able to monitor the location and use of all existing dual-use process equipment. This provided Iraq the ability to rapidly reallocate key equipment for proscribed activities, if required by the Regime.

- One effect of UN monitoring was to implement a national level control system for important dual-use process plants.

Iraq's historical ability to implement simple solutions to weaponization challenges allowed Iraq to retain the capability to weaponize CW agent when the need arose. Because of the risk of discovery and consequences for ending UN sanctions, Iraq would have significantly jeopardized its chances of having sanctions lifted or no longer enforced if the UN or foreign entity had discovered that Iraq had undertaken any weaponization activities.

- ISG has uncovered hardware at a few military depots, which suggests that Iraq may have prototyped experimental CW rounds. The available evidence is insufficient to determine the nature of the effort or the timeframe of activities.
- Iraq could indigenously produce a range of conventional munitions, throughout the 1990s, many of which had previously been adapted for filling with CW agent. However, ISG has found ambiguous evidence of weaponization activities.

Saddam's Leadership Defense Plan consisted of a tactical doctrine taught to all Iraqi officers and included the concept of a "red-line" or last line of defense. However, ISG has no information that the plan ever included a trigger for CW use.

- Despite reported high-level discussions about the use of chemical weapons in the defense of Iraq, information acquired after OIF does not confirm the inclusion of CW in Iraq's tactical planning for OIF. We believe these were mostly theoretical discussions and do not imply the existence of undiscovered CW munitions.

Discussions concerning WMD, particularly leading up to OIF, would have been highly compartmentalized within the Regime. ISG found no credible evidence that any field elements knew about plans for CW use during Operation Iraqi Freedom.

- Uday [Husayn, Saddam's son]—head of the Fedayeen Saddam—attempted to obtain chemical weapons for use during OIF, according to reporting, but ISG found no evidence that Iraq ever came into possession of any CW weapons.

ISG uncovered information that the Iraqi Intelligence Service (IIS) maintained throughout 1991 to 2003 a set of undeclared covert laboratories to research and test various chemicals and poisons, primarily for intelligence operations. The network of laboratories could have provided an ideal, compartmented platform from which to continue CW agent R&D or small-scale production efforts, but we have no indications this was planned.

- ISG has no evidence that IIS Directorate of Criminology (M16) scientists were producing CW or BW agents in these laboratories. However, sources indicate that M16 was planning to produce several CW agents including sulfur mustard, nitrogen mustard, and Sarin.
- Exploitations of IIS laboratories, safe houses, and disposal sites revealed no evidence of CW-related research or production, however many of these sites were either sanitized by the Regime or looted prior to OIF. Interviews with key IIS officials within and outside of M16 yielded very little information about the IIS' activities in this area.
- The existence, function, and purpose of the laboratories were never declared to the UN.
- The IIS program included the use of human subjects for testing purposes.

ISG investigated a series of key pre-OIF indicators involving the possible movement and storage of chemical weapons, focusing on 11 major depots assessed to have possible links to CW. A review of documents, interviews, available reporting, and site exploitations revealed alternate, plausible explanations for activities noted prior to OIF which, at the time, were believed to be CW-related.

- ISG investigated pre-OIF activities at Musayyib Ammunition Storage Depot— the storage site that was judged to have the strongest link to CW. An extensive investigation of the facility revealed that there was no CW activity, unlike previously assessed.

BIOLOGICAL

Key Findings

The Biological Warfare (BW) program was born of the Iraqi Intelligence Service (IIS) and this service retained its connections with the program either directly or indirectly throughout its existence.

- The IIS provided the BW program with security and participated in biological research, probably for its own purposes, from the beginning of Iraq's BW effort in the early 1970s until the final days of Saddam Husayn's Regime.

In 1991, Saddam Husayn regarded BW as an integral element of his arsenal of WMD weapons, and would have used it if the need arose.

- At a meeting of the Iraqi leadership immediately prior to the Gulf war in 1991, Saddam Husayn personally authorized the use of BW weapons against Israel, Saudi Arabia and US forces. Although the exact nature of the circumstances that would trigger use was not spelled out, they would appear to be a threat to the leadership itself or the US resorting to *"unconventional harmful types of weapons."*
- Saddam envisaged all-out use. For example, all Israeli cities were to be struck and all the BW weapons at his disposal were to be used. Saddam specified that the *"many years"* agents, presumably anthrax spores, were to be employed against his foes.

ISG judges that Iraq's actions between 1991 and 1996 demonstrate that the state intended to preserve its BW capability and return to a steady, methodical progress toward a mature BW program when and if the opportunity arose.

- ISG assesses that in 1991, Iraq clung to the objective of gaining war-winning weapons with the strategic intention of achieving the ability to project its power over much of the Middle East and beyond. Biological weapons were part of that plan. With an eye to the future and aiming to preserve some measure of its BW capability, Baghdad in the years immediately after Desert Storm sought to save what it could of its BW infrastructure and covertly continue BW research, hide evidence of that and earlier efforts, and dispose of its existing weapons stocks.
- From 1992 to 1994, Iraq greatly expanded the capability of its Al Hakam facility. Indigenously produced 5 cubic meter fermentors were installed, electrical and water utilities were expanded, and massive new construction to house its desired 50 cubic meter fermentors were completed.
- With the economy at rock bottom in late 1995, ISG judges that Baghdad abandoned its existing BW program in the belief that it constituted a potential embarrassment, whose discovery would undercut Baghdad's ability to reach its overarching goal of obtaining relief from UN sanctions.

In practical terms, with the destruction of the Al Hakam facility, Iraq abandoned its ambition to obtain advanced BW weapons quickly. ISG found no direct evidence that Iraq, after 1996, had plans for a new BW program or was conducting BW-specific work for military purposes. Indeed, from the mid-1990s, despite evidence of continuing interest in nuclear and chemical weapons, there appears to be a complete absence of discussion or even interest in BW at the Presidential level.

Iraq would have faced great difficulty in re-establishing an effective BW agent production capability. Nevertheless, after 1996 Iraq still had a significant dual-use capability—some declared—readily useful for BW if the Regime chose to use it to pursue a BW program. Moreover, Iraq still possessed its most important BW asset, the scientific know-how of its BW cadre.

- Any attempt to create a new BW program after 1996 would have encountered a range of major hurdles. The years following Desert Storm wrought a steady degradation of Iraq's industrial base: new equipment and spare parts for existing machinery became difficult and expensive to obtain, standards of maintenance declined, staff could not receive training abroad, and foreign technical assistance was almost impossible to get. Additionally, Iraq's infrastructure and public utilities were crumbling. New large projects, particularly if they required special foreign equipment and expertise, would attract international attention. UN monitoring of dual-use facilities up to the end of 1998, made their use for clandestine purpose[s] complicated and risk laden.

Depending on its scale, Iraq could have re-established an elementary BW program within a few weeks to a few months of a decision to do so, but ISG discovered no indications that the Regime was pursuing such a course.

- In spite of the difficulties noted above, a BW capability is technically the easiest WMD to attain. Although equipment and facilities were destroyed under UN supervision in 1996, Iraq retained technical BW know-how through the scientists that were involved in the former program. ISG has also identified civilian facilities and equipment in Iraq that have dual-use application that could be used for the production of agent.

ISG judges that in 1991 and 1992, Iraq appears to have destroyed its undeclared stocks of BW weapons and probably destroyed remaining holdings of bulk BW agent. However ISG lacks evidence to document complete destruction. Iraq retained some BW-related seed stocks until their discovery after Operation Iraqi Freedom (OIF).

- After the passage of UN Security Council Resolution (UNSCR) 687 in April 1991, Iraqi leaders decided not to declare the offensive BW program and in consequence ordered all evidence of the program erased. Iraq declared that BW program personnel sanitized the facilities and destroyed the weapons and their contents.
- Iraq declared the possession of 157 aerial bombs and 25 missile warheads containing BW agent. ISG assesses that the evidence for the original number of bombs is uncertain. ISG judges that Iraq clandestinely destroyed at least 132 bombs and 25 missiles. ISG continued the efforts of the UN at the destruction site but found no remnants of further weapons. This leaves the possibility that the fragments of up to 25 bombs may remain undiscovered. Of these, any that escaped destruction would probably now only contain degraded agent.
- ISG does not have a clear account of bulk agent destruction. Official Iraqi sources and BW personnel, state that Al Hakam staff destroyed stocks of bulk agent in mid-1991. However, the same personnel admit concealing details of the movement and destruction of bulk BW agent in the first half of 1991. Iraq continued to present information known to be untrue to the UN up to OIF. Those involved did not reveal this until several months after the conflict.
- Dr. Rihab Rashid Taha Al 'Azzawi, head of the bacterial program, claims she retained BW seed stocks until early 1992 when she destroyed them. ISG has not found a means of verifying this. Some seed stocks were retained by another Iraqi official until 2003 when they were recovered by ISG.

ISG is aware of BW-applicable research since 1996, but ISG judges it was not conducted in connection with a BW program.

- ISG has uncovered no evidence of illicit research conducted into BW agents by universities or research organizations.
- The work conducted on a biopesticide (*Bacillus thuringiensis*) at Al Hakam until 1995 would serve to maintain the basic skills required by scientists to produce and dry anthrax spores (*Bacillus anthracis*) but ISG has not discovered evidence suggesting this was the Regime's intention. However in 1991, research and production on biopesticide and single cell protein (SCP) was selected by Iraq to provide cover for Al Hakam's role in Iraq's BW program. Similar work conducted at the Tuwaitha Agricultural and Biological Research Center (TABRC) up to OIF also maintained skills that were applicable to BW, but again, ISG found no evidence to suggest that this was the intention.
- Similarly, ISG found no information to indicate that the work carried out by TABRC into Single Cell Protein (SCP) was a cover story for continuing research into the production of BW agents, such as *C. botulinum* and *B. anthracis,* after the destruction of Al Hakam through to OIF.
- TABRC conducted research and development (R&D) programs to enable indigenous manufacture of bacterial growth media. Although these media are suitable for the bulk production of BW agents, ISG has found no evidence to indicate that their development and testing were specifically for this purpose.
- Although Iraq had the basic capability to work with variola major (smallpox), ISG found no evidence that it retained any stocks of smallpox or actively conducted research into this agent for BW intentions.

The IIS had a series of laboratories that conducted biological work including research into BW agents for assassination purposes until the mid-1990s. ISG has not been able to establish the scope and nature of the work at these laboratories or determine whether any of the work was related to military development of BW agent.

- The security services operated a series of laboratories in the Baghdad area. Iraq should have declared these facilities and their equipment to the UN, but they did not. Neither the UN Special Commission (UNSCOM) nor the UN Monitoring, Verification, and Inspection Commission (UNMOVIC) were aware of their existence or inspected them.
- Some of the laboratories possessed equipment capable of supporting research into BW agents for military purposes, but ISG does not know whether this occurred although there is no evidence of it. The laboratories were probably the successors of the Al Salman facility, located three kilometers south of Salman Pak, which was destroyed in 1991, and they carried on many of the same activities, including forensic work.
- Under the aegis of the intelligence service, a secretive team developed assassination instruments using poisons or toxins for the Iraqi state. A small group of scientists, doctors and technicians conducted secret experiments on human beings, resulting in their deaths. The aim was probably the development of poisons, including ricin and aflatoxin to eliminate or debilitate the Regime's opponents.

It appears that testing on humans continued until the mid 1990s. There is no evidence to link these tests with the development of BW agents for military use.

In spite of exhaustive investigation, ISG found no evidence that Iraq possessed, or was developing, BW agent production systems mounted on road vehicles or railway wagons.

- Prior to OIF there was information indicating Iraq had planned and built a break-out BW capability, in the form of a set of mobile production units, capable of producing BW agent at short notice in sufficient quantities to weaponize. Although ISG has conducted a thorough investigation of every aspect of this information, it has not found any equipment suitable for such a program, nor has ISG positively identified any sites. No documents have been uncovered. Interviews with individuals suspected of involvement have all proved negative.
- ISG harbors severe doubts about the source's credibility in regards to the break-out program.
- ISG thoroughly examined two trailers captured in 2003, suspected of being mobile BW agent production units, and investigated the associated evidence. ISG judges that its Iraqi makers almost certainly designed and built the equipment exclusively for the generation of hydrogen. It is impractical to use the equipment for the production and weaponization of BW agent. ISG judges that it cannot therefore be part of any BW program.

SOURCE: "Comprehensive Report of the Special Advisor to the DCI on Iraq's WMD: Key Findings," October 6, 2004, https://www.cia.gov/library/reports/general-reports-1/iraq_wmd_2004/chap1.html.

Iraq's New Government

DOCUMENT IN CONTEXT

During the latter years of the dictatorship headed by Saddam Hussein, Iraq held occasional elections, but had nothing close to the substance of democracy. In 2005—two years after the United States ousted Hussein from power—Iraqis went to the polls three times and elected two new governments and ratified a new constitution. Even so, it remained unclear whether real democracy had taken root and could survive the daily onslaught of violence that kept the country on the edge of civil war.

Iraq after Hussein's ouster became a large-scale experiment for those in the Bush administration and elsewhere who believed democracy to be a viable form of government in Middle Eastern lands that previously had been ruled by empires, colonial powers, and dictators. With help from elections experts at the United Nations, Iraqis and

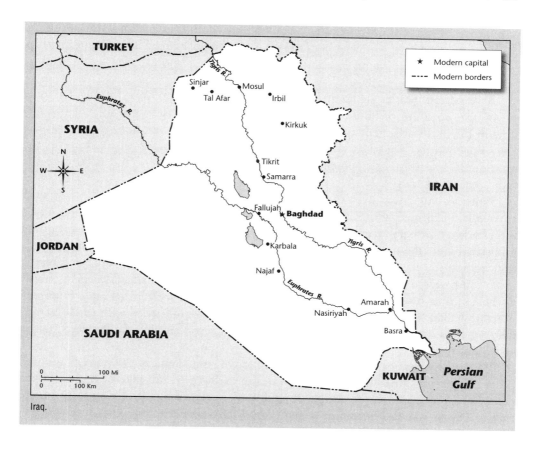

Iraq.

their political tutors from the United States in 2004 devised a process for the three elections held in 2005 followed by the formation of a permanent government bridging the country's sectarian divide. This process began with an election in January 2005 for a Transitional National Assembly, which governed Iraq temporarily and wrote a new democratic constitution, which voters approved in an October 2005 referendum. Iraqis returned to the polls in December 2005 to elect a permanent parliament—or Council of Representatives—which chose a new government after intense bargaining early in 2006.

Each step of this process came fraught with numerous difficulties and was overshadowed by the daily toll of deaths and injuries from car bombings, suicide bombings, kidnappings, assassinations, and other forms of violence. A basic problem at the outset was persuading minority Sunni Muslims—who previously had governed Iraq and still thought of themselves as the country's natural leaders—to accept the fact that they were a minority and would no longer exercise unilateral power. Sunnis boycotted the first elections in January 2005, but some Sunni leaders later realized that this had been a mistake because it left them without a voice at the table where decisions were made. Many Sunnis also believed that the process of writing the new constitution was rigged against them, so many of them boycotted the referendum on that document the following October.

The real test of Iraq's new experiment with representative government began with the December 2005 elections. In technical terms, these elections went smoothly and were generally fair and relatively free from violence. Political bargaining following the elections was, however, intense because the stakes were high: The resulting government would serve for four years and receive increasingly more power as the United States handed control to Iraqis.

As expected, parties representing majority Shiite Muslims won the biggest share of votes. A coalition of Shiite parties, the United Iraqi Alliance won 128 of the 275 seats in the new parliament (just short of a majority), and a coalition of Kurdish parties won 53 seats. Together, these groups, which had combined their efforts in the transitional assembly, had enough votes to choose a government and determine the future course of Iraq.

Political bargaining over the new government proved to be more difficult than anyone had expected. Not until mid-April 2006, five months after the election, did a little-known Shiite politician, Nuri al-Maliki, emerge as the consensus choice for prime minister, by far the most powerful post in the new government. Maliki got the position because he had the support of legislators loyal to Muqtada al-Sadr, one of the most controversial figures in post-Hussein Iraq and one who had parlayed his status as the son of a revered Shiite cleric into a prominent role for himself after Hussein's overthrow. Sadr formed the Mahdi Army, a militia that had battled with the U.S. military in 2004 and would later play a major role in sectarian violence between Shiites and Sunnis.

The year of transitional government following the January 2005 elections had given Maliki and other Iraqi politicians a taste of the give-and-take of representative democracy but had not prepared them for the stresses of running a country in the midst of what was fast becoming a civil war. Maliki and his colleagues found themselves under pressure from sectarian groups—particularly the Shiites and Kurds—that insisted the government meet their narrowly focused demands. Countervailing pressure came from the United States, which repeatedly urged Maliki to make compromises benefiting the Sunnis to give them a stake in policymaking by government rather than by violence.

Maliki responded to these pressures with a far-reaching proposal he called the National Reconciliation and Dialogue Project. Introduced in parliament on June 25, 2006, the twenty-four point plan offered something for each of Iraq's major sects in hopes of turning them away from violence. A central component, aimed mainly at Sunnis, offered a limited amnesty for insurgents who renounced violence and had not been involved in attacks on Iraqis or foreign troops. Other key aspects included reforms in the legal and judicial systems, increased government aid to the Sunni heartland areas where much of the violence was occurring, and the opening of a "dialogue" on changes demanded by the Sunnis to the constitution that voters had approved the previous October. The plan also talked of "disbanding" militias but offered no specifics.

"To those who want to rebuild our country, we present an olive branch," Maliki told parliament when describing the plan. "And to those who insist on killing and terrorism, we present a fist with the power of law to protect our country and people."

The U.S. government quickly endorsed the plan, as did important leaders from the major sects. Parliament then recessed for most of the summer, however, and by the time it returned to work in September the increasing violence had further dimmed the prospects of reconciliation. Maliki repeatedly revised his reconciliation plan to gain more support, but none of the changes made it any easier for parliament to act.

Later in 2006, senior officials of the Bush administration expressed doubt that Maliki had the will power or the political clout to carry out his reconciliation plan and govern Iraq on behalf of all Iraqis. By then, Washington's options had become limited. Even with some 150,000 troops in Iraq, it could no longer dictate who would be in power in Iraq or what actions those officials should take.

Following is the text of the National Reconciliation and Dialogue Project, as presented to the Iraqi National Assembly on June 25, 2006, by Prime Minister Nuri al-Maliki.

DOCUMENT

Iraqi National Reconciliation and Dialogue Project

JUNE 25, 2006

In The Name of God
The National Reconciliation and Dialogue project

In order to confirm the coherence between the Iraqi people, establishing the basis of national unity among their different components, to treat the remains of terrorism and administrative corruption, spreading the spirit of the loyal nationality to Iraq in order to build [a] wide national front to confront challenges and to regain the pioneer position of Iraq regionally and internationally . . . for all that we release the initiative of national reconciliation and dialogue that depends on two basic elements:

1. The reliable procedure.
2. Principles and required policies.

First: Procedures

A. Forming national head committee (the head National Committee of National Reconciliation and Dialogue project) contains representatives from the three authorities, the state minister of the national dialogue and representatives from the parliamentary slates.

B. Forming sub-committees in the governorates by the head national committee, it takes over the tasks of the committee to expand the reconciliation horizontally.

C. Forming field committees to put horizontal cultural and media conceptions, follow up the process of reconciliation and evaluating it[s] stages.

D. [Holding] conferences for the different slices of life such as:

1. Conference to the religious leaders to support the reconciliation process and announcing (Fatwa) to convince people.

2. Conference to the heads of tribes issues covenant of honor to confront the state fighting and fighting terrorism.

3. Conference to the effective political parties pledge to support the government, protect the political process and confront the terrorist challenge and corruption.

4. Calling all the NGOs to carry out activities, conferences, education campaigns to achieve the aims of reconciliation plan.

Second: The Principles and Policies Required

1. Adopting a political reasonable address by the political powers that take part in the political process, and by the government to bring back the alternating currents and to achieve media neutralism.

2. Adopting an honest national dialogue in dealing with all political visions and stances, which are opposite to those of the government in the political process.

3. Adopting the legal and constitutional legitimacy to solve the country's problems and to put an end to the assassination phenomenon.

4. The political powers, involved in the government should take a rejecting stance against the terrorists and Saddam's followers.

5. Issuing an amnesty to the prisoners who are not involved in crimes against humanity or terrorist acts and forming committees to set them free immediately. The insurgent who seeks to gain the amnesty opportunity has to denounce violence, support the national government and to obey the rule of law.

6. Preventing human rights violations, working on reforming the prisons and punishing those responsible for torture crimes and allowing the international organizations to visit the prisons.

7. Dealing with the MNF to put mechanisms to prevent human rights violations and the civilians' abuses through military operations.

8. Finding solutions for the personnel of the dissolved departments, especially in relation to economic part and to take benefits of their expertise.

9. Reconsidering the Debaathification Board according to the Constitution, the judicial authorities and the Law to take a constitutional and vocational pattern.

10. Taking prompt procedures to improve the services, especially in the hot areas.

11. Activating the preparatory committees, emanated from the Cairo Conference for National Accord, in coordination with the UN and the Arab League and encouraging the Baghdad Peace Initiative.

12. The government should make a balanced Islamic-Arabic-Regional movement to make the other government be acquainted with what is going on in Iraq and gain their support to the National Accord Process, especially those enhancing terrorism or overlooking it.

13. Taking a serious and quick step towards establishing the armed forces which will take the responsibility of managing Iraq's security in preparation of withdrawal of the MNF.

14. Taking a serious and quick step towards establishing the armed forces in both Ministry of Defence and Ministry of Interior on professional and national bases for

they will take the responsibility of managing Iraq's security instead of the MNF before they withdraw.

15. Activating the decisions that support victims of the former regime through compensations and making available all potentials to improve their living standards all over Iraq.

16. Removing all obstacles facing the Iraqi citizens or organizations to take part in building Iraq according to the Constitution if they did not commit any crime.

17. Giving compensations for those who have been suffering from terrorist acts, military operations or violence.

18. Activating the role of judiciary to punish the criminals, making it the only reference in dealing with crimes, former regime's top officials, terrorists and gangs of kidnapping and killing.

19. Making the armed forces independent on the influence of the competing political powers, disbanding the militias and illegal armed groups and treat them according to politics, economy and security.

20. Gathering the visions and stances towards the anti-Iraq terrorist and expiatory groups.

21. Starting a wide-scaled construction campaign all over Iraq to treat the unemployment phenomenon.

22. The elections led to the forming [of a] Parliament, constitution and a government of national unity as the only legal representative of the Iraqi peoples' will in dealing with sovereignty and the existence of MNF.

23. Make the deportees get back home. The government and the security systems are responsible for their return and safety to prevent the terrorists from harming them in addition to compensating them for all the damages they have and adopt a firm security plan that ensures protecting people and prevents them from being subject to blackmail.

24. Search and arrest operations happen according to judiciary orders before the raid or arrest. These orders should follow certain information, not vexatious one[s] and should be in conformity with human rights. The military operations should also occur on the basis of official orders.

SOURCE: Government of Iraq, "The Prime Minister Announces the National Reconciliation Project before the Parliament," press release, June 25, 2006, www.iraqigovernment.org/msalhaa.htm.

U.S. Policy in Iraq

DOCUMENT IN CONTEXT

All of the shortcomings of the George W. Bush administration's policies in Iraq appeared to coalesce in 2006 when sectarian violence exploded into a civil war and the new government—created through U.S.-sponsored elections—proved unable to overcome increasingly dangerous sectarian divisions. In the United States, voters signaled their unhappiness with Bush's Iraq policies by stripping his fellow Republicans of control of Congress. An independent, high-level commission recommended subtle but important changes in these policies, and Bush acknowledged in January 2007 that the situation in Iraq had become "unacceptable." Rather than withdrawing from Iraq, however, as many Democrats and even some Republicans were urging, Bush chose to increase the U.S. military presence there, at least in the short-term, in hopes of calming the violence in Baghdad so Iraq's government could gain its footing.

Before the invasion of Iraq in 2003, the Bush administration had assumed that the removal of the country's autocratic leader, Saddam Hussein, would unleash the pent-up desire of Iraqis for democracy, which in turn would overcome any lingering resistance on the part of minority Sunni Muslims, who had formed the base of Hussein's government. Iraqis did exhibit a desire for democracy, or at least elections, but their expectations for democracy proved different from what planners in Washington had assumed. For the majority Shiites, democracy meant having political power for the first time. For many Sunnis—reluctant to acknowledge their minority status—democracy meant trying to hold on to the power they had exercised for centuries. For the other large minority, the Kurds, democracy meant controlling their own destiny in the three northern provinces they called Kurdistan—preferably outside Iraq as an independent country, but inside Iraq, with a great deal of autonomy, if necessary.

These differing expectations influenced the course of events as the United States, with help from the United Nations, negotiated and then implemented a process of holding elections and forming numerous governing structures in the years after the 2003 invasion. Just as important, the fact that Iraqis did not share a universal vision of the country's future meant that some of them would try to reach their own goals via violence, the customary route of the past (Iraq's New Government, p. 526).

Violent opposition to the U.S. occupation of Iraq began to spread in the summer of 2003 after the Bush administration's representatives in Baghdad dismantled the military and the Baath Party—the key elements of Hussein's former power structure. At first, officials in Washington blamed the violence on criminals and "dead-enders" from the overthrown regime. Bush even appeared to invite these opponents to throw themselves against the U.S. military. "There are some who feel that the conditions are such that they can attack us there," he said on July 2, 2003. "My answer is: bring 'em on. We've got the force necessary to deal with the security situation." Later in 2003, after a series of high-profile bombings that targeted the United Nations and Iraqis working with the U.S. occupation, the Bush administration concluded that elements associated with the al-Qaida network had moved into Iraq.

The level of violence ebbed and flowed during 2003, 2004, and 2005, often in response to political developments, such as the three elections held in 2005. Most attacks were small in scale, primarily roadside bombs that each killed a handful of U.S. or Iraqi soldiers. Massive car bombs or suicide bombs, often against such civilian targets as mosques or open-air markets, heightened the sense of insecurity, however, and led Iraqis to wonder whether their country would ever again be safe.

The Samarra Mosque Bombing

The Bush administration hoped that elections in December 2005 would give all Iraqis a sense of ownership of their new government and thus eliminate the incentive for violence and any residual public support for those who committed violent acts. Even before the newly elected government could take its place, however, a spectacular act of violence in February 2006 flattened these hopes. Early in the morning of February 22, gunmen disguised as police took control of the Askariya mosque in Samarra, about sixty miles north of Baghdad. As the burial site of two of the most important leaders in the early years of Shiite Islam, the mosque with a famed gold dome was a revered shrine for Shiites. The gunmen set off explosives that collapsed the dome into rubble and destroyed most of the rest of the mosque.

Enraged Shiites responded to this bombing with violent rampages through Sunni neighborhoods in Baghdad and other cities, and Sunnis attacked Shiites, establishing a pattern of sectarian violence that would continue for the rest of 2006 and into 2007. The Shiites formed militias that attacked Sunnis in a campaign of terror intended to force them from mixed neighborhoods. Most of the Sunni violence took the form of roadside bombs aimed at Iraqi and U.S. security forces or car bombs and suicide bombs intended to kill large numbers of Shiites as they shopped or worshiped.

By the end of 2006, the UN mission in Iraq had compiled figures estimating that at least 34,000 Iraqis had died from various forms of violence in 2006 and another 36,000-plus had been injured. Academic experts, human rights groups, and others estimated that the total number of Iraqis killed since the U.S. invasion was at least 50,000 and possibly as many as a half-million. The United Nations also estimated that about 10 percent of Iraq's 26 million people had fled their homes since 2003, most of them taking refuge in neighboring Syria and Jordan, where they became a major burden despite UN refugee assistance.

In the United States, the figure that captured attention was the number of U.S. service personnel who had died since the invasion. That number grew steadily from the toll of roadside bombings and other attacks specifically aimed at the U.S. occupation. The total of U.S. deaths reached 1,000 in September 2004, then 2,000 in October 2005, and 3,000 at the end of 2006. These numbers are small when compared to U.S. casualties in other long wars, but the steady climb in deaths contributed to a growing sense in the United States that Americans were dying in Iraq for a cause already lost. The bombings also wounded thousands of U.S. personnel, many of them with life-debilitating injuries. Roadside bombs proved especially effective weapons against the U.S. military, which found itself spending billions of dollars to protect the troops as they patrolled Iraq's cities and countryside.

Searching for a New Policy

Responding to voter concerns about Iraq, members of Congress in 2005 proposed the creation of a blue-ribbon commission to study the situation in Iraq and recommend policy alternatives. The ten-member, bipartisan Iraq Study Group began work early in 2006 under the chairmanship of former secretary of state James A. Baker III (a long-time associate of the Bush family) and former House member Lee H. Hamilton, an Indiana Democrat who had chaired the foreign affairs and intelligence committees and was widely respected in Washington. The commission held several hearings and traveled to Iraq, but announced that it would withhold publishing its recommendations until after November 2006 midterm congressional elections to keep its findings out of the partisan spotlight.

The Baker-Hamilton report, issued on December 6, 2006, confirmed the obvious—that the situation in Iraq was "grave and deteriorating"—and it raised serious questions about whether the use of military force would succeed in bringing the violence in Iraq under control. The report offered seventy-nine recommendations, most of which involved minor shifts in policy or bureaucratic procedures in Washington. The single most controversial recommendation suggested that the administration conduct negotiations with Iraq's neighbors, including Iran and Syria, as part of an international conference to find a political solution to the violence. The Bush administration had refused to have high-level contacts with Syria in recent years and had embraced the long-running U.S. policy of shunning Iran.

President Bush politely accepted the Iraq Study Group report from Baker and Hamilton, but White House aides made clear that the president was unlikely to accept its key policy prescriptions. One month later, on January 10, 2007, Bush gave a televised speech outlining what he called a "new strategy" for Iraq. The heart of this strategy consisted of a short-term increase, or "surge," in the number of U.S. troops in Iraq. The surge would involve an additional 21,000 combat troops, most of whom would be deployed to Baghdad in an effort to bring the security situation there under control. The additional troops would bring the total U.S. armed presence in Iraq to nearly 170,000.

The president offered this explanation: "Our troops will have a well-defined mission: to help Iraqis clear and secure neighborhoods, to help them protect the local population, and to help ensure that the Iraqi forces left behind are capable of providing the security that Baghdad needs." Bush said the extra troops were necessary to ensure that "we'll have the force levels we need to hold the areas that have been cleared" of antigovernment insurgents and sectarian militias.

The first contingents of additional U.S. troops began arriving in Iraq early in February 2007, but the full complement of 21,000 new troops was not in place until June. Neither the president nor his aides would say how long this surge of extra troops would last or when they expected to begin a gradual withdrawal of all U.S. troops from Iraq. The new Democratic-led Congress in April 2007 sent Bush legislation setting a timetable for such a withdrawal, but he vetoed the measure.

> *Following are excerpts from "The Way Forward—A New Approach," the recommendations section of the report by the Iraq Study Group, made public on December 6, 2006, and a speech by President George W. Bush, on January 10, 2007, announcing his plans for a "surge" of additional U.S. troops in Iraq.*

DOCUMENT

Recommendations of the Iraq Study Group

DECEMBER 6, 2006

II
THE WAY FORWARD—A NEW APPROACH

Progress in Iraq is still possible if new approaches are taken promptly by Iraq, the United States, and other countries that have a stake in the Middle East.

To attain the goals we have outlined, changes in course must be made both outside and inside Iraq. Our report offers a comprehensive strategy to build regional and international support for stability in Iraq, as it encourages the Iraqi people to assume control of their own destiny. It offers a responsible transition.

Externally, the United States should immediately begin to employ all elements of American power to construct a regional mechanism that can support, rather than retard, progress in Iraq. Internally, the Iraqi government must take the steps required to achieve national reconciliation, reduce violence, and improve the daily lives of Iraqis. Efforts to implement these external and internal strategies must begin now and must be undertaken in concert with one another.

This responsible transition can allow for a reduction in the U.S. presence in Iraq over time.

A. THE EXTERNAL APPROACH:
BUILDING AN INTERNATIONAL CONSENSUS

The United States must build a new international consensus for stability in Iraq and the region.

In order to foster such consensus, the United States should embark on a robust diplomatic effort to establish an international support structure intended to stabilize Iraq and ease tensions in other countries in the region. This support structure should include every country that has an interest in averting a chaotic Iraq, including all of Iraq's neighbors—Iran and Syria among them. Despite the well-known differences between many of these countries, they all share an interest in avoiding the horrific consequences that would flow from a chaotic Iraq, particularly a humanitarian catastrophe and regional destabilization.

A reinvigorated diplomatic effort is required because it is clear that the Iraqi government cannot succeed in governing, defending, and sustaining itself by relying on U.S. military and economic support alone. Nor can the Iraqi government succeed by relying only on U.S. military support in conjunction with Iraqi military and police capabilities. Some states have been withholding commitments they could make to support Iraq's stabilization and reconstruction. Some states have been actively undermining stability in Iraq. To achieve a political solution within Iraq, a broader international support structure is needed.

1. The New Diplomatic Offensive

Iraq cannot be addressed effectively in isolation from other major regional issues, interests, and unresolved conflicts. To put it simply, all key issues in the Middle East—the Arab-Israeli conflict, Iraq, Iran, the need for political and economic reforms, and extremism and terrorism—are inextricably linked. In addition to supporting stability in Iraq, a comprehensive diplomatic offensive—the New Diplomatic Offensive—should address these key regional issues. By doing so, it would help marginalize extremists and terrorists, promote U.S. values and interests, and improve America's global image.

Under the diplomatic offensive, we propose regional and international initiatives and steps to assist the Iraqi government in achieving certain security, political, and economic milestones. Achieving these milestones will require at least the acquiescence of Iraq's neighbors, and their active and timely cooperation would be highly desirable.

The diplomatic offensive would extend beyond the primarily economic "Compact for Iraq" by also emphasizing political, diplomatic, and security issues. At the same time, it would be coordinated with the goals of the Compact for Iraq. The diplomatic offensive would also be broader and more far-reaching than the "Gulf Plus Two" efforts currently being conducted, and those efforts should be folded into and become part of the diplomatic offensive.

States included within the diplomatic offensive can play a major role in reinforcing national reconciliation efforts between Iraqi Sunnis and Shia. Such reinforcement would contribute substantially to legitimizing of the political process in Iraq. Iraq's leaders may not be able to come together unless they receive the necessary signals and support from abroad. This backing will not materialize of its own accord, and must be encouraged urgently by the United States.

In order to advance a comprehensive diplomatic solution, the Study Group recommends as follows:

RECOMMENDATION 1: The United States, working with the Iraqi government, should launch the comprehensive New Diplomatic Offensive to deal with the problems of Iraq and of the region. This new diplomatic offensive should be launched before December 31, 2006.

RECOMMENDATION 2: The goals of the diplomatic offensive as it relates to regional players should be to:

i.   Support the unity and territorial integrity of Iraq.
ii. Stop destabilizing interventions and actions by Iraq's neighbors.
iii. Secure Iraq's borders, including the use of joint patrols with neighboring countries.
iv. Prevent the expansion of the instability and conflict beyond Iraq's borders.
v.   Promote economic assistance, commerce, trade, political support, and, if possible, military assistance for the Iraqi government from non-neighboring Muslim nations.
vi. Energize countries to support national political reconciliation in Iraq.
vii. Validate Iraq's legitimacy by resuming diplomatic relations, where appropriate, and reestablishing embassies in Baghdad.

viii. Assist Iraq in establishing active working embassies in key capitals in the region (for example, in Riyadh, Saudi Arabia).

ix. Help Iraq reach a mutually acceptable agreement on Kirkuk.

x. Assist the Iraqi government in achieving certain security, political, and economic milestones, including better performance on issues such as national reconciliation, equitable distribution of oil revenues, and the dismantling of militias.

RECOMMENDATION 3: As a complement to the diplomatic offensive, and in addition to the Support Group discussed below, the United States and the Iraqi government should support the holding of a conference or meeting in Baghdad of the Organization of the Islamic Conference or the Arab League both to assist the Iraqi government in promoting national reconciliation in Iraq and to reestablish their diplomatic presence in Iraq.

2. The Iraq International Support Group

This new diplomatic offensive cannot be successful unless it includes the active participation of those countries that have a critical stake in preventing Iraq from falling into chaos. To encourage their participation, the United States should immediately seek the creation of the Iraq International Support Group. The Support Group should also include all countries that border Iraq as well as other key countries in the region and the world.

The Support Group would not seek to impose obligations or undertakings on the government of Iraq. Instead, the Support Group would assist Iraq in ways the government of Iraq would desire, attempting to strengthen Iraq's sovereignty—not diminish it.

It is clear to Iraq Study Group members that all of Iraq's neighbors are anxious about the situation in Iraq. They favor a unified Iraq that is strong enough to maintain its territorial integrity, but not so powerful as to threaten its neighbors. None favors the breakup of the Iraqi state. Each country in the region views the situation in Iraq through the filter of its particular set of interests. For example:

- Turkey opposes an independent or even highly autonomous Kurdistan because of its own national security considerations.
- Iran backs Shia claims and supports various Shia militias in Iraq, but it also supports other groups in order to enhance its influence and hedge its bets on possible outcomes.
- Syria, despite facilitating support for Iraqi insurgent groups, would be threatened by the impact that the breakup of Iraq would have on its own multiethnic and multiconfessional society.
- Kuwait wants to ensure that it will not once again be the victim of Iraqi irredentism and aggression.
- Saudi Arabia and Jordan share Sunni concerns over Shia ascendancy in Iraq and the region as a whole.
- The other Arab Gulf states also recognize the benefits of an outcome in Iraq that does not destabilize the region and exacerbate Shia-Sunni tensions.
- None of Iraq's neighbors especially major countries such as Egypt, Saudi Arabia, and Israel see it in their interest for the situation in Iraq to lead to aggrandized

regional influence by Iran. Indeed, they may take active steps to limit Iran's influence, steps that could lead to an intraregional conflict.

Left to their own devices, these governments will tend to reinforce ethnic, sectarian, and political divisions within Iraqi society. But if the Support Group takes a systematic and active approach toward considering the concerns of each country, we believe that each can be encouraged to play a positive role in Iraq and the region.

SAUDI ARABIA. Saudi Arabia's agreement not to intervene with assistance to Sunni Arab Iraqis could be an essential quid pro quo for similar forbearance on the part of other neighbors, especially Iran. The Saudis could use their Islamic credentials to help reconcile differences between Iraqi factions and build broader support in the Islamic world for a stabilization agreement, as their recent hosting of a meeting of Islamic religious leaders in Mecca suggests. If the government in Baghdad pursues a path of national reconciliation with the Sunnis, the Saudis could help Iraq confront and eliminate al Qaeda in Iraq. They could also cancel the Iraqi debt owed them. In addition, the Saudis might be helpful in persuading the Syrians to cooperate.

TURKEY. As a major Sunni Muslim country on Iraq's borders, Turkey can be a partner in supporting the national reconciliation process in Iraq. Such efforts can be particularly helpful given Turkey's interest in Kurdistan remaining an integral part of a unified Iraq and its interest in preventing a safe haven for Kurdish terrorists (the PKK).

EGYPT. Because of its important role in the Arab world, Egypt should be encouraged to foster the national reconciliation process in Iraq with a focus on getting the Sunnis to participate. At the same time, Egypt has the means, and indeed has offered, to train groups of Iraqi military and security forces in Egypt on a rotational basis.

JORDAN. Jordan, like Egypt, can help in the national reconciliation process in Iraq with the Sunnis. It too has the professional capability to train and equip Iraqi military and security forces.

RECOMMENDATION 4: As an instrument of the New Diplomatic Offensive, an Iraq International Support Group should be organized immediately following the launch of the New Diplomatic Offensive.

RECOMMENDATION 5: The Support Group should consist of Iraq and all the states bordering Iraq, including Iran and Syria; the key regional states, including Egypt and the Gulf States; the five permanent members of the United Nations Security Council; the European Union; and, of course, Iraq itself. Other countries for instance, Germany, Japan and South Korea—that might be willing to contribute to resolving political, diplomatic, and security problems affecting Iraq could also become members.

RECOMMENDATION 6: The New Diplomatic Offensive and the work of the Support Group should be carried out with urgency, and should be conducted by and organized at the level of foreign minister or above. The Secretary of State, if not the President, should lead the U.S. effort. That effort should be both bilateral and multilateral, as circumstances require.

RECOMMENDATION 7: The Support Group should call on the participation of the office of the United Nations Secretary-General in its work. The United Nations Secretary-General should designate a Special Envoy as his representative.

RECOMMENDATION 8: The Support Group, as part of the New Diplomatic Offensive, should develop specific approaches to neighboring countries that take into account the interests, perspectives, and potential contributions as suggested above.

3. Dealing with Iran and Syria

Dealing with Iran and Syria is controversial. Nevertheless, it is our view that in diplomacy, a nation can and should engage its adversaries and enemies to try to resolve conflicts and differences consistent with its own interests. Accordingly, the Support Group should actively engage Iran and Syria in its diplomatic dialogue, without preconditions.

The Study Group recognizes that U.S. relationships with Iran and Syria involve difficult issues that must be resolved. Diplomatic talks should be extensive and substantive, and they will require a balancing of interests. The United States has diplomatic, economic, and military disincentives available in approaches to both Iran and Syria. However, the United States should also consider incentives to try to engage them constructively, much as it did successfully with Libya.

Some of the possible incentives to Iran, Syria, or both include:

i. An Iraq that does not disintegrate and destabilize its neighbors and the region.
ii. The continuing role of the United States in preventing the Taliban from destabilizing Afghanistan.
iii. Accession to international organizations, including the World Trade Organization.
iv. Prospects for enhanced diplomatic relations with the United States.
v. The prospect of a U.S. policy that emphasizes political and economic reforms instead of (as Iran now perceives it) advocating regime change.
vi. Prospects for a real, complete, and secure peace to be negotiated between Israel and Syria, with U.S. involvement as part of a broader initiative on Arab-Israeli peace as outlined below.

RECOMMENDATION 9: Under the aegis of the New Diplomatic Offensive and the Support Group, the United States should engage directly with Iran and Syria in order to try to obtain their commitment to constructive policies toward Iraq and other regional issues. In engaging Syria and Iran, the United States should consider incentives, as well as disincentives, in seeking constructive results.

IRAN. Engaging Iran is problematic, especially given the state of the U.S.-Iranian relationship. Yet the United States and Iran cooperated in Afghanistan, and both sides should explore whether this model can be replicated in the case of Iraq.

Although Iran sees it in its interest to have the United States bogged down in Iraq, Iran's interests would not be served by a failure of U.S. policy in Iraq that led to chaos and the territorial disintegration of the Iraqi state. Iran's population is slightly more than 50 percent Persian, but it has a large Azeri minority (24 percent of the population) as well as Kurdish and Arab minorities. Worst-case scenarios in Iraq could inflame sectarian tensions within Iran, with serious consequences for Iranian national security interests.

Our limited contacts with Iran's government lead us to believe that its leaders are likely to say they will not participate in diplomatic efforts to support stability in Iraq. They attribute this reluctance to their belief that the United States seeks regime change in Iran.

Nevertheless, as one of Iraq's neighbors Iran should be asked to assume its responsibility to participate in the Support Group. An Iranian refusal to do so would demonstrate to Iraq and the rest of the world Iran's rejectionist attitude and approach, which could lead to its isolation. Further, Iran's refusal to cooperate on this matter would diminish its prospects of engaging with the United States in the broader dialogue it seeks.

RECOMMENDATION 10: The issue of Iran's nuclear programs should continue to be dealt with by the United Nations Security Council and its five permanent members (i.e., the United States, United Kingdom, France, Russia, and China) plus Germany.

RECOMMENDATION 11: Diplomatic efforts within the Support Group should seek to persuade Iran that it should take specific steps to improve the situation in Iraq.

Among steps Iran could usefully take are the following:

- Iran should stem the flow of equipment, technology, and training to any group resorting to violence in Iraq.
- Iran should make clear its support for the territorial integrity of Iraq as a unified state, as well as its respect for the sovereignty of Iraq and its government.
- Iran can use its influence, especially over Shia groups in Iraq, to encourage national reconciliation.
- Iran can also, in the right circumstances, help in the economic reconstruction of Iraq.

SYRIA. Although the U.S.-Syrian relationship is at a low point, both countries have important interests in the region that could be enhanced if they were able to establish some common ground on how to move forward. This approach worked effectively in the early 1990s. In this context, Syria's national interests in the Arab-Israeli dispute are important and can be brought into play.

Syria can make a major contribution to Iraq's stability in several ways. Accordingly, the Study Group recommends the following:

RECOMMENDATION 12: The United States and the Support Group should encourage and persuade Syria of the merit of such contributions as the following:

- Syria can control its border with Iraq to the maximum extent possible and work together with Iraqis on joint patrols on the border. Doing so will help stem the flow of funding, insurgents, and terrorists in and out of Iraq.
- Syria can establish hotlines to exchange information with the Iraqis.
- Syria can increase its political and economic cooperation with Iraq.

4. The Wider Regional Context

The United States will not be able to achieve its goals in the Middle East unless the United States deals directly with the Arab-Israeli conflict.

There must be a renewed and sustained commitment by the United States to a comprehensive Arab-Israeli peace on all fronts: Lebanon, Syria, and President Bush's June 2002 commitment to a two-state solution for Israel and Palestine. This commitment must include direct talks with, by, and between Israel, Lebanon, Palestinians (those who accept Israel's right to exist), and particularly Syria—which is the principal transit point for shipments of weapons to Hezbollah, and which supports radical Palestinian groups.

The United States does its ally Israel no favors in avoiding direct involvement to solve the Arab-Israeli conflict. For several reasons, we should act boldly:

- There is no military solution to this conflict.
- The vast majority of the Israeli body politic is tired of being a nation perpetually at war.
- No American administration—Democratic or Republican—will ever abandon Israel.
- Political engagement and dialogue are essential in the Arab-Israeli dispute because it is an axiom that when the political process breaks down there will be violence on the ground.
- The only basis on which peace can be achieved is that set forth in UN Security Council Resolutions 242 and 338 and in the principle of "land for peace."
- The only lasting and secure peace will be a negotiated peace such as Israel has achieved with Egypt and Jordan.

This effort would strongly support moderate Arab governments in the region, especially the democratically elected government of Lebanon, and the Palestinian Authority under President Mahmoud Abbas.

RECOMMENDATION 13: There must be a renewed and sustained commitment by the United States to a comprehensive Arab-Israeli peace on all fronts: Lebanon and Syria, and President Bush's June 2002 commitment to a two-state solution for Israel and Palestine.

RECOMMENDATION 14: This effort should include—as soon as possible—the unconditional calling and holding of meetings, under the auspices of the United States or the Quartet (i.e., the United States, Russia, European Union, and the United Nations), between Israel and Lebanon and Syria on the one hand, and Israel and Palestinians (who acknowledge Israel's right to exist) on the other. The purpose of these meetings would be to negotiate peace as was done at the Madrid Conference in 1991, and on two separate tracks—one Syrian/Lebanese, and the other Palestinian.

RECOMMENDATION 15: Concerning Syria, some elements of that negotiated peace should be:

- Syria's full adherence to UN Security Council Resolution 1701 of August 2006, which provides the framework for Lebanon to regain sovereign control over its territory.

- Syria's full cooperation with all investigations into political assassinations in Lebanon, especially those of Rafik Hariri and Pierre Gemayel.
- A verifiable cessation of Syrian aid to Hezbollah and the use of Syrian territory for transshipment of Iranian weapons and aid to Hezbollah. (This step would do much to solve Israel's problem with Hezbollah.)
- Syria's use of its influence with Hamas and Hezbollah for the release of the captured Israeli Defense Force soldiers.
- A verifiable cessation of Syrian efforts to undermine the democratically elected government of Lebanon.
- A verifiable cessation of arms shipments from or transiting through Syria for Hamas and other radical Palestinian groups.
- A Syrian commitment to help obtain from Hamas an acknowledgment of Israel's right to exist.
- Greater Syrian efforts to seal its border with Iraq.

RECOMMENDATION 16: In exchange for these actions and in the context of a full and secure peace agreement, the Israelis should return the Golan Heights, with a U.S. security guarantee for Israel that could include an international force on the border, including U.S. troops if requested by both parties.

RECOMMENDATION 17: Concerning the Palestinian issue, elements of that negotiated peace should include:

- Adherence to UN Security Council Resolutions 242 and 338 and to the principle of land for peace, which are the only bases for achieving peace.
- Strong support for Palestinian President Mahmoud Abbas and the Palestinian Authority to take the lead in preparing the way for negotiations with Israel.
- A major effort to move from the current hostilities by consolidating the cease-fire reached between the Palestinians and the Israelis in November 2006.
- Support for a Palestinian national unity government.
- Sustainable negotiations leading to a final peace settlement along the lines of President Bush's two-state solution, which would address the key final status issues of borders, settlements, Jerusalem, the right of return, and the end of conflict.

Afghanistan

At the same time, we must not lose sight of the importance of the situation inside Afghanistan and the renewed threat posed by the Taliban. Afghanistan's borders are porous. If the Taliban were to control more of Afghanistan, it could provide al Qaeda the political space to conduct terrorist operations. This development would destabilize the region and have national security implications for the United States and other countries around the world. Also, the significant increase in poppy production in Afghanistan fuels the illegal drug trade and narco-terrorism.

The huge focus of U.S. political, military, and economic support on Iraq has necessarily diverted attention from Afghanistan. As the United States develops its approach toward Iraq and the Middle East, it must also give priority to the situation in Afghanistan. Doing so may require increased political, security, and military measures.

RECOMMENDATION 18: It is critical for the United States to provide additional political, economic, and military support for Afghanistan, including resources that might become available as combat forces are moved from Iraq.

B. THE INTERNAL APPROACH: HELPING IRAQIS HELP THEMSELVES

The New Diplomatic Offensive will provide the proper external environment and support for the difficult internal steps that the Iraqi government must take to promote national reconciliation, establish security, and make progress on governance.

The most important issues facing Iraq's future are now the responsibility of Iraq's elected leaders. Because of the security and assistance it provides, the United States has a significant role to play. Yet only the government and people of Iraq can make and sustain certain decisions critical to Iraq's future.

1. Performance on Milestones

The United States should work closely with Iraq's leaders to support the achievement of specific objectives—or milestones—on national reconciliation, security, and governance. Miracles cannot be expected, but the people of Iraq have the right to expect action and progress. The Iraqi government needs to show its own citizens—and the citizens of the United States and other countries—that it deserves continued support.

The U.S. government must make clear that it expects action by the Iraqi government to make substantial progress toward these milestones. Such a message can be sent only at the level of our national leaders, and only in person, during direct consultation.

As President Bush's meeting with Prime Minister Maliki in Amman, Jordan demonstrates, it is important for the President to remain in close and frequent contact with the Iraqi leadership. There is no substitute for sustained dialogue at the highest levels of government.

During these high-level exchanges, the United States should lay out an agenda for continued support to help Iraq achieve milestones, as well as underscoring the consequences if Iraq does not act. It should be unambiguous that continued U.S. political, military, and economic support for Iraq depends on the Iraqi government's demonstrating political will and making substantial progress toward the achievement of milestones on national reconciliation, security, and governance. The transfer of command and control over Iraqi security forces units from the United States to Iraq should be influenced by Iraq's performance on milestones.

The United States should also signal that it is seeking broad international support for Iraq on behalf of achieving these milestones. The United States can begin to shape a positive climate for its diplomatic efforts, internationally and within Iraq, through public statements by President Bush that reject the notion that the United States seeks to control Iraq's oil, or seeks permanent military bases within Iraq. However, the United States could consider a request from Iraq for temporary bases.

RECOMMENDATION 19: The President and the leadership of his national security team should remain in close and frequent contact with the Iraqi leadership. These contacts must convey a clear message: there must be action by the Iraqi government to make substantial progress toward the achievement of milestones. In public diplomacy, the President should convey as much detail as possible about the substance of these exchanges in order to keep the American people, the Iraqi people, and the countries in the region well informed.

RECOMMENDATION 20: If the Iraqi government demonstrates political will and makes substantial progress toward the achievement of milestones on national reconciliation, security, and governance, the United States should make clear its willingness to continue training, assistance, and support for Iraq's security forces, and to continue political, military, and economic support for the Iraqi government. As Iraq becomes more capable of governing, defending, and sustaining itself, the U.S. military and civilian presence in Iraq can be reduced.

RECOMMENDATION 21: If the Iraqi government does not make substantial progress toward the achievement of milestones on national reconciliation, security, and governance, the United States should reduce its political, military, or economic support for the Iraqi government.

RECOMMENDATION 22: The President should state that the United States does not seek permanent military bases in Iraq. If the Iraqi government were to request a temporary base or bases, then the U.S. government could consider that request as it would in the case of any other government.

RECOMMENDATION 23: The President should restate that the United States does not seek to control Iraq's oil.

Milestones for Iraq

The government of Iraq understands that dramatic steps are necessary to avert a downward spiral and make progress. Prime Minister Maliki has worked closely in consultation with the United States and has put forward the following milestones in the key areas of national reconciliation, security and governance:

NATIONAL RECONCILIATION

By the end of 2006–early 2007:
- Approval of the Provincial Election Law and setting an election date
- Approval of the Petroleum Law
- Approval of the De-Baathification Law
- Approval of the Militia Law

By March 2007:
- A referendum on constitutional amendments (if it is necessary)

By May 2007:
- Completion of Militia Law implementation
- Approval of amnesty agreement
- Completion of reconciliation efforts

By June 2007:
- Provincial elections

SECURITY (pending joint U.S.-Iraqi review)

By the end of 2006:
- Iraqi increase of 2007 security spending over 2006 levels

By April 2007:
- Iraqi control of the Army

By September 2007:
- Iraqi control of provinces

By December 2007:
- Iraqi security self-reliance (with U.S. support)

GOVERNANCE

By the end of 2006:
- The Central Bank of Iraq will raise interest rates to 20 percent and appreciate the Iraqi dinar by 10 percent to combat accelerating inflation.
- Iraq will continue increasing domestic prices for refined petroleum products and sell imported fuel at market prices.

RECOMMENDATION 24: The contemplated completion dates of the end of 2006 or early 2007 for some milestones may not be realistic. These should be completed by the first quarter of 2007.

RECOMMENDATION 25: These milestones are a good start. The United States should consult closely with the Iraqi government and develop additional milestones in three areas: national reconciliation, security, and improving government services affecting the daily lives of Iraqis. As with the current milestones, these additional milestones should be tied to calendar dates to the fullest extent possible.

2. National Reconciliation

National reconciliation is essential to reduce further violence and maintain the unity of Iraq.

U.S. forces can help provide stability for a time to enable Iraqi leaders to negotiate political solutions, but they cannot stop the violence—or even contain it—if there is no underlying political agreement among Iraqis about the future of their country.

The Iraqi government must send a clear signal to Sunnis that there is a place for them in national life. The government needs to act now, to give a signal of hope. Unless Sunnis believe they can get a fair deal in Iraq through the political process, there is no prospect that the insurgency will end. To strike this fair deal, the Iraqi government and the Iraqi people must address several issues that are critical to the success of national reconciliation and thus to the future of Iraq.

Steps for Iraq to Take on Behalf of National Reconciliation

RECOMMENDATION 26: Constitution review. Review of the constitution is essential to national reconciliation and should be pursued on an urgent basis. The United Nations has expertise in this field, and should play a role in this process.

RECOMMENDATION 27: De-Baathification. Political reconciliation requires the reintegration of Baathists and Arab nationalists into national life, with the leading figures of Saddam Hussein's regime excluded. The United States should encourage the return of qualified Iraqi professionals—Sunni or Shia, nationalist or ex-Baathist, Kurd or Turkmen or Christian or Arab—into the government.

RECOMMENDATION 28: Oil revenue sharing. Oil revenues should accrue to the central government and be shared on the basis of population. No formula that gives control over revenues from future fields to the regions or gives control of oil fields to the regions is compatible with national reconciliation.

RECOMMENDATION 29: Provincial elections. Provincial elections should be held at the earliest possible date. Under the constitution, new provincial elections should have been held already. They are necessary to restore representative government.

RECOMMENDATION 30: Kirkuk. Given the very dangerous situation in Kirkuk, international arbitration is necessary to avert communal violence. Kirkuk's mix of Kurdish, Arab, and Turkmen populations could make it a powder keg. A referendum on the future of Kirkuk (as required by the Iraqi Constitution before the end of 2007) would be explosive and should be delayed. This issue should be placed on the agenda of the International Iraq Support Group as part of the New Diplomatic Offensive.

RECOMMENDATION 31: Amnesty. Amnesty proposals must be far-reaching. Any successful effort at national reconciliation must involve those in the government finding ways and means to reconcile with former bitter enemies.

RECOMMENDATION 32: Minorities. The rights of women and the rights of all minority communities in Iraq, including Turkmen, Chaldeans, Assyrians, Yazidis, Sabeans, and Armenians, must be protected.

RECOMMENDATION 33: Civil society. The Iraqi government should stop using the process of registering nongovernmental organizations as a tool for politicizing or stopping their activities. Registration should be solely an administrative act, not an occasion for government censorship and interference.

Steps for the United States to Take on Behalf of National Reconciliation

The United States can take several steps to assist in Iraq's reconciliation process.

The presence of U.S. forces in Iraq is a key topic of interest in a national reconciliation dialogue. The point is not for the United States to set timetables or deadlines for withdrawal, an approach that we oppose. The point is for the United States and Iraq to make clear their shared interest in the orderly departure of U.S. forces as Iraqi forces take on the security mission. A successful national reconciliation dialogue will advance that departure date.

RECOMMENDATION 34: The question of the future U.S. force presence must be on the table for discussion as the national reconciliation dialogue takes place. Its inclusion will increase the likelihood of participation by insurgents and militia leaders, and thereby increase the possibilities for success.

Violence cannot end unless dialogue begins, and the dialogue must involve those who wield power, not simply those who hold political office. The United States must try to talk directly to Grand Ayatollah Sistani and must consider appointing a high-level American Shia Muslim to serve as an emissary to him. The United States must also try to talk directly to Moqtada al-Sadr, to militia leaders, and to insurgent leaders. The United Nations can help facilitate contacts.

RECOMMENDATION 35: The United States must make active efforts to engage all parties in Iraq, with the exception of al Qaeda. The United States must find a way to talk to Grand Ayatollah Sistani, Moqtada al-Sadr, and militia and insurgent leaders.

The very focus on sectarian identity that endangers Iraq also presents opportunities to seek broader support for a national reconciliation dialogue. Working with Iraqi leaders, the international community and religious leaders can play an important role in fostering dialogue and reconciliation across the sectarian divide. The United States should actively encourage the constructive participation of all who can take part in advancing national reconciliation within Iraq.

RECOMMENDATION 36: The United States should encourage dialogue between sectarian communities, as outlined in the New Diplomatic Offensive above. It should press religious leaders inside and outside Iraq to speak out on behalf of peace and reconciliation.

Finally, amnesty proposals from the Iraqi government are an important incentive in reconciliation talks and they need to be generous. Amnesty proposals to once-bitter enemies will be difficult for the United States to accept, just as they will be difficult for the Iraqis to make. Yet amnesty is an issue to be grappled with by the Iraqis, not by Americans. Despite being politically unpopular—in the United States as well as in Iraq—amnesty is essential if progress is to take place. Iraqi leaders need to be certain that they have U.S. support as they move forward with this critical element of national reconciliation.

RECOMMENDATION 37: Iraqi amnesty proposals must not be undercut in Washington by either the executive or the legislative branch.

Militias and National Reconciliation

The use of force by the government of Iraq is appropriate and necessary to stop militias that act as death squads or use violence against institutions of the state. However, solving the problem of militias requires national reconciliation.

Dealing with Iraq's militias will require long-term attention, and substantial funding will be needed to disarm, demobilize, and reintegrate militia members into civilian society. Around the world, this process of transitioning members of irregular military forces from civil conflict to new lives once a peace settlement takes hold is familiar. The disarmament, demobilization, and reintegration of militias depends on national reconciliation and on confidence-building measures among the parties to that reconciliation.

Both the United Nations and expert and experienced nongovernmental organizations, especially the International Organization for Migration, must be on the ground with appropriate personnel months before any program to disarm, demobilize, and reintegrate militia members begins. Because the United States is a party to the conflict, the U.S. military should not be involved in implementing such a program. Yet U.S. financial and technical support is crucial.

RECOMMENDATION 38: The United States should support the presence of neutral international experts as advisors to the Iraqi government on the processes of disarmament, demobilization, and reintegration.

RECOMMENDATION 39: The United States should provide financial and technical support and establish a single office in Iraq to coordinate assistance to the Iraqi government and its expert advisors to aid a program to disarm, demobilize, and reintegrate militia members.

3. Security and Military Forces

A Military Strategy for Iraq

There is no action the American military can take that, by itself, can bring about success in Iraq. But there are actions that the U.S. and Iraqi governments, working together, can and should take to increase the probability of avoiding disaster there, and increase the chance of success.

The Iraqi government should accelerate the urgently needed national reconciliation program to which it has already committed. And it should accelerate assuming responsibility for Iraqi security by increasing the number and quality of Iraqi Army brigades. As the Iraqi Army increases in size and capability, the Iraqi government should be able to take real responsibility for governance.

While this process is under way, and to facilitate it, the United States should significantly increase the number of U.S. military personnel, including combat troops, imbedded in and supporting Iraqi Army units. As these actions proceed, we could begin to move combat forces out of Iraq. The primary mission of U.S. forces in Iraq should evolve to one of supporting the Iraqi army, which would take over primary responsibility for combat operations. We should continue to maintain support forces, rapid-reaction forces, special operations forces, intelligence units, search-and-rescue units, and force protection units.

While the size and composition of the Iraqi Army is ultimately a matter for the Iraqi government to determine, we should be firm on the urgent near-term need for significant additional trained Army brigades, since this is the key to Iraqis taking over full responsibility for their own security, which they want to do and which we need them to do. It is clear that they will still need security assistance from the United States for some time to come as they work to achieve political and security changes.

One of the most important elements of our support would be the imbedding of substantially more U.S. military personnel in all Iraqi Army battalions and brigades, as well as within Iraqi companies. U.S. personnel would provide advice, combat assistance, and staff assistance. The training of Iraqi units by the United States has improved and should continue for the coming year. In addition to this training, Iraqi combat units need supervised on-the-job training as they move to field operations. This on-the-job training could be best done by imbedding more U.S. military personnel in Iraqi deployed units. The number of imbedded personnel would be based on the recommendation of our military commanders in Iraq, but it should be large enough to accelerate the development of a real combat capability in Iraqi Army units. Such a mission could involve 10,000 to 20,000 American troops instead of the 3,000 to 4,000 now in this role. This increase in imbedded troops could be carried out without an aggregate increase over time in the total number of troops in Iraq by making a corresponding decrease in troops assigned to U.S. combat brigades.

Another mission of the U.S. military would be to assist Iraqi deployed brigades with intelligence, transportation, air support, and logistics support, as well as providing some key equipment.

A vital mission of the U.S. military would be to maintain rapid-reaction teams and special operations teams. These teams would be available to undertake strike missions against al Qaeda in Iraq when the opportunity arises, as well as for other missions considered vital by the U.S. commander in Iraq.

The performance of the Iraqi Army could also be significantly improved if it had improved equipment. One source could be equipment left behind by departing U.S. units. The quickest and most effective way for the Iraqi Army to get the bulk of their equipment would be through our Foreign Military Sales program, which they have already begun to use.

While these efforts are building up, and as additional Iraqi brigades are being deployed, U.S. combat brigades could begin to move out of Iraq. By the first quarter of 2008, subject to unexpected developments in the security situation on the ground, all combat brigades not necessary for force protection could be out of Iraq. At that time, U.S. combat forces in Iraq could be deployed only in units embedded with Iraqi forces, in rapid-reaction and special operations teams, and in training, equipping, advising, force protection, and search and rescue. Intelligence and support efforts would continue. Even after the United States has moved all combat brigades out of Iraq, we would maintain a considerable military presence in the region, with our still significant force in Iraq and with our powerful air, ground, and naval deployments in Kuwait, Bahrain, and Qatar, as well as an increased presence in Afghanistan. These forces would be sufficiently robust to permit the United States, working with the Iraqi government, to accomplish four missions:

- Provide political reassurance to the Iraqi government in order to avoid its collapse and the disintegration of the country.
- Fight al Qaeda and other terrorist organizations in Iraq using special operations teams.
- Train, equip, and support the Iraqi security forces.
- Deter even more destructive interference in Iraq by Syria and Iran.

Because of the importance of Iraq to our regional security goals and to our ongoing fight against al Qaeda, we considered proposals to make a substantial increase (100,000 to 200,000) in the number of U.S. troops in Iraq. We rejected this course because we do not believe that the needed levels are available for a sustained deployment. Further, adding more American troops could conceivably worsen those aspects of the security problem that are fed by the view that the U.S. presence is intended to be a long-term "occupation." We could, however, support a short-term redeployment or surge of American combat forces to stabilize Baghdad, or to speed up the training and equipping mission, if the U.S. commander in Iraq determines that such steps would be effective.

We also rejected the immediate withdrawal of our troops, because we believe that so much is at stake.

We believe that our recommended actions will give the Iraqi Army the support it needs to have a reasonable chance to take responsibility for Iraq's security. Given the ongoing deterioration in the security situation, it is urgent to move as quickly as possible to have that security role taken over by Iraqi security forces.

The United States should not make an open-ended commitment to keep large numbers of American troops deployed in Iraq for three compelling reasons.

First, and most importantly, the United States faces other security dangers in the world, and a continuing Iraqi commitment of American ground forces at present levels will leave no reserve available to meet other contingencies. On September 7, 2006, General James Jones, our NATO commander, called for more troops in Afghanistan, where U.S. and NATO forces are fighting a resurgence of al Qaeda and Taliban forces. The United States should respond positively to that request, and be prepared for other security contingencies, including those in Iran and North Korea.

Second, the long-term commitment of American ground forces to Iraq at current levels is adversely affecting Army readiness, with less than a third of the Army units currently at high readiness levels. The Army is unlikely to be able to meet the next rotation of troops in Iraq without undesirable changes in its deployment practices. The Army is now considering breaking its compact with the National Guard and Reserves that limits the number of years that these citizen-soldiers can be deployed. Behind this short-term strain is the longer-term risk that the ground forces will be impaired in ways that will take years to reverse.

And finally, an open-ended commitment of American forces would not provide the Iraqi government the incentive it needs to take the political actions that give Iraq the best chance of quelling sectarian violence. In the absence of such an incentive, the Iraqi government might continue to delay taking those difficult actions.

While it is clear that the presence of U.S. troops in Iraq is moderating the violence, there is little evidence that the long-term deployment of U.S. troops by itself has led or will lead to fundamental improvements in the security situation. It is important to recognize that there are no risk-free alternatives available to the United States at this time. Reducing our combat troop commitments in Iraq, whenever that occurs, undeniably creates risks, but leaving those forces tied down in Iraq indefinitely creates its own set of security risks.

RECOMMENDATION 40: The United States should not make an open-ended commitment to keep large numbers of American troops deployed in Iraq.

RECOMMENDATION 41: The United States must make it clear to the Iraqi government that the United States could carry out its plans, including planned redeployments, even if Iraq does not implement its planned changes. America's other security needs and the future of our military cannot be made hostage to the actions or inactions of the Iraqi government.

RECOMMENDATION 42: We should seek to complete the training and equipping mission by the first quarter of 2008, as stated by General George Casey on October 24, 2006.

RECOMMENDATION 43: Military priorities in Iraq must change, with the highest priority given to the training, equipping, advising, and support mission and to counterterrorism operations.

RECOMMENDATION 44: The most highly qualified U.S. officers and military personnel should be assigned to the imbedded teams, and American teams should be present with Iraqi units down to the company level. The U.S. military should establish suitable career-enhancing incentives for these officers and personnel.

RECOMMENDATION 45: The United States should support more and better equipment for the Iraqi Army by encouraging the Iraqi government to accelerate its Foreign Military Sales requests and, as American combat brigades move out of Iraq, by leaving behind some American equipment for Iraqi forces.

Restoring the U.S. Military

We recognize that there are other results of the war in Iraq that have great consequence for our nation. One consequence has been the stress and uncertainty imposed on our military—the most professional and proficient military in history. The United States will need its military to protect U.S. security regardless of what happens in Iraq. We therefore considered how to limit the adverse consequences of the strain imposed on our military by the Iraq war.

U.S. military forces, especially our ground forces, have been stretched nearly to the breaking point by the repeated deployments in Iraq, with attendant casualties (almost 3,000 dead and more than 21,000 wounded), greater difficulty in recruiting, and accelerated wear on equipment.

Additionally, the defense budget as a whole is in danger of disarray, as supplemental funding winds down and reset costs become clear. It will be a major challenge to meet ongoing requirements for other current and future security threats that need to be accommodated together with spending for operations and maintenance, reset, personnel, and benefits for active duty and retired personnel. Restoring the capability of our military forces should be a high priority for the United States at this time.

The U.S. military has a long tradition of strong partnership between the civilian leadership of the Department of Defense and the uniformed services. Both have long benefited from a relationship in which the civilian leadership exercises control with the advantage of fully candid professional advice, and the military serves loyally with the understanding that its advice has been heard and valued. That tradition has frayed, and civil-military relations need to be repaired.

RECOMMENDATION 46: The new Secretary of Defense should make every effort to build healthy civil-military relations, by creating an environment in which the senior military feel free to offer independent advice not only to the civilian leadership in the Pentagon but also to the President and the National Security Council, as envisioned in the Goldwater-Nichols legislation.

RECOMMENDATION 47: As redeployment proceeds, the Pentagon leadership should emphasize training and education programs for the forces that have returned to the continental United States in order to "reset" the force and restore the U.S. military to a high level of readiness for global contingencies.

RECOMMENDATION 48: As equipment returns to the United States, Congress should appropriate sufficient funds to restore the equipment to full functionality over the next five years.

RECOMMENDATION 49: The administration, in full consultation with the relevant committees of Congress, should assess the full future budgetary impact of the war in Iraq and its potential impact on the future readiness of the force, the ability to recruit and retain high-quality personnel, needed investments in procurement and in research and development, and the budgets of other U.S. government agencies involved in the stability and reconstruction effort.

4. Police and Criminal Justice

The problems in the Iraqi police and criminal justice system are profound.

The ethos and training of Iraqi police forces must support the mission to "protect and serve" all Iraqis. Today, far too many Iraqi police do not embrace that mission, in part because of problems in how reforms were organized and implemented by the Iraqi and U.S. governments.

Recommended Iraqi Actions

Within Iraq, the failure of the police to restore order and prevent militia infiltration is due, in part, to the poor organization of Iraq's component police forces: the Iraqi National Police, the Iraqi Border Police, and the Iraqi Police Service.

The Iraqi National Police pursue a mission that is more military than domestic in nature—involving commando-style operations—and is thus ill-suited to the Ministry of the Interior. The more natural home for the National Police is within the Ministry of Defense, which should be the authority for counterinsurgency operations and heavily armed forces. Though depriving the Ministry of the Interior of operational forces, this move will place the Iraqi National Police under better and more rigorous Iraqi and U.S. supervision and will enable these units to better perform their counterinsurgency mission.

RECOMMENDATION 50: The entire Iraqi National Police should be transferred to the Ministry of Defense, where the police commando units will become part of the new Iraqi Army.

Similarly, the Iraqi Border Police are charged with a role that bears little resemblance to ordinary policing, especially in light of the current flow of foreign fighters, insurgents, and weaponry across Iraq's borders and the need for joint patrols of the border with foreign militaries. Thus the natural home for the Border Police is within the Ministry of Defense, which should be the authority for controlling Iraq's borders.

RECOMMENDATION 51: The entire Iraqi Border Police should be transferred to the Ministry of Defense, which would have total responsibility for border control and external security.

The Iraqi Police Service, which operates in the provinces and provides local policing, needs to become a true police force. It needs legal authority, training, and equipment to control crime and protect Iraqi citizens. Accomplishing those goals will not be easy, and the presence of American advisors will be required to help the Iraqis determine a new role for the police.

RECOMMENDATION 52: The Iraqi Police Service should be given greater responsibility to conduct criminal investigations and should expand its cooperation with other elements in the Iraqi judicial system in order to better control crime and protect Iraqi civilians.

In order to more effectively administer the Iraqi Police Service, the Ministry of the Interior needs to undertake substantial reforms to purge bad elements and highlight best practices. Once the ministry begins to function effectively, it can exert a positive influence over the provinces and take back some of the authority that was lost to local governments through decentralization. To reduce corruption and militia infiltration, the Ministry of the Interior should take authority from the local governments for the handling of policing funds. Doing so will improve accountability and organizational discipline, limit the authority of provincial police officials, and identify police officers with the central government.

RECOMMENDATION 53: The Iraqi Ministry of the Interior should undergo a process of organizational transformation, including efforts to expand the capability and reach of the current major crime unit (or Criminal Investigation Division) and to exert more authority over local police forces. The sole authority to pay police salaries and disburse financial support to local police should be transferred to the Ministry of the Interior.

Finally, there is no alternative to bringing the Facilities Protection Service under the control of the Iraqi Ministry of the Interior. Simply disbanding these units is not an option, as the members will take their weapons and become full-time militiamen or insurgents. All should be brought under the authority of a reformed Ministry of the Interior. They will need to be vetted, retrained, and closely supervised. Those who are no longer part of the Facilities Protection Service need to participate in a disarmament, demobilization, and reintegration program (outlined above).

RECOMMENDATION 54: The Iraqi Ministry of the Interior should proceed with current efforts to identify, register, and control the Facilities Protection Service.

U.S. Actions

The Iraqi criminal justice system is weak, and the U.S. training mission has been hindered by a lack of clarity and capacity. It has not always been clear who is in charge of the police training mission, and the U.S. military lacks expertise in certain areas pertaining to police and the rule of law. The United States has been more successful in training the Iraqi Army than it has the police. The U.S. Department of Justice has the expertise and capacity to carry out the police training mission. The U.S. Department of Defense is already bearing too much of the burden in Iraq. Meanwhile, the pool of expertise in the United States on policing and the rule of law has been underutilized.

The United States should adjust its training mission in Iraq to match the recommended changes in the Iraqi government—the movement of the National and Border Police to the Ministry of Defense and the new emphasis on the Iraqi Police Service within the Ministry of the Interior. To reflect the reorganization, the Department of Defense would continue to train the Iraqi National and Border Police, and the Department of Justice would become responsible for training the Iraqi Police Service.

RECOMMENDATION 55: The U.S. Department of Defense should continue its mission to train the Iraqi National Police and the Iraqi Border Police, which should be placed within the Iraqi Ministry of Defense.

RECOMMENDATION 56: The U.S. Department of Justice should direct the training mission of the police forces remaining under the Ministry of the Interior.

RECOMMENDATION 57: Just as U.S. military training teams are imbedded within Iraqi Army units, the current practice of imbedding U.S. police trainers should be expanded and the numbers of civilian training officers increased so that teams can cover all levels of the Iraqi Police Service, including local police stations. These trainers should be obtained from among experienced civilian police executives and supervisors from around the world. These officers would replace the military police personnel currently assigned to training teams.

The Federal Bureau of Investigation has provided personnel to train the Criminal Investigation Division in the Ministry of the Interior, which handles major crimes. The FBI has also fielded a large team within Iraq for counterterrorism activities.

Building on this experience, the training programs should be expanded and should include the development of forensic investigation training and facilities that could apply scientific and technical investigative methods to counterterrorism as well as to ordinary criminal activity.

RECOMMENDATION 58: The FBI should expand its investigative and forensic training and facilities within Iraq, to include coverage of terrorism as well as criminal activity.

One of the major deficiencies of the Iraqi Police Service is its lack of equipment, particularly in the area of communications and motor transport.

RECOMMENDATION 59: The Iraqi government should provide funds to expand and upgrade communications equipment and motor vehicles for the Iraqi Police Service.

The Department of Justice is also better suited than the Department of Defense to carry out the mission of reforming Iraq's Ministry of the Interior and Iraq's judicial system. Iraq needs more than training for cops on the beat: it needs courts, trained prosecutors and investigators, and the ability to protect Iraqi judicial officials.

RECOMMENDATION 60: The U.S. Department of Justice should lead the work of organizational transformation in the Ministry of the Interior. This approach must involve Iraqi officials, starting at senior levels and moving down, to create a strategic plan and work out standard administrative procedures, codes of conduct, and operational measures that Iraqis will accept and use. These plans must be drawn up in partnership.

RECOMMENDATION 61: Programs led by the U.S. Department of Justice to establish courts; to train judges, prosecutors, and investigators; and to create institutions and practices to fight corruption must be strongly supported and funded. New and refurbished courthouses with improved physical security, secure housing for judges and judicial staff, witness protection facilities, and a new Iraqi Marshals Service are essential parts of a secure and functioning system of justice.

5. The Oil Sector

Since the success of the oil sector is critical to the success of the Iraqi economy, the United States must do what it can to help Iraq maximize its capability.

Iraq, a country with promising oil potential, could restore oil production from existing fields to 3.0 to 3.5 million barrels a day over a three- to five-year period, depending on evolving conditions in key reservoirs. Even if Iraq were at peace tomorrow, oil production would decline unless current problems in the oil sector were addressed.

Short Term

RECOMMENDATION 62:

- As soon as possible, the U.S. government should provide technical assistance to the Iraqi government to prepare a draft oil law that defines the rights of regional and local governments and creates a fiscal and legal framework for investment. Legal clarity is essential to attract investment.
- The U.S. government should encourage the Iraqi government to accelerate contracting for the comprehensive well work-overs in the southern fields needed to increase production, but the United States should no longer fund such infrastructure projects.
- The U.S. military should work with the Iraqi military and with private security forces to protect oil infrastructure and contractors. Protective measures could include a program to improve pipeline security by paying local tribes solely on the basis of throughput (rather than fixed amounts).

- Metering should be implemented at both ends of the supply line. This step would immediately improve accountability in the oil sector.
- In conjunction with the International Monetary Fund, the U.S. government should press Iraq to continue reducing subsidies in the energy sector, instead of providing grant assistance. Until Iraqis pay market prices for oil products, drastic fuel shortages will remain.

Long Term

Expanding oil production in Iraq over the long term will require creating corporate structures, establishing management systems, and installing competent managers to plan and oversee an ambitious list of major oil-field investment projects.

To improve oil-sector performance, the Study Group puts forward the following recommendations.

RECOMMENDATION 63:

- The United States should encourage investment in Iraq's oil sector by the international community and by international energy companies.
- The United States should assist Iraqi leaders to reorganize the national oil industry as a commercial enterprise, in order to enhance efficiency, transparency, and accountability.
- To combat corruption, the U.S. government should urge the Iraqi government to post all oil contracts, volumes, and prices on the Web so that Iraqis and outside observers can track exports and export revenues.
- The United States should support the World Bank's efforts to ensure that best practices are used in contracting. This support involves providing Iraqi officials with contracting templates and training them in contracting, auditing, and reviewing audits.
- The United States should provide technical assistance to the Ministry of Oil for enhancing maintenance, improving the payments process, managing cash flows, contracting and auditing, and updating professional training programs for management and technical personnel. . . .

SOURCE: U.S. United States Institute of Peace, Iraq Study Group, "The Iraq Study Group Report," www.usip.org/isg/iraq_study_group_report/report/1206/iraq_study_group_report.pdf.

DOCUMENT

Bush Announces His Plan for a Troop "Surge" in Iraq

JANUARY 10, 2007

THE PRESIDENT: Good evening. Tonight in Iraq, the Armed Forces of the United States are engaged in a struggle that will determine the direction of the global war on terror—and our safety here at home. The new strategy I outline tonight will change America's course in Iraq, and help us succeed in the fight against terror.

When I addressed you just over a year ago, nearly 12 million Iraqis had cast their ballots for a unified and democratic nation. The elections of 2005 were a stunning achievement. We thought that these elections would bring the Iraqis together, and that as we trained Iraqi security forces we could accomplish our mission with fewer American troops.

But in 2006, the opposite happened. The violence in Iraq—particularly in Baghdad—overwhelmed the political gains the Iraqis had made. Al Qaeda terrorists and Sunni insurgents recognized the mortal danger that Iraq's elections posed for their cause, and they responded with outrageous acts of murder aimed at innocent Iraqis. They blew up one of the holiest shrines in Shia Islam—the Golden Mosque of Samarra—in a calculated effort to provoke Iraq's Shia population to retaliate. Their strategy worked. Radical Shia elements, some supported by Iran, formed death squads. And the result was a vicious cycle of sectarian violence that continues today.

The situation in Iraq is unacceptable to the American people—and it is unacceptable to me. Our troops in Iraq have fought bravely. They have done everything we have asked them to do. Where mistakes have been made, the responsibility rests with me.

It is clear that we need to change our strategy in Iraq. So my national security team, military commanders, and diplomats conducted a comprehensive review. We consulted members of Congress from both parties, our allies abroad, and distinguished outside experts. We benefited from the thoughtful recommendations of the Iraq Study Group, a bipartisan panel led by former Secretary of State James Baker and former Congressman Lee Hamilton. In our discussions, we all agreed that there is no magic formula for success in Iraq. And one message came through loud and clear: Failure in Iraq would be a disaster for the United States.

The consequences of failure are clear: Radical Islamic extremists would grow in strength and gain new recruits. They would be in a better position to topple moderate governments, create chaos in the region, and use oil revenues to fund their ambitions. Iran would be emboldened in its pursuit of nuclear weapons. Our enemies would have a safe haven from which to plan and launch attacks on the American people. On September the 11th, 2001, we saw what a refuge for extremists on the other side of the world could bring to the streets of our own cities. For the safety of our people, America must succeed in Iraq.

The most urgent priority for success in Iraq is security, especially in Baghdad. Eighty percent of Iraq's sectarian violence occurs within 30 miles of the capital. This violence is splitting Baghdad into sectarian enclaves, and shaking the confidence of all Iraqis. Only Iraqis can end the sectarian violence and secure their people. And their government has put forward an aggressive plan to do it.

Our past efforts to secure Baghdad failed for two principal reasons: There were not enough Iraqi and American troops to secure neighborhoods that had been cleared of terrorists and insurgents. And there were too many restrictions on the troops we did have. Our military commanders reviewed the new Iraqi plan to ensure that it addressed these mistakes. They report that it does. They also report that this plan can work.

Now let me explain the main elements of this effort: The Iraqi government will appoint a military commander and two deputy commanders for their capital. The Iraqi government will deploy Iraqi Army and National Police brigades across Baghdad's nine districts. When these forces are fully deployed, there will be 18 Iraqi Army and National Police brigades committed to this effort, along with local police. These Iraqi forces will operate from local police stations—conducting patrols and setting up checkpoints, and going door-to-door to gain the trust of Baghdad residents.

This is a strong commitment. But for it to succeed, our commanders say the Iraqis will need our help. So America will change our strategy to help the Iraqis carry out their campaign to put down sectarian violence and bring security to the people of Baghdad. This will require increasing American force levels. So I've committed more than 20,000 additional American troops to Iraq. The vast majority of them—five brigades—will be deployed to Baghdad. These troops will work alongside Iraqi units and be embedded in their formations.

Our troops will have a well-defined mission: to help Iraqis clear and secure neighborhoods, to help them protect the local population, and to help ensure that the Iraqi forces left behind are capable of providing the security that Baghdad needs.

Many listening tonight will ask why this effort will succeed when previous operations to secure Baghdad did not. Well, here are the differences: In earlier operations, Iraqi and American forces cleared many neighborhoods of terrorists and insurgents, but when our forces moved on to other targets, the killers returned. This time, we'll have the force levels we need to hold the areas that have been cleared. In earlier operations, political and sectarian interference prevented Iraqi and American forces from going into neighborhoods that are home to those fueling the sectarian violence. This time, Iraqi and American forces will have a green light to enter those neighborhoods—and Prime Minister Maliki has pledged that political or sectarian interference will not be tolerated.

I've made it clear to the Prime Minister and Iraq's other leaders that America's commitment is not open-ended. If the Iraqi government does not follow through on its promises, it will lose the support of the American people—and it will lose the support of the Iraqi people. Now is the time to act. The Prime Minister understands this. Here is what he told his people just last week: "The Baghdad security plan will not provide a safe haven for any outlaws, regardless of [their] sectarian or political affiliation."

This new strategy will not yield an immediate end to suicide bombings, assassinations, or IED attacks. Our enemies in Iraq will make every effort to ensure that our television screens are filled with images of death and suffering. Yet over time, we can expect to see Iraqi troops chasing down murderers, fewer brazen acts of terror, and growing trust and cooperation from Baghdad's residents. When this happens, daily life will improve, Iraqis will gain confidence in their leaders, and the government will have the breathing space it needs to make progress in other critical areas. Most of Iraq's Sunni and Shia want to live together in peace—and reducing the violence in Baghdad will help make reconciliation possible.

A successful strategy for Iraq goes beyond military operations. Ordinary Iraqi citizens must see that military operations are accompanied by visible improvements in their neighborhoods and communities. So America will hold the Iraqi government to the benchmarks it has announced.

To establish its authority, the Iraqi government plans to take responsibility for security in all of Iraq's provinces by November. To give every Iraqi citizen a stake in the country's economy, Iraq will pass legislation to share oil revenues among all Iraqis. To show that it is committed to delivering a better life, the Iraqi government will spend $10 billion of its own money on reconstruction and infrastructure projects that will create new jobs. To empower local leaders, Iraqis plan to hold provincial elections later this year. And to allow more Iraqis to re-enter their nation's political life, the government will reform de-Baathification laws, and establish a fair process for considering amendments to Iraq's constitution.

America will change our approach to help the Iraqi government as it works to meet these benchmarks. In keeping with the recommendations of the Iraq Study Group, we will increase the embedding of American advisers in Iraqi Army units, and partner a coalition brigade with every Iraqi Army division. We will help the Iraqis build a larger and better-equipped army, and we will accelerate the training of Iraqi forces, which remains the essential U.S. security mission in Iraq. We will give our commanders and civilians greater flexibility to spend funds for economic assistance. We will double the number of provincial reconstruction teams. These teams bring together military and civilian experts to help local Iraqi communities pursue reconciliation, strengthen the moderates, and speed the transition to Iraqi self-reliance. And Secretary Rice will soon appoint a reconstruction coordinator in Baghdad to ensure better results for economic assistance being spent in Iraq.

As we make these changes, we will continue to pursue al Qaeda and foreign fighters. Al Qaeda is still active in Iraq. Its home base is Anbar Province. Al Qaeda has helped make Anbar the most violent area of Iraq outside the capital. A captured al Qaeda document describes the terrorists' plan to infiltrate and seize control of the province. This would bring al Qaeda closer to its goals of taking down Iraq's democracy, building a radical Islamic empire, and launching new attacks on the United States at home and abroad.

Our military forces in Anbar are killing and capturing al Qaeda leaders, and they are protecting the local population. Recently, local tribal leaders have begun to show their willingness to take on al Qaeda. And as a result, our commanders believe we have an opportunity to deal a serious blow to the terrorists. So I have given orders to increase American forces in Anbar Province by 4,000 troops. These troops will work with Iraqi and tribal forces to keep up the pressure on the terrorists. America's men and women in uniform took away al Qaeda's safe haven in Afghanistan—and we will not allow them to re-establish it in Iraq.

Succeeding in Iraq also requires defending its territorial integrity and stabilizing the region in the face of extremist challenges. This begins with addressing Iran and

Syria. These two regimes are allowing terrorists and insurgents to use their territory to move in and out of Iraq. Iran is providing material support for attacks on American troops. We will disrupt the attacks on our forces. We'll interrupt the flow of support from Iran and Syria. And we will seek out and destroy the networks providing advanced weaponry and training to our enemies in Iraq.

We're also taking other steps to bolster the security of Iraq and protect American interests in the Middle East. I recently ordered the deployment of an additional carrier strike group to the region. We will expand intelligence-sharing and deploy Patriot air defense systems to reassure our friends and allies. We will work with the governments of Turkey and Iraq to help them resolve problems along their border. And we will work with others to prevent Iran from gaining nuclear weapons and dominating the region.

We will use America's full diplomatic resources to rally support for Iraq from nations throughout the Middle East. Countries like Saudi Arabia, Egypt, Jordan, and the Gulf States need to understand that an American defeat in Iraq would create a new sanctuary for extremists and a strategic threat to their survival. These nations have a stake in a successful Iraq that is at peace with its neighbors, and they must step up their support for Iraq's unity government. We endorse the Iraqi government's call to finalize an International Compact that will bring new economic assistance in exchange for greater economic reform. And on Friday, Secretary Rice will leave for the region, to build support for Iraq and continue the urgent diplomacy required to help bring peace to the Middle East.

The challenge playing out across the broader Middle East is more than a military conflict. It is the decisive ideological struggle of our time. On one side are those who believe in freedom and moderation. On the other side are extremists who kill the innocent, and have declared their intention to destroy our way of life. In the long run, the most realistic way to protect the American people is to provide a hopeful alternative to the hateful ideology of the enemy, by advancing liberty across a troubled region. It is in the interests of the United States to stand with the brave men and women who are risking their lives to claim their freedom, and to help them as they work to raise up just and hopeful societies across the Middle East.

From Afghanistan to Lebanon to the Palestinian Territories, millions of ordinary people are sick of the violence, and want a future of peace and opportunity for their children. And they are looking at Iraq. They want to know: Will America withdraw and yield the future of that country to the extremists, or will we stand with the Iraqis who have made the choice for freedom?

The changes I have outlined tonight are aimed at ensuring the survival of a young democracy that is fighting for its life in a part of the world of enormous importance to American security. Let me be clear: The terrorists and insurgents in Iraq are without conscience, and they will make the year ahead bloody and violent. Even if our new strategy works exactly as planned, deadly acts of violence will continue—and we must expect more Iraqi and American casualties. The question is whether our new strategy will bring us closer to success. I believe that it will.

Victory will not look like the ones our fathers and grandfathers achieved. There will be no surrender ceremony on the deck of a battleship. But victory in Iraq will bring something new in the Arab world—a functioning democracy that polices its territory, upholds the rule of law, respects fundamental human liberties, and answers to its people. A democratic Iraq will not be perfect. But it will be a country that fights terrorists instead of harboring them—and it will help bring a future of peace and security for our children and our grandchildren.

This new approach comes after consultations with Congress about the different courses we could take in Iraq. Many are concerned that the Iraqis are becoming too dependent on the United States, and therefore, our policy should focus on protecting Iraq's borders and hunting down al Qaeda. Their solution is to scale back America's efforts in Baghdad—or announce the phased withdrawal of our combat forces. We carefully considered these proposals. And we concluded that to step back now would force a collapse of the Iraqi government, tear the country apart, and result in mass killings on an unimaginable scale. Such a scenario would result in our troops being forced to stay in Iraq even longer, and confront an enemy that is even more lethal. If we increase our support at this crucial moment, and help the Iraqis break the current cycle of violence, we can hasten the day our troops begin coming home.

In the days ahead, my national security team will fully brief Congress on our new strategy. If members have improvements that can be made, we will make them. If circumstances change, we will adjust. Honorable people have different views, and they will voice their criticisms. It is fair to hold our views up to scrutiny. And all involved have a responsibility to explain how the path they propose would be more likely to succeed.

Acting on the good advice of Senator Joe Lieberman and other key members of Congress, we will form a new, bipartisan working group that will help us come together across party lines to win the war on terror. This group will meet regularly with me and my administration; it will help strengthen our relationship with Congress. We can begin by working together to increase the size of the active Army and Marine Corps, so that America has the Armed Forces we need for the 21st century. We also need to examine ways to mobilize talented American civilians to deploy overseas, where they can help build democratic institutions in communities and nations recovering from war and tyranny.

In these dangerous times, the United States is blessed to have extraordinary and selfless men and women willing to step forward and defend us. These young Americans understand that our cause in Iraq is noble and necessary—and that the advance of freedom is the calling of our time. They serve far from their families, who make the quiet sacrifices of lonely holidays and empty chairs at the dinner table. They have watched their comrades give their lives to ensure our liberty. We mourn the loss of every fallen American—and we owe it to them to build a future worthy of their sacrifice. Fellow citizens: The year ahead will demand more patience, sacrifice, and resolve. It can be tempting to think that America can put aside the burdens of freedom. Yet times of testing reveal the character of a nation. And throughout our history, Americans have always defied the pessimists and seen our faith in freedom redeemed. Now America is engaged in a new struggle that will set the course for a new century. We can, and we will, prevail.

We go forward with trust that the Author of Liberty will guide us through these trying hours. Thank you and good night.

SOURCE: The White House, Office of the Press Secretary, www.whitehouse.gov/news/releases/2007/01/20070110-7.html.

Afghanistan

CHAPTER 7 DOCUMENTS

                                                                 CHAPTER 7

Overview

During the last two decades of the twentieth century, Afghanistan certainly would have appeared on any list of the world's most conflicted countries. Since a political coup in 1973, Afghanistan has experienced almost unending political turmoil, foreign occupation, and civil war. Something of a respite arrived early in the twenty-first century, when a new, democratically elected government took office and obtained international support for reconstruction of the country. A resurgence of violence in 2006, however, raised new doubts about whether Afghanistan could escape the demons of its past.

From Alexander the Great in ancient times to the British and the Soviets more recently, Afghanistan has been the target of empire builders, not for its natural resources—of which it has none of significant commercial value—but because of its location at the intersections of Central Asia, East Asia, South Asia, and the Middle East. For a century, between the mid-1700s and the mid-1800s, Afghanistan and the rest of Central Asia stood at the center of the "Great Game," a geopolitical contest between Britain and czarist Russia. The Russians looked to expand to the south, in part to reach warm-water ports, and the British wanted to protect India, the recently acquired crown jewel of their empire. The Russians gained some control over most of Central Asia—the area now consisting of Kazakhstan, Kyrgyzstan, Tajikistan, Turkmenistan, and Uzbekistan—but the British held much of Afghanistan into the early twentieth century, punctuated by three bloody Anglo-Afghan wars.

Despite, or perhaps partly because of, its geographic desirability, Afghanistan developed a well-deserved reputation as a place that most rulers, especially outsiders, found difficult to control. In recent times, nearly everyone who tried to govern Afghanistan ultimately came to grief. Only the local Pashtun kings, the Durrani, who created Afghanistan as an independent country in the mid-eighteenth century, endured for long. The last Durrani king, Mohammad Zahir Shah, ruled for forty years until ousted by his cousin Mohammad Daoud in 1973. The deposed king lived a long life, however, and returned as the symbolic "father of the nation" in 2002 to bless the new democratic government, headed by Hamid Karzai, a fellow Pashtun. Zahir Shah died in 2007, at the age of ninety-two.

                                                                                      565

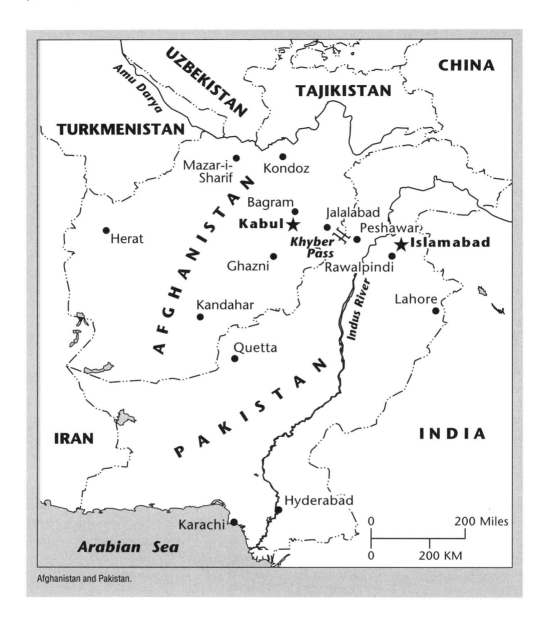

Afghanistan and Pakistan.

The 1973 coup that send Zahir Shah into exile in Italy proved to be the beginning of Afghanistan's most recent descent into tragedy. Daoud at first turned Afghanistan leftward but was himself pushed from power five years later by local communist leaders under the strong influence of Moscow. After these leaders turned against one another in 1979, the Soviet Union intervened to save the teetering communist regime on its southern flank.

In what turned out to be the last gasp of the cold war, Kremlin leaders sent tens of thousands of troops into Afghanistan, where they became mired in a hopeless conflict to save an unpopular government. The United States and an unlikely array of allies, including China, India, Pakistan, and Saudi Arabia, provided weapons and logistical support to thousands of Afghan guerrillas who battled the Soviet army to a standoff. Many of these guerrillas were radical Islamists who accepted the outside aid as a matter of expediency and later turned on their benefactors, particularly the United States.

Moscow withdrew its last soldiers from Afghanistan in February 1989, six months before the fall of the Berlin Wall, the climactic event that led two years later to the collapse of the Soviet Union itself. The Soviet withdrawal, however, brought more war, not peace, to Afghanistan. The communist government that Moscow had propped up for eight years managed to hold on for three more years, largely with Soviet economic and military assistance. A fractious coalition of Afghan guerrillas pushed the communists from Kabul in 1992, only to create another period of civil war in which various factions battled for power and territory.

The ultimate victor of that conflict was perhaps the most unlikely: a group of Muslim students, many from Pakistan, known as the Taliban. United by religious fervor, and armed and guided by Pakistan's military intelligence service, the Taliban scored one victory after another during 1995 and 1996 and finally succeeded in capturing Kabul in September 1996. Once in power, the Taliban imposed their extreme interpretations of Islam on the 90 percent or so of the country they ruled, barring women from working or attending school, for example, and measuring the worth— that is, piety—of a man by the length of his beard. (The Taliban considered shaving to be an expression of vanity and therefore an affront to Islam.) Pakistan emerged as the key outside actor in Afghanistan's affairs during the rule of the Taliban. Military aid from Pakistan's army helped keep the Taliban in power, and Pakistan tried to use its limited influence to protect the Taliban diplomatically, notably when critics in the West questioned their adherence to contemporary human rights standards. For a time, this relationship put to rest a dispute arising from the nineteenth century, when the British drew a border that put some ethnic Pashtuns in Afghanistan and the rest of them in the northern part of India that later became Pakistan. Because the Taliban were Pashtuns, and because they were so heavily dependent on Pakistan, the old border dispute no longer seemed quite as important.

Even Pakistan, however, could not protect the Taliban against the wrath of the United States. Washington first became irate about the Taliban in 1998, not so much because of the government's domestic policies, but because it allowed the al-Qaida network to operate freely on Afghan territory. In August 1998, al-Qaida members bombed the U.S. embassies in Kenya and Tanzania, killing more than 250 people, most of them Africans. President Bill Clinton retaliated by ordering the bombing of al-Qaida training camps in Afghanistan. The bombing destroyed camps and killed about two dozen people, but al-Qaida leader Osama bin Laden and his top aides escaped unharmed. Two years later, on October 12, 2000, al-Qaida operatives bombed the USS *Cole* in the harbor of Aden, Yemen, killing seventeen American sailors and wounding thirty-seven others. U.S. officials later alleged that the bombing was, at least in part, revenge for Clinton's attack on al-Qaida camps in Afghanistan.

Al-Qaida carried out an even bigger attack against the United States on September 11, 2001, destroying the World Trade Center towers in New York City and damaging the Pentagon outside Washington. In response, President George W. Bush ordered the Taliban to hand over bin Laden and his al-Qaida colleagues to the United States. The Taliban refused, and Bush ordered an invasion of Afghanistan, quickly forcing the Taliban from power. The invasion failed to achieve a key objective, however: bin Laden and top al-Qaida and Taliban officials, along with many of their fighters, escaped into the mountains of eastern and southern Afghanistan and into Pakistan as well.

Aided by the United Nations, with financing from the United States and other countries, leaders of Afghanistan's ethnic and tribal groups in December 2001 agreed on an arrangement for an interim government, to be followed by elections for a permanent new government. Karzai, a leader of one of the most prominent Pashtun families and a man well known in Western circles, emerged as the leader of the new government, winning the presidency in 2004 in Afghanistan's first truly free elections. In balloting the following year, Afghans chose a diverse group of representatives for a new two-house parliament. When the legislators convened in December 2005, former warlords sat next to Western-educated intellectuals, several dozen women, and a few former members of the Taliban.

Even with billions of dollars in Western aid, the new government struggled to overcome decades of destruction and provide the services necessary to make the society whole. Meanwhile, Taliban fighters, who had been pushed from power but not defeated in 2001, gradually regrouped. By 2006 the Taliban had reemerged as a major threat, particularly in their home base in southern Afghanistan. The United States and its NATO allies, who still provided most of Afghanistan's security, suddenly found themselves deploying more troops in an attempt to prevent the country from sliding into chaos once again.

Soviet Invasion of Afghanistan

DOCUMENT IN CONTEXT

Afghanistan's role in the closing chapters of the cold war began in July 1973, when Mohammad Daoud mounted a coup against the government led by King Mohammad Zahir Shah, his cousin. Daoud, who had served as prime minister for ten years before the king ousted him in 1963, had backing for his coup from army officers trained in the Soviet Union and one of the two main factions in the local communist party, the People's Democratic Party of Afghanistan (PDPA). This faction, headed by Babrak Karmal, was known as the Parcham, or Red Banner. After the coup, Daoud headed a coalition government that included Karmal and several ministers from the Parcham faction.

For a variety of reasons, Daoud gradually pushed his communist colleagues from government and sought to distance Afghanistan from the Soviet Union. At the same time, in the mid-1970s, Moscow pressured the two competing communist factions in Afghanistan to unite, presumably to strengthen the possibility of their taking power. The Soviets' effort succeeded, at least superficially, when in July 1977 Karmal's Parcham faction united with the opposing Kalq (Masses) faction headed by Mohammad Taraki, who became the leader of the unified PDPA party. Another central actor, Hafizullah Amin, the number two figure in the Kalq faction, became head of the party's military wing.

On April 27, 1978, the united communist party ousted Daoud's government. The exact origins of the coup remain in dispute, but in any case, the Soviet Union moved quickly to take advantage of the situation by sending several hundred military advisors to Kabul, along with hundreds of millions of dollars worth of military supplies. Moscow later signed a "friendship and cooperation" treaty with the new government in Kabul.

A split soon developed between the communist factions along old lines, however, and by the middle of 1978 Karmal and several other leaders of the Kalq faction had been ousted from power. Karmal was sent into exile as ambassador to Czechoslovakia. Meanwhile, Taraki's government faced a rapidly growing insurgency from tribal leaders and other conservative factions in the countryside who had been angered by a series of decrees that flouted traditional Afghan and Islamic customs on such matters as land ownership and family and marriage practices. These decrees appeared to be the work primarily of Amin, the Kalq faction official who by this time had become a senior leader in Taraki's government.

In February 1979, antigovernment insurgents kidnapped and then killed Adolph Dubs, the U.S. ambassador to Kabul. The administration of President Jimmy Carter, accusing the Afghan government of failing to protect Dubs, cut off the limited aid it had been providing Kabul. Over the summer of 1979, the Carter administration secretly began providing medical supplies and other nonmilitary aid to antigovernment insurgents in Afghanistan. Most of this aid flowed through Pakistan and was accompanied by public warnings from the White House against direct Soviet intervention on behalf of the Kabul government.

In mid-September 1979, however, Amin ousted Taraki as head of the Kabul government. This angered Soviet officials, who blamed Amin for the decrees that had led to the insurgency, which by this time was gaining in strength and threatening the communist government's hold on Afghanistan. In response to Amin's takeover, Moscow began boosting its already sizable military presence in the country in late November 1979. By mid-December three battalions of the Soviet army (totaling more than 5,000 troops) were in Afghanistan, and U.S. intelligence agencies observed heightened activity at Soviet military bases in Central Asia.

The level of Soviet intervention suddenly jumped on December 24, 1979, when several thousand Soviet paratroopers began landing in Kabul for what was called a military exercise. Two days later, Soviet special forces troops took control of Kabul, killed Amin, and installed Babrak Karmal as prime minister. A much larger invasion of Soviet ground forces began on December 27, reaching at least 40,000 troops by early January 1980 and more than double that number by the end of 1980. (Their numbers would continue to grow.) In a statement delivered over Kabul Radio on December 27, Karmal made no mention of the Soviet presence and insisted that a wide range of Afghan people had risen up against Amin and his fellow "agents of United States imperialism."

In the immediate aftermath of the invasion, the Kremlin appeared to be satisfied with the outcome. On December 31, four senior officials sent their fellow Politburo members a secret memorandum reporting that "broad masses" of the Afghan people had greeted the overthrow of Amin with "unconcealed joy." The memo—made public in the early 1990s—also offered a detailed justification for the invasion, stating that under Amin, "dictatorial methods of running the country, repressions, mass executions, and disregard for legal norms have produced widespread discontent in the country." These events made it necessary for Moscow "to render additional military assistance to Afghanistan," the memo said.

International Reaction

To much of the world, the Soviet invasion of Afghanistan at first appeared to be a mystifying event involving the replacement of one communist government with another. It quickly became apparent, however, that officials in the Kremlin had acted to avert increasing instability in Afghanistan that might lead to the collapse of the pro-Soviet government there. In a January 12, 1980, interview with TASS, the Soviet news agency, Soviet leader Leonid Brezhnev said that a "well advanced plot by external forces of reaction created a real threat that Afghanistan would lose its independence and be turned into an imperialist military bridgehead on our country's southern border."

Kremlin officials probably believed that they were acting at an opportune moment: the taking of American diplomats as hostages in Iran the previous month continued to occupy Washington's attention in December 1979. With President Carter and his administration focused intently on events in Tehran, which directly threatened U.S. interests in an important part of the world, officials in Moscow may have assumed that the invasion of Afghanistan would not cause a major international uproar. In his TASS interview, Brezhnev insisted that the United States and its allies should not be concerned because their interests "are not affected in any way by the events in Afghanistan" (Iranian Hostage Crisis, p. 383).

Carter was, however, concerned about the events in Afghanistan, and said so loudly and repeatedly, even stating that the Soviet invasion had changed his thinking about the Kremlin's overall intentions. A week after the invasion, Carter asked the Senate to delay consideration of the pending U.S.-Soviet SALT II arms control treaty "so that the Congress and I can assess Soviet actions." The treaty—which already faced strong opposition in the Senate—went unratified. (It was replaced by other treaties during the 1980s.)

On January 4, 1980, Carter addressed the nation from the White House, denouncing the Soviet invasion as "an extremely serious threat to peace because of the threat of further Soviet expansion into neighboring countries in Southwest Asia and also because such an aggressive military policy is unsettling to other peoples throughout the world." Carter continued to ratchet up the rhetoric, saying in a January 20, 1980, television interview that the Soviet invasion was "the most serious threat to peace since the second world war."

Three days later, in his State of the Union address on January 23, Carter directly warned Moscow against attempting to expand its reach into the Persian Gulf, an area of greater concern to the United States than Afghanistan. In what became known as the Carter Doctrine, the president said, "An attempt by any outside force to gain control of the Persian Gulf region will be regarded as an assault on the vital interests of the United States of America, and such an assault will be repelled by any means necessary, including military force." Carter also declared Pakistan to be a "front-line state" facing communist aggression because of the Soviet presence in Afghanistan. This assessment meant Pakistan could again receive U.S. military aid, which Washington had suspended early in 1979 to punish Islamabad for its apparent efforts to acquire nuclear weapons. The invasion of Afghanistan brought the Soviets condemnation from around the world, not just from Washington. Leaders of the Organization of the Islamic Conference, a group of majority-Muslim nations, denounced the invasion twice during 1980, in January calling it a "flagrant violation of international law" and the following May calling for international mediation to restore local rule in Afghanistan. With veto power on the UN Security Council, the Soviet Union blocked criticism of the invasion in that forum, but it could not head off action by the General Assembly, which repeatedly passed resolutions calling for a Soviet withdrawal.

Aid to the Afghan Resistance

Over the long term, the most effective opposition to the Soviet presence in Afghanistan proved not to be rhetoric, but fierce resistance by rebels in Afghanistan supplied with a large amount of military assistance from the United States and other countries. Throughout the 1980s, Afghan fighters representing a variety of ethnic and political groups mounted guerrilla attacks against the Soviet army. These relentless operations caused thousands of deaths and severely undermined the determination of Kremlin officials and public morale in the Soviet Union. Just as the United States had gotten itself into a quagmire in Vietnam two decades earlier, the Soviet Union found itself facing a similarly hopeless situation in Afghanistan.

Brezhnev had ruefully noted in his January 12 TASS interview defending the invasion that guerrillas opposed to the communist government in Kabul had been active since shortly after the April 1978 coup. Seeking to defend their homeland against the foreign invaders, thousands more Afghans flocked to the rebel groups. Starting in 1980, the United States and an unlikely coalition including China, Egypt, Iran, and Saudi Arabia provided money, weapons, and logistical support to the guerrillas, who called themselves the *mujahidin,* or freedom fighters. Most of this aid flowed through Pakistan's military intelligence service. The effectiveness of the guerrillas increased markedly after May 1985, when seven diverse groups, all based in Peshawar, Pakistan, agreed to coordinate their anti-Soviet activities in Afghanistan (Soviet Withdrawal from Afghanistan, p. 580).

> *Following are a memorandum, dated December 31, 1979, from four senior Soviet officials—Defense Minister Dmitri Ustinov, KGB chairman Yuri Andropov, Foreign Minister Andrei Gromyko, and Central Committee International Department chairman Boris Ponomarev—reporting on events in Afghanistan on December 27–28, 1979; a televised speech delivered on January 4, 1980, by U.S. president Jimmy Carter on the Soviet invasion of Afghanistan; and an interview of Communist Party general secretary Leonid Brezhnev conducted by the Soviet Union's news agency, Tass, on January 12, 1980, on the invasion.*

DOCUMENT

Soviet Memorandum on the Invasion of Afghanistan

DECEMBER 31, 1979

After a coup-d'etat and the murder of the CC PDPA [Central Committee of the Peoples Democratic Party of Afghanistan] General and Secretary and Chairman of the Revolutionary Council N. M. [Nur Muhammad] Taraki, committed by H. [Hafizullah] Amin in September of this year, the situation in Afghanistan has been sharply exacerbated and taken on crisis proportions.

H. Amin has established a regime of personal dictatorship in the country, effectively reducing the CC PDPA and the Revolutionary Council to the status of entirely nominal organs. The top leadership positions within the party and the state were filled with appointees bearing family ties or maintaining personal loyalties to H. Amin. Many members from the ranks of the CC PDPA, the Revolutionary Council and the Afghan government were expelled and arrested. Repression and physical annihilation were for the most part directed toward active participants in the April revolution [a coup that brought Taraki to power the previous April], persons openly sympathetic to the USSR, those defending the Leninist norms of intra-party life. H. Amin deceived the party and the people with his announcements that the Soviet Union had supposedly approved of Taraki's expulsion from party and government.

By direct order of H. Amin, fabricated rumors were deliberately spread throughout the DRA [Democratic Republic of Afghanistan], smearing the Soviet Union and casting a shadow on the activities of Soviet personnel in Afghanistan, who had been restricted in their efforts to maintain contact with Afghan representatives.

At the same time, efforts were made to mend relations with America as part of the "more balanced foreign policy strategy" adopted by H. Amin. H. Amin held a series of confidential meetings with the American charge d'affaires in Kabul. The DRA government began to create favorable conditions for the operation of the American cultural center; under H. Amin's directive, the DRA special services have ceased operations against the American embassy.

H. Amin attempted to buttress his position by reaching compromises with leaders of internal counter-revolution. Through trusted persons he engaged in contact with leaders of the Moslem fundamentalist opposition.

The scale of political oppression was taking on increasingly mass proportions. Just during the period following the events of September, more than 600 members of the PDPA, military personnel and other persons suspected of anti-Amin sentiments were executed without trial or investigation. In effect, the objective was to liquidate the party.

All this, in conjunction with objective difficulties and conditions specific to Afghanistan, put the progress of the revolutionary process in extremely difficult circumstances and emerged the counter-revolutionary forces which have effectively disestablished their control in many of the country's provinces. Using external support, which has taken on increasingly far-reaching proportions under Amin, they strived to bring about radical change in the country's political-military situation and liquidate the revolutionary gains.

Dictatorial methods of running the country, repressions, mass executions, and disregard for legal norms have produced widespread discontent in the country. In the capital numerous leaflets began to appear, exposing the anti-people nature of the current regime and containing calls for unity in the struggle with "H. Amin's clique." Discontent also spread to the army. A significant number of officers have expressed dismay at the domination of H. Amin's incompetent henchmen. In essence, a broad anti-Amin front was formed in the country.

Expressing alarm over the fate of the revolution and the independence of the country, and reacting keenly to the rise of anti-Amin sentiments in Afghanistan, Karmal Babrak [sic] and Asadulla Sarwari, both living abroad as émigrés, have undertaken to unite all anti-Amin groups in the country and abroad, in order to save the motherland and the revolution. In addition, the currently underground group "Parcham," [one faction of the communist party] under the leadership of an illegal CC [central committee], has carried out significant work to rally all progressive forces, including Taraki supporters from the former "Kalq" group [the other faction of the communist party].

All earlier disagreements were eliminated and the previously existing schism in the PDPA has been liquidated. Kalqists (represented by Sarwari) and Parchamists (represented by Babrak) have announced the final unification of the party. Babrak was elected leader of the new party, and Sarwari his deputy.

In this extremely difficult situation, which has threatened the gains of the April revolution and the interests of maintaining our national security, it has become necessary to render additional military assistance to Afghanistan, especially since such requests had been made by the previous administration in the DRA. In accordance with the provisions of the Soviet-Afghan treaty of 1978, a decision has been made to send the necessary contingent of the Soviet Army to Afghanistan.

Riding the wave of patriotic sentiments that have engaged fairly large numbers of the Afghan population in connection with the deployment of Soviet forces which has been carried out in strict accordance with the provisions of the Soviet-Afghan treaty of 1978, the forces opposing H. Amin organized an armed operation which resulted in the overthrow of H. Amin's regime. This operation has received broad support from the working masses, the intelligentsia, significant sections of the Afghan army, and the state apparatus, all of which welcomed the formation of a new administration of the DRA and the PDPA.

The new government and the Revolutionary Council have been forced on a broad and representative basis, with the inclusions of representatives from former "Parcham" and "Kalq" factions, military representatives, and non-party members. . . .

Brood masses of people met the announcement of the overthrow of H. Amin's regime with unconcealed joy and express[ed] their eagerness to support the new administration's program. The commanders of all key formations and units of the Afghan army have already announced their support of the new leadership of the party and the government. Relations with Soviet soldiers and specialists continue to remain friendly overall. The situation in the country is normalizing.

In Kabul's political circles it is noted that the Babrak government, evidently, must overcome significant difficulties, inherited by him from the previous regime, in establishing order in domestic politics and economy; however, they express hope that PDPA, with USSR's help, will be able to solve these problems. Babrak can be described as one of the more theoretically equipped leaders of PDPA, who soberly and objectively evaluates the situation in Afghanistan; he was always distinguished by his sincere sympathies for the Soviet Union, and commanded respect within party masses and the country at large. In this regard, the conviction can be expressed that the new leadership of DRA will find effective ways to stabilize completely the country's situation.

[signature]   [signature]
Yu. Andropov   A. Gromyko

[signature]   [signature]
D. Ustinov   B. Ponomarev

31 December 1979
No. 2519-A

[Note: The signers of the memorandum were Defense Minister Dmitri Ustinov; KGB chairman Yuri Andropov; Foreign Minister Andrei Gromyko; and Central Committee International Department chairman Boris Ponomarev.]

SOURCE: "Regarding Events in Afghanistan during 27–28 December 1979," *Documents on the Soviet Invasion of Afghanistan,* e-Dossier no. 4, *Cold War International History Project* (Washington, D.C.: Woodrow Wilson International Center for Scholars, 2001), 55–56, www.wilsoncenter.org/topics/pubs/e-dossier_4.pdf.

DOCUMENT

Carter Address on the Soviet Invasion of Afghanistan

JANUARY 4, 1980

I come to you this evening to discuss the extremely important and rapidly changing circumstances in Southwest Asia.

I continue to share with all of you the sense of outrage and impatience because of the kidnaping of innocent American hostages and the holding of them by militant terrorists with the support and the approval of Iranian officials. Our purposes continue to be the protection of the longrange [sic] interests of our Nation and the safety of the American hostages.

We are attempting to secure the release of the Americans through the International Court of Justice, through the United Nations, and through public and private diplomatic efforts. We are determined to achieve this goal. We hope to do so without bloodshed and without any further danger to the lives of our 50 fellow Americans. In these efforts, we continue to have the strong support of the world community. The unity and the common sense of the American people under such trying circumstances are essential to the success of our efforts.

Recently, there has been another very serious development which threatens the maintenance of the peace in Southwest Asia. Massive Soviet military forces have invaded the small, nonaligned, sovereign nation of Afghanistan, which had hitherto not been an occupied satellite of the Soviet Union.

Fifty thousand heavily armed Soviet troops have crossed the border and are now dispersed throughout Afghanistan, attempting to conquer the fiercely independent Muslim people of that country.

The Soviets claim, falsely, that they were invited into Afghanistan to help protect that country from some unnamed outside threat. But the President, who had been the leader of Afghanistan before the Soviet invasion, was assassinated—along with several members of his family—after the Soviets gained control of the capital city of Kabul. Only several days later was the new puppet leader even brought into Afghanistan by the Soviets.

This invasion is an extremely serious threat to peace because of the threat of further Soviet expansion into neighboring countries in Southwest Asia and also because such an aggressive military policy is unsettling to other peoples throughout the world.

This is a callous violation of international law and the United Nations Charter. It is a deliberate effort of a powerful atheistic government to subjugate an independent Islamic people.

We must recognize the strategic importance of Afghanistan to stability and peace. A Soviet-occupied Afghanistan threatens both Iran and Pakistan and is a steppingstone to possible control over much of the world's oil supplies.

The United States wants all nations in the region to be free and to be independent. If the Soviets are encouraged in this invasion by eventual success, and if they maintain their dominance over Afghanistan and then extend their control to adjacent countries, the stable, strategic, and peaceful balance of the entire world will be changed. This would threaten the security of all nations including, of course, the United States, our allies, and our friends.

Therefore, the world simply cannot stand by and permit the Soviet Union to commit this act with impunity. Fifty nations have petitioned the United Nations Security Council to condemn the Soviet Union and to demand the immediate withdrawal of all Soviet troops from Afghanistan. We realize that under the United Nations Charter the Soviet Union and other permanent members may veto action of the Security Council. If the will of the Security Council should be thwarted in this manner, then immediate action would be appropriate in the General Assembly of the United Nations, where no Soviet veto exists.

In the meantime, neither the United States nor any other nation which is committed to world peace and stability can continue to do business as usual with the Soviet Union.

I have already recalled the United States Ambassador from Moscow [b]ack to Washington. He's working with me and with my other senior advisers in an immediate and comprehensive evaluation of the whole range of our relations with the Soviet Union.

The successful negotiation of the SALT II treaty has been a major goal and a major achievement of this administration, and we Americans, the people of the Soviet Union, and indeed the entire world will benefit from the successful control of strategic nuclear weapons through the implementation of this carefully negotiated treaty.

However, because of the Soviet aggression, I have asked the United States Senate to defer further consideration of the SALT II treaty so that the Congress and I can assess Soviet actions and intentions and devote our primary attention to the legislative and other measures required to respond to this crisis. As circumstances change in the future, we will, of course, keep the ratification of SALT II under active review in consultation with the leaders of the Senate.

The Soviets must understand our deep concern. We will delay [the] opening of any new American or Soviet consular facilities, and most of the cultural and economic exchanges currently under consideration will be deferred. Trade with the Soviet Union will be severely restricted.

I have decided to halt or to reduce exports to the Soviet Union in three areas that are particularly important to them. These new policies are being and will be coordinated with those of our allies. I've directed that no high technology or other strategic items will be licensed for sale to the Soviet Union until further notice, while we revise our licensing policy.

Fishing privileges for the Soviet Union in United States waters will be severely curtailed.

The 17 million tons of grain ordered by the Soviet Union in excess of that amount which we are committed to sell will not be delivered. This grain was not intended for human consumption but was to be used for building up Soviet livestock herds.

I am determined to minimize any adverse impact on the American farmer from this action. The undelivered grain will be removed from the market through storage and price support programs and through purchases at market prices. We will also increase amounts of grain devoted to the alleviation of hunger in poor countries, and we'll have a massive increase of the use of grain for gasohol production here at home.

After consultation with other principal grain-exporting nations, I am confident that they will not replace these quantities of grain by additional shipments on their part to the Soviet Union.

These actions will require some sacrifice on the part of all Americans, but there is absolutely no doubt that these actions are in the interest of world peace and in the interest of the security of our own Nation, and they are also compatible with actions being taken by our own major trading partners and others who share our deep concern about this new Soviet threat to world stability.

Although the United States would prefer not to withdraw from the Olympic games scheduled in Moscow this summer, the Soviet Union must realize that its continued aggressive actions will endanger both the participation of athletes and the travel to Moscow by spectators who would normally wish to attend the Olympic games.

Along with other countries, we will provide military equipment, food, and other assistance to help Pakistan defend its independence and its national security against the seriously increased threat it now faces from the north. The United States also stands ready to help other nations in the region in similar ways.

Neither our allies nor our potential adversaries should have the slightest doubt about our willingness, our determination, and our capacity to take the measures I have outlined tonight. I have consulted with leaders of the Congress, and I am confident they will support legislation that may be required to carry out these measures.

History teaches, perhaps, very few clear lessons. But surely one such lesson learned by the world at great cost is that aggression, unopposed, becomes a contagious disease.

The response of the international community to the Soviet attempt to crush Afghanistan must match the gravity of the Soviet action.

With the support of the American people and working with other nations, we will deter aggression, we will protect our Nation's security, and we will preserve the peace. The United States will meet its responsibilities.

SOURCE: "Soviet Invasion of Afghanistan Address to the Nation, January 4th, 1980," from John Woolley and Gerhard Peters, The American Presidency Project, University of California, Santa Barbara, www.presidency. ucsb.edu/ws/?pid=32911.

DOCUMENT

Brezhnev on the Invasion of Afghanistan

JANUARY 12, 1980

. . . Today the opponents of peace and detente are trying to speculate on the events in Afghanistan. Mountains of lies are being built up around these events, and a shameless anti-Soviet campaign is being mounted. What has really happened in Afghanistan?

A revolution took place there in April 1978. The Afghan people took their destiny into their hands and embarked on the road of independence and freedom. As it has always been in history, the forces of the past ganged up against the revolution. The people of Afghanistan, of course, could have coped with them themselves. But from the very first days of the revolution it encountered an external aggression and rude interference from outside into their internal affairs.

Thousands and tens of thousands of insurgents, armed and trained abroad, and whole armed units were sent into the territory of Afghanistan. In effect, imperialism, together with its accomplices, launched an undeclared war against revolutionary Afghanistan.

Afghanistan persistently demanded an end to the aggression and that it be allowed to build its new life in peace. Resisting the external aggression, the Afghan leadership, during the lifetime of President [Nur Mohammad] Taraki and then later, repeatedly asked the Soviet Union for assistance. On our part, we warned those concerned that if the aggression did not stop, we would not abandon the Afghan people at a time of trial. As is known, we stand by what we say.

The actions of the aggressors against Afghanistan were assisted by [Hafizullah] Amin, who, upon seizing power, launched cruel repressions against broad segments of Afghan society, against party and military cadres, against representatives of the intelligentsia and the Moslem clergy, that is, exactly against those segments on which the April Revolution relied. And the people under the leadership of the People's Democratic Party headed by Babrak Karmal rose against this Amin tyranny and put an end to it. Now in Washington and some other capitals they are mourning over Amin. This exposes their hypocrisy with particular clarity. Where were these mourners when Amin was conducting his mass repressions, when he forcibly removed and unlawfully murdered Taraki, the founder of the new Afghan State?

The unceasing armed intervention, the well advanced plot by external forces of reaction created a real threat that Afghanistan would lose its independence and be turned into an imperialist military bridgehead on our country's southern border. In other words, the time came when we could no longer fail to respond to the request of the government of friendly Afghanistan. To have acted otherwise would have meant leaving Afghanistan prey to imperialism and allowing the aggressive forces to repeat in that country what they had succeeded in doing, for instance, in Chile where the people's freedom was drowned in blood. To act otherwise would have meant to watch passively the origination on our southern border of a seat of serious danger to the security of the Soviet state.

When making the request to us, Afghanistan proceeded from clear-cut provisions of the Treaty of Friendship, Good-Neighborliness and Cooperation, concluded by Afghanistan with the USSR on December 1978, on the right of each state, in accordance with the United Nations Charter, to individual or collective self-defense, a right that other states have exercised more than once.

It was no simple decision for us to send Soviet military contingents to Afghanistan. But the party's Central Committee and the Soviet Government acted in full awareness of their responsibility and took into account the entire sum total of circumstances. The only task given to the Soviet contingents is to assist the Afghans in repulsing the aggression from outside. They will be fully withdrawn from Afghanistan once the causes that made the Afghan leadership request their introduction disappear.

It is deliberately and unscrupulously that the imperialist and also the Peking propaganda distort the Soviet Union's role in Afghan affairs.

It goes without saying that there has been no Soviet "intervention" or "aggression" at all. Oh, there is another thing: We are helping the new Afghanistan, on the request of its government, to defend the national independence, freedom and honor of its country from armed aggressive actions from outside.

The national interests or security of the United States of America and other states are not affected in any way by the events in Afghanistan. All attempts to portray matters otherwise are sheer nonsense. These attempts are being made with ill intent, with the aim of making the fulfillment of their own imperialist plans easier.

Also absolutely false are the allegations that the Soviet Union has some expansionist plans in respect to Pakistan, Iran or other countries of that area. The policy and psychology of colonialists is alien to us. We are not coveting the lands or wealth of others. It is the colonialists who are attracted by the smell of oil.

Outright hypocritical are the attempts to talk at length about the "Soviet threat of peace" and to pose as observers of international morals by those whose record includes the "dirty war" against Vietnam, who did not move a finger when the Chinese aggressors made their armed intrusion into Socialist Vietnam, who for decades have kept a military base on Cuban soil contrary to the will of its people and government, who are engaged in saber-rattling, who are threatening to impose a blockade and are exerting open military pressure on the revolutionary Iranian people by sending to the shores of Iran a naval armada armed with atomic weapons and including a considerable part of the U.S. carrier force.

And one last point must be made in this connection. Interference in the internal affairs of Afghanistan is really taking place, and even such an august and respected institution as the United Nations organization is being used for this. Indeed, can the discussion of the so-called "Afghan question" at the United Nations, contrary to objections by the government of Afghanistan, be described in any other way than a rude flouting of the sovereign rights of the Afghan state?

For the Afghan government and its responsible representative in the United Nations organization are stating for all to hear: Leave us alone; the Soviet military contingents were brought in at our request and in accordance with the Soviet-Afghan Treaty and Article 51 of the United Nations Charter.

Meantime, under the cover of the clamor, assistance is being increased to those elements that are intruding into Afghanistan and perpetrating aggressive actions against the legitimate government. The White House recently openly announced its decision to expand the supply to these elements of military equipment and everything necessary for hostile activities. The Western press reports that during his talks in Peking the U.S. Defense Secretary colluded with the Chinese leadership on the coordination of such actions.

Concluding the Afghan theme, it must be said that there is nothing surprising in the hostile reaction of imperialist forces to the events in Afghanistan. The crux of the matter is that the card on which the imperialists and their accomplices had counted was trumped there.

In short, the events in Afghanistan are not the true cause of the present complication of the international situation. If there were no Afghanistan, certain circles in the United States and in NATO would have surely found another pretext to aggravate the situation in the world. . . .

SOURCE: "Islamic Parleys on Afghan Crisis," *Historic Documents of 1980* (Washington, D.C.: CQ Press, 1981), 9–15.

Soviet Withdrawal from Afghanistan

DOCUMENT IN CONTEXT

The Soviet Union's occupation of Afghanistan lasted slightly more than eight years, causing a large number of deaths and widespread destruction in Afghanistan and contributing to the demise of the Soviet Union. Kremlin officials had hoped that the military intervention would bolster the weak communist regime in Afghanistan and ensure the continued existence of a friendly power along part of its long southern border. Those goals could be achieved only as long as Moscow provided direct support for the government in Kabul. Once that support was withdrawn, after the collapse of the Soviet Union at the end of 1991, all semblance of communist government in Afghanistan disappeared, and a new era of chaos began.

After the December 1979 invasion, the Soviet Union installed a new government headed by Babrak Karmal, the leader of one of two factions of the Afghan communist party. Karmal put his own allies in key positions in the new government, but neither he nor the Soviet army were able to make much progress toward defeating an antigovernment insurgency that had been gaining strength since early 1979. The Kremlin replaced Karmal in May 1986 with Muhammad Najibullah, a former head of the Afghan secret police. Najibullah changed the country's name from the Democratic Republic of Afghanistan to the Republic of Afghanistan and offered the insurgents, or *mujahidin,* tentative concessions, such as conceding a greater role for Islam in society. They rejected his offers.

Aid to the Mujahidin

The battle for Afghanistan during the 1980s was a classic guerrilla war except for one major factor—the absence of a united antigovernment guerrilla army with a single political agenda. Instead, the anti-Soviet insurgency in Afghanistan consisted of dozens of local guerrilla commanders, some of whom were affiliated with but not necessarily controlled by a coalition of seven political parties headquartered in the city of

Peshawar, across the border in Pakistan. These commanders and political groups shared the goal of ousting the Soviet Union and the government it supported in Kabul, but they had varying other agendas, usually based on the needs of the ethnic or tribal groups they represented. In 1985 the seven parties in Pakistan formed a united front, the Islamic Alliance of Afghanistan Mujahidin, which helped attract international aid for their cause but disintegrated after the Soviets withdrew.

According to most analysts, the mujahidin fell into two broad groups: Islamic fundamentalists (or Islamists) and traditionalists. The Islamists embraced a religious agenda—a *jihad* (or holy war) to drive out the infidel invader. Most of these fighters were native Afghans, but hundreds of Muslims from other countries joined the fight against the communist "infidels" in Afghanistan, a pattern that would be repeated in later conflicts in the Balkans, Chechnya, and Iraq. The term *traditionalists* covered an array of conservative forces in Afghanistan, all of whom were Muslim and most of whom simply wanted to force the Soviet army from their territory in favor of traditional tribal or ethnic rule.

Early on, following the Soviet invasion, China, Egypt, Iran, Pakistan, Saudi Arabia, and the United States provided limited amounts of military aid to the mujahidin. Most of this aid they funneled through Interservices Intelligence (ISI), the Pakistani intelligence agency run by the military as a virtual government within a government, bypassing civilian leaders in Islamabad.

In March 1985 the administration of Ronald Reagan decided to escalate U.S. military support for the mujahidin, by increasing the quantity of weapons it supplied. In another step, in 1986, the United States began providing portable high-tech antiaircraft Stinger missiles to the Afghan fighters. These missiles deprived the Soviet air force of air superiority, and just as important, made Soviet pilots more cautious, thus reducing their effectiveness in combat. The United States gave the mujahidin several hundred, possibly as many as nine hundred, Stinger missiles in 1986 and 1987.

According to information compiled by Barnett Rubin, a U.S. scholar on Afghanistan, U.S. aid to the mujahidin began in 1980 at $30 million, rose to $80 million in 1983, jumped to $470 million in 1986, and reached $630 million annually for 1987 and 1988. The *Washington Post* reported in 1992 that covert U.S. aid totaled more than $2 billion during the 1980s, and was matched by funds provided by Saudi Arabia through ISI. China also provided substantial quantities of weapons to the mujahidin, as did Iran.

The mujahidin carried out thousands of classic guerrilla hit-and-run attacks against the Soviet army and a small Afghan army loyal to the Kabul government. At its peak in 1987, the Soviet presence in Afghanistan stood at just under 120,000 troops, with another 30,000 or so providing support from Uzbekistan, across the border. The mujahidin never inflicted a major military defeat on the Soviet army, but their constant attacks prevented the Soviets from establishing long-term control over more than a small fraction of Afghan territory.

Prolonged Negotiations

For nearly six years, between June 1982 and April 1988, United Nations diplomat Diego Cordovez mediated a series of negotiating sessions that eventually produced an agreement giving the Kremlin a degree of diplomatic cover for a withdrawal from

Afghanistan. The initial participants were the governments of Afghanistan and Pakistan, whose representatives did not meet face to face, but instead exchanged ideas through Cordovez in so-called proximity talks, with the diplomats nearby but not in the same room. By the mid-1980s, the Soviet Union and the United States had joined the negotiations, but the mujahidin never had direct representation at the talks, relying on Pakistan and the United States to represent their interests. This lack of a direct role for the mujahidin proved to be a weakness for the eventual agreement because the Afghan fighters had no direct ownership of it.

A drawn-out political transition in Moscow—hastened by the failure of the adventure in Afghanistan—became a central factor in the Soviet withdrawal. Soviet leader Leonid Brezhnev died in 1982 and was succeeded by two short-term replacements, neither of whom brought any energy or imagination to the task of governing the Soviet Union in what turned out to be its declining years. In March 1985, Mikhail Gorbachev took office as the youngest Soviet leader and gradually launched a series of reforms intended to bolster the communist system but instead had the effect of exposing its inherent structural weaknesses. By 1987 Gorbachev and his foreign minister, Eduard Shevardnadze, seemed determined to bring an end to the costly occupation of Afghanistan. In addition to being a drain on Moscow's treasury, the occupation was increasingly unpopular, with thousands of Soviet families burying sons killed in Afghanistan.

At a summit in Washington with President Reagan on December 10, 1987, Gorbachev announced that the Soviet Union would withdraw from Afghanistan. His announcement spurred the UN negotiations toward a final agreement, which was concluded in Geneva on April 14, 1988. The agreement consisted of five major documents calling for "noninterference" in the internal affairs of Afghanistan and Pakistan by the Soviet Union and the United States; requiring all regional states to allow Afghan refugees to return to their homes without fear of persecution; and setting a timetable for the Soviet Union to withdraw its military forces from Afghanistan by February 15, 1989. At a news conference shortly after the treaty signing, Shevardnadze drew particular attention to the noninterference clause. "The entire spectrum of possible activities and actions to meddle in the affairs of Afghanistan has finally been all blocked," he said.

The last Soviet soldiers left Afghanistan on the February 15, 1989, a date set by the Geneva accords. The Soviet military command issued a statement rejecting widespread comparisons between Moscow's withdrawal from Afghanistan and the U.S. retreat from Vietnam nearly fourteen years earlier. The Kremlin later acknowledged that more than 14,000 Soviet soldiers had died during the eight years of the Soviet military occupation, and at least another 11,000 seriously wounded. No official accounting was ever made of how many Afghan and foreign fighters and civilians died, but most estimates put the number at 1 million to 1.5 million. In addition, at least 5 million Afghan citizens fled into neighboring countries during the 1980s, most of them to Pakistan (about 3 million) and Iran (about 2 million). Few of the refugees returned until after the United States invaded Afghanistan in 2001 (Rise of the Taliban, p. 593; U.S. Invasion of Afghanistan, p. 598).

Following are three documents, all dated April 14, 1988: the two main agreements, known as the Geneva Accords, providing for the withdrawal of Soviet military forces from Afghanistan and excerpts from remarks by Soviet foreign minister Eduard Shevardnadze at a news conference.

DOCUMENT

Geneva Accords

APRIL 14, 1988

[Following are main portions of the documents comprising the negotiated settlement regarding Afghanistan]

BILATERAL AGREEMENT ON PRINCIPLES OF MUTUAL RELATIONS

The Republic of Afghanistan and the Islamic Republic of Pakistan, hereinafter referred to as the High Contracting Parties,

Desiring to normalize relations and promote good-neighbourliness and co-operation as well as to strengthen international peace and security in the region,

Have agreed as follows:

Article I

Relations between the High Contracting Parties shall be conducted in strict compliance with the principle of non-interference and non-intervention by States in the affairs of other States.

Article II

For the purpose of implementing the principles of non-interference and non-intervention each High Contracting Party undertakes to comply with the following obligations:

1. to respect the sovereignty, political independence, territorial integrity, national unity, security and non-alignment of the other High Contracting Party, as well as the national identity and cultural heritage of its people;
2. to respect the sovereign and inalienable right of the other High Contracting Party freely to determine its own political, economic, cultural and social systems, to develop its international relations and to exercise permanent sovereignty over its natural resources, in accordance with the will of its people, and without outside intervention, interference, subversion, coercion or threat in any form whatsoever;
3. to refrain from the threat or use of force in any form whatsoever so as not to violate the boundaries of each other, to disrupt the political, social or eco-

nomic order of the other High Contracting Party, to overthrow or change the political system of the other High Contracting Party or its Government, or to cause tension between the High Contracting Parties;

4. to ensure that its territory is not used in any manner which would violate the sovereignty, political independence, territorial integrity and national unity or disrupt the political, economic and social stability of the other High Contracting Party;

5. to refrain from armed intervention, subversion, military occupation or any other form of intervention and interference, overt or covert, directed at the other High Contracting Party, or any act of military, political or economic interference in the internal affairs of the other High Contracting Party, including acts of reprisal involving the use of force;

6. to refrain from any action or attempt in whatever form or under whatever pretext to destabilize or to undermine the stability of the other High Contracting Party or any of its institutions;

7. to refrain from the promotion, encouragement or support, direct or indirect, of rebellious or secessionist activities against the other High Contracting Party, under any pretext whatsoever, or from any other action which seeks to disrupt the unity or to undermine or subvert the political order of the other High Contracting Party;

8. to prevent within its territory the training, equipping, financing and recruitment of mercenaries from whatever origin for the purpose of hostile activities against the other High Contracting Party, or the sending of such mercenaries into the territory of the other High Contracting Party and accordingly to deny facilities, including financing for the training, equipping and transit of such mercenaries;

9. to refrain from making any agreements or arrangements with other States designed to intervene or interfere in the internal and external affairs of the other High Contracting Party;

10. to abstain from any defamatory campaign, vilification or hostile propaganda for the purpose of intervening or interfering in the internal affairs of the other High Contracting Party;

11. to prevent any assistance to or use of or tolerance of terrorist groups, saboteurs or subversive agents against the other High Contracting Party;

12. to prevent within its Territory the presence, harbouring, in camps and bases or otherwise, organizing, training, financing, equipping and arming of individuals and political, ethnic and any other groups for the purpose of creating subversion, disorder or unrest in the territory of the other High Contracting Party and accordingly also to prevent the use of mass media and the transportation of arms, ammunition and equipment by such individuals and groups;

13. not to resort to or to allow any other action that could be considered as interference or intervention.

Article III

The present Agreement shall enter into force on 15 May 1988.

Article IV

Any steps that may be required in order to enable the High Contracting Parties to comply with the provisions of Article II of this Agreement shall be completed by the date on which this Agreement enters into force.

Article V

This Agreement is drawn up in the English, Pashtu and Urdu languages, all texts being equally authentic. In case of any divergence of interpretation, the English text shall prevail.

(Signed by Afghanistan and Pakistan)

DECLARATION ON INTERNATIONAL GUARANTEES

The Governments of the Union of Soviet Socialist Republics and of the United States of America,

Expressing support that the Republic of Afghanistan and the Islamic Republic of Pakistan have concluded a negotiated political settlement designed to normalize relations and promote good-neighbourliness between the two countries as well as to strengthen international peace and security in the region;

Wishing in turn to contribute to the achievement of the objectives that the Republic of Afghanistan and the Islamic Republic of Pakistan have set themselves, and with a view to ensuring respect for their sovereignty, independence, territorial integrity and non-alignment;

Undertake to invariably refrain from any form of interference and intervention in the internal affairs of the Republic of Afghanistan and the Islamic Republic of Pakistan and to respect the commitments contained in the bilateral agreement between the Republic of Afghanistan and the Islamic Republic of Pakistan on the Principles of Mutual Relations, in particular on Non-Interference and Non-Intervention;

Urge all States to do likewise.

The present Declaration shall enter into force on 15 May 1988.

(Signed by the USSR and the USA)

BILATERAL AGREEMENT ON THE VOLUNTARY RETURN OF REFUGEES

The Republic of Afghanistan and the Islamic Republic of Pakistan, hereinafter referred to as the High Contracting Parties,

Convinced that voluntary and unimpeded repatriation constitutes the most appropriate solution for the problem of Afghan refugees present in the Islamic Republic of Pakistan and having ascertained that the arrangements for the return of the Afghan refugees are satisfactory to them,

Have agreed as follows:

Article I

All Afghan refugees temporarily present in the territory of the Islamic Republic of Pakistan shall be given the opportunity to return voluntarily to their homeland in accordance with the arrangements and conditions set out in the present Agreement.

Article II

The Government of the Republic of Afghanistan shall take all necessary measures to ensure the following conditions for the voluntary return of Afghan refugees to their homeland:
  a. All refugees shall be allowed to return in freedom to their homeland;
  b. All returnees shall enjoy the free choice of domicile and freedom of movement within the Republic of Afghanistan;
  c. All returnees shall enjoy the right to work, to adequate living conditions and to share in the welfare of the State;
  d. All returnees shall enjoy the right to participate on an equal basis in the civic affairs of the Republic of Afghanistan. They shall be ensured equal benefits from the solution of the land question on the basis of the Land and Water Reform;
  e. All returnees shall enjoy the same rights and privileges, including freedom of religion, and have the same obligations and responsibilities as any other citizens of the Republic of Afghanistan without discrimination.

The Government of the Republic of Afghanistan undertakes to implement these measures and to provide, within its possibilities, all necessary assistance in the process of repatriation.

Article III

The Government of the Islamic Republic of Pakistan shall facilitate the voluntary, orderly and peaceful repatriation of all Afghan refugees staying within its territory and undertakes to provide, within its possibilities, all necessary assistance in the process of repatriation.

Article IV

For the purpose of organizing, co-ordinating and supervising the operations which should effect the voluntary, orderly and peaceful repatriation of Afghan refugees, there shall be set up mixed commissions in accordance with the established international practice. For the performance of their functions the members of the commissions and their staff shall be accorded the necessary facilities, and have access to the relevant areas within the territories of the High Contracting Parties.

Article V

With a view to the orderly movement of the returnees, the commissions shall determine frontier crossing points and establish necessary transit centres. They shall also establish all other modalities for the phased return of refugees, including registration and communication to the country of return to the names of refugees who express the wish to return.

Article VI

At the request of the Governments concerned, the United Nations High Commissioner for Refugees will co-operate and provide assistance in the process of voluntary repatriation of refugees in accordance with the present Agreement. Special agreements may be concluded for this purpose between UNHCR and the High Contracting Parties.

Article VII

The present Agreement shall enter into force on 15 May 1988. At that time the mixed commissions provided in Article IV shall be established and the operations for the voluntary return of refugees under this Agreement shall commence.

The arrangements set out in Articles IV and V above shall remain in effect for a period of eighteen months. After that period the High Contracting Parties shall review the results of the repatriation and, if necessary, consider any further arrangements that may be called for.

Article VIII

This Agreement is drawn up in the English, Pashtu and Urdu languages, all texts being equally authentic. In case of any divergence of interpretation, the English text shall prevail.

(Signed by Afghanistan and Pakistan)

AGREEMENT ON INTERRELATIONSHIPS

[Articles 1 through 6 omitted]

7. To consider alleged violations and to work out solutions to questions that may arise in the implementation of the instruments comprising the settlement representatives of

the Republic of Afghanistan and the Islamic Republic of Pakistan shall meet whenever required.

A representative of the Secretary-General of the United Nations shall lend his good offices to the Parties and in that context he will assist in the organization of the meetings and participate in them. He may submit to the Parties for their consideration and approval suggestions and recommendations for prompt, faithful and complete observance of the provisions of the instruments.

In order to enable him to fulfil his tasks, the representative shall be assisted by such personnel under his authority as required. Any report submitted by the representative to the two Governments shall be considered in a meeting of the Parties no later than forty-eight hours after it has been submitted.

The modalities and logistical arrangements for the work of the representative and the personnel under his authority as agreed upon with the Parties are set out in the Memorandum of Understanding which is annexed to and is part of this Agreement.

[Article 8 omitted]

(Signed by Afghanistan and Pakistan)

In witness thereof, the representatives of the States-Guarantors affixed their signatures hereunder:

(Signed by the USSR and USA)

Annex

Memorandum of Understanding

[Parts I and II omitted]

III. Modus Operandi and Personnel Organization
The Secretary-General will appoint a senior military officer as Deputy to the Representative who will be stationed in the area, as head of two small headquarters units, one in Kabul and the other in Islamabad, each comprising five military officers, drawn from existing United Nations operations, and a small civilian auxiliary staff.

The Deputy to the Representative of the Secretary-General will act on behalf of the Representative and be in contact with the Parties through the Liaison Officer each Party will designate for this purpose.

The two headquarters units will be organized into two Inspection Teams to ascertain on the ground any violation of the instruments comprising the settlement. Whenever considered necessary by the Representative of the Secretary-General or his Deputy, up to 40 additional military officers (some 10 additional Inspection Teams) will be redeployed from existing operations within the shortest possible time (normally around 48 hours).

The nationalities of all the Officers will be determined in consultation with the Parties.

Whenever necessary the Representative of the Secretary-General, who will periodically visit the area for consultations with the Parties and to review the work of his personnel, will also assign to the area members of his own Office and other civilian personnel from the United Nations Secretariat as may be needed. His Deputy will alternate between the two Headquarters units and will remain at all times in close communication with him.

[Part IV omitted]

V. Duration

The Deputy to the Representative of the Secretary-General and the other personnel will be established in the area not later than twenty days before the entry into force of the instruments. The arrangements will cease to exist two months after the completion of all time-frames envisaged for the implementation of the instruments.

VI. Financing

The cost of all facilities and services to be provided by the Parties will be borne by the respective Governments. The salaries and travel expenses of the personnel to and from the area, as well as the costs of the local personnel assigned to the headquarters units, will be defrayed by the United Nations.

U.S. STATEMENT

The United States has agreed to act as a guarantor of the political settlement of the situation relating to Afghanistan. We believe this settlement is a major step forward in restoring peace to Afghanistan, in ending the bloodshed in that unfortunate country, and in enabling millions of Afghan refugees to return to their homes.

In agreeing to act as a guarantor, the United States states the following:

1. The troop withdrawal obligations set out in paragraphs 5 and 6 of the Instrument on Interrelationships are central to the entire settlement. Compliance with those obligations is essential to achievement of the settlement's purposes, namely, the ending of foreign intervention in Afghanistan and the restoration of the rights of the Afghan people through the exercise of self determination as called for by the United Nations Charter and the United Nations General Assembly resolutions on Afghanistan.

2. The obligations undertaken by the guarantors are symmetrical. In this regard, the United States has advised the Soviet Union that, if the USSR undertakes, as consistent with its obligations as guarantor, to provide military assistance to parties in Afghanistan, the U.S. retains the right, as consistent with its own obligations as guarantor, likewise effectively to provide such assistance.

3. By acting as a guarantor of the settlement, the United States does not intend to imply in any respect recognition of the present regime in Kabul as the lawful Government of Afghanistan.

SOURCE: "Agreements on Afghanistan," *Historic Documents of 1988* (Washington, D.C.: CQ Press, 1989), 259–266.

DOCUMENT

Shevardnadze Statements on the Afghanistan Peace Accord

APRIL 14, 1988

Representatives of the Republic of Afghanistan, the Islamic Republic of Pakistan, the Union of Soviet Socialist Republics and the United States of America today affixed their signatures to agreements on a political settlement regarding Afghanistan.

The presence of the UN secretary general, Mr. Perez de Cuellar, and his personal envoy, Mr. Diego Cordovez, at the ceremony reflected not only their role in attaining the long-sought goal, but also the immense possibilities of the United Nations in settling regional and other conflicts.

But even given all their tireless and purposeful peacemaking activities, today's result would have been impossible without the wisdom, good will and readiness for a sensible compromise in the supreme interest of peace and security, which has been demonstrated by the sides.

This result has been predetermined by my country's policy of solving acute international problems exceptionally by political means, which has been proclaimed by Mikhail Gorbachev, general secretary of the CPSU [Communist Party of the Soviet Union] Central Committee.

The "Afghan knot" can be untied by dint of what is nowadays the most efficient tool, which we call new political thinking.

Two dates have, in our view, been of utterly exceptional significance in the calendar of the Geneva negotiations on Afghanistan. One was 8 February 1988, when Mikhail Gorbachev in Moscow and President Najibullah in Kabul issued statements that led the talks to the level of practical solutions. The other was 7 April 1988, when in Tashkent the leaders of the two friendly countries ushered in a new phase in the relationship of friendship and good-neighborliness between the Soviet and Afghan peoples, which dates back to dozens of years ago.

The pivotal idea of the new phase is every kind of support for the success of the national reconciliation policy in every field essential to Afghanistan—be it aid with creating satisfactory conditions for the return of refugees or help with economic rehabilitation and socioeconomic development in Afghanistan.

Speaking of the national reconciliation policy, which is by right associated with President Najibullah, we are convinced that it is this policy that has lent a strong impetus to the Geneva process. No outside actions can promise any worthy result if not backed up with adequate efforts inside the country. The President's course for national accord has definitely contributed to the success of the talks.

It has been facilitated, especially at the finishing stretch, by the compromise decisions of the sides, the realistic position of the Pakistani leaders and their readiness to take account of the opinions of the whole Afghan people. This approach, just as, of course, unfailing compliance by Pakistan with the signed agreements, will furnish a sound basis for improving Soviet-Pakistani relations.

The Soviet Union does justice to the United States consent to become a guarantor of the Geneva accords together with it.

We hail the signature of the Geneva agreements because they put an end to outside interference in the affairs of Afghanistan and give the Afghan people a possibility to achieve peace and accord in their land.

The sides—Afghanistan and Pakistan—today made legal commitments in treaty form, which exclude interference in any form in each other's affairs.

They pledged:

— Not to make their territories available for hostile actions against the other side,

— To refrain from any form of intervention, overt or covert, and from any act of military, political or economic interference,

— To refrain from assistance, encouragement or support for any insurgent or separatist activity,

— Not to allow the training, outfitting, funding, and recruitment of mercenaries of any origins in their territories,

— To refrain from concluding any agreements or accords with other states, which would be aimed at intervention or interference in the domestic or external affairs of the other side,

— Not to allow any aid to, use of or tolerance to terrorist groups, saboteurs or wreckers acting against the other side.

Please pay attention to this: The entire spectrum of possible activities and actions to meddle in the affairs of Afghanistan has finally been all blocked.

This is precisely what has been needed for the Afghan people to be able to determine its destiny itself. Now it will get down to this and will be able to do away with the war and achieve peace in its lead [land?] on the basis of national reconciliation and the unity of all the patriotic forces.

Another most acute problem, that of refugees, is being solved as well. They will have the possibility to return to their fatherland as equal citizens of Afghanistan. Assistance with repatriating refugees will be given by the U.N. High Commissioner for Refugees. Mixed commissions to deal with issues connected with their return will also be formed.

In keeping with the agreements signed today, special U.N. personnel will investigate any violation of any commitment by the sides.

So a mechanism is being established also for verification, which adds to the conviction that the agreements will be observed.

Now that they have been signed and acquired the force of international legal instruments, the responsibility of the sides has grown dramatically. It is only irresponsible people that can ignore, reject or violate norms and principles of the settlement.

The Geneva agreements are a touchstone testing the sincerity of intentions with regard to Afghanistan. Those who really wish peace for the Afghan people and seek sincerely to help it heal its wounds will back these accords.

After not so rare visits to Kabul and conversations with representatives of most diverse social currents in that country, I have become convinced that they can and want to get into the single mainstream of a revived, neutral and non-aligned Afghanistan. This goal, as we see it, is above all pretensions and ambitions and above ideological irreconcilability or claims to power.

A new counting out of time began in Geneva today. It has begun not only for Afghanistan and Pakistan. The Geneva agreements have been unanimously supported by the Soviet people and we have signed them with its mandate in hand.

But this does not exhaust our contribution to the settlement. It is with these thoughts that we are returning home. . . .

Question: Some political figures in the West as well as mass media assert that the signing of the Geneva accords does not mean an end to the armed struggle in Afghanistan, and that the opposition will continue its struggle, getting as it does its weapons from the USA. What is the rationale behind this propagandist campaign?

Answer: I would answer your question as follows: Those who are opposed to the Geneva accords, to the implementation of the principles laid down in these documents, are in essence opposed to peace in the long-suffering Afghan land.

These people have their self-seeking interests. This is one aspect of the matter.

The other is: I think it must be stressed that the accords signed today by the representatives of four states in the presence of the U.N. secretary general and his personal envoy, create all the necessary conditions for the final political settlement of the Afghan problem. It goes without saying that this will be so only if the principles which are proclaimed by these accords will be honestly complied with. And we hope that the accords will be observed, for they provide for the creation of a single and coherent system of control through the U.N. framework. . . .

SOURCE: Foreign Broadcast Information Service, "Shevardnadze Press Conference," *Daily Report: Soviet Union,* April 14, 1988, 33–37. Originally published in *Pravda* (in Russian), April 15 1988, second edition, p. 6.

Rise of the Taliban

After the Soviet Union withdrew its last soldiers from Afghanistan in February 1989, observers widely assumed that the communist government in Kabul led by Muhammad Najibullah would collapse under the weight of the *mujahidin* insurgency. Although it enjoyed little popular support, Najibullah's government had two important advantages: the Soviet Union continued to provide the government with a large arsenal of military equipment (much of it recalled from Eastern European countries after the fall of the Berlin Wall later in 1989); and one of the country's most important guerrilla commanders, the Uzbek leader Abdurrashid Dostum, used his militia to help keep Najibullah in power. Early in 1992, shortly after the Soviet Union's collapse, Najibullah lost both these sources of support.

In March 1992, Najibullah announced that he was stepping down in favor of an "interim" government, and in late April forces loyal to Ahmed Shah Massoud, one of the most successful mujahidin commanders, took control of Kabul. The sudden collapse of Najibullah's government left mujahidin political leaders, based in Peshawar, Pakistan, unprepared to exercise power through a united government. Instead, the politicians and guerrilla fighters decided to alternate power through a series of interim governments. In June 1992, Burhannuddin Rabbani took office as interim president, a position he was supposed to hold for only a few months. In December, however, Rabbani arranged for a council of elders to extend his term for two years—a move that angered rival mujahidin leaders and set off a civil war among the former anti-Soviet allies. Much of the fighting centered around ethnic loyalties. Massoud and Rabbani were ethnic Tajiks, for example, while many of their rivals were ethnic Pashtuns (the largest group in Afghanistan), Uzbeks, or members of other groups.

For the better part of three years—from early 1993 through much of 1996—rival groups, in constantly shifting alliances, battled for control of Kabul and other strategic areas. By early 1994, the capital had been largely destroyed by rocket fire, much of it from forces loyal to Gulbuddin Hekmatyar, who claimed he—rather than Rabbani—was the rightful president.

Taliban Take Power

While the rival mujahidin forces battered each other, in south-central Afghanistan, a group of ethnic Pashtun students from Islamic schools (*madaris*) in Afghanistan and Pakistan organized as a military force, with support from the governments of Pakistan and Saudi Arabia. The students were known as the Taliban (*talib* means student), and their promise to restore traditional, rural Islamic values to Afghanistan won them widespread popularity.

In November 1994, the Taliban captured Kandahar, the country's second-largest city, then moved quickly to the north and west, seizing the town of Wardak, just south of Kabul, in early February 1995. By this time, the Taliban and Massoud, who still controlled Kabul and much of the north of the country, had become the main combatants. The Taliban took control of western Herat province in September 1995, defeating a regional warlord who had strong backing from Iran. (Although they shared some of the same conservative Islamic values as the Shiite clerics who ruled Iran, the Taliban were Sunni Muslims. Iran considered the Taliban to be an enemy.)

The big break for the Taliban came in September 1996, when they captured the eastern city of Jalalabad, thus nearly encircling Kabul. After three surrounding provinces fell to the Taliban, Massoud ordered his forces to withdraw from the capital. The Taliban moved into Kabul on September 26, completing an extraordinary sweep for an organization that had been in existence for only two years and whose leaders had little military command experience. Mullah Mohammad Omar, who emerged as leader of the Taliban, had taught at a rural Islamic school and then joined the mujahidin to fight against the Kabul government after the Soviet withdrawal.

In one of their first acts after gaining control of Kabul, the Taliban seized Najibullah and his brother from a UN compound, dragged them around town behind a jeep, shot them, and hung their bodies for public display. Of more lasting significance was the issuance of a series of decrees based on extreme interpretations of Islamic law and rural Pashtun customs. Many of the rules concerned women and girls, including a requirement that all females wear full-body coverings when outside the home and prohibitions on women working outside the home or attending school. All men were required to wear full beards. Other decrees banned all sports and entertainment, including music and games, such as chess, and kite flying (a popular diversion in Afghanistan). The Taliban also cracked down, at least temporarily, on cultivation of opium poppies, one of the country's most successful agricultural crops. Afghanistan traditionally had been one of the world's largest sources of the opium paste used to make heroin, but production plummeted under Taliban rule.

By the end of 1998, the Taliban had gained control of at least 80 percent of the country, with the most significant resistance coming from an alliance of Tajik and Uzbek forces in northern Afghanistan, headed by Massoud and Dostum. These forces, which eventually became known as the Northern Alliance, carried out numerous guerrilla attacks against the Taliban but had neither the military power nor the popular support to make serious inroads until they received the backing of the United States in 2001.

Bin Laden in Afghanistan

Even before the Taliban seized control of Kabul, a little-noticed event took place that would ultimately lead to the end of the Taliban's hold on Afghanistan: Osama bin Laden, a wealthy Saudi Arabian exile of Yemeni descent, arrived in Jalalabad, via a chartered jet in May 1996. Bin Laden, whose family ran one of the biggest contracting firms in the Middle East, had served with the mujahidin in the 1980s, for the most part running logistical operations out of Peshawar, Pakistan. Angered by the continuing U.S. military presence in Saudi Arabia after the 1990–1991 Persian Gulf War, bin Laden moved to Sudan in 1992 as a volunteer for Hassan Turabi, the new Islamist leader there. Bin Laden had several businesses in Sudan, where he also was largely responsible for creating al-Qaida (the Base), a network consisting for the most part of fellow veterans from the war in Afghanistan with the intention of opposing U.S. and Western influence in the Middle East.

In 1994 Saudi Arabia revoked bin Laden's citizenship because of his extremist connections, and the next year Saudi authorities and the Clinton administration began pressing the Sudanese government to expel him for the same reason. Bin Laden moved to Jalalabad in May 1996 along with several dozen supporters and family members. The following August he issued a *fatwa,* or decree, calling on Muslims to stage a holy war, or jihad, against the U.S. military presence in Saudi Arabia, the birthplace of Islam. Bin Laden moved in 1997 to Kandahar, the home region of the Taliban, and set up several camps for training and selecting al-Qaida recruits for jihad.

On August 7, 1998, near-simultaneous suicide bombings destroyed the U.S. embassies in Nairobi, Kenya, and Dar-es-Salaam, Tanzania, killing more than 250 people, most of them Africans. The Clinton administration immediately accused bin Laden of sponsoring the attacks, and on August 20 U.S. warships fired dozens of Cruise missiles that destroyed al-Qaida training camps near the cities of Jalalabad and Khost. Several dozen people died in the attacks, but bin Laden and his top aides were not at the camps at the time.

Having failed to kill bin Laden, the Clinton administration sought to apply the same pressure on the Taliban that had worked in Sudan. In November 1999, the United States sponsored, and the UN Security Council approved, Resolution 1267 freezing the international assets of the Taliban government and barring international flights by Ariana, the Afghan national airline. A year later, in December 2000, the Security Council adopted Resolution 1333, imposing additional sanctions against Afghanistan, including an arms embargo, in an unsuccessful attempt to force the Taliban to hand over bin Laden to the United States. By that time, planning already was well under way for al-Qaida's September 11, 2001, attacks, which would lead to the U.S. invasion of Afghanistan and overthrow of the Taliban the following October (U.S. invasion of Afghanistan, p. 598).

Following are the English-language texts of three decrees issued by the Taliban government in Kabul, Afghanistan, in November and December 1996, governing personal and social activities in that country.

DOCUMENT

Taliban Decrees

1996

[These translations were handed out to reporters in Kabul.]

1. Decree announced by the General Presidency of Amr Bil Maruf and Nai Az Munkar (Religious Police.) Kabul, November 1996.

Women you should not step outside your residence. If you go outside the house you should not be like women who used to go with fashionable clothes wearing much cosmetics and appearing in front of every men before the coming of Islam.

Islam as a rescuing religion has determined specific dignity for women. Islam has valuable instructions for women. Women should not create such opportunity to attract the attention of useless people who will not look at them with a good eye. Women have the responsibility as a teacher or co-ordinator for her family. Husband, brother, father have the responsibility for providing the family with the necessary life requirements (food, clothes, etc). In case women are required to go outside the residence for the purposes of education, social needs or social services they should cover themselves in accordance with Islamic Sharia regulation. If women are going outside with fashionable, ornamental, tight, and charming clothes to show themselves, they will be cursed by the Islamic Sharia and should never expect to go to heaven.

All family elders and every Muslim have responsibility in this respect. We request all family elders to keep tight control over their families and avoid these social problems. Otherwise these women will be threatened, investigated, and severely punished as well as the family elders by the forces of the Religious Police (*Munkrat*).

The Religious Police (*Munkrat*) have the responsibility and duty to struggle against these social problems and will continue their effort until evil is finished.

2. Rules of work for the State Hospitals and private clinics based on Islamic Sharia principles. Ministry of Health, on behalf of Amr ul Momineen Mullah Mohammed Omar. Kabul, November 1996.

1. Female patients should go to female physicians. In case a male physician is needed, the female patient should be accompanied by her close relative.
2. During examination, the female patients and male physicians both should be dressed with Islamic *hijab* (veil).
3. Male physicians should not touch or see the other parts of female patients except for the affected part.
4. Waiting room for female patients should be safely covered.
5. The person who regulates turn for female patients should be a female.
6. During the night duty, in what rooms which female patients are hospitalized, the male doctor without the call of the patient is not allowed to enter the room.
7. Sitting and speaking between male and female doctors are not allowed, if there be need for discussion, it should be done with *hijab*.
8. Female doctors should wear simple clothes, they are not allowed to wear stylish clothes or use cosmetics or make-up.
9. Female doctors and nurses are not allowed to enter the rooms where male patients are hospitalized.
10. Hospital staff should pray in mosques on time.
11. The Religious Police are allowed to go for control at any time and nobody can prevent them.

Anybody who violates the order will be punished as per Islamic regulations.

3. General Presidency of Amr Bil Marnuf. Kabul, December 1996.
1. To prevent sedition and female uncovers (Be Hejabi). No drivers are allowed to pick up women who are using Iranian *burqa.* In case of violation the driver will be imprisoned. If such kind of female are observed in the street their

house will be found and their husband punished. If the women use stimulating and attractive cloth and there is no accompany of close male relative with them, the drivers should not pick them up.

2. To prevent music. To be broadcasted by the public information resources. In shops, hotels, vehicles and rickshaws cassettes and music are prohibited. This matter should be monitored within five days. If any music cassette found in a shop, the shopkeeper should be imprisoned and the shop locked. If five people guarantee the shop should be opened the criminal released later. If cassette found in the vehicle, the vehicle and the driver will be imprisoned. If five people guarantee the vehicle will be released and the criminal released later.

3. To prevent beard shaving and its cutting. After one and a half months if anyone observed who has shaved and/or cut his beard, they should be arrested and imprisoned until their beard gets bushy.

4. To prevent keeping pigeons and playing with birds. Within ten days this habit/hobby should stop. After ten days this should be monitored and the pigeons and any other playing birds should be killed.

5. To prevent kite-flying. The kite shops in the city should be abolished.

6. To prevent idolatry. In vehicles, shops, hotels, room and any other place pictures/portraits should be abolished. The monitors should tear up all pictures in the above places.

7. To prevent gambling. In collaboration with the security police the main centres should be found and the gamblers imprisoned for one month.

8. To eradicate the use of addiction. Addicts should be imprisoned and investigation made to find the supplier and the shop. The shop should be locked and the owner and user should be imprisoned and punished.

9. To prevent the British and American hairstyle. People with long hair should be arrested and taken to the Religious Police department to shave their hair. The criminal has to pay the barber.

10. To prevent interest on loans, charge on changing small denomination notes and charge on money orders. All money exchangers should be informed that the above three types of exchanging the money should be prohibited. In case of violation criminals will be imprisoned for a long time.

11. To prevent washing cloth by young ladies along the water streams in the city. Violator ladies should be picked up with respectful Islamic manner, taken to their houses and their husbands severely punished.

12. To prevent music and dances in wedding parties. In the case of violation the head of the family will be arrested and punished.

13. To prevent the playing of music drum. The prohibition of this should be announced. If anybody does this then the religious elders can decide about it.

14. To prevent sewing ladies cloth and taking female body measures by tailor. If women or fashion magazines are seen in the shop the tailor should be imprisoned.

15. To prevent sorcery. All the related books should be burnt and the magician should be imprisoned until his repentance.

16. To prevent not praying and order gathering pray at the bazaar. Prayer should be done on their due times in all districts. Transportation should be strictly

prohibited and all people are obliged to go to the mosque. If young people are seen in the shops they will be immediately imprisoned.

Source: Ahmed Rashid, *Taliban: Militant Islam, Oil and Fundamentalism in Central Asia* (New Haven: Yale University Press, 2001).

U.S. Invasion of Afghanistan

DOCUMENT IN CONTEXT

Following the September 11, 2001, al-Qaida attacks against the United States, President George W. Bush launched what he called a "global war on terror." It would begin with an attack on al-Qaida, which was based in Afghanistan under the protection of the Taliban government. The Bush administration decided on a full-scale invasion of Afghanistan requiring the support of neighboring Pakistan.

Pakistan's military and intelligence services long had been the principal source of outside support for the Taliban, because the Pakistanis considered the Taliban to be reliable allies who would not threaten Pakistani interests. Since 1999 Pakistan had been led by Gen. Pervez Musharraf, the head of the military who had ousted the civilian government in a coup. Senior U.S. diplomats visited Musharraf in the days after the September 11 attacks and demanded that he provide support for a U.S. military operation against the Taliban, including intelligence information about the Taliban's military formations and permission for U.S. planes to use Pakistani airspace. Musharraf reportedly agreed to these demands reluctantly and only under considerable pressure.

In a televised speech on September 19, Musharraf told the Pakistani people of the U.S. requests and made clear that he had agreed to them, but he did so while also suggesting that a decision remained pending. "The decision we can take today can have far-reaching and wide-ranging consequences," he said. "The crisis is formidable and unprecedented." He added, "We are trying our best to come out of this critical situation without any damage to Afghanistan and Taliban."

In a speech to a joint session of Congress the day after Musharraf's speech, President Bush announced the launch of his global war on terror. He presented no specific actions for this war, but he did lay down a series of demands for the Taliban, whom he noted harbored Osama bin Laden and al-Qaida. His demands included turning bin Laden and his colleagues over to the United States, closing down al-Qaida's training camps, and opening the camps to U.S. inspection. "These demands are not open to negotiation or discussion," Bush said. "The Taliban must act and act immediately. They will hand over the terrorists, or they will share in their fate."

Ousting the Taliban

Bush made his demands in the midst of a rapid U.S. military buildup in the Middle East and Indian Ocean, supported by Great Britain. U.S. special forces and intelligence agents also moved into northern Afghanistan to coordinate war plans with commanders of the Northern Alliance, the last major guerrilla group still fighting five years after the Taliban took power. The Northern Alliance, however, recently had lost its most successful commander, Ahmed Shah Massoud, who had been killed in a terrorist-type bombing two days before the September 11 attacks.

The Taliban took none of the steps demanded by Bush, so on October 7, U.S. and British forces launched air attacks against military targets in Afghanistan while Northern Alliance forces moved south from their camps into the valleys of northern Afghanistan. In coordinated speeches from Washington and London, Bush and British prime minister Tony Blair announced the start of combat in Afghanistan and set out what appeared to be limited goals for it. Bush said the "carefully targeted actions are designed to disrupt the use of Afghanistan as a terrorist base of operations, and to attack the military capability of the Taliban regime." Blair said the war's objectives were "to eradicate Osama bin Laden's network of terror and to take action against the Taliban regime that is sponsoring it." Neither leader specifically listed removing the Taliban from power as a goal, though this clearly was their intent.

Taliban forces put up fierce resistance for several weeks in the face of unrelenting U.S. bombing, but the tide of war eventually turned against them. On November 9 the Northern Alliance captured Mazar e-Sharif, a city that had been a center of fighting throughout the late 1990s. Four days later, on November 13, the Taliban abandoned Kabul, and units from the Northern Alliance moved into the capital, greeted by cheering crowds. Taliban forces retreated to Kandahar, the group's original base in southern Afghanistan, but were forced from that city on December 9, ending the last vestiges of Taliban rule.

Ousted from power but not destroyed as a force, thousands of Taliban fighters—along with members of al-Qaida—disappeared into the mountains of southern and eastern Afghanistan or crossed the ill-defined border into neighboring Pakistan. The U.S. military mounted a major effort to locate bin Laden and Mullah Mohammad Omar, the Taliban leader, but to no avail. During the fighting, bin Laden was believed to have taken refuge in a rugged area of eastern Afghanistan known as Tora Bora, but an intense manhunt failed to find him. For years afterward, U.S. officials said they believed bin Laden and his key aides were still in hiding along the Afghanistan-Pakistan border. Frustrated U.S. officials offered a $25 million reward for information leading to bin Laden's capture, but as of 2007 had no takers.

Bonn Agreement

With fighting ongoing, UN officials and diplomats from the United States and other countries began the process of putting together a new government for Afghanistan. An initial meeting took place in October in Pakistan, the base of numerous anti-Taliban groups. In late November, the German government flew more than thirty representatives of major Afghan ethnic, tribal, and political groups to Bonn for a conference to develop an interim government. Lakhdar Brahimi, a former Algerian foreign minister who often served as a troubleshooter for UN secretary-general Kofi Annan, was the chief mediator. Brahimi was widely respected, especially for his ability to coax enemies into compromising.

Despite the long history of sectarian and tribal conflict in Afghanistan, the delegates reached agreement on a government framework and interim leaders in just two weeks. Their agreement, signed and announced on December 5, called for an interim government to serve for six months, followed by the convening of a *loya jirga,* a traditional assembly of notables. This meeting was to be presided over by former king Mohammad Zahir Shah, who had been ousted from power in 1973, had since lived in Italy, but still retained wide support in Afghanistan. The loya jirga would appoint a "transitional government" to serve two years, during which period, another loya jirga would draft a constitution under which national elections would be held for a permanent government.

As Afghanistan's temporary leader the delegates chose Hamid Karzai, the head of a prominent family among the Pashtuns, the country's largest ethnic group. Karzai was not a famed guerrilla fighter—as were many of the delegates and those angling for power—but he was well-known in Western capitals and, the Afghan leaders believed, would be able to secure the financial backing that Afghanistan clearly would need after decades of war.

The UN Security Council endorsed the Afghan agreement on December 6, giving it a legal imprimatur. Karzai obtained the backing of Zahir Shah and key Northern Alliance commanders who still controlled Kabul and took office on December 22. Among those pledging to support his interim government were two men who had not attended the sessions in Bonn and had been critical of the resulting agreement: Burhanuddin Rabbani, who had been president of Afghanistan after the communist government fell in 1992 and for years afterward was recognized as president by the United Nations, and Abdurrashid Dostum, an Uzbek warlord who was one of the most important of the Northern Alliance commanders. In the past, Dostum had been famous for shifting allegiances according to the prevailing winds of Afghanistan. His grudging endorsement of Karzai was widely seen as a good sign for the new government, at least for the moment (The Karzai Government, p. 615).

Military Decisions and Financial Assistance

After the Taliban's removal from power, no single authority fully controlled the majority of Afghan territory. The Northern Alliance controlled Kabul and much of the northern part of the country; the U.S. military and U.S. allies had some control over Kandahar and other key cities in the east and south; and the country's many warlords and ethnic commanders emerged to reassert control over their home territories.

UN officials and numerous experts on peacekeeping in postconflict situations recommended the creation of a large nationwide peacekeeping force to stabilize Afghanistan while Karzai's new government gained its footing and put together a new army. The Bush administration, however, argued that such a peacekeeping force would interfere with its ongoing military operations to track down remnants of the Taliban and al-Qaida fighters. Key administration officials, from Bush on down, also had an ideological aversion to international peacekeeping operations, which they insisted usually ended in failure. As a result, the Bonn agreement and UN Security Council Resolution 1386 approved on December 20 called for a peacekeeping force limited to Kabul and "its surrounding areas." Britain and other NATO countries—excluding the United States—contributed troops to this new force, the International Security Assistance Force (ISAF), which initially was under U.S. command but essentially amounted to little more than a palace guard for Karzai and his new government in Kabul. As the Taliban reemerged and the security situation deteriorated, the Bush administration gradually relented in its opposition to a nationwide peacekeeping force. The Security Council in 2003 authorized ISAF to expand its operations outside the Kabul region, but the expansion took place slowly because of continuing U.S. resistance. It was not until 2006 that the peacekeeping force operated on a truly nationwide basis and came under the command of NATO. Meanwhile, thousands of American troops remained in Afghanistan under a separate U.S. command, with the objective of tracking down Taliban and al-Qaida fighters.

The United States and other countries poured billions of dollars in emergency relief supplies and long-term development aid into Afghanistan in the years after 2001. By the beginning of 2005, total aid had reached approximately $9 billion, just short of the $10 billion the United Nations had estimated in 2002 would be necessary to meet the country's immediate needs. Afghanistan was in such terrible shape after a quarter-century of war, however, that even this large infusion of foreign assistance did little to improve the lives of most Afghan residents. Kabul was transformed into a relatively cosmopolitan city, with a few luxury hotels and a high-end shopping district, but millions of refugees who had sought shelter in the capital and other cities during the years of conflict still lived in shacks without electricity or running water. Karzai's government struggled to keep up with the demand for services from its citizens and the demands from Western governments for accountability in the use of aid money. In January 2006, international donors agreed to support another $10 billion aid effort to help Afghanistan meet its needs.

Following are excerpts from a speech to the people of Pakistan by President Pervez Musharraf delivered on September 19, 2001, concerning U.S. requests for Pakistani cooperation in an impending invasion of Afghanistan; texts of statements made October 7, 2001, by U.S. president George W. Bush and British prime minister Tony Blair announcing the start of military operations against the Taliban regime and the al-Qaida network in Afghanistan; and excerpts from the "Agreement on Provisional Arrangements in Afghanistan Pending the Re-Establishment of Permanent Government Institutions," signed on December 5, 2001, in Bonn, Germany, by representatives of major political, ethnic, and tribal factions from Afghanistan.

DOCUMENT

President Musharraf Speech to the People of Pakistan

SEPTEMBER 19, 2001

My dear countrymen, Asslam-o-Alaikum:
The situation confronting the nation today and the international crisis have impelled me to take the nation into confidence. First of all, I would like to express heartfelt sympathies to the United States for the thousands of valuable lives lost in the United States due to horrendous acts of terrorism. We are all the more grieved because in this incident people from about 45 countries from all over the world lost their lives. People of all ages old, children, women and people from all and every religion lost their lives. Many Pakistanis also lost their lives. These people were capable Pakistanis who had gone to improve their lives.

On this loss of lives I express my sympathies with those families. I pray to Allah to rest their souls in peace. This act of terrorism has raised a wave of deep grief, anger and retaliation in the United States. Their first target from day one is Osama bin Laden's movement Al-Qaeda, about which they say that it is their first target. The second target are Taliban and that is because Taliban have given refuge to Osama and his network. This has been their demand for many years. They have been demanding their extradition and presentation before the international court of justice. Taliban have been rejecting this.

The third target is a long war against terrorism at the international level. The thing to ponder is that in these three targets nobody is talking about war against Islam or the people of Afghanistan. Pakistan is being asked to support this campaign. What is this support? Generally speaking, these are three important things in which America is asking for our help. First is intelligence and information exchange, second support is the use of our airspace and the third is that they are asking for logistic support from us.

I would like to tell you now that they do not have any operational plan right now. Therefore we do not have any details on this count but we know that whatever are the United States' intentions they have the support of the UN Security Council and the General Assembly in the form of a resolution. This is a resolution for war against terrorism and this is a resolution for punishing those people who support terrorism. Islamic countries have supported this resolution. This is the situation as it prevailed in the outside world.

Now I would like to inform you about the internal situation. Pakistan is facing a very critical situation and I believe that after 1971, this is the most critical period. The decision we take today can have far-reaching and wide-ranging consequences. The crisis is formidable and unprecedented. If we take wrong decisions in this crisis, it can lead to worst consequences. On the other hand, if we take right decisions, its results will be good. The negative consequences can endanger Pakistan's integrity and solidarity. Our critical concerns, our important concerns can come under threat. When I say critical concerns, I mean our strategic assets and the cause of Kashmir. If these come under threat it would be a worse situation for us.

On the other hand, we can re-emerge politically as a responsible and dignified nation and all our difficulties can be minimized. I have considered all these factors and held consultations with those who hold different opinions. I met the corps commanders, National Security Council and the Federal Cabinet. I interacted with the media. I invited the religious scholars and held discussions with them. I met politicians. I also invited intellectuals. I will be meeting with the tribal chiefs and Kashmiri leaders tomorrow. This is the same process of consultation that I held earlier. I noted that there was difference of opinion but an overwhelming majority favors patience, prudence and wisdom. Some of them, I think about ten percent, favored sentimental approach. . . .

Pakistan's armed forces and every Pakistani citizen is ready to offer any sacrifice in order to defend Pakistan and secure its strategic assets. Make no mistake and entertain no misunderstanding. At this very moment our Air Force is at high alert; and they are ready for "Do or die" Missions My countrymen! In such a situation, a wrong decision can lead to unbearable losses. What are our critical concerns and priorities? These are four:

First of all is the security of the country and external threat.
Second is our economy and its revival.
Third are our strategic nuclear and missile assets.
And Kashmir cause.

The four are our critical concerns. Any wrong judgment on our part can damage all our interests. While taking a decision, we have to keep in mind all these factors. The decision should reflect supremacy of righteousness and it should be in conformity with Islam. Whatever we are doing, it is according to Islam and it upholds the principle of righteousness. . . .

Some of our friends seem to be much worried about Afghanistan. I must tell them that I and my government are much more worried about Afghanistan and Taliban. I have done everything for Afghanistan and Taliban when the entire world is against them. I have met about twenty to twenty five world leaders and talked to each of them in favor of the Taliban. I have told them that sanctions should not be imposed on Afghanistan and that we should engage them. I have been repeating this stance before all leaders but I am sorry to say that none of our friends accepted this.

Even in this situation, we are trying our best to cooperate with them. I sent Director General ISI [Pakistani intelligence service] with my personal letter to Mullah Omar [head of the Taliban]. He returned after spending two days there. I have informed Mullah Omar about the gravity of the situation. We are trying our best to come out of this critical situation without any damage to Afghanistan and Taliban. This is my earnest endeavor and with the blessings of Allah I will continue to seek such a way out.

We are telling the Americans too that they should be patient. Whatever their plans, they should be cautious and balanced. We are asking them to come up with whatever evidence they have against Osama bin Laden. What I would like to know is how do we save Afghanistan and Taliban. And how do we ensure that they suffer minimum losses. I am sure that you will favor that we do so and bring some improvement by working with the nations of the world. At this juncture, I am worried about Pakistan only. I am the Supreme Commander of Pakistan and I give top priority to the defense of Pakistan. Defense of any other country comes later.

We want to take decisions in the interest of Pakistan. I know that the majority of the people favor our decisions. I also know that some elements are trying to take unfair advantage of the situation and promote their personal agenda and advance the interests of their parties. They are poised to create dissensions and damage the country. There is no reason why this minority should be allowed to hold the sane majority as a hostage.

I appeal to all Pakistanis to display unity and solidarity and foil the nefarious designs of such elements who intend to harm the interests of the country. At this critical juncture, we have to frustrate the evil designs of our enemies and safeguard national interests. Pakistan is considered a fortress of Islam. God forbid, if this fortress is harmed in any way it would cause damage to the cause of Islam. My dear countrymen, have trust in me the way you reposed trust in me before going to Agra. I did not disappoint the nation there.

We have not compromised on national honor and integrity and I shall not disappoint you on this occasion either. This is firm pledge to you. In the end before I take your leave, I would like to end with the prayer of Hazrat Musa (A.S)(Prophet Moses) as given in Sura-e-Taha: "May Allah open my chest, make my task easier, untie my tongue so that they may comprehend my intent."

May Allah be with us in our endeavors.

Pakistan Paindabad.

SOURCE: "Statement by President of Pakistan," *Historic Documents of 2001* (Washington, D.C.: CQ Press, 2002), 632–636.

DOCUMENT

Bush on the Start of Military Strikes against Afghanistan

OCTOBER 7, 2001

Good afternoon. On my orders, the United States military has begun strikes against al Qaeda terrorist training camps and military installations of the Taliban regime in Afghanistan. These carefully targeted actions are designed to disrupt the use of Afghanistan as a terrorist base of operations, and to attack the military capability of the Taliban regime.

We are joined in this operation by our staunch friend, Great Britain. Other close friends, including Canada, Australia, Germany and France, have pledged forces as the operation unfolds. More than 40 countries in the Middle East, Africa, Europe and across Asia have granted air transit or landing rights. Many more have shared intelligence. We are supported by the collective will of the world.

More than two weeks ago, I gave Taliban leaders a series of clear and specific demands: Close terrorist training camps; hand over leaders of the al Qaeda network; and return all foreign nationals, including American citizens, unjustly detained in your country. None of these demands were met. And now the Taliban will pay a price. By destroying camps and disrupting communications, we will make it more difficult for the terror network to train new recruits and coordinate their evil plans.

Initially, the terrorists may burrow deeper into caves and other entrenched hiding places. Our military action is also designed to clear the way for sustained, comprehensive and relentless operations to drive them out and bring them to justice.

At the same time, the oppressed people of Afghanistan will know the generosity of America and our allies. As we strike military targets, we'll also drop food, medicine and supplies to the starving and suffering men and women and children of Afghanistan.

The United States of America is a friend to the Afghan people, and we are the friends of almost a billion worldwide who practice the Islamic faith. The United States of America is an enemy of those who aid terrorists and of the barbaric criminals who profane a great religion by committing murder in its name.

This military action is a part of our campaign against terrorism, another front in a war that has already been joined through diplomacy, intelligence, the freezing of financial assets and the arrests of known terrorists by law enforcement agents in 38 countries. Given the nature and reach of our enemies, we will win this conflict by the patient accumulation of successes, by meeting a series of challenges with determination and will and purpose.

Today we focus on Afghanistan, but the battle is broader. Every nation has a choice to make. In this conflict, there is no neutral ground. If any government sponsors the outlaws and killers of innocents, they have become outlaws and murderers, themselves. And they will take that lonely path at their own peril.

I'm speaking to you today from the Treaty Room of the White House, a place where American Presidents have worked for peace. We're a peaceful nation. Yet, as we have learned, so suddenly and so tragically, there can be no peace in a world of sudden terror. In the face of today's new threat, the only way to pursue peace is to pursue those who threaten it.

We did not ask for this mission, but we will fulfill it. The name of today's military operation is Enduring Freedom. We defend not only our precious freedoms, but also the freedom of people everywhere to live and raise their children free from fear.

I know many Americans feel fear today. And our government is taking strong precautions. All law enforcement and intelligence agencies are working aggressively around America, around the world and around the clock. At my request, many governors have activated the National Guard to strengthen airport security. We have called up Reserves to reinforce our military capability and strengthen the protection of our homeland.

In the months ahead, our patience will be one of our strengths—patience with the long waits that will result from tighter security; patience and understanding that it will take time to achieve our goals; patience in all the sacrifices that may come.

Today, those sacrifices are being made by members of our Armed Forces who now defend us so far from home, and by their proud and worried families. A Commander-in-Chief sends America's sons and daughters into a battle in a foreign land only after the greatest care and a lot of prayer. We ask a lot of those who wear our uniform. We ask them to leave their loved ones, to travel great distances, to risk injury, even to be prepared to make the ultimate sacrifice of their lives. They are dedicated, they are honorable; they represent the best of our country. And we are grateful.

To all the men and women in our military—every sailor, every soldier, every airman, every coastguardsman, every Marine—I say this: Your mission is defined; your objectives are clear; your goal is just. You have my full confidence, and you will have every tool you need to carry out your duty.

I recently received a touching letter that says a lot about the state of America in these difficult times—a letter from a 4th-grade girl, with a father in the military: "As much as I don't want my Dad to fight," she wrote, "I'm willing to give him to you."

This is a precious gift, the greatest she could give. This young girl knows what America is all about. Since September 11, an entire generation of young Americans has gained new understanding of the value of freedom, and its cost in duty and in sacrifice.

The battle is now joined on many fronts. We will not waver; we will not tire; we will not falter; and we will not fail. Peace and freedom will prevail.

Thank you. May God continue to bless America.

SOURCE: The White House, Office of the Press Secretary, "Presidential Address to the Nation," www.whitehouse .gov/news/releases/2001/10/20011007-8.html.

DOCUMENT

Blair Statement on Military Action in Afghanistan

OCTOBER 7, 2001

As you will know from the announcement by President Bush military action against targets inside Afghanistan has begun. I can confirm that UK forces are engaged in this action. I want to pay tribute if I might right at the outset to Britain's armed forces. There is no greater strength for a British Prime Minister and the British nation at a time like this than to know that the forces we are calling upon are amongst the very best in the world.

They and their families are, of course, carrying an immense burden at this moment and will be feeling deep anxiety as will the British people. But we can take pride in their courage, their sense of duty and the esteem with which they're held throughout the world.

No country lightly commits forces to military action and the inevitable risks involved but we made it clear following the attacks upon the United States on September 11th that we would take part in action once it was clear who was responsible.

There is no doubt in my mind, nor in the mind of anyone who has been through all the available evidence, including intelligence material, that these attacks were carried out by the al Qaeda network masterminded by Osama bin Laden. Equally it is clear that his network is harbored and supported by the Taliban regime inside Afghanistan.

It is now almost a month since the atrocity occurred, it is more than two weeks since an ultimatum was delivered to the Taliban to yield up the terrorists or face the consequences. It is clear beyond doubt that they will not do this. They were given the choice of siding with justice or siding with terror and they chose to side with terror.

There are three parts all equally important to the operation of which we're engaged: military, diplomatic and humanitarian. The military action we are taking will be targeted against places we know to be involved in the operation of terror or against the military apparatus of the Taliban. This military plan has been put together mindful of our determination to do all we humanly can to avoid civilian casualties.

I cannot disclose, obviously, how long this action will last but we will act with reason and resolve. We have set the objectives to eradicate Osama bin Laden's network of terror and to take action against the Taliban regime that is sponsoring it. As to the precise British involvement I can confirm that last Wednesday the U.S. Government made a specific request that a number of UK military assets be used in the operation which has now begun. And I gave authority for these assets to be deployed. They include the base at Diego Garcia, reconnaissance and flight support aircraft and missile firing submarines. Missile firing submarines are in use tonight. The air assets will be available for use in the coming days.

The United States are obviously providing the bulk of the force required in leading this operation. But this is an international effort as well as UK, France, Germany, Australia and Canada have also committed themselves to take part in the operation.

On the diplomatic and political front in the time I've been Prime Minister I cannot recall a situation that has commanded so quickly such a powerful coalition of support and not just from those countries directly involved in military action but from many others in all parts of the world. The coalition has, I believe, strengthened not weakened in the twenty six days since the atrocity occurred. And this is in no small measure due to the statesmanship of President Bush to whom I pay tribute tonight.

The world understands that whilst, of course, there are dangers in acting the dangers of inaction are far, far greater. The threat of further such outrages, the threat to our economies, the threat to the stability of the world.

On the humanitarian front we are assembling a coalition of support for refugees in and outside Afghanistan which is as vital as the military coalition. Even before September 11th four million Afghans were on the move. There are two million refugees in Pakistan and one and a half million in Iran. We have to act for humanitarian reasons to alleviate the appalling suffering of the Afghan people and deliver stability so that people from that region stay in that region. Britain, of course, is heavily involved in this effort.

So we are taking action therefore on all those three fronts: military, diplomatic and humanitarian. I also want to say very directly to the British people why this matters so much directly to Britain. First let us not forget that the attacks of the September 11th represented the worst terrorist outrage against British citizens in our history. The murder of British citizens, whether it happens overseas or not, is an attack upon Britain. But even if no British citizen had died it would be right to act.

This atrocity was an attack on us all, on people of all faiths and people of none. We know the al Qaeda network threaten Europe, including Britain, and, indeed, any nation throughout the world that does not share their fanatical views. So we have a direct interest in acting in our own self defence to protect British lives. It was also an attack not just on lives but on livelihoods. We can see since the 11th of September how economic confidence has suffered with all that means for British jobs and British industry. Our prosperity and standard of living, therefore, require us to deal with this terrorist threat.

We act also because the al Qaeda network and the Taliban regime are funded in large part on the drugs trade. Ninety per cent of all the heroin sold on British streets originates from Afghanistan. Stopping that trade is, again, directly in our interests.

I wish to say finally, as I've said many times before, that this is not a war with Islam. It angers me, as it angers the vast majority of Muslims, to hear bin Laden and his associates described as Islamic terrorists. They are terrorists pure and simple. Islam is a peaceful and tolerant religion and the acts of these people are wholly contrary to the teachings of the Koran.

These are difficult and testing times therefore for all of us. People are bound to be concerned about what the terrorists may seek to do in response. I should say there is at present no specific credible threat to the UK that we know of and that we have in place tried and tested contingency plans which are the best possible response to any further attempts at terror.

This, of course, is a moment of the utmost gravity for the world. None of the leaders involved in this action want war. None of our nations want it. We are a peaceful people. But we know that sometimes to safeguard peace we have to fight. Britain has learnt that lesson many times in our history. We only do it if the cause is just but this cause is just. The murder of almost seven thousand innocent people in America was an attack on our freedom, our way of life, an attack on civilized values the world over. We waited so that those responsible could be yielded up by those shielding them. That offer was refused, we have now no choice so we will act. And our determination in acting is total. We will not let up or rest until our objectives are met in full.

Thank you.

SOURCE: 10 Downing Street, "Prime Minister's Statement on Military Action in Afghanistan," www.number-10.gov.uk/output/Page1615.asp.

DOCUMENT

Bonn Agreement

DECEMBER 5, 2001

The participants in the UN Talks on Afghanistan,
In the presence of the Special Representative of the Secretary-General for Afghanistan,

Determined to end the tragic conflict in Afghanistan and promote national reconciliation, lasting peace, stability and respect for human rights in the country,

Reaffirming the independence, national sovereignty and territorial integrity of Afghanistan,

Acknowledging the right of the people of Afghanistan to freely determine their own political future in accordance with the principles of Islam, democracy, pluralism and social justice,

Expressing their appreciation to the Afghan mujahidin who, over the years, have defended the independence, territorial integrity and national unity of the country and have played a major role in the struggle against terrorism and oppression, and whose sacrifice has now made them both heroes of jihad and champions of peace, stability and reconstruction of their beloved homeland, Afghanistan,

Aware that the unstable situation in Afghanistan requires the implementation of emergency interim arrangements and expressing their deep appreciation to His Excellency Professor Burhanuddin Rabbani for his readiness to transfer power to an interim authority which is to be established pursuant to this agreement,

Recognizing the need to ensure broad representation in these interim arrangements of all segments of the Afghan population, including groups that have not been adequately represented at the UN Talks on Afghanistan,

Noting that these interim arrangements are intended as a first step toward the establishment of a broad-based, gender-sensitive, multi-ethnic and fully representative government, and are not intended to remain in place beyond the specified period of time,

Recognizing that some time may be required for a new Afghan security force to be fully constituted and functional and that therefore other security provisions detailed in Annex I to this agreement must meanwhile be put in place,

Considering that the United Nations, as the internationally recognized impartial institution, has a particularly important role to play, detailed in Annex II to this agreement, in the period prior to the establishment of permanent institutions in Afghanistan,

Have agreed as follows:

THE INTERIM AUTHORITY

I. General provisions

1) An Interim Authority shall be established upon the official transfer of power on 22 December 2001.

2) The Interim Authority shall consist of an Interim Administration presided over by a Chairman, a Special Independent Commission for the Convening of the Emergency Loya Jirga, and a Supreme Court of Afghanistan, as well as such other courts as may be established by the Interim Administration. The composition, functions and governing procedures for the Interim Administration and the Special Independent Commission are set forth in this agreement.

3) Upon the official transfer of power, the Interim Authority shall be the repository of Afghan sovereignty, with immediate effect. As such, it shall, throughout the interim period, represent Afghanistan in its external relations and shall occupy the seat of Afghanistan at the United Nations and in its specialized agencies, as well as in other international institutions and conferences.

4) An Emergency Loya Jirga shall be convened within six months of the establishment of the Interim Authority. The Emergency Loya Jirga will be opened by His Majesty Mohammed Zaher, the former King of Afghanistan. The Emergency Loya Jirga shall decide on a Transitional Authority, including a broad-based transitional administration, to lead Afghanistan until such time as a fully representative government can be elected through free and fair elections to be held no later than two years from the date of the convening of the Emergency Loya Jirga.

5) The Interim Authority shall cease to exist once the Transitional Authority has been established by the Emergency Loya Jirga.

6) A Constitutional Loya Jirga shall be convened within eighteen months of the establishment of the Transitional Authority, in order to adopt a new constitution for Afghanistan. In order to assist the Constitutional Loya Jirga prepare the proposed Constitution, the Transitional Administration shall, within two months of its commencement and with the assistance of the United Nations, establish a Constitutional Commission.

II. Legal framework and judicial system

1) The following legal framework shall be applicable on an interim basis until the adoption of the new Constitution referred to above:

    i)   The Constitution of 1964, a/ to the extent that its provisions are not inconsistent with those contained in this agreement, and b/ with the exception of those provisions relating to the monarchy and to the executive and legislative bodies provided in the Constitution; and

    ii) existing laws and regulations, to the extent that they are not inconsistent with this agreement or with international legal obligations to which Afghanistan is a party, or with those applicable provisions contained in the Constitution of 1964, provided that the Interim Authority shall have the power to repeal or amend those laws and regulations.

2) The judicial power of Afghanistan shall be independent and shall be vested in a Supreme Court of Afghanistan, and such other courts as may be established by the Interim Administration. The Interim Administration shall establish, with the assistance of the United Nations, a Judicial Commission to rebuild the domestic justice system in accordance with Islamic principles, international standards, the rule of law and Afghan legal traditions.

III. Interim Administration

A. *Composition*

1) The Interim Administration shall be composed of a Chairman, five Vice Chairmen and 24 other members. Each member, except the Chairman, may head a department of the Interim Administration.

2) The participants in the UN Talks on Afghanistan have invited His Majesty Mohammed Zaher, the former King of Afghanistan, to chair the Interim Administration. His Majesty has indicated that he would prefer that a suitable candidate acceptable to the participants be selected as the Chair of the Interim Administration.

3) The Chairman, the Vice Chairmen and other members of the Interim Administration have been selected by the participants in the UN Talks on Afghanistan, as listed in Annex IV to this agreement. The selection has been made on the basis of

professional competence and personal integrity from lists submitted by the participants in the UN Talks, with due regard to the ethnic, geographic and religious composition of Afghanistan and to the importance of the participation of women.

4) No person serving as a member of the Interim Administration may simultaneously hold membership of the Special Independent Commission for the Convening of the Emergency Loya Jirga.

B. *Procedures*

1) The Chairman of the Interim Administration, or in his/her absence one of the Vice Chairmen, shall call and chair meetings and propose the agenda for these meetings.

2) The Interim Administration shall endeavour to reach its decisions by consensus. In order for any decision to be taken, at least 22 members must be in attendance. If a vote becomes necessary, decisions shall be taken by a majority of the members present and voting, unless otherwise stipulated in this agreement. The Chairman shall cast the deciding vote in the event that the members are divided equally.

C. *Functions*

1) The Interim Administration shall be entrusted with the day-to-day conduct of the affairs of state, and shall have the right to issue decrees for the peace, order and good government of Afghanistan.

2) The Chairman of the Interim Administration or, in his/her absence, one of the Vice Chairmen, shall represent the Interim Administration as appropriate.

3) Those members responsible for the administration of individual departments shall also be responsible for implementing the policies of the Interim Administration within their areas of responsibility.

4) Upon the official transfer of power, the Interim Administration shall have full jurisdiction over the printing and delivery of the national currency and special drawing rights from international financial institutions. The Interim Administration shall establish, with the assistance of the United Nations, a Central Bank of Afghanistan that will regulate the money supply of the country through transparent and accountable procedures.

5) The Interim Administration shall establish, with the assistance of the United Nations, an independent Civil Service Commission to provide the Interim Authority and the future Transitional Authority with shortlists of candidates for key posts in the administrative departments, as well as those of governors and uluswals, in order to ensure their competence and integrity.

6) The Interim Administration shall, with the assistance of the United Nations, establish an independent Human Rights Commission, whose responsibilities will include human rights monitoring, investigation of violations of human rights, and development of domestic human rights institutions. The Interim Administration may, with the assistance of the United Nations, also establish any other commissions to review matters not covered in this agreement.

7) The members of the Interim Administration shall abide by a Code of Conduct elaborated in accordance with international standards.

8) Failure by a member of the Interim Administration to abide by the provisions of the Code of Conduct shall lead to his/her suspension from that body. The decision to suspend a member shall be taken by a two-thirds majority of the membership of the Interim Administration on the proposal of its Chairman or any of its Vice Chairmen.

9) The functions and powers of members of the Interim Administration will be further elaborated, as appropriate, with the assistance of the United Nations.

IV. The Special Independent Commission for the Convening of the Emergency Loya Jirga

1) The Special Independent Commission for the Convening of the Emergency Loya Jirga shall be established within one month of the establishment of the Interim Authority. The Special Independent Commission will consist of twenty-one members, a number of whom should have expertise in constitutional or customary law. The members will be selected from lists of candidates submitted by participants in the UN Talks on Afghanistan as well as Afghan professional and civil society groups. The United Nations will assist with the establishment and functioning of the commission and of a substantial secretariat.

2) The Special Independent Commission will have the final authority for determining the procedures for and the number of people who will participate in the Emergency Loya Jirga. The Special Independent Commission will draft rules and procedures specifying (i) criteria for allocation of seats to the settled and nomadic population residing in the country; (ii) criteria for allocation of seats to the Afghan refugees living in Iran, Pakistan, and elsewhere, and Afghans from the diaspora; (iii) criteria for inclusion of civil society organizations and prominent individuals, including Islamic scholars, intellectuals, and traders, both within the country and in the diaspora. The Special Independent Commission will ensure that due attention is paid to the representation in the Emergency Loya Jirga of a significant number of women as well as all other segments of the Afghan population.

3) The Special Independent Commission will publish and disseminate the rules and procedures for the convening of the Emergency Loya Jirga at least ten weeks before the Emergency Loya Jirga convenes, together with the date for its commencement and its suggested location and duration.

4) The Special Independent Commission will adopt and implement procedures for monitoring the process of nomination of individuals to the Emergency Loya Jirga to ensure that the process of indirect election or selection is transparent and fair. To pre-empt conflict over nominations, the Special Independent Commission will specify mechanisms for filing of grievances and rules for arbitration of disputes.

5) The Emergency Loya Jirga will elect a Head of the State for the Transitional Administration and will approve proposals for the structure and key personnel of the Transitional Administration.

V. Final provisions

1) Upon the official transfer of power, all mujahidin, Afghan armed forces and armed groups in the country shall come under the command and control of the Interim Authority, and be reorganized according to the requirements of the new Afghan security and armed forces.

2) The Interim Authority and the Emergency Loya Jirga shall act in accordance with basic principles and provisions contained in international instruments on human rights and international humanitarian law to which Afghanistan is a party.

3) The Interim Authority shall cooperate with the international community in the fight against terrorism, drugs and organized crime. It shall commit itself to respect

international law and maintain peaceful and friendly relations with neighbouring countries and the rest of the international community.

4) The Interim Authority and the Special Independent Commission for the Convening of the Emergency Loya Jirga will ensure the participation of women as well as the equitable representation of all ethnic and religious communities in the Interim Administration and the Emergency Loya Jirga.

5) All actions taken by the Interim Authority shall be consistent with Security Council resolution 1378 (14 November 2001) and other relevant Security Council resolutions relating to Afghanistan.

6) Rules of procedure for the organs established under the Interim Authority will be elaborated as appropriate with the assistance of the United Nations.

This agreement, of which the annexes constitute an integral part, done in Bonn on this 5th day of December 2001 in the English language, shall be the authentic text, in a single copy which shall remain deposited in the archives of the United Nations. Official texts shall be provided in Dari and Pashto, and such other languages as the Special Representative of the Secretary-General may designate. The Special Representative of the Secretary-General shall send certified copies in English, Dari and Pashto to each of the participants. . . .

ANNEX I
INTERNATIONAL SECURITY FORCE

1. The participants in the UN Talks on Afghanistan recognize that the responsibility for providing security and law and order throughout the country resides with the Afghans themselves. To this end, they pledge their commitment to do all within their means and influence to ensure such security, including for all United Nations and other personnel of international governmental and non-governmental organizations deployed in Afghanistan.

2. With this objective in mind, the participants request the assistance of the international community in helping the new Afghan authorities in the establishment and training of new Afghan security and armed forces.

3. Conscious that some time may be required for the new Afghan security and armed forces to be fully constituted and functioning, the participants in the UN Talks on Afghanistan request the United Nations Security Council to consider authorizing the early deployment to Afghanistan of a United Nations mandated force. This force will assist in the maintenance of security for Kabul and its surrounding areas. Such a force could, as appropriate, be progressively expanded to other urban centres and other areas.

4. The participants in the UN Talks on Afghanistan pledge to withdraw all military units from Kabul and other urban centers or other areas in which the UN mandated force is deployed. It would also be desirable if such a force were to assist in the rehabilitation of Afghanistan's infrastructure.

ANNEX II
ROLE OF THE UNITED NATIONS DURING THE INTERIM PERIOD

1. The Special Representative of the Secretary-General will be responsible for all aspects of the United Nations' work in Afghanistan.

2. The Special Representative shall monitor and assist in the implementation of all aspects of this agreement.

3. The United Nations shall advise the Interim Authority in establishing a politically neutral environment conducive to the holding of the Emergency Loya Jirga in free and fair conditions. The United Nations shall pay special attention to the conduct of those bodies and administrative departments, which could directly influence the convening and outcome of the Emergency Loya Jirga.

4. The Special Representative of the Secretary-General or his/her delegate may be invited to attend the meetings of the interim Administration and the Special Independent Commission on the Convening of the Emergency Loya Jirga.

5. If for whatever reason the Interim Administration or the Special Independent Commission were actively prevented from meeting or unable to reach a decision on a matter related to the convening of the Emergency Loya Jirga, the Special Representative of the Secretary-General shall, taking into account the views expressed in the Interim Administration or in the Special Independent Commission, use his/her good offices with a view to facilitating a resolution to the impasse or a decision.

6. The United Nations shall have the right to investigate human rights violations and, where necessary, recommend corrective action. It will also be responsible for the development and implementation of a programme of human rights Education to promote respect for and understanding of human rights.

ANNEX III
REQUEST TO THE UNITED NATIONS BY THE PARTICIPANTS AT THE UN TALKS ON AFGHANISTAN

The participants in the UN Talks on Afghanistan hereby

1. Request that the United Nations and the international community take the necessary measures to guarantee the national sovereignty, territorial integrity and unity of Afghanistan as well as the non-interference by foreign countries in Afghanistan's internal affairs;

2. Urge the United Nations, the international community, particularly donor countries and multilateral institutions, to reaffirm, strengthen and implement their commitment to assist with the rehabilitation, recovery and reconstruction of Afghanistan, in coordination with the Interim Authority;

3. Request the United Nations to conduct as soon as possible (i) a registration of voters in advance of the general elections that will be held upon the adoption of the new constitution by the constitutional Loya Jirga and (ii) a census of the population of Afghanistan.

4. Urge the United Nations and the international community, in recognition of the heroic role played by the mujahidin in protecting the independence of Afghanistan and the dignity of its people, to take the necessary measures, in coordination with the Interim Authority, to assist in the reintegration of the mujahidin into the new Afghan security and armed forces;

5. Invite the United Nations and the international community to create a fund to assist the families and other dependents of martyrs and victims of the war, as well as the war disabled;

6. Strongly urge that the United Nations, the international community and regional organizations cooperate with the Interim Authority to combat international terrorism, cultivation and trafficking of illicit drugs and provide Afghan farmers with financial, material and technical resources for alternative crop production. . . .

SOURCE: United Nations, "Agreement on Provisional Arrangements in Afghanistan Pending the Re-Establishment of Permanent Government Institutions," www.un.org/News/dh/latest/afghan/afghan-agree.htm.

The Karzai Government

DOCUMENT IN CONTEXT

A quarter-century of political upheaval—including Soviet military occupation, civil war, and Taliban rule—had left Afghanistan a national wreck by the end of 2001. At least 5 million of the country's 25 million or so citizens had become refugees, with more than 1 million others killed. Military operations had largely destroyed its major cities and ruined large swaths of agricultural areas. Cultivation of opium poppies stood out as a rare functioning part of the economy. Regional warlords controlled all parts of the country except Kabul, where a small international peacekeeping force had been deployed, and the handful of areas where the U.S. military operated. An interim government, headed by Hamid Karzai, took office at the end of 2001, but his writ was so limited that critics derided him as the mayor of Kabul.

Over the next five years, Afghans and the international community made remarkable progress in reviving parts of Afghanistan. The United Nations sponsored a series of negotiations and two successful elections that led to the installation of the country's first democratic government. International aid projects rebuilt much of Kabul and several other cities, helped millions of refugees return to their homes, put millions of children in school, and helped jump-start economic development, particularly in Kabul. Even so, much of Afghanistan remained in ruins, and in 2006 guerrillas associated with the former Taliban regime regained enough strength to pose a significant security challenge to Karzai's government and to the NATO peacekeeping force protecting it. By 2007 Afghanistan once again teetered on the brink of renewed chaos.

Electing a New Government

Afghanistan's first post-2001 election emerged from a complex process negotiated by Afghan notables, with UN assistance, in December 2001. In the first genuine national election in Afghan history, held on October 9, 2004, Karzai defeated fifteen other candidates to win the presidency of the new permanent government. The balloting went remarkably smooth considering the country's recent conflicts and the lack of roads, telecommunications, and other infrastructure to support such an undertaking.

Elections for a two-chamber parliament, the National Assembly, were supposed to take place the following April or May, but continuing insecurity and other problems forced their postponement, until September 18, 2005. As in the presidential election, voting proceeded smoothly in determining seats in parliament and provincial councils, especially considering that more than 5,000 candidates ran for office, and voters cast their ballots at some 26,000 polling places. An estimated 6.7 million citizens went to the polls for the legislative elections, a drop of about 10 percent from the presidential election a year earlier.

The new parliament convened for the first time on December 19, 2005, using a hall in Kabul that had served as the seat of a legislature during the reign of King Mohammad Zahir Shah, who was ousted from power in 1973. U.S. vice president Dick Cheney and several other notables attended. In an hour-long speech marking the occasion, Karzai asked the legislators to set aside their past differences and work together for the sake of the country as a whole rather than for narrow ethnic or tribal interests. "Cooperation, competitions and efforts all need to happen but for the service of the people and strengthening the Government," he said. Karzai and his new government experienced numerous rocky moments, notably because cabinet members and legislators had trouble following the president's request to act on behalf of the national interest. Karzai also struggled to control regional warlords, some of whom had gained seats in the parliament and were reluctant to dismantle their private militias.

Taliban Resurgence

The Taliban had disappeared into the mountains in 2001 after being pushed from power, but they had not been thoroughly defeated. Over the next few years, the Taliban carried out regular attacks against the government and international peacekeepers, but in the early months of 2006 they launched a full-scale insurgency, thus becoming the greatest danger facing the Karzai government. Thousands of new recruits flocked to fight for the Taliban, having seen little or no improvement in their lives under the Karzai government. Many also were angered by the continuing presence of troops from the United States and other Western countries, some of whom demonstrated a lack of sensitivity to local cultural values. Many Afghans also were angered by the U.S. practice of detaining indefinitely, and reportedly torturing, suspected Taliban and al-Qaida fighters at the Bagram air base, the prison at Guantanamo Bay, Cuba, and other, secret locations. In addition, several cases of mistaken bombings by U.S. warplanes, resulting in the deaths of dozens of Afghan civilians, inflamed passions and aided recruitment by the Taliban. Karzai repeatedly expressed frustration about international military operations in his country, stating in June 2007 that "indiscriminate and imprecise" bombings had killed many civilians. As he had in the past with little effect, Karzai demanded that NATO forces coordinate their actions with his government.

In 2006, fighting killed an estimated 4,000 people in Afghanistan, nearly three times as many as during the previous year. According to official U.S. estimates, most of the dead were guerrillas from the Taliban and other antigovernment groups, but about 1,000 civilians and 105 Western soldiers also died. The George W. Bush administration, which at first had scorned the role of peacekeeping in Afghanistan, began embracing the concept in response to the Taliban's resurgence. By late 2006, NATO had assumed command of most of the nearly 40,000 Western troops in the country. NATO officials estimated that a large peacekeeping presence would be needed in Afghanistan for another three to five years.

Following are excerpts from a speech by Afghan president Hamid Karzai at the inaugural session of his country's new parliament on December 19, 2005.

DOCUMENT

Speech by President Karzai before the Afghan Parliament

DECEMBER 19, 2005

With wishes for prosperity and dignity of the Afghan nation, I inaugurate the first session and the first legislative period of the National Assembly of the Islamic Republic of Afghanistan.

Praise be to God for providing our nation the opportunity to be in control of its own destiny. This gathering represents the assumption of full sovereignty by the great people of Afghanistan and Almighty God's blessing. Over the course of our long history and during difficult days, the women and men of our country have stood steadfastly for defense of their homeland and religion and have saved their fellow countrymen and their country's historic destiny. This soil has been inherently stable for thousands of years and will last forever.

Respectable representatives of the People of Afghanistan,

With the establishment of the parliament, the main pillars of the state of Afghanistan as per the Constitution are now in place. It is an opportunity to remember those men and women who have sacrificed their lives to pave the way for this historic event. Hundreds of thousands of men and women of this country have lost their lives for freedom and we cherish their memories and pray for their souls. The enemies of our country's security resorted to killing the electoral staff, security forces and the candidates during the parliamentary elections. We pray for the souls of these victims of freedom and peace. Afghans will always cherish their memories.

Respectable Senators

Completion of pillars of the State doesn't mean full execution of the government's duties; more difficult responsibilities are lying ahead of us. Separation of powers and performance of responsibilities of each of the three powers are among the duties lying ahead. At this historic juncture, the role of parliament as a legislative power and mirror of democracy is highly critical and significant. Political institutions must demonstrate their loyalty to the Government (state) of Afghanistan. So long as the difference of opinions and sound competition among political trends are at the service of the people of Afghanistan, the country will benefit. The principle of loyalty to the Government of Afghanistan, state in the context of people, sovereignty and democracy are the principles that can't be ignored. Cooperation, competitions and efforts all need to happen but for the service of the people and strengthening the Government. The competition of different visions to adopt best approaches to give the people of Afghanistan the chance for free choice would lead to further safety of the society as well as political system.

I want to assure the people of Afghanistan and their elected representatives that the Government of the Islamic Republic of Afghanistan is the servant of the nation subject to the law and will fully abide by the decisions of the state.

It is very difficult to strengthen state institutions, ensure the maintenance of law and order, end interference, beat terrorism, fight corruption and reduce poverty unless we improve coordination among state entities and harmonize the national and international resources.

Dear distinguished members of the National Assembly,

When the Interim Administration was established, the state system was in a complete state of disarray. The political, economic, social and cultural infrastructures of the country were totally destroyed. Different parts of the country were ruled by various armed factions and had their own styles of administration. Administration system was dismantled. Roads were in state of disrepair. There were no health services and the status of education system was of most concern. The government treasury was empty and public funds and property had lost its true sense. In such a situation came very worrying the Interim administration taking control of the political leadership.

From the day one, despite all these challenges, we have tried our utmost to implement the Bonn Agreement [reached by various Afghan factions meeting in Bonn, Germany, in December 2001] with full integrity. This Agreement involved two committed sides: Afghanistan to pave the ground and facilitate implementation of the Agreement and the international community to support in military, security, economic and political areas. With support from [the] international community, Afghanistan has had the following achievements in the last four years:

Rule of Law

The convention of the Emergency Loya Jirga [a conclave of senior leaders in June 2002] was the first step towards participation of Afghan citizens in the political life of their country. This Loya Jirga to some extent filled the legal vacuum and kick-started the realization of the Bonn agreement based on the predetermined timeline. The establishment of the Constitution Drafting and Review commissions, the drafting of the constitution and subsequently the convention of the Constitutional Loya Jirga [a conclave of senior leaders in December 2003 that drafted a new constitution] for final approval were part of our concerted efforts towards building a state based on rule of law.

Approval of the constitution based on the wishes of our people legitimized our government. The constitution provides a legal and political framework for our polity and moves our country towards a democratic and sovereign state after years of devastating war.

After the establishment of the Interim Administration, the government passed several laws and issued many legislative decrees to fill the existing legal vacuum. All this was done in an effort to legitimize the working procedures of the government. In accordance with the constitution, all these laws and decrees will shortly be submitted to the National Assembly.

The presidential and parliamentary elections were two other major achievements towards building a democratic state in Afghanistan. Adherence to the principles of participation and election showed that the people of Afghanistan are taking courageous steps towards ensuring democratic rule.

Peace and Security

To expand the legitimate control of the central government throughout Afghanistan was a crucial issue in our state-building efforts. In our security policy, the demobilization, disarmament and disintegration of illegal armed groups were very problematic tasks.

The demobilization, disarmament and Reintegration (DDR) of armed groups from one side and the building and training of a national army, national police and security forces from the other, were two major tasks that needed to be accomplished.

In the first phase of the DDR program, thirty-six thousand light weapons and ten thousand heavy weapons were collected from a number of 63380 individuals out of which 61533 have been included in the reintegration process. 28157 persons have taken reintegration courses and 23370 have been provided with employment opportunities after graduation. The disarmament process continues under the DIAG program [disbandment of illegal armed groups, a process of demobilizing fighters in illegal militias] and so far sixteen thousand light and heavy weapons have been collected.

The building of a national army, police and armed forces loyal to the constitution is ongoing and so far around 34591 national army soldiers and more than fifty-thousand police and security forces have received trainings. The human and institutional capacities of the armed forces have expanded and have also been equipped technically. Their leadership and management have improved considerably.

Education

We have had visible achievements in the area of education during the past four years. Approximately 6.5 million girls and boys are attending schools and higher education institutions. 35% of these students are girls. During the Taliban regime, even one higher educational institution was not fully functioning but now there are 19 functional institutions in the country out of which 10 are universities.

Human rights, women's rights and civil society

In the last three decades, the human rights of our people especially of the women's were widely violated. In other words, Afghanistan was the home of prisons, torture and destruction. Rule of law was missing. Pluralism was opposed and the women were marginalized in the society. Now, in accordance with our constitution, the civil and human rights of all our citizens are safeguarded. The Afghan Independent Human Rights Commission and thousands of other organizations are assessing human rights issues and freely operate in our country. Today we have a free media. Around 300 papers are published inside the country. There are five TV and more than 20 radio stations. There are dozens of civil society organizations operating in the country. The emergence of civil society is an important sign of political development in our society. . . .

Esteemed representatives of the nation!
With all the success and strides, we have a long road ahead. We need to put even more efforts forward in building a stable and self-reliant Afghanistan. We must be ready to give sacrifices to protect our freedom, independence and territorial integrity. I would like to say to the nation's representatives that in spite of the success achieved in the past four years, we have not been able to fulfill all of the legitimate demands of our people.

Allow me to explain to you issues which are at the spotlight of the government's future working policy for accomplishment of which are required strong efforts.

Defending cultural values, promoting political and civil freedoms
Defending the cherished values of the sacred religion of Islam and promoting our culture are the prime objectives. We strongly believe in promoting culture of tolerance in accordance with cherished values of Islam and accepted moral principles. Adequate attention should be paid to rebuilding of mosques and religious centers, to promoting cultural values, and to appropriately utilizing of religious allocated properties. Our cultural policy recommends safeguarding of historical sites and relics as well as prevention of illegal excavation of historical sites.

Campaign against terrorism
Terrorism is still a problem to our country. To eliminate this menace, we have to address the roots and prime sources of this menace. The root of terrorism in Afghanistan has originated from outside. Those, who carry out destructive efforts and kill our religious scholars, elders, school teachers and road workers and other innocent people, and destroy our hospitals, and set ablaze schools, should keep in mind that the Afghan people are determined and united against them.

Afghanistan will not be place of terrorists, and with the grace of Allah, the Almighty, it will be safe from foreign invasion.

Two days ago in southern province of Helmand, the terrorists killed a student and a janitor of a school. These inhumane and anti-Islamic acts can well reveal the ill intentions of the terrorists.

Counter-Narcotics
To fight against cultivation, production and trafficking of narcotics is of vital importance to Afghanistan. Our farmers gain the minimum benefit of production of narcotics while utmost benefit of narcotic-trade goes to international traffickers. The main

victims of narcotics are our own youths. The drug-economy is deemed to be crime and it greatly impedes economic growth. The fund, which comes out of drug economy, disburses to help training of our enemies. Narcotic swell moral and social corruptions. Where there is tradition of narcotics, it has no place within the international community and will stay isolated.

We have pledged to our people and the international community that we will seriously fight this menace [narcotics]. Because; our religion orders fighting narcotics, so we will continue our fight for the sake of prosperity of future generations. We will continue to conduct a comprehensive program against this social threat; provision of alternative livelihood would be a part of this program.

I urge all government officials to take active part in the process of our combat for elimination of this menace. . . .

Defense and Security Policy

Security is not merely a military issue. True security can only be achieved when our people are protected against terror and violence and when they are provided with at least minimum social security. We consider security as integral parts of both our defense and social policy. Only pursuing military objectives is not rational. The policy of consolidating peace in our country should be maintained. This policy is an opportunity for those of our compatriots who are ready to abandon violence. We should not deprive our compatriots of the opportunity to return to a peaceful life. Availing this opportunity, I renew my invitation to those who love the religion and culture of our people and Afghanistan to join the peace process so that they are no longer victimized by the whims of the foreign enemies.

Peace and security cannot be achieved in this chaotic world with mere statements of morality. Afghanistan should be able to possess such a strong army equipped with patriotic aspirations so that our bitter history is not repeated. Having strong armed forces is not enough, defense and security forces should realize that they are the soldiers of this Republic and the defenders of this soil. The tradition of sacrifice and devotion of our people should always be alive and sustained by our armed forces.

Preferring national interests over partisan, ethnic and regional interests and other divisive aims should become the real belief and aspiration of Afghanistan army. The sad experiences of the last thirty years and the planned downfall of Afghanistan army by foreign countries were made possible by those who lacked such a national aspiration.

The establishment of ground and air defense forces able to defend our borders is indispensable. The Islamic Republic will do everything possible in this direction. The establishment of a professional army is not contradictory to the objective of recruitment of the youth of the country for defense and social services. The government of Afghanistan will seriously consider recruiting youth to serve under Afghanistan flag. The Afghan army and other security forces should be equipped with modern weaponry. Police and the border forces as well as other security forces should realize that they are the servants of this country and the guardians of their borders. Ensuring security and defending the liberties of our people are the prime tasks of our security forces. Security forces should not mistreat people. People are the owner of the state and the real source of political power. Combating violence, torture and mistreatment of the citizens is one of the main reasons for the legitimacy of our government and state.

Foreign Policy
Our foreign policy is based upon the principle of non-interference, peaceful resolution of disputes, acceptance of national sovereignty and national integrity of countries. Afghanistan is committed to the Charter of the United Nations, International Declaration of Human Rights, and all other international bilateral and multilateral treaties. Our policy of friendship and cooperation with all countries is based on respect to our national sovereignty and integrity. The reality of this new world is that it is shrinking day by day. In such a world, time and place take on a different meaning. Cultures are coming closer. In such a world, the foreign and domestic policies of the countries should be based on existing realities. We do not want to live in an isolated civilization and consider other cultures as foreign and enemy. Rather, we would like to consciously find our place in this globalizing process.

Today, Afghanistan is a country where countries of different cultures and beliefs are cooperating with each other in its reconstruction. From my perspective, this is the cooperation of the civilizations. The collaboration of international community in the peace-building and reconstruction process in our country is a magnificent experience for strengthening co-existence and understanding among us all. This is a historic opportunity for us to compile lessons of this experience and present them to the global community.

Our foreign policy is founded based on the following three principles: formidable loyalty to the family of Islamic countries, strategic cooperation with the Western countries, loyalty to continued friendship and belief in vital common interests with the countries of the region.

The convention of the London conference [a conference planned for January 2006 to deal with Afghanistan's development needs] with the objective of continuation of international assistances as the Bonn process is over is of paramount importance to our country. Afghanistan has the determining role in setting the agenda and discussions in this conference. . . .

Distinguished parliamentarians and representatives of the people,
The success of the Afghan people in the last few years is the output of sacrifices and aspirations of our people for a country based on peace and international support. Our people honestly and sincerely began to defend their country's reconstruction, national government and strengthening stability for which the international community offered cordial support. I take the opportunity to express my gratitude and thankfulness to all the countries and organizations which have always stood by our people in such difficult situations.

Distinguished members of the National Assembly,
We want to guide our country towards the contemporary world civility. We want to found a progressive country based on the wishes of our people. To have a strong secure

and peaceful Afghanistan with vibrant economy is the historic task that we have under-taken in the court of God, history and our people. To discharge this noble duty, we need honesty, sacrifice and concerted efforts. We will not be able to do our duty if we do not consider the love of our country and religion superior to anything else. We aspire that our black, red and green flag will always be fluttering throughout Afghanistan. We aspire that our people with full abandonment of ethnic and regional prejudice will remain united as the citizens of this Republic in the reconstruction and development of this great land.

We Afghans have the right to stand with full dignity and self-confidence in front of the people of the world and say that this immortal phoenix, this beloved Afghanistan, once again rose from the ashes of invasion and subjugation; we have the right to declare to all those who aspire the destruction of our soil, that this country will never vanquish.

May God bless you all.

SOURCE: Islamic Republic of Afghanistan, Embassy of Afghanistan in Canada, "Speech of H.E. Hamid Karzai at the Opening Session of the Parliament of Afghanistan," www.afghanemb-canada.net/en/events_activities/2005/special/parliament/speech_english_karzai.php.

Turkey

CHAPTER 8 DOCUMENTS

Overview

O ver the past century, ethnic and national identities have played crucial roles throughout the Middle East. Turkey, however, has struggled with its identities to an unusual degree. Is Turkey a Middle Eastern country, a European country, or both? What should be the status of the minority of residents—notably the Kurds and the Armenians—who are not ethnic Turks? Is Turkey an Islamic society, or is it a secular society where more than 90 percent of the people are Muslims? Is Turkey a genuine democracy in the modern, Western sense, or does the military's influence in national life mean that Turkey's democracy has yet to mature? Since the rise of Turkish nationalism in the late nineteenth century and the collapse of the Ottoman Empire following World War I, Turkey has grappled with these and similar questions about its identity as a nation. It continues to look for answers today.

Starting with Mustafa Kemal, or Ataturk, the dynamic founder of modern Turkey, Turkish leaders, have pointed the country westward, in the direction of Europe. Geographically, however, all but a sliver of Turkey is on the Asian continent. Many elements of Turkey's history, particularly its past as a great empire, also point primarily eastward, toward the Middle East.

The role of religion in society remains a core issue for Turkey. In the 1920s and 1930s, Ataturk declared Turkey to be a secular society. In it, the state and religion were not necessarily separated, but the state controlled religion, not the other way around. In 2002, Turks elected the Justice and Development Party (AKP), an avowedly Islamist political party, to lead the government. The AKP governed with moderate policies for more than four years with widespread support, but it ran into opposition from the military in 2007 when its leaders moved to take control of the presidency, the position that Ataturk had used to impose his personal stamp on Turkey. The party prevailed in 2007 by calling early elections and winning a renewed mandate to govern. How the party chooses to use that mandate could determine whether, and how far, Turkey might stray from Ataturk's secular legacy.

The political drama in 2007 concerning the presidency resurrected old disputes about the state and religion at an especially sensitive time, with Turkey and Europe

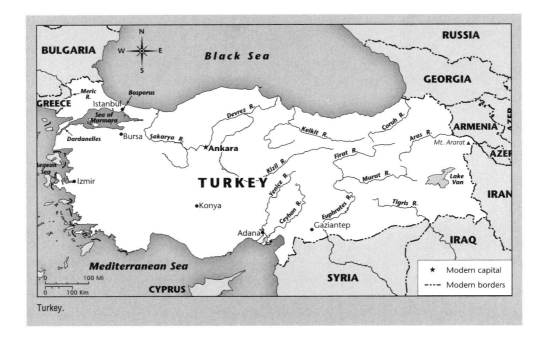

Turkey.

beginning to confront the persistent issue of Turkey's role in Europe. Although none of Turkey's territory lies along the Atlantic Ocean, Turkey had joined the North Atlantic Treaty Organization in 1952 and within a decade had begun seeking membership in the pan-European organizations that eventually evolved into the European Union. Year after year, the Europeans rebuffed Turkey, asserting that it was not really part of Europe or that it was too poor or too undemocratic to qualify.

Left unspoken by most European leaders was that Turkey had too many Muslims to be part of a Europe that still considered itself Christian, at least in name. Over the years, Europe's ambivalence about Turkey increasingly could be seen in Turkey itself. For example, it became acceptable in Turkey to suggest that the country stop yearning to join the West and instead embrace its Eastern heritage, including Islam and all the other cultural and social aspects of its location in the Middle East. Ironically, it was the AKP-led Islamist government that in 2004 finally convinced Europe to consider Turkey's application seriously. If that process stays on track, Turkey could become an EU member in another ten or fifteen years.

Mustafa Kemal, who in 1934 became known as Ataturk ("father of the Turks"), believed that he had resolved Turkey's identity issues during his long hold on power. Ataturk formally took leadership of Turkey in 1923, when he became the first president of the new republic that succeeded the Ottoman state's collapse. He had emerged as the dominant figure in Turkey four years earlier, in 1919, when he took control of a nationalist movement that rebelled against the harsh terms imposed on Turkey by the victorious Western Allies of World War I. In September 1919, Ataturk guided the writing of the Turkish National Pact, a manifesto renouncing the old Ottoman claims to Arab lands but insisting on retention of the core of Turkey—all of the Anatolian peninsula (Asia Minor) and the portion of historic Thrace surrounding Constantinople (later Istanbul).

The republic that Ataturk and his allies built on the ashes of the Ottoman Empire had the appearance, but not the reality, of a democracy. The government rested in the hands of an elected national assembly that had appointed Ataturk as president, but only the Republican People's Party, founded by Ataturk, was allowed to contest elections; Ataturk himself held nearly all real political power. In addition, Ataturk developed a series of ideas for the Turkish nation-state that guided the development of Turkey. To one degree or another, his ideas remain the core concepts of the Turkish state. Referred to as Kemalism, or the Six Arrows, the ideas are reformism, republicanism, secularism, nationalism, populism, and etatism (or stateism, a guiding role for the state in the economy).

Democracy, absent from Ataturk's ideas, did not make an appearance in Turkey in any genuine form until 1950—a dozen years after Ataturk's death and the year an opposition party swept the Republican People's Party from power. Since that time, multiparty elections have been the norm in Turkey, often with so many parties involved that no single party managed to win a majority of parliamentary seats. The result has been a series of unstable coalition governments that failed to deal with the challenges facing Turkey, especially modernizing the economy to meet the needs of global competition.

Four times—in 1960, 1971, 1980, and 1997—Turkey's military has intervened to remove governments that the generals determined to be ineffective or heading in the wrong direction. The last of these interventions, in 1997, was what Turks call a "soft coup" to force the resignation of the country's first prime minister from an openly Islamist political party, the Welfare Party. The military long had considered itself the guardian of Ataturk's legacy, so its actions in 1997 were widely seen as upholding the principle of secularism. Five years later, however, Turkey's voters gave a much stronger mandate to another Islamist party, the AKP, while at the same time ousting from office nearly all the traditional politicians who had governed in preceding decades. The AKP, led by Recep Tayyip Erdogan, a former mayor of Istanbul, established one of the most competent governments in years. In 2007, however, the generals again intervened in politics, trying this time to block Erdogan's preferred candidate for president. This action prompted Erdogan to call the early elections that his party won, a victory widely viewed as a public rebuke to the generals.

Nationalism has also been a driving force in modern Turkish history, besmirching the international reputation of Turks for nearly a century. During the last decades of the Ottoman Empire, a new generation of leaders who called themselves the Young Turks emerged to proclaim the virtues of the Turkish nation. The Young Turks seized power in 1908 and six years later dragged the empire into World War I on what would prove to be the losing side. A consequence of the Ottomans' entry into the war was a movement by ethnic Armenians in eastern Turkey to align themselves with czarist Russia on the opposing side in the war. The Young Turks reacted in 1915 by forcing the Armenians out of Turkey and into what is present-day Syria. Hundreds of thousands of Armenians died of starvation, disease, and maltreatment during the forced deportations. The exact number of deaths remains in dispute, with Armenians insisting that approximately 1.5 million people died, and most Turkish sources putting the figure at 200,000 or less. These deaths—which Armenians call the first genocide of the twenty-first century—trigger such emotion that successive Turkish governments have threatened to suspend diplomatic relations with countries that endorse the Armenian version of what occurred.

Turkish nationalists also have failed to come to terms with ethnic Kurds, particularly those who insist on a national right to an independent Kurdistan. For eight decades under Ataturk's edicts, Turkey barred public use of the Kurdish language. A rebellion by a radical Kurdish separatist group, the Kurdistan Workers' Party (PKK), raged from 1984 until 1999 and resulted in thousands of deaths. The rebellion sputtered in 1999 after Turkey captured and imprisoned PKK leader Abdullah Ocalan, but several thousand PKK loyalists remain in the Kurdish region of northern Iraq, posing what Turkish officials say is a serious threat.

Turkey's ability to deal with the Kurdish issue and the other questions posed by its history and its location at the intersection of Europe and the Middle East will determine its success in becoming the modern state that Ataturk envisioned three generations ago.

Turkey Emerges from World War I

DOCUMENT IN CONTEXT

Most Western histories of World War I emphasize its importance in ending the so-called old order in Europe—the political map of the continent in place at least since the Congress of Vienna, which restructured Europe after the final defeat of Napoleon a century earlier. World War I also demolished the considerably older order of the Ottoman Empire, which had dominated much of the Middle East for six centuries and parts of southeastern Europe for more than three centuries.

Ottoman rulers signed what turned out to be the death warrant of the empire by aligning with Germany and the Austro-Hungarian empire in August 1914 at the start of World War I. After the conflict concluded, the victorious Allies, notably Britain and France, quickly implemented their plans to carve up the Ottoman Empire by dividing the Arabic-speaking lands among themselves and splitting off key portions of Anatolia, the empire's Turkish-speaking heartland. The Treaty of Sèvres, signed in August 1920, gave France the rights to Syria and much of the eastern Mediterranean coast (including modern-day Lebanon and the southeastern coast of Anatolia); gave Italy control of the southwestern coast of Anatolia and the Dodecanese Islands (including Rhodes); awarded Greece the region of western Anatolia around the city of Smyrna (present-day Izmir) and the southeastern European region of Thrace; placed Istanbul and the strategic Dardanelles and the Bosphorus Strait under international control; created an independent country for the Armenians; and promised an autonomous area of eastern Anatolia for the Kurds (a non-Arab, Muslim people).

These harsh terms were intended to preserve the Ottoman Empire, though under the virtual control of the Allies and stripped of its most economically and strategically important territories. The harshness of the postwar settlement also had the unintended effect of stimulating an embryonic Turkish nationalist movement, which found its champion in the person of Mustafa Kemal, a dynamic former Ottoman general.

The specific events that led to the collapse of the Ottoman Empire and the creation of the modern state of Turkey began before the Treaty of Sèvres was formally signed. In May 1919, in anticipation of the treaty, a division of the Greek army landed at the coastal city of Smyrna, which had a large Greek-speaking population. Backed by the Allies, the Greek forces quickly conquered much of the surrounding countryside, often massacring the Turkish inhabitants.

In September 1919, with this Greek conquest under way, Kemal convened Turkish nationalist representatives in the town of Sivas. Delegates adopted a platform that later developed into the National Pact (or Misak-i Milli). Based in large part on President Woodrow Wilson's call for "self-determination" by the world's nationalities, the pact in essence asserted that Turks should rule over themselves but not over people of other nationalities, notably the Arabs, who for centuries had been under Ottoman rule and at the time were succumbing to European domination.

In addition to renouncing Turkish claims to the Arabic-speaking regions of the Ottoman Empire, the main points of the pact included maintaining the territorial integrity of all areas with a majority of Turkish Muslim residents; respecting the rights of minorities; restoring Istanbul and the region of the strategic straits (including Eastern Thrace) to Turkish control; and rejecting the so-called capitulations, or special legal and financial privileges for Europeans living in or doing business in Turkey. Although the pact's nationalist tenets stood at odds with the restraints imposed by the Allies on the government in Istanbul, the Ottoman parliament adopted it on January 28, 1920. The pact remains a cornerstone of Turkish policy. The Allies reacted to the adoption of the pact by imposing even tighter control on the weakened Ottoman government.

The words of the National Pact would have meant nothing if not backed by action. Kemal, a preeminent man of action, pieced together an army from former elements of the Ottoman military, and by June 1920 this new Turkish army had blocked Greek advances into Anatolia. Two years later, after a brutal war, Kemal's army pushed the Greeks out of Smyrna and firmly established his nationalist regime as the de facto successor to the Ottomans. The last act of the Greek-Turkish drama was the forced transfer in 1922–1923 of some 1.3 million ethnic Greeks from Turkey to Greece and of about 400,000 ethnic Turks from Greece back to Turkey.

Recognizing the new realities in Turkey, the Allies convened a peace conference in Lausanne, Switzerland, to renegotiate the terms of the Sèvres treaty and award Turkey control over all the territories claimed in the National Pact with the exceptions of the province of Mosul (which Britain had incorporated into the new country of Iraq) and the Mediterranean port city of Alexandretta (present-day Iskenderun, which was given to Syria but later returned to Turkey, in 1939). The Treaty of Lausanne was signed on July 24, 1923, and three months later, on October 29, 1923, the nationalist Grand National Assembly proclaimed the establishment of the Republic of Turkey, with Kemal as its president. The Ottoman Empire, one of the world's oldest political institutions, officially ceased to exist.

Meanwhile, Kemal's government joined with leaders of the recently formed Soviet Union to crush the independent Armenia that had been proposed by the World War I Allies. Moscow incorporated the bulk of Armenia into an "autonomous republic," while Turkey occupied the western portion around the city of Kars. The Kurds never received the autonomous region the Allies had promised them, and most of the region they called Kurdistan was split by the Allies between Iraq and Turkey.

Following are the declaration by Turkish nationalists at the Congress of Sivas on September 8, 1919, and a summary of the key points of the Turkish National Pact, adopted on January 28, 1920, by the last parliament of the Ottoman Empire.

DOCUMENT

Declaration of the Congress of Sivas

SEPTEMBER 8, 1919

In view of the exterior and interior perils which threaten our country, the national conscience has become awakened and gave birth to our congress, which has reached the following decision:

I. All of the Turkish territory within the frontier outlined 30 October, 1334 (1918), between the Ottoman Government and the Allies, and inhabited by a preponderate majority of Turk population, will form an undivided and inseparable whole. All the Mussulman [Muslim] elements living in said territories are filled with mutual sentiments of respect and devotion for the social conditions of the country and form a veritable fraternity.

II. In order to assure the integrity of our country and our national independence, as well as to assure the conservation of the Sultanat [*sic*] and supreme Califat [*sic*], it is indispensable to place in action the national forces and the absolute will of the people.

III. Against all intermeddling or occupation of no matter what part of the Ottoman territory, and in particular against every movement tending toward the formation, at the expense of the mother country, of an independent Armenia and of an independent Greece on the Aidin, Magnesie, and Balikessir [regions of the former Ottoman Empire] fronts, we are absolutely resolved to resist and to defend our rights.

IV. It is inadmissible that privileges be accorded all non-Mussulman elements who, for ages, have lived from the breast of the same country and who enjoy of the same rights of equality; such privileges would tend to trouble our political government and break the social equilibrium.

V. All methods and all means are taken with a view to safeguard the Sultanat, the supreme Califat, and the integrity of the country in the case where the Turkish Government, under foreign pressure, should be called upon to abandon no matter what part of our territory.

VI. We await a decision which will conform with right and with such justice as will annul the initiatives that are contrary to our historic, ethnic, and religious rights; a decision relative to the annulling of the project of the separation of our territory situated within the line of demarcation traced by the armistice treaty, 30 October, 1334, and inhabited by a preponderate majority of Mussulman population having an intellectual preponderance and economic superiority and forming an absolutely indivisible brotherhood which is inseparable of race and religion.

VII. Our people honor and respect humanitarian and contemporary purposes and take in consideration our scientific, industrial, and economic needs; in consequence whereof, on condition that the interior and exterior independence of our people and of our State, and on condition that the territorial integrity of our country shall be conserved intact, we will accept with pleasure the scientific, industrial, and economic assistance of every State which will not set forth imperialistic tendencies with respect to our country and which will respect the principles of nationality within the limits indicated under Article VI. We await in the name of the preservation of humanity and universal peace the urgent signature of a peace based on the aforenamed equitable and humanitarian conditions which we consider to be our great national objective.

VIII. In the course of historic events which fix the destinies of nations, it is indispensible that our central Government shall submit itself to the national will, for the arbitrary decision, emanating from a government which treats lightly of the supreme will of the people not only causes that government not to be respected but, again, it could not be taken into consideration; the history of our past is proof. In consequence, it is absolutely urgent that before taking the means to remedy the anguish which exists within the very breast of the nation, our central Government shall proceed without delaying further to convoke the Nationalist Assembly and submit all the decisions to take with a view to safeguarding the interests of the nation.

IX. The sufferings and the calamities of the nations have given birth to a federal assembly called "the assembly to defend the rights and the interests of the Provinces of Anatolia and of Roumelia." That assembly abstracts all the tendencies of the political parties so that all our Mussulman compatriots as such can be considered as legitimate members of that assembly.

X. The congress of that assembly, named "the assembly to defend the rights and the interests of the Provinces of Anatolia and of Roumelia," which met at Sivas 4 September, 1335 (1919), has chosen a representative corps charged to push on the proposed sacred cause and to direct such similar organizations as well in the smaller communities as in the larger centers of the vilayets [provinces].

THE CONGRESS.

SOURCE: James G Harbord, *Conditions in the Near East: Report of the American Military Mission to Armenia* (Washington, D.C.: Government Printing Office, 1920), 39–39. Also available at http://armenianhouse.org/harbord/conditions-near-east.htm.

DOCUMENT

Turkish National Pact

JANUARY 28, 1920

The Members of the Ottoman Chamber of Deputies recognise and affirm that the independence of the State and the future of the Nation can be assured by complete respect for the following principles, which represent the maximum of sacrifice which can be undertaken in order to achieve a just and lasting peace, and that the continued existence of a stable Ottoman Sultanate and society is impossible outside of the said principles:

First Article.—Inasmuch as it is necessary that the destinies of the portions of the Turkish Empire which are populated exclusively by an Arab majority, and which on the conclusion of the armistice of the 30th October 1918 were in the occupation of enemy forces, should be determined in accordance with the votes which shall be freely given by the inhabitants, the whole of those parts whether within or outside the said armistice line which are inhabited by an Ottoman Moslem majority, united in religion, in race and in aim, imbued with sentiments of mutual respect for each other and of sacrifice, and wholly respectful of each other's racial and social rights and surrounding conditions, form a whole which does not admit of division for any reason in truth or in ordinance.

Second Article.—We accept that, in the case of the three Sandjaks [Ottoman provinces] which united themselves by a general vote to the mother country when they first were free, recourse should again be had, if necessary, to a free popular vote.

Third Article.—The determination of the juridical status of Western Thrace also, which has been made dependent on the Turkish peace, must be effected in accordance with the votes which shall be given by the inhabitants in complete freedom.

Fourth Article.—The security of the city of Constantinople [Istanbul], which is the seat of the Caliphate of Islam, the capital of the Sultanate, and the headquarters of the Ottoman Government, and of the Sea of Marmora must be protected from every danger. Provided this principle is maintained, whatever decision may be arrived at jointly by us and all other Governments concerned, regarding the opening of the Bosphorus to the commerce and traffic of the world, is valid.

Fifth Article.—The rights of minorities as defined in the treaties concluded between the Entente Powers and their enemies and certain of their associates shall be confirmed and assured by us—in reliance on the belief that the Moslem minorities in neighbouring countries also will have the benefit of the same rights.

Sixth Article.—It is a fundamental condition of our life and continued existence that we, like every country, should enjoy continued existence that we, like every country, should enjoy complete independence and liberty in the matter of assuring the means of our development, in order that our national and economic development should be rendered possible and that it should be possible to conduct affairs in the form of a more up-to-date regular administration.

For this reason we are opposed to restrictions inimical to our development in political, judicial, financial, and other matters.

The conditions of settlement of our proved debts shall likewise not be contrary to these principles.

January 28th, 1920.

SOURCE: Arnold J. Toynbee, *The Western Question in Greece and Turkey: A Study in the Contact of Civilisations* (London: Constable and Company, 1922), 209–210. This translation is from the text of the National Pact as printed in the *Proceedings of the Turkish Chamber of Deputies*, of February 17, 1920. Used with permission from the author's estate.

Modern Turkey's Founding Principles

No country is the creation of a single person, but one man left an extraordinary imprint, still very much visible, on Turkey. During a two-decade period, Mustafa Kemal—named Ataturk, or "father of the Turks" by his compatriots in 1934—dragged Turkey from a collapsed empire into nationhood, drafted a set of principles that continue to guide Turkey, shifted the country's fundamental outlook from the East to the West, and altered the daily lives of Turks by implementing changes in areas as diverse as the alphabet and clothing.

Ataturk used dictatorial means to reach the ends he sought. Only a dozen years after his death in 1938 did Turkey have its first change of government through open elections. Even so, Turkey's advance toward democracy, which remains turbulent early in the twenty-first century, might have been even more uncertain had not Ataturk imposed his will on his country at a crucial time in its history.

After leading the 1919–1920 revolt against Greece and the Western powers—a revolt considered by Turks to be their war of independence—Ataturk emerged as the dominant figure in the Turkish world following the Ottoman Empire's collapse. He then set out to transform Turkey from a backward society into a modern, Western-oriented secular country along the lines of Britain, France, or even the defeated Germany. Ataturk led Turkey from 1923 until his death, but his formal position as president fails to adequately acknowledge his role as the initiator and promoter of Turkey's march toward modernity.

Many of the changes that Ataturk implemented in Turkey represent the rapid acceleration of a reform process that began in the late nineteenth century, during the final decades of Ottoman rule. Ataturk was one of the so-called Young Turks, who seized effective control of the Ottoman Empire in 1908 and sought to modernize it, only to push it into collapse by aligning with Germany at the outset of World War I. Among the Young Turks' contributions was their advocacy of the concept of ethnic Turks as a nation, rather than mere residents of an empire ruled over by the Ottoman dynasty. Ataturk incorporated Turkish nationalism into a series of ideas that came to be known as Kemalism, or the Six Arrows.

Six Principles of Kemalism

The six principles of Kemalism usually are listed in the following order: reformism, republicanism, secularism, nationalism, populism, and etatism (stateism). These ideas, even when taken together, do not constitute a formal political theory. In fact, Ataturk never fully explained Kemalism. Rather, it evolved through the various decrees and laws that he used to implement the policies that flowed from his ideas. In 1931, these principles were incorporated into the platform of the ruling Republican People's Party, founded by Ataturk. Six years later, they were included in the constitution as the country's "fundamental and unchanging principles." The most recent version of the constitution, adopted in 2001, does not include the six principles specifically, but requires members of the Grand National Assembly to take an oath of office swearing to uphold "Ataturk's principles and reforms."

The principle that Ataturk called reformism—or "revolutionism" depending on the version of the Six Arrows text—lies at the heart of his entire program. According to him, it means a willingness by the Turkish people and national institutions to accept change, even if it breaks sharply with the imperial past. Republicanism signifies Turkey having become a republic, with a representative government, rather than a monarchy as in the past.

Secularism represents one of the clearest breaks with the past. Its implementation led to some of the most obvious changes in the national and daily lives of ordinary Turks. On a political level, secularism in Turkey generally has meant eliminating Islam as the principle guide for public affairs. Among other things, its implementation entailed the abolition of institutions that had been at the heart of the Ottoman Empire, notably the sultan's dual position as the *caliph* (protector) of Islam, the national religious schools, the Ministry of Religious Endowments, and the use of *sharia* (Islamic law) as the basis of the legal code. Secularism also affected how Turks worshiped and what they wore. Ataturk's regulations banned the mystical Sufi and Dervish orders of Islam, prohibited religious ceremonies at tombs, and barred men from wearing the traditional fez and discouraged women from wearing the veil in public. Ataturk also switched the day of rest from Friday—the traditional day of prayer for Muslims—to Sunday. One illustration of the often contradictory nature of Ataturk's reforms was that a new constitution written by his government in 1924 declared that "the religion of the Turkish state is Islam," a status that had never been accorded it even during the Ottoman era. Changes to the constitution in 1928 and 1937 deleted this language, however. Some scholars contend that Ataturk's fundamental goal was to have the state control the mosque, rather than vice versa.

Ataturk's concept of nationalism basically meant creating a sense of Turkish national identity, beginning with translating the Quran into Turkish and replacing Arabic with the Roman alphabet. Ataturk fundamentally sought to make the people of Turkey proud to be called *Turks,* a term that over the years had been used (especially in Western countries) as one of disparagement. An important aspect of Ataturk's nationalism was a conscious attempt to absorb ethnic minorities into the mainstream of Turkish life by eliminating their distinctiveness. Turkey's Kurdish population, residing primarily in the southeastern part of the country, became the chief target of this policy. For example, until 2003, the government prohibited the use of the Kurdish language in schools and other public forums and regularly cracked down on Kurdish separatist groups. The status of Kurds remains one of the most sensitive subjects in Turkey.

Populism represents Ataturk's notion of equality of citizenship for Turks—at least for all Turkish males, who were entitled to vote; women could not vote until 1934. Insisting on a classless society, Ataturk abolished the system of nobility developed under the Ottomans. Etatism, or stateism, refers to the government's guiding role in managing the economy, including its ownership of large-scale industrial enterprises. Ataturk wanted to avoid control by foreign interests by keeping most of the economy in Turkish hands.

The Kemalist Legacy

In a thirty-six-hour oration to his party spread out over five days in October 1927, Ataturk barely mentioned his political ideas. Instead, he presented an extended justification of the actions he had taken since the war of independence in 1919–1920. At the end of the speech, Ataturk appealed to subsequent generations of Turks to defend the "national independence" that he and his colleagues had won. In the future, he warned, "there will be ill-will, both in the country itself and abroad, which will try to tear this treasure from you."

The six principles of Kemalism remain at the core of Turkish public life although most of them have been diluted to one degree or another over the years. Some aspects of secularism, for example, were modified during the 1950s after the defeat of Ataturk's Republican People's Party, and the election of 2007 was widely viewed, in part, as a referendum on how strictly Turkey should adhere to Ataturk's secularist philosophy. State intervention in the economy was curtailed under mandates from the International Monetary Fund, which extended a major loan to Turkey in 1999 after the economy went into a deep recession. Economic reforms to reduce the government's role in the economy also were key to the governing philosophy of the Justice and Development Party when it first came to office in 2002.

Democracy was notably not among Ataturk's six principles. Under his autocratic rule, Turkey had just one political party—his Republican People's Party—and the Grand National Assembly essentially acted as a rubber stamp for the president. Ataturk's party continued to govern for a dozen years after his death, but lost its solitary on power in 1950, when the Democratic Party won the country's first multiparty elections. The Democratic Party would govern until its ouster by Turkey's first military coup in 1960 (Military Intervention in Politics, p. 639).

Following is an excerpt from a speech delivered over five days, from October 15 to October 20, 1927, by Ataturk to the ruling Republican People's Party, meeting in Angora, Turkey. In this excerpt, Ataturk calls on his colleagues to defend Turkish independence against domestic and foreign challenges.

DOCUMENT

Ataturk's 1927 Speech to the Republican People's Party

OCTOBER 1927

The result we have attained [today] is the fruit of teachings which arose from centuries of suffering, and the price of streams of blood which have drenched every foot of the ground of our beloved Fatherland.

This holy treasure I lay in the hands of the youth of Turkey.

Turkish Youth! Your primary duty is ever to preserve and defend the National independence, the Turkish Republic.

That is the only basis of your existence and your future. This basis contains your most precious treasure. In the future, too, there will be ill-will, both in the country itself and abroad, which will try to tear this treasure from you. If one day you are compelled to defend your independence and the Republic, then, in order to fulfil your duty, you will have to look beyond the possibilities and conditions in which you might find yourself. It may be that these conditions and possibilities are altogether unfavourable. It is possible that the enemies who desire to destroy your independence and your Republic represent the strongest force that the earth has ever seen; that they have, through craft and force, taken possession of all the fortresses and arsenals of the Fatherland; that all its armies are scattered and the country actually and completely occupied.

Assuming, in order to look still darker possibilities in the face, that those who hold the power of Government within the country have fallen into error, that they are fools or traitors, yes, even that these leading persons identify their personal interests with the enemy's political goals, it might happen that the nation came into complete privation, into the most extreme distress; that it found itself in a condition of ruin and complete exhaustion.

Even under those circumstances, Turkish child of future generations! It is your duty to save the independence, the Turkish Republic. The strength that you will need for this is mighty in the noble blood which flows in your veins.

SOURCE: *A Speech Delivered by Ghazi Mustapha Kemal, President of the Turkish Republic, October 1927* (Leipzig: K. F. Koehler, 1929), www.archive.org/details/speechdeliveredg010347mbp.

Military Intervention in Politics

DOCUMENT IN CONTEXT

Since the collapse of the Ottoman Empire, the Turkish military rarely has been called on to fight in foreign wars, but the country's generals have intervened repeatedly in domestic politics. In each case, the military labeled its actions an effort to stabilize a precarious political situation and to ensure the country's status as a secular democracy. Also in each case, the generals returned the government to civilian leaders after accomplishing their stated mission.

Mustafa Kemal, or Ataturk, a prominent general largely responsible for creating modern Turkey, established the military's role in Turkish politics. Ataturk exercised dictatorial powers for most of his thirteen years as Turkey's president, and Turkey remained a one-party state for a dozen years after his death in 1938. The one party was the Republican People's Party, founded by Ataturk.

Rapid urbanization and other changes following World War II created widespread demands for more political openness. Disgruntled members of the ruling party formed an opposition party, the Democratic Party, which contested the 1946 parliamentary elections and won about one-seventh of the total seats, a significant showing for the country's first multiparty election. Four years later, in May 1950, the Democratic Party swept the long-ruling Republican People's Party from power, an event that appeared to herald a new era for Turkey as a genuine democracy.

The Democrats won two more elections during the 1950s but proved unable to adequately deal with rising social discontent when the economy went into a sharp tail-spin in the latter part of the decade. The government cracked down on dissent by stifling criticism in the news media, attempting to undermine the Republican People's Party, and eventually imposing martial law. These repressive measures backfired by emboldening protesters, including university students and military cadets.

With the country in political crisis, the military intervened. On May 27, 1960, the army took control of Ankara and Istanbul, ousted the government, and arrested top Democratic Party leaders, including President Celal Bayar, Prime Minister Adnan Menderes, and most of the party's members of parliament. Under Gen. Cemal Gursel, the military established the Committee of National Unity, which forcibly halted the civil disorder. The generals also staged trials of nearly 600 politicians from the former government and convicted about three-fourths of them on various counts of corruption, mismanagement, and other charges. Menderes was hanged in September 1961.

The military government also drafted a new constitution that drastically reshaped the government, notably by dividing the legislature into two chambers and by shoring up civil liberties. The first elections under this constitution took place in October 1961. The military suffered a setback when voters forced the Republican People's Party, which the generals openly favored, to share power in a coalition government.

The right-leaning Justice Party, a successor to the deposed Democratic Party, won the next elections, in 1965. Suleiman Demirel took office as prime minister, beginning a long career in government that would see him serve repeatedly as head of government and later as president. The Justice Party held power throughout the 1960s, but it gradually lost members to several splinter parties, part of a broader fracturing process in which numerous groups created their own parties to represent their special interests.

In 1971 another wave of civil unrest—involving competition between extreme left-wing and extreme right-wing groups—led to Turkey's second military coup. In this case, military leaders gave President Cevdet Sunay and legislative leaders a three-point memorandum stating that the parliament and government had "driven our country into anarchy, fratricidal strife, and social and economic unrest" and demanding the formation of a "strong and credible government." It warned that the military would take power if they failed to act "quickly."

Prime Minister Demirel and his government immediately resigned, effectively allowing the military to achieve what observers called a "coup by memorandum." A series of unstable coalition cabinets then served throughout the 1970s, marking yet another period in which Turkish politicians failed to address the country's underlying problems (particularly a faltering economy) and to suppress violence by the left and the right.

The 1980 Coup

In December 1979, the military warned the government that it needed to act against ongoing unrest, but Prime Minister Demirel—back in office at the head of a minority government—lacked the political clout to take effective measures. During the first eight months of 1980, some 1,800 people died in several rounds of political violence and terrorism. Events came to a head in September 1980, when opposition parties forced the resignation of the foreign minister, and advocates of Islamic law staged a huge public rally.

On September 12, 1980, the military seized control of the government, dismissed parliament, and created the National Security Council, a five-member junta headed by chief of staff Gen. Kenan Evren. In a statement, the military said it had suspended all political activity but would govern only until it could restore order. The generals pledged "a speedy restoration of the democratic process."

In a sweeping crackdown intended to halt the violence, the military began arresting thousands of political activists, including leaders of opposition parties, students, trade union leaders, and others. The arrests eventually totaled around 30,000, according to most sources. The military's repression brought international protests, including from European countries, which suspended Turkey's participation in the Council of Europe, a human rights monitoring agency. The military implemented an economic reform program, first proposed by Demirel's government, that succeeded in reducing inflation and reviving the economy. Breaking with its past support for strict secularist policies, the military also introduced several measures promoting religious instruction in schools. These measures were intended to reduce public support for leftist groups but instead created opportunities for advocates of greater Islamic influence in public life.

The military government drafted, and in 1982 voters approved by referendum, a new constitution providing for a strong presidency. Also as part of the constitutional referendum, voters ratified the appointment of General Evren as president. Under this new constitutional arrangement, Turgut Ozal emerged as Turkey's most successful politician during the 1980s as leader of the conservative Motherland Party. He had launched the economic stabilization program under the generals. His party won elections in 1983 and 1987, enabling him to serve six years as prime minister, the longest of any prime minister since Menderes during the 1950s. Ozal went on to succeed Evren as president in 1989, a position he held until he died of a heart attack in 1993.

A "Soft Coup"

Turkey's next experience with military intervention in politics came in 1997, two years after an Islamic party, the Welfare Party, finished first in parliamentary elections. Welfare Party leader Necmettin Erbakan became prime minister in a coalition government, making him the first avowedly Islamic leader since Ataturk assumed power seven decades earlier. After Erbakan took several steps—such as encouraging women to wear headscarves in public—that offended Turkey's secularists, the military acted. In what became known as a "soft coup," the generals on February 28, 1997, demanded that Erbakan sign a statement that included a commitment to secularism. The prime minister signed the statement but was slow to carry out the pledges. He finally gave in to the military's pressure and resigned on June 18. A year later, the Constitutional Court banned the Welfare Party and prohibited seven of its leaders, including Erbakan, from engaging in political activity for seven years.

The military's intervention restored secular politicians to office but did not succeed in making them any more effective in dealing with the country's problems. After another period of indecisive leadership, Turkish politics experienced one of its most revolutionary moments in 2002, when a new Islamic party, the Justice and Development Party (AKP), finished first in that year's parliamentary elections and swept into power (Rise of the Justice and Development Party, p. 647).

Pressure via Internet

Led by Recep Tayyip Erdogan, the charismatic former mayor of Istanbul, the AKP governed effectively and maintained broad public support. In 2007, however, Turkey's generals argued that the party had overstepped what they viewed as a significant boundary between religion and politics. With the term of President Ahmet Necdet Sezer about to expire, Erdogan negotiated with other political leaders on a successor, eventually settling on his closest political ally, Foreign Minister Abdullah Gul. A U.S.-educated economist, Gul was one of the most sophisticated leaders in the AKP, but the military viewed an Islamist party leader as too divisive a figure to be president.

On April 27, the military high command posted a notice on its Web site, complaining about recent incidents that it said endangered the country's secularist underpinnings and indirectly warning the parliament not to appoint Gul as president. "It must not be forgotten that the Turkish Armed Forces do take sides in this debate and are the sure and certain defenders of secularism," the statement read. It continued, "Moreover, the Turkish Armed Forces are definitely on the receiving end of the debates being argued and the negative commentary, and they will make their position and stance perfectly clear if needs be. Let nobody have any doubt about this."

Gul withdrew his candidacy amid large demonstrations, some favoring the military's intervention on behalf of secularism and others opposing it. Prime Minister Erdogan sought to override the generals by putting the final decision on Turkey's next president into the hands of the public. He therefore called for early parliamentary elections in July 2007, and at his request, the parliament passed legislation calling for the popular election of the president. Outgoing president Sezer vetoed the legislation, but parliament overrode the veto. In this case, however, the voters, rather than the generals, had the ultimate say in the dispute. In the elections held on July 22, 2007, Erdogan's party scored an impressive victory, winning 47 percent of the vote—an unusually high percentage for any party in modern Turkish elections—and retaining its large majority in parliament.

These events of 2007 had the potential to affect Turkey's pending application for membership in the European Union (EU). After decades of knocking at Europe's door, Turkey won an invitation to negotiate the terms for its membership in the EU in 2004. Even under the best of circumstances, it was likely that Turkey would not win actual admission for another ten or fifteen years. The military's political intervention in 2007 at first appeared to hand ammunition to those in Europe opposed to allowing Turkey into the EU. The election in July, however, was widely seen as a setback for the military and a major step toward the consolidation of democracy in Turkey—possibly boosting Turkey's long-delayed quest for a seat at the EU table.

Following is the text of a memorandum, signed by General Memduh Tagmac, chief of the General Staff and the commanders of the Turkish air, naval, and ground forces, delivered on March 12, 1971, to President Cevdet Sunay and the presidents of the National Assembly and Senate; excerpts from a press release on the military takeover in Turkey issued September 12, 1980, by the Turkish Embassy in Washington, D.C.; and the text of a statement by the General Staff posted on the military's Web site on April 27, 2007, warning against a plan by the ruling Justice and Development Party to nominate Foreign Minister Abdullah Gul as the next president.

DOCUMENT

Coup Memorandum by the General Staff (1971)

MARCH 12, 1971

1. Parliament and the government, through their sustained policies, views, and actions, have driven our country into anarchy, fratricidal strife, and social and economic unrest. They have caused the public to lose all hope of rising to the level of contemporary civilization, which Ataturk established as our goal. They have failed to realize the reforms stipulated by the constitution. Thus, the future of the Turkish Republic is seriously threatened.

2. Parliament's assessment, in a spirit above partisan considerations, of the solutions needed to eliminate the concern and disillusionment of the Turkish armed forces, which have emerged from the bosom of the Turkish nation, over this grave situation, and the formation, within the framework of democratic principles, of a strong and credible government that will neutralize the current anarchistic situation and, inspired by Ataturk's views, will implement the reformist laws envisioned by the constitution are considered essential.

3. Unless this is done quickly, the Turkish armed forces are determined to take over the administration of the state in accordance with the powers invested in them by the laws to protect and preserve the Turkish Republic.

Please be informed.

Signed: Gen Memduh Tagmac, chief of the General Staff and member of the National Security Council; Gen Faruk Gurler, commander of the Ground Forces and member of the National Security Council; Adm Celal Eyicioglu, commander of the Naval Forces and member of the National Security Council; Gen Muhsin Batur, commander of the Air Force and member of the National Security Council.

SOURCE: Library of Congress, Foreign Affairs Division, *A Select Chronology and Background Documents Relating to the Middle East* (Washington, D.C.: Government Printing Office, 1975), 275. Prepared for the Senate Committee on Foreign Relations. This document originally appeared in Foreign Broadcast Information Service, *Daily Report,* March 12, 1971, p. L12.

DOCUMENT

Turkish Embassy Announcement of a Coup (1980)

SEPTEMBER 12, 1980

A military takeover has taken place in Turkey in the early hours of September 12, Turkish time.

A National Security Council under the Chairmanship of General Kenan Evren, Chief of General Staff, has been established. Members of this Council are the Chiefs of the four Services, Ground, Air, Naval and Gendarmerie. General Haydar Saltik has been appointed as the Secretary General of this Council. Martial Law has been declared throughout the country.

The following are the highlights from the Communiqués issued by this Council, as well as the statement of General Evren to the nation:

The Turkish Armed Forces, in face of the vital dangers confronting the territorial integrity and national unity of the Republic of Turkey has taken over the Government and has established complete control of the entire country. The Turkish Armed Forces has undertaken this historic task, which the overwhelming majority of the Turkish nation expected and yearned, with a great responsibility and love for the country. This historic task is entrusted to the Turkish Army by the Internal Service Law.

In carrying out this task the members of the Armed Forces have acted and will act free from all personal interests and ambitions, with a superior sense of discipline, and great determination to strive and succeed for the preservation of a free and independent Turkish Republic based on Ataturk's principles.

The Republic of Turkey, committed to all its alliances and treaties including NATO, is resolved to develop economic, social and cultural relations on the principles of equality and reciprocal respect for independence and non-interference in the internal affairs of others with all countries, in particular with her neighbors.

The present Parliament and the Government have been abolished. The Turkish Armed Forces are devoted to the free democratic parliamentary system. Therefore they commit themselves to a speedy restoration of the democratic process.

A new Constitution, electoral law and a law on political parties, befitting the Turkish nation, will be prepared and parallel arrangements to these will be taken so that the degeneration of the free democratic parliamentary system, as has recently been the case, prevented. It will transfer the administration of the country to a freely elected Government.

Until these preparation[s] are completed, all political activities at all levels are suspended. Political activities will resume . . . sufficiently ahead of time before the elections, the time and conditions of which will be later announced. No action will be taken against the members of the Parliament unless they adopt an attitude constituting a crime against the new Administration. However, those members of the Parliament who in the past have under the laws committed crime, will be prosecuted. Leaders of the Justice Party, Republican Peoples Party, National Salvation Party, National Action Party, for their personal safety, are under protective custody. When conditions so permit they will be set free.

SOURCE: *Historic Documents of 1980* (Washington, D.C.: CQ Press, 1981), 809–810.

DOCUMENT

Statement by the General Staff on Founding Principles and Religion (2007)

APRIL 27, 2007

[The following is an unofficial translation.]

It is being observed that certain circles that are waging a relentless struggle to erode the founding principles of the Turkish Republic starting with secularism have recently increased their efforts. These activities, which are constantly being brought to the attention of the pertinent authorities in an appropriate manner, encompass a broad spectrum of activities ranging from their wish to question and redefine the founding principles to the creation of alternative celebrations to our national holidays, which are the symbol of our state's independence and the unity and integrity of our nation.

The people engaged in these activities do not hesitate to exploit our people's sacred religious sentiments, and they work to conceal their true aims by dressing up these efforts, which have become an open challenge to the state, in the apparel of religion. The way they use women and children in particular in the front line of their activities carries striking similarities to the destructive and separatist activities being conducted against our country's unity and integrity.

In connection with this:

A Koran recital competition had been organized in Ankara for the same day as the National Sovereignty and Children's Holiday on 23 April, but was cancelled thanks to pressure brought to bear by the sensitive media and public.

In Sanliurfa on 22 April 2007 a chorus made up of young girls dressed in outmoded clothing that was inappropriate to their ages and at an hour at which they should have long been in their beds was made to recite Islamic hymns with the participation of certain groups from the provinces of Mardin, Gaziantep and Diyarbakir. The true motives and intentions of the people organizing the evening became apparent when they attempted to take down pictures of Ataturk and the Turkish flag.

Furthermore, there has been disturbing news to the effect that all the school principles in Ankara's Altindag district were ordered to attend a "Sacred Birth Celebration," that Islamic hymns were sung by primary school girls wearing Islamic headscarves during an event arranged jointly by the Denizli Provincial Muftu's Office and a political party, and that despite there being four mosques in the borough of Nikfer in Denizli's Tavas district a sermon and religious talk directed at women were held in the Ataturk Primary School.

The activities to be celebrated in schools are specified in the pertinent Ministry of Education directives. However, despite the fact that these kinds of events were arranged according to non-directive instructions and the fact that the General Staff notified the pertinent authorities it has been observed that no preventative measures have been taken.

The fact that the above mentioned activities took place with the permission and knowledge of the authorities whose duty it is to intercede in and prevent them makes the issue all the more serious. It is possible to list more examples.

This reactionary mindset, which is opposed to our Republic and has no other aim than to undermine the founding principles of our state, has been encouraged by certain developments and rhetoric in recent days and is broadening the scope of its activities.

Developments in our region are replete with examples that should be heeded of the disasters that can be caused by playing with religion and exploiting faith for political rhetoric and ends. It can be seen in both our country and abroad that when a sacred faith is used to try and carry political rhetoric or ideology it changes into something by taking faith out of the picture. The incident in Malatya can be said to be a striking example of this. It goes without saying that the only condition under which the state of the Turkish Republic may live in peace and stability as a modern democracy is to stand up for the founding qualities of the state as specified in the Constitution.

It is a clear fact that this behavior and these actions contradict entirely the principle of "being loyal to the Republic regime in spirit and not in word and of acting in such a way as to show this" as stated by the Chief of Staff in a news conference on 12 April 2007, and that they violate the founding qualities and provisions of the Constitution.

The question that has come to the fore in the recent run up to the presidential elections is focused on the secularism debate. This situation is being watched in trepidation by the Turkish Armed Forces. It must not be forgotten that the Turkish Armed Forces do take sides in this debate and are the sure and certain defenders of secularism. Moreover, the Turkish Armed Forces are definitely on the receiving end of the debates being argued and the negative commentary, and they will make their position and stance perfectly clear if needs be. Let nobody have any doubt about this.

In short, anybody who opposes the idea as stated by the founder of the Republic the Great Leader Ataturk of "Happy is the man who says I am a Turk!" is an enemy of the Turkish Republic and will stay that way.

The Turkish Armed Forces remain steadfast in their unwavering commitment to carry out in full the duties given to them by law to protect these qualities. Its allegiance to and faith in this commitment is certain.

The public has been respectfully informed.

SOURCE: Courtesy of the U.S. Embassy, Ankara, Turkey.

Rise of the Justice and Development Party

DOCUMENT IN CONTEXT

Despite numerous crises and repeated interventions by the military, Turkey's political system remained fairly stable for the five decades after the introduction of multiparty elections in 1950. Political parties came and went over the years, and the generals ousted governments of which they disapproved, but some of the same leaders returned to office repeatedly. Government policies varied only by a matter of degree.

A harbinger of chance arrived in 1995–97, when the Welfare Party, an Islamic-oriented party, won a plurality of seats in parliamentary elections and formed a coalition government. This was the first major break with the secular politics mandated for Turkey by its founder, Mustafa Kemal (or Ataturk). The Welfare-led government lasted less than a year before the military—having declared itself the guarantor of Ataturk's legacy—pressured it to resign, leading to a series of weak governments led by the traditional parties.

Another turning point of more enduring significance occurred in the 2002 elections. As Prime Minister Bulent Ecevit's health failed him, Turkey's traditional parties on the left and the right proved themselves unable to assuage growing public dissatisfaction with a sagging economy. Into this vacuum stepped Recep Tayyip Erdogan, a charismatic politician able to generate enthusiasm across the political spectrum. Erdogan, a former mayor of Istanbul, headed the Justice and Development Party (AKP), a successor to the ousted and disbanded Welfare Party. Erdogan was himself ineligible to run for election in 2002 because of a criminal conviction for "religious incitement" stemming from his publicly reading a poem that the authorities considered to be overtly Islamic.

The AKP scored an astonishing victory in the elections held on November 3, 2002, winning 34 percent of the vote, enough to give it an overwhelming majority of seats in the Grand National Assembly. The AKP thus became the first party in nearly fifteen years to win an outright majority in parliament. The traditional parties that in various guises had governed Turkey in recent decades all failed to obtain the 10 percent of the vote necessary to acquire seats in the legislature. The only other party to win seats was a revamped Republican People's Party, Ataturk's old ruling party, which had not held power by itself since its ouster in the landmark elections of 1950.

Immediately after the election, Erdogan and the AKP moved to dispel fears that they intended to transform Turkey into an Islamist state. In a program published on November 23—five days after the new government took office—the AKP pledged to respect the country's tradition of secularism as well as freedom of religion. The party also said it would govern responsibly and would cooperate with other segments of society. "We will respect pluralistic democracy, human rights and the supremacy of law and we will do our best to achieve social consensus when tackling with important issues, for we know very well that numerical superiority does not mean everything," the party announced.

The new government selected as prime minister Abdullah Gul, a Western-educated economist who had been the AKP's deputy chairman. Erdogan took over as prime minister in March 2003 after he won a parliamentary seat; parliament had adopted a constitutional change lifting the ban on Erdogan's political involvement. Gul became foreign minister.

Under Erdogan's guidance, the new AKP government embarked on an ambitious program to stabilize the sagging economy and put Turkey on the road to membership in the European Union (EU). Erdogan traveled to European capitals, pleading Turkey's long-delayed case for joining the EU. He won a surprising degree of support from Western leaders who might otherwise have been leery of the leader of an Islamist party. In November 2004, EU leaders voted to open formal negotiations for Turkey's admission.

The Europeans' decision represented a major personal achievement for Erdogan, but it also meant that Turkey would have to carry out numerous economic and political reforms to meet the EU's criteria for membership. Erdogan's government moved to implement many of these reforms, including eliminating the death penalty, easing restrictions on Kurdish culture and language, and opening Turkey's economy to foreign trade and investment. Even so, opposition to Turkish membership in the EU grew in several European countries, angering many Turks and embarrassing Erdogan. By 2007, it had become unclear whether the initial goal of Turkey entering the EU by 2015 or 2020 could be met, or whether Turkey might ever take a seat at the European table.

Erdogan and his party won a second, even more solid, electoral victory in 2007—this one resulting from a failed political intervention by the military. In April of that year the generals moved to block a plan by Erdogan to have parliament elect Foreign Minister Gul to the presidency, a step that would have put an avowed Islamist in Ataturk's old post for the first time. Calling the generals' bluff, Erdogan advanced the date of parliamentary elections to July 22. His party scored an overwhelming victory in that voting and retained its strong majority in parliament, gaining the support even of many secular moderates impressed with the government's success in reviving the economy and governing efficiently (Military Intervention in Politics, p. 639).

Following are excerpts from the government program published on November 23, 2002, by the leadership of Turkey's Justice and Development Party, which had captured a majority of parliamentary seats in elections held on November 3, 2002.

DOCUMENT

Program of the Fifty-eighth Turkish Government

NOVEMBER 23, 2002

Turkey, in the aftermath of the November 3 General Elections, has achieved stability with a bipartisan parliament and a one-party government. We, as the Parliament and the Government, are well aware of our responsibility to do our best in order to introduce genuine and swift solutions to the problems which have been confronting us. While we try to find urgent solutions to problems, we will also undertake structural changes and reforms to make sure that such problems would never face us again. We are well aware of the fact that the current conditions cannot be overcome by superficial measures.

Both our Electoral Manifesto and the Emergency Action Plan, which was announced by our leader Recep Tayyip Erdogan, the result of a coherent, responsible and reformist understanding, were appreciated by the public opinion. Therefore, our Government Programme has been prepared along these lines to fulfil the commitments we had given to the people before the elections.

The Government will not get involved into unnecessary political discussions and polemics and it expects to receive the trust and support of the nation. We will work in dialogue and cooperation with the opposition party and all sectors of the society in a democratic and transparent way. We will respect pluralistic democracy, human rights and the supremacy of law and we will do our best to achieve social consensus when tackling with important issues, for we know very well that numerical superiority does not mean everything.

We will strengthen the ties between the state and the society, broaden the political field, reinstall the trust between the politics and the society and respond to the demands of the people.

Following the announcement of the November 3 election results, interest rates began to decrease, the stock exchange began to rally and foreign exchange rates started to fall down because of the positive expectations and the climate of confidence in both domestic and international markets. It is imperative to maintain this climate of confidence to solve urgent social and economic problems. We will never forget the demands and expectations of the people. Our success will not only belong to us, it will be the success of all political and state institutions, and, above all, it will belong to the nation.

While the world was undergoing radical transformations, Turkey, unfortunately, has wasted her time and energy tackling internal problems. Although [a] multiparty system was adopted 50 years ago, Turkey is still among the countries which could not become fully democratic, where basic rights and freedoms cannot be fully enjoyed. Despite its young and dynamic population and rich natural [re]sources, Turkey has been unable to increase her level of welfare and establish a truly competitive production sector.

The state's role in the economy could not conform with the changing conditions due to wrong policies that were being implemented and the injustice in the distribution of wealth among the parts of the community and regions could not be corrected. A sound privatization scheme could not be carried out. The country could not rid itself of [its] cumbersome, overcentralist administrative system, impoverishment and political corruption.

The economic policies of recent coalition governments have failed and the worst economic crisis in its history hit the country. As a result, unprecedented poverty has struck our people. Hundreds of thousands have lost their jobs and tens of thousands of business[es] had to be closed down. People have lost their hope for the future.

The government, however, believes that Turkey has the potential to be a rightful member of the new world with its young population, unique geographical location, rich natural resources and cultural aspects. The government has set off a course to establish a secure future and meet the people's demands with a comprehensive program, an honest leadership and well-educated and experienced personnel.

Most of the issues mentioned in the program are actually those which have been discussed for [a] long time. These issues will be taken up in an atmosphere of social dialogue and constructive relations between the government and the opposition. The motto of Mustafa Kemal Ataturk, the founder of the Republic and our great leader, to surpass the level of contemporary civilization, will form the basis of the steps we will take.

The government will create a democratic, credible and dynamic Turkey enjoying economic stability, competitive market structure, sustainable development environment, justice in welfare, peace, freedom and integration with the modern world. We will make this vision come true.

Basic Rights and Freedoms

People enjoy inalienable and nontransferable basic rights and freedoms. The individual will be the center of our policies which will take all international democratic standards as a basis.

Our country, which made [the] European Convention on Human Rights and Universal Declaration of Human Rights a part of its internal law, will put these values into practice and reach universal standards in the field of basic rights and freedoms, under our leadership.

Therefore, we will introduce all necessary amendments to the Constitution and the laws to upgrade the basic rights and freedoms to the level in international conventions and the Copenhagen criteria [conditions for membership in the European Union], in particular.

We will put these basic rights and freedoms into practice and make them an established dimension of our political culture.

No double standards and political manipulation will be permitted in basic rights and freedoms of individuals.

We will wage a determined struggle against violations of human rights and torture in particular. . . .

We will also prepare a new Constitution which will underline freedoms and participatory aspects. The new Constitution will enjoy powerful social legitimacy and conform with the international norms. It will feature the understanding of the democratic rule of law based on individual rights and freedoms as well as pluralist and participatory democracy. . . .

A New Economic Programme To Be Implemented

Taking into account the deficient and problematic aspects of the current economic program, the Government will implement a new economic programme, which would receive the support of the people, [in] order to reach a high and stable growth performance to decrease public debt stock and to reduce [the] inflation rate.

It is evident that a growth model based on foreign loans and public deficits can no longer be sustained. Therefore, the finance policy of our Government will aim to reduce the debt stock and ensure non-interest surplus which would protect macro stability. The scale of non-interest surplus would be formed by taking its composition, economic feasibility as well as the growth and social policies into consideration. The public debt stock would be reduced to a sustainable level.

The public sector will be restructured, privatization will be speeded up, and an encouraging atmosphere will be created for domestic and foreign investors. We will also see to it that the productivity in the agriculture sector would be restructured as well.

The Government will continue the floating exchange rate policy but [the] Central Bank would intervene in a more sensitive way in case of speculative floatings which have no macro economic bases.

The Government will implement the economic development policies in a balanced way together with social policies.

We believe that it is necessary to put individuals at the centre of economic development in order to have successful policies to fight . . . poverty and to improve the distribution of income.

The basic priority in removing poverty will be to clean the politics and public administration [of] corruption. On the other hand, the tax burden on employees will be lessened gradually. . . .

Education and Secularism

The government will make the principle of secularism as well as the freedom of religion and conscience defined in the Constitution more tangible and functional. We will attach importance to a religious education and teaching which will prevent manipulation of religion, religious feelings, and things considered "holy" by the religion for political and individual interests. Thus, the expectations of the citizens in the field of religious education and teaching will be met and also manipulations in this field will be over.

The government will lift the impediments in front of exercising the right to education and [to] be educated. Universities will turn into free forums where there are no prohibitions and restrictions. . . .

Despite the most difficult economic problems, we have managed to survive. This is mainly due to our strong family structure. The Government will support efforts which aim to protect the family.

The women will have the equal status which would [allow] them to have social responsibility in every field with that of men. Violence against women will be prevented.

The youth, besides the treasure of the country, is the source of our dynamism and potential for change. We will support cultural, artistic and supporting activities for our youth. The central administration should play a regulating and coordinating role in such services. Local administrations, cooperating with the private sector and volunteer organisations will provide these services. . . .

Foreign Policy

The government will pursue an objective, unbiased and realist foreign policy based on reciprocal interests, and it will respect the territorial integrity and sovereignty of all countries.

Turkey has to redefine its foreign policy priorities in line with changing regional and global realities and set up a new balance with these realities and national interests.

Turkey has close relations with Europe both in respect of geography and also in respect of history. Therefore, the relations with European countries will continue to occupy the highest level at Turkey's foreign policy agenda.

Turkey's full EU membership is the fundamental goal of our administration. Therefore, the government will endeavour to start accession talks with the EU after Turkey's candidacy in [the] EU enlargement process is reconfirmed. It is without doubt that Turkey's getting the place it deserves in the EU family will bring benefits to both sides and create positive results for the peace, stability and security beyond the European continent as well.

Within this framework, the EU adjustment laws adopted by the Parliament will be strengthened in respect to basic rights and freedoms. We will also attach importance to training studies to fully put these reforms into practice. . . .

The government will launch efforts to decrease the tension between religions and cultures which started to escalate following the September 11 attack and it will actively be involved in endeavours to form an atmosphere of global peace.

Our cooperation with the U.S.[,] which exists for a long time and which deals mainly with defense issues, will continue. This cooperation will also spread to economy, investment, science and technology. . . .

Turkey has concerns regarding the uncertainty vis-á-vis its neighbour Iraq. The government attributes particular importance to the territorial integrity of Iraq and the protection of its political unity. Spoiling Iraq's territorial integrity will change all the balances in the Middle East. The Government wants [the] Iraqi administration to fully implement the U.N. resolutions and a peaceful solution to this problem. . . .

SOURCE: Office of the Prime Minister of Turkey, Directorate General of Press and Information, www.byegm. gov.tr/hukumetler/58hukumet/governmentprogramme.htm.

Chronology of the Middle East, 1914–2007

1914

August: World War I begins. The Ottoman Empire sides with the Central Powers (Germany and the Austro-Hungarian Empire).

December 18: Britain declares a "protectorate" over Egypt, enhancing its effective control of the country.

1915

July 14: Sharif Hussein ibn Ali, the amir of Mecca, and Sir Henry McMahon, the British high commissioner in Cairo, begin corresponding. Their correspondence, which continues into 1916, leads to the "Arab revolt" against the Ottoman Empire in exchange for a British promise to support an independent Arab state.

1916

May 16: British and French diplomats exchange letters incorporating the Sykes-Picot Agreement for the division of the Arab lands of the Ottoman Empire following World War I. Under this agreement, Britain was to control most of Iraq, France was to oversee Lebanon and coastal Syria, and most of Palestine was to be under international control.

1917

November 2: In a letter to Lionel Walter Lord Rothschild of the Zionist Federation, British foreign secretary Arthur Balfour offers his government's support for a "national home for the Jewish people" in Palestine. This British endorsement becomes known as the Balfour Declaration.

December 9: A British force under Gen. Edmund Allenby captures Jerusalem, which had been under Ottoman control.

1918

October 2: A combined British and Arab force under General Allenby captures Damascus from the Ottomans.

October 30: The Ottomans sign an armistice with the Entente allies, ending their participation in World War I.

1919
January: Chaim Weizmann of the World Zionist Organization and Amir Faisal ibn Hussein sign an agreement calling for cooperation between Arabs and Jews.

May 14: Greek forces land at Smyrna, on the coast of Turkey, to claim the region for Greece. This leads to a series of battles in which Turkish nationalists under Mustafa Kemal defeat the Greeks and gain control of all of Anatolia.

July 2: The Syrian General Congress, a meeting of Arab notables in Damascus, issues a declaration calling for the creation of an independent Syrian state, or failing that, temporary administration of Syrian territory by the United States.

August 18: Afghanistan declares independence from Great Britain.

September 9: Led by Mustafa Kemal, Turkish nationalists meeting in Sivas issue a declaration insisting on Turkish control of all of Anatolia and the region around Istanbul. Their declaration later becomes the Turkish National Pact.

1920
January 28: Ottoman parliament adopts the Turkish National Pact, setting out the proposed borders of the Turkish state.

March 11: Meeting in Damascus, the Syrian National Congress declares Faisal ibn Hussein the ruler of Syria and Palestine.

April 24: Meeting at San Remo, the League of Nations awards mandates for Iraq and Palestine to Britain and a mandate for Lebanon and Syria to France.

June: In Iraq, a brief but widespread revolt begins against British rule.

July 1: Britain installs Herbert Samuel as the first civilian high commissioner in Palestine.

July 24: A French army force captures Damascus and forces Faisal ibn Hussein from the throne.

August 10: The Treaty of Sèvres is signed, stripping the Ottoman Empire of its Arab provinces and portions of Anatolia and placing Istanbul and the strategic straits under international control.

August: The French high commissioner in Damascus creates "Greater Lebanon" by separating the Mount Lebanon region from Syria and annexing to Lebanon the coastal regions of Beirut and Tripoli.

1921
February 22: Reza Khan, an army commander, seizes power in Iran.

March 15: A British government conference in Cairo results in the appointment of Faisal ibn Hussein as king of Iraq and Abdallah ibn Hussein as amir of Transjordan.

1922
February 28: Britain ends its protectorate over Egypt but in a declaration known as the Four Reserved Points retains control of matters related to communications links, security, the protection of foreigners, and the future of Sudan.

March 15: Britain recognizes Egypt as an independent country under King Fuad.

July 24: The Council of the League of Nations approves the mandates under which

Britain will control Iraq, Transjordan, and Palestine; and France will control Lebanon and Syria.

November 1: The Turkish Grand National Assembly declares the abolition of the sultanate.

November 17: Mohammed VI, the last sultan, leaves Istanbul.

1923

May 26: Britain establishes Transjordan as an autonomous state under Amir Abdallah ibn Hussein.

July 24: The Treaty of Lausanne is signed, modifying the terms of the Treaty of Sèvres and allowing sovereignty for Turkey over all of Anatolia and eastern Thrace (including Istanbul). In a related agreement, Greece and Turkey decide to "exchange" nationals on each other's territory, leading to the forced relocation of more than 1 million ethnic Greeks from Turkey and more than 400,000 ethnic Turks from Greece.

September 29: Britain officially assumes control of Palestine under the League of Nations mandate.

October 29: Mustafa Kemal declares the establishment of a republic in Turkey. He will become its first president.

1924

February 2: Turkish Grand National Assembly abolishes the caliphate, which had been held by a relative of the deposed sultan.

1925

December 12: The Iranian parliament approves the establishment of the Pahlavi dynasty under Reza Khan, who becomes Reza Shah Pahlavi.

December 16: The League of Nations awards most of the region of Mosul to Iraq, rebuffing a claim by Turkey.

1926

January 8: Having defeated Sharif Hussein to gain control of the Hijaz in the western Arabian Peninsula, Abd al-Aziz ibn Saud (or Ibn Saud) declares himself king of the Hijaz in a major step toward the unification of the Hijaz and Najd regions in the creation of Saudi Arabia.

May 23: France officially establishes Greater Lebanon as a republic.

1927

May 20: Britain recognizes Ibn Saud as king of the Hijaz and Najd on the Arabian Peninsula.

October 15–20: President Mustafa Kemal of Turkey delivers a thirty-six-hour-long speech to political supporters recounting events since the beginning of the Turkish war of independence in 1919.

December 14: Britain signs a treaty promising to recognize Iraq as an independent country by 1932 in exchange for the right to maintain three airbases there.

1928

February 28: Britain grants limited independence to Transjordan.

1929

August 6: Britain and Egypt reach agreement providing for the end of British military occupation, but with British forces still stationed at key points along the Suez Canal. Egypt would be admitted as an independent member of the League of Nations.

August 8: Arabs in Jerusalem riot against Jews as the result of a dispute over Jewish access to the so-called "Wailing Wall."

1930

June 30: Britain and Iraq sign a formal treaty promising eventual independence for Iraq (in 1932).

October 20: Britain publishes the Passfield White Paper limiting Jewish immigration to Palestine and imposing restrictions on land sales to Jews.

1932

September 22: Ibn Saud changes the name of his domain to the Kingdom of Saudi Arabia (from the Kingdom of Hijaz and Najd).

October 3: Iraq is admitted to the League of Nations, ending the British mandate.

1935

March 21: Reza Shah changes the name of Persia to Iran.

1936

January: Widespread rioting erupts in Syria following the French administration's disbanding of the Nationalist Party. The French impose martial law.

April: An Arab revolt against British rule begins in Palestine; it will continue, intermittently, for nearly three years and result in hundreds of deaths, most of them of Arabs.

September 6: France and Syria sign a treaty of friendship intended to lead to Syrian independence within three years.

November 13: France and Lebanon sign an agreement asserting that Lebanon will remain independent of Syria.

1937

May 26–27: Egypt is admitted to the League of Nations.

July 7: The Palestine Royal Commission (also known as the Peel Commission) recommends to the British government that Palestine be partitioned into Arab and Jewish sectors.

1938

November 9: The Woodhead Commission reports that the partitioning of Palestine would be impractical. As a result, the British government will abandon partition as a policy.

1939

May 17: The British government issues a white paper calling for an independent Palestinian state within ten years and imposing limits on Jewish immigration to Palestine. Parliament will approve this policy on May 23.

1941

May 2: Britain intervenes in Iraq to overthrow a new government that had aligned itself with Nazi Germany. British forces will gain control of Baghdad by the end of May and of Mosul province by early June.

June 8: British and Free French forces invade Syria to quell a nationalist uprising.

September 16: Reza Shah is forced to abdicate following an invasion of Iran by armed forces from Britain and the Soviet Union. He is succeeded by his son, Mohammad Reza Pahlavi.

1942

January: Britain and the Soviet Union pledge to respect the sovereignty of Iran and withdraw their forces after the end of World War II.

May 11: American Zionists, meeting at the Biltmore Hotel in New York City, adopt a program calling for the establishment of a Jewish state in Palestine and rejecting Britain's policy of limiting Jewish immigration into Palestine.

1943

November 22: Under British and U.S. pressure, France releases imprisoned Lebanese leaders. (This date is celebrated in Lebanon as independence day.) Later in the month, Lebanese leaders agree on an unwritten National Pact dividing political power among the communities of Christians and Shiite and Sunni Muslims.

1945

March 22: The founding charter of the League of Arab States is adopted in Cairo.

1946

March 22: Britain signs a treaty ending its mandate over Transjordan and acknowledging the independence of that country.

April 15: Britain and France withdraw their remaining troops from Syria.

May 6: Under U.S. pressure, the Soviet Union withdraws its forces from Iran. The Kremlin previously had refused to honor a 1941 agreement under which Britain and the Soviet Union were both to withdraw from Iran following the end of World War II.

October 4: The White House publishes a letter from President Harry Truman to the British government supporting the creation of a "viable Jewish state" in Palestine.

1947

February 14: Following the failure of a conference in London on the future of Palestine, the British government says it will refer the question of Palestine to the United Nations.

August 31: A special committee of the United Nations issues a report recommending the partition of Palestine into Arab and Jewish states by September 1949. The recommendation is later endorsed by Britain, the United States, and the Soviet Union, but a group of Arab leaders known as the Arab Higher Committee rejects it.

November 29: The UN General Assembly adopts Resolution 181, partitioning Palestine into Arab and Jewish sectors. Representatives of Arab nations denounce the action.

1948

May 13: Britain ends its mandate over Palestine, and the Arab League declares that a state of war exists between itself and the Jews of Palestine.

May 14: David Ben-Gurion proclaims the State of Israel. The United States becomes the first country to recognize the new state.

May 15: Egypt, Iraq, Lebanon, Syria, and Transjordan attack Israel, beginning a war that will last until the signing of cease-fire agreements in 1949. Israel survives the attack and gains control over more territory than UN Resolution 181 had awarded it.

December 11: The UN General Assembly adopts Resolution 194, establishing a Palestine Conciliation Commission and calling for the "right of return" by Palestinians to their former homes in the new state of Israel.

1949

January 6: Egypt and Israel sign the first cease-fire ending the Arab-Israeli war; Other cease-fire agreements are signed subsequently: between Israel and Transjordan on March 11 and Israel and Syria on July 20. The other combatants, Iraq and Lebanon, do not sign cease-fire agreements with Israel.

January 25: The Labor Party, led by Prime Minister David Ben-Gurion, wins the first elections held in Israel.

March 21: The UN Palestine Conciliation Commission holds its first meeting, in Beirut. Subsequent sessions are held in 1950 and 1951 but end in failure in November 1951.

April 26: King Abdallah changes the name of his country from Transjordan to Jordan.

April 28: Israel says it will not allow Arab refugees to return to their former homes inside Israel.

July 27: UN mediator Ralph Bunche says the "military phase" of the war between Arabs and Israel has ended.

December 13: The Israeli Knesset approves a proposal by Prime Minister David Ben-Gurion to move government offices, including those of the Knesset, to Jerusalem, from Tel Aviv.

1950

March 9: Turkey becomes the first majority Muslim state to recognize Israel.

March 15: Iran recognizes Israel.

April 1: The Arab League demands that Israel return captured lands that exceed the boundaries set by the 1947 UN partition resolution and votes to expel any member country that negotiates a separate peace with Israel.

April 24: Jordan annexes the West Bank, including the Old City of Jerusalem.

1951

April 28: The Iranian parliament votes to nationalize the Anglo-Iranian Oil Company (owned by the British government).

July 20: Jordan's King Abdallah is assassinated. His son Talal will be crowned king on September 6.

September 13: The UN Palestine Conciliation Commission opens a final round of talks in Paris with delegates from Israel and several Arab countries. During the talks,

Israel offers to sign "nonaggression" agreements with its four Arab neighbors and to compensate (but not accept the return of) Palestinian refugees. The talks end in a deadlock.

October 8: Egypt says it will expel British troops from the Suez Canal area. Britain refuses to evacuate, setting off skirmishes between British troops and Egyptian rioters.

November 21: The UN Palestine Conciliation Commission suspends its work.

December 24: The independent country of Libya is established as kingdom. Britain and the United States plan to keep military bases there.

1952

July 23: A military coup in Egypt ousts King Farouk, who goes into exile in Italy. His infant son is named King Fuad II.

August 11: The Jordanian parliament declares King Talal unfit to rule and proclaims Crown Prince Hussein as king.

August 11: Iran's parliament gives Prime Minister Mohammad Mosaddeq dictatorial powers to deal with an economic and political crisis resulting from a Western boycott of Iranian oil.

October 22: Iran cuts diplomatic ties with Britain because of a dispute over the nationalization of the Anglo-Iranian Oil Company.

1953

August 19: Iranian prime minister Mosaddeq is ousted by troops loyal to the shah, with assistance from the CIA. Maj. Gen. Gazollah Zahedi, the leader of the coup, is named prime minister. In December, a military court will convict Mossaddeq of attempted rebellion and sentences him to three years of solitary confinement.

September 2: Israel begins work on a project to divert water from the Jordan River. The project becomes a regular source of tension between Israel and Jordan.

1954

April 18: Col. Gamal Abdel Nasser is named prime minister of Egypt, replacing Mohammed Naguib, who is given the ceremonial post of president.

July 27: Britain and Egypt sign an agreement ending a dispute over control of the Suez Canal; Britain agrees to remove its military forces from the canal area within twenty months but retains the right to use the military base at the canal to repel aggression against another Arab state or Turkey.

November 13: Nasser becomes president of Egypt, after deposing President Naguib.

1955

February 24: Iraq and Turkey sign the Baghdad Pact, a mutual defense treaty. Britain will sign it on April 4, Pakistan on September 23, and Iran on November 3, after which the five nations announce the creation of the Middle East Treaty Organization (later called the Central Treaty Organization, or CENTO).

1956

May 9: The United States rejects an Israeli request to buy weapons, declaring that arming Israel would increase the prospect for conflict in the Middle East. Israel will later turn to France for weapons.

June 13: Britain ends its military occupation of the Suez Canal.

June 24: Egyptian president Nasser wins an uncontested election to remain in office.

July 20: The United States announces that it will not provide financing for Egypt's project to build the Aswan High Dam on the Nile River. Britain also withdraws its offer to help finance the dam.

July 27: Reacting to U.S. and British refusals to fund the Aswan dam, Nasser announces the nationalization of the Suez Canal, setting off an international crisis over access to and control of the waterway.

October 24: British, French, and Israeli officials sign a secret agreement in Sévres, France, providing for an invasion of Egypt to seize control of the Suez Canal.

October 29: In keeping with its agreement with Britain and France, Israel attacks Egyptian forces in the Sinai.

November 2: The UN General Assembly adopts Resolution 997, demanding a halt to the fighting in Egypt.

November 5: British and French forces attack Egypt. The UN General Assembly adopts Resolution 1000, again calling for a halt to fighting and proposing creation of a UN Emergency International Force to monitor the withdrawal of foreign forces.

November 6: Israel completes its occupation of the Sinai Peninsula (except for the canal zone).

November 7: The UN General Assembly adopts Resolution 1001 demanding that Britain, France, and Israel withdraw from Egypt. U.S. president Dwight D. Eisenhower sends a letter to Israeli prime minister David Ben-Gurion on November demanding that Israel comply with the UN resolution.

November 15: The first contingents of the UN emergency force arrive in Egypt.

November 21: British and French forces begin withdrawing from Egypt.

December 24: Israel begins withdrawing its forces from Egypt. Britain and France had completed their withdrawals three days earlier.

1957

January 4: The Suez Canal reopens for medium-size ships.

January 5: In an address to a joint session of Congress, President Eisenhower says the United States will use military force, if necessary, to prevent communist domination of the Middle East. His declaration becomes known as the Eisenhower Doctrine.

March 13: Britain and Jordan cancel a 1958 mutual defense treaty, and Britain agrees to withdraw its troops from Jordan within six months.

March 15: Egypt says Israeli ships will not be allowed to pass through the Suez Canal.

April 24: In response to a leftist rebellion against Jordan's King Hussein, the United States says it considers the "independence and integrity of Jordan as vital."

September 5: In keeping with the Eisenhower Doctrine, the United States announces plans to send weapons to Iraq, Jordan, Lebanon, and Turkey.

1958

February 1: Egypt and Syria agree to form a single country called the United Arab Republic.

February 14: Iraq and Jordan announce the formation of the Arab Federation, with Iraq's King Faisal II as head of state. King Hussein remains head of state in Jordan.

February 21: Voters in Egypt and Syria approve their countries' merger in plebiscites. Yemen will later join the union.

July 14: King Faisal of Iraq and leaders of his government are overthrown and killed in a military coup. Brig. Gen. Abd al-Karim al-Qasim becomes prime minister. Relations between Iraq and Jordan are severed, thus ending the five-month-old Arab Federation.

July 15: The United States sends 5,000 marines to Lebanon to bolster the government of President Camile Chamoun, who has come under attack from Muslim forces aligned with Nasser of Egypt. The marines will begin withdrawing one month later and complete the operation on October 25.

August 13: President Eisenhower gives the UN General Assembly a "framework" for a Middle East peace plan, calling for a UN peacekeeping force and the economic development of Arab nations.

1959

January 17: Britain and Egypt sign an agreement ending their dispute over the Suez Canal.

March 24: Iraq withdraws from the Baghdad Pact.

August: The Middle East Treaty Organization is renamed the Central Treaty Organization (CENTO), with Britain, Iran, Pakistan, and Turkey as full members and the United States participating as a nonmember.

1960

September 15: Meeting in Baghdad, delegates from Iran, Iraq, Kuwait, Saudi Arabia, and Venezuela agree to form the Organization of the Petroleum Exporting Countries (OPEC) to help stabilize world oil prices.

1961

June 19: Britain grants independence to Kuwait. Iraq will later claim Kuwait as an "integral part" of its territory, and at Egypt's instigation, the Arab League will send troops to Kuwait to protect its independence.

September 29: One day after a military coup in Damascus, the new government of Syria announces its withdrawal from the United Arab Republic, which had been composed of Egypt, Syria, and Yemen.

December 26: Egyptian president Nasser dissolves the union with Yemen but retains the name United Arab Republic for Egypt.

1963

January 26: The shah of Iran begins the White Revolution, a program of modernization and land reform. It will lead to protests and the eventual arrest and deportation to Iraq (in 1964) of protest leader Ayatollah Ruhollah Khomeini.

February 8: Members of the Iraqi branch of the Baath Party and other nationalist leaders overthrow Prime Minister Qasim, who is killed the following day.

November 18: The Syrian government that seized power in February is ousted.

1964

May 28: The Palestine National Council (PNC) holds its first meeting, in East Jerusalem, under Arab League sponsorship.

June 1: The PNC establishes the Palestine Liberation Organization (PLO).

November 2: King Saud of Saudi Arabia is deposed and replaced by his half-brother Crown Prince Faisal.

1967

May 19: At the request of Egypt, the United Nations withdraws its Emergency Force, which has been monitoring the post–Suez crisis cease-fire in the Gaza Strip and Gulf of Aqaba.

May 22: Egypt closes the Strait of Tiran (at the entrance to the Gulf of Aqaba) to Israeli shipping.

May 29: Egyptian president Nasser tells the National Assembly that Egypt is prepared for war against Israel. Minor skirmishes are reported between Egyptian and Israeli forces along the Gaza Strip.

June 5: Jordan launches an artillery attack against western Jerusalem and central Israel. In anticipation of a broader Arab attack, Israel bombs airfields in Egypt, Jordan, and Syria, virtually eliminating those countries' air forces. The UN Security Council calls for a cease-fire.

June 6: Israeli ground forces capture the Gaza Strip and much of the Sinai Peninsula. The Egyptian and Jordanian armies order retreats. In a lengthy speech to the UN Security Council, Israeli foreign minister Abba Eban defends Israel's preemptive strike.

June 7: Israel captures the Old City of Jerusalem and Bethlehem and Jericho on the West Bank. Jordan accepts the UN cease-fire.

June 8: Egypt accepts the cease-fire. Israeli warplanes attack the U.S. Navy's *Liberty* in the Mediterranean, killing at least thirty-four sailors. Israel later apologizes for what it says was a mistake, but many continue to suspect that the attack was deliberate.

June 9: Israeli forces reach the Suez Canal and begin to push onto the Golan Heights. Egyptian president Nasser offers his resignation, but the National Assembly refuses to accept it.

June 10: Israel captures the Golan Heights from Syria, completing its conquests of Arab territory. Late in the day Israel and Syria accept a cease-fire, ending the war after six days.

June 19: In a decision not made public at the time, the Israeli cabinet agrees to return most of the territory Israel had just captured in return for peace and normal relations with its Arab neighbors. The offer will later be spurned by the Arabs and withdrawn by Israel. In a speech in Washington, President Lyndon B. Johnson outlines a "peace plan" for the Middle East.

June 28: Israel says it has merged the eastern and western sectors of Jerusalem under its control.

July 26: Israeli cabinet minister Yigal Allon submits a draft plan calling for Israel to hold onto East Jerusalem and the strategic portions of the West Bank permanently while accepting autonomy for the Palestinians in other portions of the West Bank. Although never officially adopted by the government, subsequent versions of the so-called Allon Plan will become the basis for Israel's policy of building settlements and military posts in the territories captured from the Arabs.

September 1: Meeting in Khartoum, Arab leaders declare "three noes": no peace with, no recognition of, and no negotiation with Israel.

September 24: Israel says it will move civilian settlers into East Jerusalem and the Golan Heights.

November 22: The UN Security Council adopts Resolution 242 calling for peace in the Middle East based on the exchange of land captured by Israel in the June war for peace with its Arab neighbors.

1968

January: The British government announces its intention to withdraw its remaining military posts from the Persian Gulf region by 1971.

April 10: Jewish activists attempt to establish a settlement in the Palestinian city of Hebron. This leads to a prolonged political battle in which the activists will ultimately prevail.

July 1–18: The Palestine National Council adopts the Palestine National Charter, expressing a Palestinian national identity and calling for "armed struggle" to "liberate" Palestine from Israeli control.

July 17: The Baath Party returns to power in Iraq in a bloodless coup. Ahmad Hassan al-Bakr is named president and prime minister on July 31; Saddam Hussein is a senior member of the Revolutionary Command Council, the ruling body.

1969

February 1–4: At a meeting in Cairo, the Fatah faction gains control of the Palestine National Council, and its leader Yasir Arafat becomes chairman of the PLO Executive Committee. He will remain the Palestinian leader until his death in 2004.

March: Egyptian attacks on Israeli positions signal the start of a "war of attrition" that will last until July 1970.

July 3: The UN Security Council adopts Resolution 267, with the strongest wording yet censuring Israel for unilateral actions changing the legal status of Jerusalem.

August 3: Israel announces that it will keep the Gaza Strip, the Golan Heights, and the Sinai Peninsula. Left unclear are Israeli intentions toward the occupied West Bank.

September 1: Libya's King Idris is ousted in a coup. Army officer Muammar al-Qadhafi, head of the Revolutionary Command Council, emerges as the leading figure in the new government.

October 22: Nine emirates on the east coast of the Arabian Peninsula announce the formation of the Federation of Persian Gulf Emirates.

October 28: The new government in Libya orders the United States to withdraw from Wheelus Air Force Base by the end of 1970. The United States will complete the withdrawal by June 1970.

December 9: U.S. secretary of state William Rogers unveils a peace plan calling for Israeli withdrawal from occupied Arab lands in exchange for peace treaties with its neighbors.

December 12: Israel rejects the Rogers plan.

1970

January 21: Renewed fighting breaks out between Israel and some of its Arab neighbors.

August 7: A U.S.-sponsored cease-fire in the "war of attrition" between Israel and its Arab neighbors goes into effect.

September 1: In the midst of a conflict between Palestinian guerrillas and the Jordanian army, Jordan's King Hussein narrowly escapes assassination in Amman. In subsequent weeks, guerrillas from the Popular Front for the Liberation of Palestine will hijack five commercial jets and fly three of them (including some 300 hostages) into the desert of Jordan.

September 16: Amid fighting between Jordanian forces and Palestinian guerrillas, King Hussein declares martial law. A week later, Jordan defeats a Syrian army unit that had crossed the border in support of the Palestinians.

September 27: Arab leaders sign an agreement in Cairo ending the crisis in Jordan that becomes known as Black September. All the remaining hostages from the hijacked airplanes will be released within the next three days.

September 28: Egyptian president Nasser dies of a heart attack after mediating the crisis in Jordan. He is succeeded by Vice President Anwar al-Sadat.

November 13: Syrian air force Lt. Gen. Hafiz al-Asad seizes power in a bloodless coup, ousting a rival faction of the Baath Party.

1971

February 4: Egyptian president Sadat offers a peace agreement with Israel, if Israel returns all Arab lands captured in the June 1967 War.

March 12: The Turkish military issues a memorandum demanding immediate action by the civilian government to deal with the country's political crises. In response, the government resigns, and the military takes over.

March 13: Prime Minister Hafiz al-Assad is named president of Syria.

April 17: Egypt, Libya, and Syria agree to form the Federation of Arab Republics, a successor to the failed United Arab Republic. The merger will be approved in plebiscites in September and Egypt's Sadat chosen in October as the first president.

December 1: Britain completes its military withdrawal from the Persian Gulf.

December 2: Six of the Persian Gulf emirates form the United Arab Emirates. A seventh will join later.

1972

March 15: King Hussein announces a plan to convert Jordan and the West Bank into a federation of two autonomous regions. Israel and most of Jordan's Arab neighbors denounce the plan, effectively killing it.

July 18: Egyptian president Sadat orders all 15,000 Soviet military "advisors" to leave the country, ending Egypt's heavy reliance on the Soviet Union for military support.

September 5: Arab guerrillas from an organization called Black September seize Israeli athletes at the Olympics in Munich, West Germany. Eleven Israelis and five Arabs will die in the crisis. Israel will retaliate by bombing Palestinian guerrilla bases in Lebanon and Syria.

September 13: The Soviet Union and Syria agree to extensive military cooperation, making Syria Moscow's chief Arab ally in the region.

1973

April 12: In a speech to the Labor Party, Israeli prime minister Golda Meir says that Palestinians looking for a state of their own could find it in Jordan.

July 17: In Afghanistan, King Zahir Shah is overthrown by his cousin, Prime Minister Mohammad Daoud.

October 6: Egypt and Syria attack Israel.

October 15: In the midst of the Middle East war, the United States announces that it is providing large quantities of military supplies and weapons to Israel in response to resumed Soviet aid to Egypt.

October 17: The Organization of Arab Petroleum Exporting Countries announces that it will cease deliveries to the United States, the Netherlands, and South Africa because of their support for Israel and cut back shipments to other countries. The embargo will continue until March 1974 and contribute to a major international economic downturn.

October 22: The UN Security Council adopts Resolution 338, demanding a cease-fire in the Arab-Israeli war and reaffirming the "land for peace" concept of its Resolution 242 from November 1967.

October 25: A cease-fire takes effect in the Arab-Israeli war. The Arabs fail to achieve their goal of winning back territory captured by Israel in 1967, but they do achieve a psychological victory. President Nixon orders a worldwide alert of the U.S. military because of concerns that the Soviet Union might intervene in the Middle East war.

November 11: Egypt and Israel sign a cease-fire providing for prisoner exchanges and negotiations on returning to the battle lines in effect when the Security Council adopted Resolution 338 on October 22.

December 21: Representatives from Egypt, Israel, and Jordan meet in Geneva with officials from the Soviet Union, the United Nations, and the United States. Syria boycotts the sessions, which make no progress. For the next several years, resuming the "Geneva talks" is a main goal of international diplomacy.

1974

January 18: After rounds of "shuttle diplomacy" mediated by U.S. secretary of state Henry Kissinger, Egypt and Israel sign Sinai I, a disengagement agreement calling for Israel to pull back from the eastern bank of the Suez Canal and for a UN force to patrol a buffer zone between Egyptian and Israeli forces in the Sinai.

March 18: Most Arab oil-producing countries—Libya is the major exception—agree to lift the oil embargo imposed against the United States during the October 1973 war.

April 10: After a political dispute over assigning blame for Israel's failure to anticipate the Arab attack the previous October, Prime Minister Golda Meir resigns. Yitzhak Rabin, a former general, succeeds her.

May 29: Israel and Syria agree on a Kissinger-negotiated plan to disengage their armies.

June 9: The Palestine National Council resolves to "employ all means, and first and foremost armed struggle, to liberate Palestinian territory and to establish the independent combatant national authority for the people over every part of Palestinian territory that is liberated."

July 31: Israeli prime minister Yitzhak Rabin, following a decision by the Israeli cabinet on July 26, announces that only the government can determine whether and when Jewish settlements will be established in the West Bank. This is in response to an attempt by members of the Gush Emunim movement to move into Sebastia, an abandoned railway station near the city of Nablus on the West Bank.

October 28: Arab leaders, meeting in Rabat, Morocco, recognize the Palestine Liberation Organization as the "sole legitimate representative" of the Palestinian people. Jordan's King Hussein, who previously had been a voice for the Palestinians, agrees to honor the PLO's claim.

November 13: PLO chairman Yasir Arafat addresses the UN General Assembly and calls for the creation of a Palestinian state.

November 22: The UN General Assembly grants the PLO observer status.

December 1: Israeli president Ephraim Katzir offers the first official acknowledgment that Israel is capable of producing nuclear weapons. Subsequent reports will assert that Israel had possessed this capability for several years.

1975

March 5: Iran and Iraq sign the Algiers Accord, an agreement mediated by Algeria, resolving conflicting boundary claims to the Shatt al-Arab waterway and pledging not to interfere in each other's domestic affairs. A year-long Kurdish rebellion will quickly collapse after Iran, under the agreement, suspends its support for Kurdish separatists in Iraq.

March 25: King Faisal of Saudi Arabia is assassinated by a nephew and is succeeded by Crown Prince Khalid. This is the first violent transfer of power in Saudi Arabia since the kingdom's founding four decades earlier.

April 13: An attack by unknown gunmen on Christian worshipers in a Beirut suburb results in riots and retaliatory attacks. The ongoing conflict will develop into a civil war lasting until 1990.

July 1: After the deaths of nearly 300 people, factions in Lebanon sign a truce, but it fails to halt fighting.

September 4: Egyptian and Israeli officials sign Sinai II, an "interim agreement" negotiated by Kissinger providing for additional Israeli withdrawals from the Sinai Peninsula.

November 10: The UN General Assembly adopts Resolution 3379, declaring that Zionism is a form of racism.

1976

March 23: William Scranton, the U.S. ambassador to the United Nations, calls Israeli settlements in the occupied territories "an obstacle to the success of the negotiations for a just and final peace." This is the first of many similar official U.S. statements on the settlements, which Israel continues to build.

October 25: The Arab League, except for Iraq and Libya, approves a plan calling for an end to the Lebanese civil war and the deployment of a 30,000-man Arab peacekeeping force. This plan will become the legal basis for Syria's long-term military occupation of Lebanon.

November 11: The UN Security Council issues a statement deploring Israel's settlements in the occupied territories and declaring Israel's annexation of East Jerusalem to be "invalid." The United States in March had vetoed a somewhat stronger Security Council resolution on these matters.

1977

March 16: President Carter endorses a Palestinian "homeland," becoming the first president to do so.

May 17: The right-wing Likud Party wins in Israeli elections, ending the domination of the Labor Party since 1948. Likud leader Menachem Begin will become prime minister.

November 9: Egyptian president Anwar al-Sadat tells the National Assembly that "I am ready to go to the Israeli parliament" to discuss peace.

November 17: Sadat accepts an invitation from Israeli prime minister Begin to address the Knesset in Jerusalem.

November 19: Sadat arrives in Israel, becoming the first Arab leader to visit the country officially since its creation in 1948.

November 21: A day after addressing the Knesset, Sadat holds a joint news conference with Israeli prime minister Begin, during which both men express a desire for peace.

November 26: Sadat invites leaders of other Arab countries, Israel, the United States, and the Soviet Union to attend a peace conference in Cairo. Israel and the United States accept, but the others refuse.

December 2: Arab leaders, meeting in Libya, denounce Egypt's peace efforts.

December 5: Egypt severs diplomatic relations with Algeria, Iraq, Libya, South Yemen, and Syria.

December 14: Representatives from Egypt, Israel, the United States, and the United Nations meet in Cairo to prepare for resumption of long-stalled peace talks in Geneva.

December 25: Begin and Sadat meet in Ismailia, Egypt, but reach no substantive agreements.

1978

January: Iranian security forces kill several dozen student protesters in the religious center of Qom, sparking a series of protests that escalate throughout the year.

March 14: Israel conducts its largest invasion to date of southern Lebanon in retaliation for a Palestinian cross-border raid that killed thirty Israelis. Israel will withdraw by June 13 but leave the territory it had occupied under the control of a pro-Israeli Lebanese military commander.

April 27: Afghan president Daoud is ousted in a communist coup. A communist government headed by Muhammad Taraki will order numerous modernization programs that alienate conservative forces, who launch a widespread rebellion.

August 13: An estimated 200 people are killed when a bomb destroys a nine-story building in Beirut housing the Fatah faction of the PLO and the Iraqi Palestine Liberation Front (a rival group).

September 8: The Iranian military fires on antigovernment demonstrators in Tehran, killing several hundred people.

September 17: After a series of meetings with President Jimmy Carter at Camp David, Israeli prime minister Menachem Begin and Egyptian president Anwar al-Sadat sign two documents: a Framework for the Conclusion of a Peace Treaty Between Egypt and Israel and a Framework for Peace in the Middle East. Negotiations on the text of an Egypt-Israel treaty continue all through the rest of 1978 and into early 1979.

October 31: Thousands of Iranian oil workers go on strike to protest the government crackdown on protests by students and others.

November 6: The shah imposes martial law in Iran in a failed attempt to halt the protests.

December 29: The shah of Iran appoints opposition politician Shapour Bakhtiar as head of a new government.

1979

January 16: The shah of Iran flees the country—he says for a "vacation"—after his concessions fail to calm widespread disturbances.

February 1: Ayatollah Ruhollah Khomeini returns to Iran from exile in France.

February 14: Leftist forces briefly occupy the U.S. embassy in Tehran. U.S. personnel are freed by armed supporters of Khomeini.

March 26: In a ceremony at the White House, Israeli prime minister Menachem Begin and Egyptian president Anwar al-Sadat sign the first formal peace treaty between Israel and an Arab nation.

March 31: Arab League foreign ministers vote for an economic boycott of Egypt and oust it from the league because of its peace treaty with Israel. In subsequent months, most Arab countries will break diplomatic relations with Egypt, and the Organization of the Islamic Conference will suspend its membership.

April 1: Ayatollah Khomeini proclaims an Islamic Republic in Iran after its endorsement by plebiscite.

May 25: Israel begins withdrawing from the Sinai Peninsula, a process that it will complete in 1982.

July 16: Iraqi president Ahmad Hasan al-Bakr suddenly resigns (citing ill health) and is replaced by Vice President Saddam Hussein.

August: The new Islamic government of Iran faces its most intense opposition yet as the result in major riots in Tehran.

September 16: Israel revokes a law barring Israeli citizens and businesses from buying Arab-owned land in the Gaza Strip and West Bank, an action that will accelerate the process of Jewish settlement in the territories.

September 24: Israeli planes down four Syrian planes in a confrontation over Lebanon.

October 22: The United States admits the former shah of Iran for medical treatment in New York, sparking anti-U.S. protests in Iran.

November 4: A group of Iranian students seize the U.S. embassy in Tehran and take hostage sixty-five Americans there, marking the beginning of a diplomatic crisis that will last until the last hostages are released in January 1981.

December 24: The Soviet Union launches an invasion of Afghanistan.

December 27: Babrak Karmal is installed as prime minister of Afghanistan.

1980

January 23: President Carter announces in his State of the Union Address that an attempt by "any outside force" to gain control of the Persian Gulf would be considered an assault on the vital interests of the United States and would be repelled "by any means necessary, including military force." This declaration, known as the Carter Doctrine, is aimed at the Soviet Union because of its invasion of Afghanistan in December.

January 26: The border between Egypt and Israel is opened.

April 7: The United States severs diplomatic relations with Iran because of the embassy hostage crisis.

April 8: Iranian leader Ayatollah Khomeini calls for the ouster of Iraqi leader Saddam Hussein.

April 25: A U.S. military attempt to rescue the embassy hostages in Iran fails and results in the deaths of eight service personnel in a crash between an airplane and helicopter.

June 22: Israel announces that the offices of the prime minister and other cabinet members will be moved from West Jerusalem to East Jerusalem, another step toward unifying Jerusalem under its control.

July 30: The Knesset passes a law affirming Israel's claim to Jerusalem. The measure will prompt protests from Egypt and the UN Security Council (on August 20).

July 27: The former shah of Iran dies of cancer in Cairo.

September 12: The Turkish military ousts the civilian government.

September 17: Iraqi president Saddam Hussein announces the abrogation of the 1975 border agreement with Iran.

September 22: Iraq invades Iran, starting a war that is to last for eight years. Iraq will make initial military gains into western Iran, but an Iranian counterattack in March 1982 will then drive the Iraqi army back across the border.

1981

January 20: Minutes after Ronald Reagan is inaugurated as U.S. president, Iran releases the remaining fifty-two Americans who had been held hostage in Tehran since November 1979. Their release results from an agreement, mediated by Algeria, under which the United States frees $8 billion in Iranian assets that had been frozen.

April 29: Syria installs surface-to-air missiles in the Bekaa Valley of Lebanon in response to an Israeli attack on Syrian helicopters in Lebanon.

May 25: Bahrain, Kuwait, Oman, Qatar, Saudi Arabia, and the United Arab Emirates form the Gulf Cooperation Council to deter threats to the Persian Gulf region.

June 7: Israeli warplanes bomb and destroy a nuclear reactor under construction at Osirak, near Baghdad. Israel accuses Iraq of intending to use the reactor to build nuclear weapons. The raid is condemned by most countries, including the United States, which temporarily suspends the delivery of several warplanes to Israel.

June 30: The Likud Party headed by Prime Minister Menachem Begin wins a narrow victory in Israeli elections. It will establish a coalition government on August 5.

July 17: Israeli warplanes bomb PLO headquarters in downtown Beirut, killing an estimated 300 people.

July 24: After mediation by the United States and Saudi Arabia, a cease-fire between Israel and the PLO takes effect along the Israeli-Lebanese border.

August 3: Egypt and Israel agree to the establishment of an international peacekeeping force in the Sinai following the completion of Israel's withdrawal, scheduled for April 1982.

August 7: Crown Prince Fahd of Saudi Arabia presents an eight-point plan calling for peace with Israel, provided that it withdraw to borders as they existed before the June 1967 War. Israel rejects the plan, but President Reagan will express support for it in October.

October 6: Islamist extremists assassinate Egyptian president Sadat. Vice President Hosni Mubarak is elected to succeed him on October 13.

November 30: Israel and the United States sign a "strategic memorandum of understanding" to counter Soviet threats to the Middle East.

December 14: Israel extends its laws to the Golan Heights, effectively annexing the strategic plateau, which it had captured in 1967 from Syria.

December 18: To protest Israel's annexation of the Golan Heights, the Reagan administration suspends the strategic memorandum with Israel signed weeks earlier.

1982

February: After guerrillas from the Muslim Brotherhood take control of Hama in northern Syria, the army counterattacks and destroys much of the city, killing a reported 10,000 people.

March 22: Iran launches a counteroffensive against Iraq, driving Iraqi forces out of the positions they had held inside Iran since the Iran-Iraq War began in late 1980.

April 25: Israel completes its withdrawal from the Sinai Peninsula after demolishing Jewish settlements there.

June 6: Israel invades Lebanon to attack Palestinian guerrillas who have been launching cross-border raids into northern Israel.

June 8: In a speech to the Knesset, Prime Minister Menachem Begin says Israel seeks a twenty-five-mile-deep security zone inside Lebanon to protect itself against Palestinian attacks launched from Lebanese territory.

June 13: King Khalid of Saudi Arabia dies and is succeeded by his half-brother Crown Price Fahd. Prince Abdallah ibn Abd al-Aziz becomes crown prince.

August 4: Israeli forces reach Beirut.

August 18: The Lebanese government and the PLO approve a U.S.-mediated plan for PLO leaders and thousands of fighters to be evacuated from Lebanon.

August 21: The evacuation of the PLO begins in Lebanon as the first French troops arrive as part of an international peacekeeping force. The Palestinian withdrawal will be completed on September 2, and international peacekeepers will later also leave.

September 1: President Ronald Reagan announces a Middle East peace plan, calling for Jordan to exercise responsibility over the West Bank.

September 9: Meeting in Fez, Morocco, Arab leaders adopt a statement that for the first time implies recognition of Israel. Echoing a Saudi peace plan from August 1981, the Fez statement calls on Israel to withdraw to the pre-June 1967 borders and for peace among "all states" of the region. The United States praises the statement but Israel rejects it.

September 14: Lebanese president-elect Bashir Gemayel is assassinated when a bomb destroys the headquarters of the Christian Phalange Party in East Beirut.

September 16: On the outskirts of Beirut, Israeli forces allow Phalange fighters to enter the Sabra and Shatila refugee camps, where the Phalangists kill several hundred Palestinians, causing an international uproar.

September 20: In response to the Sabra and Shatila killings, the Lebanese government requests the return of international peacekeepers. France, Italy, and the United States agree to provide the peacekeepers, who will begin arriving later in the month. President Reagan explains that the peacekeepers will be in Lebanon for "a limited period" with a limited mission of bolstering the government.

December 1: At Lebanon's request, the United States agrees to expand the international peacekeeping force there.

1983

February 8: An Israeli commission finds that several officials, including Defense Minister Ariel Sharon, neglected their duty when they allowed Lebanese Phalange militiamen into the Sabra and Shatila refugee camps the previous September. Sharon resigns as defense minister but remains in the cabinet as a minister without portfolio.

April 18: The U.S. embassy in Beirut is destroyed by a large car bomb; 63 people (including 17 Americans) are killed and more than 100 wounded. Islamic Jihad, a pro-Iranian group, claims responsibility.

May: Factional conflicts erupt between Palestinian fighters who have re-infiltrated into Lebanon.

May 17: Israel and Lebanon sign the second treaty between Israel and an Arab nation.

June 24: PLO chairman Yasir Arafat is expelled from Damascus, where he had gone after leaving Lebanon in the previous December, and heads to Tripoli, Lebanon, where his Fatah faction is based.

August 28: Israeli prime minister Begin says he will resign for personal reasons.

September 12: In Israel, coalition partners agree on a new cabinet under Yitzhak Shamir.

October 23: Near-simultaneous bomb attacks in Beirut kill 241 U.S. service personnel and 58 French servicemen serving in the international peacekeeping force in Lebanon. U.S. officials blame Islamist guerrillas backed by Iran.

November 4: A truck bomb hits Israeli military headquarters in Tyre, Lebanon, killing 60 people, including Israeli soldiers and Arab prisoners.

November 23: PLO factions battling since May agree to a Saudi-brokered cease-fire that allows Arafat and his supporters to evacuate Tripoli, Lebanon.

November 24: Israel swaps 4,500 Lebanese and Palestinian prisoners for 6 Israeli soldiers held by the PLO.

December 4: One day after a Syrian attack on U.S reconnaissance planes, the United States attacks Syrian positions in eastern Lebanon. Two U.S. planes are shot down; one pilot is killed and another captured.

December 14: U.S. warships extensively shell Syrian positions in Lebanon.

December 20: Aboard Greek ships flying UN flags, Arafat and about 4,000 Palestinian fighters leave Tripoli, Lebanon, for Tunis, where the PLO will be based for more than ten years.

1984

February 7: Less than four months after saying U.S. peacekeepers would remain in Lebanon, President Reagan announces that U.S. troops have been "redeployed" to ships off the Lebanese coast. The last U.S. troops will leave Beirut on February 21. Britain and Italy also withdraw their forces from the international peacekeeping force.

March 5: Lebanon abrogates the treaty signed with Israel in May 1983.

June 23: The Lebanese government restructures the national army to make it more representative of Christian and Muslim communities.

July 4: A revamped Lebanese army begins taking control of Beirut from the various militias and destroys a wall, known as the Green Line, that had separated Christian and Muslim neighborhoods.

July 23: Israeli elections end in a virtual deadlock, with neither Labor nor Likud winning enough seats to form a stable coalition.

September 13: After July's inconclusive elections in Israel, the Labor and Likud parties agree to share power. Labor leader Shimon Peres will be prime minister for two years, and then Likud leader (and former prime minister Yitzhak Shamir) will take over for two years.

September 25: Jordan becomes the first Arab country to renew diplomatic relations with Egypt.

1985

February 22: Jordan's King Hussein and PLO leader Arafat announce their agreement on the Amman Accord, a peace plan calling for a Jordanian-Palestinian "confederation." Israel rejects the plan.

March: Iran and Iraq escalate bomb and missile attacks against each other's cities. This "war of the cities," which began in February 1984, will continue intermittently until the Iran-Iraq War ends in 1988.

March: Under a plan announced in January, Israel begins withdrawing from most of Lebanon except for a self-declared "security zone" in southern Lebanon.

June 14: TWA Flight 847, from Athens to Rome, is hijacked and forced to land in Beirut. After prolonged negotiations, the last of the passengers will be released on June 30.

October 1: After the killing of three Israelis by Palestinians in Cyprus in late September, Israel bombs PLO headquarters in Tunis. More than seventy people die from the bombing, which brings widespread criticism.

October 7: Four Palestinian gunmen hijack the *Achille Lauro,* an Italian cruise ship, in the Mediterranean. They will kill an American, Leon Klinghoffer, before surrendering and releasing other hostages. The hijackers are said to be associated with the Palestine Liberation Front, headed by Abul Abbas.

November 7: PLO chairman Arafat renounces the use of terrorism.

December 27: At the Rome and Vienna airports, Palestinians from Fatah–Revolutionary Council, headed by Abu Nidal, attack travelers at check-in counters for El Al, the Israeli airline. Eighteen people are killed, plus four of the gunmen.

1986

January 7: The United States imposes economic and trade sanctions against Libya, accusing it of supporting Abu Nidal's Palestinian faction.

February 11: Iran captures the Faw Peninsula in Iraq, including the oil-export terminal there, marking the beginning of an unsuccessful Iranian drive to capture Basra and other cities in southern Iraq.

February 17: Lebanese guerrillas capture two Israeli soldiers along the Israel-Lebanon border.

February 19: Jordan's King Hussein renounces the Amman Accord he reached one year earlier with PLO chairman Arafat, charging the Palestinian leader with failing to cooperate in carrying out the agreement, specifically his ongoing refusal to accept UN Resolution 242. Jordan closes PLO offices in the country.

April 14: The United States carries out an air attack against Libya, killing some fifteen people, including an infant daughter of Libyan leader Muammar al-Qadhafi. President Reagan had accused Libya of sponsoring the April 5 bombing of a Berlin discotheque in which a U.S. soldier and a woman from Turkey died.

May 4: Muhammad Najibullah, a former chief of the secret police, replaces Babrak Karmal as president of Afghanistan.

May 25: A delegation of White House officials arrive in Tehran on a secret mission intended to gain the freedom of U.S. hostages in Lebanon. This mission is an opening element of what became known as the Iran-contra affair: the United States provided weapons to Iran (for use in its war with Iraq) in exchange for Iranian promises to help free U.S. citizens held hostage in Lebanon by groups supported by Iran. The first public report of the U.S.-Iran arms-for-hostages deal will appear on November 3.

July 22: Israeli prime minister Shimon Peres and Morocco's King Hassan II hold meetings in Ilfrane, Morocco, in the only public meeting to date of Arab and Israeli leaders except for those between Egyptians and Israelis.

October 5: The *Sunday Times* (London) quotes former Israeli nuclear technician Mordechai Vanunu as saying that Israel has been building nuclear weapons for two decades and possesses as many as 200 such weapons. Vanunu will later be captured in Rome and charged by Israeli authorities with espionage.

October 20: Under the power-sharing arrangement following 1984 elections, Yitzhak Shamir becomes prime minister of Israel, swapping jobs with Shimon Peres, who becomes foreign minister.

1987

January 20: Anglican Church envoy Terry Waite, who had been negotiating the release of Western hostages in Lebanon, disappears. He is later confirmed to have been taken hostage himself.

January 24: Three American and one Indian professor at the American University of Beirut are taken hostage.

April 20–26: The Palestine National Council, meeting in Algiers, reelects Arafat as chairman of the PLO; the meeting is called to end feuding among the group's various factions. Arafat accepts a demand by extremist factions to take a harder line against Israel.

May 19: After months of hesitation, the United States signs an agreement to re-flag Kuwaiti oil tankers and protect them from Iranian attack in the Persian Gulf. The first U.S. escort of tankers will take place on July 22.

June 1: Lebanese prime minister Rashid Karami, who had announced his resignation in May because of the country's political gridlock, is killed when a bomb explodes in his helicopter. Selim al-Hoss is appointed acting prime minister.

July 20: The UN Security Council adopts Resolution 598 demanding a cease-fire between Iran and Iraq. Iraq will accept the resolution the following day, but Iran rejects it.

July 31: A riot by Iranian pilgrims near the Grand Mosque in Mecca leads to the death of more than 400 people. Iranians attack the Saudi and Kuwaiti embassies in Tehran the following day.

November 11: Meeting in Amman, Arab leaders take their strongest stand yet on the Iran-Iraq War, condemning Iran for its "procrastination" in responding to calls for a cease-fire.

December 8: Four Palestinians are killed when a vehicle driven by an Israeli accidentally runs into theirs at a checkpoint.

December 9: Funerals for the Palestinians killed the preceding day in Gaza turn into demonstrations against the Israeli occupation, marking the start of the first intifada. The uprising will last, intermittently, until the Israeli-PLO peace process begins in 1993.

December 22: The UN Security Council adopts a resolution that "strongly deplores" the harsh response by Israel to the Palestinian intifada, including the "excessive use of live ammunition" against protesters. The United States abstains, allowing the resolution to be adopted.

1988

February: Iraq launches the Anfal campaign to move tens of thousands of Kurds out of areas the government has declared off-limits to them. It will continue until September. A subsequent investigation by Human Rights Watch claims that more than 100,000 Kurds, most of them men and boys, were trucked to remote sites and executed.

February 27: Iraq bombs an Iranian oil refinery near Tehran, setting off another round of reciprocal attacks in the "war of the cities" between the two countries.

February 29: Iran hits Baghdad with long-range missiles.

March 16: The Iraqi army uses chemical weapons to bomb the Kurdish town of Halabja, in northern Iraq, after Iran captures it. Later investigations by human rights groups will put the death toll at 3,000.

April 14: Afghanistan and Pakistan sign the Geneva Accords settling differences between them and providing for the withdrawal of Soviet military forces from Afghanistan. The United States and the Soviet Union are witnesses to the agreement.

April 16: In Tunis, an Israeli commando team assassinates Khalil Wazir, also known as Abu Jihad, the second-ranking official in the Fatah faction of the PLO.

May 15: Soviet forces begin withdrawing from Afghanistan.

July 3: The U.S. warship *Vincennes* shoots down a civilian Iranian airliner, killing all 290 people on board. The ship's captain says the plane was mistaken for an Iranian warplane, but Iran maintains that the downing was deliberate murder.

July 18: Iran accepts UN Security Council Resolution 598 demanding a cease-fire in the Iran-Iraq War. Iraq had accepted the resolution in 1987.

July 20: In a national speech, Iranian supreme leader Ayatollah Khomeini calls the decision to accept UN Resolution 598 "more lethal for me than poison."

July 31: As the intifada continues, King Hussein of Jordan renounces his claim to the West Bank, cutting all legal and administrative ties to the territory it had administered until Israel captured it in June 1967.

August 4: Jordan announces that it will stop paying the salaries of thousands of Palestinian teachers and other civil servants on the West Bank.

August 18: Hamas, the Islamic Resistance Movement, issues its "covenant," or program, calling for resistance to Israel by all necessary means.

August 20: Iran and Iraq formally agree to a cease-fire, ending their eight-year war.

September 22: With the Lebanese parliament having failed to appoint a new president, outgoing president Amin Gemayel appoints Gen. Michel Aoun to head a provisional government hours before stepping down at the end of his term.

September 23: Muslims refuse to recognize the Aoun government and form a rival government headed by previous prime minister Selim al-Hoss.

September 29: Ending a long dispute, an international arbitration panel awards Egypt control of Taba in the Sinai Peninsula. Israel had occupied Taba during the June 1967 War and had built a seaside resort there. Egypt demanded that Israel return it as part of the 1979 peace treaty.

November 1: The Likud Party scores a narrow victory in Israeli elections, enabling Prime Minister Shamir to hold on to power.

November 15: Meeting in Algiers, the Palestine National Council issues a statement declaring a Palestinian state, with its capital in Jerusalem and Arafat as president. Earlier, the council also had voted limited acceptance of UN Resolutions 242 and 338.

December 14: Under pressure from the United States, PLO chairman Yasir Arafat again renounces terrorism and directly accepts UN Resolutions 242 and 338. This enables the United States to say that Arafat has met its conditions for direct contacts.

December 21: Pan Am Flight 203 from London to New York explodes and crashes in Lockerbie, Scotland, after a bomb explodes onboard. All 259 passengers and crew on the plane are killed, along with 11 people on the ground. British authorities will later charge that Libyan government agents planted the bomb.

1989

February 14: Iran's Ayatollah Khomeini issues a *fatwa,* or decree, calling on all Muslims to kill author Salman Rushdie because his novel *The Satanic Verses* allegedly blasphemes Islam. Rushdie goes into hiding.

February 15: The last Soviet soldiers leave Afghanistan, ending an occupation of more than nine years. The Soviet departure will intensify battles for power among factions in Afghanistan, including the communist government supported by Moscow and various groups of Islamist guerrillas, or *mujahidin.*

March 14: A new round of conflict between Christian and Muslim militias in Lebanon erupts into a major artillery battle killing several dozen people and marking the start of several months of fighting.

March 15: Israel evacuates Taba, which returns to Egyptian sovereignty.

April 2: Hamas kidnaps and murders two Israeli soldiers, its first such attack. Israel will arrest dozens of Hamas members and leaders, including spiritual leader Shaykh Ahmad Yasin, and later declare Hamas an illegal organization.

April 6: Israeli prime minister Shamir proposes a plan for Palestinians to elect representatives who would negotiate with Israel toward a limited autonomy. Palestinian officials will denounce the plan, which goes nowhere.

May 22: Secretary of State James A. Baker III tells the American Israel Public Affairs Committee that Israel should give up "the unrealistic vision of a greater Israel" and negotiate an agreement with the Palestinians. The speech is one of the toughest ever given by a senior U.S. official criticizing Israeli policies.

May 22: Meeting in Casablanca, the Arab League formally readmits Egypt a decade after its suspension following the signing of its peace treaty with Israel.

June 3: Iranian supreme leader Ayatollah Khomeini dies.

June 4: The Iranian Assembly of Experts names President Ali Khamenei as the country's new supreme leader.

July 28: Israeli commandos abduct Shaykh Abd al-Karim Obeid, leader of the Shiite group Hizballah in Lebanon. Officials will later reveal that they had planned to trade Obeid for Israeli hostages in Lebanon. A Lebanese group called the Organization of the Oppressed on Earth will announce that in retaliation for the kidnapping it has killed U.S. Marine Corps Lt. Col. William Higgins, who had been held hostage in Lebanon since February 1988.

October 24: After three weeks of meetings in Taif, Saudi Arabia, members of the Lebanese parliament sign an agreement for political reconciliation. The agreement provides for equal representation of Christians and Muslims in parliament (even though Muslims are a majority) and allows Syria to continue its military presence in Lebanon.

November 5: The Lebanese parliament elects Rene Muawwad as president under the terms of the new Taif accord.

November 22: Lebanese prime minister Muawwad is assassinated by a large bomb blast in Beirut. Elias Hrawi will be selected to replace him.

1990

March 15: After the Labor Party withdraws from the coalition government in Israel, Prime Minister Yitzhak Shamir loses a no-confidence motion in parliament, a first for an Israeli leader.

May 22: Ending years of conflict followed by negotiations, North and South Yemen agree to merge into a unified country.

May 25: PLO chairman Yasir Arafat addresses a special meeting of the UN Security Council in Geneva.

June 20: The United States suspends diplomatic contacts with the PLO, conducted since December 1988, because of the PLO's failure to condemn a May 30 attack against Israelis by the Palestine Liberation Front, led by Abul Abbas.

August 2: Iraq invades and occupies Kuwait. The UN Security Council adopts Resolution 660, condemning the invasion.

August 6: The UN Security Council adopts Resolution 661, imposing economic sanctions against Iraq.

   King Fahd of Saudi Arabia agrees to the stationing of U.S. forces in the kingdom after a meeting in Riyadh during which U.S. secretary of defense Dick Cheney presents satellite photographs of Iraqi forces massed along the border with Saudi Arabia.

August 8: Iraq announces that it has annexed Kuwait as its nineteenth province.

August 10: Most countries of the Arab League vote to support Saudi Arabia and other countries resisting the Iraqi occupation of Kuwait.

August 12: Iraqi leader Saddam Hussein states in a televised speech that Iraq invaded Kuwait to reverse the ill of "colonialism" when Britain separated Kuwait from Iraq. He also says that Iraq will withdraw from Kuwait if Israel withdraws from the Palestinian territories and Syria withdraws from Lebanon.

August 25: The UN Security Council adopts Resolution 665, authorizing member nations to enforce UN sanctions against Iraq.

September 9: In response to Iran's invasion of Kuwait, President George H. W. Bush and Soviet president Mikhail Gorbachev pledge to take whatever actions are necessary to show "beyond any doubt that aggression cannot and will not pay."

September 10: Iran and Iraq agree to restore diplomatic relations, which were severed after the outbreak of their war in 1980.

October 8: In one of the most violent incidents of the Palestinian intifada, Israeli police use live ammunition to suppress a demonstration in Jerusalem, killing an estimated twenty Palestinians.

October 12: The UN Security Council adopts Resolution 672, condemning Israel's use of violence on October 8 against Palestinian demonstrators in Jerusalem and condemning the use of violence by the demonstrators. The resolution also calls for a UN fact-finding mission to investigate the violence, but Israel refuses to accept such a mission. The Israelis' reaction will lead the Security Council to adopt another resolution, on October 24, critical of Israel. These resolutions are noteworthy because they are supported by the United States, which customarily blocks criticism of Israel in the Security Council.

October 13: In Beirut, after Syria bombs the presidential palace, the base of Gen. Michel Aoun's "provisional" Lebanese government, Aoun admits defeat and takes refuge in the French embassy. Aoun will later go into exile in France and remain there until 2005.

November 29: The UN Security Council adopts Resolution 678, authorizing the use of military force to expel Iraq from Kuwait. It is the first such authorization since the Korean War in 1950.

1991

January 4: The United States votes at the UN Security Council to denounce Israel's use of violence against Palestinians in the fourth resolution condemning Israel since October 1990.

January 13: UN secretary-general Javier Pérez de Cúellar meets in Baghdad with Saddam Hussein but fails to persuade the Iraqi leader to withdraw his forces from Kuwait.

January 17: A U.S.-led multinational coalition launches a massive aerial assault to force Iraq to withdraw from Kuwait.

January 18: Attempting to draw Israel into the war, Iraq fires medium-range Scud missiles at Haifa and Tel Aviv, injuring fifteen people. Israel, under intense pressure from the United States to stay out of the war, does not retaliate.

February 24: The U.S.-led coalition launches a ground offensive to force Iraqi troops from Kuwait. In a classic pincer attack, one wing moves against Iraqi positions in Kuwait while another wing moves into Iraq.

February 27: President Bush announces that Iraqi forces have been pushed out of Kuwait and a cease-fire has taken effect.

March 1: Following Iraq's defeat, Shiites in southern Iraq and Kurds in northern Iraq launch uncoordinated uprisings against the government of Saddam Hussein. The uprisings will continue through March, but are brutally suppressed by the Iraqi army. Thousands of Kurds flee across the border into Iran and Turkey.

March 3: Iraq accepts the U.S.-led coalition's terms for ending the conflict.

April 3: The UN Security Council adopts Resolution 687, imposing tough conditions on Iraq, including prohibitions against the possession of biological, chemical, or nuclear weapons and long-range missiles and a requirement that Iraq submit to UN inspections of its weapons programs.

April 17: The U.S., British, and French militaries create what they call a "safe haven" for Kurds in northern Iraq.

May 15: The first UN weapons inspectors arrive in Iraq.

October 11: The UN Security Council adopts Resolution 715, demanding that Iraq comply "unconditionally" with UN weapons inspections.

October 30: A peace conference opens in Madrid between representatives of Israeli and Arab nations. The United States and the Soviet Union are co-sponsors.

December 2–4: The last three American hostages in Lebanon are freed. The longest-held is Terry Anderson, a reporter for the Associated Press kidnapped in March 1985.

December 10: Peace talks between Israeli and Arab delegations begin in Washington, D.C., as a follow-up to the Madrid conference. The talks, opened late because of delays, will adjourn on December 18 with little or no progress to report.

December 16: The UN General Assembly repeals its 1975 resolution equating Zionism with racism.

1992

February 16: Israeli helicopters fire missiles at a convoy in southern Lebanon, killing Hizballah leader Abbas al-Musawi along with his wife and son. Musawi's deputy, Hassan Nasrallah, assumes leadership of the organization.

March 31: The UN Security Council adopts Resolution 748, imposing sanctions against Libya unless it extradites officials indicted for the December 1988 bombing of Pan Am Flight 103 over Lockerbie, Scotland.

April 15: Mujahidin rebel factions occupy Kabul. President Najibullah takes refuge in a UN compound.

April 25: Afghan mujahidin agree on a power-sharing arrangement, and rebel commander Burhannuddin Rabbani takes office in June as interim president.

June 23: The Labor Party wins elections in Israel in its first outright victory since 1974.

July 13: Yitzhak Rabin takes office as Israeli prime minister and says he is committed to advancing peace talks with Arabs.

August 23–October 11: Lebanon holds its first elections since 1972.

August 26: The United States, Britain, and France establish a "no-fly" zone in southern Iraq to protect Shiites against aerial attacks by the Iraqi air force.

September 9: Syrian president Hafiz al-Assad publicly states that he is willing to negotiate a peace agreement with Israel. A round of talks between Israeli and Syrian diplomats later in September will make little headway.

October 22: Rafiq Hariri, a construction magnate, takes office as the new prime minister of Lebanon.

1993

January 13: U.S., British, and French warplanes bomb military targets in Baghdad in response to Iraq's stationing of antiaircraft missiles in the "no-fly" zone of southern Iraq.

January 20: Israeli and PLO representatives hold secret talks in Norway under Norwegian government sponsorship. The preceding day, the Israeli Knesset had revoked a law banning official and unofficial contact with members of the PLO.

June 26: The United States launches cruise missiles against Iraqi intelligence agency headquarters in Baghdad, charging that Iraq had supported an unsuccessful assassination attempt against former president George H. W. Bush during a visit to Kuwait in mid-April.

September 9: Israeli prime minister Yitzhak Rabin and PLO leader Yasir Arafat sign letters of mutual recognition.

September 13: At a White House ceremony, Israeli foreign minister Shimon Peres and PLO negotiator Mahmoud Abbas sign the Declaration of Principles on Interim Self-

Government Arrangements, worked out in the secret negotiations mediated by Norway. During the same ceremony, Israeli prime minister Yitzhak Rabin and PLO leader Yasir Arafat shake hands for the first time. Popularly known as the Oslo Accords, the declaration is intended to bring peace between Israel and the Palestinians and to provide for self-governance by the Palestinians of parts of the Gaza Strip and West Bank. The Israeli parliament will approve the accord on September 23, and the PLO Central Committee will follow suit on October 11. The Israelis and Palestinians will sign subsequent major agreements in May 1994, September 1995, January 1997, and October 1998.

September 14: Israeli and Jordanian officials conclude a "common agenda" intended to lead to a permanent peace agreement.

October 1: International donors meeting in Washington pledge $2 billion in aid for the new quasi-governmental Palestinian agency to be formed as a result of the Oslo Accords.

October 22: Hizballah launches a major attack on Israeli positions in southern Lebanon.

October 25: Israel launches a large air and ground attack in southern Lebanon that forces more than 200,000 people from their homes.

November 16: Israel offers to withdraw from southern Lebanon if Hizballah is disarmed and brought under the control of the Lebanese government.

November 26: Iraq agrees to accept UN Security Council Resolution 715 (of October 1991), requiring it to comply with UN weapons inspections.

1994

January: Renewed fighting among factions in Afghanistan results in the large-scale destruction of Kabul.

January 16: After meeting in Geneva with President Bill Clinton, Syrian president Hafez al-Assad says Syria would be willing to negotiate a peace treaty with Israel if Israel withdraws from the Golan Heights.

February 25: Baruch Goldstein, an American-born Israeli settler on the West Bank, kills twenty-nine Palestinians worshiping at the Ibrahimi Mosque in Hebron. Goldstein is then killed by Palestinians at the mosque, and ensuing clashes between Palestinians and Israeli security forces result in more deaths.

April 6: The Izzedine al-Qassam Brigades, the armed wing of Hamas, carries out its first car bombing, killing eight people in Afula, Israel.

April 21: Israeli prime minister Yitzhak Rabin says Israel would be willing to withdraw from the Golan Heights in exchange for a peace treaty with Syria.

May 4: PLO chairman Yasir Arafat and Israeli prime minister Rabin sign an agreement establishing a Palestinian civil authority to govern parts of the Gaza Strip and the West Bank city of Jericho, the first step to implementing the Oslo Accords of September 1993.

May 7: A simmering dispute between the two main Kurdish political factions in Iraq breaks into an open conflict that will drag on for more than two years, killing an estimated 3,000 people.

May 13: Israeli security forces withdraw from Jericho and are replaced by Palestinian forces.

May 18: Israel withdraws from much of the Gaza Strip, except for areas containing settlements and military installations.

July 1: Arafat arrives in the Gaza Strip after twenty-seven years in exile.

July 5: Arafat assumes office as the first president of the new Palestinian Authority.

July 11: Rolf Ekeus, head of UN weapons inspectors in Iraq, reports to the Security Council that all illegal weapons acknowledged by Iraq have been destroyed. Ekeus says Iraq could, however, still be hiding other weapons.

July 25: In Washington, Israeli prime minister Rabin and Jordan's King Hussein sign the Washington Declaration, calling for an end to the state of war between their countries.

October 14: Arafat, Rabin, and Israeli foreign minister Shimon Peres are named recipients of the 1994 Nobel Peace Prize for of their participation in the Oslo peace process.

October 26: At the Arava/Araba border crossing between Israel and Jordan, Israeli prime minister Rabin and Jordan's King Hussein sign a formal peace treaty.

November 5: The Taliban, an Islamist guerrilla group, captures Kandahar, the largest city in southern Afghanistan, in an ongoing struggle among anticommunist factions following the overthrow of the Soviet-backed government in 1992.

1995

January 22: Two car bombs explode in Bet Lid, a coastal town in northern Israel, killing 19 Israelis and wounding more than 60 others. Islamic Jihad claims responsibility for the attack. The Israeli government temporarily suspends negotiations with the Palestinians.

March 20: Turkish military forces invade the Kurdish areas of northern of Iraq in pursuit of the Kurdistan Worker's Party (PKK), which has been fighting for a separate Kurdish area in Turkey.

April 14: The UN Security Council adopts Resolution 986, creating an oil-for-food program through which Iraq can sell limited quantities of oil on world markets with the proceeds used to buy food and other humanitarian supplies for the Iraqi people, to pay reparations to Kuwait, and to reimburse UN agencies for their expenses. The oil sales are limited to $2 billion every 180 days.

April 17: Iraq rejects Resolution 986, creating an oil-for-food program.

August 8: Two sons-in-law of Iraqi leader Saddam Hussein, along with their wives and some family members, defect to Jordan, taking with them crates of documents alleged to show that Iraq is continuing to hide weapons from UN inspectors. The defectors will be killed after being convinced to return to Iraq in February 1996.

September 28: At the White House, Israeli prime minister Yitzhak Rabin and PLO chairman Yasir Arafat sign the Interim Agreement on the West Bank and the Gaza Strip, also known as Oslo II, expanding on the previous Oslo Accords by broadening Palestinian rule in the West Bank. President Bill Clinton, Egyptian president Hosni Mubarak, and Jordan's King Hussein act as witnesses.

October 10–11: Israel hands control of several West Bank towns to the Palestinian Authority as part of the Oslo II agreement. Israel also releases about 900 Palestinians who had been held in Israeli jails.

November 4: A Jewish extremist assassinates Rabin during a peace rally in Tel Aviv.

November 22: Shimon Peres takes over as Israeli prime minister.

December: Israel withdraws from the main West Bank towns of Tulkarm (on December 9), Nablus (December 12), Bethlehem (December 21), and Ramallah (December 27).

December 24: The Welfare Party wins a plurality in Turkey's parliamentary elections, marking the best showing yet for an Islamist party in Turkey.

1996

January 20: Palestinians go to the polls to elect a president for the first time and give Arafat an overwhelming victory with 88 percent of the vote. Arafat's Fatah Party wins all but 20 seats in parallel elections for the 88-member Palestinian Legislative Council.

February 25: A Hamas suicide bomber attacks a bus in downtown Jerusalem, killing 22 people in the first of a series of such attacks that kill several dozen people and appear to be aimed at influencing Israeli elections scheduled for May 29. The Israeli government declares war on Hamas and pressures the Palestinian Authority to arrest more than 100 Hamas activists.

April 11: Israel launches Operation Grapes of Wrath into Lebanon. The fighting will continue for more than two weeks, forcing several hundred thousand Lebanese from their homes.

April 18: Israeli artillery hit a UN refugee camp in Qana, killing 107 people and wounding more than 100 others. Israel says the attack was a mistake, but a later investigation by the UN will assert that the attack was deliberate.

April 21–24: Meeting for the first time in Gaza, the Palestine National Council votes to endorse the Oslo peace accords and to remove language from the Palestinian national charter that runs counter to the accords.

May: Al-Qaida leader Osama bin Laden and an entourage of supporters arrive in Jalalabad, Afghanistan, after Sudan expels them as a result of U.S. pressure.

May 22: Iraq accepts the UN oil-for-food program established under Security Council Resolution 986 in April 1995.

May 29: The Likud Party, under Binyamin Netanyahu, wins a narrow victory in Israeli elections. Netanyahu collects 50.4 percent of the vote against acting prime minister Shimon Peres in Israel's first-ever direct election of a prime minister. The Labor Party wins a tiny plurality of 33 seats in parliamentary elections, but Netanyahu assembles a coalition of religious and right-wing parties for a majority.

June 6: Welfare Party leader Necmettin Erbakan becomes prime minister of Turkey after the collapse of a minority coalition government. He is the first Islamist to hold that post since the creation of the Turkish republic in 1923.

June 25: A truck bomb explodes outside the Khobar Towers military housing complex near Dhahran, Saudi Arabia, killing 19 U.S. airmen and wounding about 400 others. U.S. officials will later blame the attack on Shiite Muslims from Saudi Arabia who had been trained in Lebanon and financed by Iran.

June 26: An attempted coup against Iraqi leader Saddam Hussein fails. Dozens of alleged coup plotters will be executed in subsequent days. The coup was sponsored by the Iraqi National Accord, an exile group, allegedly with help from the CIA.

August 31: Iraq intervenes militarily in the ongoing conflict between the two main Kurdish factions in northern Iraq. The government supports the Kurdistan Democratic Party of Massoud Barzani against the Patriotic Union of Kurdistan, headed by Jalal Talabani, which had received support from Iran. The Iraqi army briefly takes over Irbil and attacks Talbani's forces.

September 24: Israel reopens an ancient tunnel in the Old City of Jerusalem near the al-Aqsa Mosque, setting off violent protests by Palestinians. More than sixty

Palestinians and fifteen Israelis will die in subsequent rioting, the worst of which takes place in Ramallah.

September 26: The Taliban occupy Kabul, thus securing effective control of most of Afghanistan.

October 23: French president Jacques Chirac becomes the first foreign head of state to address the Palestinian legislature. He says that France supports a Palestinian state.
    The two rival Iraqi Kurdish parties agree to end their fighting, which has killed an estimated 3,000 people and forced tens of thousands of Kurds to flee their homes.

December 10: Iraq pumps the first oil for legal export under the UN's oil-for-food program after announcing an agreement with the Security Council on November 25.

1997

January 17: Israeli and Palestinian officials sign a long-delayed agreement providing for the Israeli military to withdraw from most of the West Bank town of Hebron, a flashpoint for violence between Israeli settlers and Palestinian residents. Israeli forces begin leaving Hebron immediately.

February 28: Turkey's top generals issue a statement demanding that Prime Minister Necmettin Erbakan sign a statement that includes a commitment to secularism.

May 23: Mohammad Khatami, a mid-level cleric generally considered a reformer, scores a landslide victory in Iranian presidential elections, with about 69 percent of the vote.

June 18: Turkey's Islamist prime minister Erbakan resigns under pressure from the military. He is succeeded by Mesut Yilmaz, president of the secular Motherland Party.

June 26: Turkey withdraws most of the soldiers sent into northern Iraq in April as part of Operation Hammer to destroy the Kurdistan Workers Party (PKK), which had taken refuge there.

July 31: Palestinian legislature demands that members of the Palestinian Authority cabinet resign because of corruption allegations. Arafat appoints a commission to investigate the charges, but its findings are suppressed.

September: The Turkish army returns to Iraq for an operation that will continue into May 1998.

September 5: Israeli prime minister Binyamin Netanyahu says Israel is suspending its obligations under the various Oslo agreements to protest two suicide bombings in a Jerusalem market on July 30 that killed thirteen people.

September 25: In Amman, Israeli agents carrying Canadian passports inject a lethal poison into the left ear of Khaled Meshel, the political leader of Hamas. Israel provides an antidote for the poison after King Hussein demands it. Meshel recovers.

October 1: At King Hussein's insistence, Israel releases from prison Hamas spiritual leader Shaykh Ahmad Yasin, who is flown to Jordan. He eventually will return to the Gaza Strip.

October 29: Iraq's government demands the departure from Iraq of all Americans working for the UN weapons agency. The inspectors will leave in November but return later in the month after the Russian government pressures Baghdad on the issue.

November 17: Gunmen from the Islamic Group attack a group of tourists near an ancient temple in Egypt's Luxor Valley and kill about seventy people, most of them foreign tourists. It is the second major attack on foreign tourists in two months.

The Islamic Group says the attack is in retaliation for the U.S. imprisonment of the group's founder, Shaykh Umar Abd al-Rahman, who was convicted on charges related to the 1993 bombing of the World Trade Center in New York.

December 14: Iranian president Khatami says in his first news conference that he hopes for a "thoughtful dialogue with the American people."

1998

January 7: In an interview with CNN, Iranian president Mohammad Khatami proposes a "dialogue between civilizations and cultures" involving Iran and the United States, citing for example exchanges of scholars, journalists, and others.

January 16: Ayatollah Ali Khamenei, Iran's supreme leader, says Iran will not engage in any dialogue with the U.S. government, but praises Khatami's offer of a dialogue with the American people. Turkey's Constitutional Court bans the Welfare Party of former prime minister Erbakan. Many party members will later form the Virtue Party.

February 20: The previous limit of $2 billion worth of oil that Iraq can sell every six months is increased by the UN Security Council to $5.2 billion.

February 23: UN secretary-general Kofi Annan brokers a compromise to allow UN weapons inspectors to visit so-called presidential sites in Iraq, including some palaces of President Saddam Hussein. The government previously had barred the inspectors from them.

June 17: U.S. secretary of state Madeleine Albright calls for the United States and Iran to develop a "road map leading to normal relations." Weeks later, on July 1, Iranian president Khatami will praise the "tone" of Albright's remarks but add that Iran wants to see more positive action by the United States.

August 7: The U.S. embassies in Nairobi, Kenya, and Dar es Salaam, Tanzania, are destroyed by powerful car bombs, resulting in the deaths of more than 200 people, most of them Africans. The United States blames al-Qaida.

August 20: The United States fires missiles at an alleged al-Qaida training camp in Khost, Afghanistan, and at a plant in Khartoum, Sudan, alleged to produce chemical weapons. Subsequent evidence suggests that the plant in Khartoum made pharmaceuticals, not chemical weapons.

September 17: The United States says it has brokered a peace agreement between the two main Kurdish political factions in Iraq, the Kurdistan Democratic Party and the Patriotic Union of Kurdistan. Under the deal, the two parties will share power in the northern provinces of Iraq that they call Kurdistan. A cease-fire in October 1996 had failed to end the conflict.

October 23: At the White House, PLO chairman Yasir Arafat and Israeli prime minister Binyamin Netanyahu sign the Wye River Memorandum, pledging to carry out several delayed steps in the peace process. Provisions include Israel's phased withdrawal from 13 percent of the West Bank and a pledge by the Palestinians to arrest suspects wanted by Israel and to remove anti-Israeli statements from the PLO charter.

October 31: President Bill Clinton signs the Iraq Liberation Act (PL 105-338), calling for the removal of Iraqi leader Saddam Hussein from power and pledging support for Iraqi opposition groups. Iraq announces that it is ending all cooperation with UN weapons inspectors.

November 20: In limited compliance with the Wye River agreement, Israel withdraws from about 220 square miles in the vicinity of the West Bank town of Jenin and releases 250 Palestinians from Israeli jails.

December 14: The Palestine National Council votes to eliminate clauses in the PLO charter demanding the destruction of Israel. President Clinton attends the council meeting in Gaza and praises the Palestinian leaders for the action.

December 15: After failing to reach agreement with Iraq on procedures for continued weapons inspections, the United Nations withdraws all of its inspectors from the country.

December 16: The U.S. and British militaries begin four days of air strikes in Operation Desert Fox, targeting suspected weapons facilities, intelligence agencies, and other military targets in Iraq. This is the most extensive attack against Iraq since the Persian Gulf War of January–February 1991.

December 20: Prime Minister Netanyahu suspends Israeli compliance with the October 23 Wye River agreement, citing what he calls the failure of Palestinians to carry out their promises, including collecting unlicensed weapons and restraining incitement against Israel.

December 21: Netanyahu's government loses a "no-confidence" vote in the Knesset. New elections will take placed in May 1999.

1999

January 11: Former prime minister Shimon Peres becomes the first Israeli to address the Palestinian Legislative Council. He expresses support for a Palestinian state.

January 25: Richard Butler, head of the UN weapons inspection commission in Iraq, sends a final report to the Security Council stating that many of Iraq's illegal weapons have been destroyed but that the Iraqi government's repeated lack of cooperation means that the United Nations cannot be sure how many and what types of weapons the country might still have.

February 7: Jordan's King Hussein dies after a long battle with cancer. He was the longest-serving ruler in the Middle East, having taken power in August 1952. He is succeeded by a son, Abdallah II.

February 16: Turkish agents in Nairobi, Kenya, capture Abdallah Ocalan, the leader of the Kurdistan Workers Party who had been charged with numerous counts of terrorism by the Turkish government.

April 5: The UN Security Council suspends international sanctions against Libya after the government hands over to Scottish authorities two suspects in the December 1988 bombing of Pan Am Flight 103 over Lockerbie, Scotland.

April 12: President Bill Clinton says the United States should abandon its "total denial" of Iranian grievances about past U.S. behavior toward Iran, just as Iran should accept that the United States has grievances about its behavior. This statement is seen as part of the Clinton administration's ultimately fruitless attempt to reach out to Iran's government.

April 29: The Palestine Liberation Organization decides to delay plans (which had been announced the previous fall) to formally declare establishment of Palestinian state.

May 17: Ehud Barak, the new leader of Israel's Labor Party, wins election as prime minister, defeating incumbent Netanyahu. One of his key campaign promises was to withdraw Israeli military forces from southern Lebanon.

June 29: Abdallah Ocalan, leader of the Kurdistan Workers Party, is convicted of treason and sentenced to death. After legal appeals and international intervention, his sentence will be reduced in 2002 to life in prison.

July 8: Iranian police attack student protesters at Tehran University, sparking a series of riots that spread to other cities and continue into September. The police attack and subsequent suppression of student demonstrations indicate that President Khatami does not have effective control of the security services.

July 23: Morocco's King Hassan II dies and is succeeded by his son, Muhammad VII.

September 4: Israeli prime minister Barak and PLO chairman Yasir Arafat sign an agreement in Sharm el-Sheikh, Egypt, calling for further Israeli withdrawals from the West Bank, the release of 350 prisoners held by Israel, and the construction of a "safe passage" route between Gaza and the West Bank. The agreement also calls for conclusion of a final peace agreement between Israel and the Palestinians by September 2000. The so-called final status talks will begin on September 13.

December 15: Israel and Syria resume formal peace negotiations that had been suspended in 1996. The talks will end on January 11, 2000, without an agreement.

December 17: The UN Security Council adopts Resolution 1284, establishing a new agency, the UN Monitoring, Verification, and Inspection Commission (UNMOVIC), to investigate Iraq's illegal weapons. The resolution offers a suspension of sanctions after Iraq has cooperated with the inspections for four months. Iraq already had announced that it would not allow weapons inspections to resume until after economic sanctions are eliminated or substantially reduced.

2000

February 18: Reform parties backing Iranian president Mohammad Khatami win a strong majority of seats in parliamentary elections.

March 5: the Israeli cabinet approves a plan by Prime Minister Ehud Barak to withdraw Israeli military forces from southern Lebanon by July.

March 17: Secretary of State Madeleine Albright acknowledges that the United States played a "significant role" in the August 1953 coup that ousted Iranian prime minister Mohammad Mosaddeq. Albright also announces the lifting of a U.S. ban on importation of some consumer goods from Iran, including carpets, nuts, dried fruit, and caviar. Eight days later, Iran's supreme leader, Ayatollah Khamenei will reject the U.S. initiative toward improved relations.

March 26: During a meeting in Geneva, Syrian president Hafiz al-Assad tells President Bill Clinton that he will not accept a peace agreement with Israel in exchange for Israel's surrendering of the Golan Heights after Israel refuses to cede a strip of land bordering the Sea of Galilee.

May 23: Israel completes its withdrawal from southern Lebanon six weeks earlier than planned. The Shiite militia Hizballah had launched an attack on the Israeli-backed South Lebanon Army, which collapsed.

May 24: Hizballah gains full control of southern Lebanon.

June 10: Syrian president Assad dies of a heart attack. He had been the country's leader since November 1970. He will be succeeded on July 11 by his son, Bashar, a Western-educated eye doctor.

June 18 : The UN Security Council endorses a report by the secretary-general verifying Israel's withdrawal from Lebanon. Hizballah and Syria insist that Israel continues an illegal occupation of the Shabaa Farms area.

July 25: A twelve-day summit at Camp David between the Israelis and Palestinians
ends in failure. President Clinton, who mediated, places most of the blame on PLO
chairman Yasir Arafat for refusing to accept an offer by Israeli prime minister Barak
for Israel to withdraw from most of the West Bank. Arafat's aides play down the
significance of Barak's offer.

September 28: Ariel Sharon, leader of Israel's Likud Party, leads a large delegation of
lawmakers, and a huge security contingent, on a tour of the Haram al-Sharif in the
Old City of Jerusalem.

September 29: Palestinian protests against Sharon's visit to the Haram al-Sharif flare
into violence in Gaza and the West Bank, including East Jerusalem. The violence
grows in succeeding days, and many Palestinians proclaim a second intifada, or
uprising, against Israeli occupation.

October 12: A suicide attack on the USS *Cole,* docked in the port of Aden, Yemen, kills
seventeen U.S. sailors. The Clinton administration blames the attack on al-Qaida.

October 17: After a meeting in Sharm el-Sheikh, Egypt, Arafat and Barak agree on a
cease-fire and limited steps to end ongoing Israeli-Palestinian violence. Neither side
follows through on its promises, however, and the violence continues. One outcome
of the meeting is an agreement by President Clinton to appoint an international
panel, headed by former U.S. senator George J. Mitchell, to examine the causes of
the violence.

December 10: Israeli prime minister Barak, politically weakened by the failure of the
Camp David talks and the second intifada, calls for early elections to be held in
February.

December 19: The UN Security Council adopts Resolution 1333, imposing sanctions
against the Taliban government of Afghanistan because of its refusal to hand over
al-Qaida leader Osama bin Laden to the United States. The sanctions include a ban
on military aid.

December 23: In Washington, U.S. diplomats present proposals known as the Clinton
parameters to the Israelis and Palestinians in a last attempt at a peace agreement.
The Israeli cabinet will accept the proposals, but with "reservations," on December 27. Palestinian leader Arafat will decline to accept the proposals after a personal
meeting with Clinton at the White House on January 2, 2001.

2001

January 7: President Bill Clinton publicly outlines his plan for a final peace settlement
between the Israelis and Palestinians. Clinton says the plan entails "real pain and
sacrifices" by both sides but is the best way to establish a Palestinian state that can
live in peace with Israel.

January 21: In a last-ditch effort to secure a peace agreement before scheduled Israeli
elections, Israeli and Palestinian negotiators meet in Taba, Egypt. They make
progress based on Clinton's proposals but fail to reach agreement before negotiations are suspended on January 28 because of the elections.

January 31: A special Scottish court convicts Libyan agent Abd al-Baset Ali al-Megrahi
on charges related to the bombing of Pam Am Flight 103 in December 1988. He

receives a sentence of life in prison. The court acquits a second defendant on all charges.

February 6: Ariel Sharon, of the Likud Party, wins early elections to become Israel's next prime minister, soundly defeating the incumbent, Ehud Barak. Sharon promises tough action against the ongoing Palestinian violence.

May 21: The U.S.-appointed panel headed by former senator George J. Mitchell reports that Israel and the Palestinians are both to blame for the current round of violence, which began in September. The panel calls for "confidence-building" steps by both sides, including a freeze in Jewish settlement in the occupied territories and efforts to end Palestinian violence against Israelis. Prime Minister Sharon will reject the call for a freeze on settlements.

June 8: Iranian president Mohammad Khatami is reelected with 77 percent of the vote, but support among his core constituencies (reformers and the youth) appears to have cooled since his first election in 1997.

June 13: Israelis and Palestinians agree to a cease-fire, mediated by CIA director George Tenet, but both sides will soon violate it.

August 9: A Palestinian suicide bomber kills fourteen Israelis at a Jerusalem restaurant. In response, the Israeli army occupies Orient House in East Jerusalem, an historic building used by the Palestinian leadership.

August 13: The Israeli army reoccupies much of the West Bank Palestinian town of Jenin, destroying a police station, in part of a broader Israeli offensive that will eventually involve the takeover of all or parts of several Palestinian towns, including Bethlehem, Hebron and Ramallah, along with parts of the Gaza Strip.

September 9: Suicide bombers, posing as journalists, kill Afghan resistance leader Ahmed Shah Massoud.

September 11: Nineteen members of al-Qaida commandeer four civilian airliners in the United States and fly two of them into the World Trade Center towers in New York City and a third into the Pentagon, outside Washington. The fourth plane crashes in rural Pennsylvania. Nearly 3,000 people die in attacks, most of them as the result of the collapse of the World Trade Center towers.

September 19: Pakistani president Pervez Musharraf, in a speech to the nation, suggests that he will agree to support an impending U.S. military campaign against the Taliban in Afghanistan. Pakistan had been the Taliban's strongest supporter.

September 20: President George W. Bush tells Congress that the United States will conduct a "war on terror" that will target all terrorist groups with a "global reach." He cites al-Qaida in particular.

October 7: U.S. and British armed forces launch an invasion of Afghanistan to oust the Taliban government because of its support for al-Qaida. The invasion has crucial backing from neighboring Pakistan and from the Northern Alliance, an Afghan militia.

November 13: The Northern Alliance captures Kabul. Although driven from power and dispersed into the mountain ranges between Afghanistan and Pakistan, the Taliban are not destroyed as a fighting force. U.S. forces fail to capture either Taliban leader Mullah Mohammad Omar or al-Qaida leader Osama bin Laden.

November 21: President Bush warns that Iraq might give biological, chemical, or nuclear weapons to terrorist groups. He does not provide evidence for this claim.

November 27: Anthony Zinni, appointed by President Bush as the U.S. envoy to the Middle East, arrives in the region. He will soon depart after another upsurge of violence, including a December 2 suicide bombing in Haifa that kills fifteen bus passengers.

December 5: After a meeting in Bonn, Germany, leaders of Afghanistan's various political and ethnic factions agree on a plan for a transitional government leading to a permanent government. They select Hamid Karzai, a leader of the Pashtun ethnic group, as the first interim leader.

December 17: Responding to pressure from European countries and the United States, Palestinian leader Yasir Arafat calls for an end to armed attacks, including suicide bombings, against Israelis.

December 21: Hamas announces that it will suspend its attacks in response to Arafat's request to do so.

2002

January 18: As part of its continuing crackdown against the Palestinians, the Israeli military establishes a blockade around the Palestinian Authority's Ramallah compound, confining Yasir Arafat to it. He will remain there almost continuously until he becomes ill in late 2004 and is allowed to travel to France for medical treatment.

January 29: In his State of the Union Address, President George W. Bush says that Iran, Iraq, and North Korea, along with "their terrorist allies," constitute an "axis of evil" that is "arming to threaten the peace of the world."

March 27: A Palestinian suicide bomber kills twenty-nine people and wounds more than 100 during a Passover observance at a hotel in Netanya, in northern Israel.

March 28: Meeting in Beirut, Arab leaders endorse a peace plan, authored by Crown Prince Abdallah of Saudi Arabia, calling for the exchange of land for peace between Israel and the Arab states.

March 29: Israel launches Operation Defensive Shield, a major military occupation of Palestinian cities and refugee camps.

April 9: Israeli troops engage in a fierce battle with Palestinian militants in Jenin. Thirteen Israeli soldiers are killed when they enter a building booby-trapped with bombs. The Israelis then bulldoze parts of the town. Palestinian officials allege an Israeli "massacre," but this claim will be refuted by subsequent investigations that reveal slightly more than 50 Palestinian deaths.

June 24: President Bush endorses the eventual creation of a Palestinian state, but he demands that the Palestinians replace Arafat as their leader.

June 30: A *loya jirga,* a council of Afghan notables, selects Hamid Karzai to continue as head of state.

August 26: Vice President Dick Cheney says "there is no doubt" that Iraq has rebuilt its illegal weapons program, is working to build nuclear weapons, and has ties to terrorist groups.

September 8: Long-feuding Iraqi Kurdish leaders Massoud Barzani and Jalal Talabani meet for the first time in two years and agree to reestablish the Kurdish National Assembly, which had been disbanded in 1994.

September 12: In a speech to the UN General Assembly, President Bush demands that the UN enforce its many resolutions requiring Iraq to eliminate its weapons of mass destruction and says that if the United Nations fails to act against the "gathering danger" of Iraq, the United States will.

September 19: After a Palestinian suicide bomber kills five people in Tel Aviv, Israel launches a new military operation in Ramallah that destroys nearly all of the Palestinian Authority compound. Palestinian leader Arafat and others remain holed up in the only building not totally destroyed.

September 29: Under strong international pressure, the Israeli army withdraws from the area of the Palestinian Authority compound, but Israel continues to bar Arafat from leaving Ramallah.

October 7: In a nationally televised speech to build public support for a war against Iraq, President Bush warns that Iraq poses a direct threat to the United States because of its weapons programs and collaboration with terrorist groups.

October 11: The U.S. Congress adopts a resolution authorizing the president to use force against Iraq.

November 3: Voters in Turkey hand an overwhelming victory to the Justice and Development Party (AKP), making it the first avowedly Islamist party to control the parliament.

November 8: In a unanimous vote, the UN Security Council adopts Resolution 1441, demanding that Iraq cooperate with UN weapons inspections. The resolution warns Iraq of unspecified "serious consequences" should it refuse to do so.

November 26: UN weapons inspectors return to Iraq for the first time since they were withdrawn in December 1998.

December 8: Iraq gives UN inspectors thousands of pages of documents allegedly showing that it does not have illegal weapons of mass destruction.

December 14: Iraqi opposition groups begin a four-day meeting in London to plan for a new government in Baghdad based on the expectation that the United States will force Saddam Hussein from power.

*December 20:*The United States accuses Iraq of a "material breach" of UN Resolution 1441 by failing to provide a complete and accurate inventory of its weapons.

2003

January 5: Simultaneous suicide bombs in Tel Aviv kill twenty-three Israelis and foreign workers and wound more than 100 people. Israel bars Palestinian officials from attending a conference in London on Palestinian government reform and possible peace overtures.

January 27: UN weapons inspection chief Hans Blix faults Iraq for failing to cooperate, telling the Security Council that "Iraq appears not to have come to a genuine acceptance, not even today, of the disarmament that was demanded of it." Blix will issue subsequent reports on February 14 and March 7, his last before the U.S.-led invasion of Iraq.

February 24: Britain, Spain, and the United States submit a draft resolution to the Security Council asserting that Iraq "has failed" to meet the demands of Resolution 1441. France and Russia block action, and the resolution never comes to a formal vote.

March 17: President Bush sets a forty-eight-hour deadline for Iraqi leader Saddam Hussein and his two sons to leave the country or face an invasion. Addressing the people of Iraq, Bush says: "The tyrant will soon be gone. The day of your liberation is near."

March 19 (U.S. time; March 20 local time): The United States, Britain, and their allies begin air strikes against Iraq; this will be followed shortly by a ground invasion launched primarily from Kuwait.

March 20: Under strong U.S. pressure, Palestinian leader Arafat appoints Mahmoud Abbas, a long-time aide, as the first prime minister of the Palestinian Authority. Abbas accepts the post only after receiving assurances from Arafat that he will have independent power.

April 9: U.S. marines help Iraqis pull down a giant statue of Saddam Hussein in central Baghdad, an event widely viewed as symbolizing the fall of the Hussein's Baathist government.

April 30: The United States releases A Performance-Based Roadmap to a Permanent Two-State Solution to the Israeli-Palestinian Conflict, detailing steps to be taken by the Israelis and Palestinians to resolve their conflict. The plan had been drafted by diplomats in mid-2002 but was withheld from formal public release until after the Iraq invasion and the creation of a new Palestinian government.

May 1: President Bush declares an end to major combat operations in Iraq.

May 12: Four simultaneous suicide bombings in Riyadh, Saudi Arabia, target residential compounds for foreigners, killing twenty-five people (in addition to the attackers), including seven Americans. The Saudi government blames al-Qaida for the attacks.

May 16: More than forty people are killed in five bombings in Casablanca, Morocco. The government blames al-Qaida for the attacks.

May 22: The UN Security Council adopts Resolution 1483, recognizing the United States and Britain as occupying powers in Iraq. The resolution also ends international sanctions against Iraq, phases out the oil-for-food program, and allows occupation forces to spend an estimated $20 billion in Iraqi oil revenues under the United Nations' control.

June 3: Israeli prime minister Ariel Sharon, Palestinian prime minister Mahmoud Abbas, and U.S. president George W. Bush meet in Aqaba, Jordan, and pledge to work to implement the "road map" to peace, which was released on April 30.

July 2: Responding to an upsurge of violent attacks against the U.S. occupation in Iraq, President Bush says, "My answer is: bring 'em on. We've got the force necessary to deal with the security situation."

July 13: The U.S. occupation authority in Iraq names a twenty-five-member Iraqi Governing Council to serve as its local liaison.

July 22: Saddam Hussein's two sons, Qusay and Uday, are killed in a firefight with U.S. forces in Mosul, Iraq.

August 13: Libya accepts an agreement, brokered by Britain and the United States, under which it accepts responsibility for the December 1988 bombing of Pan Am Flight 103 over Lockerbie, Scotland. Libya will pay $2.7 billion into a fund to compensate the victims' families.

August 19: A truck bomb destroys the UN headquarters in Baghdad, killing twenty-three people, including Sergio Vieira de Mello, the head of the UN delegation in Iraq. The bombing will come to be viewed as the beginning of an escalation of opposition to the U.S. occupation by Iraqi Sunnis.

August 29: A bomb destroys the historic Imam Ali mosque in Najaf, Iraq, killing dozens of people, notably Muhammad Baqir al-Hakim, a leading Shiite cleric and political leader who had advocated cooperation with the U.S. occupation.

September 10: After less than six months in office, Palestinian prime minister Abbas resigns, stating that Arafat had not given him enough independence. Arafat names Ahmad Qurei, speaker of the Palestinian legislature, to succeed Abbas.

October 16: The UN Security Council adopts Resolution 1511, endorsing the interim Iraqi Governing Council and calling on other countries to contribute troops to help stabilize Iraq.

November 15: U.S. authorities in Iraq issue a plan for handing political power to an appointed Iraqi government by June 30, 2004, with national elections to be held by the end of 2005. The plan comes under sharp attack from Shiite leaders, notably Ayatollah Ali al-Sistani, who demands elections no later than the end of 2004.

December 14: U.S. Army troops capture former Iraqi leader Saddam Hussein hiding in a hole in his home region of Tikrit, north of Baghdad.

December 18: Israeli prime minister Sharon announces tentative plans for "unilateral disengagement" from the Palestinians, starting with the probable withdrawal of at least some Jewish settlements from the Gaza Strip.

December 19: British, Libyan, and U.S. officials announce that Libya has agreed to abandon all programs to develop biological, chemical, and nuclear weapons. The United States subsequently will remove substantial material from Libya's weapons programs and in the process uncover evidence of the illicit trade in nuclear weapons material by "A.Q." Kahn, a scientist often called the father of Pakistan's nuclear bomb.

2004

February 1: Simultaneous suicide bombings in Irbil target the headquarters of the two main Iraqi Kurdish political parties, killing more than 100 people and wounding more than 200 others.

February 24: Conservative candidates win a majority of seats in Iran's parliamentary elections. Most reformists had withdrawn their candidacies in protest after the Council of Guardians disqualified several thousand candidates, including some incumbent legislators. The election is widely seen as ending, for the time being, any prospect of serious political reform in Iran.

March 2: Suicide bombs and other attacks at Shiite shrines in Baghdad and Karbala kill more than 180 people, the highest single-day toll since the U.S.-led invasion.

March 8: The Iraqi Governing Council formally approves an interim constitution called the Transitional Administrative Law. Shiite members had resisted the law, arguing that it failed to provide enough representation for Shiites.

March 21: An Israeli air strike kills Shaykh Ahmad Yasin, the founder and spiritual leader of the Palestinian movement Hamas.

March 31: Mobs in Fallujah, Iraq, mutilate the bodies of four civilian U.S. contractors and hang them from a bridge. This action will prompt a major U.S. operation against Fallujah that will be called off by the White House just as gets under way on April 9.

April 4: U.S. forces in Iraq and the Mahdi Army militia of Shiite cleric Muqtada al-Sadr engage in combat, which lasts for two months; the militia withdraws from Kufa and Najaf.

April 17: Israel kills Hamas leader Abd al-Aziz Rantisi, who had succeeded Shaykh Ahmad Yasin.

April 23: The United States lifts most remaining economic sanctions against Libya.

April 28: CBS News airs photographs of U.S. Army Reserve soldiers humiliating Iraqi detainees at Abu Graib prison outside Baghdad. The photographs prompt a series of investigations and news reports that result in worldwide outrage about the treatment of Iraqi detainees by some U.S. prison guards, severely damaging the United States' image.

June 6: The Israeli cabinet approves the disengagement plan by Prime Minister Ariel Sharon to withdraw Jewish settlements and Israeli military posts from the Gaza Strip.

June 28: The U.S.-led Coalition Provisional Authority disbands and hands national sovereignty in Iraq to an interim administration headed by President Ghazi al-Yawar and prime minister Iyad Allawi.

June 30: Israel's High Court rules that portions of the separation barrier under construction in and around the West Bank violate the rights of Palestinians and therefore orders changes in the route.

July 6: Iraqi prime minister Allawi signs a law giving himself broad powers to impose martial law and to take other steps in the name of restoring security.

July 9: The World Court rules that the separation barrier being built by Israel violates international law and must be dismantled. Israel rejects this ruling and continues construction of the barrier.

July 28: In one of the most violent days to date in Iraq since the U.S.-led invasion, a suicide bomber explodes a car bomb in Baquba, killing 70 people and wounding more than 50, and more than 40 people are killed in clashes south of Iraq.

September 2: The UN Security Council adopts Resolution 1559, demanding the withdrawal from Lebanon of all foreign forces, a measure aimed at Syria, the only country with a substantial military presence in Lebanon. The United States and other sponsors express hope that adoption of the resolution will block a Syrian attempt to force an extension of the term of Lebanese president, Emile Lahoud.

September 3: Acquiescing to Syrian pressure, the Lebanese parliament agrees to extend the term of President Lahoud for three additional years.

October 6: Charles A. Duelfer, head of the U.S. agency searching for weapons of mass destruction in Iraq, reports publicly that all such weapons appear to have been destroyed shortly after the 1991 Persian Gulf War. Duelfer says that Iraq had "strategic intent" to rebuild its weapons but had not done so, contrary to U.S. claims.

October 9: Afghanistan holds its first genuine presidential election, of which leader Hamid Karzai is declared the winner on November 3. The election had been delayed for several months because of security concerns; parliamentary elections were delayed until 2005 because of similar concerns and for technical reasons.

October 25: The Knesset approves the Sharon disengagement plan.

November 9: The U.S. military launches a major assault on Fallujah, in central Iraq, which had been taken over by insurgent forces resisting the U.S. occupation.

November 13: U.S. commanders announce that they have gained effective control of Fallujah, much of which had been destroyed in the fighting, the heaviest since the U.S. invasion in 2003.

November 11: Palestinian leader Yasir Arafat dies in a French hospital, where he had been taken the previous month after falling ill from unexplained causes.

2005

January 9: Mahmoud Abbas wins the election to succeed Yasir Arafat as president of the Palestinian Authority.

January 30: Iraq holds its first parliamentary elections since the ouster of Saddam Hussein nearly two years earlier. The United Iraqi Alliance, a coalition of Shiite parties, wins about 48 percent of the vote and will dominate the transitional parliament, the chief responsibility of which is to draft a constitution. An alliance of Kurdish parties finishes second with 26 percent of the vote. Most Sunni politicians boycott the election.

February 8: Israeli prime minister Sharon and Palestinian president Abbas declare a mutual cease-fire, which Abbas has persuaded Hamas and other groups to observe.

February 9: Saudi Arabia holds its first elections—for city council seats in Riyadh— the first round of municipal elections promised by Saudi leaders in 2004.

February 14: Former Lebanese prime minister Rafiq Hariri is assassinated by a car bomb in Beirut that kills another 16 people and sparks a series of massive demonstrations against Syria, which is widely assumed to be behind the killing.

April 26: Syria announces that it has completed its withdrawal of military forces and intelligence operatives from Lebanon. Syria had begun the withdrawal in March, after a presence of almost thirty-years, as a result of the intense international pressure generated in large part by the February 14 assassination of former prime minister Hariri.

April 28: The transitional Iraqi parliament approves a still-incomplete list of government officials, headed by President Jalal Talabani (a Kurd) and prime minister Ibrahim al-Jaafari (a Shiite and head of the al-Dawa Party).

May 3: An Iraqi cabinet led by Prime Minister Jaafari is sworn in.

May 4: The UN Security Council praises Syria's "significant and noticeable progress" toward compliance with its Resolution 1559, demanding the withdrawal of foreign forces from Lebanon.

May 29: Lebanon begins parliamentary elections, the first held since 1972 without the threat of civil war or the military presence of outside powers, notably, Syria and Israel. A coalition of anti-Syrian parties wins a majority of seats, but the Shiite militia Hizballah (aligned with Syria) wins a sizable minority.

June 23: Mahmoud Ahmadinejad, the mayor of Tehran, is the surprise winner of presidential elections in Iran, defeating former president Ali Akbar Hashemi Rafsanjani.

July 20: Speaking in Cairo, Secretary of State Condoleezza Rice calls for political reforms in Egypt and other Arab countries and says democracy is a chief goal of U.S. policy in the Middle East: "For sixty years, my country, the United States, pursued stability at the expense of democracy in this region here in the Middle East, and we achieved neither," she says.

August 15: Israel begins closing Jewish settlements in the Gaza Strip, part of a plan for total Israeli withdrawal from that territory. The last civilian settlers will leave Gaza on August 23, and the Israeli military will closes all its posts there by September 12. Palestinians engage in widespread looting of property the Israelis left behind, hampering international plans to revive the Gazan economy.

August 31: In Baghdad, hundreds of people die in a stampede at a bridge over the Tigris River when rumors spread of a suicide bomber in the crowd. Some reports put the death toll at close to 1,000.

September 7: Egypt holds its first multi-candidate presidential elections, although restrictions on opposition candidates minimize the degree of competition. Incumbent president Hosni Mubarak receives 88.6 percent of the vote, but turnout is less than 25 percent.

September 18: Afghanistan holds its first parliamentary elections under the new political system in place since early 2004. Allies of President Hamid Karzai do well, but so do warlords and former Islamist guerrillas who have turned to politics.

October 15: In a national referendum, nearly 79 percent of Iraqi voters approve a new constitution drafted by the transitional parliament. Most Sunni politicians opposed the constitution until the last minute, when Shiite and Kurdish leaders agreed to future negotiations on amending the constitution to assuage Sunni concerns that the document discriminated against their interests.

October 19: Former Iraqi leader Saddam Hussein and seven codefendants go on trial, charged with responsibility for the 1982 killings of 148 Shiite boys and men in Dujail, north of Baghdad.

October 20: A preliminary report by a UN-sponsored investigation appears to blame Syria for the assassination of former Lebanese prime minister Hariri on February 14.

October 26: Iranian president Ahmadinejad says that Israel should be "wiped off the map." The remark sparks international outrage.

November 10: Bombs explode at three hotels in Amman, Jordan, killing 57 people. Jordanian authorities blame al-Qaida in Mesopotamia (or Iraq), an Iraqi insurgent group headed by Abu Musab al-Zarqawi, a Jordanian.

November 17: Rep. John Murtha, D-Penn., calls for the start of U.S. troop withdrawal from Iraq. A respected voice on military matters, Murtha sets off a debate in the United States about Bush administration policies in Iraq. President Bush will respond on November 30 with a speech defending his policies and warning against a U.S. withdrawal from Iraq.

December 7: Egypt concludes parliamentary elections. Candidates representing the banned Muslim Brotherhood win 88 seats, which is 19 percent of the total but represents a psychological boost for the banned group.

December 15: Iraq's voters select a new parliament, called the Council of Representatives. Sunni politicians and voters participate in this election after opposing the year's two previous elections (in January for a transitional parliament and in October on a new constitution). Preliminary results, announced on December 19–20, will indicate a strong majority to the Shiite coalition called the United Iraqi Alliance.

2006

January 4: Israeli prime minister Ariel Sharon suffers a debilitating stroke. He is succeeded by his deputy, Ehud Olmert, who will later win previously scheduled parliamentary elections on March 28.

January 25: Hamas scores a surprisingly strong win in the first Palestinian legislative elections since 1996, gaining majority control of the Palestinian Legislative Council. The vote is a stunning defeat for Fatah, which had dominated Palestinian politics for four decades.

January 30: The Middle East Quartet—the United States, the United Nations, the European Union, and Russia—announces that future international aid to the Palestinian Authority will be determined by that government's "commitment to the principles of nonviolence, recognition of Israel, and acceptance of previous agreements and obligations, including the roadmap." As a result, most direct aid to the Hamas-led government is suspended, except for food and humanitarian supplies provided through the United Nations.

February 1: Meeting in London, international donors agree to provide more than $10 billion in aid to Afghanistan over the next five years. As part of a "compact" with donors, the government of President Hamid Karzai pledges specific steps, including cracking down on corruption and mismanagement.

February 22: Gunmen dressed as policemen detonate bombs that destroy most of the famed Golden Dome shrine in Samarra, one of the most important Shiite shrines. The bombing escalates sectarian violence between Shiites and Sunnis that continues throughout 2006 and into 2007.

April 21: Members of the Shiite majority bloc in the new Iraqi parliament select Nuri al-Maliki of the al-Dawa Party as prime minister.

May 4: A new coalition government headed by Ehud Olmert takes office in Israel as the result of March 28 elections.

May 15: Secretary of State Condoleezza Rice announces that the United States will restore full diplomatic relations with Libya, completing a process of reconciliation that began in December 2003 with Libya's renunciation of weapons of mass destruction. Washington had suspected diplomatic ties with Tripoli in 1979.

June 7: The U.S. military bombs a house in Baquba, north of Baghdad, killing Abu Musab al-Zarqawi, the head of a Sunni insurgent group calling itself al-Qaida in Mesopotamia. President Bush claims the killing of Zarqawi is an important victory.

June 25: Iraqi prime minister Maliki presents a National Reconciliation and Dialogue Project to the parliament. It calls for a limited amnesty and other provisions to reduce sectarian tensions.

June 25: Palestinian guerrillas cross into Israel from Gaza and capture an Israeli soldier. Two soldiers and three Palestinians are killed in an ensuing gun battle. Israel then launches air attacks, lasting into late July, against the Gaza Strip but fails to secure the release of the captured soldier.

July 12: Hizballah guerrillas cross from Lebanon into Israel, where they kill three Israeli soldiers and capture two others. In a subsequent skirmish, five more Israeli soldiers and an unknown number of Hizballah fighters are killed. Israel launches a broad air attack on Hizballah targets in Lebanon, leading to a month-long war that will kill more than 1,000 Lebanese and nearly 150 Israelis.

July 31: The United States hands the NATO alliance command of coalition forces in southern Afghanistan.

August 14: All sides in the Hizballah-Israeli war accept UN Security Council Resolution 1701, adopted on August 11, calling for a cease-fire.

November 6: Former Iraqi leader Saddam Hussein is found guilty of murder and other charges in connection with the killing of 148 Shiite boys and men in Dujail in 1982. He is sentenced to death.

November 23: More than 280 people are killed in numerous attacks in Iraq, including five car bombs that kill 215 people in the Shiite neighborhood of Sadr City in Baghdad. This is one of the bloodiest days in Iraq since the U.S.-led invasion.

November 28: The *New York Times* publishes a leaked memo, written by national security advisor Stephen Hadley, that questions the abilities and political will of Iraqi prime minister Maliki. President Bush will meet with Maliki, in Jordan on November 30, and affirm his support for him.

December 1: Hizballah mounts large demonstrations in Beirut calling for the resignation of Prime Minister Fouad Siniora. The demonstrations will continue for several weeks and increase political tensions between anti- and pro-Syrian factions in Lebanon.

December 6: The Iraq Study Group issues a detailed report on the failures of U.S. policy in Iraq, characterizing the situation there as "grave and deteriorating." The panel offers dozens of recommendations for policy changes, notably, the opening of diplomatic talks with Iran and Syria. President Bush thanks the group for its work but makes clear that he will not embrace most of its recommendations.

December 16: Palestinian president Mahmoud Abbas threatens to call early elections to break a political deadlock between Fatah, which he leads, and Hamas, which controls the government.

December 23: The UN Security Council adopts Resolution 1737, demanding that Iran halt its work to enrich uranium and imposing an international freeze on the assets of individuals and agencies linked to Iran's suspected nuclear weapons program.

December 30: Former Iraqi leader Saddam Hussein is executed by hanging in Baghdad. Videos showing Saddam being taunted by guards cause widespread outrage.

December 31: The toll of U.S. service personnel killed since the beginning of the Iraq war reaches 3,000.

2007

January 10: President George W. Bush announces that he plans to sends an additional 21,000-plus soldiers to Iraq as part of a "surge" intended to suppress violence, particularly in Baghdad. He also says that he will hold the Iraqi government accountable for meeting several "benchmarks," such as adoption of a law governing oil production.

February 8: After negotiations mediated by Saudi Arabia, Fatah and Hamas agree to form a unity Palestinian government. The Palestinian legislature will approve the deal on March 17.

February 21: British prime minister Tony Blair announces that about 1,600 of the 7,000 British troops remaining in Iraq will be withdrawn in the coming months. Britain has had principle responsibility for securing the area around Basra, Iraq's second-largest city.

March 24: The UN Security Council adopts Resolution 1696, tightening sanctions against Iran because of its refusal to suspend uranium enrichment. The sanctions include a ban on Iranian arms exports and financial sanctions against officials associated with Iran's Revolutionary Guard.

March 27: About 200 people are killed in several attacks or found dead in Iraq. Tal Afar, in northwestern Iraq, suffers the greatest toll when truck bombs explode in markets, killing more than 150 people.

March 29: At an Arab League summit, leaders reaffirm the 2002 Saudi-sponsored plan offering to recognize Israel provided that it relinquish the territories it captured in the June 1967 War.

April 9: Iranian president Mahmoud Ahmadinejad says his country can now produce enriched uranium on an industrial scale. Most experts say his claim is exaggerated.

April 12: A suicide bomber attacks the Iraqi parliament, killing eight people, including two legislators. It is the deadliest attack to date inside the heavily fortified Green Zone of Baghdad.

April 18: More than 230 people are killed, or found dead, from violence in Iraq. More than 180 of the deaths occur in Shiite neighborhoods of Baghdad as the result of four bombings.

April 27: The Turkish military declares its objections to plans by the openly Islamist Justice and Development Party to appoint Foreign Minister Abdullah Gul as the next president. Gul will eventually withdraw his candidacy, but the military's intervention, as the self-declared defenders of secularism, sparks a political crisis resulting in early elections in July.

April 30: A fact-finding panel in Israel issues a preliminary report blaming top government officials—including Prime Minister Ehud Olmert, Defense Minister Amir Peretz, and former army chief of staff Dan Halutz—for failures during the war with Hizballah in July–August 2006.

May 1: President Bush vetoes a bill sent to him by Congress establishing a deadline for the start of U.S. withdrawals from Iraq. Congress on May 24 will send Bush another bill funding U.S. military operations in Iraq but without the deadline he had opposed.

May 3: U.S. secretary of state Condoleezza Rice meets with Syrian foreign minister Walid al-Moallem during a regional conference in Egypt and asks him to prevent foreign fighters from crossing the border into Iraq. It is the highest-level meeting between U.S. and Syrian officials in nearly four years.

May 20: Fighting breaks out in Lebanon between the army and Fatah al-Islam, an Islamist guerrilla group that has taken up positions in a Palestinian refugee camp outside Tripoli.

May 28: The U.S. and Iranian ambassadors to Iraq—Ryan Crocker and Hassan Kazemi Qumi, respectively—meet at the office of Iraqi prime minister Nuri al-Maliki to discuss ways of improving security in Iraq. It is a rare diplomatic exchange between the two countries, which have not had formal diplomatic relations since 1980.

May 30: The UN Security Council adopts Resolution 1757, creating a special tribunal to prosecute those responsible for the killing of former Lebanese prime minister Rafiq Hariri in February 2005.

June 13: After five days of violence between supporters of Fatah and Hamas in the Gaza Strip, Hamas prevails and gains effective control over the territory. Fatah continues to control the West Bank.

June 13: Iraqi insurgents attack the Golden Dome shrine in Samarra, which had been largely destroyed by a bombing in February 2006. The mosque's two remaining minarets fall in this latest attack.

   The Israeli Labor Party elects former prime minister Ehud Barak as its leader, replacing Amir Peretz, whose service as defense minister in the coalition government had been widely criticized. Barak will take over from Peretz as defense minister on June 19. The Knesset elects Shimon Peres as Israel's president. He succeeds Moshe Katsav, who had been on a leave of absence because of charges of sexual improprieties.

June 15: Palestinian president Abbas swears in an "emergency" government of technocrats, all of whom are independents or belong to Fatah. The preceding day he had dissolved the Palestinian Authority government headed by Prime Minister Ismail Haniyeh of Hamas.

June 17: A suicide bomber attacks a police academy in Kabul, killing thirty-five people, most of them police instructors, in one of the deadliest days in Afghanistan since the Taliban's ouster in 2001.

June 25: Egyptian president Hosni Mubarak, Israeli prime minister Olmert, King Abdallah II of Jordan, and Palestinian president Abbas meet in Sharm el-Sheikh, Egypt, to develop a unified response to the Hamas takeover of Gaza. They pledge support for Abbas and Fatah; Israel says it will release to Abbas several hundred million dollars in Palestinian tax revenues that Israel had collected but had withheld after Hamas won parliamentary elections in January 2006.

June 27: On British prime minister Tony Blair's last day in office, the Middle East Quartet—the European Union, Russia, the United Nations, and the United States—announces that he will serve as its UN envoy for Middle East peace negotiations.

July 22: Turkey's ruling Justice and Development Party achieves a major victory in early parliamentary elections, capturing 47 percent of the popular vote (a landslide by recent Turkish standards) and winnings 340 of the 550 seats in parliament. The vote is a setback for the military, which sought to block the party from appointing Foreign Minister Gul as president.

Bibliography

One could spend several lifetimes studying the literature about the Middle East and still only have skimmed the surface. This bibliography lists many of the works consulted in preparing this book. It is not comprehensive, but many such bibliographies are available elsewhere. For example, the library of the Middle East Institute in Washington, D.C., has posted several excellent bibliographies, arranged by country and topic, at www.mideasti.org.

In addition to the books listed below, the well-written and reasonably detailed Country Notes prepared by the U.S. Library of Congress were consulted for this volume. The historical studies for Middle Eastern countries are available online at www.loc.gov/rr/amed. Note that some studies are reasonably current while several have not been updated since the late 1980s or early 1990s. The U.S. Department of State provides regularly updated reports, including historical background and current developments, on individual countries in its Background Notes series available at www.state.gov/r/pa/ei/bgn.

Dozens of think tanks, universities, and special interest groups around the world have programs devoted to studying the Middle East. Many of these produce useful information for novices and experts alike. Many of these programs, however, promote specific points of view, often under the guise of independent analysis. Finding nonpartisan, unbiased information about the Middle East—particularly on the Internet—can be almost as difficult as finding peace and harmony in the region.

Books

Ajami, Fouad. *The Arab Predicament: Arab Political Thought and Practice since 1967.* Updated ed. New York: Cambridge University Press, 1992.

Brumberg, Daniel. *Reinventing Khomeini: The Struggle for Reform in Iran.* Chicago: University of Chicago Press, 2001.

Cleveland, William L. *A History of the Modern Middle East.* 3rd ed. Boulder, Colo.: Westview Press, 2004.

Congressional Quarterly. *The Iran-Contra Puzzle*. Washington, D.C.: Congressional Quarterly, 1987.

———. *The Middle East*. 11th ed. Washington, D.C.: CQ Press, 2007.

Dawisha, Adeed. *Arab Nationalism in the Twentieth Century: From Triumph to Despair*. Princeton: Princeton University Press, 2003.

Friedman, Thomas L. *From Beirut to Jerusalem*. New York: Farrar, Straus and Giroux, 1989.

Fromkin, David. *A Peace to End All Peace: The Fall of the Ottoman Empire and the Creation of the Modern Middle East*. New York: Henry Holt and Company, 2001.

Gelvin, James L. *The Modern Middle East: A History*. New York: Oxford University Press, 2005.

Gettleman, Marvin E., and Stuart Schaar, eds. *The Middle East and Islamic World Reader*. New York: Grove Press, 2005.

Goodwin, Jason. *Lords of the Horizons: A History of the Ottoman Empire*. New York: Henry Holt and Company, 1998.

Gorenberg, Gerson. *The Accidental Empire: Israel and the Birth of the Settlements, 1967–1977*. New York: Henry Holt and Company, 2006.

Hirst, David. *The Gun and the Olive Branch: The Roots of Violence in the Middle East*. New York: Thunder's Mouth Press/Nation Books, 2003.

Hourani, Albert. *A History of the Arab Peoples*. New York: Warner Books, 1992.

Hourani, Albert, Philip Khoury, and Mary C. Wilson, eds. *The Modern Middle East: A Reader*. 2nd ed. London: I. B. Tauris, 2005.

Jankowski, James. *Egypt: A Short History*. Oxford: Oneworld Publications, 2000.

Hurewitz, J. C. *Diplomacy in the Near and Middle East: A Documentary Record*. Vol. 2, *1914–1956*. Princeton: D. Van Nostrand, 1956.

———. *The Middle East and North Africa in World Politics: A Documentary Record*. 2 vols. New Haven: Yale University Press, 1975–1979.

Kamrava, Mehran. *The Modern Middle East: A Political History since the First World War*. Berkeley: University of California Press, 2005.

Khalidi, Rashid. *Resurrecting Empire: Western Footprints and America's Perilous Path in the Middle East*. Boston: Beacon Press, 2005.

Laqueur, Walter, and Barry Rubin, eds. *The Israel-Arab Reader: A Documentary History of the Middle East Conflict*. 6th ed. New York: Penguin Books. 2001.

Leverett, Flynt. *Inheriting Syria: Bashar's Trial by Fire*. Washington, D.C.: Brookings Institution Press, 2005.

Lewis, Bernard. *The Middle East: A Brief History of the Last 2,000 Years*. New York: Touchstone, 1997.

Lukacs, Yehuda. *The Israeli-Palestinian Conflict: A Documentary Record, 1967–1990*. Cambridge: Cambridge University Press, 1992.

Lustick, Ian. *For the Land and the Lord: Jewish Fundamentalism in Israel*. New York: Council on Foreign Relations, 1988.

MacMillan, Margaret. *Paris 1919: Six Months That Changed the World*. New York: Random House, 2002.

Makiya, Kanan. *Republic of Fear: The Politics of Modern Iraq*. Updated ed. Berkeley: University of California Press, 1998.

Marr, Pebe. *The Modern History of Iraq*. 2nd ed. Boulder, Colo.: Westview Press, 2004.

Morris, Benny. *Righteous Victims: A History of the Zionist-Arab Conflict, 1881–2001*. New York: Vintage Books, 2001.

Oren, Michael B. *Six Days of War: June 1967 and the Making of the Modern Middle East.* New York: Ballantine Books, 2003.

Pollack, Kenneth M. *The Persian Puzzle Palace: The Conflict between Iran and America.* New York: Random House, 2004.

Quandt, William B. *Peace Process: American Diplomacy and the Arab-Israeli Conflict since 1967.* Washington, D.C.: Brookings Institution Press, 2001.

Al-Rasheed, Madawi. *A History of Saudi Arabia.* Cambridge: Cambridge University Press, 2002.

Rashid, Ahmed. *Taliban: Militant Islam, Oil, and Fundamentalism in Central Asia.* New Haven: Yale University Press, 2001.

Ricks, Thomas. *Fiasco: The American Military Adventure in Iraq.* New York: Penguin Books, 2006.

Ross, Dennis. *The Missing Peace: The Inside Story of the Fight for Middle East Peace.* New York: Farrar, Straus, and Giroux, 2005.

Sachar, Howard M. *A History of Israel: From the Rise of Zionism to Our Time.* New York: Knopf, 1996.

Schiff, Zeev, and Ehud Ya'ari. *Israel's Lebanon War.* New York: Simon and Schuster, 1984.

Segev, Tom. *One Palestine Complete: Jews and Arabs under the British Mandate.* New York: Henry Holt and Company, 2001.

Shipler, David. *Arab and Jew: Wounded Spirits in a Promised Land.* Rev. ed. New York: Penguin Books, 2002.

Shlaim, Avi. *The Iron Wall: Israel and the Arab World.* New York: W. W. Norton and Company, 2001.

Sick, Gary. *All Fall Down: America's Tragic Encounter with Iran.* New York: Penguin Books, 1986.

Tripp, Charles. *A History of Iraq.* Cambridge: Cambridge University Press, 2005.

United Nations, Division for Palestinian Rights. *The Origins and Evolution of the Palestine Problem: 1917–1988.* New York: United Nations, 1990.

Yambert, Karl, ed. *The Contemporary Middle East.* Boulder, Colo.: Westview Press, 2006.

Zurcher, Erik J. *Turkey: A Modern History.* London: I. B. Taurus, 2004.

Journal Articles and Reports

Allon, Yigal. "Israel: The Case for Defensible Borders." *Foreign Affairs* 55, no. 1 (1976).

Earle, Edward Mead. "The New Constitution of Turkey." *Political Science Quarterly* 40, no. 1 (March 1925).

Gold, Dore. "Defensible Borders for Israel." *Jerusalem Letter/Viewpoints,* no. 500, June 15–July 1, 2003.

Karsh, Efraim. "The Unbearable Lightness of My Critics." *Middle East Quarterly* (Summer 2002).

Lewis, Bernard. "Why Turkey Is the Only Muslim Democracy." *Middle East Quarterly* (March 1994).

MacEachin, Douglas. "Predicting the Soviet Invasion of Afghanistan: The Intelligence Community's Record." Central Intelligence Agency, Center for the Study of Intelligence, 2002. www.cia.gov/csi/monograph/afghanistan/csi.gif.

Migdalovitz, Carol. "Israeli-Arab Negotiations: Background, Conflicts, and U.S. Policy." Congressional Research Service, November 14, 2006.

Rubin, Barnett R. "Afghanistan's Uncertain Transition from Turmoil to Normalcy."
    Council on Foreign Relations, Center for Preventive Action, New York, March 2006.
Shlaim, Avi. "The Protocol of Sevres, 1956: Anatomy of a War Plot." *International Affairs*
    73, no. 3 (1997).
United Nations Information System on the Question of Palestine. *The Origin and Evo-
    lution of the Palestine Problem: 1917–1988.* http://domino.un.org/UNISPAL.NSF/
    561c6ee353d740fb8525607d00581829/aeac80e740c782e4852561150071fdb0!
    OpenDocument.

Credits

Index

Surnames starting with "al-" or "ibn" are alphabetized by the following part of the name